CHRISTIANITY IN

# Sub-Saharan Africa

# Editorial Team

**Editors**
Kenneth R. Ross
J. Kwabena Asamoah-Gyadu
Todd M. Johnson

**Associate Editor**
Albert W. Hickman

**Managing Editor**
Jennifer Lee

**Editorial Advisory Board**
Jehu H. Hanciles
Nicta Makiika Lubaale
Laurenti Magesa
Tinyiko Maluleke
Philomena Mwaura
Isabel Apawo Phiri
John S. Pobee

**Demographic Profile**
Editor: Gina A. Zurlo
Data Analyst: Peter Crossing
Layout and Design: Justin Long
Cartography: Bryan Nicholson

CHRISTIANITY IN

# Sub-Saharan Africa

Edited by Kenneth R. Ross,
J. Kwabena Asamoah-Gyadu, and Todd M. Johnson

CENTER FOR THE STUDY OF GLOBAL CHRISTIANITY

HENDRICKSON PUBLISHERS

**Christianity in Sub-Saharan Africa**

Hendrickson Publishers Marketing, LLC
P. O. Box 3473
Peabody, Massachusetts 01961-3473
www.hendrickson.com



Originally published in 2017 in Edinburgh, UK [under the title Christianity in Sub-Saharan Africa], by Edinburgh University Press Ltd
The Tun – Holyrood Road
12 (2f) Jackson's Entry
Edinburgh EH8 8PJ



*Printed in the United States of America*

*First Printing — January 2020*

Cover image: Photograph taken, by kind permission, from the private collection of Dr. Martin Ott. It shows the African Pietà by the late Jesuit and Cameroonian artist Engelbert Mveng, painted as the 13th station of his "Stations of the Cross" for the chapel of Hekima College, Nairobi, Kenya.

Cover and title page map image by PytyCzech via Getty Images.
Cover design by Karol Bailey.

# Contents

# Series Preface

While a number of compendia have recently been produced on the study of worldwide Christianity, the distinctive quality of this series arises from its examination of global Christianity through a combination of reliable demographic information and original interpretative essays by indigenous scholars and practitioners. This approach was successfully pioneered by the *Atlas of Global Christianity 1910–2010*, published by Edinburgh University Press on the occasion of the centenary of the epoch-making Edinburgh 1910 World Missionary Conference.

Using the same methodology, the Edinburgh Companions to Global Christianity take the analysis to a deeper level of detail and explore the context of the twenty-first century. The series considers the presence of Christianity on a continent-by-continent basis worldwide. Covering every country in the world, it maps patterns of growth and/or decline and examines current trends. The aim of the series is to comprehensively map worldwide Christianity and to describe it in its entirety. Country-specific studies are offered, all the major Christian traditions are analysed and current regional and continental trends are examined.

Each volume is devoted to a continent or sub-continent, following the United Nations classifications. Through a combination of maps, tables, charts and graphs, each of the successive volumes presents a comprehensive demographic analysis of Christianity in the relevant area. Commentary and interpretation are provided by essays on key topics, each written by an expert in the field, normally an indigenous scholar. By the use of these various tools each volume provides an accurate, objective and incisive analysis of the presence of Christian faith in the relevant area.

The projected volumes in the series are:

1. Christianity in Sub-Saharan Africa
2. Christianity in North Africa and West Asia
3. Christianity in South and Central Asia
4. Christianity in East and Southeast Asia
5. Christianity in the Pacific
6. Christianity in Latin America
7. Christianity in North America
8. Christianity in Western and Northern Europe

9. Christianity in Eastern and Southern Europe
10. Compact Atlas of Global Christianity

As series editors, we rely heavily on the regional expertise of the dedicated third editor who joins us for each volume. Furthermore, each volume has its own editorial advisory board, made up of senior scholars with authoritative knowledge of the field in question. We work together to define the essay topics for the volume, arrange for compilation of the required demographic data, recruit the authors of the essays and edit their work. Statistical and demographic information is drawn from the highly regarded *World Christian Database* maintained by the Center for the Study of Global Christianity at Gordon-Conwell Theological Seminary (South Hamilton, MA, USA) and published by Brill. For each volume, a team of 35–40 authors will be recruited to write the essays, and it is ultimately upon their scholarship and commitment that we depend in order to create an original and authoritative work of reference.

Each volume in the series will be, we hope, a significant book in its own right and a contribution to the study of Christianity in the region in question. At the same time, each is a constituent part of a greater whole – the 10-volume series, which aims to provide a comprehensive analysis of global Christianity that will be groundbreaking in its demographic quality and analytical range. Our hope is that the Companions will be of service to anyone seeking a fuller understanding of the worldwide presence of the Christian faith.

*Kenneth R. Ross and Todd M. Johnson*
*Series Editors*

# Volume Preface

It is fitting that the Edinburgh Companions to Global Christianity, which aim to offer an authoritative account of Christianity in every part of the world, should begin with Sub-Saharan Africa, for this sub-continent is a new heartland of the Christian faith, having experienced the fastest growth rate for Christian faith in any part of the globe during the past century. As a result, it offers a dynamic and fast-changing field of study. It has become impossible to understand contemporary Christianity without some knowledge of Africa, just as it is impossible to understand contemporary Africa without some knowledge of Christianity.

In pursuit of such understanding, this volume offers four angles of analysis. The first is demographic, using the methodology of the highly successful *Atlas of Global Christianity* (Edinburgh University Press, 2009) to present accurate statistical information in an attractive, user-friendly format. Maps and charts depict the status of Christianity continentally, regionally and in terms of the principal church traditions.

The second angle of analysis is at the country level. Account is taken of the presence and influence of Christianity in each of the 51 countries in Sub-Saharan Africa. Indigenous scholars have contributed interpretative essays that offer a 'critical insider' perspective on the way in which Christianity is finding expression in their context. Where possible, a number of neighbouring countries are considered together in a full-length essay. In other cases, a shorter essay is devoted to a single country. Where several countries are considered by one essay, some authors treat them sequentially while others adopt a thematic frame of reference to consider Christianity across neighbouring countries in an integrated way. Given the range and diversity of the nations that make up Sub-Saharan Africa, this flexible approach allows due proportion to be applied to an analysis that offers readers a profile of Christianity in every country.

Thirdly, Christianity in Sub-Saharan Africa is considered in terms of its principal ecclesial forms or traditions. Five types of church are considered: Anglican, Independent, Orthodox, Protestant and Roman Catholic; in addition, the Evangelical and Pentecostal/Charismatic movements, which cut across ecclesial affiliation, are examined. It must be acknowledged that the African context presents challenges in terms of definition and dual identification, where a given individual might have more than one ecclesial identity. Nonetheless, it is clear that today's African Christianity, in all its variety, flows in these broad streams, and close examination of each advances our understanding of the whole.

Fourthly, selected themes are considered. Eight of these run right through the Edinburgh Companions series: faith and culture, worship and spirituality, theology, social and political context, mission and evangelism, gender, religious freedom, and inter-religious relations. A further three have been selected specifically for this volume on account of their salience in the African context: the Bible in African Christianity, the anthropology of evil, and migration. Each of these themes is examined on a continent-wide basis, deepening our understanding of features that are definitive for Christianity in Sub-Saharan Africa.

As is evident from the short bibliography offered at the end of each essay, this book rests on the body of scholarship that has illumined our understanding of African Christianity, particularly the burgeoning literature of the past 25 years. Besides many detailed local studies, much insight has been derived from such attempts at comprehensive analysis as Adrian Hastings's *The Church in Africa 1450–1950* (Oxford University Press, 1994), John Baur's *2000 Years of Christianity in Africa: An African Church History* (Paulines, 1994), Elizabeth Isichei's *A History of Christianity in Africa: From Antiquity to the Present* (Eerdmans, 1995), Bengt Sundkler and Christopher Steed's *A History of the Church in Africa* (Cambridge University Press, 2004), Ogbu U. Kalu's (as editor) *African Christianity: An African Story* (Africa World Press, 2007), Elias K. Bongmba's (as editor) *The Routledge Companion to Christianity in Africa* (Routledge, 2015) and Isabel Apawo Phiri, Dietrich Werner, Chammah Kaunda and Kennedy Owino's (as editors) *Anthology of African Christianity* (Regnum, 2016). While resting on the preceding scholarship, this volume breaks new ground through its reliable demographic analysis, its contemporary focus, the indigenous authorship of its essays and the originality of the analyses. The essay authors employ a variety of disciplinary approaches – historical, theological, sociological, missiological, anthropological – as appropriate to their topics. Taken together, the volume offers a deeply textured and highly authoritative account of Christianity in Sub-Saharan Africa, one that will reward the attention of any who wish to deepen their knowledge of this subject.

*Kenneth R. Ross*
*J. Kwabena Asamoah-Gyadu*
*Todd M. Johnson*

June 2016

# Contributors

**Afe Adogame** holds the Maxwell M. Upson Chair as Professor of Christianity and Society, Princeton Theological Seminary, New Jersey, USA. He is the Secretary General of the International Association for the History of Religions.
*The Anthropology of Evil*

**James N. Amanze** is Professor in Systematic Theology at the University of Botswana and Editor-in-Chief of the *Boleswa Journal of Theology, Religion and Philosophy*. He is Secretary of the Association of Theological Institutions in Southern and Central Africa, having also served as Secretary of the World Conference of the Association of Theological Institutions from 2010 to 2015.
*Botswana, Lesotho, Namibia and Swaziland*

**Jacqueline Andoche** is an anthropologist and Lecturer at the University of La Réunion. Trained in social and cultural anthropology at the University of Paris–Sorbonne, her research concentrates on the close links between medicine and religion, as well as issues related to the coexistence of religions and the emergence of new spiritualities in Réunion and in the wider world.
*Réunion*

**Solomon Andriatsimialomananarivo**, originally from Madagascar, is Langham Partnership Coordinator for Literature in Francophone Africa. Since 1997 he has also served as Lecturer in Systematic Theology at the Faculté de Théologie Evangélique de l'Alliance Chrétienne in Abidjan, Côte d'Ivoire.
*Madagascar*

**J. Kwabena Asamoah-Gyadu**, Fellow of the Ghana Academy of Arts and Sciences, is Baëta-Grau Professor of Contemporary African Christianity and Pentecostal/Charismatic Theology at the Trinity Theological

Seminary, Legon, Accra, Ghana. He has published widely on Christianity and Christian religious innovation in Africa.
*Christianity in Sub-Saharan Africa*

**Valérie Aubourg** holds a doctorate in anthropology and ethnology and is Researcher at the Groupe Sociétés, Religions, Laïcités at the Centre national de la recherché scientifique and Professor at the Catholic University of Lyon. She is author of *Christianismes charismatiques à l'île de la Réunion* (Karthala, 2014).
*Réunion*

**Deji Isaac Ayegboyin**, the immediate past President of the Nigerian Baptist Theological Seminary, Ogbomosho, is Professor and Head of the Department of Religious Studies, University of Ibadan, Nigeria. He is co-author (with S. Ademola Ishola) of *African Indigenous Churches: An Historical Perspective* (Greater Heights Publications, 1997).
*Pentecostals/Charismatics*

**Anthony Balcomb** is Senior Research Associate in the School of Religion, Philosophy and Classics at the University of KwaZulu-Natal, South Africa. He is the author of *Third Way Theology – Reconciliation, Revolution, and Reform in the South African Church During the 1980s* (Cluster, 1993) and *Journey into the African Sun – Soundings in Search of Another Way of Being in the World* (UNISA, 2014).
*Evangelicals*

**Elias Kifon Bongmba** holds the Harry and Hazel Chavanne Chair in Christian Theology and is Professor of Religion at Rice University, Houston, Texas, USA. He served as President of the African Association for the Study of Religion from 2010 to 2015. He edited *The Wiley Blackwell Companion to African Religions* (Wiley, 2012) and *The Routledge Companion to Christianity in Africa* (Routledge, 2015).
*Central African Republic, Togo, Côte d'Ivoire, Benin and Cameroon*

**Luciano Chanhelela Chianeque** is an ordained minister of the Evangelical Congregational Church in Angola and Associate Professor in the Faculty of Human Sciences at the Catholic University of Angola. He earned a BTheol and an MA at the University of Durban–Westville and a PhD in religion and social transformation at the University of KwaZulu-Natal, South Africa.
*Angola and São Tomé and Príncipe*

**Evaristi Magoti Cornelli** is Lecturer in the Department of Philosophy and Religious Studies at the University of Dar es Salaam, Tanzania. He is the author of *Nyerere's Ujamaa: Its Foundation and Values* (Lambert Academic, 2015) and co-editor (with Jesse Mugambi) of *Endless Quest: Essays in Honour of Laurenti Magesa* (Acton, 2014).
*Inter-religious Relations*

**Rodney Curpanen** is an ordained pastor of the Presbyterian Church of Mauritius and served for 10 years as its moderator. He coordinates outreach campaigns and church growth programmes, is currently Vice-President of Prison Fellowship Mauritius and lectures in various institutions.
*Mauritius*

**Simon Kossi Dossou**, formerly Professor of Old Testament Theology at the Faculty of Protestant Theology, Yaoundé, Cameroon, is currently the All Africa Conference of Churches' Special Envoy to West and Central Africa. An ordained minister of the Benin Methodist Church, he served as Africa President of the World Council of Churches from 2006 to 2013.
*Senegal, the Gambia, Guinea, Guinea-Bissau and Cape Verde*

**Musa W. Dube** is a scholar of the New Testament at the University of Botswana and research affiliate of the University of South Africa. She is coeditor (with Gerald O. West) of *The Bible in Africa: Transactions, Trajectories and Trends* (Brill, 2000).
*Social and Political Context*

**Anthony Egan, SJ,** works at the Jesuit Institute South Africa and the Steve Biko Centre for Bioethics, University of the Witwatersrand, Johannesburg, South Africa. Ordained in 2002, he has written books, chapters and journal and popular articles on ethics and on the religious history of South Africa.
*Roman Catholics*

**Amélé Adamavi-Aho Ekué**, originally from Togo, is Professor of Ecumenical Ethics at the Ecumenical Institute at the Château de Bossey, Switzerland. A Protestant theologian with a specialisation in intercultural and ecumenical theology, she is the author of 'Migrant Christians: Believing Wanderers Between Cultures and Nations' (*Ecumenical Review*, vol. 61, no. 4, 2009, pp. 387–99) and coeditor of the quarterly journal *Ökumenische Rundschau*.
*Migration*

**Tibebe Eshete** is Assistant Professor in the Departments of History and Religious Studies at Michigan State University, USA. He previously taught at the University of Asmara, Addis Ababa University and Missouri State University and is the author of *The History of the Evangelical Movement in Ethiopia: Resistance and Resilience* (Baylor University Press, 2009).
*Ethiopia, Eritrea, Somalia and Djibouti*

**Emmanuel Foro** is a Jesuit from the West Africa Province. He obtained a master's degree in geography at the University of Ouagadougou, Burkina Faso. After his initial religious formation he earned a doctorate in sacred theology at the Jesuit School of Theology of Santa Clara University, California, USA. He is currently Dean and teaches systematic theology at Hekima University College in Nairobi, Kenya.
*Niger, Mauritania, Mali, Chad and Burkina Faso*

**Tharcisse Gatwa** is Associate Research Professor of Ethics and Missiology and Director of Research at the Protestant Institute of Arts and Social Sciences, Butare, Rwanda. He is author of *The Churches and Ethnic Ideology in the Rwandan Crises, 1900–1994* (Regnum, 2005) and coeditor (with Laurent Rutinduka) of *Histoire du Christianisme au Rwanda. Des origines à nos jours* (CLÉ, 2014).
*Rwanda and Burundi*

**Mary N. Getui** teaches in the Department of Religious Studies at the Catholic University of Eastern Africa in Kenya. A Seventh-day Adventist, she has published widely on religion, culture, education, gender and health.
*Faith and Culture*

**Wanjiru M. Gitau** completed her PhD in intercultural studies in world Christianity at Africa International University, Nairobi, Kenya, in 2015. She served for 10 years at Nairobi Chapel, combining pastoral leadership with service in dynamic urban congregations, and also as a researcher on global Christian revitalisation with the Center for the Study of World Christian Revitalization Movements, Asbury Theological Seminary, Wilmore, Kentucky, USA, and a researcher with the Africa Leadership Survey.
*Kenya and Tanzania*

**Todd M. Johnson** is Associate Professor of Global Christianity and Director of the Center for the Study of Global Christianity at Gordon-Conwell Theological Seminary in South Hamilton, Massachusetts, USA.

He is also Visiting Research Fellow at Boston University's Institute for Culture, Religion and World Affairs, leading a research project on international religious demography.

*Seychelles, Comoros, Mayotte and Saint Helena; Methodology and Sources of Christian and Religious Affiliation*

**Chammah J. Kaunda**, from Zambia, is Postdoctoral Research Fellow in Christian Spirituality at the University of South Africa, Pretoria. He is particularly interested in how African religio-cultural heritage can inform African Christianity within theological education, African Pentecostal theology, missiology and ecumenical theology.

*Gender*

**Malebogo Kgalemang** is a scholar of the New Testament at the University of Botswana, Department of Theology and Religious Studies. She is a well known feminist theologian who has published on illness-based stigma, especially as it relates to HIV/AIDS.

*Social and Political Context*

**Ralph Lee** worked and lived in Ethiopia for many years, most recently teaching at the Holy Trinity Theological College of the Ethiopian Orthodox Church in Addis Ababa. He has research interests in historical and contemporary Ethiopian Christianity and in particular is part of a major research project on the Book of Enoch at the Ludwig Maximilians University in Munich, Germany.

*Orthodox*

**Hany Longwe** is Lecturer in the Faculty of Education at the University of Livingstonia, Malawi. An ordained Baptist minister, he is the author of *Christians by Grace – Baptists by Choice: A History of the Baptist Convention of Malawi* (Mzuni Press, 2013) and *Identity by Dissociation: A History of Achewa Providence Industrial Mission* (Mzuni Press, 2013).

*Zimbabwe, Zambia and Malawi*

**Nicta Lubaale** is General Secretary of the Organisation of African Instituted Churches (OAIC), having earlier served as Director for the OAIC Development Programme. His major areas of interest include faith and development and the place of the theology of African Independent churches in Africa's socioeconomic and political realities.

*Independents*

**Tinyiko Maluleke** is Professor of Theology at the University of Pretoria, where he is Director for the Centre for African Spirituality and Culture. He is also responsible for the University's Africa Strategy in the Office of the Principal and Vice-Chancellor of the University of Pretoria, South Africa.
*South Africa*

**Ukachukwu Chris Manus** is Professor of Biblical Studies (New Testament) and African Christian Theology in the Department of Theology and Religious Studies at the National University of Lesotho. He is the author of *Christ, the African King: New Testament Christology* (Peter Lang, 1993) and *Intercultural Hermeneutics: Methods and Approaches* (Acton, 2003).
*The Bible in African Christianity*

**Esther Mombo** is Lecturer in the Faculty of Theology at St Paul's University, Limuru, Kenya. She teaches courses in African church history, with a focus on women and mission, interfaith relations, gender and theology and African women's theologies.
*Mission and Evangelism*

**Jean-Gottfried Mutombo** is a co-worker of the United Evangelical Mission in the Department of Missionary Services of the Evangelische Kirche von Westfalen, Dortmund, Germany. A pastor of the Church of Christ in Congo (CCC), he has served as Permanent Secretary of the Theological Commission and Director of the Office of the National President of the CCC.
*Gabon, Equatorial Guinea, Republic of Congo and Democratic Republic of Congo*

**Richard Nnyombi** is a Ugandan Catholic priest and a member of the Society of the Missionaries of Africa. He has served in Algeria, Tanzania, Kenya, Italy and Uganda, and is presently Director of the John Paul II Justice and Peace Centre in Kampala, Uganda.
*Uganda and South Sudan*

**Setri Nyomi**, a Ghanaian theologian, is currently Senior Pastor at the Evangelical Presbyterian Church, Ghana – Adenta District. From 2000 to 2014 he was General Secretary of the World Communion of Reformed Churches.
*Protestants*

**Elijah Obinna** is a minister of the Church of Scotland and a former Senior Lecturer and Director of Research and Postgraduate Studies at Hugh Goldie Lay/Theological Training Institution, Arochukwu, Nigeria. The immediate past national Director of the Directorate of Lay Development and Leadership Training of the Presbyterian Church of Nigeria, he is the author of *Scottish Missionaries in Nigeria: Foundation, Transformation and Development Among the Amasiri (1927–1944)* (Edwin Mellen Press, 2013).
*Nigeria*

**Francis Anekwe Oborji**, a Nigerian diocesan priest, is Professor of Missiology at the Pontifical Urban University in Rome, Italy. He is a founding officer of the International Association of Catholic Missiologists and author of *Concepts of Mission: The Evolution of Contemporary Missiology* (Orbis, 2006) and *Towards a Christian Theology of African Religion* (Gaba Publications, 2005).
*Theology*

**Mercy Amba Oduyoye** is founder and Director of the Institute of African Women in Religion and Culture at Trinity Theological Seminary, Accra, Ghana. A former Deputy General Secretary of the World Council of Churches, she is a pioneer of African women's theology and founder of the Circle of Concerned African Women Theologians.
*The Future of Christianity in Sub-Saharan Africa*

**Michael Adeleke Ogunewu** is Senior Lecturer in the Faculty of Theological Studies, Nigerian Baptist Theological Seminary, Ogbomosho, Nigeria. He teaches church history, with specialisation in Pentecostalism and African Christianity. He has contributed extensively to the *Dictionary of African Christian Biography* (a digital resource hosted by the Center for Global Christianity and Mission at Boston University School of Theology).
*Pentecostals/Charismatics*

**Cephas N. Omenyo** is Professor of African Christianity and Missions, and Provost, College of Education, University of Ghana, Legon, and Extra-ordinary Professor, Faculty of Theology, University of Stellenbosch, South Africa. He is an ordained minister of the Presbyterian Church of Ghana and member of the advisory board of *Exchange: Journal of Missiological and Ecumenical Research.*
*Ghana, Liberia and Sierra Leone*

**Isabel Apawo Phiri** is Associate General Secretary for Public Witness and Diakonia of the World Council of Churches and Honorary Professor in the School of Religion, Philosophy and Classics at the University of KwaZulu-Natal. She is a Presbyterian layperson from Malawi.
*Gender*

**John S. Pobee**, an ordained Anglican priest, is Professor Emeritus of New Testament at the University of Ghana and a Fellow of the Ghana Academy of Arts and Sciences. He has served as Director of the Programme on Ecumenical Theological Education at the World Council of Churches and as President of the International Association for Mission Studies.
*Worship and Spirituality*

**Kenneth R. Ross,** formerly Professor of Theology at the University of Malawi, is parish minister at Netherlorn in Argyll, Honorary Fellow of the Edinburgh University School of Divinity and Chair of the Scotland Malawi Partnership. Over the last three decades he has published extensively on global Christianity. He was awarded the OBE in the UK New Year Honours of 2016.
*Seychelles, Comoros, Mayotte and Saint Helena*

**Christof Sauer** is Professor of Religious Studies and Missiology at Evangelische Theologische Facultiet, Leuven, Belgium, and Co-director of the International Institute for Religious Freedom. An ordained Lutheran pastor in Germany, he is coeditor of *Freedom of Belief and Christian Mission* (Wipf and Stock, 2015) and Editor of the *International Journal for Religious Freedom*.
*Religious Freedom*

**Daniel Seifemichael** has both traditional Ethiopian and academic training in theology, serves as Deputy Head of the Ecumenical Relations Office of the Ethiopian Orthodox Church and is Head of Public and External Relations for the Ethiopian Orthodox Church Development and Inter-Church Aid Commission in Addis Ababa, Ethiopia.
*Orthodox*

**James Tengatenga** is a former Bishop of the Anglican Diocese of Southern Malawi, former Chair of the Anglican Consultative Council and the Distinguished Visiting Professor of Global Anglicanism at the School of Theology, University of the South, Sewanee, Tennessee, USA.
*Anglicans*

**Isaias Paulo Titoce** is Lecturer in New Testament Theology at the United Seminary of Ricatla in Mozambique. He is an ordained pastor of the United Methodist Church.
*Mozambique*

**Frans Veerman** is Director of the World Watch Research Unit of Open Doors International. He has a strong connection to Africa by his previous service in Christian rural development in Zaire (now Democratic Republic of Congo) and Mozambique, and as consultant to Wycliffe Bible Translators in Africa.
*Religious Freedom*

**Gina A. Zurlo** is Assistant Director of the Center for the Study of Global Christianity at Gordon-Conwell Theological Seminary, South Hamilton, Massachusetts, USA, as well as a PhD candidate at Boston University School of Theology. She is Coeditor of the *World Christian Database* (Brill) and Associate Editor of the *World Religion Database* (Brill).
*A Demographic Profile of Christianity in Sub-Saharan Africa; Methodology and Sources of Christian and Religious Affiliation*

# Introduction

# A Demographic Profile of Christianity in Sub-Saharan Africa

## Gina A. Zurlo

*Majority Religion by Province, 2015*

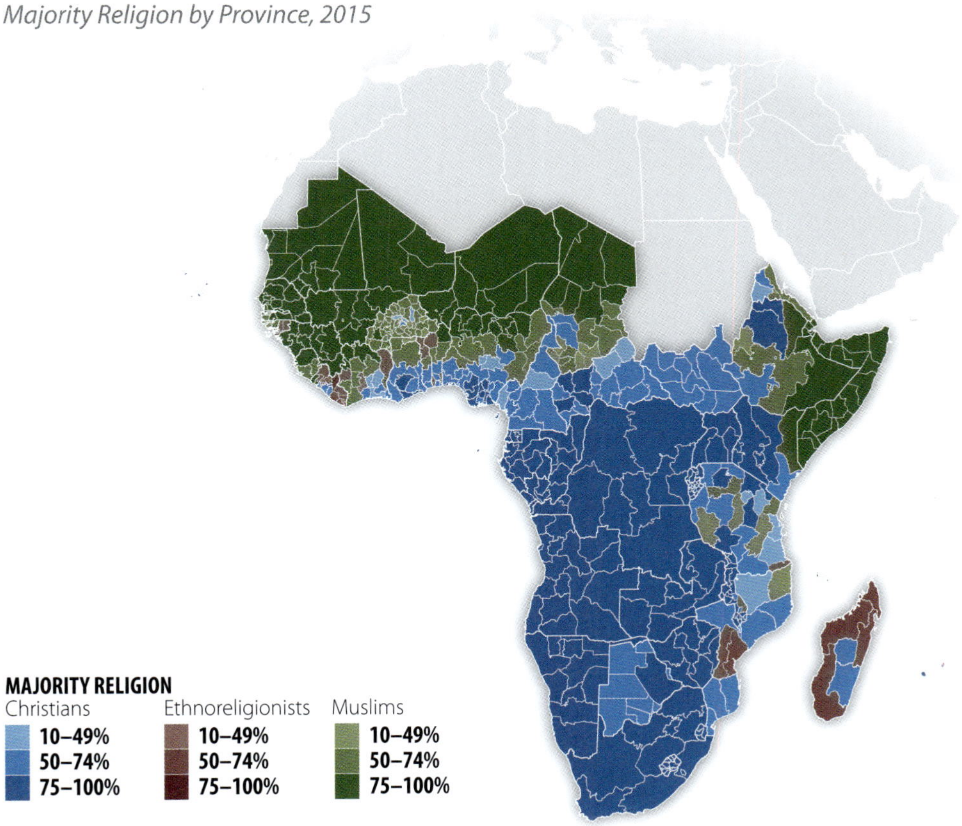


Christianity, Islam and ethnoreligions (African traditional religions) are the largest religions in Sub-Saharan Africa. Christianity and Islam have increased their shares since 1970, while ethnoreligions have declined. However, many people observe elements of African traditional religion alongside Christian or Muslim practices.

*Religions in Sub-Saharan Africa, 1970 and 2015*

| | 1970 | | 2015 | |
|---|---|---|---|---|
| Religion | Adherents | % | Adherents | % |
| Christians | 134,235,000 | 47.5% | 564,536,000 | 58.7% |
| Muslims | 71,714,000 | 25.4% | 283,042,000 | 29.4% |
| Ethnoreligionists | 74,443,000 | 26.3% | 101,704,000 | 10.6% |
| Other | 2,351,000 | 0.8% | 13,005,000 | 1.4% |
| **Total** | **282,743,000** | **100.0%** | **962,287,000** | **100.0%** |

Source: Todd M. Johnson and Gina A. Zurlo (eds), *World Christian Database* (Leiden/Boston: Brill), accessed March 2016.

## Christianity in Sub-Saharan Africa, 1970–2015

*Christians by Country, 2015*

*565 Million Christians, 58.7% of Population*

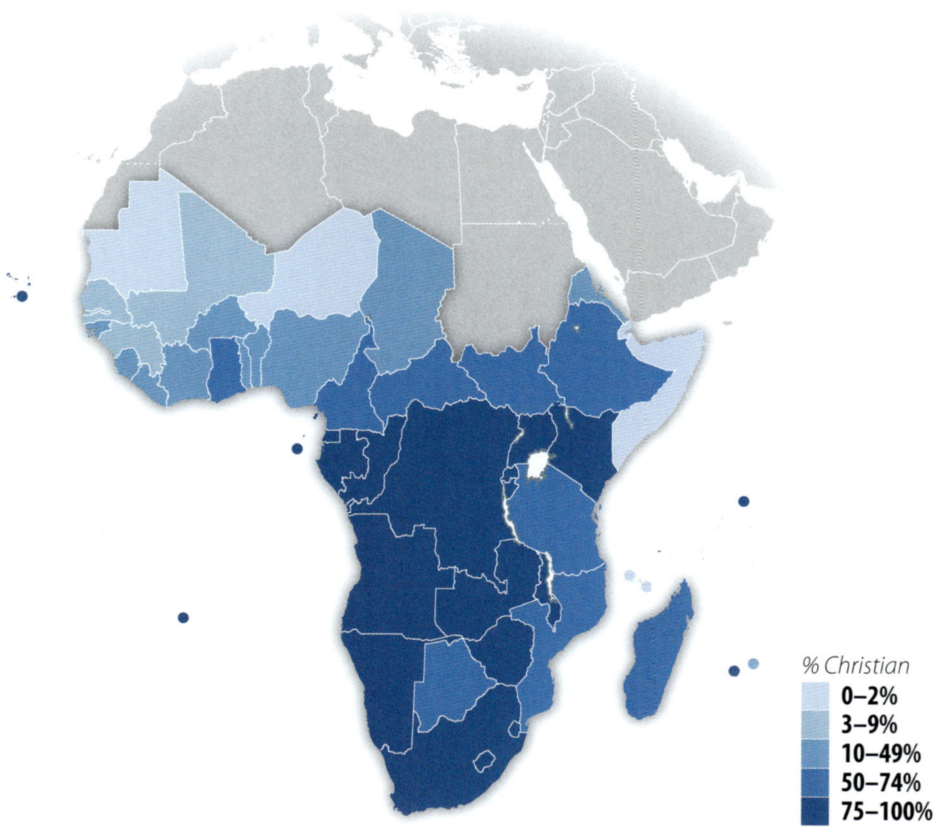


Overall, Christianity in Sub-Saharan Africa has been growing. From 1970 to 2015 the region's Christian population grew from 47.5% (134 million) of the total population to 58.7% (565 million), an average annual growth rate of 3.2%. Muslims represent around half that (29.4% in 2015; 283 million). Some of the least-Christian areas in Sub-Saharan Africa are found in Western Africa (which was 36.1% Christian in 2015), including Muslim-majority countries the Gambia, Guinea, Guinea-Bissau, Mali, Mauritania, Niger, Senegal and Sierra Leone.

Christianity grew the fastest between 1970 and 2015 in Benin (averaging 5.1% per year), Guinea (5.0%) and Burkina Faso (4.8%). The only countries where Christianity declined as a percentage of the population are Saint Helena (from 99.4% to 95.8% Christian), Djibouti and Somalia. Decline in Saint Helena is due to natural demographic causes. In Djibouti it is because of emigration, and in Somalia Christians have been persecuted, leading to death and emigration.

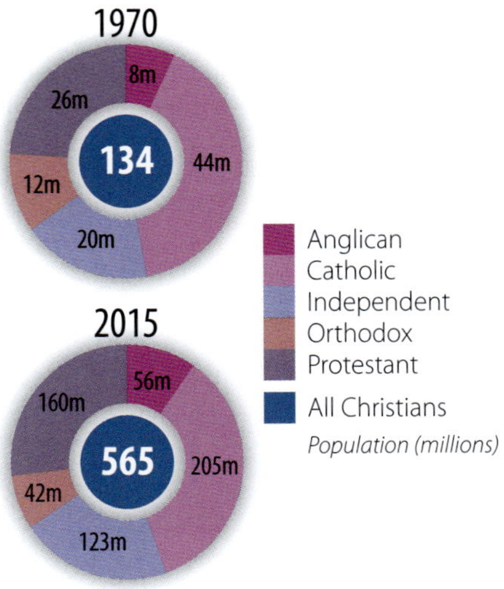


*Major Christian Traditions, 1970 and 2015*

Between 1970 and 2015, Catholics grew from 44 million to 205 million, now representing 36.3% of all Christians in the region. Independents have also increased, now representing 21.8% of all Christians. It is likely that these two traditions' shares will continue to grow in the future.

*Christians, 1970–2015*

Christianity in Sub-Saharan Africa had impressive growth throughout the twentieth century, with growth anticipated to level off into the twenty-first century. While less than 50% of the region's population in 1970, Christianity could represent more than three-fifths by 2050. Much of this growth will likely be due to high birth rates among Christians and more conversions from African traditional religions.

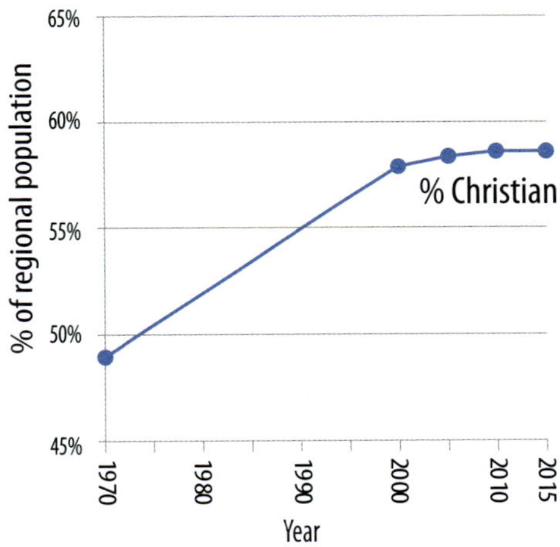


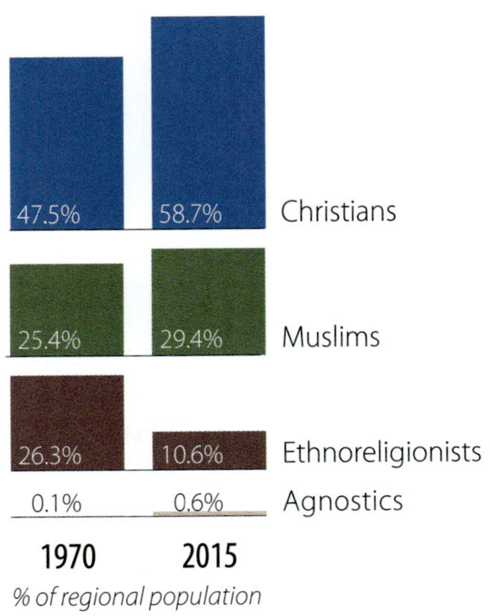


*Religious Affiliation, 1970 and 2015*

Both Christianity and Islam have made significant gains in the last 45 years, although conversions to Christianity in Middle Africa have given Christianity a slight edge. Ethnoreligions (African traditional religions) have been on the decline as more people switch to Christianity or Islam. Agnosticism is growing only slightly, and mainly in urban areas with the arrival of foreigners.

*Note:* Throughout this profile, traditions will not add up to total Christians in each region because of double-affiliation and the unaffiliated. Only the four largest religions are depicted.

## Major Christian Traditions, 1970 and 2015

*Christians*

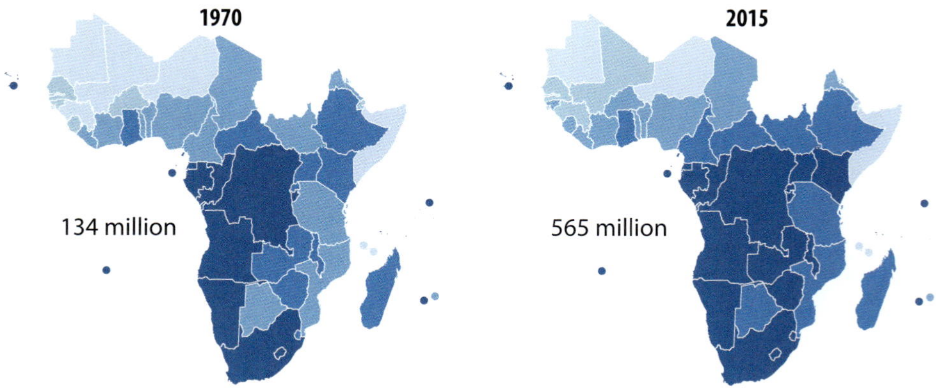


*% of country population*
- **0–2%**
- **3–9%**
- **10–49%**
- **50–74%**
- **75–100%**

Christianity continues to grow in Sub-Saharan Africa. Most Christians are concentrated in the South, Middle and East, while the West is more closely affiliated with Islam. There were no significant changes between 1970 and 2015 except a deepening of Christian affiliation in Middle, Eastern and Southern Africa.

*Anglicans*

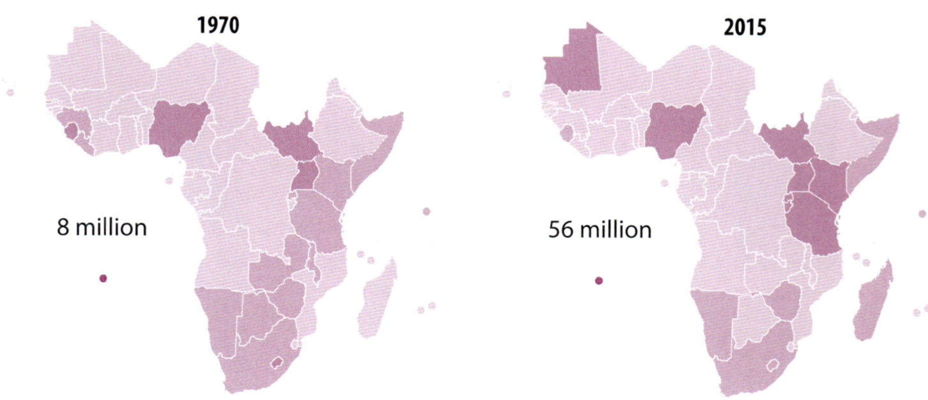


*% of Christian population*
- **0–2%**
- **3–9%**
- **10–49%**
- **50–74%**
- **75–100%**

Anglicanism has grown substantially in the region since 1970. Some of the largest Anglican congregations in the world are currently found in Kenya, Uganda and Tanzania. The number of Anglicans in Africa far outnumbers that in Europe and North America, and this trend is likely to continue in the future.

*Catholics*

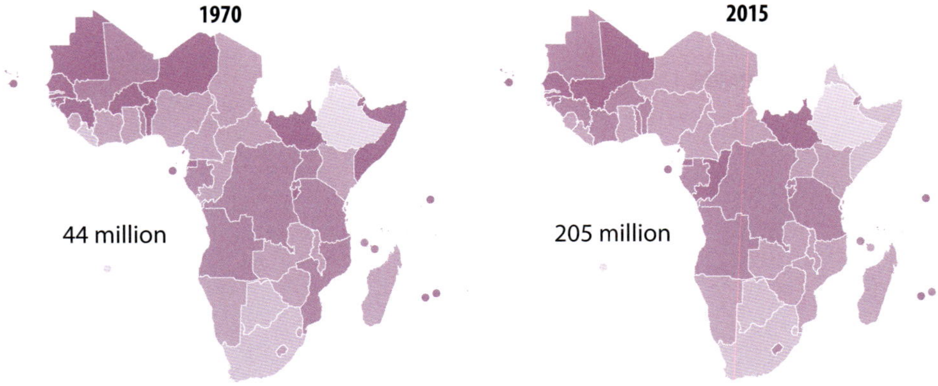


*% of Christian population*
- 0–2%
- 3–9%
- 10–49%
- 50–74%
- 75–100%

Catholicism has grown in Sub-Saharan Africa because the tradition has adapted to local culture; since the Second Vatican Council, the Catholic Church has stressed that one does not need to cease being African to become Catholic. Africa is home to many historical Catholic churches as well as newer ones introduced during the colonial period.

*Independents*

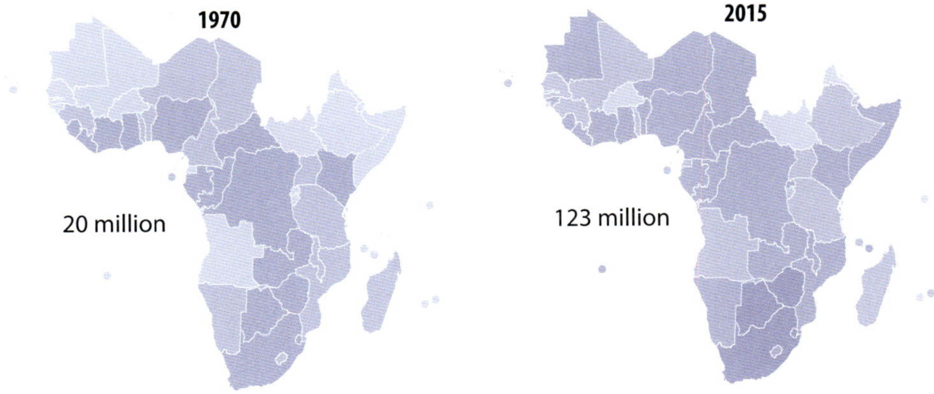


*% of Christian population*
- 0–2%
- 3–9%
- 10–49%
- 50–74%
- 75–100%

Independent Christianity continues to represent a large portion of Christians in Sub-Saharan Africa (22%, up from 15% in 1970). Botswana had the highest percentage of Independent Christians in 2015, at 61%, followed by Swaziland at 54% and Zimbabwe at 51%.

## Major Christian Traditions, 1970 and 2015

*Orthodox*

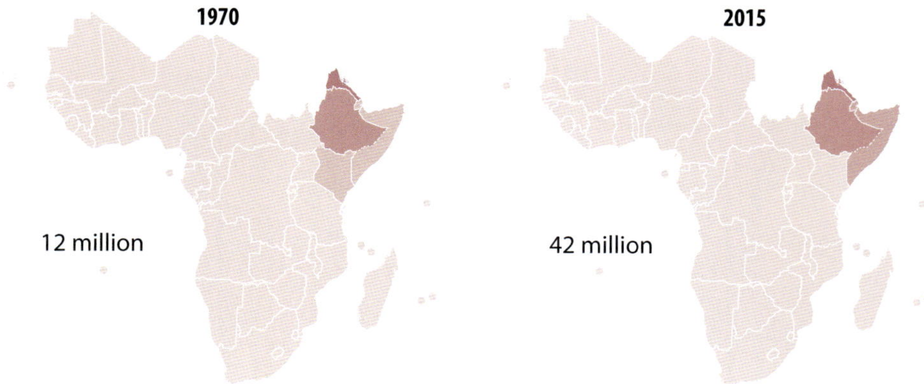


*% of Christian population*
- 0–2%
- 3–9%
- 10–49%
- 50–74%
- 75–100%

Orthodox Christianity in Sub-Saharan Africa is concentrated in the east (16% of all Christians in Eastern Africa). Ethiopia and Eritrea have the largest Orthodox populations by percentage of all Christians, 91% and 67%, respectively. There has been recent migration of Orthodox Christians in Eastern Africa due to drought and famine, which explains the increase seen in Somalia and Djibouti.

*Protestants*

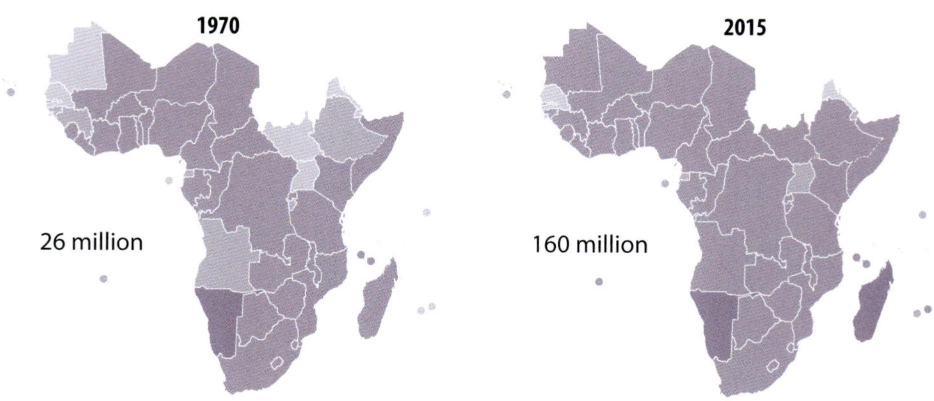


*% of Christian population*
- 0–2%
- 3–9%
- 10–49%
- 50–74%
- 75–100%

Protestants' share has declined in some countries—such as Botswana, Congo and the Democratic Republic of the Congo—due to faster growth of Independents, Anglicans and Catholics. The country with the highest Protestant percentage (among all Christians) in 2015 was Namibia (67%). Eastern Africa has more than five times as many Protestants as Southern Africa.

## Movements Within Christianity, 1970 and 2015

*Evangelicals*

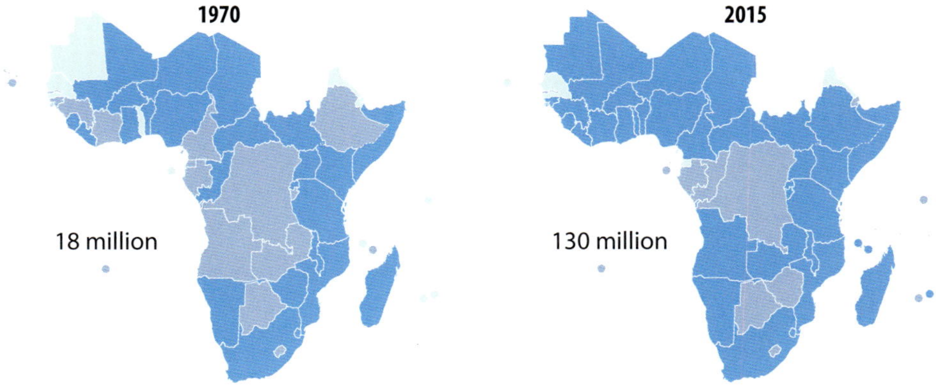


*% of Christian population*
- **0–2%**
- **3–9%**
- **10–49%**
- **50–74%**
- **75–100%**

Evangelicals grew substantially between 1970 and 2015, from 6% of the population to 14%. This corresponds with the growth of Independent churches, which are typically Evangelical in theology and outlook. Some of the most dramatic growth of Evangelical Christianity has occurred in Ghana (from 5% to 20% Evangelical), Angola (3% to 18%) and Rwanda (6% to 20%).

*Pentecostals/Charismatics*

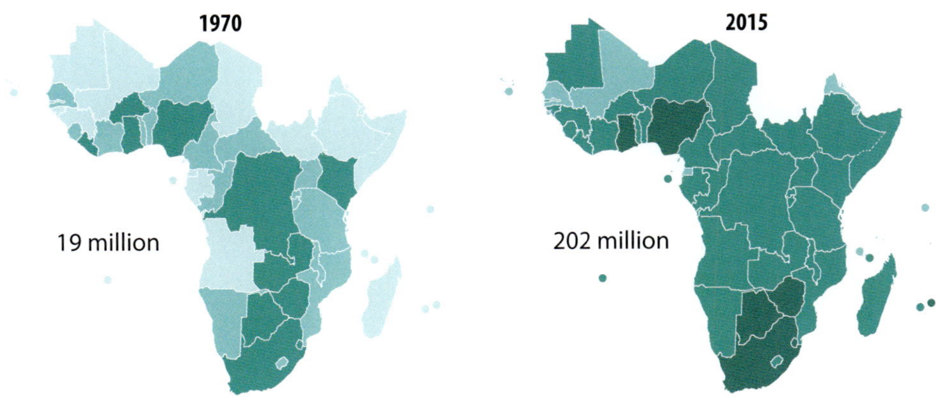


*% of Christian population*
- **0–2%**
- **3–9%**
- **10–49%**
- **50–74%**
- **75–100%**

In 1970 Sub-Saharan Africa was 7% Pentecostal/ Charismatic, growing to 21% by 2015. Southern Africa has a historical presence of Pentecostals/ Charismatics, particularly in South Africa, but still saw Pentecostals/Charismatics grow to 56% of all Christians by 2015. The largest relative growth was in Southern Africa, where Pentecostals/Charismatics jumped from 18% of the population in 1970 to 46% in 2015.

## Christianity In Eastern Africa, 1970–2015

*Christians by Country, 2015*

*260 Million Christians, 65.9% of Population*

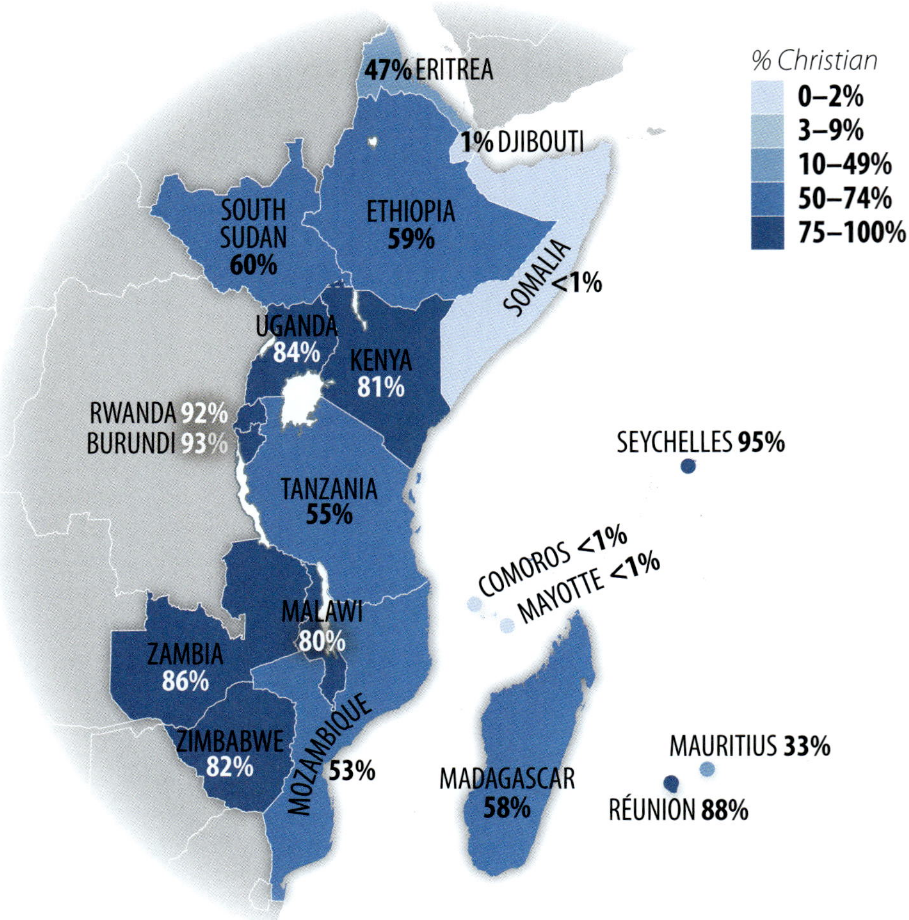


Eastern Africa's population, which has tripled since 1970, is now nearly 395 million, 65.9% of whom are Christian in 2015 (up from 49.7% in 1970). One major political change has been the creation of South Sudan, which split from Muslim-majority Sudan in 2009. South Sudan has a long history of Catholic and Anglican missionary work and is 60% Christian (7.5 million) in 2015.

Eastern Africa is home to several countries that are 80% or more Christian including Kenya, Malawi, Uganda, Rwanda, Burundi, Zambia and Zimbabwe. Yet it is also home to Muslim-majority countries such as Somalia and Djibouti, where minority Christians are under great persecution from extremist groups. Ethiopia is the largest country in the region with nearly 100 million people, most of whom are Orthodox (39%) or Muslim (34%).

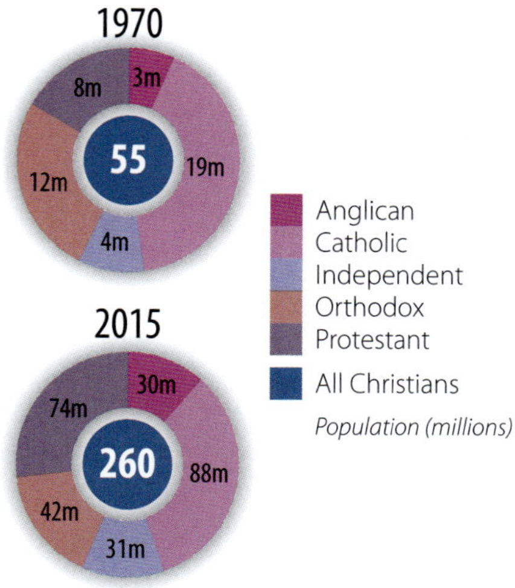


*Major Christian Traditions, 1970 and 2015*

Catholicism is the largest Christian tradition in Eastern Africa (34% of all Christians). There has been significant growth of Anglicans (from 5.6% in 1970 to 11.5% in 2015), who have an increasingly prominent voice in the global Anglican Communion. Independent Christianity has also grown, from 8.0% of all Christians to 11.8%.

*Christians, 1970–2015*

Eastern Africa has had a substantial Christian population since at least the fourth century, and looking to the future it is likely to remain so. The region is likely to grow from 65.9% Christian in 2015 to nearly 70% Christian by 2050, mostly due to Christian births in already majority-Christian countries.

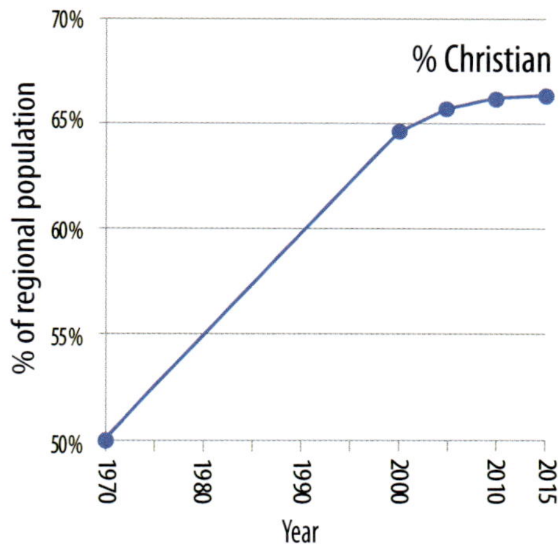


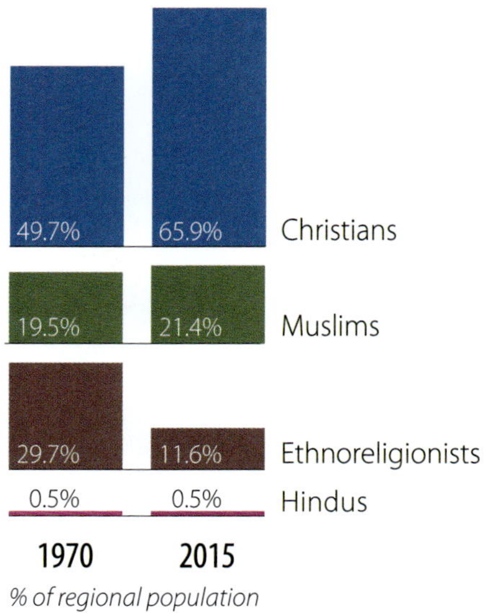


*Religious Affiliation, 1970 and 2015*

In 2015 the largest religions in the region are Christianity (65.9%), Islam (21.4%) and ethno-religions (11.6%). Traditional African religions are decreasing in share because of conversions to Christianity and Islam, though many adherents continue to hold on to some traditional beliefs and practices.

## Christianity in Middle Africa, 1970–2015

*Christians by Country, 2015*

*125 Million Christians, 82.5% of Population*

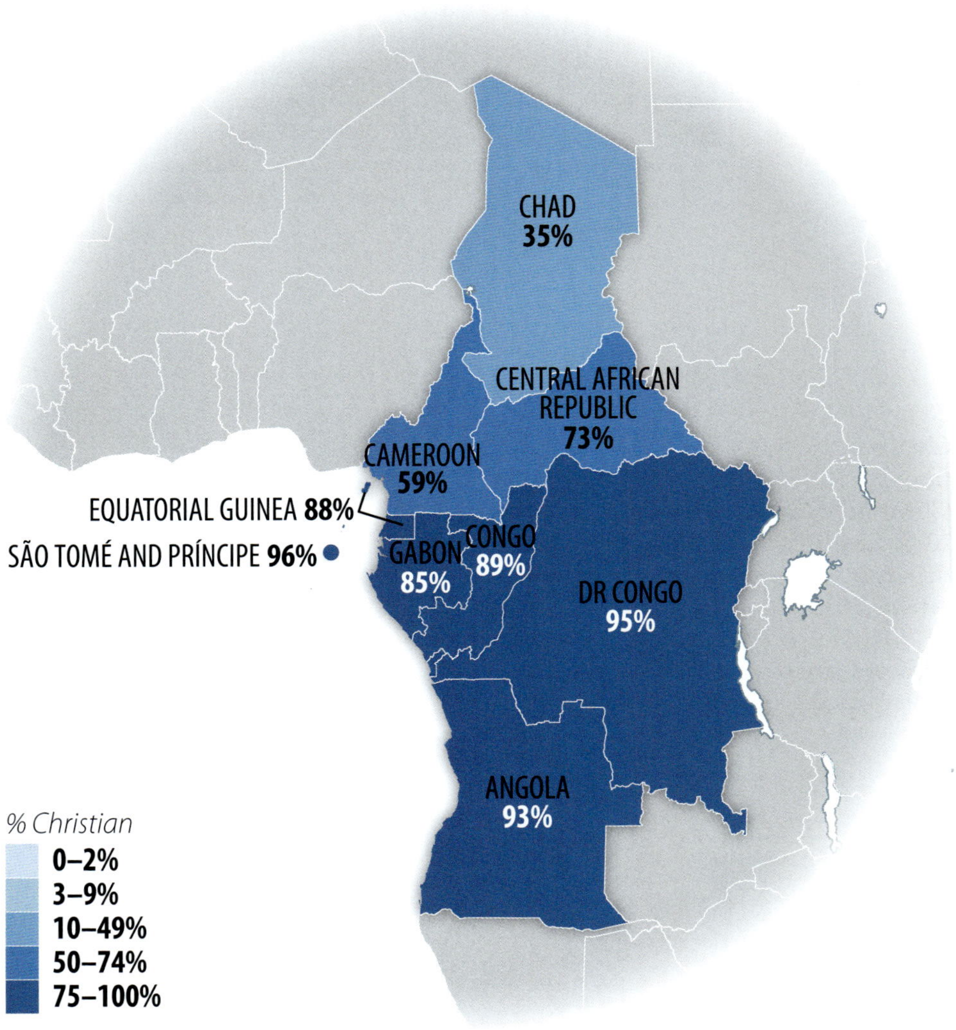


Middle Africa is the most Christian region on the continent: 82.5% of the population, or more than 125 million adherents. Catholicism is the largest tradition (56.2% of all Christians), with longstanding Catholic involvement starting with missionaries and colonisers in the fifteenth century in Angola and the Democratic Republic of the Congo (DRC). Despite being more than 95% Christian, the DRC is one of the most violent nations in Africa. Both Catholic and Protestant Christians, especially in the east, have faced extreme persecution—including rape and murder—in recent years by rebel groups. Many refugees have fled to Burundi, Rwanda and Uganda, and at least 2.7 million are internally displaced within the country.

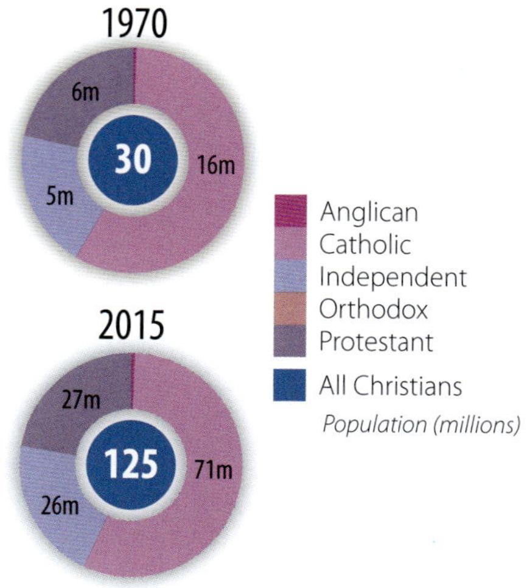


*Major Christian Traditions, 1970 and 2015*

Catholicism remains the largest Christian tradition in Middle Africa, growing from 16 million to 71 million between 1970 and 2015. Independents and Protestants have also experienced growth, in particular Kimbanguists in the DRC.

*Christians, 1970–2015*

Christianity in Middle Africa grew from 73.2% of the population in 1970 (30 million) to 82.5% (125 million) in 2015. The fastest Christian growth in the region was Chad, which grew at a rate of 4.0% per year between 1970 and 2015. Chad is now home to nearly 5 million Christians, although they only represent 35% of the population.

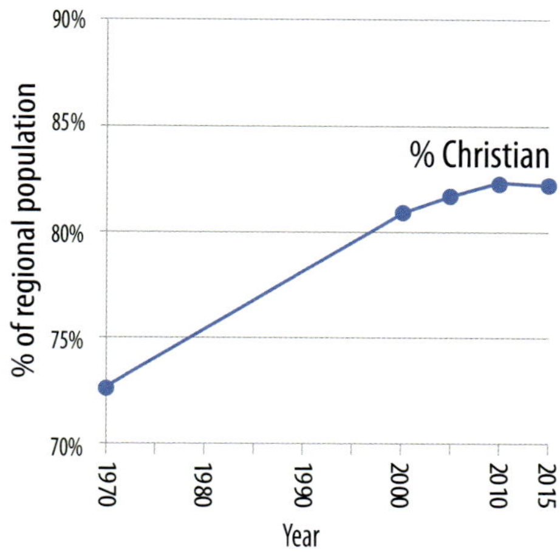


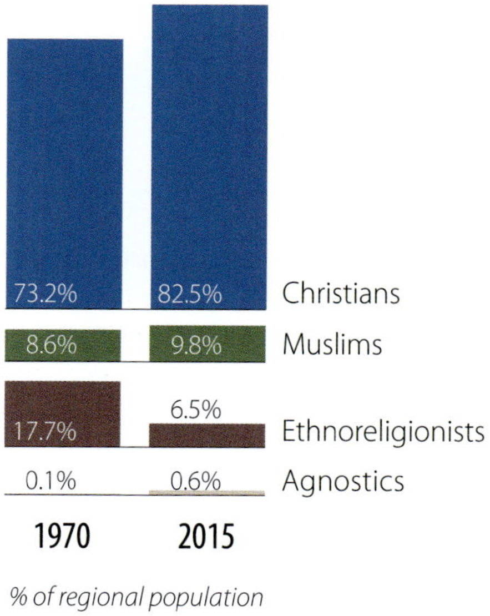


*Religious Affiliation, 1970 and 2015*

Ethnoreligionists' share of the region's population is continuing to decline as more people convert to Christianity. By 2050 it is likely that the region will be less than 3% ethnoreligionist, down from nearly 18% in 1970. Christianity and Islam had average growth rates that were similar (between 3.2% and 3.3%) over the period 1970–2015 and are predicted to continue (averaging between 2.6 and 2.7% per year) over the period 2015–50.

## Christianity in Southern Africa, 1970–2015

*Christians by Country, 2015*

*52 Million Christians, 82.4% of Population*

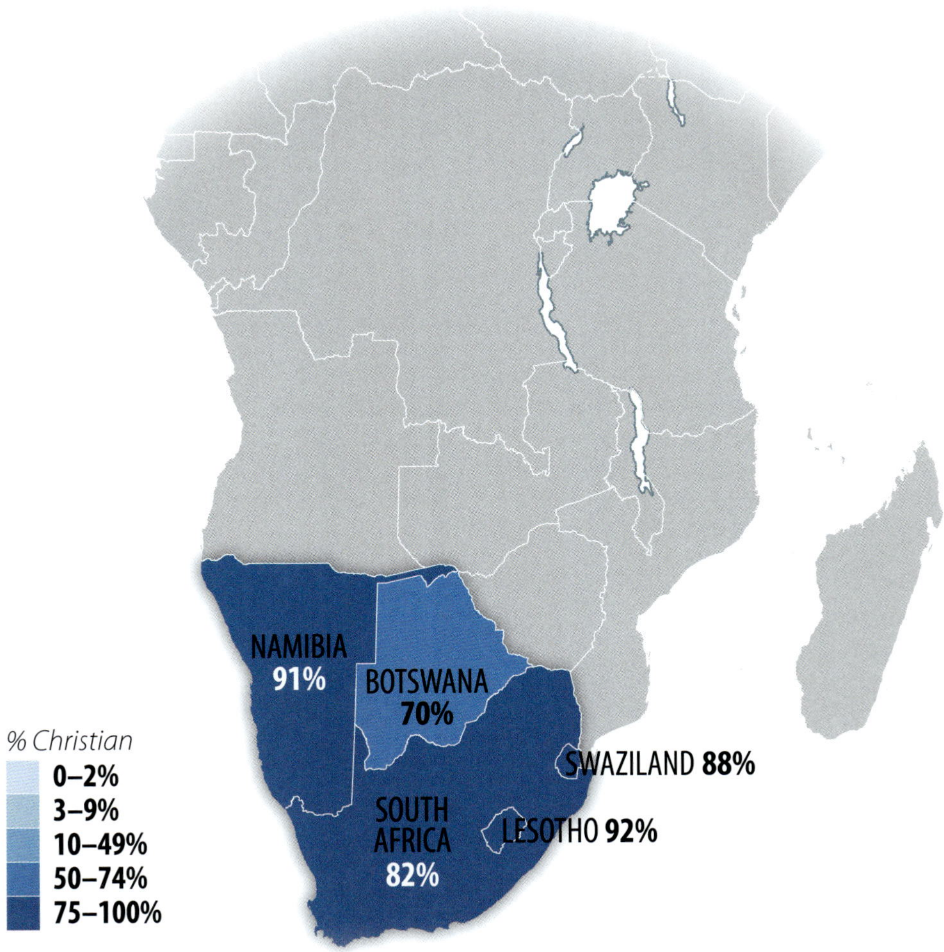


Christianity in Southern Africa grew from 75.8% of the population in 1970 (19 million) to 82.4% (52 million) in 2015, with anticipated growth into the future (84.5% in 2050). The religion has been growing at almost the same rate as the general population (2.2% per year versus 2.0%), and all five of the countries in the region are at least 70% Christian. There is much less inter-religious diversity in the region (only 7.9% ethnoreligionist) as well as intra-religious diversity. Independents make up more than 47% of all Christians there, and almost 25% are Protestant. Southern Africa has fewer Catholics than any other region in Sub-Saharan Africa; the Anglican share of the population is also low. Nearly 56% of all Christians in the region are Pentecostal or Charismatic.

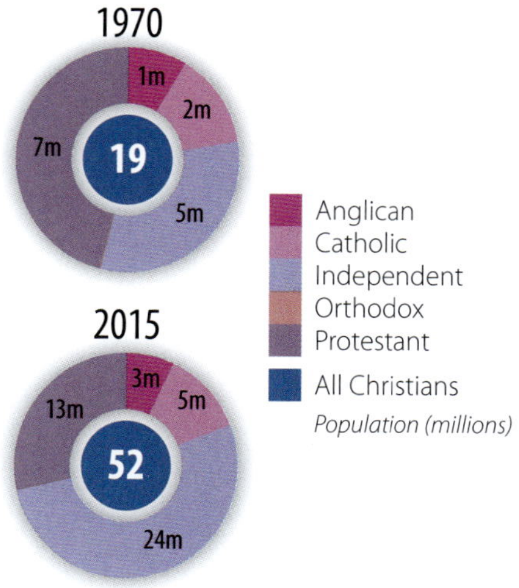


*Major Christian Traditions, 1970 and 2015*
The largest share of Christians in Southern Africa are Independents and many are members of Zion churches, Assemblies of God congregations or other Holiness–Pentecostal denominations. The percentages of Protestants, Anglicans and Orthodox have declined since 1970.

*Christians, 1970–2015*
Southern Africa was the most Christian region (75.8%) in Sub-Saharan Africa in 1970. Christianity has continued to gain in proportional share of the population, although Middle Africa was the most Christian region in 2015. Looking toward 2050, Christian growth is likely to continue but could plateau as the pool of potential converts diminishes.

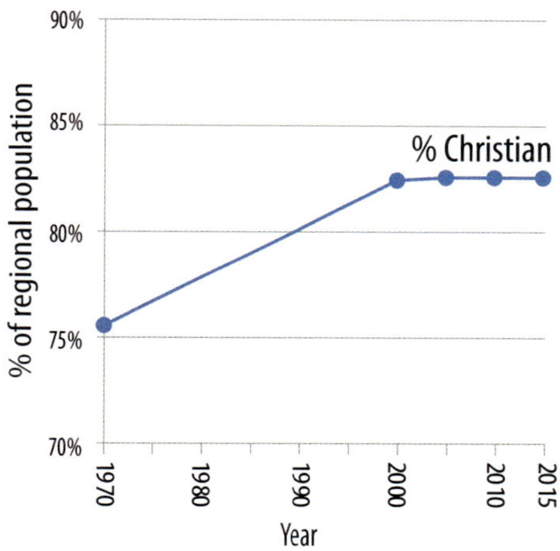


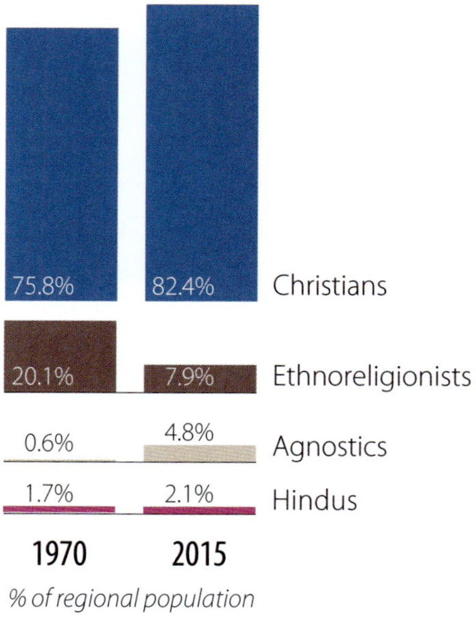


*Religious Affiliation, 1970 and 2015*
Southern Africa has the highest percentage of both agnostics and atheists in Sub-Saharan Africa. Together they comprise 5.0% of the population. There is also a sizeable Hindu population due to the Indian presence in South Africa. Smaller populations of other religions also exist, including Jews, Sikhs and New Religionists.

## Christianity in Western Africa, 1970–2015

*Christians by Country, 2015*

*128 Million Christians, 36.1% of Population*

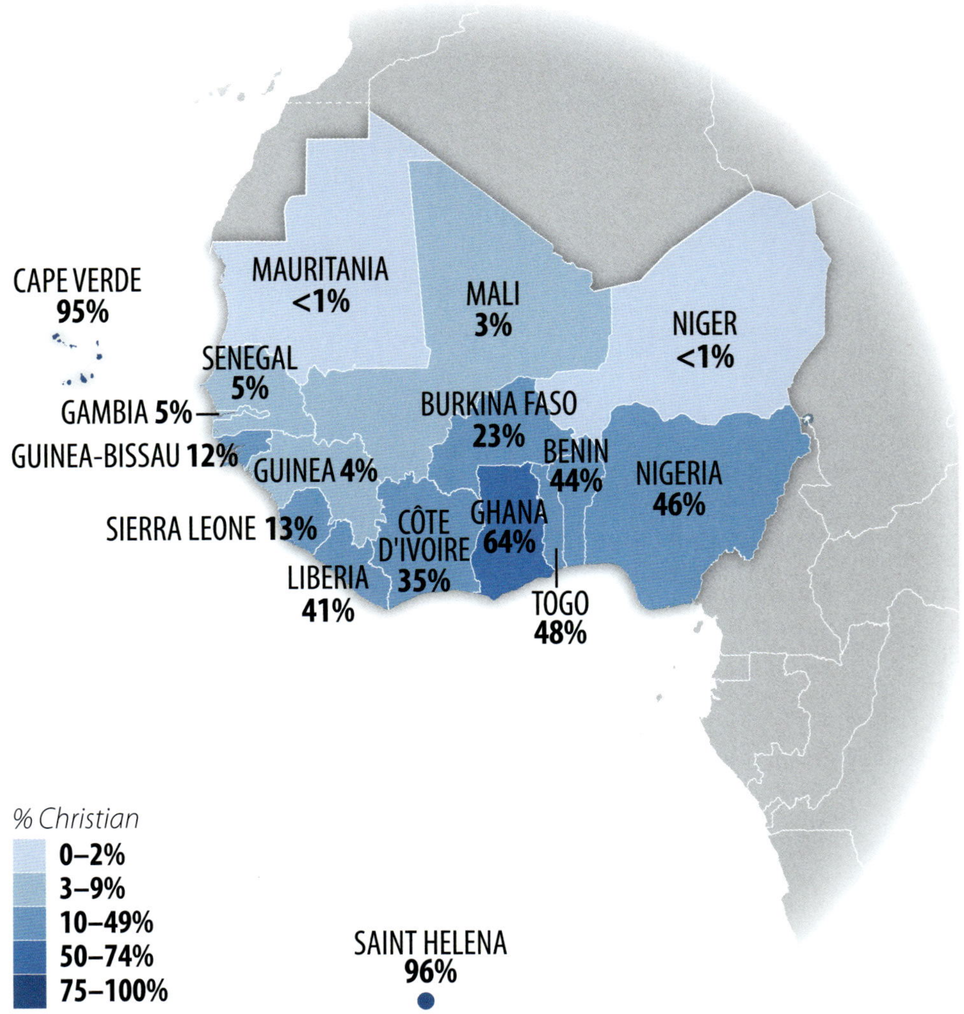


Western Africa is the least Christian region of Sub-Saharan Africa, only 36.1% Christian (128 million) in 2015 (although up from 28.4%, 30 million, in 1970). Most Western Africans are Muslims (183 million) and many countries have extremely small Christian proportions, such as Mauritania (<1%), Mali (3%) and Niger (<1%). Having positive Christian–Muslim relations is absolutely critical in Western Africa since these two religions exist intimately side by side. This proximity has caused violence in many cases, such as in Nigeria, where extremist groups have targeted Christian churches and kidnapped young girls from Christian families. Nigeria is nearly evenly split between Muslims in the north and Christians in the south, making it a particularly important place in terms of inter-religious relations.

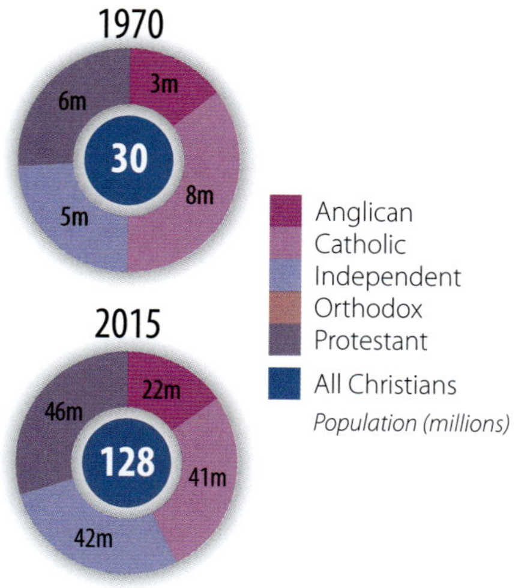


*Major Christian Traditions, 1970 and 2015*
Western Africa has a more even distribution of Catholics, Independents and Protestants than other regions in Africa. Each of these traditions represents 11–13% of the total population. Independents made great gains between 1970 and 2015, now representing a third of all Christians. Nearly 60% of all Christians are Pentecostal or Charismatic, spanning all major traditions.

*Christians, 1970–2015*
Growth of Christianity in the region has been due to high birth rates in countries like Ghana and Nigeria and Evangelical mission church-planting efforts in Muslim-majority countries. The region's Christian growth between 2015 and 2050 is likely to remain at the same rate as the general population's, averaging 2.4% per year, compared to Muslim growth of 2.7%.

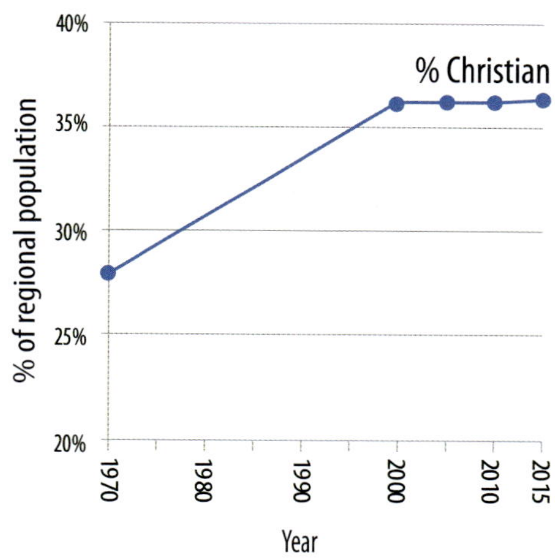


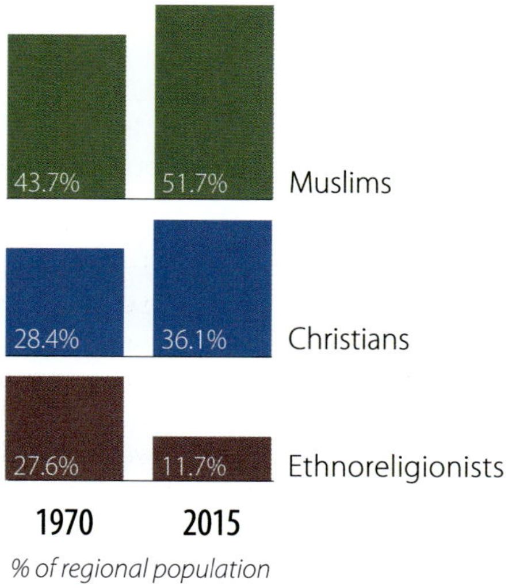


*Religious Affiliation, 1970 and 2015*
Muslims are the majority in Western Africa (51.7%), followed by Christians (36.1%) and then ethnoreligionists (11.7%). Between 1970 and 2015 Christianity grew at a faster rate than Islam (because of conversion), but looking toward 2050 it is likely that Islam will grow faster because of higher birth rates.

## Future of Christianity in Sub-Saharan Africa, 2015–2050

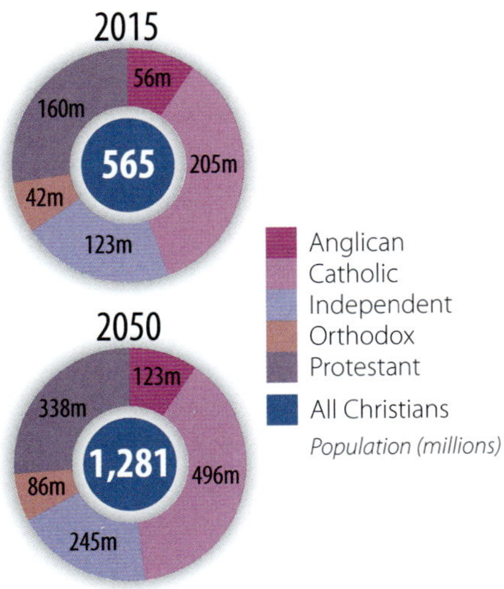


*Major Christian Traditions, 2015 and 2050*

Looking toward 2050, it is anticipated that the proportions of major Christian traditions in Sub-Saharan Africa will largely remain the same. Catholics are expected to grow the fastest over the 35-year period, at an annual rate of 2.6%. Independents are expected to grow the slowest, at 2.0% per year.

*Christians, 2015–2050*

Christianity is expected to increase slightly in Sub-Saharan Africa between 2015 and 2050, from 59% (565 million) to 60% (1.3 billion). There is little regional variation in this trend, although Eastern and Middle Africa are expected to grow slightly faster. In 2050, Middle Africa will have the highest percentage Christian (86%), followed by Southern Africa (84%).

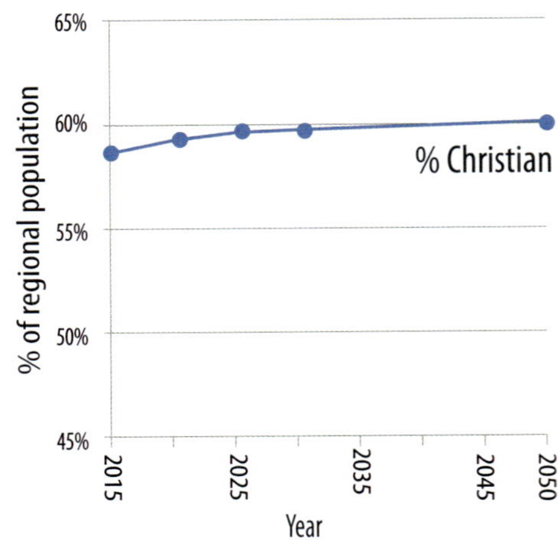


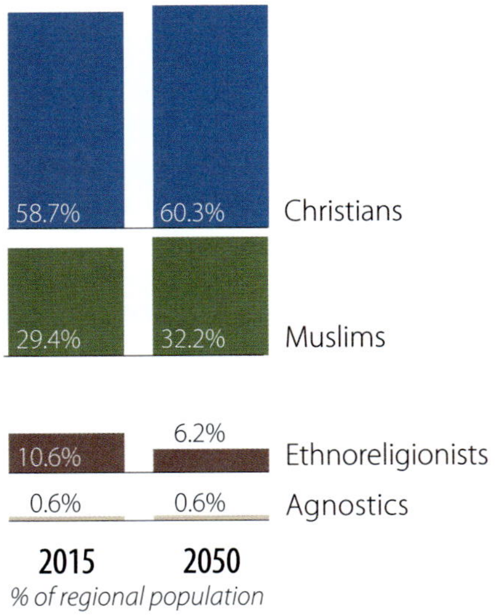


*Religious Affiliation, 2015 and 2050*

In 2050, Christianity and Islam will have slightly larger proportions of Sub-Saharan Africa's population, largely due to continued conversions from ethnoreligions. Ethnoreligionists are expected to decline from 10.6% of the population in 2015 to 6.2% in 2050. Christianity is likely to remain the largest religion in Sub-Saharan Africa in 2050, with 60.3% of the population.

# Christianity in Sub-Saharan Africa

## J. Kwabena Asamoah-Gyadu

Christianity has assumed a central role in African life and thought, and the essays in this volume speak to various aspect of that development. (In addition to the resources mentioned in this introductory essay and those that make up the volume, *African Christianity Rising,* a documentary film on the history on Christianity on the continent produced by Jim Ault and available on DVD, is also an invaluable resource for understanding the developments discussed here.) This introduction does not necessarily discuss or summarise the contents of the individual essays that follow because they speak for themselves. Instead, it attempts to provide in broad strokes insights into some of the non-quantitative indices that serve to illustrate the importance of Africa as a geographical centre of world Christianity. We begin from the Edinburgh 1910 World Missionary Conference and the early Western missionary evangelisation of Africa, moving through early attempts at African initiatives in Christianity to the rise of contemporary Pentecostalism. At each stage this introduction also draws attention to conferences and writings on Christianity in Africa as evidence of the growing importance, significance and impact of the faith through the twentieth century. The essay also pays attention to some of the new issues in ecclesiology, such as the debates over gay/lesbian ordination and the contentious matter of the prosperity gospel, and their implications for understanding the growth of Christianity in Africa. In doing this, the introduction spotlights Africans as leading some of the faith's most important innovations, on the continent and beyond, without taking the rich mission history in Africa's Christian heritage for granted.

The sheer numbers of its professing Christians today represent one important reason for taking Africa seriously. Even the lands of the former missionaries now play host to different kinds of non-Western immigrant Christian communities, many of them formed by Africans operating in their midst. Historically, it has been impossible to ignore Christianity in the making and development of the African continent into the modern nation-states we have today. Virtually all of Sub-Saharan Africa's post-colonial political leaders were educated and trained through Christian mission schools and, following the military dictatorship regimes of the 1970s and 1980s, the historic mission denominations of Africa in particular played key roles in the transitions to democratic systems of government. The recent example of South Sudan is a classic case. Whether we talk of development in terms of education, political democratisation, health systems or other forms of social development, therefore, the influence of the church has loomed large in African public life. Literacy in colonial languages for conducting business in the modern world and the reduction of vernaculars into writing are also in Africa traceable to the presence of Christianity, although they are hardly bereft of indigenous collaboration.

Fifteenth-century Sub-Saharan Africa had already encountered Christianity in various locations through the work of Portuguese Roman Catholic merchants and the chaplains who accompanied them. In places where the slave trade took hold, every fort or castle had a chapel, and so indigenous people, in spite of the negative witness and effects of trade in human beings, knew that white slave masters prayed to a Supreme Being who was supposed to be loving and caring.

It is important, however, to establish from the outset that Christianity has had a much longer history on the continent than in the regions of Europe and North America that later became known as the traditional heartlands of the faith. The New Testament account of Pentecost lists Libya and Egypt as locations from which people had assembled in Jerusalem when the Holy Spirit fell, leading to the formation of the church. When persecution broke out a little later, Philip found himself in the Samaritan regions under the compulsion of the Holy Spirit, and there he ministered to and baptised an Ethiopian eunuch of important political standing. In the early post-biblical history of Christianity in Africa, a number of important church fathers, including Tertullian, Cyprian and Augustine, were of African descent. Because of these historical links between the church in North Africa and that of the ancient world, Christianity in Africa can by no means be treated as merely a colonial legacy. Important as these ancient and early histories may be, that which engages our attention here is the development and growth of Christianity in Africa from the closing decades of the twentieth century.

## Indigenous Agency and Christian Growth

Our interest is in indigenous agency and the religious impact of Christian religious innovation in Africa. This is because although nineteenth-century European missions obviously played their part in the spread of the faith, modern African Christianity has been sustained and developed primarily as a result of African ingenuities. The individual mission histories of Christianity across the continent reveal that the church has spread principally through lay activities, with civil servants, settler farmers and itinerant traders – many without formal education – establishing preaching posts and communities of worship wherever they have been. When their message has taken root, they have either requested trained support from mission stations in urban towns or, in some cases, called for missionary support. One of the biggest churches in Africa today, the Church of Pentecost – a Classical Pentecostal denomination with branches in virtually every African country – has its roots in the relationship between Peter Anim of the Gold Coast (Ghana since 1957) and the British Pentecostal missionary James McKeown. This goes back to the late 1920s, when Anim invited the British Apostolic Church to send a missionary to help with a small prayer fellowship he had started. The British church sent McKeown and the collaboration resulted in the formation of at least three apostolic churches, with the Church of Pentecost as the largest. Given such developments, the future of world Christianity, in terms of growth, seems likely to belong to the non-Western regions of the world.

This development is a surprising element in world Christianity, because virtually no one saw it coming. For many years Sub-Saharan Africa was the recipient of Western missionaries, to the point that the word 'mission' became synonymous with Christians from the global North heading southward, with a good proportion tasked with the Christianisation (and, by implication, civilisation) of the then 'dark' continent. The efforts of the Church Missionary (now Mission) Society, together with those of mission agencies from Bremen, Basel, London, Hamburg and Rome, are fairly well known and documented, and there is no need for them to be discussed here. Today, a number of modern Western interpreters of world Christianity, including the late David B. Barrett, Richard Gray, Philip Jenkins and Wesley Granberg-Michaelson, join their African compatriots in speaking of Africa as a major Christian heartland. Even many countries with large Muslim populations, such as Senegal, the Gambia, Nigeria and Sudan and South Sudan, have a noticeable Christian presence. On the documentation process from the African side, but not in any particular order, we can mention the following: Lamin Sanneh, Ogbu U. Kalu, Jesse N. K. Mugambi, Mercy A. Oduyoye, Emmanuel Bolaji Idowu, John S. Mbiti, Jean-Marc Éla, Christian G. Baëta, Kwesi A. Dickson, John S. Pobee and Kwame Bediako. They are among those who have devoted much of their writings to the interpretation of Africa's emergence as a leading player in world Christianity. In the closing decades of the twentieth century, when the continent had clearly become a major centre of Christian activities, these voices, along with many others, drew attention to the roles that Africans, as agents of Christian religious adaptations, have played; indeed, Africans have been of greater importance in the spread of the faith than missionaries from the West, whose roles as historical transmitters were often exaggerated in the literature.

## Christianity as Africa's Religion

The sheer numbers of publications in the last half-century dealing with developments within contemporary African Christianity collectively testify to the importance of Africa in world Christianity. Four of these and how they sought to capture and articulate developments within twentieth-century Christianity in Africa set the tone for what followed. These seminal works are: *Christianity in Tropical Africa* (C. G. Baëta, ed.; Oxford University Press, 1968), *Christianity in Independent Africa* (Edward Fasholé-Luke et al., eds; Rex Collings, 1978), *African Theology En Route* (Kofi Appiah-Kubi and Sergio Torres, eds; Orbis Books 1979) and *African Christianity: An African Story* (Ogbu Kalu, ed.; Africa World Press, 2007). Three important points should be noted about these publications: firstly, the essays were mainly published papers from conferences on African Christianity; secondly, they spanned a period of almost half a century; and thirdly, all these publications brought together carefully edited essays by both Western and African scholars. The texts are indicative of the awareness that Christianity in Africa had started developing as a non-Western religion at the time. In the time span in which these books were published, a number of publications from scholars on both sides of the Atlantic also emerged. Some of these not only reflected on Christianity as a Western missionary enterprise but also challenged the inability of missionaries to promote a Christianity that took African cultural values seriously. One of the consequences of Western Christian hegemonic tendencies in Africa was the exclusion of South Africa from conferences deliberating on African Christianity, because of apartheid.

The four publications listed above amount to a historical collection that points to the growing importance of Christianity on the continent. Virtually all of them refer to the settlement of freed slaves in Sierra Leone at the end of the eighteenth century and the work of Samuel Ajayi Crowther of the Niger Mission as significant developments in the history of African Christian mission. What the essays in the present volume do is demonstrate that in spite of the strong presence of Islam and a multiplicity of non-Christian new religious movements, Christianity remains an influential faith in twenty-first-century Africa. What gives us the African Christianity brand is that – whether they belong to historical Western mission denominations or one of the multitudes of African Initiated Churches, including the Pentecostal/Charismatic traditions – ordinary Christians have, since the late nineteenth century, been fashioning expressions of faith that can appropriately be called post-Western and post-Enlightenment. So, in many ways, what we are witnessing is the pilgrimage of Christianity as it weaves its path out of the dominance of modern Western culture and beyond the framework of the modern Enlightenment, with its anti-supernatural worldviews, which threatens to edge God out of His own creation.

The overall tenor of the essays in this Sub-Saharan Africa volume of the Edinburgh Companions to Global Christianity is that ordinary African Christians continue to seek to demonstrate that, as Christianity becomes a non-Western religion, it goes through religious metamorphoses of immersion in the prevailing cultures of the societies in which it finds itself. This important point was completely lost on the delegates at the Edinburgh 1910 World Missionary Conference, a landmark in world Christianity to which we now turn.

## Edinburgh 1910 and Africa

The Edinburgh 1910 World Missionary Conference, which shut out African voices as far as indigenous Christian agency was concerned, was a turning point in the history of world Christianity. However, by the time of that gathering, the developments that were to lead to Africa becoming a major Christian heartland had already started. Ethiopianist and nationalist churches had started in Western and Southern Africa, and independent itinerant prophetic figures were at work in Liberia, Ghana, Côte d'Ivoire, Kenya, Uganda, the Belgian Congo and virtually all of Southern Africa. The absence of African representation at the Edinburgh 1910 Conference did not mean that Africa was not discussed. There were missionaries at the Conference who were supposed to represent the continent. It is the exclusion of Africans that has made the current growth in Christian presence even more surprising. The churches in Africa were deemed insufficiently advanced to merit their own representatives. This was not simply because African churches were young in years, but also because their members were thought to be starting from much further back in the process of human development than were Christian converts from Asia. The Western European construction of Africa as a dark and backward continent affected many things, including thoughts on mission. At the time when the Edinburgh 1910 Conference was in session, however, African Christians had already taken charge of their own spiritual destiny through religious innovation.

This is significant because the fear at the Edinburgh 1910 Conference was that Africa was going to develop into a 'Muhammadan' continent. To some extent this fear was not unfounded. One of the prime motivations for Evangelical revivalism in Ethiopia, for example, was to halt the spread of Islam in the region. A number of more recent Islamic initiatives across Africa – such as the use of electronic media for disseminating Qur'anic teachings, the establishment of Islamic international schools and universities, and the conscious efforts at political participation – are indirect responses to and contestations of the presence of Christianity within the public sphere. Even the heightened activities of some forms of militant and extremist Islam could in some senses be construed and explained as a response to the overwhelming presence of Christianity within the public sphere.

In the imagination of the developed world, Africa remains a tragedy, a continent still reeling from the effects of slavery and colonialism while now locked up in an economic quagmire that is evident in endemic poverty, systemic corruption, squalor, depressing medical infrastructure and economic deprivation. In the midst of this gloomy socio-economic outlook is one area in which the continent has within the last century developed as a shining example: the growth and influence of Christianity as a non-Western religion. The schools and institutes of world Christianity that have emerged across the Western world usually have a strong orientation towards the study of Christianity in Africa. Africans staff many of their professorial chairs. Much of this success has come through the Christian religious innovations that led to the rise of the independent church movement just around the time of the Edinburgh 1910 Conference.

## Evangelisation, Formal Education and Christianity

The provision of formal education was the principal means by which Western missions undertook the task of evangelisation. Evangelisation through formal education helped to open up the continent of Africa to modern development and participation in the processes of globalisation. From the middle of the nineteenth century, West African Christianity, for example, had become synonymous with English culture because the new African elite were virtually all people who had been 'civilised' by passing through the portals of the church. The key African names included Samuel Lewis, Samuel Ajayi Crowther, Samuel Johnson, Thomas Babington Macaulay, James Johnson, Nathaniel King and James Africanus Beale Horton. Here we find English nomenclature, English language, English manners and modes of dress adopted in Africa rather than imposed. An indigenous clergy was soon to develop with the ordination of Crowther, a former Yoruba slave boy, of the Church Missionary Society, as the first African bishop of the Anglican Church. The numbers increased in the next four decades, with several receiving training at Fourah Bay College in Sierra Leone. Others had the opportunity of training in Britain. The early political leadership of post-independence Africa, to cite but one critical example, was made up almost entirely of people who passed through Christian mission schools: Kwame Nkrumah of Ghana, Félix Houphouët-Boigny of Côte d'Ivoire, Jomo Kenyatta of Kenya and Kenneth Kaunda of Zambia are notable examples. Houphouët-Boigny expressed eternal gratitude to the Catholic Church by putting up the world's largest Catholic basilica – the Basilica of Our Lady of Peace – in Yamoussoukro, his home town.

Western Christian missionaries might have provided the resources and impetus for the Christian evangelisation of Africa, but the spreading of the message outside the mission stations was always the work of indigenous lay people. In Sub-Saharan African countries like Ghana, Nigeria, Malawi, Botswana and Kenya, for example, catechist training was an integral part of the teacher training curriculum. Lusophone African countries like Mozambique had the same experience. The idea was that since schools had been established in most rural communities, teachers serving these institutions needed to be trained so that they could double as church catechists and caretakers. Public schools – primary, middle and secondary – thus became the main source of members for the churches. Children attending a particular mission school grew up with a set denominational identity, as Catholic, Presbyterian, Lutheran or Anglican. Until the middle of the twentieth century, when private schools started in several Sub-Saharan African countries, it was impossible to find any civil or public servant without some connection to a historic mission denomination through education. The downside was that there was little emphasis on Christian conversion in the conservative Evangelical sense. The rise of non-denominational educational institutions has therefore meant that denominational loyalties are being gradually eroded, and although by no means comparable to the situation in Europe, historic mission denominations can no longer count on their schools as ready sources of automatic church membership. The transformation of mission schools into government-sponsored institutions means that church control over them has waned. Unless they make a vigorous attempt at direct evangelisation, the historic mission denominations might not be able to sustain the numbers that made them a force in post-colonial African public life.

## Ethiopia and Ethiopianist/nationalist churches

The story of Christian innovation in Africa following the work of early-nineteenth-century Western missionaries has often been told from the viewpoint of the African Independent Church movement. Ethiopia, a country that was never colonised, took the lead in becoming an icon of African religious innovation. The early result of the attempts to 'Africanise' Christianity in terms of leadership was the rise of the Ethiopianist or nationalist churches as they were called in South Africa and Western Africa respectively. Their emergence was triggered by questions of ecclesiastical control, often prompted by poor race relations between missionaries and African clergy. This was the first African response to European missionary work. The point at issue in the rise of Christian Ethiopianism in Africa was that, after a century of missionary work on the continent, Africa's Christian leaders began decrying the fact that indigenous peoples bore the brunt of the Christian mission enterprise but they remained nameless, as unsung heroes, in a missionary historiography that placed the missionary at the centre of the story. In Nigeria, a certain David Vincent Brown seceded from the mission-related Baptist Church to start the Native Baptist Church in 1888. To give some bite to his African Christian affirmative action, Brown even changed his name, dropping the colonial Christian tag and becoming known simply as Mojola Agbebi. In the then Gold Coast (Ghana), highly educated Methodist ministers Samuel Solomon and Mark Hayford became leaders in the nationalist church movement. Samuel Solomon, for instance, followed Agbebi in changing his name to a local one, Attoh Ahumah. The desire to 'Africanise' Christianity thus started with Christian elites, originating from the continent, who detested the European religious hegemony in Africa. Thus, when in 1892 Mangena Mokone, the Wesleyan minister in Johannesburg, resigned in opposition to racial segregation to establish a new 'Ethiopian Church', it became part of something very significant that had already started happening in African church life.

The Ethiopianist movement was biggest in South Africa because of its racial policies. Throughout the continent, the Ethiopianist/nationalist churches offered a Christian religious dimension to the political movements that were agitating for independence. It is the ecclesial statement made by the establishment and presence of the new churches that is important for our purposes here. The Ethiopianists were ahead of their time in their perception of Christianity as a non-Western religion and their desire to fashion an authentic African response to the good news of the gospel of Jesus Christ. A number of the Ethiopianist/nationalist churches disseminated their ideas through church newspapers. It is the agitation for the abrogation of the colonial project that gave rise to these Ethiopianist/nationalist Christian religious movements in Africa towards the end of the nineteenth century. Africa's Christian elite, seeking religious independence, accepted an Ethiopian identity first because of the statement of the Psalmist, 'Ethiopia shall stretch out her hands to God' (Psalm 68: 31). Added to the biblical note was the fact that Ethiopia, on account of its resistance to colonisation by Italy at the end of the nineteenth century, had become a symbol of African liberation. Ethiopia, then, gave to Africans a natural sense of cultural, political and ecclesial identity.

Ethiopia is significant in the history of Christianity in Africa in other respects. The place of the Orthodox Church as a state institution means Evangelical movements, including their Pentecostal/Charismatic variants, have often been viewed as fringe phenomena. Yet Evangelicalism is very significant in Ethiopian Christianity today. Evangelical Christians, said to constitute less than 1% of the Ethiopian population in the early 1960s, now number in the millions. Ethiopia offers a different scenario when it comes to Christian religious innovation. In other African countries, new religious movements emerged as an encounter between Christianity and primal religions, but in Ethiopia the encounter was between the Orthodox tradition and European Protestant missions. Today, several centuries later, the Evangelical movement in Ethiopia has come to the fore by contesting the ground held by an Orthodox Church that has enjoyed state patronage for the greater part of its history. The result is that independent Christianity in Ethiopia continues to blossom in the midst of persecution from the Orthodox Church as a state institution.

Protestant missionaries introduced Evangelical Christianity to Ethiopia from the West, but its growth and expansion resulted mainly from indigenous efforts. This growth is linked to the rise of a radical Pentecostal movement in the 1960s. By the early years of the twentieth century, a new Christian movement with a strong Evangelical orientation had already emerged within the Orthodox tradition. The Ethiopian Evangelical Mekane Yesu Church stressed personal salvation in Jesus Christ and openly questioned traditional church practices such as the Mass for the dead, which in the Orthodox Church was believed to possess the power of redeeming souls from *seol*, the Amharic equivalent of purgatory. It questioned the theological validity of the intercessory role of Mary, and although saints were honoured, the Mekane Yesu Church did not share the theological position that saints could be invoked to act on behalf of believers. The growth of Pentecostalism as a largely independent initiative of young educated Ethiopian Christians has been an important factor in the expansion of Evangelicalism in Ethiopia.

If the rise of Ethiopianist/nationalist churches was the first response to Western Christian hegemonies in Sub-Saharan Africa, the second was found in the rise of indigenous independent church movements that became known in the academic literature simply as African Independent/Initiated/Instituted Churches.

## African Independent/Initiated/Instituted Churches

Coming on the heels of the historic mission denominations and the Ethiopianist/nationalist churches, the African Independent Churches (AICs) started emerging in the second decade of the twentieth century. By the 1930s, the East African Revival had already broken out in Kenya, Rwanda and neighbouring regions and the Independent church movement had become symbolic representatives of what it meant to be an African church, with possible lessons for world Christianity. Again, to use publications on religious history and phenomena as a barometer of importance, some of the most important works on the Independent church movement came from Europeans who were amazed at the level and impact of

African-initiated Christianity on the continent. The list includes Harold W. Turner's *History of an African Independent Church: The Church of the Lord Aladura* (two volumes, Clarendon Press, 1967), David B. Barrett's *Schism and Renewal in Africa: An Analysis of Six Thousand Contemporary Religious Movements* (Oxford University Press, 1968), Bengt Sundkler's *Bantu Prophets in South Africa* (Oxford University Press, 1948, 1961), John Peel's *Aladura: A New Religious Movement Among the Yoruba* (Oxford University Press, 1968), Marie-Louise Martin's *Simon Kimbangu: An African Prophet and His Church* (Blackwell, 1975) and Sheila S. Walker's *The Religious Revolution in the Ivory Coast: Prophet Harris and the Harrist Church* (University of North Carolina Press, 1983). David Shank's 1994 book *Prophet Harris: The 'Black Elijah' of West Africa* (published by E. J. Brill) includes much informative data not available to previous writers on this iconic Charismatic prophet.

These historical and theological works focused on their subjects' ingenuity as religious reformers on the continent and provided clear evidence that Christianity in Africa had, through the AICs, become a genuinely African experience. Furthermore, the AICs had provided the 'raw materials' out of which the discipline of African theology developed. This movement was especially significant in South Africa, where European forms of the faith had excluded Africans from fellowship on account of the various apartheid regimes. Academic discussions on theological incarnation, contextualisation, inculturation and oral/grassroots theology used the ministry of the Independent church movement as a practical example of what Africans considered important in the Christian experience. In Southern Africa the churches associated with that movement were known collectively as Zionist churches and in Eastern African countries like Kenya as Roho (Holy Spirit) churches. In Ghana the AICs referred to their movement as Spiritual churches and in Nigeria as the *Aladura* (people of prayer). The single most important factor defining these new religious movements was the integration of Charismatic experiences – especially healing, prophecy and ecstatic dances – into Christian worship. These churches have been so important to the transformation of the religious landscape of Sub-Saharan Africa that they remain some of the best-studied movements in the Christian history of the continent.

In the rest of Sub-Saharan Africa, the origins of the AICs lay in the work of African itinerant prophets – William Wadé Harris of Liberia, Garrick Sokari Braide of Nigeria, Simon Kimbangu of the Congo and Isaiah Shembe of South Africa. The impact of these charismatic prophets on Christianity in Sub-Saharan Africa has been phenomenal. Laying claim to different crisis-related conversions and Holy Spirit-inspired Charismatic experiences and graces, many travelled within their countries with large followings, preaching the gospel and challenging people to abandon traditional resources of supernatural succour in favour of belief in Jesus Christ as Lord. The ministries of such itinerant prophets were deemed a threat to the existing mission churches; for example, the Catholic Church in the Belgian Congo persecuted Prophet Kimbangu until he died in prison. Healing and prophecy remained the stock in trade of the Independent churches that emerged from the work of indigenous itinerant prophets and changed the face of Christianity in Africa. In a theological sense, the AICs are critical in demonstrating the real spiritual hunger that Christianity encountered in Africa and sought to satisfy. The movement 'Charismatised' the religious landscape of Sub-Saharan Africa and tilled the soil in which contemporary Pentecostal Christianity has developed.

### Pentecostal/Charismatic Movements

There is a relationship between the rise of Ethiopianism, the emergence of the Independent church movement and contemporary African Pentecostalism. When Mensa Otabil, a Ghanaian Pentecostal, wrote *Beyond the Rivers of Ethiopia* in 1992 (Pneuma Life Publishing), he was recalibrating the ideals of an older generation for our contemporary period. In spite of any continuities between the theological emphases of the AICs and Pentecostalism, Pentecostal/Charismatic churches and movements challenged their compatriots to move away from the traditional religio-cultural symbols and idioms in which their Christianity was expressed. It was only a matter of time, however, for the Pentecostals in Africa to be seen as contemporary versions of the same old thing. The biblical emphases on speaking in tongues, prophecy, healing, visions, revelations, exorcism and the like that characterised the AICs have continuities in the spirituality of both the Classical and contemporary Pentecostal movements of indigenous origin. The major areas of contention, as far as the Christianity of the AICs was concerned, included the use of sacramentals such as holy water and anointed oils as therapeutic substances. Even these have been incorporated into contemporary Pentecostalism, with the rise of healing and deliverance ministries taking care of the shortfalls of the gospel of prosperity. If the material prosperity that must accompany the exercise of faith and the faithful payment of tithes and offerings does not occur, the popular contemporary hermeneutics goes, then it means witches and demons are holding back one's blessing and need to be taken care of in ever-developing rites of exorcism, healing and deliverance.

The characteristics of the new Pentecostals are clear: a charismatic, gifted and entrepreneurial leadership; urban-centred mega-sized congregations, an attraction for Africa's educated and upwardly mobile youth; innovative and extensive use of modern media technologies; and the preaching of a gospel of prosperity. The ministry of the prophet, which was an important hallmark of the classical Independent churches, is now also a central feature of contemporary Pentecostalism. Prophet T. B. Joshua of Nigeria is perhaps one of the most popular examples of a modern-day Pentecostal prophet. Prophesying and conducting exorcism services on television is new in African Pentecostalism. Add that to the use that the new churches make of other media resources, such as the Internet, with their professionally designed and constantly updated web pages, and the saturation of the airwaves with church services and Pentecostal gospel music, and one gets a sense of how Christianity in Africa has been transformed into a public religion. Within the public sphere, contemporary Pentecostal pastors exert their influence on Africa politics. Several politicians consult T. B. Joshua. Much attention was paid in 2010 to pictures of Goodluck Jonathan, the then President of Nigeria, kneeling in public for prayer as he received blessings from Pastor Enoch A. Adeboye. An attempt by the late President of Zambia, Frederick Chiluba, to publicly bring his Charismatic Christianity to bear on political life backfired on several fronts. Nevertheless, it is public knowledge that Africa's political leaders now count on the spiritual services of Pentecostal/Charismatic pastors in the same ways that traditional chiefs sought the help of Muslim clerics and shrine priests to shore up their power bases.

## African Christianity and the African Worldview

This volume's rich diversity of essays, exploring the histories, development, theological orientations and impact of Christianity in Africa, collectively tell an important story, describing what may conveniently be termed African Christianity. We have argued so far that this is Christianity that partly owes its culture to the Western missionary enterprise but which in many places on the continent has resulted from indigenous initiatives and primal realities. At the time of the Edinburgh 1910 Conference, the historic mission denominations had started coming under African leadership and new Christian religious innovations were occurring under the inspiration of indigenous Christian leaders. This melting pot of churches and new Christian movements means the continent now boasts a massive Christian presence, unparalleled in the history of the faith, with Africans at the heart of developments. The recognition of the historical influence of European Christianity is visible in the numbers of churches, educational institutions and medical facilities bearing the names of Christians from those parts of the world. In virtually every African country, one can encounter, in a remote village or town, mausoleums where the mortal remains of white Christians who laboured and passed on in Africa have been interred. Such burial places are still in use, as leading clergy take their places of rest alongside missionaries – for example at an old Baptist missionary cemetery on the campus of the Nigerian Baptist Theological Seminary in Ogbomosho and in several Presbyterian strongholds in Ghana.

The growth of Christianity in Africa means that it has become impossible to sustain the sharp distinctions by which Westerners defined the faith in terms of liberals, Evangelicals, Pentecostals and Charismatics. The religio-cultural world within which African churches operate is one with emphasis on the manifestations of supernatural power and the integration of Charismatic renewal into worship. This approach is, for example, changing the nature of ecclesiology as defined in the Western world, making a strict typology virtually impossible. For most people, as long as their existential queries are being answered satisfactorily, one system of worship and belief would not necessarily negate another in their experience of Christianity. Africans are notorious for accumulating in their personal worlds different streams of Christianity without regard to their types, doctrinal differences or emphases. The Western missionary influence on Christianity in Africa has by no means waned completely. The traditional Western mission denominations maintain their historical links with 'mother churches' in Europe in particular. New Independent churches and Classical Pentecostal denominations of various kinds also develop strategic fraternal ecumenical relationships with churches across the North Atlantic for whatever benefits they hope to obtain. By and large, however, Christianity in Africa remains the product of African initiatives in religious innovation and evangelisation.

Whatever its origins, the one thing that is common to the histories and trajectories of Christianity in Africa is the way in which traditional worldviews have influenced the appropriations and expressions of Christian spirituality. In other words, Christianity in Africa has been expressed primarily through African cultural values, presuppositions and idioms, making it a truly and genuinely African endeavour. The options for the pneumatic versions of the faith in Christian religious innovations, for example, has always resulted from an amalgamation of the biblical and African worlds and their sensitivities to the presence of supernatural realities behind and within the universe. In short, the African universe is one that is alive with the presence of supernatural powers, and when access to vernacular translations of the Bible indicated that this was so also in the biblical world, it was only a matter of time before African Christians were claiming encounters with the Holy Spirit and breaking free from the apron strings of mission Christianity to start new ecclesial communities that took indigenous worldviews seriously.

In the past, Roman Catholicism was considered the most foreign of the historic mission denominations in Africa. Most of its agents remained white Western fathers until early in the twentieth century. The Mass was said in Latin and liturgical accoutrements and regalia were all visibly

Roman in appearance. Today, through the writings of the late historian of African Christianity Adrian Hastings of the UK, Archbishop Emeritus Peter K. Sarpong of the Kumasi Archdiocese in Ghana, the Presbyterian scholar of Ghanaian Catholicism Pashington Obeng and Catholic scholar Laurenti Magesa of Tanzania, we have abundant documentation of the successful inculturation of Catholicism across the continent. A number of other studies produced by Catholic insiders underscore the fact that, through a systematic vernacularisation of the Catholic faith since the Second Vatican Council (1962–5), Africans have built their own brand of the worldwide Catholic faith that is recognisably Catholic and African at the same time. In *Asante Catholicism* (1996), Obeng demonstrates how Archbishop Sarpong, himself an Oxford-trained religious anthropologist, translates his anthropological ideas on the ground with African traditional songs, religious symbols, gestures, modes of worship and other paraphernalia introduced into the Catholic Mass among the Asante. During Corpus Christi processions, for example, the body of Christ is now enthroned in a chief palanquin to indicate that Christ is King of Kings.

An important constant in African Christianity is the reality of the supernatural as inseparable from everyday life. Divine healing thus remains an important category in all forms of Christianity in Africa. Thus African Catholic grottos have acquired a non-denominational character, with Christians of all traditions patronising them as places of intercession for their health and related problems. On the streets of Africa, popular Catholicism is expressed through a loose devotion to Mary, seen in her image portrayed through art in public places and in the rosary, which people carry in their cars and on their persons for spiritual protection against evil. The strong belief in the power of the supernatural also explains why prophecy, divine healing and visionary ideas that have fallen out of fashion in traditional Western Christianity still permeate the religious practices of both old and new churches in Africa. Further, the oral nature of African cultures means, for example, that indigenous Christians are able to respond rather more quickly and easily to various forms of Evangelical Christianity, which emphasise on the experiential aspects of the faith.

## Bible Translation and Religious Innovation

The emphasis in this volume on the indigenous dynamics that underlie the growth of African Christianity does not mean that European contributions have not been significant. One of these is in Bible translation. As they translated the Bible into non-European languages, Western missionaries and their African collaborators became champions of non-Western cultures, emancipating indigenous languages to literary levels and enabling people to apprehend the gospel in their mother tongues. The translated Scriptures helped African Christians to appreciate the affinities between the biblical and their own primal worldviews and inspirit new ways of viewing the gospel. This commenced a process of reflection that impacted the personal and cultural spheres of life, enabling the renewal of Christianity. Thus Andrew Walls, Lamin Sanneh and Kwame Bediako, in their influential writings on this issue, make a connection between the translation of the Bible into various vernaculars and the growth of Christianity in Africa and its translation into African Christianity. It is to the undying credit of the modern missionary enterprise from the West, and to the lasting benefit of the newer churches that have resulted, that the value of the vernacular Bible for converts was recognised quite early. There is probably no more important single explanation for the massive presence of Christianity on the African continent, it is often asserted, than the availability of the Scriptures in many different vernaculars.

### African Migrants and Christianity

Africans have also carried the gospel beyond the continent. Migrant Christians and their churches have, since the closing decades of the twentieth century, emerged as the representative face of the faith in Europe and North America. Many have referred to this development as 'reverse mission' or the church 'beyond Christendom' and there are cogent reasons for that. African Catholics, Methodists, Anglicans and Presbyterians have established versions of these denominational churches in the lands of the missionaries who first evangelised the continent. In Western Europe, for example, Ghanaian Methodist and Nigerian Anglican congregations constitute some of the largest religious communities. That some Westerners do not recognise the new African mission churches as authentically Methodist or Anglican only reinforces our earlier observation that African Christian innovation must not be limited to the formation of Independent churches. Distinctive forms of Methodism, Anglicanism and Lutheranism, qualitatively different from those initially received, have taken shape in African societies. Now African migrants in Western countries are establishing branches of these denominations, offering forms of worship that have been developed in the African context. Additionally, a number of such historic mainline denominations with white European membership are now led by African pastors. If one adds to the African presence and involvement in historic mission denominations the numbers of independent Pentecostal/Charismatic churches that have formed in Europe and North America over the last 30 years, we gain a sense of the seismic change that has occurred in the Western Christian religious landscape due to migration.

The point here is that when we talk about African Christianity today, it is important to have in mind both the growth of the church on the continent and the establishment of diaspora churches by Africans living abroad; the development of Christianity as an African religion is also seen in the lives of African Christians living abroad, who constitute much of what is described as immigrant Christianity in the Northern continents today. Not only are abandoned industrial sites, cinemas and warehouses now housing churches in Africa, but also in the various Western diasporas Africans have reclaimed and refurbished empty church buildings, restoring them to their former sacred purposes as places of worship. In many senses African Christians, through a process of religious globalisation, have helped to reshape what it means to be Christian in the modern West. To that end, there is wisdom in calls for a new understanding of migrants' churches, not as ethnic enclaves but rather as conscious attempts to re-sacralise the West through active Christian witness. This is evident in a number of ways. In British Columbia, Canada, Samuel Owusu, a Ghanaian, leads one of the largest ethnically mixed congregations, the 1,000-member Calvary Worship Centre, with members from 75 nations. In London, Pastor Matthew Ashimolowo's 12,000-member Kingsway International Christian Centre is the single largest Christian community in Western Europe, with members drawn mainly from the African immigrant community. In Eastern Europe that honour belongs to another Nigerian pastor, Sunday Adelaja, whose Embassy of the Blessed Kingdom of God for All Nations boasts a congregation of more than 25,000 members, overwhelmingly made up of white Eastern Europeans.

Thus we cannot talk about world Christianity today without reference to the African Christian presence in the modern West and East. The scholarship African migrant Christianity has attracted within the last two decades is testimony to its extensive influence on the world stage. In the rise of African migrant Christianity we have a taste of its grassroots and popular influence. As often happens in both rural and urban Africa, the majority of African migrant Christian congregations have been started by ordinary lay people seeking a more enchanted religious context in which to express their faith. The demystification of the Bible and the transformation of sacred spaces for secular and mundane purposes in the developed world leave new African immigrants traumatised. The reason for this trauma is not difficult to find. The 'fact' that Christianity is a white man's religion and it is through him that God reached out to those living on the 'dark' continent is firmly etched in the popular mind. So to travel as migrants – whether in search of work or education or simply to visit on a short-term basis – and to find that the church buildings in 'God's continent' are now brothels, old people's homes, Buddhist and Hindu temples, mosques and restaurants is a trauma that many an African Christian is not able to come to terms with. African Christians leading churches in the West today see their efforts, born out of a deep-seated sense of calling and purpose, in terms of a rescue mission to the secular industrialised world.

## Contemporary Issues in Ecclesiology

The changing face of Christianity in Africa has placed quite a number of new and challenging issues on the agenda of the church. Some of them were made 'challenges' due to an initial hostile attitude towards African traditions and cultures on the part of Western missionaries. One of these is the matter of polygyny, which has always been a fact of African cultural life. Two centuries after the encounter with Western Christianity, the church in Africa has not been able to articulate a solid theological response to this issue. Churches still exclude polygynists and their extra wives from receiving Communion. Additionally, marriages rooted in elaborate traditional systems involving whole communities and bringing two spouses and their extended families together – which were considered valid before the arrival of Western missionaries and colonial administrators – are today not considered proper unions until they have been brought under the authority of the church in Western-style weddings. Shaming (through immediate excommunication) young women who get pregnant outside marriage is quite common in African churches. In almost all the major denominations, those who have not 'blessed' their marriages through church weddings are excluded from leadership, and the church is struggling to articulate a solid biblical and theological direction on these matters.

Although it might have chosen an independent path in many ways, including the incorporation of traditional ideas and practices into Christian worship, the church in Africa has not been impervious to the influences of cultural changes in the West. A critical area in which this Western influence has been evident is the issue of homosexuality. The worldwide Anglican Communion has had a tough time working together since the Episcopal Church (USA) ordained its first openly gay bishop, Gene Robinson, in 2003. Members of the Anglican Communion in Africa have on the whole rejected any attempt to get them to endorse the practice of homosexuality as an alternative sexual lifestyle, and much less to accept practising homosexuals as priests. A critical voice in the debate has been Nigerian Archbishop Peter Akinola. The Working Committee for the Primates of the Global South has been 'appalled' that the Episcopal Church ignored the pleas of non-Western compatriots not to consecrate openly gay bishops. Archbishop Benjamin Nzimbi of the Anglican Church of Kenya said the consecration of a gay bishop had created an avenue for 'the devil to enter the church'. What has contributed to the importance of Africa in the debate are the numbers of Anglicans on the continent. The figures from Nigeria alone indicate that the UK has ceased to be the heartland of world Anglicanism.

When in 2008 the Global Anglican Futures Conference (GAFCON), an Evangelical group intended to rival the Lambeth Conference, met in Jerusalem, a majority of the bishops attending came from Africa. Today, a number of Episcopal bishops in the USA hold themselves accountable to African compatriots because they are unable to accept the ordination of practising homosexuals.

A third contemporary ecclesial concern is the preaching of a gospel of materialism, also known as the prosperity gospel, by sections of the contemporary Pentecostal movement. It has become a major issue for the church in Africa. The prosperity gospel reflects the influence of North American televangelism on African Christianity, although in the African context existential values have always remained a religious concern. The popularity of these teachings (that God rewards the faithful practice of Christianity with spiritual and material blessings) has had a snowball effect on the church in Africa. Versions of prosperity preaching can now be found in virtually all churches – both mainline Protestant and Pentecostal – leading to much anxiety among level-headed church leaders regarding how to respond to such a message. The fruits of the prosperity gospel are most evident in the lives of the pastors who preach it. This has led to a widespread concern in Africa that Christian ministry has degenerated into an institution for personal enrichment among those claiming the call of God upon their lives. In many situations, the promise of prosperity, which is supposed to be made possible by the positive confession of faith and faithful discharge of tithing obligations, has come unstuck. One of the problems of the prosperity message is that faithful Christianity is assessed primarily on the basis of success. It therefore has a very weak theology of suffering, with hardly any pastoral message for Christians living in situations of persecution.

In response, a new theology of witchcraft and demons has emerged to offset the shortfalls of the prosperity gospel. Independent prophetic ministries that specialise in diagnosing spiritual problems have arisen across Sub-Saharan Africa, and have invented new interventionist rites and rituals to deal with the fallout of the prosperity gospel. Witchcraft is, thus, still a big problem in African societies, with the churches perpetuating witch-hunting and accusations by explaining calamity and misfortunes in terms of its activities. The exorcism ministry of Emmanuel Milingo, former Archbishop of the Roman Catholic Archdiocese of Lusaka in Zambia, in the late 1970s and early 1980s served only to make the point that these phenomena were not limited to the Independent churches. The reality of the demonic in Africa today is reinforced through a burgeoning African video industry in which storylines deal overwhelmingly with the omnipresence of witchcraft as the single most important cause of personal and communal problems. The articulation of a theology of evil to respond to African beliefs in witchcraft is certainly an important contribution to world Christianity, but the obsession with interpreting every problem in terms of the workings of demons and witches has played its part in destroying important communal values. This issue, in one way or another, affects the nature of ecclesiology in the African church, as even non-Evangelical churches are now forced to take up issues concerning healing, exorcism and deliverance because of the popular nature of these ministries on the continent.

## African Christianity and Development

Developments in Africa with respect to Christian growth and expansion and the importance of the public role of the faith within the civil sphere are indicative of the critical role the continent now plays in world Christianity. The church in Africa has generally acquired and maintained a very conservative Evangelical character. The Bible is regarded as a sacred text – the word of God. We have seen how on issues of homosexuality, for example, the churches in Africa have taken what they consider a more biblical stance, one which protects a conservative understanding of marriage. Many church and even political leaders have been willing to break their historical links with Western denominations in the face of accusations that they are attempting to adulterate the teachings of the Bible for their own self-aggrandisement. This has been so because African Christians have a much greater respect for the Bible, which they are willing to accept as the authoritative word of God in a literal manner.

The supernatural element in its miraculous stories is also taken seriously and, most of the time, informs the African church's open and receptive attitude to miracles, prophecies, visions, healing and exorcism as workings of the Spirit that are good for the life of the church today. The supernatural worldview of the Bible resonates with traditional understandings of causality and how to deal with evil in particular, using the resources given by the Holy Spirit. Among Africans, the Bible has found a congenial home because people identify with the socio-economic and political realities it portrays. For the growing churches of Africa and the African diaspora, the Bible speaks an existential language that is no different from everyday experiences of poverty and debt, famine and urban crises and, in some places, political and religious persecution. Making all allowances for generalisation, then, Christians of the global South retain a strong supernatural orientation and are by and large far more interested in personal salvation than in radical politics. In many ways this has led to shortfalls in the contribution of the church to social development on a continent within which poverty and infrastructural deficits are still of great concern.

On a visit to any African city, even the casual observer can miss neither the still-in-active-use cathedrals built by Western missionaries in the early decades of the twentieth century nor the new theatre-like 'cathedroms' of the contemporary Pentecostal and prosperity-preaching Charismatic ministries. Their imposing billboards (often featuring their founders or leaders) compete with those mounted by corporate establishments like Coca-Cola and Adidas. In between the two types of worship places are those of the older AICs and the Classical Pentecostal denominations, ranging from simple shed-like structures to renovated warehouses and recognisably modest church buildings of different sizes and colours. The overall negative effects on African economies are hard to estimate, but most of the industrial properties and sites that have been closed down in Sub-Saharan Africa have now been transformed into meeting places for mega-sized Charismatic ministries. One of these, named simply the Quodesh ('the Lord's Holy Hill'), belonging to the Lighthouse Chapel International in Ghana, has a 5,000-seat cathedral and four smaller chapels on the same property that accommodate between 300 and 500 persons each. Much bigger facilities of that kind exist in Zimbabwe, South Africa, Kenya and Nigeria. Two of the most impressive belong to the Redeemed Christian Church of God, led by Enoch A. Adeboye, and the Living Faith Church Worldwide, led by David O. Oyedepo. Additionally, conservative Evangelical para-church movements like the Scripture Union are still functional in Africa's high schools and universities, helping to put on the table a 'religious buffet' that even the best of typologies and quantitative data find difficult to capture in its entirety.

The significance of the church in Africa is evident in other respects as well. Church leaders have been vociferous in arguing that projects sponsored by Western institutions are often left in the hands of foreign experts paid disproportionately high salaries and allowances but with little knowledge of the issues on the ground. In response, it is very instructive to note that when the World Bank was looking for alternative partners for the management of resources for development in Africa, religious institutions, including churches, became the obvious choice. African governments of both the military dictatorial and democratic types are known to be very corrupt. The church, although not completely absolved from blame in this direction, is seen as a more dependable partner in social and economic development. This is not simply due to moral considerations but also because the allegiance to the church of ordinary Africans tends to be much stronger than to the state.

A new phenomenon that has developed in African Christianity and which we can safely consider in the arena of development is private higher education. In addition to the efforts of the historic mission denominations in various countries, contemporary Pentecostal churches are also involved. The Central University College of the International Central Gospel Church in Ghana and the Covenant University of the Living Faith Church Worldwide in Nigeria are two of the best examples in this area.

## Conclusion

When we consider Christianity in Africa, the qualitative indices that help us to identify it are many, but perhaps at the core are the ways in which the African traditional worldview or primal imagination has remained resilient in the expressions of the faith across denominations. Vestiges remain of Western European mission influence on Christianity in Africa, but through a combination of factors, including access to the Bible in vernacular languages and indigenous initiatives in Christianity, Africans have taken the faith to different levels. Christianity today is a non-Western religion and Africa has been a key player in that development. In keeping with its pneumatic orientation, for example, healing camps in Africa function as spiritual medical centres where the sick, afflicted and physically and emotionally troubled are quarantined for extensive prayer sessions in bouts of exorcism and deliverance. All these developments must be considered in any discussion of Christianity in Africa. In other words, it is impossible to describe any form of indigenous Christianity in Africa without reference to the ways in which it has been influenced by traditional religious ideas and the independent trans- and non-denominational institutions and structures that operate within the religious environment. Even the historic mission denominations have been stirred into emulative action, and their previously rigid liturgical services have now been relaxed to accommodate informal praise and worship services with mass spontaneous extempore forms of praying introduced into Christian worship by the African Independent Churches.

There have been failures along the way, as the churches in Rwanda and Burundi in particular attempt to come to terms with the roles they played in the genocidal conflicts of recent years. Many have also pointed to the endemic corruption, unhygienic communities and political and other socio-economic quagmires in which the continent finds itself, in spite of the dynamic presence of Christianity. After all, as we have noted, it is impossible to talk about any kind of development in Africa without reference to the presence of Christianity. Much needs to be done if Christianity is to sustain its credibility as a God-given blessing to a continent with its fair share of endowments. The hope is that numerical growth and dynamism will be translated into concrete action, so that the abundance of life promised by Jesus Christ for those who come to Him may be realised in lives and communities to the glory of God and the blessing of His people.

## Bibliography

Bediako, Kwame, *Christianity in Africa: The Renewal of a Non-Western Religion* (Edinburgh: Edinburgh University Press, 1995).

Eshete, Tibebe, *The Evangelical Movement in Ethiopia: Resistance and Resilience* (Waco, TX: Baylor University Press, 2009).

Fasholé-Luke, Edward, Richard Gray, Adrian Hastings and Godwin Tasie (eds), *Christianity in Independent Africa* (Bloomington, IN: Indiana University Press, 1978).

Kalu, Ogbu U. (ed.), *African Christianity: An African Story* (Trenton, NJ, and Asmara, Eritrea: Africa World Press, 2007).

Sanneh, Lamin, *Translating the Message: The Missionary Impact on Culture*, revised and expanded edition (Maryknoll, NY: Orbis Books, 2009).

# Countries

# South Africa

## Tinyiko Maluleke

Unlike in North Africa, where Christianity arrived as early as the first century, Christianity came to Southern Africa on the back of colonialism. Such Christianity had little to do with the people subjected to colonialism, at least initially: it was settler Christianity, served by settler churches and pastors who represented imperial powers and provided spiritual services to the settlers. However, such is the nature of the Christian faith that the churches serving European settlers across Southern Africa had to answer the question of whether to confine their work to the settlers or expand it to include the colonial subjects, the Africans.

When the Dutch established a permanent station at the Cape of Good Hope in 1652, they soon brought a minister of religion, but only for themselves. It took the settler church more than 100 years to start engaging in formal missionary outreach, first among the imported slaves and thereafter among the local African populations. Christian mission was not, though, one of the aims of the Dutch who settled in the Cape. Their initial interests were commercial and economic. After all, the Cape was supposed to be only a halfway station between India and the Netherlands.

### African Religion and the Reception of Christianity

African historians, religion scholars and theologians have long taken issue not so much with the historical fact or the role of the settler church and imperial religion in the transmission of Christianity to the locals but with the presumption, often unstated, that the religious history of Africans begins with the arrival of the colonial settlers. The non-acknowledgement of the religions with which the slaves came, and those of the indigenous peoples, is often experienced as an attempt to suggest that whereas Europeans came with religion, the locals had little, if any, concept of religion. Many books on Christianity in (South) Africa contain the usual disclaimer about a lack of sources on the religions of local people at the point of contact with settler Christianity. Clearly, the religions and cultures of the locals were not of much interest to either the colonial settlers or the settler church and its officials. Indeed, indigenous peoples' supposed lack of capacity for religion was an aspect of the self-serving justifications for both slavery and colonialism. What has continued to irk interested observers is the complicit and continued neglect of these religions by scholars and researchers. In part this grievance is at the heart of the emergence of African Theology, Black Theology, Contextual Theology and Feminist Theology.

Correcting this theological and historical neglect in order to show the continuities and discontinuities between Christianity and African religions has occupied the attention of many first-generation scholars, such as John Mbiti (Kenya), Bolaji Idowu (Nigeria) and Fabien Eboussi Boulaga (Cameroon), to mention but a few. In South Africa, this scholarship is eminently represented by the work of Gabriel Setiloane on the concept of God among the Sotho-Tswana and to some extent by Desmond Tutu in his emphasis on the role of *Ubuntu*. The main aim of these scholars has been to posit a rational, rich and old account of African religiosity, philosophy and cultures. Incidentally, this was also the mission of the first generation of African creative writers, including Chinua Achebe (Nigeria), Ngugi wa Thiongo (Kenya) and Ayi Kwei Armah (Ghana). In South Africa, writers such as Sol Plaatje, author of the first full-length English novel by an African (*Mhudi*, 1930), and Es'kia Mphahlele pursued a similar agenda.

They sought to portray the disruption that occurred to African life as a result of colonialism and the introduction of Christianity and Western culture. The point about pre-existent African religions is not merely to assert African religiosity, but also to point out that both the transmission and the appropriation of Christianity would not have been possible if Africans had had little or no religion before the arrival of Christianity. Christianity owes its reception and growth in South Africa to African religion and culture. Missionaries in Africa never had to invent a new word or concept for God because the locals already had an equivalent concept in their own languages.

Clearly, the biggest casualty of the growth of Christianity has been traditional African religion. Centuries of stigmatisation, harassment and structured suppression through, among others, the systems of education, health, economics and agriculture installed by successive colonial and

*Christianity in South Africa, 1970 and 2015*

| | 1970 | | 2015 | | Average annual growth rate (%), 1970–2015 |
|---|---|---|---|---|---|
| Tradition | Population | % | Population | % | |
| Christians | 17,181,000 | 76.4% | 44,690,000 | 82.0% | 2.15% |
| *Roman Catholics* | 1,589,000 | 7.1% | 3,722,000 | 6.8% | 1.91% |
| *Orthodox* | 30,000 | 0.1% | 30,100 | 0.1% | – |
| *Independents* | 4,698,000 | 20.9% | 22,240,000 | 40.8% | 3.52% |
| *Protestants* | 6,464,000 | 28.7% | 10,464,000 | 19.2% | 1.08% |
| *Anglicans* | 1,236,000 | 5.5% | 2,850,000 | 5.2% | 1.87% |
| Pentecostals | 4,358,000 | 19.4% | 26,330,000 | 48.3% | 4.08% |
| Evangelicals | 2,898,000 | 12.9% | 5,337,000 | 9.8% | 1.37% |
| **Total population** | **22,503,000** | **100.0%** | **54,490,000** | **100.0%** | **1.98%** |

Source: Todd M. Johnson and Gina A. Zurlo (eds), *World Christian Database* (Leiden/Boston: Brill), accessed March 2016.

apartheid administrations have forced traditional African religions to operate underground – in front, behind, beneath and between Christianity and other 'established' religions.

Without taking away from the contributions of famed Christian missionaries like Robert Moffat, David Livingstone and Henri-Alexandre Junod, the truth is that Christianity took off among Africans only in the twentieth century, once African evangelists and African missionaries entered the fray. It was the likes of Nicholas Benghu, Calvin Maphophe, Ntsikana, Albert Luthuli and Tiyo Soga who helped make Christianity at home in South Africa.

Strictly speaking, it makes little sense to discuss Christianity in South Africa separately from Christianity in Southern Africa. Many of the founding missionary organisations sent missionaries to more than one country in what is now known as the SADC (Southern African Development Community) region. As a result, many mainline churches are spread across the region.

Inspired by a similar movement in the United States (led by the likes of James Cone) and the Black Consciousness Movement in South Africa, South African Black Theology radicalised the discussions. The categories of race, class and gender as well as Marxist analysis were added to conventional theological methodology. The charge here was not merely that colonial Christianity had either misunderstood or neglected African religious reality but, rather, that it was wilfully complicit in the racial, class and gender marginalisation of black peoples. One area of focus for South African Black Theology has been biblical hermeneutics. For black theologians, if the Bible were not going to be one more oppressive document, new and other ways of reading it had to be found. In this regard Black Theology has developed reading methods that include reading against the grain, gendered readings, reading behind the text, reading the silences and reading in front of the text. Some of the most vocal proponents of South African Black Theology include Bonganjalo Goba, Mokgethi Mothlabi, Takatso Mofokeng, Manas Buthelezi, Madipoane Masenya, Denise Ackerman, Christina Landman, Simon Maimela, Itumeleng Mosala and Steve Biko, as well as the author of this chapter.

### The New Mainline

Perhaps the story of the largest Christian denomination in contemporary South Africa, the Zion Christian Church (ZCC), best illustrates the point about African agency in the growth of Christianity in South Africa. Travelling the 500 km stretch of road from Johannesburg to Beitbridge at the border between South Africa and Zimbabwe is precarious at the best of times. In the days leading up to Good Friday and all through the

Easter weekend, the road is extremely congested, making travel on it, slow, stressful and dangerous. This seasonal migration, first from south to north and a few days later from north to south, is a function of several factors. It is a legacy of the colonial migratory labour system, which included the targeted conscription of young men from rural South Africa and from neighbouring countries to work in the mines of Johannesburg after the discovery of gold in 1886. Similar patterns of labour migration are still in place today. There is, however, also a religious dimension to the annual Easter weekend traffic snarl. Less than 30 km outside the town of Polokwane in the province of Limpopo, on the road that connects the town of Tzaneen to Polokwane, are the headquarters of the ZCC. According to the 2001 census, the ZCC had a membership of nearly 5 million. Its headquarters, now known as Zion City of Moria, sprawl over an unremarkable hill, originally known as Thabakgone. The new name derives from the biblical place where Abraham was tested by God through the command to sacrifice his son Isaac. Moria has become a great place of pilgrimage for ZCC members. The Easter weekend is the pinnacle of several annual pilgrimage moments in the liturgical calendar of the ZCC.

Such is the importance of these pilgrimages for ZCC members that they travel in their thousands to Moria by mini-bus, bus, train, car, bicycle and on horse, donkey or foot. Over the Easter weekend, the dominance and impact of the ZCC on the road that connects Johannesburg to Polokwane is almost total. Not only does it affect traffic flow, it also impacts the businesses by the roadside and in the towns located along or near it. The periodic influx of pilgrims has a particularly strong impact on the town of Polokwane and its surrounding villages. Both small and big businesses look forward to the annual injection of patronage they receive during each pilgrimage. For the pilgrims themselves, this is the time and place for learning, edification, rejuvenation, inspiration and healing. Legend has it that when the leaders of the ZCC go banking after each pilgrimage their chosen bank is closed to the public for a whole day, in light of the amount of cash they have to deposit. This is probably nothing more than legend – but it speaks to the other power of the ZCC, its business side, its effort to forge a life and ecclesial model of healing, economic and spiritual self-reliance.

The founder of the ZCC, Engenas Lekganyane (c. 1891–1948), is an important figure in South African Christianity. Currently, the church is divided into two factions that live peacefully side by side, the main (Star) faction and the smaller St Engenas (Dove) faction, named for the badges members wear and led by the grandsons of the founder, Ramarumo and Joseph Lekganyane, respectively. Established in 1910, the ZCC is a kind of metaphor for the seismic changes that have occurred in South African Christianity over the past century and half. With roots within the Lutheran,

Apostolic Faith Mission and Presbyterian traditions, the ZCC speaks to the rise of Pentecostal, Charismatic and African Initiated Churches in African Christianity. Hundreds of other Zion-type churches also exist.

In terms of numbers at least, the churches comprising the Pentecostal, Charismatic and Zion types constitute the vast majority, and therefore the representative church type, in South African Christianity today. The pulse, energy, cadence, shape and form of South African Christianity are to be found within, between and among these churches. This is a remarkable turn of events. Over the past 100 years, conventional church classification has been turned on its head. In terms of numbers, Zion-type and Pentecostal churches have become the mainline churches, while the historic mission churches now form part of a receding minority. The explosive growth of the former types of churches in Africa and other parts of the global South is one of the major factors that accounts for the shift of Christianity's centre of gravity from North to South.

Laying aside the question of whether the political orientation of some of these churches is progressive or not, these churches could never be said to be politically or socially insignificant. They are bridge builders between the old ways of Africa and the new world Africans find themselves in, the modern and the post-modern, the despair of the present and the hope for a better future. They are on the cutting edge of current spiritual innovation and renewal. Their organising themes are those of healing and self-reliance, encompassing both the spiritual and the material realms of life.

Over the past 25 years, we have seen various politicians acknowledge, not always in so many words, the political significance of the ZCC as they have joined the pilgrims and sought the blessings, the podium or an audience with the leadership of this church. On 20 April 1992, Nelson Mandela addressed his fellow pilgrims and the ZCC church leadership in Zion City Moria, basing his speech on a passage from the fifth chapter of the book of Lamentations.

We have come a long way from the days when African Initiated Churches used to be roundly called sects, supposedly designed to transport African Christians back into the world of 'animism'. Notably, the ZCC now has branches in several neighbouring countries in Southern Africa.

### The Evangelicals

Evangelicals are generally understood as those Christians who promote conversion and missionary activism, attach a special importance to the Bible and lay a special emphasis on Christ's sacrifice on the cross. Within South Africa, Evangelicals are organised across several denominations and interdenominational organisations such as: the Church of England in South Africa (CESA), led by Bishop Frank Retief; the Rhema Church, led by Ray McCauley; Africa Enterprise, led Michael Cassidy; the Back to God Movement, led by the late Nicholas Bhengu; and the Evangelical Alliance of South Africa (TEASA), led by Moss Ntlha. Frank Chikane's Apostolic Faith Mission, the Assemblies of God denominations and the Church of the Nazarene are some of the prominent denominations among the Evangelicals.

The grouping called Evangelicals is varied. While they share, to varying degrees, the four characteristics highlighted above, their social impact and interventions are uneven. Some, such as CESA, are politically conservative. Others are more pragmatic; for instance McCauley in the apartheid years was not radically opposed to the regime and is now close to the Zuma government. Cassidy's Africa Enterprise has always sought a 'third way' position for its adherents, neither radical nor conservative. Bhengu and his Back to God movement, within and beyond the Assemblies of God Church, sought to establish an alternative community of believers beyond the divisions and exigencies of the politics and political arrangements of the time. Perhaps the best-known among the radical Evangelicals is Frank Chikane, leader of the Apostolic Faith Mission Church (closely aligned to TEASA) and former General Secretary of the South African Council of Churches, who became Director General in the Office of the President in post-apartheid South Africa.

From Bhengu's opposition to racial segregation within the Assemblies of God to Chikane's well documented opposition to apartheid and currently to Ntlha's public opposition to urban road tolling, Evangelicals have been a vociferous group within South African Christianity. With the proximity to political power that the likes of Chikane and McCauley have achieved since the advent of democracy, the Evangelicals are more powerful than ever.

## The Old Mainline

While the ZCC is numerically dominant and growing in influence, traditional mainline Christianity – the Roman Catholic Church, the Anglican Church of the Province of Southern Africa, the Methodist Church of Southern Africa, the Reformed and Presbyterian family of churches, the Pentecostal churches as well as the Charismatic churches – maintains a formidable presence in the country. Many of these churches were in the forefront of the church struggle against apartheid. These are the churches that gave us the likes of Allan Boesak, the former President of the World Alliance of Reformed Churches; Brigalia Bam, who worked for the World Council of Churches (WCC) in Geneva for 21 years; Barney Pityana, a comrade of Black Consciousness leader Steve Biko and a WCC staffer himself; Jean-François Bill, a Presbyterian and leader of the South African Council of Churches; as well as Anglican Archbishop Emeritus Desmond

Tutu, Nobel Prize laureate. Nelson Mandela was brought up as a member of the Methodist Church of Southern Africa and remained a member to his death. Combined, these churches have more members than the ZCC. More importantly, these churches continue to exercise tremendous moral influence nationally and internationally.

But there is a catch. Some of the old mainline churches, notably the Dutch Reformed Church, supported the apartheid system. While from among this group of churches came some of the fiercest opponents of the apartheid ideology, calling it a heresy, it was nevertheless from this group of churches that the apartheid ideology was created – at least its theological justification – and staunchly defended. Some churches in this group might not have defended the system, but they were embroiled in it and therefore compromised by it. It is in the light of this that the role of such church leaders as Beyers Naudé and Johan Heyns of the Dutch Reformed Church and Frank Chikane of the Apostolic Faith Mission Church becomes noteworthy, given the official stances of the churches from which they came. Similarly, the role of such Reformed theologians as Willem Saayman, David Bosch and Klippies Kritzinger, who were openly critical of the stance of their own churches, is remarkable.

The old mainline churches were therefore internally conflicted regarding not only their stance in relation to apartheid ideology but also in relation to their theologies, as well as their visions of the role of the church in society. The fact that apartheid found overt and elaborate support from at least one so-called mainline church has proved costly, as many have concluded that all of Christianity was implicated and therefore fundamentally compromised.

The period since apartheid in South Africa has been a time of serious introspection and regrouping for old mainline Christianity. A particularly thorny issue is the legacy of the role of Christianity in colonialism and apartheid. This legacy continues to haunt Christianity in South Africa.

The crisis in mainline Christianity is made worse by the waning strength of ecumenism, not only in South Africa but also internationally, since the end of both the Cold War and apartheid. The waning fortunes of ecumenism have often been described in terms of diminished funding, but the crisis is more than merely financial. Reflection on ecumenical theology has itself become impoverished. Perhaps mainline Christianity has not responded effectively to the fundamental issues of the twenty-first century, such as environmental sustainability, the HIV/AIDS pandemic, inequality, poverty and sexual orientation.

The South African Council of Churches has become a much smaller and weaker entity than it was at the height of the struggle against apartheid. Other ecumenical structures such as the Institute for Contextual Theology, which oversaw the crafting of the Kairos Document in 1985, have disappeared. The Federal Theological Seminary, in which the likes of Desmond Tutu and Khoza Mgojo (members of the Truth and Reconciliation Commission) once taught, has collapsed. With the demise of several ecumenical platforms has emerged the re-marginalisation of radical prophetic theologies such as Contextual Theology, Black Theology and African Theology.

Additionally, the past two decades have also been a time of change, as many of the older church leaders and theologians either retired or took up other positions outside the church setting. Frank Chikane became Director General in the Presidency of Thabo Mbeki. Brigalia Bam became chairperson of the country's Independent Electoral Commission. Barney Pityana became chairperson of the Human Rights Commission and later principal of the University of South Africa. Desmond Tutu became the chairperson of the Truth and Reconciliation Commission. These experienced, well known and very able leaders were suddenly no longer available to the churches. The churches had to find new, often younger, and definitely less known and less experienced leaders.

## Strangers in Our Midst: Immigrant Churches

Owing to porous borders, the exact numbers of immigrant Christians remain as elusive as the exact number of immigrants in South Africa. While the country might not have the highest number, continentally, it has one of the highest numbers of economic and war refugees from other countries. Indeed, the Johannesburg metropolis has long been a continental, global and regional magnet for immigrants – a sanctuary for refugees fleeing repression, famine and economic deprivation. For many Southern Africans it is the city of dreams, as a result of which the rate of urbanisation has been high. Since the end of apartheid, other major cities, like Pretoria, Durban and Cape Town, have become truly cosmopolitan. As a consequence, several immigrant churches have emerged in these cities. While a few of these are part of the so-called mega churches, many are smaller, ordinary churches that hire church or industrial sites, or pitch tents in open fields.

Among the more flamboyant of these is the Christ Embassy International, the church of Chris Oyakhilome, a Nigerian known as Pastor Chris, which has branches in South Africa, the UK, Nigeria and the USA. The same applies to David Oyedepo's Winners' Chapel network of churches, which is spread across several cities globally, including Pretoria and Johannesburg. The current Chief Justice of South Africa, Mogoeng Mogoeng, is a member of this church, in which he also serves as a preacher. Mogoeng is also well known for his outspokenness on matters religious. Mmusi Maimane, the leader of the Democratic Alliance (South Africa's official opposition party), is a pastor and preacher in Liberty Church, a Charismatic church established by D. J. McPhail.

These two immigrant churches of Nigerian origin are illustrative of a new breed of 'international', Charismatic and immigrant African churches making their presence felt on the South African church scene. While the vast majority of their members are immigrants, their intention is to recruit locals as well. The Synagogue Church of All Nations, of Temitope Balogun (T. B.) Joshua, is another such church with a substantial following within South Africa. However, for all their spiritual credentials, there is an intricate and fundamental business and entrepreneurial side to these churches which goes a little further than the conventional. Some of the leaders are worth millions in US dollars, if periodic *Forbes* magazine calculations are anything to go by.

Perhaps one of the best illustrations of an immigrant church in South Africa has been the Johannesburg Central Methodist Church. It was founded in the late 1880s, shortly after the discovery of gold in Johannesburg. At the height of the apartheid system, this was a whites-only church, deep in the heart of the city. After the end of apartheid, it briefly became a mixed congregation. Soon the white members left in droves and it became a black church. With the onset of inner-city decay it gradually became the church of the city's poor. This was to change, after 2008, when South Africans started attacking foreigners – the so-called xenophobic attacks. The Methodist bishop in charge of the church, Paul Verryn, opened the doors of the church as a sanctuary and refuge for immigrants and foreign nationals fleeing from attacks in South Africa and from poverty and conflict in their own countries. This situation led to the emergence of two distinct groups attached to the congregation: conventional church members and those who literally and daily lived in the church – members and dwellers. The former were mainly South Africans, while the latter were non-South African. Tensions started building between the two groups and between the church leadership and the city municipality.

This led to great controversies about what could and could not be done in church, about cleanliness and godliness, and – from the side of the local government and municipality – about safety and about crime in the city. Verryn has been unrepentant, arguing that, in welcoming refugees and immigrants, the Johannesburg Central Methodist Church was doing what all other churches and municipalities ought to be doing. The Johannesburg Central Methodist Church has become one of the largest and best-known immigrant churches in Johannesburg. Its ministry highlights the question of what it means to be church in urban South Africa in the twenty-first century, in the face of xenophobia and homelessness. Few churches have highlighted these issues as prominently in post-apartheid South Africa.

## The Future in the Present

In spite of the fact that South Africa has one of the most progressive constitutions, patriarchy, gender discrimination, homophobia and racism continue to be serious problems within the South African society and churches. The laws have changed but human behaviour lags behind. Even at the best of times, the relationship between the church and liberal democracy is fraught with tensions. These tensions are heightened in South Africa because of inequality and the legacy of legalised racism.

Few South African church leaders have demonstrated that it is possible both to be Christian and to espouse some of the so-called liberal democratic values as well as Desmond Tutu has. His faith in God and his trust in the Bible are almost child-like, but he is a fierce defender of the dignity of the gay, the women, the children, the poor and the oppressed in South Africa and beyond. It is perhaps thanks to him and his like that the role of the church in the struggle against domination, colonialism and apartheid continues to be widely acknowledged.

All four South African Nobel Peace laureates (Albert Luthuli, Desmond Tutu, F. W. de Klerk and Nelson Mandela) are protégés of Christian churches and products of missionary education. In all four of them are represented also the tensions within South African Christianity. Luthuli, de Klerk and Mandela were politicians who were nevertheless deeply influenced by the Christian traditions of Congregationalism, the Dutch Reformed Church and Methodism, respectively. Tutu, the Anglican Archbishop, was influenced also by his Methodist upbringing and the African Initiated Church in which his grandfather and uncle ministered.

To see the present and future of the church in South Africa, we must return to the traffic snarl on the road to Zion City of Moria near Polokwane. The future is on display equally among the pilgrims of the Shembe Church – the Nazareth Baptist Church – as they go to worship at EkuPhakameni in Kwazulu-Natal province. We see the ugly side of that future when members of these churches literally fight proxy succession battles outside the courts of the land, on behalf of one or the other son of the founder.

The future of the church in South Africa seems to lie between the burgeoning Pentecostal and Charismatic churches. These are the churches, mainly, of the youth. The devotion and dedication of their members has become legendary, if also tragic. The amounts of money they raise for the church leaders, and the risks they are prepared to take in the process, are enormous. We have seen the ugly side of these churches in tragedies such as that witnessed on 12 September 2014, when 84 South Africans died after a poorly constructed guesthouse belonging to T. B. Joshua collapsed on them in Lagos while on pilgrimage to Joshua's Synagogue Church of All Nations (SCOAN).

The rise of the so-called 'prosperity gospel' churches has become a key challenge. In recent times, some of them have included weird if also demeaning practices. An incident widely reported in the media during 2014–15 involved a young pastor from Garankuwa, outside Pretoria, who ordered his congregants, the vast majority of whom were young women, to eat grass and later to drink petrol as a bizarre form of proof of faith and healing. This prompted the South African Commission for Cultural Linguistic and Religious Rights to launch, during 2015, a nationwide investigation into the commercialisation of religion.

The intersection between economic desperation and religion is clearly an important area in which we may search for ways of understanding some of the extreme religious practices. We could also search for clues to these in theories about toxic leadership and the dysfunctional co-dependent relationships between leaders and followers. Similarly, collapsing cultural structures and dysfunctional state processes and institutions, as well as rampant corruption, seem to drive some African Christians towards a need for miracles and immediate signs of divine intervention, perhaps as forms of relief from the desperate situations in which they find themselves.

## A Profile

What, then, would be the profile of a representative South African Christian? She is a young woman. She is part of the overwhelming majority of the population: women and youth. She could be a member of one of the old mainline churches. She is more probably a member of the ZCC or a member of Liberty Church in Randburg, outside Johannesburg. Her Christianity is made up of various influences. In her is the influence of the spirituality of her missionary-educated mother, who died a leader of the women's group in the black part of the Dutch Reformed Church or similar. Formally, the young woman has left mainline Christianity, but the habits of mainline Christianity remain strong. The choruses that sustain her and fellow members of her Charismatic or African Initiated Church are excerpts from old hymns written or translated by the first generation of missionaries from the hymnals of their European home churches.

How and where does the young South African woman practise her faith? In several places and ways. Her Bible is permanently in her handbag. She is a member of a church that meets in a particular coach of the train in which she travels to work. In the 50 minutes from her departure to arrival, a complete church service, sometimes with Holy Communion, is held inside the moving train. Out in the open veldt, she meets with fellow members of her church every Sunday, all dressed in white, to worship and to receive faith-strengthening water and anointing oils. Maybe she attends Pastor Chris's Christ Embassy Church in Randburg. After much loud singing accompanied by musical instruments, she joins her fellow worshippers to watch Pastor Chris preach to them, dressed in his trademark suit, as his picture is beamed via satellite on a big screen. He is preaching to them from London. But the congregation act as if he is in their midst. So does he. More crucially, both assume and insist that Christ is in their midst.

But perhaps the young South African woman Christian is rural and poor. She is a member of the woman's group of her local church, a mainline church. She sings choruses as she carries water from the local fountain and collects firewood from the forest nearby. Her hope is to go to heaven. But before that, she plans to go to university in Cape Town, where she can study medicine, so she can return and serve the locals who are dying prematurely from entirely preventable diseases. And yet, the young South African Christian continues to believe deep down what her grandmother used to tell her, namely, that rivers are alive, lakes are sacred, animals are like humans and the skies can talk back when upset.

## Bibliography

Bongmba, Elias Kifon (ed.), *African Religions* (Chichester: Blackwell, 2012).

Elphick, Richard and Rodney Davenport, *Christianity in South Africa: Political and Cultural History* (Cape Town: David Philip, 1997).

Hofmeyer, J. W., J. A. Millard and C. J. J. Froneman, *History of the Church in South Africa: A Document Source Book* (Pretoria: UNISA, 1991).

Isichei, Elizabeth, *A History of Christianity in Africa: From Antiquity to the Present* (London: Society for Promoting Christian Knowledge, 1995).

Villa-Vicencio, Charles and Peter Grassow, *Christianity and the Colonisation of South Africa: A Documentary History*, vols 1 and 2 (Pretoria: UNISA, 2009).

# Botswana, Lesotho, Namibia and Swaziland

## James N. Amanze

This chapter examines the status of Christianity in four countries in Southern Africa: Botswana, Lesotho, Namibia and Swaziland. The four countries share a Christian history going back to the first half of the nineteenth century. Much of the missionary work that was undertaken in the four countries was pioneered by missionary societies from Europe and America. Their legacies in the missionary field linger to the present day. Brief consideration will be given to the history of the churches in each of the four countries before turning to their current status and their contribution to socio-economic development, with a focus on education and health, as they work in partnership with their respective governments. The chapter also examines the ecumenical efforts made by the churches to work together in order to promote church unity in their respective countries.

### Botswana

Botswana is a predominantly Christian country situated immediately north of South Africa. It came under the influence of Christianity in the first half of the nineteenth century through the missionary activities of Robert Moffat, David Livingstone and other representatives of the London Missionary Society (from 1817). They succeeded in establishing what is known today as the United Congregational Church in Southern Africa (UCCSA). Their arrival opened the missionary field to other churches, namely the Dutch Reformed Church (1871), the Lutheran Church (1891), the Anglican Church (1900s), the Seventh-day Adventists (1922), the Roman Catholic Church (1928), Pentecostal churches (1930s) and the Methodist Church (1940s). It should be noted that though Christian values have permeated every aspect of Tswana society, Batswana Christians continue to observe many African traditional religious practices alongside Christianity, especially during such crises as sickness and death. This is particularly the case among African Independent Churches (AICs), which have been formed by Africans in order to worship God and practise their Christianity in African ways.

Christianity in Botswana is growing by leaps and bounds, especially among the youth. The majority of those who attend church services are women, while men spend a lot of time at their cattle posts, where they keep their livestock. It is common to have churches full of people on Sundays, confirming the view that Christianity's centre of gravity is now in Sub-Saharan Africa. Despite a high rate of church membership, however, Botswana does not consider itself a Christian state: there is no state church. The constitution of the country provides freedom of worship. According to Chapter 2 of the Constitution, Section 11:

> Except with his own consent, no person shall be hindered in the enjoyment of his freedom of conscience, and for the purposes of this section the said freedom includes freedom of thought and of religion, freedom to change his religion or belief, and freedom, either alone or in community with others, and both in public and in private, to manifest and propagate his religion or belief in worship, teaching, practice and observance.

As a result, the churches in Botswana are many and varied. According to the latest government gazette, there are more than 1,500 registered churches, with many more still waiting to be registered.

It should be noted that in the interest of public safety, public order, public morality and public health, and for the purpose of protecting the rights and freedoms of other persons, the government enacted the 1972 Societies Act. This Act requires all churches in Botswana to be registered with the Registrar of Societies at the Ministry of Labour and Home Affairs (MLHA) in the Department of Civil and National Registration. Until recently, one of the requirements for registration was that a new church should have a minimum of 10 people. For reasons that we shall see below, this number has now been increased to 250. Other requirements include submission of a letter of intention to form a church, minutes of the meeting that led to the

*Christianity in Botswana, 1970 and 2015*

| | 1970 | | 2015 | | Average annual growth rate (%), 1970–2015 |
|---|---|---|---|---|---|
| Tradition | Population | % | Population | % | |
| Christians | 259,000 | 37.4% | 1,585,000 | 70.0% | 4.11% |
| *Roman Catholics* | 21,200 | 3.1% | 88,200 | 3.9% | 3.22% |
| *Orthodox* | 50 | 0.0% | 80 | 0.0% | 1.05% |
| *Independents* | 45,200 | 6.5% | 969,000 | 42.8% | 7.05% |
| *Protestants* | 102,000 | 14.7% | 231,000 | 10.2% | 1.84% |
| *Anglicans* | 7,000 | 1.0% | 10,000 | 0.4% | 0.80% |
| Pentecostals | 47,300 | 6.8% | 1,042,000 | 46.1% | 7.11% |
| Evangelicals | 22,700 | 3.3% | 119,000 | 5.3% | 3.75% |
| **Total population** | **693,000** | **100.0%** | **2,262,000** | **100.0%** | **2.66%** |

Source: Todd M. Johnson and Gina A. Zurlo (eds), *World Christian Database* (Leiden/Boston: Brill), accessed March 2016.

formation of the said church, a list of those who participated, with their signatures and identity numbers, and possible names for the new church, reflecting its nature and objectives.

The different churches that operate in Botswana today can be grouped into three categories or typologies. In the first instance we have the mainline churches, sometimes also known as mission churches or historic churches. These comprise the Roman Catholic Church, Anglican Church, Lutheran Church, Methodist Church, Dutch Reformed Church and Seventh-day Adventists. These churches were introduced to Botswana from Europe and America. They are essentially the local representation of the mother churches overseas on matters of church doctrine, spirituality, church practice, church organisation and liturgical observances. In some instances, they receive financial support and missionaries.

The second category consists of the Pentecostal churches. Good examples of this type of church are the Assemblies of God Church, the Church of God in Christ, the Church of Prophecy, Apostolic Faith Mission and Forward in Faith International. These churches are currently growing rapidly, particularly among young people in urban areas.

The third group consists of African Independent Churches. They normally have an entirely African membership and practise their Christianity in conjunction with African traditional beliefs and practices. They are self-regulating and financially self-supporting. They are considered part of the larger Christian family because the majority of them subscribe to the teachings of the doctrine of the Trinity and believe in Jesus Christ as their Lord and personal Saviour. From the second half of the twentieth century until a decade ago they constituted a gigantic Christian movement. They attracted into their rank and file thousands of people through faith healing and the use of African traditional medicines.

One of the most interesting developments in recent years has been the emergence of 'Fire Churches', which are essentially Pentecostal revivalist Charismatic movements. They are manifested in the form of 'ministries'. Their success is attributed to their emphasis on healing miracles and promises of abundant wealth here and now. It appears that because of high levels of unemployment and poverty in the country, many Batswana flock to the Fire Churches with the hope of becoming rich almost instantly. As a result, Fire Churches are making a lot of money from people who attend their services based on the promise that the more one gives in the form of 'seed' money, the more one gets in return in one's bank account and business success. Unfortunately, much of the money earned in this way is abused and misused by the 'prosperity gospel' preachers.

As a result, the government of Botswana has taken strong action to control the proliferation of churches in the country, by amending the 1972

Societies Act so that it now requires a membership 250 people in order for a new church to qualify for registration. This is a steep increase from the previous figure of 10, as noted above. The move is intended to curb the mushrooming of churches and the emergence of self-styled pastors who, from the government's perspective, 'abuse God, the people and push their agendas'.

Another interesting phenomenon in the country has been the rise to prominence and influence of two Nigerians: Prophet T. B. Joshua, of the Synagogue Church of all Nations (SCOAN), and Pastor Chris Oyakhilome, of Christ Embassy. Daily, many Batswana, disgruntled by what they perceive as 'the failure of local churches to perform instant healing miracles', travel to Nigeria seeking anointing and healing from Prophet Joshua and Pastor Oyakhilome, both of whom claim to have direct access to God. Both ministries have strong representation in Botswana.

Churches in Botswana are contributing significantly to the socio-economic development of the country, especially in the area of formal education and provision of health services. As regards the latter, churches in Botswana both individually and ecumenically provide badly needed medical services to people in many parts of the country through clinics and hospitals at which people are treated for various diseases. For instance, the Bamalete Hospital in Ramotswa (Lutheran), the Deborah Retief Memorial Hospital in Mochudi (Dutch Reformed), the Seventh-day Adventist Hospital in Kanye, the Livingstone Hospital in Molepolole (Presbyterian), St Peter's Hospital in Mmadinare (founded by the Anglican Church) and the Ramotswa Clinic (Roman Catholic) play significant roles in the provision of health services to the nation as a whole.

In the field of formal education, such schools as St Joseph's College and Mater Spei Secondary School in Francistown (Roman Catholic) and Moeding College at Otse (UCCSA) are contributing significantly to the educational system of the country. Ecumenically, the mainline churches established the Urban Industrial School, the Building and Carpentry School and Amogelang Primary School, all in Selebi-Phikwe, in order to reduce high levels of unemployment and curb crime committed by young people who drop out of school.

Churches in Botswana have also taken a strong lead in ecumenical relations in order to minimise religious conflicts, which were rampant among the churches before independence in 1966. At present, there are four ecumenical bodies whose aim is to promote unity among the churches. One of these is the Botswana Council of Churches (BCC), which was formed in 1966. Its membership consists largely of the mainline churches, with a few African Independent Churches as well as some Pentecostal churches. The BCC has contributed significantly to the socio-economic development of Botswana, by taking an active part in the provision of health services, education and poverty eradication, and in the fight against the HIV/AIDS pandemic.

Apart from the BCC, there is also the Evangelical Fellowship of Botswana (EFB), which was founded in 1974. Its membership consists of the majority of Pentecostal and Charismatic churches. It is also actively engaged in socio-economic activities that promote the welfare of the nation as a whole.

Mention should also be made of the Organisation of African Instituted Churches Southern Region, which was formed in 1980s. A majority of African Independent Churches are members. Its mission is to be the mouthpiece of all the African Independent Churches in the country, which are, by and large, marginalised by both mainline churches and Pentecostal churches.

Last but not least it is important to note the ecumenical work of the Ministers' Fraternals, which are found in practically all the villages, towns and cities of Botswana. Their membership consists of pastors in a given locality working together to promote the ecumenical agenda. They operate on the principles of 'receptive ecumenism', since no church imposes its ecumenical agenda on the other.

## Lesotho

Lesotho is another predominantly Christian country. It is completely surrounded by South Africa. The history of Christianity in the country is traced back to the first half of the nineteenth century, when King Moshoeshoe requested missionaries of the Paris Evangelical Missionary Society (PEMS) to come to his country (1833) to start missionary work there. This led to the establishment of what is called today the Lesotho Evangelical Church. Their arrival opened the doors for the establishment of other churches, such as the Roman Catholic Church (1862), the Anglican Church (1875), the African Methodist Episcopal Church (1908), the Assemblies of God Church (1912) and a host of others. There are also many African Independent Churches in Lesotho, of different types and sizes. These churches practise their Christianity in conjunction with their African traditional religious beliefs and practices, a feature that is common in churches across the spectrum.

There is no state church in Lesotho. All churches are equal before the law. People's freedom of conscience, including freedom of thought and of religion, is well protected by the constitution. Unlike other countries in Southern Africa, the government of Lesotho has not imposed specific registration requirements on churches. For example, unlike the situation in Botswana, where churches can face legal charges for failing to register with the Registrar of Societies, in Lesotho there are no hard-and-fast rules for the churches to register. Those that opt for registration are asked to submit their leadership committee and constitution. However, if a religious group is not registered, it may not qualify for government benefits, such as a waiver of taxes and duties on charitable donations received from outside the country.

As is the case in many other African countries, fear of losing members to Pentecostal churches has become a strong motivation among mainline churches to Pentecostalise in their style of worship and witness. In recent years, the emergence of revivalist Pentecostal churches that promise people fantastic healing miracles and abundant wealth has become a threat to traditional churches, which preach the theology of the cross as a way to go to heaven. Events in South Africa, where some revivalist Charismatic ministries make their followers eat grass, snakes and rats and drink petrol as means of miraculous healing, are perceived in Lesotho as a serious threat to the well-being of the people. Currently, there is much debate about how to deal with this threat.

The churches play a very important role in the socio-economic development of the country, especially in the areas of education and provision of health services. As regards education, there is a strong partnership between the government and the churches. From the time of their inception, churches in Lesotho established primary schools and later secondary schools as a means of bringing people into the church. People were taught how to read and write. This created job opportunities for them and raised their social status. Those who attended such schools became civil servants, administrators, court clerks, police officers, teachers, medical doctors and church ministers in their respective churches. Such schools also produced the politicians who led the country to independence on 4 October 1966.

In modern times, the churches have continued to provide education to the majority of people in Lesotho. The Ministry of Education maintains overall responsibility for the overall educational and training needs of

*Christianity in Lesotho, 1970 and 2015*

| | 1970 | | 2015 | | Average annual growth rate (%), 1970–2015 |
|---|---|---|---|---|---|
| Tradition | Population | % | Population | % | |
| Christians | 841,000 | 81.5% | 1,967,000 | 92.1% | 1.91% |
| *Roman Catholics* | 411,000 | 39.8% | 1,106,000 | 51.8% | 2.23% |
| *Independents* | 63,100 | 6.1% | 227,000 | 10.7% | 2.89% |
| *Protestants* | 224,000 | 21.7% | 425,000 | 19.9% | 1.44% |
| *Anglicans* | 80,000 | 7.8% | 115,000 | 5.4% | 0.81% |
| Pentecostals | 67,100 | 6.5% | 379,000 | 17.8% | 3.93% |
| Evangelicals | 49,500 | 4.8% | 172,000 | 8.1% | 2.80% |
| **Total population** | **1,032,000** | **100.0%** | **2,135,000** | **100.0%** | **1.63%** |

Source: Todd M. Johnson and Gina A. Zurlo (eds), *World Christian Database* (Leiden/Boston: Brill), accessed March 2016.

the country as a whole but various churches, such as the Roman Catholic Church, the Anglican Church and the Methodist Church, operate primary schools under its management. In order to expand the broad base of educated citizenry, the government introduced free primary education in 2000. This move led to the establishment of new non-denominational schools and reduced the number of church-affiliated schools.

In order to ensure and promote high standards of education, the churches also set up tertiary education institutions. One good example is the National University of Lesotho (NUL), which was established in 1945. This initiative was taken by the Synod of Catholic Bishops in South Africa as early as 1938. The intention was to provide African Catholic students with post-matriculation and religious guidance. From its humble beginnings in a temporary primary school building at Roma, 34 km from Maseru, the National University of Lesotho (NUL) has produced an educated elite who have contributed significantly to the socio-economic development of the country. Professors and graduates from NUL eventually set up university campuses in Swaziland and Botswana, thus making a major contribution to the overall development of the southern African region.

Apart from their involvement in education, the churches also play a very important role in the provision of health services, in the form of hospitals, health centres, clinics and outposts. Many of these operate under the auspices of the Christian Health Council of Churches. It is estimated that this organisation provides 40% of the health care services in the country. This shows the extent of the commitment made by the churches to the ministry of healing.

Christian churches in Lesotho are wholly involved in the ecumenical movement. There is harmony and concord between Christians and people of other faiths, such as Muslims, Hindus and Baha'i. A number of churches, including the Roman Catholic Church, are members of the Christian Council of Lesotho. Besides its spiritual agenda, the Council is also involved, from time to time, in conflict resolution with regard to matters of governance. For example, in 2007 the Council successfully intervened in a dispute between the government and the opposition parties regarding the allocation of proportional representational seats in the national assembly. In this regard, the churches play a significant role at national level.

### Namibia

Namibia is located on the western side of Africa, along the shores of the Atlantic Ocean. It shares borders with South Africa in the South, Angola in the north and Botswana in the east. Historically, the introduction of Christianity in Namibia is attributed to the missionary activities of the London Missionary Society (LMS), which sent the first missionaries in 1806. In 1840 the LMS decided to transfer all its mission work to the Rhenish Missionary Society (RMS). This marked the beginning of the missionary era in Namibia and led to the establishment of many churches.

Churches carrying out missionary work in the country include the Evangelical Lutheran Church (1830), the Methodist Church (1832), the Roman Catholic Church (1892), the Dutch Reformed Church (1870s) and the Anglican Church (1916). It should be noted that Namibia is also home to many Pentecostal churches, especially Pentecostal and Charismatic churches from Nigeria, Ghana, Zimbabwe, Zambia and the USA. Many of these arrived after the country gained independence from South Africa, on 21 March 1990, and they are a religious force to reckon with.

Namibia is a predominantly Christian country. At independence it adopted a constitution that recognises religious freedom. This is clearly expressed in Article 10, according to which all Namibians have the freedom to profess and practise their religion freely and without discrimination. The Lutheran, Roman Catholic and Anglican are considered to be the largest churches. Apart from these, there are also a number of others that are operating in the Namibian missionary field. These include the Baptists, Methodists, Pentecostals, Evangelicals and Charismatic churches. Mention should also be made here of the Church of Jesus Christ of Latter-Day Saints (Mormons), which was formally organised in the country in 1973.

Namibia is also home to many African Independent Churches, many of which were introduced from South Africa and Botswana. These churches integrate biblical teaching and beliefs with African traditional beliefs and practices. Recent scholarship shows that, despite their incorporation of traditional beliefs, they are genuinely Christian.

As in the case of Lesotho, there is no state church in Namibia. All denominations are consulted when the government is deciding on a major national policy. It should also be noted here that church leaders are expected to register their churches with the government. This enables them

*Christianity in Namibia, 1970 and 2015*

| | 1970 | | 2015 | | Average annual growth rate (%), 1970–2015 |
|---|---|---|---|---|---|
| Tradition | Population | % | Population | % | |
| Christians | 709,000 | 90.9% | 2,232,000 | 90.8% | 2.58% |
| *Roman Catholics* | 116,000 | 14.9% | 517,000 | 21.0% | 3.37% |
| *Independents* | 63,900 | 8.2% | 297,000 | 12.1% | 3.47% |
| *Protestants* | 402,000 | 51.5% | 1,487,000 | 60.5% | 2.95% |
| *Anglicans* | 20,000 | 2.6% | 75,000 | 3.1% | 2.98% |
| Pentecostals | 37,300 | 4.8% | 384,000 | 15.6% | 5.32% |
| Evangelicals | 67,400 | 8.6% | 325,000 | 13.2% | 3.56% |
| **Total population** | **780,000** | **100.0%** | **2,459,000** | **100.0%** | **2.58%** |

Source: Todd M. Johnson and Gina A. Zurlo (eds), *World Christian Database* (Leiden/Boston: Brill), accessed March 2016.

to acquire land and property as charitable associations. Once registered, a church acquires tax-exempt status and can purchase land at a discounted rate. Thus, in order to obtain land and other properties, churches are required to submit evidence of their registration to the Ministry of Local Government, Housing and Rural Development. They must also show their affiliation to the Council of Churches of Namibia (CCN).

As in many other African countries, it has been observed that differences among the leaders of various churches had led to the formation of many break-away churches, the number of which has consequently mushroomed. This phenomenon and the emergence of so-called 'false prophets' are seen as a problem for Namibia. In order to curb the proliferation of churches, the Council of Churches of Namibia adopted a policy of requiring churches to have a membership of at least 5,000 before they can register with the CCN.

Churches in Namibia play a very important role in the socio-economic development of the country, particularly in formal education and the provision of health services. They work in partnership with government institutions. The Roman Catholic Church and other churches own schools at all levels of the educational system. Religious and moral education is taught in church schools and there has been an attempt to reintroduce this in state schools, something that has not been accepted by the Ministry of Education because of the secular nature of the state as set out in the constitution.

Churches in Namibia are also at the forefront in the provision of health services, through hospitals, clinics and health centres. For example, the Evangelical Lutheran Church in Namibia runs the Onandjokwe Lutheran Hospital in the northern part of the country; it provides medical services to a large sector of the population, and its activities extend to malaria prevention and control, for example. In the face of the HIV/AIDS pandemic, the churches established religiously affiliated non-governmental organisations such as Catholic Aids Action, the Bernhard Nordkamp Centre and the Evangelical Lutheran Church's Aids Program. These organisations are well known for their caring and counselling.

Churches in Namibia have also developed a strong ecumenical spirit, which led to the formation of the CCN. Practically all major churches in the country, such as the Anglican Diocese of Namibia, the Evangelical Lutheran Church in Namibia, the Roman Catholic Church and the African Methodist Episcopal Church, are members of the CCN. This helps them to cooperate with one another on a number of issues pertaining to the socio-economic development of the Namibian people.

## Swaziland

Swaziland is mostly surrounded by South Africa but in the east it shares a border with Mozambique. The introduction of Christianity in the country goes back to King Somhlolo (King Sobhuza I), who ruled the country from 1815 to 1836. The first missionaries arrived in Swaziland at the invitation of King Mswati II (Somhlolo's son and successor) in 1844. This marked the introduction of the Methodist Church in the country. It was soon followed by Anglican missionaries, who began missionary work in the 1880s.

Missionary work was also undertaken by the South African General Mission (established in 1890), the Seventh-day Adventists (1892), the Scandinavian Alliance Mission (1892), the Church of the Nazarene (1910) and the Pentecostal churches (1910). Other attempts to establish missionary work in Swaziland was undertaken by German missionaries (from 1920). In addition to these missionary undertakings, the Roman Catholic Church began its mission in 1912 and grew very rapidly. The Church of Jesus Christ of Latter-Day Saints (the Mormons) also established its presence in the country.

It should be noted that Swaziland has a large number of African Independent Churches, the majority of which are of the Zionist type. They have very strong ties with the royal family. This led to the formation of the League of African Churches in Swaziland (LAC) by Sobhuza II in 1937. Zionist churches have a great deal of political influence in the country because of their closeness to the royal family. They provide the theological legitimacy of Swazi Kingship in gratitude for what the King does for them.

Swaziland is a predominantly Christian nation with a wide variety of churches. However, the government does not recognise any one church as a state church. At independence on 6 September 1968 the country adopted a constitution that guaranteed freedom of conscience and religion to all. This was affirmed in the new constitution adopted in 2006. It recognises and protects freedom of thought, conscience and religion. It also advocates equality of all citizens before the law. It does not allow discrimination of persons on the basis of gender, race, colour, ethnic origin or tribe, and so on. Interestingly, despite all this, minority religious groups seem to enjoy

*Christianity in Swaziland, 1970 and 2015*

| | 1970 | | 2015 | | Average annual growth rate (%), 1970–2015 |
|---|---|---|---|---|---|
| Tradition | Population | % | Population | % | |
| Christians | 300,000 | 67.3% | 1,137,000 | 88.3% | 3.00% |
| *Roman Catholics* | 34,000 | 7.6% | 58,000 | 4.5% | 1.19% |
| *Independents* | 88,200 | 19.8% | 619,000 | 48.1% | 4.42% |
| *Protestants* | 65,300 | 14.6% | 137,000 | 10.6% | 1.65% |
| *Anglicans* | 3,600 | 0.8% | 28,000 | 2.2% | 4.64% |
| Pentecostals | 86,800 | 19.5% | 649,000 | 50.5% | 4.57% |
| Evangelicals | 60,700 | 13.6% | 157,000 | 12.2% | 2.13% |
| **Total population** | **446,000** | **100.0%** | **1,287,000** | **100.0%** | **2.38%** |

Source: Todd M. Johnson and Gina A. Zurlo (eds), *World Christian Database* (Leiden/Boston: Brill), accessed March 2016.

fewer protections under traditional laws and customs as exercised by traditional courts and traditional chiefs.

Because of the multiplicity of churches, the Protection of Names and Badges Act requires that churches register with the government. This is done through the Registrar General's Office in the Ministry of Justice and Constitutional Affairs. For registration, churches are required to have a recommendation from one of the country's ecumenical bodies, namely the League of African Churches in Swaziland, the Swaziland Conference of Churches or the Council of Swaziland Churches. Registered religious organisations are exempt from taxation. In order to build a new church in an urban or rural area, churches are required to obtain permission from the government and chiefs, respectively.

In recent years, the country has experienced a mushrooming of churches because it is easy to establish a new one. This has caused a great deal of concern in government circles. Members of Parliament in particular see the proliferation of churches as potentially disastrous for Swaziland's well-being. Another concern has been the emergence of controversial pastors, who make people drink petrol or eat grass, snakes and rats for healing. This has created the need to put in place a mechanism that controls church activities. Many of the controversial churches are linked to the Swaziland Conference of Churches. Fear of the uncontrolled proliferation of churches prompted the government in 2014 to consider putting in place measures to regulate their registration. This, however, is still a matter of much debate.

As suggested above, although the government does not recognise any church as a state church, there are indications that the monarchy and the government support many of the activities of the Zionist type of churches. This is evidenced by the fact that both the King and the Queen Mother, as well as other members of the royal family, attend Good Friday and Easter services organised by the Zionist churches, during which the King is invited to preach. By and large, the King acts as a patron ensuring that politically nothing goes wrong for the Zionist churches.

The churches play a very important role in the socio-economic development of the country. The Roman Catholic Church, the Church of the Nazarene and the Anglican Church run many schools. Religious instruction is mandatory in primary schools and is an elective subject in secondary schools. Although schools teach religion predominantly from a Christian perspective, the Ministry of Education includes a multi-religion component in the religious curriculum. Apart from schools, the above churches also run many hospitals and clinics.

Ecumenically, churches in Swaziland work together through three ecumenical bodies. The League of African Churches in Swaziland, mentioned above, is a kind of a federation of all African Independent Churches in the country, particularly Zionist churches. The Council of Swaziland Churches (CSC) consists of the mainline churches, namely the Roman Catholics, Lutherans, Anglicans, Methodists and Congregationalists. It was founded in 1976 in order to assist the victims of the apartheid system in South Africa who flocked into Swaziland as refugees before independence. One of its objectives is to further the unity of God's church as the body of Christ. The third ecumenical body is the Swaziland Conference of Churches (SCC), formed in 1929. It is made up of Evangelical churches. It works side by side with other Evangelical associations in the world such as the Evangelical Churches of Africa and the World Evangelical Alliance. This is because their theological ethos and mission are the same.

## Conclusion

This chapter has discussed the status of Christianity in Botswana, Lesotho, Namibia and Swaziland. It has considered how Christianity was introduced in the four countries and noted its legal position today. The relationship between the church and the state has been discussed. The chapter has also examined the emergence of the revival Charismatic ministries that promise instant wealth and healing in their churches. It has noted that their unconventional practices of making people eat grass, rats and snakes for healing are perceived as threats to the well-being of the people in all four countries, thereby forcing some governments to take drastic measures to stop such practices. The chapter has also discussed the role played by the churches in the socio-economic development of their respective countries, thus contributing significantly to the well-being of the people at large.

## Bibliography

Amanze, James N., *African Christianity in Botswana* (Gweru: Mambo Press, 1998).

Buys, G. L. and Skekutaamba V. V. Nambala, *History of the Church in Namibia 1805–1990: An Introduction* (Gamsberg: Macmillan, 2003).

Kumalo, R. Simangaliso, *Religion and Politics in Swaziland* (Bloemfontein: Sun Press, 2013).

Nkomazana, Fidelis and Laurel Lanner (eds), *Aspects of the History of the Church in Botswana* (Pietermaritzburg: Cluster Publications, 2007).

Stotler, Pat, *The Mountain Kingdom: Claiming Lesotho for Christ* (Kansas City, MO: Nazarene Publishing House, 2000).

# Mozambique

## Isaias Paulo Titoce

Mozambique is a country marked by great diversity, as evidenced by the 25 indigenous languages that are spoken. Its unity as a nation was forged through the shared experience of Portuguese colonial rule. Portuguese remains the official language, although it is spoken only by a minority of the population. With some 2,800 km of Africa's south-eastern coastline, Mozambique historically has been exposed to external influences from both Arab traders and European travellers seeking to reach India. Its natural harbours offered a base for trade with inland Africa and a staging post for the journey eastward to India. Along with trade came religious influence: first Islam through the Arabs and then Roman Catholic Christianity through the Portuguese. African traditional religions and Hinduism are also practised, with the result that religious plurality is built into the fabric of national life. Christianity, too, finds diverse expression, taking three main forms: Catholic, Protestant and Pentecostal.

### Roman Catholics

Catholics have been present in Mozambique for about five centuries, arriving some three centuries earlier than their Protestant counterparts. Today, Catholic communities can be found in every district of Mozambique and around one-fifth of the population is Catholic, though the proportion regularly participating in church life may be considerably lower. This applies not only to the Catholic Church but also to other denominations. The number of Christians enrolled in church records greatly exceeds those who are really connected.

The Catholic Church came to Mozambique hand in hand with Portuguese colonial rule. For this reason it met with initial resistance and it was only when the Portuguese conquered the indigenous kingdoms that it found an opportunity to establish itself. Many churches were built throughout the country, but at first no attempt was made to provide educational, social or health services. It was only when Portugal was questioned about the legitimacy of its occupation of African countries that it gave its colonies the status of 'ultramarine provinces'. The Catholic Church was then charged with the basic education of the natives and given authority to confer Portuguese citizenship on those who complied with its educational requirements. To get a basic education in the country, one had to become a Catholic.

With the advent of independence in 1975 and the anti-religion policy introduced by the Frente de Libertação de Moçambique ('Frelimo'; the Mozambique Liberation Front) now in office, the Catholic Church suffered a major setback. For the first three years after independence, religion – and Christianity in particular – was seen as a means of alienating people. The new government aimed to eradicate it. Many churches were closed and some church institutions were seized. Schools, hospitals and other key institutions were nationalised. This brought a new challenge to the Catholic Church in Mozambique. Until this time it had not been actively engaged in evangelism. The Mass was conducted using the Latin language in communities where the local people could not understand a single word. Even when the Mass in Portuguese was introduced it still excluded the more than 90% of attenders who did not understand Portuguese either. Stripped of its privileged position and no longer holding magisterial responsibility, the Catholic Church was running the risk of becoming irrelevant to local people. During this period church attendance dropped drastically.

From this point of crisis the Catholic Church became much more active in evangelism and social action. When the government began to ease its relations with religious communities and to return nationalised institutions, the Catholic Church used them as orphanages, technical schools and learning centres (particularly for girls). After the civil war (1975–91), the government allowed private institutions to be involved in education, including higher education. The Catholic Church was the first to open a university. The Catholic University, known as UCM, is located in Beira, but it has branches in the northern provinces. The Church then established other higher education institutions and facilities around the country.

Presently, the Catholic Church has 12 dioceses. Candidates for priestly formation are recruited at a young age and enrol first in a seminary

*Christianity in Mozambique, 1970 and 2015*

| | 1970 | | 2015 | | Average annual growth rate (%), 1970–2015 |
|---|---|---|---|---|---|
| Tradition | Population | % | Population | % | |
| Christians | 2,611,000 | 28.2% | 14,818,000 | 53.0% | 3.93% |
| *Roman Catholics* | 1,553,000 | 16.8% | 6,409,000 | 22.9% | 3.20% |
| *Orthodox* | 2,000 | 0.0% | 710 | 0.0% | -2.28% |
| *Independents* | 99,300 | 1.1% | 3,684,000 | 13.2% | 8.36% |
| *Protestants* | 378,000 | 4.1% | 3,567,000 | 12.8% | 5.11% |
| *Anglicans* | 45,000 | 0.5% | 149,000 | 0.5% | 2.70% |
| Pentecostals | 142,000 | 1.5% | 5,445,000 | 19.5% | 8.44% |
| Evangelicals | 285,000 | 3.1% | 2,826,000 | 10.1% | 5.23% |
| **Total population** | **9,262,000** | **100.0%** | **27,978,000** | **100.0%** | **2.49%** |

Source: Todd M. Johnson and Gina A. Zurlo (eds), *World Christian Database* (Leiden/Boston: Brill), accessed March 2016.

close to their village before going on to a major seminary elsewhere and often finishing their studies in Italy. Worship in the Catholic Church in Mozambique follows exactly the pattern of its European counterpart, being focused on the sacraments. The liturgy lacks cultural resonance since it follows a prescribed order and is delivered in Portuguese, a language in which less than 25% of Mozambicans are competent and which is completely unknown to some 50%. The exclusion of indigenous languages from worship and educational programmes has meant that local communities have little opportunity to adopt the faith. Being a Catholic was, for many, a mere formality. The relatively high membership of the Catholic Church in Mozambique is due to the Portuguese colonial history. For example, during the colonial period in order to get the status of a citizen one would have to prove that one had been baptised in the Catholic Church; to pass the elementary school one was required to have a Catholic baptism certificate. It is power, privilege and coercion, rather than evangelism and free adherence, that account for the relatively large number of Catholics in Mozambique.

This sense of Catholic power and privilege is still present subconsciously in Mozambican society today. Christian festivals such as Easter and Christmas are often called Catholic feasts by the government and media. Despite this dominance, new movements, such as Pentecostal 'prosperity gospel' churches, draw their membership mainly from the Catholic community. Nonetheless, the future looks bright for the Catholics. In the social and political dimensions they are using their huge infrastructure for professional education, thus making a positive impact on Mozambican society. Particularly through their Episcopal Conference, they are more vocal than other Christian traditions with regard to the misuse of power by the government. The use of Portuguese as the Church's official language might be beneficial in the long term, since many children are learning Portuguese at school at a time when local communities are becoming ever more heterogeneous in terms of native languages, due to intense internal migration. In spite of the Catholic Church's great potential, a key issue for the future is how proactive it can be with regard to indigenous culture.

## Protestants

The main Protestant traditions in Mozambique are Methodist, Anglican, Presbyterian, Lutheran and Congregationalist. Some of these are divided into several denominations. Methodism includes the United Methodist Church, the Wesleyan Methodist Church and the Free Methodist Church. Presbyterianism includes the Presbyterian Church of Mozambique and the Church of Christ in Mozambique, the latter found mainly in the northern provinces of Nampula and Zambeze. Congregationalism includes the

United Congregational Church of Mozambique and the United Church of Christ in Mozambique.

Protestant Christianity was introduced to Mozambique by migrant workers who returned from South Africa, bringing with them the Protestant faith they had adopted while working in the mines and other industries. They shared their new faith, and what it meant in their lives, within their communities and churches began to be formed. Mission boards in Europe and in the USA took this as an opportunity to expand their work to Mozambique, using these converted migrant workers as their starting point. The Presbyterian Church in Mozambique, for example, owes its origins to Josefa Mhalamala, who received the gospel while he was working in the diamond mines of Griqualand and, after receiving some education and training, returned to Mozambique and began preaching at Magude. Soon Swiss Reformed missionaries arrived and built on the foundation laid by Mhalamala. There was a 'gentleman's agreement' that the Swiss mission would concentrate its work in the provinces of Maputo and Gaza while American Methodist and Congregationalist missionaries focused their attention on Inhambane, where they established important centres at Chicuque, Cambine, Balaza and Nhamachafo.

The Portuguese government was not sympathetic to Protestant missions, but the extent of its control over the country was limited and local chiefs were welcoming in some areas. Despite government hostility, the Protestant missions proved attractive because of their use of indigenous languages. The translation of the Bible, hymns and liturgy into local languages was a major part of their work. This unleashed a dynamic process in which Mozambicans were able to play a leading role in inculturating the gospel in their context. It also equipped them with literacy and other skills that they could use in the emerging modern economy. The Protestant missions also built schools, hospitals and agricultural training centres through which many people were introduced to the gospel.

The Protestant strategy of dividing the country between different missions and grounding each church in an indigenous language and culture proved fruitful in many respects. However, a more problematic result was that each Protestant church became identified with a particular ethnic or linguistic group. For example, the Methodist Church is labelled the Church of the Vatswa, while the Presbyterian Church is labelled the Church of the Changanas and the Rongas. The Protestant churches thus took on an exclusive tribal character. This became a major issue during the civil war of 1975–91, which saw mass migration from rural areas to the towns and cities. Many Protestant migrants did not feel comfortable in the churches they found in their new urban context, since the language and culture were unfamiliar. They therefore formed their own congregations and requested their parent denominations to provide pastors for them. As a result, Protestant Christianity in the towns and cities of Mozambique today is divided largely on ethnic and linguistic lines. Evangelism is inhibited since each denomination can reach out only to those who belong to its own ethnic community. Alongside the establishment of new congregations, the Protestants have continued to build schools, hospitals and orphanages, though their financial strength has diminished since the departure of missionaries loosened their connection with funding sources in the global North.

Protestant worship is centred around the proclamation of the Word. Some denominations, such as the Presbyterians, have an ordinal to guide their conduct of worship. Often this has been inherited from the missionary period and offers orders of service in line with the Christian liturgical calendar. Others, such as the Methodists, provide models of the order of service but leave the local congregation free to determine the order it will follow. Holy Communion is celebrated infrequently. Some, such as the Methodists, have an open table, while others restrict participation in Communion to those who fulfil particular requirements.

In many cases the first leaders of the Protestant churches were migrant workers who brought the gospel with them when they returned to their home areas. Often they had no formal theological training but discovered gifts in evangelism and a charismatic authority. They laid the foundation on which the European missionaries could later build. The missionaries offered theological training to these indigenous church leaders, some of whom eventually became the first ordained pastors. As the work developed and many new congregations were established, the missionaries felt that a systematic approach to the training of pastors was needed. A number of Bible schools were founded. Later, around 1958, the four main Protestant denominations decided to create an ecumenical seminary for theological training, the United Seminary of Ricatla. Since then, five more denominations have joined the Seminary and for almost 50 years it has been the main agent of Protestant pastoral formation.

The Protestant churches understood the importance of addressing common problems together. In 1948, inspired by the foundation of the World Council of Churches that year, the missionaries of the different denominations formed the Christian Council of Mozambique. The new body aimed to organise Protestant churches in order to reach out to the whole country with Protestant evangelisation at a time when Catholicism was the official religion in Mozambique and the Protestant denominations were operating within tribal boundaries. Today, the Council has 24 member churches and acts as the arm and voice of the Protestant churches in social and political matters.

### Pentecostals

The Pentecostal churches in Mozambique fall into three main categories: historic Pentecostal churches of Western origin, historic Pentecostal churches of African origin, and recently arrived Pentecostal churches identified with the 'prosperity gospel'. Of the historic Pentecostal churches with a Western origin, the Assemblies of God are particularly influential. They trace their beginnings in Mozambique to the work of a Canadian missionary, Austin Chawner, who arrived around 1926. He trained local leaders who enabled the Assemblies of God communities to multiply and scatter throughout the country. They have been highly effective in evangelism and church growth but are not very active in social and political matters. The church's leadership is charismatic in style. Some pastoral training is offered by Bible schools and presently the Assemblies of God offer theological studies jointly with the Nazarenes.

As regards historic Pentecostal churches with African origins, the Zionist churches are prominent. There are many Zionist communities scattered around the country, especially in suburban areas. These churches came into being as a result of a reaction against a form of Christianity that privileged European culture and practices. The founders of Zionist churches were often dissidents from the missionary-founded churches. The Luso Episcopal Church, for example, was founded in 1918 by Muti Munene Sicobele, a dissident from the Episcopal Methodist Church. The Zionist churches are popular among the poor, as their worship resonates with local culture and beliefs. They will continue to grow, as their spiritual life is founded in the hearts of the people, but some theological education will be needed if the authenticity of the faith is to be sustained.

The third type of Pentecostal churches is a more recent phenomenon, distinguished by their preaching of the 'prosperity gospel'. Often these churches originate from Brazil, such as the Universal Church of the Kingdom of God. They currently enjoy great popularity and often attract members of other denominations. At first, they hired public buildings such as cinemas in which to hold their meetings. After some years they began constructing purpose-built worship centres, often close to markets or business centres in cities and towns. They are skilled in the use of modern media, particularly television and radio. Their claim to possess healing powers and the capacity to make people rich has made them very popular, attracting worshippers in large numbers. They often give the impression that generous financial giving to the church is the key to attaining the healing and prosperity that are emphasised in their preaching and practice. People have been induced to donate large sums of money, even their entire life savings. However, many have been disappointed when the promised healing or prosperity did not materialise. For this reason many members are leaving the 'prosperity' churches, feeling that they have been deceived. Some have even attempted to take legal action against their church. Indeed, such is the negative impact that this movement is becoming popularly known as the 'church of thieves'. It does continue to attract new converts, but there is also a strong element of disillusionment, leaving its future open to question.

## Conclusion

A brief account such as this cannot fully do justice to the complex mosaic of Christianity in Mozambique. The churches in Mozambique are still passing through a transitional period, in which they operate by default on the basis of the legacy left by the missionaries. They need visionary leaders to shape their vision and mission. Their biggest challenge is to achieve a shift from being churches that receive and implement policies fashioned in the West to being churches that engage in proactive ways with the dynamics of popular culture. Such a shift is needed in order to ground Christianity in the hearts of the people for the benefit of coming generations.

## Bibliography

Chamango, Simão, *A Chegada do Evangelho em Moçambique* (Maputo: SUR, 1982).

Cruz e Silva, Teresa, *Igrejas Protestantes e Consciência Política no Sul de Moçambique* (Maputo: Promédia, 2001).

van Butselaar, Jan, *Africanos, Missionários e Colonialistas: As Origens da Igreja Presbiteriana de Moçambique (Missão Suiça), 1880–1896*, translated by Francisco da Cruz (Lausanne: Département Missionaire des Églises Protestantes de la Suisse Romande, 1987).

# Zimbabwe, Zambia and Malawi

## Hany Longwe

### Missionary Spheres of Influence

During the second half of the nineteenth century, white traders, concession seekers and missionaries arrived in Zimbabwe, Zambia and Malawi in small parties. Before long, missionaries became agents in a complex transformation process of the region that was closely related to the extensive transformations that followed the impact of capitalism and colonialism. Each missionary organisation entering the region chose a specific area in which to begin its work. At the end of 1859, the London Missionary Society (LMS) established a mission at Inyati in Zimbabwe, though the evangelistic efforts were not to bear fruit for many years. It was the first permanent European outpost that also provided a home for travellers. In Zimbabwe, as in Zambia and Malawi, the missionary presence both eased and critiqued the colonial advance.

The missionary work also demonstrates the speed and shape of the ecclesiastical scramble. In mid-1861, the Anglican Church's Universities' Mission to Central Africa (UMCA) started work at Magomero in Malawi, only to withdraw to Zanzibar due to several difficulties. It was back in Malawi in 1882. In the meantime, the Scottish Presbyterian Livingstonia Mission established itself in northern Malawi. Its area of influence included central Malawi and north-eastern Zambia. Its success owed much to the work of Zulu evangelists, including Shadrach Ngunana and William Koyi. In 1889, Livingstonia transferred central Malawi to the Dutch Reformed Church Mission from South Africa. Blantyre Mission, also Scottish Presbyterian, took southern Malawi, which left the lakeshore areas for the UMCA. After an abortive attempt to establish a mission in southern Malawi in 1889–91, the Catholics returned to Malawi only in 1901. In the comity of missions in Malawi there was no place for the Catholics, whom the Presbyterians viewed as intruders into a country already divided up. That has since changed. The comity agreement between Nkhoma Synod (formerly the Dutch Reformed Mission) and Livingstonia Synod has also ended, with Livingstonia starting congregations in Nkhoma's territory in central Malawi.

It was not until the founding of the Zambezi Industrial Mission at Blantyre in 1892 that the challenge to the Scottish missions' hegemony began in earnest. The next nine years saw the founding of four smaller missions: Nyasa Industrial Mission (NIM) in 1893 (now the Evangelical Church of Malawi); the Scottish Baptist Industrial Mission (BIM) at Gowa in 1896; the Providence Industrial Mission (PIM) of John Chilembwe in 1900; and the Seventh-day Baptist (SDB) Mission at Malamulo in Makwasa in 1901, which two years later became Seventh-day Adventist (SDA). The BIM became the Churches of Christ in 1929. It also opened the door into Malawi for other Baptist individuals and mission organisations.

In 1885 the LMS was the first to establish a mission station in Zambia, based at Niamikolo, close to Lake Tanganyika; and it was followed by other missions throughout Zambia. One of the reasons for the rapid spread of mission stations was that smaller tribes in the area believed that the missionaries would provide protection from their attackers, such as the powerful Bemba. The Paris Mission established itself in 1892 and achieved considerable success among the Lozi, largely due to the Sotho evangelists on its team. In the same year, the Primitive Methodists settled among the Illa. The Scottish Presbyterians settled at Mwenzo in 1894. The four missions were to merge their work in 1965 and become known as the United Church of Zambia (UCZ).

The Catholics established a mission among the Bemba in 1895. As a result, the Catholic Church later became by far the most influential denomination in Zambia. Catechists played an important part in the rapid proliferation of Catholic stations. In 1899, the LMS started work in the north-east of Zambia. In 1905, the NIM opened a mission station at Kafulafuta, south-east of Ndola, which later became the nucleus of the Zambia Baptist Association. In 1911, Leonard Kamungu, a priest from Malawi, established the first Anglican mission at Msoro, near Chipata, under the UMCA, which held to a strict Anglo-Catholic theology.

The Catholics offended the LMS by starting a mission station near the LMS station in the north-east. The Catholics strongly opposed the spheres

*Christianity in Zimbabwe, 1970 and 2015*

| | 1970 | | 2015 | | Average annual growth rate (%), 1970–2015 |
|---|---|---|---|---|---|
| Tradition | Population | % | Population | % | |
| Christians | 2,719,000 | 52.2% | 12,740,000 | 81.7% | 3.49% |
| *Roman Catholics* | 557,000 | 10.7% | 1,983,000 | 12.7% | 2.86% |
| *Orthodox* | 8,000 | 0.2% | 5,400 | 0.0% | −0.87% |
| *Independents* | 704,000 | 13.5% | 6,516,000 | 41.8% | 5.07% |
| *Protestants* | 730,000 | 14.0% | 3,338,000 | 21.4% | 3.44% |
| *Anglicans* | 153,000 | 2.9% | 420,000 | 2.7% | 2.27% |
| Pentecostals | 604,000 | 11.6% | 6,944,000 | 44.5% | 5.58% |
| Evangelicals | 282,000 | 5.4% | 1,191,000 | 7.6% | 3.25% |
| **Total population** | **5,206,000** | **100.0%** | **15,603,000** | **100.0%** | **2.47%** |

Source: Todd M. Johnson and Gina A. Zurlo (eds), *World Christian Database* (Leiden/Boston: Brill), accessed March 2016.

of influence, though they did not like other missions to come close to 'their' area. They opposed the Anglicans who wanted to open a mission in Bangweulu. The Anglicans also found resistance in eastern Zambia from the Reformed Mission. Later on, however, the Catholic, Anglican and Adventist missions rejected the allocation of land to different missions, which was loosened in the 1930s because of the growth of towns and of labour migration, whereby people 'brought' their church and denominational identifications to their new locations. Among missions such as Baptist, there existed mutual agreements that if one church was already established in a place, other churches would not start new work there. That also later changed.

In Zimbabwe, the white settler regime gave missionary groups land, half of which went to the Catholics, who had returned to the country in 1890. Catholics selected land for stations and for mission farms. The Anglicans established themselves at Penhalonga in Manicaland. The mission was successful in evangelising the Shona because it used mainly catechists, including Bernard Mizeki. Together with one of his converts, Shoniwa Kapuya, Mizeki was also involved in the translations of the Scriptures and liturgy. Mizeki was later martyred and he is officially an Anglican saint. Anglicans experienced most acutely the tensions arising from the encounter of races and cultures because they had a sizeable portion of whites who were either practising or lapsed members. Due to the comparative independence of the Anglican missions, the white members met the bulk of the Church's expenses without the need for large subsidies from missionary societies. That solved some problems but raised others.

In 1891 the Salvation Army, the Wesleyan (British) Methodists and the Dutch Reformed Church of South Africa arrived, each occupying part of the central province. In 1893 the American Board of Commissioners for Foreign Missions of the Congregational Christian Churches established a mission in the south-east. The Seventh-day Adventists arrived in

*Christianity in Zambia, 1970 and 2015*

| | 1970 | | 2015 | | Average annual growth rate (%), 1970–2015 |
|---|---|---|---|---|---|
| Tradition | Population | % | Population | % | |
| Christians | 2,825,000 | 67.5% | 13,858,000 | 85.5% | 3.60% |
| *Roman Catholics* | 923,000 | 22.1% | 5,339,000 | 32.9% | 3.98% |
| *Orthodox* | 5,200 | 0.1% | 7,700 | 0.0% | 0.86% |
| *Independents* | 844,000 | 20.2% | 2,924,000 | 18.0% | 2.80% |
| *Protestants* | 296,000 | 7.1% | 5,144,000 | 31.7% | 6.55% |
| *Anglicans* | 85,000 | 2.0% | 294,000 | 1.8% | 2.80% |
| Pentecostals | 293,000 | 7.0% | 3,676,000 | 22.7% | 5.78% |
| Evangelicals | 239,000 | 5.7% | 2,939,000 | 18.1% | 5.74% |
| **Total population** | **4,185,000** | **100.0%** | **16,212,000** | **100.0%** | **3.05%** |

Source: Todd M. Johnson and Gina A. Zurlo (eds), *World Christian Database* (Leiden/Boston: Brill), accessed March 2016.

Matabeleland in 1894. The Methodist Episcopal Church (MEC), also known as the American Methodists, arrived in Manicaland and began work in the east, around Mutare, in 1897. The British Methodists and MEC made a territorial agreement in order not to be in each other's way.

These territorial agreements, or spheres of influence or comity, played a large role in the spread of churches. Although they were not meant to restrict people's faith, the agreements could be seen as narrowing their religious freedom. Comity agreements also meant leaders felt no need to settle doctrinal differences between the missions. It is therefore no surprise that some ethnic or language groups identified themselves with a particular mission or church in their area. Speaking against another denomination, consequently, could be seen as being hostile to another ethnic group.

Throughout the region, although white missionaries served well by staying for a long time at some mission stations, very soon African missionaries were doing most of the missionary work. The involvement of local people in mission work perhaps reflects an aspect of Christianity that set it apart from many of the other structures of colonialism (which severely limited the ability of the local population to participate in what was basically for the white people). In addition to African involvement in evangelism, the participation of the Bemba people and the use of their language throughout the country helped a Zambia-wide growth of Roman Catholicism. Political and economic considerations did, and still do, play a major role in the response to Christianity.

The early missions followed the typical mission station approach in which the mission constructed buildings to house church, school and dispensary. The principal aim was to attract the local people to a central place. The later missions took a different approach. Evangelical missions, in particular, began by teaching the Bible in the areas where people lived. The idea of a personal relationship with Jesus became attractive for many people. The message about a new birth struck a chord with many who were

*Christianity in Malawi, 1970 and 2015*

| | 1970 | | 2015 | | Average annual growth rate (%), 1970–2015 |
|---|---|---|---|---|---|
| Tradition | Population | % | Population | % | |
| Christians | 2,664,000 | 57.9% | 13,735,000 | 79.8% | 3.71% |
| *Roman Catholics* | 993,000 | 21.6% | 5,901,000 | 34.3% | 4.04% |
| *Orthodox* | 1,000 | 0.0% | 3,600 | 0.0% | 2.89% |
| *Independents* | 249,000 | 5.4% | 2,406,000 | 14.0% | 5.17% |
| *Protestants* | 960,000 | 20.9% | 4,972,000 | 28.9% | 3.72% |
| *Anglicans* | 76,500 | 1.7% | 331,000 | 1.9% | 3.31% |
| Pentecostals | 103,000 | 2.2% | 3,711,000 | 21.6% | 8.30% |
| Evangelicals | 304,000 | 6.6% | 3,045,000 | 17.7% | 5.26% |
| **Total population** | **4,604,000** | **100.0%** | **17,215,000** | **100.0%** | **2.97%** |

Source: Todd M. Johnson and Gina A. Zurlo (eds), *World Christian Database* (Leiden/Boston: Brill), accessed March 2016.

adapting to new circumstances. Some members from mainline churches have founded other churches because they felt their churches did not focus enough on being 'born again'.

Apart from spiritual formation, missions and churches have been providing social welfare, including education and health care. Biblical principles of care for the weak and provision of alternative medical care to traditional healing motivated the churches' provision of health care. Through health care, churches have generally tried to change or discourage cultural practices that are contrary to Christian beliefs. Schools were often associated with mission stations and they retained the ethos of their parent denomination. Mission schools soon became centres where the aspiration for national independence was nurtured.

## Pentecostal and Charismatic Churches

Over the years, many Pentecostal-type denominational missions established themselves in this region. Pentecostalism has also contributed to the birth of some major Zionist African Instituted Church movements. Some have understood the 'messianic' leadership among the Shona African Instituted Churches in Zimbabwe, for example, as a 'translation and interpretation of Christ' and, within the processes of fragmentation and fission of independent church groups, they have seen seeds for Christian unity. The result was the founding of the Conference of Shona Independent Churches, popularly known as Fambidzano, in 1972. Prophetic-healing churches have a mythical understanding of biblical Zion (believed to have come from heaven) in their own Zion mountain-top centres. Samuel Mutendi founded Mutendi Zion Church in Zimbabwe. Other famous Zimbabwean Zion Church leaders include Yohane Masowe and Yohane Maranke.

In Malawi, Pentecostal churches established themselves rather late, in the mid-twentieth century. After they started, they progressed slowly for at least two decades. The beginnings were all attributable to returning *machona* (migrant workers). The Apostolic Faith Mission and the Assemblies of God came from Tanzania, Zimbabwe and South Africa. After 1960 the Pentecostal section of Malawian Christianity experienced a major expansion. The 'old' Pentecostal *machona* churches started to grow much faster and new missions came in, like the Pentecostal Assemblies of Canada, the Foursquare Gospel Church and the Apostolic Faith Church.

In contrast to the earlier missions, the Charismatic churches often came into existence after a period of germination in the form of interdenominational fellowships or within interdenominational para-church movements. In contrast to all the earlier denominational families that had a rural base in Africa, the Charismatic movement began its ministry in the cities and in institutions of higher learning. There is no doubt that its success has been great, especially among the urban population, and that most of those who join come from mainline or from other Evangelical denominations.

Charismatic piety is in high demand among the better-off urban people, and it gives convincing answers to the deep traditional African quests for power, wealth and health. Although most Charismatic churches are still predominantly urban and wealthy, they have started to spread to the poor suburbs of the cities and to the rural areas. On the other hand, the Charismatic movement spans both traditional and modern socio-cultural elements. Charismatic ministries address issues such as witchcraft and spirit possession while simultaneously responding to modern issues, with street children ministries, electronic music or entrepreneurial seminars. This sensitivity to the African worldview is evident in the Charismatic movement's concern with witchcraft, healing and prosperity. Furthermore, modernisation has not eradicated ancient beliefs, as is evident from witchcraft stories that constantly feature in the media.

With many people living with HIV/AIDS and malaria and dysfunctional health care systems, the need for healing has never been greater. This is aggravated by the grinding poverty in which many people find themselves. Consequently, the Charismatic practice of deliverance from evil spirits, curses, sickness and poverty finds an audience ready to receive a solution. The Charismatic influence is such that many non-Charismatic churches have adopted the Charismatic style of worship.

## Church and State

Up until national independence, churches usually took the middle of the road by ministering to the needs of the people without antagonising the colonial administration, although at times they became a means through which to oppose colonial rule. As the demand for political independence deepened, supporters of independence looked to the church as a welcome ally. Church sympathy for the nationalist cause aroused strong resentment among white Christians and the governments. In order to achieve their goal, the churches made use of their para-church agencies or organisations to engage the state on economic, political and social issues.

After independence, the established churches faced widespread suspicion due to their association with the former colonial regimes. For this reason, churches generally sought legitimacy through endorsing state-directed development at the expense of promoting multi-party democracy. The established churches embarked on a policy of appeasement due to the fear that their compromised relationship with colonial powers would cause the new government to prefer independent churches at their expense. In Zimbabwe, for example, after independence in 1980, the protection of an individual against the excesses of the state received inadequate attention and the democratic role of civic organisations was ignored. More recently, however, the churches have stood as a voice of morality by condemning political violence and lack of political tolerance. The democratic space for association has been at the centre of conflict between the churches and the government.

Whereas some politicians rebuked the dissenting voices of the clergy, and sought to limit the church to prayers and offering guidance on moral issues, the leaders of the national Catholic bishops' conferences, the national Evangelical Fellowships and National Councils of Churches, including the Public Affairs Committee in the case of Malawi, embarked on a strategy to give dialogue a chance. The churches have been strong in issuing periodic criticism of government on various issues. Not only have the churches been prominent as one of the key actors in the transition process from one-party state to multi-party political governance, they have also continued to be vocal politically. Even when they have held divergent and conflicting views on some issues, they have avoided division. The churches have also played a leading role in empowering and coordinating civil society.

Since many people identify with the Christian faith, this gives the churches legitimacy in their advocacy role. The joint working of the churches' national councils and associations, the Catholic Commissions for Justice and Peace, and the ecumenical Public Affairs Committee in Malawi, gives weight to the voice of the churches and therefore increases their influence. Although ecumenical bodies have played very important advocacy roles, they face a common dilemma in the need to expend a great deal of energy in order to reach consensus, a process often complicated by their own cumbersome structures. Despite the difficulties, joint work of the churches has been effective in advocating political change.

Whereas nationalist movements played a major role in the decolonisation process, and mainline church leaders were deeply involved in the democratisation efforts of the 1990s, more recently the Pentecostals and Charismatics have become increasingly important political actors. Pentecostals speak of praying for and electing Christians into power so that government and society should be transformed into a 'Christian nation'. Zambian President Frederick Chiluba, an avowed Pentecostal, after taking office invited a group of Pentecostal ministers to 'cleanse' the presidential palace of evil spirits and publicly dedicated Zambia and its government to 'the Lordship of Jesus Christ'. Chiluba's declaration of Zambia as a 'Christian nation' was not only anti-democratic but also was soon discredited.

Zimbabwean President Robert Mugabe, facing deepening political crises and increasing criticism from mainline church leaders, turned to Pentecostals for religious and moral legitimation, which some Pentecostal leaders have been eager to provide. Despite being a Roman Catholic, he sought closer ties to some Charismatic and Pentecostal leaders, in which he was assisted by the fact that his wife and sister are members of the Zimbabwe Assemblies of God Africa (ZAOGA). On 26 June 2006, Mugabe presided at a Zimbabwe National Day of Prayer in Harare. The event was boycotted by prominent Catholic and Anglican leaders but it included representatives of the Evangelical Fellowship of Zimbabwe and the Zimbabwe Council of Churches, because both include Pentecostal members. In Malawi, the current Malawi Congress Party President, Dr Lazarus Chakwera, the former President of the Assemblies of God in Malawi and founding pastor of the International Christian Assembly, is aiming to be the next President of the country. Although the church does its best to provide effective leadership in a heavily divided political environment, this has not had the desired impact. Divisions within the church and lack of radical theologies have compromised the church's efforts.

## The Inculturation of the Faith

The missions and churches have been able to make the Bible accessible to the people by translating it into many of the local languages, though there are still some smaller ethnic groups lacking a Bible in their own language. For almost all churches, translations of religious instruction material into local African languages were done from the missions' catechisms with little or no adaptation. This is an area that requires more indigenising effort. There is a need for African theological writers to produce instruction material that replaces the Western methodology of questions and answers with one of stories and proverbs. Unless theological teaching becomes rooted in African culture, the African church will not be able to develop its own theology. It will not be able to respond to its own context. Non-Christian contexts will remain unchallenged and the theology taught will be of marginal relevance to African issues. If the African church is to develop indigenous roots, then written theology in local languages needs to be encouraged to reflect the oral theologising already going on.

Of late, the Catholic Church has promoted the idea of the church as the family of God, an ecclesiastical structure that is more African. The model of 'family' tends to promote interpersonal relationships between people in the church. This allows for shared responsibilities, rather than leaving all initiative with the clergy or lay leaders. Some churches want to see full involvement of all members and this finds expression particularly in strengthening the role of women. Women's organisations are a strong branch of many churches. Their visibility and strong character have caused them to be seen as 'the face' of the church or 'a church within a church'. In the context of a patriarchal society, the church has proved to be a sphere in which women find liberation and engage themselves actively in religious and social life. In Malawi, churches began establishing these organisations around 1940. They blossomed from sewing clubs and Bible study and prayer groups to become national organisations. Through their evangelistic programmes, pastoral care and social work, churches have expanded tremendously.

For a long time, churches have tended to place the youth and children under the wings of the women's organisations, but that is changing. Churches have developed children's Bible study programmes and youth groups in churches, schools and colleges. There are denominational as well as interdenominational materials and groups. Subjects being discussed include femininity and masculinity, love and marriage, gender-based violence, the importance of education in relation to the Bible and how to apply biblical teaching in an African context. Churches that do not prepare their youth spiritually and mentally through such programmes lose them to other churches or non-Christian groups. With such support and as their lives are shaped by the gospel, Christian young people can exercise great influence on their peers. In many churches, the youth have moved from being the driven to being the drivers. The issue of gender, however, remains very significant. When it comes to decision-making, power is in the hands of men, and therefore decisions tend to benefit men more than women. Many girls have internalised a sense of inferiority and therefore do not aspire to leadership. As a result, their avenue of service tends to be through women's organisations, which offer a space where they can develop and exercise their gifts.

A major concern for the churches in these three countries is that Christians live in two worlds. When they are within the church premises they behave in one way, but when they are out of those premises their behaviour is quite different. There is a need to develop integrity of faith and life rather than looking on Christianity as a list of things to do and not to do. There is a great need in this region for the churches to proclaim the Christian message to people from within the perspective of their culture, in order for them to live a Christian life that is grounded in their own context. Many claim to be Christians, but most of their life does not portray their faith. The problem is compounded by the large number of church members per minister and the large number of prayer houses (chapels) for a minister to visit. It becomes difficult for the clergy to apply appropriate methods of evangelism that would ground members in biblical teaching in order for them to be true representatives of Christ in their way of life.

One area where considerable progress has been made is inculturation of the liturgy. Mainline churches have tolerated dancing or even tried to integrate it into the liturgy of a congregation. The Catholic Church recognised from the beginning that most of its converts, who were unschooled and from an oral culture, sought a literal embodiment of religion in song, word and gesture. Liturgy was its most powerful tool and the means by which the community would live and express its own history and faith experience. African music and styles of worship permeate even English-language services in the urban context.

One prominent champion of inculturation is the former Catholic Archbishop of Lusaka, Emmanuel Milingo. He argued for the development of an authentic African Christianity growing out of African values, including spiritual ones, and challenged Western control of African Christianity. Controversially, Milingo insisted that people of colour are not inferior but that they have wisdom that the West neither possesses nor acknowledges. The Catholic Church hierarchy criticised Milingo for exorcism and faith-healing practices not approved by the church. It was also disturbed by his argument that Catholic priests should be allowed to marry, and he was eventually deposed.

One way of indigenising the faith has been through theological education. This started with denominational Bible schools and colleges, but then interdenominational and non-denominational colleges were founded. The universities also introduced Theology and Religious Studies (TRS) departments. Recently, a number of Christian universities have been opened. The great majority of theology students have been men. Because clericalism empowers the pastor over the laity, it also disempowers women in theological education. That has created a shortage of theologically trained women in the churches.

## Theology

Theological issues are apparent in the popular experience of Christian faith. Christology is one area where there is active discussion. Many Christians struggle to defend the belief that Jesus was not only human but divine as well. Others stress Christ's divinity and tend towards the view that Jesus only appears to have taken on our human condition. Stressing the difference between Jesus's humanity and ours can be a way of limiting the ethical demands of the faith. Many also find it hard to believe in the Trinity and this is further complicated by the African belief in spirits.

Marriage and family life is another common area of concern. Most churches hold to a biblical theology of marriage that regards polygamy as a violation of God's norm of a monogamous and indissoluble marriage. Very few attempts have been made to baptise converted polygamists without their first divorcing the 'surplus' wives. A combination of Western missionary theology and loyalty to some African traditional cultural values has tended to create a male-dominated church and society. Only ordained men were recognised as clergy and church leaders. Women were expected to play supportive roles. Although many churches believe in the priesthood of all believers, historically they have not accepted the ordination of women as clergy. Since the 1990s, however, a growing number of Protestant mainline and Pentecostal and Charismatic churches have begun ordaining women – a significant development for the theology of gender.

The interface of church and society is another area that attracts theological reflection. Most churches' theology does not exclude cooperation with the government, provided that sufficient distance is kept. It is believed that if the church, corporately and individually, is to impact a nation, Christian values must permeate the nation, including the political terrain. There is evidence of tension, however, between an 'ecumenical' approach that is oriented to social liberation and favours political activism, and an 'Evangelical' approach that is oriented to the spiritual dimension and stresses the personal salvation of individual souls.

Since the 1980s, the challenge of publishing local theologies has been taken up by Mambo Press in Zimbabwe and by Kachere Series and Mzuni Press in Malawi. Much theological research is done by the university TRS departments and theological colleges. MA and PhD dissertations produced in the universities and theological colleges form a basis for the development of local theology. Pioneering scholars, such as Ezra Chitando and Paul Gundani in Zimbabwe, and Patrick Kalilombe, Augustine Musopole and Isabel Apawo Phiri in Malawi, have offered theological analysis that is engaged with local cultural and social issues.

Innovative approaches to theology have been promoted by women affiliated to the Circle of Concerned African Women Theologians, such as Isabel Apawo Phiri, Francisca Chihanda and Fulata Moyo. They have argued that inherited forms of theologising are patently inadequate to respond meaningfully to the present crises, including HIV/AIDS, poverty and gender injustice, that plague continental Africa. The work of women theologians on such issues is marked by its collaborative character and its interdisciplinary nature. This creative movement is promoting women's self-expression, leadership skills and spiritual development, and space for ecumenism.

## The Church and Other Faiths

Malawi, in contrast to Zambia and Zimbabwe, has a sizeable Muslim minority. Islam attracted the Yao more than any other tribe in Malawi because they have been in constant touch with the Arabs and Swahilis since the 1800s. The Yao felt Islam seemed more suited to Africans than did Christianity because it did not oblige Africans to give up traditional practices such as polygamy. By incorporating certain Islamic elements into the traditional puberty ceremony, they made the revised version an entrance to both Yao adulthood and Islam, and thereby made a significant contribution to the identification of the Yao with Islam that has long been characteristic in Malawi. Although Islam attracted the Yao more than any other tribe, there are nonetheless more Yao Christians than Yao Muslims.

Although the numbers are rather small, there are conversions from Islam to Christianity. The Baptist Convention of Malawi has three Yao Muslim-background congregations. The Assemblies of God and the Roman Catholic Church also have members who converted from Islam. However, most converts from Islam join Evangelical churches. There are also conversions from Christianity to Islam, particularly through marriage of Christian women to Muslim men. In some cases, such women return from Islam to their original church, such as Anglican or Catholic, following divorce or the death of their Muslim husbands.

There has rarely been real friction between Christians and Muslims in Central Africa. In 2003, some Muslims torched Christian churches in Mangochi, a strongly Muslim district in Malawi. Christians retaliated by burning some mosques in several towns. The government downplayed the episodes and called on the two groups to settle their differences and agree to work alongside each other. In Zambia, Pentecostals organised public evangelistic campaigns to counter the perceived ascendancy of Muslims. They organised an effort to promote Christianity and contain Islam in the eastern part of the country.

African traditional religion (ATR) does not exist any longer as an organised entity. Nonetheless, in College textbooks on religious education it is given equal weight with Christianity and Islam. Many practising Christians or Muslims incorporate elements of ATR into their daily lives. Since ATR as such is difficult to find, traditional customs and institutions, such as chieftainship, are used to represent ATR. However, in practice chiefs are either Christians or Muslims.

One can also note the presence of Judaism, Hinduism, Sikhism and the Baha'i faith in several towns and cities throughout Central Africa. Here and there one can also meet members of marginal Christian groups such as Jehovah's Witnesses, Bible Believers, the Unification Church and the Church of Jesus Christ of Latter-Day Saints. So far there is no generally agreed method for engaging with people of other faiths. Different missiological approaches create tensions and a degree of competition. This is an area that is ripe for deeper consideration.

Protestant and Catholic missions produced an African Christianity that was mainly shaped by the respective European traditions. That changed when waves of revival brought greater diversification to the missionary effort and to the emergent churches. Pentecostals gave birth to the Zionist family of African Indigenous Churches, while interdenominational fellowships produced Charismatic churches. The remarkable growth of Christianity in the three countries is attributable not only to evangelism but also to the high level of African religiosity and to population growth. Despite divisions, the churches have made a huge contribution to national development in such areas as education, health care, political governance and the economy. Despite belief in the priesthood of all believers, in practice women are excluded from leadership positions. Christian–Muslim relations remains a delicate issue, especially in Malawi.

## Bibliography

Cheyeka, Austin, *Church and State and Political Ethics in a Post-colonial State: The Case of Zambia* (Zomba: Kachere, 2008).

Daneel, M. L., *Quest for Belonging: Introduction to a Study of African Independent Churches* (Gweru: Mambo, 1987).

Mlenga, Moses, *Polygamy in Northern Malawi: A Christian Rethinking* (Mzuzu: Luviri Press, 2015).

Phiri, Isabel Apawo, *Women, Presbyterianism and Patriarchy: Religious Experience of Chewa Women in Central Malawi* (Blantyre: CLAIM, 1997).

Weller, John and Jane Linden, *Mainstream Christianity to 1980 in Malawi, Zambia and Zimbabwe* (Gweru: Mambo, 1984).

# Madagascar

## Solomon Andriatsimialomananarivo

The history of Christianity in Madagascar begins in the seventeenth century. The Congregation of Saint Vincent de Paul, also known as the Congregation of Lazarists, sent missionaries to the southern tip of the great island in 1648, to the city of Taolagnaro in the region of the Antanosy people. Cardinal Richelieu, acting as Prime Minister to King Louis XIII of France, had encouraged conquest of the island and would have commended the Lazarists' initiative. The congregation faced major challenges, such as the difficulty of introducing the Roman alphabet when Arabic script had already made inroads; the hostility of the local people, who were strongly attached both to traditional religions and to the rule of the local monarch; and the Lazarists' own failure to master the Malagasy language, which was in fact the primary barrier to evangelism. Unable to overcome these obstacles, the Catholic mission left the island. Another attempt would not be made until the nineteenth century.

### The First Wave of Missionary Societies

Missionaries of the London Missionary Society (LMS), founded in England in 1795, landed on the eastern coast of Madagascar in August 1818. It was an independent, interdenominational mission of Welsh origin. David Jones and Thomas Bevan decided to venture as far as Antananarivo, the capital of the Kingdom of Madagascar, no doubt for strategic reasons. In their evangelistic enterprise, they persuaded the king, Radama I, to adopt the Roman alphabet, which officially replaced Arabic script on 26 March 1823, and to authorise the creation of a school, open to all and particularly to the children of the royal family.

The translation of the Bible into Malagasy by the LMS missionaries was completed in June 1835, just before the beginning of the persecution ordained by the new queen, Ranavalona I, a nationalist very attached to traditional religions. Thus the newly converted Christians had the Bible in hand. It is important to note that the Scriptures, translated into their mother tongue, would be both the weapon and the food of these Christians as they practised their faith in hiding over the next 30 years.

Beginning in 1861, when the persecution ended, new missions began to arrive to add their efforts to the work of the LMS: the Friends of Foreign

Mission Association (FFMA), commonly called Quakers; the Society for the Propagation of the Gospel (SPG) and the Church Missionary Society (CMS), both from England; and the Norwegian Missionary Society. Other societies in the Lutheran tradition followed. The missionary societies collaborated harmoniously until the advent of the French colonial regime in 1895. At this time the Jesuits arrived, with confidence and even arrogance. Since the colonising nation was Catholic, the Jesuits were quite confident in their Christianising, or perhaps Catholicising, effort and sometimes opposed the British Protestant missionaries. This was the beginning of a sort of cold war. At the invitation of the British missionaries and Malagasy Protestants, the French Protestant Société des Missions Evangéliques de Paris (SMEP), founded in 1822, sent missionaries to Madagascar in 1896 to prove to the colonial powers that there were also French Protestants. The SMEP sought to calm the tension between Protestants and Catholics in a variety of ways. Thus Christianity in Madagascar during colonisation was composed of the following: Protestant churches born of British and French missions, the Lutheran Church of Norwegian and American origins, the Anglican Church, and the Roman Catholic Church. These churches are generally known as the institutional churches.

The history of Malagasy Christianity is inseparable from the history of revival. Revival, a great spiritual movement that brings thousands of people in a region to repent and turn back to God, has left its mark on the Malagasy churches. The dynamism of the island's churches today can be explained in part by the impact of the revival movements. The first of these occurred in 1894 in the central-south part of the island. Souls were turned to God, bodies healed of various illnesses and lives delivered from spiritual bondage. In 10 years, this revival movement planted 124 new churches, which were entrusted to existing Protestant denominations.

There would be other revival movements. They would be quite different from one another in their spirituality, but essentially biblical in

*Christianity in Madagascar, 1970 and 2015*

| | 1970 | | 2015 | | Average annual growth rate (%), 1970–2015 |
|---|---|---|---|---|---|
| Tradition | Population | % | Population | % | |
| Christians | 3,326,000 | 50.6% | 14,079,000 | 58.1% | 3.26% |
| *Roman Catholics* | 1,595,000 | 24.3% | 6,220,000 | 25.7% | 3.07% |
| *Orthodox* | 540 | 0.0% | 32,600 | 0.1% | 9.54% |
| *Independents* | 146,000 | 2.2% | 1,179,000 | 4.9% | 4.75% |
| *Protestants* | 1,351,000 | 20.5% | 7,206,000 | 29.7% | 3.79% |
| *Anglicans* | 50,400 | 0.8% | 450,000 | 1.9% | 4.98% |
| Pentecostals | 60,400 | 0.9% | 1,603,000 | 6.6% | 7.56% |
| Evangelicals | 318,000 | 4.8% | 1,868,000 | 7.7% | 4.02% |
| **Total population** | **6,576,000** | **100.0%** | **24,235,000** | **100.0%** | **2.94%** |

Source: Todd M. Johnson and Gina A. Zurlo (eds), *World Christian Database* (Leiden/Boston: Brill), accessed March 2016.

their theology. The common element of these revivals is the loyalty that they displayed toward the existing Protestant churches. They had no interest in creating new churches, or African Independent Churches. They helped new converts to join existing churches, particularly Lutheran and Reformed. From a theological perspective, the revival movements brought about inculturation before the term came into common use. Their faith was biblical, inherited from the Church Fathers and the sixteenth-century Reformers, but their spirituality, the expression of faith in worship and daily life, was Malagasy.

## The Second Wave of Missionary Societies

Alongside the institutional churches that eventually created the Fédération des Églises Protestantes de Madagascar (FFPM), Evangelical churches were created as a result of a second missionary wave. These trace their roots not only to the Reformation of the sixteenth century, as do the traditional Protestant churches, but also to the European revivals of the eighteenth and nineteenth centuries. Their missionaries came from various denominations. These churches generally have Baptist tendencies and define themselves as 'believers' churches'. They explored fallow fields, where Christianity had not yet penetrated for various reasons. Surprisingly, vast regions of the island had not yet heard the gospel, and in certain localities very few had even a minimal knowledge of Jesus, of salvation and of eternal life.

Missionaries in the Pentecostal tradition arrived in Madagascar at the beginning of the 1960s. After a number of evangelistic and miracle-working campaigns, churches were planted in the capital and in the provinces. The Pentecostal 'family' is diverse: some churches, such as the Assemblies of God, are moderate, others more radical; but, collectively, the Pentecostal churches represent a significant force on the island.

## The New Societies

Finally, we must mention the independent churches stemming from the third missionary wave, which arrived or rather were created early in the twenty-first century. These are focused on specific ethnic groups: those in the north-west part of the island, which have affinities with Islam; those still bound to traditional African religions and ancestor worship; and the ethnic groups most remote from modern society, such as the Mikea, who are anthropologically similar to the Pygmies of Central Africa. The missionary societies of the third wave are mostly of African origin, coming from the mainland, although some are Korean.

## The Components of Christianity in Madagascar

Christianity in Madagascar mainly comprises three types of church:

1. The institutional churches that form the Council of Christian Churches of Madagascar (FFKM):

- The Roman Catholic Church
- The Protestant churches, including the Church of Jesus Christ in Madagascar (FJKM), of Calvinist Reformed background, and the Lutheran Church in Madagascar (FLM), which form the Federation of Protestant Churches in Madagascar (FFPM). We should add two major dissident Protestant churches, the FMTA and METM
- The Episcopal Church of Madagascar (EEM), of Anglican heritage.

The Roman Catholic Church includes around a quarter of the country's population of some 24 million. The Protestant and Anglican churches stemming from the first missionary wave together make up another quarter of the total population. The FFKM is actively involved in the island's socio-political life, particularly in the context of national reconciliation.

2. The Evangelical churches that identify as believers' churches:

- The Bible Baptist Church (FBBM) is the oldest, with around 100 local congregations. Pentecostal churches of various tendencies can also be classified in this group. Some of these churches are of American origin, while others' origins lie in France and Switzerland. However, they all clearly affirm the fundamental truths of Scripture, prioritise evangelism, and aspire to holiness both individually and collectively.

3. The new Evangelical and Independent churches recently planted on the island, especially in remote regions and isolated villages. These churches preach the same gospel as the others but go to places where the others did not go. The number of believers in the two groups of Evangelical churches is still small, although their numerical growth is undeniable. They have a particular concern for the one in three Malagasy who still practise ancestor worship.

The Orthodox Church, from Eastern Europe, has also come to Madagascar; however, it will be several years at least before these churches occupy a significant place in the landscape of Malagasy Christianity. In addition, para-church ministries support the work of the various churches. The Malagasy Bible Society provides Bibles in a variety of versions. Indeed, since the first translation of the Bible into Malagasy in 1835, a number of editions and versions have been published. Particularly noteworthy is the ecumenical Bible translation, appreciated by the new generation of believers. Meanwhile, the Scripture Union helps families to make the Bible their own and the Christian Unions – the Union des Groupes Bibliques de Madagascar and the International Fellowship of Evangelical Students (IFES), a national movement – disciple secondary and university students through group Bible study, helping them enter into the culture of the Bible. There are many other para-church ministries, each with its own vision and mission, but they all work alongside the churches.

A fourth type of church may also be considered. For several decades, religious groups calling themselves 'Evangelical' have sprung up. These groups organise meetings in cinemas, and their very modern style attracts young people. They are led by stirring speakers with such strong personalities that their meetings seem like shows. Most preach Christ with a focus on well-being in the here and now, while others insist on signs and wonders. It is questioned, however, whether these are indeed churches in the strict interpretation of the term.

### Present-day Christianity and Society

Given the current state of Christianity in Madagascar, we may wonder about its impact. How does the church, through the denominations and Christian organisations, accomplish its mission today? Especially since the Lausanne Congress of 1974, leaders have understood that the church's mission includes two essential tasks: evangelism and social action.

The second task of the mission has been seriously addressed. The island's first leaders after its independence in 1960 were trained in Christian schools. Currently the best secondary schools are religiously affiliated. They train students in civic responsibility as well as academic instruction. To give just one example, the Norwegian Mission Society (NMS) developed special schools for the blind and the deaf and mute, which are now administered by the Lutheran Church (FLM).

These schools thus produced leaders for society: teachers, lawyers, doctors and also pastors. The island boasts two Protestant theological seminaries, offering masters level (and soon doctoral) training, as well as Bible institutes and Bible schools that train pastors for local churches. The churches urgently need well trained ministers who can teach their members and equip them to resist heresies, ever more numerous and aggressive.

Theologians trained in these institutions help to develop the church's thinking and influence society as a whole through their books. They have written on church history, the history of the revival movements and the history of the martyrs. Books by theologians such as Reverend Ravelojaona, who died in 1956, are still valued as reference books today.

Both the older traditional churches and the new ones have created and operate hospitals in the great cities as well as the most remote parts of the island. Clearly, the churches have generally understood that social action is part of their mission. The church as a fellowship of believers works to extend the Kingdom of God on earth. Both leaders and members pray for the governing authorities so that the nation may enjoy lasting peace and security. They help especially in times of crisis. The FFKM has helped restore order in the nation more than once. Like most African countries, Madagascar has known times of crisis. The FFKM has significantly contributed to national reconciliation when political leaders were having trouble getting along. It does this both by educating believers in the churches and by organising forums of debate in which opposing parties can express their views.

## The Future

The current configuration of churches may have to be reconsidered. First, the so-called institutional churches experience revival from time to time and in certain places. More and more young people are eager to deepen their faith and enrol in Bible courses, while others train as preachers. Many lead prayer and Bible study groups in their neighbourhoods and do what their pastors cannot do. Meanwhile, the churches of the second group outlined above are ageing and many need to be revitalised. Finally, the emerging Evangelical churches, those of the third type, are having an impact on the new landscape of Malagasy Christianity. Some are neo-Pentecostal, others Protestant. If the three types of churches in Madagascar can work together, expressing spiritual unity in Christ, they can effectively confront the danger of the proliferation of groups that preach the so-called 'prosperity gospel', widely viewed as a distortion of the Christian faith.

The churches face great challenges in the resurgence of ancestor worship and the advance of Islam. For a long time Madagascar was, surprisingly, one of the few countries that had not been significantly influenced by Islam; until recently, Muslims comprised less than 7% of the total population, even though the Malagasy had lived side by side with Arab traders for centuries and had adopted certain elements of Arab culture, such as the Arabic calendar and script, while older people were familiar with Arabic astrology. Today, however, Islamic influence is increasing. Without at least some degree of fellowship between the institutional and newer churches, Christianity could decline, at least numerically.

Malagasy Christianity, one of the oldest in French-speaking Africa, numbers fewer believers than is often assumed. Just about 25% of Malagasy are in regular contact with the Bible and have a church life and first-hand knowledge of Christian teaching. For both quantitative and qualitative growth there is great need for preaching and teaching that will deepen understanding of the Bible among the people of Madagascar.

## Bibliography

Callet, F., *Histoire des rois* (Tananarive: Éditions de la Librairie de Madagascar, 1974).

Congrégation de la mission (Lazaristes) (ed.), *Le Christianisme dans le Sud de Madagascar 1896–1996* (Fianarantsoa: Ambozontany, 1996).

Mondain, Georges, *Un Siècle de Mission Protestante à Madagascar* (Paris: Sociétés de Missions Evangéliques, 1922).

Raison-Jourde, Françoise, *Bible et Pouvoir à Madagascar, Invention d'une Identité Chrétienne et Construction de l'État* (Paris: Karthala, 1991).

Ralibera, Daniel, *Les Disciples du Seigneur* (Paris: Mémoire présenté à la Faculté Libre de Théologie Protestante de Paris, 1953).

# Mauritius

## Rodney Curpanen

The Dutch landed on the island in September 1598 and named it Mauritius. No church was set up with this first Christian presence. Roman Catholics established a permanent presence from 1721, when the island was under French occupation. The British captured it in 1810 and two years later the Anglicans started a chaplaincy. In 1814 the London Missionary Society (LMS) started an Evangelical Independent Church (later the Church of Scotland and from 1979 the Presbyterian Church), followed by Swedenborgians (1846) and Seventh-day Adventists (1914). Baptist churches and the Assemblies of God started in the 1960s. Chinese Presbyterians formed the Chinese Christian Fellowship in 1981. Several dissident churches are offshoots of the Assemblies of God: the Full Gospel Church of God, the Église de Pentecôte Unie and the Centre Evangélique Charismatique. Others grew independently; L'Église Chrétienne is a breakaway from Charismatic Catholics. The Roman Catholic, Anglican, Presbyterian and Seventh-day Adventist denominations are recognised by Act of Parliament, while others are seeking official recognition.

The Mauritian church reflects the variety of ethnic groups, with Asian, African and European roots. Creole is the major preaching language; French maintains a strong liturgical presence, while other languages like Bhojpuri, Hindi, Marathi, Telugu, Tamil and Hakka Chinese are accommodated. Due to the influx of overseas students and foreign labour, English is regaining ground.

In this multi-religious and multicultural nation are found both admirable harmony and constant tensions. Many Christians have family members and relatives of different religions due to conversion and mixed marriages. Strong Hindu voices are requesting laws against conversion. Muslims (the majority of whom are Sunnis) are active in outreach, as are Christians. An inter-faith council ensures there is dialogue to promote peace. Only three of the mainline denominations are members.

There is no national council of churches. The earliest collaboration between churches was for the purpose of initiating the British Bible Society auxiliary during the first days of British occupation. The Anglicans, Presbyterians and Roman Catholics formed the Ecumenical Working Group in the latter half of the twentieth century. Today it includes the Assemblies of God and the Fellowship of Christian Churches. Since the mid-1990s several federations have been formed by churches, based on affinities. Individual initiatives with very loose inter-church partnership gave rise to Youth for Christ, the Young Men's Christian Association (YMCA), Gideons, Scripture Union, Campus Crusade, Youth With A Mission (YWAM) and others.

Methods of church planting during the days of slavery varied from education and preaching conversion to social justice. From the 1960s to 1980s, missionaries started new churches by tapping into established mainline churches, resulting in the constant decline of the latter. Evangelism was practised extensively within the Hindu community, less among the Muslims. Later patterns of church planting and growth did not target specific ethnic groups. The mainline Protestant churches have maintained steady growth through conferences, home-based small groups and campaigns, just enough to balance decline. The striking success of independent churches can be attributed to healing services and deliverance tent meetings, often with speakers and artists from overseas. The *Jesus* film (about the life of Christ, based on the Gospel of Luke) in various Asian languages (but mostly in Creole) contributes tremendously to outreach to diverse language groups.

The country's multicultural wealth has not influenced the development of liturgy or theology, however. Artistic expressions are gaining ground but are not rooted enough to stand out and mark a strong local identity. Instead, Western music ensures the church keeps up with current occidental culture and theological thinking. The use of local languages, especially Creole, only gives a Mauritian colouring but so far has not led to the development of local theologies drawing on Mauritian cultural values and symbols. Local productions are limited to translations of the New Testament and the Psalms into Mauritian Creole.

The Roman Catholics, Anglicans and Seventh-day Adventists run secondary educational institutions while individual Christians have formed associations to launch primary schools. However, Christian schools have not promoted church growth. Similarly, involvement in social matters such as HIV/AIDS, gender issues, environmental justice, displaced peoples/

*Christianity in Mauritius, 1970 and 2015*

| | 1970 | | 2015 | | Average annual growth rate (%), 1970–2015 |
|---|---|---|---|---|---|
| Tradition | Population | % | Population | % | |
| Christians | 296,000 | 35.9% | 422,000 | 33.2% | 0.79% |
| *Roman Catholics* | 280,000 | 33.9% | 267,000 | 21.0% | −0.10% |
| *Independents* | 2,900 | 0.4% | 19,200 | 1.5% | 4.26% |
| *Protestants* | 5,900 | 0.7% | 149,000 | 11.7% | 7.45% |
| *Anglicans* | 8,000 | 1.0% | 5,200 | 0.4% | −0.95% |
| Pentecostals | 1,600 | 0.2% | 312,000 | 24.5% | 12.50% |
| Evangelicals | 3,000 | 0.4% | 142,000 | 11.2% | 8.93% |
| **Total population** | **826,000** | **100.0%** | **1,273,000** | **100.0%** | **0.96%** |

Source: Todd M. Johnson and Gina A. Zurlo (eds), *World Christian Database* (Leiden/Boston: Brill), accessed March 2016.

migrants or justice issues has never been reckoned as Christian mission. Often these were concerns of the traditional mainline churches but were of no interest to Evangelicals and Pentecostals. One exception was Youth for Christ, which ran drug rehabilitation programmes. The twenty-first century presents a different scenario, in which many churches and youth organisations have missions that address social issues, mainly poverty, health and education.

Women in leadership is still a major issue. Only one church has female pastors, moderators and presidents of sessions. A few churches now allow women on committees. Since women are most often limited to children's ministries, they look outside, to para-church organisations or non-governmental organisations (NGOs), to use their gifts and training.

Theological training and leadership development are increasing in all major denominations, although degree studies are mostly done overseas. The Presbyterians, Roman Catholics and Anglicans launched Theological Education by Extension in 1983 and offer Bible studies as optional modules at the University of Mauritius.

The Mauritian churches share a rich history of responding to constantly changing contexts, from slavery days, the period of indentured labour from India, and seeing a minority Asian population overtake others to become the major political force, to modernity and post-Christianity. Churches consolidate by ecumenism, accentuating discipleship and leadership. Christians live and work alongside people of other faiths, always facing the challenge of how to maintain a Christian witness while allowing others to share their faith stories. Some Christians will not participate in functions of other faiths, while others willingly attend weddings and festivals without fear of compromise. Today, the mission field is much closer to home. Mauritians are still involved in cross-cultural mission and this forces them to approach Islam, Hinduism and other faiths with fresh eyes. Great opportunities are opening for church and para-church organisations to develop new ministries in a world challenged by secularity and technology, as well as economic and justice issues.

## Bibliography

Burrun, Breejun, *Histoire des Religions des îles Maurice et Rodrigue* (Vacoas: Éditions le Printemps, 2002).

Burrun, Breejun, *1914–2014: 100 ans de L'Église Adventiste à Maurice, Vol. 1* (Rose Hill: Cube Printing, 2014).

Emmanuel, Ghislain, *A History of the Anglican Diocese of Mauritius (1810–1973)* (Rose Hill: Édition de l'Océan Indien, 1975; 2nd edn 2014).

Palmyre, Danielle, *Culture créole et foi chrétienne* (Brussels: Lumen Vitae, 2007).

Quenette, L. Rivaltz, *L'Oeuvre du Révérend Jean Le Brun à l'île Maurice* (Moka: Institut Mahatma Gandhi, 1982; 2nd edn 2014).

# Réunion

## Jacqueline Andoche and Valérie Aubourg

The multi-confessional configuration of Réunion is a result of the European, African, Malagasy and Asian migrations that have populated the island over the past 350 years. Originally deserted, this island in the Indian Ocean became an official French colony in 1665. Until the end of the nineteenth century, the foundations of its society and the identity of the population were fundamentally marked by slavery. Roman Catholicism, made the official religion by a declaration of the King of France, is the dominant religion. From 1712 to 1850 the island was an apostolic prefecture. The clergy were tasked with catechising the enslaved Africans and the Malagasy population. The religion of these groups, based on ancestor worship, was forbidden. Nevertheless, it was not until the abolition of slavery in 1848 that the African population underwent mass conversion to Catholicism.

In 1850 Réunion became a diocese. At the same time, a large influx of workers from southern India, newly arrived to replace emancipated slaves, introduced various types of Hinduism. As subjects of the British crown, Indians were protected by British legislation. Although the colony was required to respect their religious customs, they were subject to evangelism. Thus they practised their religion clandestinely and in opposition to the majority. Their encounters with emancipated plantation slaves promoted a cross-breeding of the faiths, which gave birth to the distinctive synthesis of Réunion religiosity.

In 1901, the construction of the first French mosque by Muslims from Gujarat confirmed the multi-religious character of the island. This original Réunion Islam is Hanafi Sunni. Only after 1970 were Shiite and Sunni Shafi'i branches established by the Karana of Madagascar and the Comorians, respectively. The nineteenth and twentieth centuries saw the free migration of Chinese families. Quickly evangelised, Chinese families nevertheless continued to venerate their ancestors and practise Taoist and Confucian rituals. European immigrants introduced Buddhism during the 1980s.

The end of the colonial period was marked by the arrival of the first Protestants. In 1946 Réunion became a French department. Then in 1992 it became a European region. These changes opened the door to globalisation, affirmation of identity and secularisation, favourable to the emergence of non-institutionalised religions. The re-establishment of ancestor worship among Africans and Malagasy, the Rastafarian movement, neo-Hinduism and trans-national esotericism emerged, increasing the complexity of the island's religious landscape. Since 1970, a small Jewish community has remained discreet, while the mystical trends at the heart of other religions (Sufi Islam and Christian Charismatic movements) asserted themselves.

While Catholicism seemed to hold on to a confessional monopoly, it had to deal with new forms of religiosity. In the spirit of adaptation and willingness to live together, representatives of the major religions formed the Group for Inter-religious Dialogues in 2000, under the leadership of the Bishop of Réunion and the Imam of Saint Denis. It brings together representatives of the major religions but does not recognize ancestral worship or some mystical currents because it is suspicious of sectarian aberrations. However, any observer can see that the different religions live in harmony on this small Creole territory.

## Establishment and Development of the Protestant Churches in Réunion

Facing a Catholicism that promised a single religion and still dominates the religious landscape of the island, Protestantism has only recently taken root. In 1936 Pastor Paul Girard founded the Adventist Mission. This was the first non-Catholic Christian church to be established in Réunion. In 1966 Aimé Cizeron (1916–2003), a pastor of the Assemblies of God (AG) from mainland France, opened the Salvation and Healing Mission. The movement quickly gained momentum. While strongly condemning the Creole religious system, the Assemblies of God revived specific traits of popular religiosity: ecstatic experiences, miracles and deliverance.

The American Baptist pastor Paul White (1937–2014) settled in Réunion in 1971. His arrival on the island was preceded by the local radio broadcast of 'The Voice of the Gospel'. Paul White centred his work on Bible distribution and calling the Réunionnais to conversion. He opened the way for missionaries to come from Australia, Canada, the USA, England,

*Christianity in Réunion, 1970 and 2015*

| | 1970 | | 2015 | | Average annual growth rate (%), 1970–2015 |
|---|---|---|---|---|---|
| Tradition | Population | % | Population | % | |
| Christians | 446,000 | 96.6% | 754,000 | 87.5% | 1.17% |
| *Roman Catholics* | 428,000 | 92.7% | 684,000 | 79.4% | 1.05% |
| *Independents* | 1,000 | 0.2% | 11,400 | 1.3% | 5.56% |
| *Protestants* | 2,200 | 0.5% | 57,400 | 6.7% | 7.47% |
| *Pentecostals* | 800 | 0.2% | 88,000 | 10.2% | 11.01% |
| Evangelicals | 1,200 | 0.3% | 53,800 | 6.2% | 8.84% |
| **Total population** | **462,000** | **100.0%** | **861,000** | **100.0%** | **1.39%** |

Source: Todd M. Johnson and Gina A. Zurlo (eds), *World Christian Database* (Leiden/Boston: Brill), accessed March 2016.

Switzerland and mainland France and establish Baptist, Evangelical and Brethren groups. They also created two libraries and the Centre for Information and Evangelical Training (CIFEM). Evangelical missionaries also engaged in prison ministry.

In 1976, Protestant civil servants and military personnel from mainland France, along with a few Malagasy, created the Religious Association of the Reformed Church of the Department of Réunion (ACERDR), which in 1989 became the Protestant Church of Réunion. In 1978 the first pastor was sent by the Protestant Federation of France. In the last decade of the twentieth century, the Reformed Church experienced a massive influx of believers from Madagascar. Since then it has experienced divisions, fragmenting into several different churches.

From 1983, the Pentecostal landscape of Réunion was turned upside down by a process of fragmentation. Multiple divisions occurred within the Assemblies of God under the aegis of local leaders. This resulted in the creation of about 30 different assemblies. Some are autonomous local organisations while others are affiliated to international networks of neo-Pentecostal or Charismatic churches. These churches struck a chord with traditional Creole religious culture, such as through their insistence on demonology and the importance of sensory experience.

With some 20,000 having been baptised, the Salvation and Healing Mission represents the largest non-Catholic Christian denomination on the island. It has 47 places of worship, 40 or so pastors and two missionaries: one in Mayotte and the other in Madagascar. It also has its own ministry training.

The Adventist Church, the non-Charismatic Evangelical churches, and the Lutheran-Reformed Protestant churches, each with around 1,500 members, have tended to stagnate. However, the last two groups play an important role in the local religious scene. Indeed, their leaders are actively promoting the networking of various Christian organisations on the island (including Catholic) while also establishing links with other religious groups on the island. Conversely, the Adventist Church and the Assemblies of God are more resistant to inter-religious dialogue. They participate only occasionally in meetings with other Protestant churches.

Members and pastors of the Evangelical churches, Adventist Church, and Pentecostals are mainly from the middle and working classes. They come from all ethnic and cultural backgrounds (Cafres, Malbars and white Creole). For the most part, they were baptised as infants in the Catholic Church. The Lutheran-Reformed churches are made up primarily of European expatriates or Protestant migrants from Madagascar. Currently, only one woman (from the United Church of Alsace) holds a post of pastor in Réunion.

## Bibliography

Aubourg, Valérie, *Christianismes charismatiques à l'île de la Réunion* (Paris: Karthala, 2014).
Boutter, Bernard, *Le pentecôtisme à l'île de la Réunion: Refuge de la religiosité populaire ou vecteur de modernité?* (Paris: L'Harmattan, 2002).
Dumas-Champion, Françoise, *Le mariage des cultures à la Réunion* (Paris: Karthala, 2008).
Mourrégot, Marie France, *L'islam à l'île de la Réunion* (Paris: L'Harmattan, 2010).
Prudhomme, Claude, *Histoire religieuse de la Réunion* (Paris: Karthala, 1984).

# Seychelles, Comoros, Mayotte and Saint Helena


## Todd M. Johnson and Kenneth R. Ross


### Seychelles

The 115-island country of Seychelles lies around 1,600 km east of Africa's south-east coast. Inhabited by fewer than 100,000 people, it has the smallest population of any independent African state. The first European settlers were Roman Catholic, and the population of Seychelles has remained overwhelmingly Catholic despite being a British crown colony from 1811 until independence in 1976. British influence did, however, result in the emergence of an Anglican Church that retains an active presence today. Other churches active in the country include Baptists, Seventh-day Adventists, Assemblies of God, the Pentecostal Church, the Pentecostal Assembly, the Orthodox Church and Jehovah's Witnesses. Although small in number, Evangelical churches are growing. A notable feature of Seychelles Christian history is that the country was an operational base of the Christian radio station FEBA (Far East Broadcasting Associates) from 1970 to 2003.

Given that a large majority of the population are professing Catholics, the Roman Catholic Church exercises great influence in society. It was shaken, however, by the coup that took place soon after independence and brought to power a regime that was rather hostile to religion. Relations between the government and the Catholic Church were strained during the 1980s but a rapprochement took place in 1990, marked by a papal audience for Seychelles President France-Albert René. Since then, church–state relations

*Christianity in Seychelles, 1970 and 2015*

| | 1970 | | 2015 | | Average annual growth rate (%), 1970–2015 |
|---|---|---|---|---|---|
| Tradition | Population | % | Population | % | |
| Christians | 51,500 | 98.3% | 91,300 | 94.7% | 1.28% |
| *Roman Catholics* | 45,300 | 86.5% | 78,300 | 81.2% | 1.22% |
| *Independents* | 100 | 0.2% | 860 | 0.9% | 4.90% |
| *Protestants* | 250 | 0.5% | 4,400 | 4.5% | 6.56% |
| *Anglicans* | 3,900 | 7.4% | 5,300 | 5.5% | 0.68% |
| Pentecostals | 0 | 0.0% | 5,300 | 5.5% | 14.96% |
| Evangelicals | 840 | 1.6% | 4,200 | 4.4% | 3.65% |
| **Total population** | **52,400** | **100.0%** | **96,500** | **100.0%** | **1.37%** |

Source: Todd M. Johnson and Gina A. Zurlo (eds), *World Christian Database* (Leiden/Boston: Brill), accessed March 2016.

have been cordial and constructive, with the Catholic Church continuing to play a major role in the national education system. Since 1985, the Diocese of Port Victoria has been part of the Episcopal Conference of the Indian Ocean (CEDOI).

Growing secularisation of society is the major current challenge faced by the churches. In this context Monsignor Denis Wiehe, the Catholic Bishop since 2001, has called for a 'new evangelisation', urging his flock to return to the source of their faith in the gospel – 'to drink the living waters of faith in Christ and to receive from him the joy and vitality of earlier days'. Liturgical renewal has advanced with the aim of achieving *une liturgie vivante, contemplative et missionnaire* (a vibrant, contemplative and missionary liturgy). Since 2004, a lay training programme, Formation à la Vie Chrétienne, has helped many Seychellois to deepen their faith, as have a variety of programmes aimed at young people. The social arm of the Catholic Church, CARITAS – Solidarité Chrétienne, is active in the distribution of food and clothes to victims of flooding or house fires, improvement of housing, and agricultural development. In 2013, the Catholic Church opened a migrants' centre to minister to the needs of foreign workers in difficulties. The Anglican Church is also very active in social outreach, for example undertaking extensive relief work after the severe flooding of 2013.

Ecumenical commitment finds expression particularly through the Bible Society of Seychelles, which brings together representatives of the Anglican, Seventh-day Adventist, Pentecostal and Catholic churches to promote Bible reading. A Creole translation of the New Testament was published in 1999 and a Kreol Seselwa translation of the entire Bible in 2014.

## Comoros

The Union of the Comoros is a group of three islands located in the northern part of the Mozambique Channel between Madagascar and the mainland. Comoros, with a population of around 788,000 in 2015, is predominantly Sunni Muslim, with Christians comprising only 0.5% of the population.

*Christianity in Comoros, 1970 and 2015*

| | 1970 | | 2015 | | Average annual growth rate (%), 1970–2015 |
|---|---|---|---|---|---|
| Tradition | Population | % | Population | % | |
| Christians | 1,500 | 0.7% | 4,000 | 0.5% | 2.24% |
| *Roman Catholics* | 1,100 | 0.5% | 2,400 | 0.3% | 1.77% |
| *Independents* | 30 | 0.0% | 250 | 0.0% | 4.82% |
| *Protestants* | 330 | 0.1% | 1,200 | 0.2% | 2.97% |
| Pentecostals | 9 | 0.0% | 280 | 0.0% | 7.95% |
| Evangelicals | 23 | 0.0% | 430 | 0.1% | 6.77% |
| **Total population** | **228,000** | **100.0%** | **788,000** | **100.0%** | **2.79%** |

Source: Todd M. Johnson and Gina A. Zurlo (eds), *World Christian Database* (Leiden/Boston: Brill), accessed March 2016.

Comoros was a French protectorate from 1886, was given internal autonomy in 1961 and gained independence from French rule in 1975.

Protestant missionaries from the African Inland Mission were sent to Comoros in 1975, but they were expelled from the country in 1978. There are also some Christian expatriates living in Comoros, both Protestants and Roman Catholics. In addition, humanitarian aid is provided by religious groups that are allowed to remain as long as they do not proselytise. Of the local Christian population, those of French descent account for the Catholics, and there is also a community of Malagasy Protestants, some of whom are seasonal workers on the islands. In addition, there is a small community of Jehovah's Witnesses.

As a result of a constitutional referendum held in 2009, Islam was established as the state religion of Comoros, resulting in governing principles and rules taken from Islamic tenets being applied to social spheres, including marriage, education and delinquency. The Council of Ulema forms one of the 'advisory bodies' expected to assist in governance of religious issues. This creates a conflict, as the constitution ostensibly supports religious freedom, upholding 'Equality of rights and duties for all without distinction of sex, origin, race, religion or belief'. Yet the penal code restricts such non-discrimination. By law, Sunni Shafi'i doctrine is the only legitimate religious practice and it is illegal to proselytise for any other religion.

In Comoros, religious discrimination in relation to Christianity comes more in the form of societal pressure than persecution. A 2013 Freedom House report mentioned 'restrictions, detentions, and harassment of non-Muslims'. There is some societal pressure on Christianity, and some reports of religious discrimination against non-Muslims, including Christian citizens lacking affiliation with an established Christian group such as the Catholic Church. This pressure was mainly at the village level and was affected by the level of influence of imams and teachers of Islam. Notably, religious discrimination was towards citizens and not foreigners, who were allowed to establish places of worship while citizens were not.

Despite this discrimination and the existence of laws restricting religious freedom, in practice, according to a 2010 International Religious Freedom report, the government generally respects religious freedom. Also, there is no evidence of either religious prisoners or forced religious conversion.

## Mayotte

Located east of the Comoros Islands, Mayotte is a French *département* comprising the two islands of Mayotte and Pamandzi, with a total population of 240,000 in 2015. Mayotte's secession from Comoros in 1974 kept the islands under the continued administration of France, as the island

*Christianity in Mayotte, 1970 and 2015*

| | 1970 | | 2015 | | Average annual growth rate (%), 1970–2015 |
|---|---|---|---|---|---|
| Tradition | Population | % | Population | % | |
| Christians | 360 | 1.0% | 1,400 | 0.6% | 3.03% |
| *Roman Catholics* | 260 | 0.7% | 510 | 0.2% | 1.51% |
| *Independents* | 0 | 0.0% | 650 | 0.3% | 9.72% |
| *Protestants* | 100 | 0.3% | 180 | 0.1% | 1.31% |
| Pentecostals | 0 | 0.0% | 400 | 0.2% | 8.51% |
| Evangelicals | 25 | 0.1% | 150 | 0.1% | 4.02% |
| **Total population** | **37,000** | **100.0%** | **240,000** | **100.0%** | **4.24%** |

Source: Todd M. Johnson and Gina A. Zurlo (eds), *World Christian Database* (Leiden/Boston: Brill), accessed March 2016.

had been a French protectorate since 1886. Because Mayotte is a French territory, French law prevails, including the separation of church and state. However, despite strong ties to France, with French as an official language and the euro as the national currency, Mayotte is a predominantly Muslim country and the majority of its people are Sunni Muslim of Malagasy origin.

Christians form a small minority in Mayotte. Most are Roman Catholics, who are served, together with the Comoros, by a missionary jurisdiction, the Apostolic Vicariate of Comoros Archipelago. Protestant Christians of Malagasy background are also found among immigrants and migrant labourers. In addition, since beginning their work in Mayotte in 1980, Jehovah's Witnesses have established a small community.

## Saint Helena

Part of the British Overseas Territory of Saint Helena, Ascension Islands, and Tristan da Cunha, Saint Helena is an island in the South Atlantic Ocean that lies midway between South America and Africa. It was uninhabited until its discovery by the Portuguese in 1502. During the seventeenth century it fell under British control, leading to it becoming a crown colony in 1834. Its population was recorded at 4,255 in 2008. Due to British influence,

*Christianity in Saint Helena, 1970 and 2015*

| | 1970 | | 2015 | | Average annual growth rate (%), 1970–2015 |
|---|---|---|---|---|---|
| Tradition | Population | % | Population | % | |
| Christians | 4,900 | 99.4% | 3,800 | 95.8% | −0.55% |
| *Roman Catholics* | 0 | 0.0% | 110 | 2.8% | 5.47% |
| *Independents* | 100 | 2.0% | 660 | 16.7% | 4.28% |
| *Protestants* | 400 | 8.1% | 490 | 12.4% | 0.47% |
| Anglicans | 4,000 | 81.9% | 3,200 | 80.8% | −0.49% |
| Pentecostals | 0 | 0.0% | 1,000 | 25.8% | 10.83% |
| Evangelicals | 140 | 2.9% | 130 | 3.4% | −0.09% |
| **Total population** | **4,900** | **100.0%** | **4,000** | **100.0%** | **−0.46%** |

Source: Todd M. Johnson and Gina A. Zurlo (eds), *World Christian Database* (Leiden/Boston: Brill), accessed March 2016.

the population of Saint Helena is predominantly Anglican. The Anglican Diocese of St Helena has its own bishop and includes Ascension Island. People on the islands belonging to other churches include Catholics (since 1958), Baptists, the Salvation Army, Seventh-day Adventists and Jehovah's Witnesses. Saint Helena has the highest proportion of Jehovah's Witnesses of any country or territory in the world: one in every 35 people.

St James Church, which was founded in 1674 in the capital, Jamestown, is the oldest Anglican church in the southern hemisphere and was rebuilt in 1774. An influential figure in Saint Helena's Christian history was the Reverend Richard Boys, who came to Saint Helena in 1811 as junior chaplain. In 1815 he became senior chaplain and held that position until 1830. He was outspoken against what he saw as 'evil living' in certain sectors of the community, particularly the upper class.

During the infamous period of Napoleon Bonaparte's exile on Saint Helena, from 1815 until his death there in 1821, there was a Christian revival on the island. The conversions mainly involved military officers on the island who were inspired by David Bogue's *Essay on the Divine Authority of the New Testament* (London: Hudson and Goodwin, 1806). There was also a significant revival stemming from the Baptist Church in the 1850s and a more localised revival in 1910.

Today, there are three Anglican parishes on Saint Helena, with 12 churches. The constitution of Saint Helena reflects the Christian identity of its people, stating that the island wishes to 'respect Christian and family values'. In 2009, a debate was raised in the UK Foreign Affairs Committee about whether Saint Helena's constitution should include such reference to Christian values. The UK government recommended removing these references, but the Governor of Saint Helena upheld the island's position, arguing that, while islanders recognised the UK as multi-faith, Christianity is the predominant religion of Saint Helena. The reference was retained.

## Bibliography

Cannan, Edward, *Churches of the South Atlantic Islands 1502–1991* (London: Anthony Nelson, 1992).

Hoarau, Gabriel and Sheila Montano, *Brève Histoire du Diocèse de Port-Victoria* (Strasbourg: Éditions du Signe, 2015).

Ottenheimer, Martin and Harriet Ottenheimer, *Historical Dictionary of the Comoro Islands* (Metuchen, NJ: Scarecrow Press, 1994).

# Kenya and Tanzania

## Wanjiru M. Gitau

### Kenya

The Kenyan nation covers a territory of 581,309 km$^2$, within which live some 42 ethnic communities. The missionary histories of Kenya and Tanzania are bound up in their beginnings. In 1498, Vasco da Gama, a mercenary of the Portuguese Prince Henry the Navigator, landed in what today is known as Malindi, not far from Mombasa. A legendary king, Prester John, was said to reside in the heart of Africa and it was believed he could help stem the spread of Islam in Europe. Following the defeat of the Portuguese by Arab Muslims at the coast, their influence faded in the seventeenth century without long-term success, except for one enduring landmark, Fort Jesus.

Johann Ludwig Krapf, a German serving with the Anglican Church Missionary (now Mission) Society, was the first Protestant missionary to arrive in East Africa. Having previously been a missionary in Ethiopia, his plan was to reach the Oromo people in southern Ethiopia by travelling up from the Kenyan coast. In 1842, when Western missionaries were expelled from Ethiopia, he and his new bride from Egypt sailed south, arriving in Mombasa in 1844. With the permission of Sultan Sayyid Said of Zanzibar, he settled at Rabai Mpya, where, within two months of their arrival, his wife and their newborn baby died of malaria. Being linguistically gifted, he wrote the first dictionary and grammar of the Swahili language. In 1846 Johannes Rebmann arrived to assist Krapf in evangelising the interior. The two produced the first Swahili New Testament and then set off to explore the interior, where they made contact with African chiefs, commenced further translation work and formulated a mission strategy. Due to ill health Krapf returned to Europe, where he wrote *Travels, Researches and Missionary Labours.* Unaware of how large Africa was, Krapf inspired the idea of an 'apostles' street', an ambitious chain of mission stations to evangelise Africa from the east coast on the Indian Ocean to the Atlantic coast in the west. Following the 'Scramble for Africa' in 1884–5, the Imperial British East Africa Company was granted trading rights in the East Africa Protectorate. Work on the Uganda railway line began in earnest in 1896 and took five years to complete. Once finished, it led to an unprecedented 'scramble' to start Krapf's proposed mission stations. The Kamba people, many of whom had been porters in the slave and ivory trades, acted as middlemen between the coast and the highlands and attracted at least eight mission societies from Germany, Britain and North America in quick succession. The geographical positioning of Kenya and the use of English as a medium of communication would turn Kenya, initially seen as a footpath to the source of the Nile and a point of access to control of Egypt, into the most evangelised nation in Eastern Africa.

Leaving Ukambani, the Kamba homeland, to the Africa Inland Mission under Peter Cameron Scott, nine Protestant missionaries and three Catholic missions settled in the Central Highlands, Rift Valley and western Kenya. The apparent competition between the missions in the environmentally friendly territory, however, had a negative impact on their witness. Plans to form a united African church were discussed at conferences involving most Protestant missions between 1911 and 1913. These discussions were the genesis of what would later become the Protestant umbrella body, the National Council of Churches of Kenya (NCCK), founded in 1913, well ahead of the formation of the World Council of Churches in 1948. The Protestants established two interdenominational schools, the Alliance High Schools for boys and girls. They also reached comity agreements which limited the number of mission stations that could be established in an area. This stamped an enduring character on Kenyan Christianity: each denomination is associated with a different tribe, and at certain times in the history of the nation this has had a negative impact on politics.

With the British colony appearing to be subdivided among and dominated by Protestant missionaries, the Catholic orders such as the Holy Ghost Fathers, Italian Fathers, Mill Hill Missionaries and Consolata Missionaries had not been party to the comity discussions. Yet in the background they quietly spread themselves throughout the country, from the heavily occupied Central Province to some of the most remote regions among the nomadic communities like the Maasai and Samburu. To date,

*Christianity in Kenya, 1970 and 2015*

| | 1970 | | 2015 | | Average annual growth rate (%), 1970–2015 |
|---|---|---|---|---|---|
| Tradition | Population | % | Population | % | |
| Christians | 7,058,000 | 62.7% | 37,275,000 | 80.9% | 3.77% |
| *Roman Catholics* | 1,936,000 | 17.2% | 10,625,000 | 23.1% | 3.86% |
| *Orthodox* | 248,000 | 2.2% | 695,000 | 1.5% | 2.32% |
| *Independents* | 1,670,000 | 14.8% | 7,548,000 | 16.4% | 3.41% |
| *Protestants* | 1,631,000 | 14.5% | 13,249,000 | 28.8% | 4.76% |
| *Anglicans* | 583,000 | 5.2% | 6,000,000 | 13.0% | 5.32% |
| Pentecostals | 1,171,000 | 10.4% | 14,153,000 | 30.7% | 5.69% |
| Evangelicals | 1,855,000 | 16.5% | 13,048,000 | 28.3% | 4.43% |
| **Total population** | **11,252,000** | **100.0%** | **46,050,000** | **100.0%** | **3.18%** |

Source: Todd M. Johnson and Gina A. Zurlo (eds), *World Christian Database* (Leiden/Boston: Brill), accessed March 2016.

the Catholics, who have a knack for establishing schools, hospitals, youth centres and numerous orders, remain the most widely spread church in Kenya, though not the largest. Catholics organise themselves under the Kenya Conference of Catholic Bishops (KCCB).

As Paul Gifford has demonstrated, Christianity has proved to be a formidable force in public life in Kenya, through both popular mobilisation and sheer size, at more than 80%. Anglicanism was seen as the church of the establishment, 'the colonial power at prayer'. In post-independent Kenya, the roles flipped, as Anglicans increasingly found themselves as leaders of the political opposition, particularly against President Daniel arap Moi's government in the 1980s and 1990s. Bishop Henry Okullu was known for his outspokenness against the government for human rights abuses, particularly following the murder of foreign minister Robert Ouko. Alexander Muge, a Kalenjin who was Anglican Bishop of Nakuru, sharply criticised tribalism, nepotism and graft in church and state. Following a public difference in the western district of Busia, Muge, who was popular for his denunciations of the political elite, was killed in a suspicious car accident in 1990, aged 42.

In the troubled decades of the 1980s and 1990s, clergymen from across the mainline denominations were prominent in advocating political reforms alongside such opposition politicians as Kenneth Matiba, Charles Rubia, and Oginga Odinga. To counter the voice of the churches pressing for a multi-party state and an end to one-party authoritarianism, the Moi government accentuated the denominational differences that had been established early on. As a result, when church leaders such as Henry Okullu, David Gitari and Timothy Njoya spoke against the government, it was not always clear whether they spoke for themselves or as representatives of their churches. They could therefore easily be contradicted by the regime. Frequently, the church leaders were denounced, threatened and publicly humiliated, as happened to Timothy Njoya, who was beaten senseless by police outside the parliament buildings.

The game changed when the Catholic Church threw its weight behind the call for reforms in 1991. Unlike the other denominations, the Catholic Church is spread throughout the country. Additionally, when the KCCB spoke, it did so with one voice. When, under the leadership of Rafael Ndigi Mwana a'Nzeki, it put its weight behind the fight for multi-party politics, Moi's government was threatened by the increasingly widespread view that it was illegitimate, and it caved in to legalise multi-party politics in December 1991. In the run-up to the elections in 1992 and 1997, mainline churches were active in mobilising popular involvement in democracy; however, on both occasions the political opposition was too divided to unseat Moi. For the rest of that decade, which turned out to have some of the worst corruption scandals, the churches were once again divided, some apparently co-opted by the government and some preoccupied with internal bureaucracy. Moi's public piety as a member of the Africa Inland Church, whose mainstay was the Kalenjin community, also dumfounded critics and made it very difficult to challenge his repressive leadership on grounds of faith.

The mainline churches also engaged in constitutional reforms through what was popularly known as the Ufungamano Initiative. This included all the religious groups in the country – Muslims, Hindus and Christians alike. Ufungamano did not succeed, because Moi's government started a rival constitutional process led by Yash pal Ghai and the reforms dragged on until after the 2002 general election. When the process resumed, the Evangelicals and Pentecostals threw their hat in the ring along with the mainline churches to form a new body, the Kenya Church. The 2005 draft national constitution had a clause that allowed Muslims to have Kadhi courts, which would decide issues related to marriage and inheritance. Although Muslims had always had Kadhi courts for themselves, their incorporation into the constitution was seen as a loophole potentially granting them special favour in an otherwise secular nation. Citing contentious clauses about abortion and homosexuality along with the Kadhi courts, the Kenya Church joined the opposition to successfully block the 2005 draft. In 2010, the church similarly opposed the second proposed constitution, over the legality of the clause on reproductive health. This time, however, the majority of politicians were preoccupied with political and economic aspects of the constitution and did not back the church, and the new constitution sailed through. None the worse for it, churches have gone back to their pre-constitutional concerns, each doing what they do best.

While Christians and Muslims have on the whole lived peacefully side by side throughout Kenyan history, the radical Muslim group Al-Shabaab, from the dysfunctional neighbour Somalia, have repeatedly attacked Kenyans in Nairobi, Mombasa and towns closer to the border with Somalia. Some attacks, like those on Westgate and Mpeketoni, were not targeted at Christians; rather, they were designed to damage the image of the nation as a tourist destination. The worst attack targeting Christians was at Garissa University in April 2015, when 148 people were killed. Churches now hire armed security to protect worshippers each Sunday.

As with mainline churches in Tanzania and other parts of Africa, theological dialogue has revolved around inculturation and indigenisation of the structures, liturgies and infrastructure that came with missionaries. John Gatu, Moderator of the Presbyterian Church of East Africa, famously called out the foreignness of mainline churches through his proposal for a moratorium on new missionaries. In his 1971 address to the Reformed

Church in America, he challenged the Western missions to withdraw foreign missionaries from many parts of the 'Third World' to allow the churches to find their own identity. He argued that the continuation of the missionary movement was a hindrance to the growth of the church that missionaries had started. Canon Burgess Carr, General Secretary of the All Africa Conference of Churches, supported Gatu in even stronger terms.

The call for a moratorium was widely debated throughout mission boards, churches and theological institutions, and while in fact it was not a new issue, the practicalities of implementation were complex. Many missionaries were in the field, and mainline churches were dependent for infrastructural and development funds especially, as this was the decade when economic crises struck African countries, drawing the sympathies of the wealthy Western churches. During the two decades that followed, dependency on foreign help became even more pronounced, as a good number of African nations imploded under political and economic failures, as well as the catastrophe of the newly discovered HIV/AIDS. Kenya – seen as the only nation in the region that was stable (Tanzania having become embroiled in Idi Amin's war) – became a haven for refugees. To date, the nation hosts two large refugee camps, Daadab in the north-eastern area for refugees from Somalia, Ethiopia and Eritrea, and Kakuma in the north-west for refugees from Sudan, Uganda, Congo, Rwanda and Burundi. Kenya became a hub for international non-governmental organisations (NGOs) responding to the crises in the region. These aid agencies often worked through the churches so that, second only to the civil service, aid agencies became a key employer for Kenyans involved in a wide variety of relief and development activities.

The NCCK, which has at least 29 member denominations and at least 17 affiliate para-church organisations, also initiated development projects for the urban and rural poor. One of their flagship programmes was village polytechnic institutes to teach primary school 'dropouts' practical income-earning skills such as masonry or metalwork. Another series of development projects, designed to provide micro-finance loans to women in the slums in the 1980s, has grown and evolved into a finance institution known as SMEP (Small and Micro Enterprise Programme), which is now an independent business. The NCCK also has a variety of other investments through the Jumuia Resorts, a hotel chain. Because of its well organised bureaucratic structures, NCCK has also been appointed to play a substantial role in running the affairs of the refugee camps.

In their turn, the Catholics, who also own substantial infrastructure run by numerous orders of European origin, have carried on quietly working in local communities, pioneering in the provision of health services, life skills education, agriculture and small-scale projects long before the government or other churches did so. There is merit to the claim that Pentecostal groups usually win their greatest harvest where the Catholics have already done the hard work of sowing the seed through service. In Nairobi there is a growing Catholic Charismatic movement led by a Vincentian congregation.

The newer Pentecostal churches, which organise themselves under the Kenya Pentecostal Church and also the Evangelical Association of Kenya (EAK), are very active in the realm of evangelism and planting churches. In 2007 the Office of the Attorney General claimed to be overwhelmed with applications for new church registrations, and in 2015 the same office instituted stricter rules to regulate the churches after a public outcry regarding rogue pastors. Pentecostals have been in Kenya since colonial times but, as in other African countries, they mostly kept a low profile, not wanting to engage in politics or to have a high-profile social presence. They began to be more visible in the 1970s as the successors to both African Independent Churches (AICs) that had their heyday in the first half of the twentieth century and the East African Revival that had revitalised the mainline churches since the 1930s but whose forcefulness as a renewing influence had faded by the 1970s. Although they define themselves against African traditions, Pentecostals are the heirs to the cultural logic of traditional practices, this time as vanquishers – hence their emphasis on healing and prosperity. Large Pentecostal churches include the Deliverance Church of Kenya, Christ Is The Answer Ministries (CITAM; formerly known as Nairobi Pentecostal Church), Jesus Is Alive Ministries (JIAM-Nairobi), Jesus Celebration Centre, Neno Evangelism Ministries, the Happy Churches, Faith Evangelistic Ministries, Jubilee Christian Centre and the Winners Chapel International Ministries, plus a wide variety of similar smaller but visible churches, many still pending registration in the Attorney General's chambers. Recently, some of these have come under public criticism for the unscrupulous practice of faking miracles. A new type of middle-class independent church, such as the Nairobi Chapel, straddle Charismatic/Pentecostal and Baptist congregational polity; they have gained public visibility because of their increasingly vocal engagement with public issues in mainstream (non-Christian) media and their ability to attract a younger middle-class demographic. Baptists, Seventh-day Adventists, Mennonites and the Salvation Army are among the many other churches with a significant spread across the country. The older AICs continue to exist minimally in rural communities; they are organised under the umbrella body the Organization of African Instituted Churches (OAIC).

Besides churches, their umbrella bodies and NGOs, Kenya is also home to many para-church organisations, including World Vision and Compassion International, World Relief, student ministries like the Fellowship of Christian Unions (FOCUs), the Navigators, Campus Crusade and African

Evangelistic Enterprise. There are also at least 16 private Christian universities and a wide range of theological training institutions. Perhaps Kenya is the New Jerusalem of Africa.

## Tanzania

As with most African countries, the trajectory of the presence and growth of Christianity in Tanzania is intricately linked to the history of the nation. Present-day Tanzania covers 947,303 km$^2$ and has a population of over 50 million (2015), comprising up to 120 ethnic communities of differing sizes and complexities. Tanzania, formerly called Tanganyika and Zanzibar, was a colonial territory of Germany until World War I, after which it became a British protectorate; it gained independence in 1961.

Christianity was first brought to Africa's east coast in the sixteenth century by the Portuguese, who established themselves at the Muslim city-states of Kilwa, Mombasa, Pate, Malindi and Lamu. They held on for a century before the ruler of Oman, Ahmed bin Said, drove them out. In 1842 Sultan Seyyid Said transferred his capital from Muscat in Oman to Zanzibar and laid claim to some 1,000 km of coastline from Somalia to Mozambique. The first Protestant missionaries to arrive in Zanzibar, Johann Ludwig Krapf and his wife Rosina in 1844, had to seek his permission to settle in Mombasa. The British signed the Treaty of Friendship, Commerce and Navigation with the Sultan of Zanzibar in 1886, guaranteeing the protection of missionaries and their followers. Inspired by Krapf's vision of a chain of mission stations across Africa and David Livingstone's call to end slavery by introducing Christianity and civilisation, a number of missionary societies arrived in quick succession. The Holy Ghost Fathers, a French Catholic mission, arrived in Zanzibar in 1868; the Universities' Mission to Central Africa (UMCA), following the vision of David Livingstone of the London Missionary Society, arrived in 1875; the Church Missionary Society

*Christianity in Tanzania, 1970 and 2015*

| | 1970 | | 2015 | | Average annual growth rate (%), 1970–2015 |
|---|---|---|---|---|---|
| Tradition | Population | % | Population | % | |
| Christians | 5,008,000 | 36.8% | 29,584,000 | 55.3% | 4.03% |
| *Roman Catholics* | 2,807,000 | 20.6% | 15,367,000 | 28.7% | 3.85% |
| *Orthodox* | 9,000 | 0.1% | 13,300 | 0.0% | 0.87% |
| *Independents* | 234,000 | 1.7% | 1,138,000 | 2.1% | 3.57% |
| *Protestants* | 1,068,000 | 7.9% | 11,870,000 | 22.2% | 5.50% |
| *Anglicans* | 386,000 | 2.8% | 3,630,000 | 6.8% | 5.11% |
| Pentecostals | 336,000 | 2.5% | 5,491,000 | 10.3% | 6.41% |
| Evangelicals | 753,000 | 5.5% | 8,337,000 | 15.6% | 5.49% |
| **Total population** | **13,606,000** | **100.0%** | **53,470,000** | **100.0%** | **3.09%** |

Source: Todd M. Johnson and Gina A. Zurlo (eds), *World Christian Database* (Leiden/Boston: Brill), accessed March 2016.

(Anglicans) came in 1876; French Catholic White Fathers came in 1878; and two German missionary societies, which later formed the Evangelical Lutheran Church in Tanzania (ELCT), arrived in the 1890s. These societies adopted Swahili as the lingua franca of instruction and evangelism. By 1905 missionaries were producing a variety of Swahili newspapers, including *Msimulizi* (UMCA), *Habari za Mwezi* by German missions and *Rafiki Yangu* by the Catholics. These papers facilitated communication with the numerous communities in the interior, and Bible translation progressed quickly. The supply of the printed Scriptures, first-time writing of grammars, liturgies and catechism excited inland communities so that evangelism progressed quickly during the colonial decades. At independence in 1961, Tanzania had a population of about 9 million, of whom roughly 25% were Christian and 25% Muslim, and 30–40% adherents of traditional religion. Today, Tanzania does not keep an official census of religion, but more than half of the population is Christian, around one-third Muslim and only a small remnant still follow traditional religions. The Catholic Church, Anglicans and Lutherans are the three main denominations in Tanzania.

Due to the work that missionaries had done, about two-thirds of all schools and half of all the hospitals belonged to the missions at independence. Julius Nyerere, the founding President of the Republic, sought to create an all-embracing national consciousness. In 1967, the Arusha Declaration turned the state into a socialist country – not a Marxist-Leninist alignment of the Cold War era, but a modern variation of Africa's age-old collective solidarity and secularity. The Ujamaa concept, named after a Swahili word for family relationship or brotherhood, drank from three key sources. The first was a return to an idealised African past, in which the land had belonged to all people, all families had the right to use it, everyone had enough work and everyone in society was cared for. Secondly, Nyerere was a staunch Catholic and former teacher with a keen sense of justice and personal ecumenical interest in the affairs of the churches, who did not want to isolate the Muslims, who had also played a significant role in the struggles for independence. Thirdly, Nyerere, who had been educated at the University of Edinburgh, was averse to the alignments of the Cold War between the capitalist West and the Marxist-Leninist socialist East. His experiment was a third way, the only one of its kind in Africa to attempt to unite the hugely diversified country with its 120 ethnic communities, numerous church groups and Muslims.

Early Christian missionaries had worried about their converts living in morally corrupting communities, so they had isolated their converts in closed mission stations, where, along with the Christian message, they trained them in literacy, artisanship, agriculture and animal husbandry. This lent the mission stations special relevance in restructuring the nascent nation for the modern world. However, this kind of privileged provision had imbued the converts with new identities – new class formations, if you will – across confessional, cultural and even ethnic gulfs, as different advantages were seen to be received by converts from different mission groups. It was to these that Nyerere took the axiomatic axe. In 1969, mission schools were turned into state schools, admitting students of all denominations and faiths. For many missionaries, the government interference with what they considered their turf and lifework as teachers and school administrators was a traumatic experience. However, considering nationalisation preferable to expulsion, as in socialist China in 1949, the missions thawed and cooperated with nationalisation and Ujamaa villagisation.

The priorities of the church under the new directive were the same as during the colonial times. They continued to provide services while missionaries remained in the background as secretaries, accountants, doctors and especially comptrollers of funds that came from overseas missions. When John Gatu's call for a moratorium came in the mid-1970s, Tanzanian churches discussed it as a good idea in principle but one they could not implement because of the complexity of not only the mission structures but also the direction the country had taken under Ujamaa.

Being seen as a unique model, and bolstered by Nyerere's personal integrity, Ujamaa attracted enthusiastic support from Western governments. Through the 1970s, Tanzania was a major recipient of aid from about 40 different bilateral donors, especially from the Nordic countries, West Germany and Canada, who were willing to encourage Tanzania's exemplary strategy of development, popular participation and social justice. It is estimated that Tanzania received US$16 billion in aid between 1967 and 1992. Using these funds, Tanzania engaged in projects to provide comprehensive welfare for its population.

However, a number of internal and external challenges unravelled this experiment before it could bear fruit. From the mid-1970s, the global oil crisis weakened commodity prices of agricultural exports such as coffee and cotton, and the value of the Tanzanian shilling dropped substantially. Secondly, the villagisation that had accompanied the Ujamaa policy had a disruptive effect on agriculture because of passive resistance from communities that did not want to relocate collectively into villages. Villagisation killed the incentive for hard work and certainly did not encourage individual enterprise. Awash with foreign aid, the effectiveness of which was nevertheless stifled by a crippling bureaucracy, the Tanzanian populace grew dependent on outside help in all socio-economic domains, including churches, and had little incentive to develop economically. Thirdly, in 1977 the East Africa Community, comprising Uganda, Tanzania and Kenya, broke up, killing all incentive for regional trade. In 1978 and

1979, Tanzania entered an economically disastrous war with Uganda to oust the latter's barbaric dictator, Idi Amin. Ujamaa buckled under the weight of these challenges, and by 1983 most of the donors, sceptical about Tanzania's policies, had withdrawn their support. In 1985 Nyerere resigned as President. His successor, Ali Hassan Mwinyi, reached an agreement with the International Monetary Fund (IMF) that required him to effect structural adjustment programmes (SAPs) as a precondition for resuming aid. SAPs, as is well known, caused more poverty and suffering for African people, and unfortunately the new aid deal returned the country to the cycle of dependence and resulted in more poverty for the masses.

In the face of these challenges, several things happened with Christianity and the missions. After the initial huff and puff about schools, the leaders of all the mainline denominations accepted the vision of Tanzania as a free nation where human dignity was protected and Christian ideals represented. Keen to participate in the new government but also uncertain, the churches never challenged any of the things that went wrong. The Christian Council, formed in 1948, always coordinated negotiations with the government. As most of the government officials had been educated in mission schools, personal contacts always played a crucial part in relationships between government and churches. They did not criticise the apparent cracks that were forming in the 1970s, including human rights violations, growing bureaucratisation and corruption. To their credit, as the government programmes failed, churches continued to perform their roles in providing services in education and health as well as help for refugees fleeing war in Burundi and Congo, albeit with donor funds. In those days, the task of mission as evangelism to unreached peoples and as quality discipleship took second place.

Since 1992, the churches have struggled to develop a new identity in a changed society. The question of autonomy and localisation lingers behind what are essentially missionary structures and never-resolved power relations between the denominational structures and individual congregations. The extraneous bureaucracy of the former stifles the creativity of local congregations. In addition, there are contradictions between the institutional wealth of the church (or at least apparent vestiges of it), which is believed to come from overseas, and a background of chronic poverty of the local masses. This apparent contradiction results in differences in the ways in which Christianity as a lived religion is perceived and performed as ritual in testing times. Marked differences remain between official doctrine and folk Christian practices. Additionally, with the end of Ujamaa-era optimism, the churches have had to face up to the reality of inept government, corruption, political bullying and a stagnant economy. The churches have attempted to redefine themselves as civil society organisations to mediate these challenges, but that means the task of evangelisation is set on the back burner, and the challenge of fragmentation hampers effectiveness.

In the face of the failure of Ujamaa and the apparent lassitude of the mainline churches, the wider society has been searching for new models to make sense of life. The rise of Pentecostalism is part of this quest. The Balakole, the saved ones, not quite Pentecostal but more revivalist, originated in Rwanda and spread to the north-west of Tanzania from the 1930s. The confession of sins, consciousness of forgiveness, commencement of a new life and rejection of traditional customs were central characteristics of this movement. It also considered mission churches not radical enough, but rather than start independent churches, the converts of the East African Revival mostly stayed in existing churches, with varying degree of tension, and imbued the popular spirituality of most mainline Protestant churches for at least a generation.

The Pentecostals had been in the country since colonial times – including the Holiness Mission, Swedish Free Mission, Elim Pentecostal Church and Assemblies of God – but they were marginal until the late 1970s. In the face of the economic crisis they became more significant, though they were not publicly visible on the national stage of politics because of their divisive power struggles. They refused to cooperate with mainline churches, which they saw as compromising the gospel, and in turn they were accused of 'stealing sheep'. Nevertheless, their fissiparous nature has actually helped them grow, since their lack of attachment to larger denominations has made it is easier to evangelise and spread, not least in the growing urban centres that have emerged since the collapse of Ujamaa-style villagisation. Their public profile and visibility have grown through large open-air evangelisation campaigns that feature international evangelists. In turn, Charismatic spirituality has significantly influenced the Evangelical Lutheran Church.

Another impact of the changed times on the Tanzanian landscape was the rise of non-governmental organisations (NGOs), particularly those focused on empowering women. Due to the historical construction of mainline churches, women have often been excluded from the male-dominated formal structures of leadership, even though they constitute the majority in the church. In turn, women have often found alternative ways of engaging through fellowships, home visits, Bible studies and choirs. After 1985, self-help development-oriented organisations mushroomed all over Africa, and Tanzania was no exception. Independent donors who were keen to empower women gravitated towards women's associations in churches, which morphed into women's credit associations, neighbourhood work groups and cottage industries. They were well intentioned and did bring a measure of relief, particularly bearing in mind how bureaucracy had formerly prevented aid from reaching women. However, since such groups were tied to mainline churches, this aid went to women who were already better off. It largely excluded women who most needed the support, the poorest of the poor and young, and therefore aggravated class differences in many rural places.

The problems of poverty, split-level Christianity and class differences have led to a unique problem that has hit the news in recent years: witchcraft accusations. Witchcraft (*uchawi*) and healers' divination (*uganga*) were part of the traditional cosmology of many African societies. However, the practices related to them were highly circumscribed by a variety of taboos and communal mechanisms of maintaining order. In the changed world of recent decades, health, financial and social problems are widely attributed to witches, and it is usually older women, widows or orphans who are accused and persecuted and even brutally killed as witches. Witchcraft practitioners (*wachawi*) and healers (*waganga*) believe that the body parts of albinos (people born without pigment in their skin) contain powerful antidotes to witchcraft. Although a variety of human rights groups decry these developments, most churches, save for a few Pentecostal groups, are yet to develop effective context-specific responses.

One more thorn in the flesh for Christians is the question of Christian–Muslim relations. Muslims were previously found along the coast, but the spread of Islam inland has coincided with that of Christianity (along with Swahili as a lingua franca). Some significant but muted tensions developed between Christians and Muslims during colonial times, including attacks on a number of mission stations and the murder of LMS missionaries. Following Nyerere's harmonisation programme, Tanzania was considered one of the African states in which there was little tension between the religious communities. In recent years there have been disruptive tendencies through BAKWATA (Baraza Kuu la Waislamu Tanzania, the Tanzania Muslim Council) and its former subunit Warsha (Warsha ya Waandishi wa Kiislam, or Islamic Writers' Workshop). Patronised by youth groups educated in Saudi Arabia and funded through the Islamic Foundation, Warsha, in a bid to give voice to what it sees as Muslim grievances against the state and domination by Christianity, has been active in preaching a form of radical Islam. Nevertheless, altercations between Christians and Muslims are rare.

## Conclusion

In the face of significant challenges and tensions, Christianity in these two East African nations continues to undergo renewal and to demonstrate vitality. It is integral to life for many citizens in both countries and exercises a formative influence on society at all levels.

## Bibliography

Gifford, Paul, *Christianity, Politics and Public Life in Kenya* (New York: Columbia University Press, 2009).

Green, Maia, *Priests, Witches and Power: Popular Christianity After Mission in Southern Tanzania* (Cambridge: Cambridge University Press, 2003).

Knighton, Ben (ed.), *Religion and Politics in Kenya: Essays in Honor of a Meddlesome Priest* (New York: Palgrave Macmillan, 2009).

Mbogoni, Lawrence Ezekiel Yona, *The Cross vs. the Crescent: Religion and Politics in Tanzania from the 1890s to the 1990s* (Dar es Salaam: Mkuki na Nyota Publishers, 2005).

NCCK Secretariat, *A Century of Ecumenism and Mission: The Story of National Council of Churches of Kenya, 1913–2013* (Nairobi: NCCK, 2013).

# Rwanda and Burundi

## Tharcisse Gatwa

### Rwanda

The story of Christianity in Rwanda began when Roman Catholic missionaries from Buganda arrived in February 1900. A team of 'White Fathers' (as Cardinal Lavigerie's Missionaries of Africa were known) and Baganda assistants led by Monsignor Jean Joseph Hirth, a French native, were received in Nyanza by King Musinga, who authorised them to start a station in Save, in the south of the country. The new faith quickly took root, with the first baptism being administered in 1903 and the first Rwandan priests ordained in 1917. The first Protestant missionaries were Germans who arrived from Tanganyika in 1907 and opened stations at Zinga in the east of Rwanda and Kirinda in the centre. Following the defeat of the Germans in Africa in 1916, the German missionaries left. Under the 1919 Treaty of Versailles, Rwanda and Burundi were given to Belgium, and the Belgian Missionary Society in Congo (SBMPC) took over the 'orphan' German missions in Rwanda. Other Protestant missions arrived in the inter-war period and opened mission stations, including the Adventists at Gitwe and Rwankeri, the Anglicans at Gahini, Shyira, Shyogwe and Kigeme, the Baptists at Nyantanga, the Pentecostals at Gihundwe and the Methodists at Kibogora.

Important revival movements influenced Christianity in Rwanda during the colonial and post-colonial eras. A key issue was the relation of the monarchy to the new faith, and a turning point was the dismissal in 1930 of King Musinga, who had been accused of opposing evangelisation, in favour of his son, Rudahigwa, a Roman Catholic convert. Exiled, King Musinga died in Moba, Belgian Congo, in 1944. The new King was enthroned in 1931 by both Monsignor Léon-Paul Classe, head of the Roman Catholic Church, and Charles Voisin, the Belgian Governor, disrespecting the historical Abiru institution customarily responsible for that function. The new King took the throne name Mutara III and was baptised together with the Queen and Queen Mother in 1943. The coming of a new King sparked a movement of mass conversion known as the 'tornado', *Irivuze Umwami* ('what the king says'), which affected both the general population and the ruling class. The conversions were 'welcomed' as the greatest Catholic missionary achievement on the continent. At the climax of the movement in 1946, King Mutara III consecrated Rwanda to Jesus Christ and the Virgin Mary. In his discourse, an extraordinary piece of contextual theology, the King publicly recognised the Lordship of Jesus and the Virgin Mary over any national religion or philosophy. From this point, the Catholic hierarchy continued to exercise great influence in society and played a significant role in colonial and post-colonial politics. Today, the Roman Catholic Church, with nine dioceses and 186 parishes, claims the allegiance of around half of the country's population.

Another spiritual revival focused on the Virgin Mary's apparitions took place from 28 November 1981, in the Kibeho girls' secondary school. Many pupils started claiming to receive messages from the 'Mother of the Word', the Virgin Mary. With great intensity, the visionaries called on church hierarchy, public authorities and the populace to repent, and to love and revere the 'Mother of God'. The Roman Catholic hierarchy was divided. Some questioned what they saw as the poor academic background of the children, their biblical illiteracy and their low moral standards, while others suspected political manipulations. Yet, on 29 June 2000, Kibeho was officially recognised as a 'holy place of apparitions of the Virgin Mary' and has since become a pilgrimage destination for believers from the region and beyond.

Within the Protestant missions a movement known as the East African Revival emerged from Gahini, an Anglican mission station, in 1933. Influenced by the Keswick Revival movement in England, the Rwandan movement, in contrast to the Catholic preoccupation with the ruling elite, focused on ordinary individuals. The missionaries attempted to emulate the Keswick teachings on the holiness of God, new birth, repentance, faith, prayer, sanctification, public confession of sins, visions and walking under the light of the Holy Spirit. After a promising beginning, the movement declined in the 1950s, a development blamed on opposition from Catholics, communists and nationalists. It was revived in the 1970s

*Christianity in Rwanda, 1970 and 2015*

| | 1970 | | 2015 | | Average annual growth rate (%), 1970–2015 |
|---|---|---|---|---|---|
| Tradition | Population | % | Population | % | |
| Christians | 2,298,000 | 61.2% | 10,624,000 | 91.5% | 3.46% |
| *Roman Catholics* | 1,684,000 | 44.9% | 5,402,000 | 46.5% | 2.62% |
| *Orthodox* | 500 | 0.0% | 1,500 | 0.0% | 2.47% |
| *Independents* | 23,200 | 0.6% | 1,118,000 | 9.6% | 8.99% |
| *Protestants* | 332,000 | 8.8% | 2,238,000 | 19.3% | 4.33% |
| *Anglicans* | 162,000 | 4.3% | 1,550,000 | 13.4% | 5.15% |
| Pentecostals | 98,700 | 2.6% | 2,202,000 | 19.0% | 7.14% |
| Evangelicals | 226,000 | 6.0% | 2,344,000 | 20.2% | 5.34% |
| **Total population** | **3,755,000** | **100.0%** | **11,610,000** | **100.0%** | **2.54%** |

Source: Todd M. Johnson and Gina A. Zurlo (eds), *World Christian Database* (Leiden/Boston: Brill), accessed March 2016.

among younger generations in missionary schools under the leadership of Peter Guillebaud (son of the Reverend Harold Guillebaud, the first Bible translator in Rwanda). The revival had far-reaching effects. The Abarokore or 'born-again' distanced themselves from politics and insisted on ethnic togetherness. Teams of evangelists sponsored by the Rwanda Mission (a branch of the Church Missionary Society) toured East Africa, Europe, Asia and the Americas, forming a worldwide fellowship.

The end of the 1994 genocide against the Tutsi was followed by the arrival of new Charismatic movements. Some returning refugees joined local churches, but many decided to start their own churches. By 2004, more than 700 new religious movements were registered. Many of these churches brought new styles of worship and witness, calling on the authorities and the people at large to publicly confess and repent for the evil that had led to the genocide. They formed their own fora, the Alliance of Evangelical Churches (AEC) and the Federation of Born Again Churches and Organisations (FOBACOR), with a determination to reshape Rwandan Christianity.

### *Evangelism, Education and Growing Influence*

The first Roman Catholic seminary was begun in 1903, in Rubya, Tanganyika, where 15 Rwandans were sent to join 43 other recruits from the rest of the Vicariate. These Rwandans included the first two Rwandan priests, Donat Rebero and Balthazar Gafuku, ordained in 1917. By this time, a new vicariate had been formed, comprising Rwanda, Burundi and Buha (western Tanzania) and a new seminary was opened at Kabgayi, Rwanda, in 1912. In 1936 the seminary was transferred to Nyakibanda, where Rwanda and Burundi continued to train priests until 1952, when Burundi opened its own major seminary, in Burasira.

Training the Protestant clergy was a matter of controversy. Formal ministerial training was suspected by some missionaries to involve absence of faith. Exceptionally, the Presbyterian Church pioneered theological formation due to Swiss missionaries like Edgard Durand, who arrived in 1924 with a master's degree in theology, and Pierre Regard, who came in the 1950s. Protestant candidates for the ministry were sent to train in theological schools abroad, starting with Naasson Hitimana and Ildephonse Muzigamfizi, who graduated from the theological seminary in Ndoungue, Cameroon, in 1958, and who were ordained to ministry in 1963, 46 years after the first Roman Catholic ordination. Hitimana became first Rwandan General Secretary of the Presbyterian Church of Rwanda, taking over from a Dutch missionary, Reverend Phildius, in 1964; then, in 1970, following constitutional reforms, he became President. During his term up to 1977, Hitimana pioneered the creation of theological and ecumenical education in Rwanda, resulting in the establishment in 1970 of the ecumenical School of Theology of Butare (later the Protestant Theological Faculty). In 2010 this was enlarged to become the Protestant Institute of Arts and Social Sciences, the country's first Protestant university. The Seventh-day Adventist Church, after years of stagnation, took steps to develop higher education, including the church-sponsored Adventist University of Central Africa and two independent lay Adventist universities, in Kigali and Gitwe.

During the colonial era and indeed up to the 1994 genocide against the Tutsi, Roman Catholic missionaries had an overwhelming influence in Rwanda. The coming of King Mutara III gave impetus to the Catholic Church, which steadily gained the allegiance of the ruling elite. It took on the status of a state church, which it maintained by defending the idea of the 'Hamite supremacy', unjustifiably equated with the Batutsi. Selected sons of chiefs were educated to become colonial and missionary subordinates. However, as the wind of change blew through Africa in the 1950s, the elite Batutsi petitioned for independence, which alienated them from the Catholic Church and the colonial power. The latter shifted its allegiance to sponsor the Bahutu, who were moderate towards the church and colonial power. The Hutu took power and held it until 1994.

By the time of the Second Vatican Council, the Catholic Church had four local bishops: Aloys Bigirumwami in Nyundo, Jean Baptiste Gahamanyi in Butare, Joseph Sibomana in Ruhengeri, and Swiss-born André Perraudin in Kabgayi as the Church's Primate. During the early years of independence, the Catholic hierarchy maintained a very close relationship with the political leaders, many of whom were former seminarians, including Gregoire Kayibanda, President of Rwanda 1962–73. The church's active role in Rwandan politics during colonial times and after independence made it complicit in policies aimed at alienating different sections of the population from one another.

The Roman Catholics' dominant position expanded to the detriment of other religious communities, including Protestantism and Islam. While adherents of African traditional religions were considered old-fashioned followers of a 'demonic' religion legally repressed, Protestants were labelled 'heretic' followers of an 'untrue' religion and their initiatives sabotaged. Converting to Catholicism was seen as a sign of cultural emancipation and progress. From the beginning, missionaries learned the language of the country, Kinyarwanda, and familiarised themselves with customs, social institutions, laws and rules so that they would be able to eradicate 'traditionalism'. Catholicism was suspicious of a religion that was integral to a Rwandan civilisation. For this reason, the missionaries preferred imported concepts like *Mungu* (God), instead of *Imana*; or *Roho Mutagatifu* (Holy Spirit) instead of *Mwuka Muziranenge*.

The promotion of literacy went hand in hand with catechism. By 1911, four books were published by the Roman Catholic missionaries in a mixture of Kinyarwanda and Luganda languages, including *Ekitabu Kyo Kufutula Bigambo Bye Dini, Okuvaku Belemye Bwi Si Okugera mu Misi Wacu* ('the book that explains faith words from the creation up to today'). At the same time, the Protestants published the four gospels in extracts called *Ifuberi ya Urunyarwanda.* The Catholic missionaries codified the Kinyarwanda language, but the result was not satisfactory until the 1960s, when Father Alexis Kagame made improvements to the phonetics and orthography.

For decades the only newspapers published in Rwanda were the Roman Catholic weekly *Kinyamateka,* begun in 1933, and *Hobe,* created by Monsignor Bigirumwami for children in 1954. In 1988, the church started a radio station, Radio Maria, which broadcast from Kabgayi. The Roman Catholic Church with its foreign and local clergy remained for a long time the leading depository of scholarly information and knowledge on the past and present of Rwanda. Prominent learned figures include Alexis Kagame, author of *La philosophie Bantu Rwandaise de l'être* (1954). A philosopher, theologian, ethno-historian and linguist, he was a leading African scholar, one of the editors of the general history of Africa published by UNESCO. Other influential figures include Monsignor Aloys Bigirumwami, first African bishop in the Belgian colonies in 1952, and author of *Imihango n'Imigenzereze ya Kinyarwanda* (Nyundo, 1922), a collection of Rwandan popular wisdom.

The creation of the Council of Protestant Churches in 1963 led to a strengthening of Protestant work in media and literacy. The Centre for Literature and Audio-visual Techniques (CELTAR) was created and run for some years under a Dutch missionary, Pastor Jaap van der Neut, offering printing services and publishing a newspaper, *Inkoramutima.* However, its activities were discontinued in 1974–5. In 2012, the present author, then General Secretary of the Protestant Council of Rwanda, launched a radio station, Inkoramutima, which broadcasts nationally from the Council's headquarters in Kigali.

From the beginning, the Roman Catholic hierarchy had a vision of schools as a key component in its strategy to influence Rwandan society. Primary and secondary schools were developed at mission stations as well as seminaries in dioceses. The missionaries controlled confessional and public schools, including the Astrida (Butare) school for sons of chiefs and the vocational school in Kicukiro, Kigali. In 1963, the National University of Rwanda, the first in the land, was created by Dominicans fathers from Canada and stood alone until the liberalisation of education in the 1990s.

Protestants had minimal resources to promote education and hence were marginalised. The first Protestant training school for primary school teachers opened in Shyogwe in 1947 while the first high school opening up to university education was inaugurated in 1965 in Kigali by the Presbyterian Church of Rwanda, assisted by the Swiss churches.

For a long time, the efforts of the Second Vatican Council and the World Council of Churches to promote dialogue and unity resulted in no concrete actions. In the 1970s, the Catholic episcopate for Zaire (now the Democratic Republic of Congo), Rwanda and Burundi were still identifying three categories of population in their respective countries: Roman Catholic converts, catechumenates and pagans. This classification totally ignored the existence of Protestants. Only in the 1980s were a few common initiatives undertaken: the ecumenical translation of the Bible, started in 1981, sponsored by the United Bible Societies and completed in 2002; the creation of an office for church medical clinics and hospitals (BUFMAR); and the creation in 1991 of the Committee of Contacts for Catholic and Protestant Hierarchies, to mediate in political turmoil and conflict between the Habyarimana regime and the Rwandan Patriotic Front rebellion.

On their side, ecumenism among Protestants included the first Protestant version of the Bible, initiated in 1925 during the Kirinda missionary conference under the British and Foreign Bible Society; the establishment in 1930 of missions' geographical limits to avoid competition and rivalry; and the formation in 1935 of the Alliance of Protestant Churches for both Rwanda and Burundi. In 1963, after independence, the Alliance of Protestant Churches of Ruanda–Urundi split into the Alliance of Churches for Burundi and the Protestant Council for Rwanda (CPR).

### *The Church and the Genocide*

The church hierarchies have been blamed for missing the opportunity to address ethnic discrimination and manipulations before and during the genocide. Many observers trace the genocide ideology to the 'hamite supremacy' ideology promoted during the colonial era. The church hierarchies had defended radical discrimination policies that promoted exclusive education and privileges for a few and supported the colonial reforms that institutionalised the 'racialisation' of the social classes (Bahutu, Batutsi and Batwa). During the crisis provoked by the movement for independence in the 1950s, the Catholic hierarchy sided with the colonial power in accusing the Batutsi elite of communism and radicalism and therefore supporting the pro-Hutu parties, seen as moderate. Many Tutsi were killed, and others were driven into exile in a period when the colonial power and the church controlled all the mechanisms of political power.

Many Tutsi remained refugees despite numerous attempts to return by force or dialogue. In 1990 the descendants of the 1959 refugees attacked from Uganda. In reaction, the Bahutu-dominated MRND (National

Revolutionary Movement for Development) exacerbated ethnic feelings against the Batutsi. From 1990, selective killings were conducted in various places, leading eventually to the genocide against the Batutsi that started on 7 April 1994 and took the lives of more than 1 million innocent people.

Trapped in its complicity with the political system, the church was unable to speak out against the perpetrators of discrimination and mass killings. There were, however, some exceptions among parish clergy, who courageously opposed the genocide and paid with their lives, such as the Presbyterian pastor of Kugituntu parish, Athanase Rwamuhizi. On the whole, the church hierarchies kept silent or spoke too little too late while hundreds of thousands of victims were being slaughtered across the country, even in church buildings. The post-genocide era was characterised by a malaise created by the size of the tragedy and the absence of a *mea culpa* from the church hierarchies.

However, some Protestant churches repented for the failure, while in 1998 the Catholic Church organised an extraordinary synod in dioceses in preparation for its centenary celebration. The synod advocated a *Gacaca* approach, a traditional mechanism of conflict resolution, but failed to repent convincingly. A more impactful initiative came in 2014.

In 2000 the Evangelicals (the AEC) and the new 'born again' (FOBACOR) persuaded the older national council, the Protestant Council of Rwanda (CPR), to form a body called the PEACE Plan. Anglican Archbishop Emmanuel Kolini was elected chairperson. Apostle Paul Gitwaza, leader of Zion Temple, one of the new churches, took over in 2013 when Archbishop Kolini retired. From 2011 the PEACE Plan organised annual crusades called Rwanda Shima Imana (Go Rwanda! Thank God!) to celebrate the country's renaissance. In 2014 under an *ad hoc* working group chaired by Augustin Mvunabandi, the Anglican Bishop of Kigeme, both Catholics and Protestants elaborated a confession repenting for past missed opportunities to stand for the truth, particularly the 1994 genocide against the Tutsi. Whether mutual recognition or realism, the joint declaration of repentance by the representatives of all Rwandan church hierarchies opened new hope for dialogue and the healing of wounds.

## Burundi

As with Rwanda, evangelisation in Burundi was pioneered by the White Fathers of Cardinal Lavigerie. Geographically, the early mission stations covered the four natural regions of the country: Imbo (Buhonga station, 1902) in the west; Kirimiro (1899) in the centre; Bunyoma (Muyaga station, 1900) in the east; and Bweru (Kanyinya, 1905, and Rugari, 1909) in the north-east. Soon a conversion movement was underway in all these areas. It was similar to Rwanda's in that emphasis was initially placed on the conversion of the youth, particularly from the ruling class. At first, the chiefs resisted conversion. At the time of the administrative and political reforms of 1926–33, out of 225 chiefs, only two were baptised: Joseph Kiraranganya in Rusengo and Joseph Menyo in Kanyinya. The situation changed with the reforms introduced by the Belgian colonial regime. Among other changes, the number of chieftaincies was reduced to only 46 and chiefs were required to be literate, to give support to missions, to be baptised and married to only one woman, to renounce traditional religion and to support their subjects' conversion. A 'chief hunt' was initiated against those who resisted conversion to Catholicism. With the creation in 1929 of the school at Astrida in Rwanda for the sons of chiefs from both countries, the Baganwa ruling dynasty in Burundi, like the Banyiginya in Rwanda, had no option but to send their children there to train. By 1954 all chiefs except one were Catholics. In contrast to the situation in Rwanda, the King of Burundi, Mwambutsa, never converted, although he never opposed conversions.

In the early period Christianity was a men's affair. From the 1930s, however, the missionaries started to force chiefs and men to bring their wives. Failure to do so was severely punished, including with exclusion from the catechumenate, which would mean losing a chieftaincy. By 1937, women outnumbered men. At first it was young people who were baptised, but following Monsignor Julien Gorju's introduction of a special catechumenate for the elderly in 1928, growing numbers of older people became Christians.

Protestantism in Burundi is represented by different branches, including Anglicans, Baptists, Free Methodists, United Methodists, Quakers, Moravians and many Evangelical and Charismatic groups. Mainline Protestantism shares parts of its history with Protestantism in Rwanda, notably the East African Revival.

*Christianity in Burundi, 1970 and 2015*

| | 1970 | | 2015 | | Average annual growth rate (%), 1970–2015 |
|---|---|---|---|---|---|
| Tradition | Population | % | Population | % | |
| Christians | 2,579,000 | 74.6% | 10,438,000 | 93.4% | 3.16% |
| *Roman Catholics* | 2,108,000 | 61.0% | 6,543,000 | 58.5% | 2.55% |
| *Orthodox* | 1,000 | 0.0% | 2,200 | 0.0% | 1.77% |
| *Independents* | 1,600 | 0.0% | 293,000 | 2.6% | 12.23% |
| *Protestants* | 147,000 | 4.2% | 1,549,000 | 13.9% | 5.38% |
| *Anglicans* | 45,000 | 1.3% | 1,080,000 | 9.7% | 7.32% |
| Pentecostals | 98,000 | 2.8% | 1,643,000 | 14.7% | 6.46% |
| Evangelicals | 124,000 | 3.6% | 1,854,000 | 16.6% | 6.19% |
| **Total population** | **3,457,000** | **100.0%** | **11,179,000** | **100.0%** | **2.64%** |

Source: Todd M. Johnson and Gina A. Zurlo (eds), *World Christian Database* (Leiden/Boston: Brill), accessed March 2016.

Its history begins with the work of the United Methodist Church, then known as 'World Gospel Church'. By 1928, it had opened mission fields in the east in Kayero, Rutana province, then in Buhonga, Murehe and Murore. The Free Methodist Church traces its origins to the same period.

Meanwhile, the Ruanda Mission of the Anglican Church set up its first mission stations, at Buhiga and Matana in 1935 and at Buye in 1936. The Anglican Church in both Rwanda and Burundi experienced much growth through medical work and education as well as through the East African Revival. The Evangelical Friends missions in Burundi began in 1934 and also saw steady growth.

### *Evangelism and Church Growth*

Following his appointment as new Head of the Catholic Church in 1922, Monsignor Gorju toured the country and convened the missionaries for a pastoral conference. This resulted in the well known *Carte de Visite* (Business Card) of the mission in Burundi. Gorju promoted 'an official directory of the catechumenate' and the *Carte de Visite* played a big role in the mass conversions. His reform of the synod statutes in 1928–9 introduced two innovations: relaxing the catechumenate for older people and emphasising a new approach to 'heathens'. This involved the missionaries in becoming familiar with traditional African beliefs and practices in order to eradicate them. Gorju instructed his missionaries to study the practices of Mizimu, the Burundi ancestor cult, Kiranga, a historic and universal figure feared by the population, as well as the Nangayivuza sect, which promoted a syncretism of Catholicism and traditional practices known as *Kubandwa,* a phenomenon known in Rwanda as well. Under Gorju, the profile of Christianity in Burundi took shape, a work pursued by his successor, Monsignor Antony Grauls.

The missionaries initiated many social activities, including rural clinics and primary and secondary schools. Yet, compared with Rwanda, the church in Burundi lagged far behind in both lay and confessional education. Only after 1945 did the network of schools spread, created and funded by missionary activities. Literacy was a condition for access to baptism. Taking advantage of the printing press in Gitega, the missionaries initiated the newspaper *Rusiziramarembe,* later renamed *Ndongozi.* For the *évolués* (the educated), the missions published *Temps Nouveaux d'Afrique* in French (1954–60), which disseminated the missionary political vision based on principles of Christian democracy.

The first ordinations of local priests took place in 1925. To assist the priests, catechists worked to great effect at local level. Under Monsignor Gorju and his colleague in Rwanda Monsignor Classe, every single detail of life for the Catholic adherents and the mission personnel was organised by the synod's *Constitution Directory*. The most talented among the clergy took university degrees in Europe to qualify for teaching in major seminaries. However, the reality of segregation was present: indigenous priests were compelled to live and eat on their own. Yet from 1933 Monsignor Gorju entrusted two missionary stations, Giheta and Murehe, to indigenous clergy.

On the Protestant side, it was not until the consecration of Bishop John Ndoricimpa in 1980 that the (Methodist) Evangelical Episcopal Church came under indigenous leadership. In 1985, the Free Methodist Church took a similar step when the Reverend Noah Nzeyimana became its local bishop. His successor, the Reverend Dr Elie Buconyori, led the denomination from 2000. He was the charismatic founder and first Chancellor of Hope African University (HAU) until his death in 2013. HAU opened in 2004 with 200 students. By 2011, the student population had increased to more than 4,000 and the university offered over 30 bachelor's programmes, including in medicine, psychology, theology, information technologies and civil engineering.

So far as the Anglican Church is concerned, in 1965 the Province of Uganda, Rwanda, Burundi and Boga-Zaire was established, and in Burundi the first national bishop was consecrated for the Diocese of Buye (covering the whole country). Today, the Anglican Church of Burundi comprises seven dioceses: Bujumbura, Buye, Gitega, Makamba, Matana, Muyinga and Rumonge. Its first primate, Samuel Sindamuka, was consecrated in 1992. He was succeeded by Samuel Ndayisenga in 1998 and Bernard Ntahoturi in 2005.

### *Christianity in Burundian Society*

The Catholic Church's Golden Jubilee was celebrated in 1948 with a major event in Gitega, attended by colonial authorities, missionaries and Vatican representatives. Both the colonial Governor of Burundi and Governor General Petillon (for Belgian Congo, Rwanda and Burundi) traced the history of the missionary movement and praised the role the church played in 'installing Christian civilisation and elevating the morality and material wealth of the indigenes' through schools, clinics and literacy. The Governor handed to the Bishop a collection of 360,830 francs from expatriates living in Burundi (colonial settlers, traders, government officials) and 887,000 francs from the indigenous population. A force to be reckoned with on account of its numbers, the Catholic Church looked to enter the decade of decolonisation with assurance. Burundi had joined Rwanda as another Christian kingdom in the centre of Africa. The Catholic leaders were confident that they would go from strength to strength, with 'heathens and Protestants' turning to the Catholic faith. In the aftermath of the celebration, the country was divided into two vicariates, Gitega for Monsignor Gorju and Ngozi for Monsignor Joseph Martin.

A major issue for the Catholic Church was the schools crisis of 1954–6. Under the 1928 and 1948 Conventions, the Roman Catholic Church was given full control of schools. This arrangement, however, was jeopardised by the advent of a liberal-socialist government in Brussels. When it announced the creation of lay schools, the episcopate of Congo, Ruanda and Urundi sent a circular letter to Christians and the clergy urging them to resist the attempt by the colonial government to create lay schools. Despite the vigorous protests of the Catholic Church, which even enlisted the support of King Mwambutsa, the lay schools were created. Although the crisis shook church–state relations, it did not stop the Christianisation of Burundi.

Like its counterpart in Rwanda, the Anglican Church of Burundi experienced the East African Revival, which did much to shape its character. Its social activities centred on schools, hospitals and clinics. In 2000, a group of church members created the Université Lumière, which had more than 2,000 students in 2003. The Church is not a member of many ecumenical bodies, not even the World Council of Churches. However, it is a member of the Anglican Global South movement, and Archbishop Bernard Ntahoturi has been involved in the Anglican realignment movement.

The United Methodist Church has been heavily affected by instability in the country. Following the 1993 military coup, the Bishop's family and many members of the church went into exile in Kenya. Challenged by the turmoil that took the lives of more than 200,000, the United Methodist leadership became involved in conflict mediation. Bishop Ndoricimpa had a significant political role. From 1989 to 1993 he was spiritual adviser and chaplain to President Pierre Buyoya and to his successor, the late Melchior Ndadaye.

### The Church and the Independence Movement

The 1955 Bandung Conference severely damaged the colonial ideology that underpinned missionary enterprise. Most African colonies gained independence between 1956 and 1962. And yet, the Catholic Church remained suspicious of African nationalists, accusing them of colluding with communism. The episcopate was urged by the Vatican to distance itself from the West if such a distance could stop the infiltration of communism. The African nationalist movement pushed the colonial government to organise elections of counsellors nationally and locally in 1952 and 1956. The results showed the dominance of the traditional elite, with a Hutu–Tutsi cleavage. However, Burundi nationalism was born. Such a move was too serious for the church to ignore.

In 1956 the Catholic episcopate of Congo, Rwanda and Burundi published a declaration evoking 'political emancipation of the indigenous' without, however, referring to 'independence'. In 1959 a pastoral letter recalled the moral supremacy of the church by reaffirming its mission and role in politics and society, towards family and in socio-economic life. The bishops acknowledged the right of Christians to belong to political parties of their choice. They called any future government to maintain such a state of affairs in 'education, medical and hospital institutions, youth movements, social actions and subsidies to missions'. Because of the absence of a central authority, the Protestant positions varied from one denomination to another and from individual to individual, marked sometimes by an annoyed silence or a volatile attitude.

Like many colonies in Africa, including Rwanda and Congo, Burundi's struggle for independence was polarised around the moderate and radical political parties. The moderate ones – MDR-Parmehutu and RADER in Rwanda; the Christian Democratic Party (PDC) in Burundi – were formed with the backing of the colonial power and the missionaries. They petitioned for independence under the care of the colonial power. Radical nationalist parties – UPRONA of Prince Louis Rwagasore in Burundi and UNAR, which supported the local monarchy, in Rwanda – that were fighting for immediate independence were formed by the elites, mostly from the Batutsi, educated and formerly privileged by the colonial power and the missionaries.

In Rwanda, the UNAR manifesto claimed immediate independence and at the same time proclaimed its intention to nationalise schools. The missionaries and the colonial power felt betrayed by their former protégés and went on to accuse them of collusion with communism. Between 25 July 1959 and October 1961, the three leaders, King Rudahigwa of Rwanda, Prince Louis Rwagasore of Burundi and Patrice Lumumba of Congo, were murdered by the hand of the colonial power.

Led by Prince Louis Rwagasore, the pro-independence UPRONA won the September 1961 elections. Unfortunately, Rwagasore, who was married to a Hutu woman, was murdered a month after winning the elections. Despite the death of its leader, the party led Burundi to independence on 1 July 1962 with a relatively high degree of Batutsi–Bahutu cooperation. The country remained a monarchy until the 1966 military putsch, when the Tutsi-dominated army led by Captain Michel Micombero proclaimed the Republic. Burundi was traumatised by the 1959 massacres of the Tutsi and subsequent massacres in Rwanda, keenly felt as a national tragedy. The Hutu–Tutsi cleavage became pronounced in Burundi, resulting in repeated tragedies on their side (1965/6; the 1972 genocide; the 1988 Ntega and Marangara's massacres against the Hutu). Above all, the murder in October

1993 of Melchior Ndadaye, the first democratically elected President, by a Tutsi-dominated army, fuelled the 'Hutu power' ideology responsible for the 1994 genocide against the Tutsi in Rwanda.

## Conclusion

In one century, both Rwanda and Burundi developed into 'Christian kingdoms'. This was reflected in many different social activities. However, the churches could not challenge public morality and political crises. During repeated traumatic events, the churches never stood as alternative mediators for peace, truth and justice in solidarity with the victims from all sides. Commenting on the 1972 genocide against the Bahutu in Burundi, historian Adrian Hastings observed that the Catholic bishops never, at any time, criticised the government's responsibility for the massacres, nor did they raise any voice of protest about the injustices perpetrated against the Hutu majority.

Dr H. H. Osborn, who served as an Anglican missionary in Rwanda, told moving stories of despair and anguish in Burundi for survivors who had experienced horror when soldiers would come day after day and systematically assemble the Bahutu elites, including pastors, evangelists, catechists, school teachers, doctors, nurses and paramedical staff, who would never be seen again; or when bulldozers would bury alive hundreds of school pupils and university students. The other shameful silence was on the part of the international community, which could have been much more robust in dealing with the Micombero dictatorship. Similar national and international shame was extensively documented following the 1994 genocide against the Tutsi in Rwanda.

Despite this history charged with painful memories, both old and new churches in Rwanda and Burundi are growing rapidly today, particularly through the influence of prophetism and the Charismatic movement. And yet, there is a growing realisation of the need for a more critical approach to church–state relations and for initiatives to heal wounds.

## Bibliography


Gatwa, Tharcisse, *Churches and Ethnic Ideology in Rwandan Crises 1900–1994* (Oxford and New Delhi: OCMS, 2005).

Gatwa, Tharcisse and Laurent Rutinduka, *Histoire du Christianisme au Rwanda des origines à nos jours* (Yaoundé: CLE, 2014).

Gatwa, Tharcisse, 'Christianity in Rwanda', in Daniel Patté (ed.), *The Cambridge Dictionary of Christianity* (Cambridge: Cambridge University Press, 2010), pp. 1116–17.

Kalibwami, Justin, *Le Catholicisme et la société Rwandaise 1900–1962* (Paris: Présence Africaine, 1991).

Mvuyekure, Augustin, *Le Catholicisme au Burundi 1922–1962: Approche historique des conversions* (Paris: Karthala, 2003).

# Uganda and South Sudan

## Richard Nnyombi MAfr

Uganda and South Sudan not only share a common border but have also been shaped by similar political and religious experiences. Both were under British rule, almost during the same period and for the same length of time – Uganda 1894–1962 and South Sudan 1898–1956. Both shared the same missionary institutions, namely the Comboni Missionaries, the Mill Hill Missionaries (MHM) and the Church Missionary Society (CMS). Both experienced the presence of Islam, which at one time or another expressed itself as the ruling political power, and both were exposed to the practice of slave trading closely linked with Arab-Muslim traders.

Christianity in Uganda dates back to 1877, when the first Protestant missionaries arrived. The 2014 census showed that Christians (Catholics, Anglicans, Orthodox, Seventh-day Adventists, Pentecostals, 'Born Again' and Evangelicals) formed more than 70% of the total population of 34.1 million. The same census showed that Muslims and Pentecostals had increased in number since the previous census, in 2002. Although the 2014 census put the followers of traditional religions at only 0.1%, the reality is that traditional religion is still lived and practised by a large proportion of Christians and Muslims. During the early years of the twenty-first century it has come out of the backyard, where it had been pushed, and moved to the courtyard and the marketplace in many parts of the country.

South Sudan as an independent country dates from 9 July 2011. However, the history of Christianity in this new state cannot be separated from the history of Christianity for the whole of Sudan before the separation. It has been greatly influenced by Arab-Islamic culture and religion. Christianity itself reached South Sudan from the north (Khartoum), along the Nile down to Gondokoro, from where it eventually reached northern Uganda. Like the pastoralist-nomadic ethnic groups of north-eastern Uganda, such as the Tepec, the Karamajong cluster and the Pokot, the South Sudan nomadic peoples such as the Dinka, the Nuer and the Toposa are very much attached to their traditional cultures and religions and therefore less open to converting to new religions such as Christianity and Islam.

### Historical Background

By the late nineteenth century, Uganda was becoming accessible to the outside world, either by land or by water: in the south on land from

Bagamoyo to Tabora and on to Mwanza, then by Lake Nalubaale (Victoria) to Uganda; in the north by the River Nile from Cairo; and in the east on land from Mombasa to Kisumu then by Lake Victoria to Uganda. These were commercial and slave-trade routes that opened up the way of evangelisation to the interior up to Uganda.

The presence of organised kingdoms and chiefdoms in Uganda – for example Buganda, Bunyoro, Toro, Busoga and Ankole – provided effective social structures for spreading Christianity. The cultural, social and political organisation of these kingdoms, from the King down to the village level, were used by the missionaries to spread Christianity and to 'plant the church'. The traditional religious and moral heritage, including belief in a 'Creator God' and such values as hospitality and charity, provided good soil for the 'gospel seed'.

The presence of Islam in Uganda was another important factor that indirectly prepared its people to receive the teachings of Christianity. The first Muslim traders from the coast and Zanzibar, Arabs and non-Arabs, arrived in the 1840s. Although they came mainly in search of ivory and slaves, they eventually Islamised the Ugandans. Through Islam, the Baganda had received new religious ideas such as beliefs in life after death in heaven or hell, sacred scriptures and the value of literacy. When the Christian missionaries taught similar ideas and beliefs, the Baganda easily understood them.

Sudan, on the other hand, during the nineteenth century was under the government of the Ottoman Empire (1820–81). The major interest in the country at that time was trade in slaves and other precious goods such as cattle and ivory. The main markets were El Obeid and Khartoum. South Sudan was then almost unknown by those in the north because of the enormous swampy area and the impossibility of navigating the White Nile. Not until the 1840s was it possible to go down the river, thus opening South Sudan to the outside world. Its population was mainly made up of independent tribes, notably the Shilluk, Dinka, Nuer and Nuba.

*Christianity in Uganda, 1970 and 2015*

| | 1970 | | 2015 | | Average annual growth rate (%), 1970–2015 |
|---|---|---|---|---|---|
| Tradition | Population | % | Population | % | |
| Christians | 6,429,000 | 68.1% | 32,958,000 | 84.4% | 3.70% |
| *Roman Catholics* | 3,395,000 | 35.9% | 16,242,000 | 41.6% | 3.54% |
| *Orthodox* | 11,200 | 0.1% | 30,500 | 0.1% | 2.25% |
| *Independents* | 260,000 | 2.7% | 1,323,000 | 3.4% | 3.69% |
| *Protestants* | 111,000 | 1.2% | 2,016,000 | 5.2% | 6.66% |
| *Anglicans* | 1,291,000 | 13.7% | 14,250,000 | 36.5% | 5.48% |
| Pentecostals | 326,000 | 3.5% | 8,396,000 | 21.5% | 7.49% |
| Evangelicals | 698,000 | 7.4% | 7,364,000 | 18.9% | 5.37% |
| **Total population** | **9,446,000** | **100.0%** | **39,032,000** | **100.0%** | **3.20%** |

Source: Todd M. Johnson and Gina A. Zurlo (eds), *World Christian Database* (Leiden/Boston: Brill), accessed March 2016.

A letter from Henry Morton Stanley published in the *Daily Telegraph* in 1875 appealing for Christian missionaries to come to Buganda and to Equatorial Africa in general, together with King Muteesa I's letter to Queen Victoria of 14 April 1875, triggered the missionary movement to this part of Africa in general and to Uganda in particular. The formation of the African International Association in 1876 was another stepping-stone. It challenged the church, and especially the missionary societies, to form concrete plans and prepare missionaries to come to Central Africa. 'The Secret Memorandum of the Evangelisation of the Equatorial Africa' prepared by Monsignor Charles Lavigerie in 1878, inspired by Father Daniel Comboni's highly influential 'Plan for the Regeneration of Africa by Africa' (1864), which was approved by the Vatican in the same year, was a response to the Association's plan. The Anglican Church Missionary Society (CMS) pioneered the evangelising mission in Uganda and for many years remained the only Protestant missionary group in Uganda.

Three major Catholic missionary institutes pioneered the evangelising mission in Uganda and Sudan: the Society of the Missionaries of Africa (White Fathers), founded in 1868 in Algiers by the future Cardinal Charles Lavigerie, the Comboni Missionaries of the Heart of Jesus (Verona Fathers), founded in 1867 in Verona (Italy) by the future Bishop Daniel Comboni, and the Mill Hill Missionaries (St Joseph Foreign Missionary Society), founded in Mill Hill in England in 1866 by the future Cardinal Herbert Vaughan. These Catholic male missionary institutes were reinforced and complemented in their work by the arrival of women missionaries. The first were the Missionary Sisters of Our Lady of Africa (MSOLA), who arrived at Lubaga on 18 October 1899. These were followed in 1903 by the Franciscan Sisters, whose apostolate was mainly in the field of education and health care. The third group was the Pious Mothers of Africa (Comboni Sisters, founded in 1872). They arrived in Gulu in December 1918. These missionary orders worked mainly with women and girls.

*Christianity in South Sudan, 1970 and 2015*

| | 1970 | | 2015 | | Average annual growth rate (%), 1970–2015 |
|---|---|---|---|---|---|
| Tradition | Population | % | Population | % | |
| Christians | 721,000 | 19.8% | 7,462,000 | 60.5% | 5.33% |
| *Roman Catholics* | 627,000 | 17.2% | 6,110,000 | 49.5% | 5.19% |
| *Orthodox* | 1,000 | 0.0% | 3,000 | 0.0% | 2.47% |
| *Independents* | 3,800 | 0.1% | 71,400 | 0.6% | 6.74% |
| *Protestants* | 6,300 | 0.2% | 1,493,000 | 12.1% | 12.92% |
| *Anglicans* | 210,000 | 5.8% | 1,750,000 | 14.2% | 4.82% |
| Pentecostals | 3,100 | 0.1% | 778,000 | 6.3% | 13.07% |
| Evangelicals | 109,000 | 3.0% | 1,639,000 | 13.3% | 6.20% |
| **Total population** | **3,647,000** | **100.0%** | **12,340,000** | **100.0%** | **2.75%** |

Source: Todd M. Johnson and Gina A. Zurlo (eds), *World Christian Database* (Leiden/Boston: Brill), accessed March 2016.

Roman Catholic missionaries were the first to arrive in Sudan. Daniel Comboni, before founding his Institutes (that for Men in 1867 and that for Women in 1872), was a missionary in this country and the Comboni missionaries played an influential role from 1842. The Mill Hill Missionaries came to Sudan in 1937 and worked among the Shilluk nomadic tribe in the territory of Malakal. Anglicans and the American Presbyterians began working in Sudan in 1899, the Anglicans through the CMS in Omdurman while the Presbyterians began in Khartoum but quickly developed ministries in both the north and the south. The Sudan Interior Mission arrived in 1937, followed by the Africa Inland Mission in 1949. The Sudan Pentecostal Church, which has grown significantly in the south, was started later by Swedish missionaries.

The presence of the British in this part of Africa and their direct rule over southern Sudan as stipulated in the Anglo-Egyptian Condominium (1898) were instrumental in the evangelising mission in South Sudan. Under this rule, there was a policy of demarcating spheres of activities to the churches and missionary institutes. Hence, the Comboni missionaries were allocated western Upper Nile Province (Rumbek), the Province of Bahr al-Ghazal (Wau) and northern Uganda; the Anglicans, Equatorial Province (Juba); and the American Presbyterians, eastern Upper Nile. The north was a monopoly of the Muslims.

### Inter-religious Encounter, Clashes and Dialogue

At the beginning of the evangelisation of Uganda, the four religions – traditional religion, Islam, Protestantism and Catholicism – met in the palaces of King Muteesa I, first at Lubaga, where the present Kampala Catholic Cathedral stands, and afterwards at Kasubi-Nabulagala, where the royal tombs *(Amasiro)* of the last four Kings (Muteesa I, Mwanga, Daudi Chwa and Muteesa II) are located. They were animated by the spirit of apologetics, polemics and rivalry that years later developed into violent clashes and wars, such as the Christian–Muslim war of 1888–90 and the Protestant–Catholic war of 1892. These conflicts and wars have left lasting marks on the social, political and religious life of the people and society of Uganda.

Although traditional religion was much less involved in the public debates carried out during the royal audiences, it was not totally absent. It was represented mainly by the *katikkiro* (Prime Minister), the royal family, the clan leaders and traditional priests, who considered the new religions a serious threat to the existence of the kingdom and Ganda cultural and religious traditions. Its resistance, often a silent one, was especially manifested in the fact that none of the Kings up to Mwanga ever fully converted to Islam or to Christianity.

Political and economic factors were to a great extent responsible for these clashes between the followers of different religions. The Anglican missionaries played a major role in making Uganda a British protectorate (1894), with all the socio-political and religious privileges that this could bring to the Protestants. Out of this encounter and contest, the Muslim community came out the least advantaged after being defeated by the combined forces of the Protestants and Catholics in 1890.

In South Sudan, too, the encounter between Christianity, Islam and traditional religion has not been without friction and clashes. In addition to the socio-political and economic causes of these conflicts and clashes, there were also racial and ethnic factors. The north was predominantly Arab and Islamic, while the south was predominantly composed of African ethnic tribes with their local traditional religions. More than in Uganda, religion was politicised in Sudan, leading to conflicts and wars. Three major political eras are outstanding in this politicisation of religion in Sudan. The first was that of the Mahdist Rebellion, led by Muhammad Ahmad ibn Abdallah, which started in 1881, a revolt that clearly associated politics and religion. This revolt forced Christian missionaries to leave Sudan. The second era was that of the Anglo-Egyptian Condominium, which followed the defeat of Mahdist rule in 1898. This Condominium gave Muslims a monopoly in the north while allocating territories in the south to the different churches for their respective missionary activities, a situation that lasted until after World War II. The third era starts from the independence of Sudan in 1956. During this period, different policies have been put in place that have provoked conflicts and wars. These policies have included: assimilation of the south through Arabisation and Islamisation; restrictions on missionary activities (1961/2); expulsion of all expatriate missionaries from the South (1964); and the imposition of Sharia law by President Jaafar Nimeiri (1983). In spite of these clashes, in both Uganda and Sudan, members of these religions and churches generally live in harmony. The social, cultural, ethnic and family bonds that bind them together are often stronger than their religious differences.

Moreover, in both countries, initiatives to establish formal ecumenical and inter-religious dialogue have been taken. In Uganda, formal ecumenical dialogue dates back to 1963 and the formation of the Uganda Joint Christian Council (UJCC). It was spearheaded by Archbishops Joseph Kiwanuka (Catholic), Theodorus Nankyama (Orthodox) and Leslie Brown (Church of Uganda). Its purpose and focus is to promote peaceful coexistence and collaboration among Christians in Uganda. The Uganda Martyrs, who came from both the Catholic and Protestant churches, are one of the sources of strength and inspiration for this Council. Inter-religious dialogue goes back to 2001, when the Inter-religious Council of Uganda (IRCU) was initiated.

It is affiliated to the World Council of Religions for Peace (WCRP) and the African Council for Religious Leaders (ACRL). The members of IRCU are the three church members of UJCC, the Muslims and the Seventh-day Adventist Uganda Union. Its mission is to promote peace, reconciliation, good governance and holistic human development through inter-faith action and collaboration, advocating the empowerment of member bodies for the common good. Although independent Pentecostal and Evangelical churches are not members of IRCU, they do participate in the implementation of its programmes. Finally, the Acholi Religious Leaders Peace Initiative (ARLPI), an inter-faith peace-building and conflict-transformation organisation in northern Uganda, was founded in 1997 by six faith communities, namely the Anglicans, Catholics, Muslims, Orthodox, Pentecostals and Seventh-day Adventists.

In South Sudan, too, initiatives have been taken to promote institutionalised ecumenical and inter-religious dialogue. Examples include the South Sudan Council of Churches (SSCC), founded in 1965; the Sudan Inter-religious Council (SIRC), founded in 2000, before the independence of South Sudan; and the New Sudan Council of Churches (NSCC), founded by Bishop Paride Taban in 1989–90. Peace-building, reconciliation and promotion of human rights are some of the key activities of these institutions in this new country, still riven by inter-tribal wars.

## Growth and Spread

The era of Muteesa I, who welcomed the pioneer missionaries, was the time of preparing the ground and sowing the seed of the gospel. During this time, the field of action was very much limited to the mission posts, Nateete for the Protestants and Lubya-Nabulagala for the Catholics, and in the palace during the royal audiences. This is the period when the first baptisms were celebrated, by Catholics in 1880 and 1882 and by Anglicans in 1882. During this time, only men could be reached by the missionaries, as evidenced by the diaries and the baptism registers of that period.

In November 1882, for unknown reasons, the Catholic missionaries voluntarily left Buganda for Mwanza, leaving behind a handful of neophytes and a few hundred catechumens, who took over the work of evangelising their fellow Ugandans, and with such great success that when the missionaries came back three years later (see below) the number of catechumens had greatly increased and now included not only men but also women.

Evangelisation in Buganda started from the elite class – the royal pages (*abagalagala*) and chiefs. They spread the message to the common people (*abakopi*). These royal pages and other palace servants were regarded as the cream of society. Only intelligent, talented and well behaved young men were chosen by the chiefs and clan leaders to serve in the palace. Moreover, many of these were destined to become future chiefs and leaders in the kingdom, depending on how they carried out their palace duties.

When Muteesa I died in October 1884, his successor, Mwanga II, at the request of the Catholic lay leaders, invited the Catholic missionaries to come back to Buganda, which they did in June 1885. He gave them a piece of land at Nalukolongo, not far from the royal palace at Mengo. Mwanga allowed some freedom of missionary work whereby the catechumens were free to go to both Catholic and Protestant missions for religious instructions and basic education. Women, too, could attend these instructions. However, this 'time of grace', as the missionaries called it, did not last long. After killing the Anglican Bishop James Hannington in October 1885, Mwanga started persecuting the Christians. The climax of this persecution was the condemning and killing of the Uganda Martyrs in May–June 1886. The majority of these were burnt to death at Nakiyinja, formerly a traditional sacrificial site and now owned by the Protestants.

The effect of this general Christian persecution was the opposite of what Mwanga had expected. More people embraced Christianity, confirming the truth enshrined in Tertullian's observation that 'the blood of the martyrs is the seed of the church'. Since that time, Christianity has never ceased to grow. Neither did the 1888–90 war between the Muslims and Christians stop this movement. In fact, the Christians who fled from the capital because of this war became evangelisers to those places where they escaped, for example in Buddu, Ankole and Busagara. And when Mwanga himself 'embraced the Catholic faith', from 1889 onwards, although he had not been baptised, hundreds of his subjects became Christians.

The coming of the British government representatives, which resulted in Uganda becoming a British protectorate in 1894, consolidated the role the Protestants played in the political life of the country. The conversion of the traditional cultural rulers and chiefs in such centres as Bunyoro, Toro and Ankole through the influence of the British administrators attracted more converts to the Protestant Church.

From 1891, the missionaries started founding missions outside the capital. What is remarkable is that in different parts of the country lay people had already started the evangelising work. In fact, lay people were precursors for both Catholic and Protestant missionaries in almost every part of the country. Still today these pioneers are revered, with Catholics inspired by the memory of figures like Yowana Kitagwana, who first brought Christianity to Kigezi (Kabale) in western Uganda in 1912, and Protestants by the work of such early leaders as Apolo Kivebulaya in Toro.

Schools and hospitals, initiated by the churches and for a long time left under their full control by the colonial government, were also means through which Christianity attracted new converts. It is significant that the name *abasomi*, given to the Christians since the beginning of their presence in the country, means 'those who know how to read and to pray'. The arrival of the twentieth century brought the era of consolidating the churches through the formation of catechists, indigenous clergy and religious. Seminaries were opened, religious institutes founded, catechetical schools started and teacher training schools established. Printing of religious materials contributed greatly to the consolidation of Christianity. New missionary societies started coming to share in the work of evangelisation. This was also the time when revival/renewal groups (*balokole* or 'saved ones') within the Protestant Church began to appear. Pentecostal, Independent and Seventh-day Adventist churches grew rapidly in the late twentieth and early twenty-first centuries.

The growth and spread of Christianity in South Sudan, compared with Uganda, encountered more natural and human obstacles. The harsh Sudanese climate, unlike that in Uganda, decimated many of the pioneer missionaries. Then the Mahdist Rebellion and rule forced the expatriate missionaries to vacate the country, leaving behind the lay people to carry on the evangelising mission. They faced such challenges as the policy of assimilation through Arabisation and Islamisation, the imposition of Sharia law, the presence of and resistance to Christian conversion of the many Nilotic pastoral ethnic tribes, and the Anglo-Egyptian Condominium policy of restricting religious influence to particular geographical areas.

However, in spite of those obstacles, profiting from the limited freedom of direct evangelisation and mostly through the indirect evangelisation of offering health and education services by both the Catholic and Protestant churches, the many pastoralists who were settling in villages and towns gradually became more open to the Christian message. In due course, this led to baptisms and slowly but steadily Christianity in South Sudan grew and spread. Also, the campaign by the Christian missionaries against the slave trade, which the southerners identified with the Arabs and Islam, opened the door of friendship with them, leading many to embrace Christianity, starting with those who had been ransomed from the slave traders by the Catholic missionaries (the Protestant missionaries were against the policy of redeeming slaves since, they reasoned, this could have encouraged the raiders and slavers to capture more slaves for selling).

## Human, Social and Political Involvement

A close look at the strategic plans of the different missionary institutes and groups, both Protestant and Catholic, for the evangelisation of both Uganda and South Sudan clearly reveals that services geared towards human and social development were an integral part of the evangelising mission in these countries. Many were inspired by David Livingstone's vision of evangelising Africa through a combination of 'commerce, Christianity and civilisation'. For the pioneer missionaries and those who came after them and eventually the established local Christian churches, these services were not only a means of getting converts, but also part of the evangelising mission in their own right.

The first activity was the fight against the slave trade, which was widely practised in this part of Africa and mostly organised by Arab-Muslims, often in connivance with local leaders. This anti-slavery campaign put Christian missionaries into direct confrontation with the Muslims. Combatting it was interpreted as hostility to Islam and Muslims. One of the means that the Catholic missionaries used, though opposed by the Protestants, was the ransoming of slaves, especially slave children, with the hope that these children once grown up and well educated would in turn fight against it.

Other activities included health services – visiting the sick and establishing clinics, dispensaries and hospitals – and formal education, both academic and professional (technical and agricultural). Female missionaries, especially the women religious in the Catholic context, played a major role in this field. In both Uganda and Sudan, the British colonial government left responsibility for these two areas entirely in the hands of the churches up until the 1950s.

Churches have been involved in activities that seek to promote justice and peace, human dignity and human rights. Justice and peace structures at national, diocesan and parish levels have been established in the different churches, although in a number of places they are dormant. At the ecumenical level, many of the activities of the Uganda Joint Christian Council have a component of this ministry. Also, the Inter-religious Council of Uganda has activities that aim to promote justice and peace.

Christianity in general and individual churches in particular, through their leaders, have played a role in the political life of these two countries. For example, in the struggle for independence in both countries, religious leaders contributed to the forging of the new constitutions of the new states, and the emerging indigenous political leaders of these states were products of church educational institutions. Church leaders have continued to influence the socio-political life of their respective countries indirectly, through their pastoral letters and acting as mediators between warring factions. However, much more could be done by the Christian community to offer a prophetic voice where the values of the gospel are wanting.

## Contemporary Challenges

Despite their rich Christian heritage, these two countries are deeply marked by hatred and rivalries, which at times lead to violent conflicts. It is in addressing the deep causes of these animosities that the churches find their most pressing challenge in the contemporary context. It is a matter of being wholly committed, as Pope Benedict XVI noted in *Africae Munus* (2011), 'to the service of true reconciliation, justice and peace'. Such service is urgently needed at a number of levels.

Family and domestic life is threatened by many negative forces, and this has led many married couples to separation and divorce. Domestic violence has been on the increase and has led to the suffering of many and to the violation of human rights, not to mention the breaking down of many families. Given the importance of the family for Christian nurture, these disturbing trends call for urgent attention. Living out the Christian faith necessarily involves cherishing family life and countering the rise of domestic violence.

There is also a pressing need for Christian engagement with social and political life. In these two countries, there is a generalised greed for power, honour and wealth (money). For many politicians, authority is seen as a matter of career progression rather than as a service to the people for the common good. Leaders hold onto power as long as they can and at whatever cost, not hesitating to use money and police and military force to achieve their ends. This has resulted in rampant corruption, impunity and violation of human rights. It has also infected the masses with the same vices. Deep animosity exists between and within political parties and this is often revealed at election times, as evidenced in the 2016 general election in Uganda. Being a Christian in such a context calls for a deeper biblical understanding of the role of politics, political parties and leaders in society: to champion a vision of politics as service to the people and the common good. A Christian ethic of selfless service and non-violence has much to contribute to the building of strong and sustainable societies in these two countries.

Also needed is a Christian witness that engages with such issues as poverty, economic development and climate change. The widening gap between the rich and the poor is another source of division and conflict among the people of these two countries. The issue of land grabbing, for example, is related to this – the rich and powerful grabbing the land of the poor. Climate change is a serious issue and the poor living in rural and slum areas suffer most from such adversities as droughts and floods. Christians need to engage in serious reflection on Jesus's preference for the poor and work towards a 'church with the poor and for the poor'.

The reality that ethnic and tribal differences underlie many conflicts must also be reckoned with. Conflicts among the many ethnic and tribal groups are often fuelled by the tribalistic practices of those in power, such as the unjust sharing of power and national natural resources. In some areas this has erupted into violent and armed conflicts, for example in South Sudan and in the Kasese region in Uganda, leading to loss of life, rape, destruction of properties, recruitment of child soldiers and displacement of peoples. Unfortunately, this problem of tribalism is also to be found within the church structures and religious institutions, seriously compromising them in their prophetic mission within the society.

Meanwhile, the societies of Uganda and South Sudan are not immune from the advance of the values of modernity, secularism and materialism. There are clear signs that, in both countries, secularism and materialism with their positive and negative effects are already at work. Christian theological institutes, universities and other learning institutions will be instrumental in helping the churches and individual Christians to face these challenges.

These two countries are in a transition period, between the traditional and the modern way of life. This has a great impact on the social and moral life of the people. Moreover, whereas there is an increase in religious adherence in general and Christian adherence in particular, there is at the same time an increase in immoral behaviour and practices. These include corruption at all levels from top to bottom, domestic violence, murder, prostitution, rape, nepotism, individualism, impunity, human trafficking and sacrifice. A Christian in this context is being challenged to work for moral regeneration at both the individual and the societal level, starting with oneself. Sunday sermons and pastoral letters from different churches have concentrated on this area, although it seems that more has to be done if real moral regeneration is to happen.

## Conclusion

These challenges call Christians to conversion and to become real ambassadors of reconciliation, justice and peace if they are to be relevant and become 'good news' to the people and societies in these countries. Christians are not alone in this mission. There are many possibilities to make common cause with people of goodwill who feel challenged by these social issues and are ready to collaborate in the search for solutions.

Christianity in both Uganda and South Sudan is now more than a century old. In both countries, the dream of the pioneer missionaries to have 'Africans evangelising Africans' is now a reality. In Uganda as well as in South Sudan, the local churches, although not present everywhere, are well established, with local religious leaders at all levels. However, in the Uganda and South Sudan of today, there are many new challenges and opportunities which call for 'new evangelisation', that is, proclaiming the 'Good News of the Kingdom of God' as lived and taught by Jesus Christ in a new way that answers the questions of today's society.

The spirit of competition and rivalry that existed between the different religions, denominations and missionary institutes at the beginning of Christianity in these countries, although not completely a thing of the past (as evidenced by religious fundamentalism and fanaticism), is counteracted by efforts, at both the national and the international levels, to promote ecumenical and inter-religious dialogue and collaboration in view of seeking together solutions to present-day social issues that affect all people, irrespective of their religious affiliation.

One of the driving forces in the first evangelisation of Uganda and South Sudan, as we have seen, was the campaign against the slave trade, which eventually was abolished. Today, new forms of slavery, including human trafficking, are on the rise. Uganda and South Sudan are not excluded from this evil. The fight against modern slavery is part and parcel of the new evangelisation.

We have noted that in the recent years there has been a revival in the practice of the traditional religions, even among the Christians. This reveals the complexity of the reality of religious conversion. It challenges Christians to deepen their understanding of what it means to be a Christian and not to be content just with numerical growth.

Finally, today in Uganda as well as in South Sudan, Africans are not only missionaries to Africans, as the pioneer missionaries dreamt, but are also missionaries in Europe and America, where the pioneer missionaries originated. Whereas Christianity is booming in Uganda and South Sudan, in the North Atlantic it appears that there is a recession of faith. Will Ugandans and South Sudanese have a role to play in meeting this fresh missionary challenge, which already is beginning to present itself in their own societies?

## Bibliography

Hastings, Adrian, *A History of African Christianity 1950–1975* (Oxford: Clarendon Press, 1994).

Tusingire, Frederick, *The Evangelization of Uganda: Challenges and Strategies* (Kisubi: Marianum, 2002).

Ward, Kevin, 'A History of Christianity in Uganda', in *Dictionary of African Christian Biography* <http://www.dacb.org/history/a%20history%20of%20christianity%20in%20uganda.html> (last accessed 11 May 2016).

Werner, Roland, William Anderson and Andrew Wheeler, *Day of Devastation, Day of Contentment: The History of the Sudanese Church across 2000 Years* (Nairobi: Paulines Publications Africa, 2000).

Wheeler, Andrew C., 'Christianity in Sudan', in *Dictionary of African Christian Biography* <http://www.dacb.org/history/christianity%20in%20sudan.html > (last accessed 11 May 2016).

# Ethiopia, Eritrea, Somalia and Djibouti

## Tibebe Eshete

### Ethiopia

Ethiopia is one of the oldest Christian nations in the world. The Aksumite Empire adopted Christianity in the fourth century AD during the reign of Emperor Ezana. The Emperor's official espousal of Christianity had serious implications, for it greatly facilitated the expansion of the faith among the populace through the institution of the Ethiopian Orthodox Church (EOC). The diffusion of Christianity in Ethiopia did not follow the pattern of the Greco-Roman world, where it was confined to the lower level of society for centuries before the rulers embraced it. In Ethiopia, it spread from top to bottom, from royal court to the people. The support that the EOC garnered from the state contributed to the expansion of its influence across culturally and geographically diverse areas. The church's close connection with the state, of course, also has a downside so far as its autonomy and freedom of initiative are concerned.

A remarkable aspect of Christianity in Ethiopia is the longstanding presence of the EOC as a national church. The EOC has, remarkably, fused the Jewish and Christian traditions into an indissoluble whole. This, coupled with its consistent claim to possess the Ark of the Covenant, has lent the people and the nation a unique sense of identity. The *tabot,* a wooden representation of the Ark, is the epicentre of the EOC, and distinguishes it from the Eastern and Oriental Orthodox churches.

The coalescence of the state and the church was firmly secured from the start. The overlapping agendas of the two institutions has been the constant refrain of Ethiopian history. The process reached its apogee in the fifteenth century during the reign of Zara Yacob (1434–68), one of the descendants of the Solomonic Dynasty. The foundation of imperial authority in Ethiopia lay in the ruler's claim of descent from the ancient line of the Queen of Sheba and King Solomon and the Jewish origin of the Ethiopian state. This claim is elaborated in the *Kebre Negest*, an epic documentary narrative that lent the Ethiopian rulers political legitimacy and divine endorsement of their kingship.

Zara Yacob made energetic attempts to bolster the missionary enterprise of the church, mainly through the consolidation of the monastic institutions through land grants to spur them to vigorously engage in evangelism.

This measure enhanced the zeal of the holy monks to venture out and proselytise. The monastic leaders who pioneered as missionaries, mostly following the footsteps and directions of the expanding state, undertook evangelistic efforts by advancing in specific areas, often alone, driven, as they often claimed, by supernatural visions.

The language factor was the deepest obstacle to the Christianisation of the ordinary people. Several languages were spoken in Ethiopia and most of the people in the newly added territories in the south were speakers of non-Semitic languages. The medium of transmission for the Orthodox faith was Ge'ez, the longstanding language of liturgy that was considered to be a sacred language to communicate the Scriptures and the tradition of worship.

This expansion of Christianity went in tandem with the territorial expansion of the Ethiopian empire through the succeeding centuries. In the same vein as in the past, the faith spread from the court to the periphery. The trajectory reached its climax in the nineteenth century, during the reign of Emperor Menelik II (1889–1913). The rise of Menelik changed the history of Ethiopia. His strong desire to reunify Ethiopia and restore its glorious history led him to conduct extensive military and diplomatic campaigns into areas that had not even remotely been connected with the central authority in the past. The result was the creation of a large empire that brought a motley collection of diverse ethnic and socio-linguistic groups under one political umbrella. As had been the case in the earlier period, the church gave ideological and functional backing to the Emperor in his expansionist endeavour. The church's missionary work involved converting key local elites (religious and secular), baptising people and building churches. Ethiopian monarchs took religion both as a source of inspiration and as a justification for territorial expansion. Menelik viewed his policy of territorial expansion in the same regard. Though its influence was uneven, the EOC laid the foundations of the Christian faith in this

*Christianity in Ethiopia, 1970 and 2015*

| | 1970 | | 2015 | | Average annual growth rate (%), 1970–2015 |
|---|---|---|---|---|---|
| Tradition | Population | % | Population | % | |
| Christians | 15,005,000 | 52.8% | 58,574,000 | 58.9% | 3.07% |
| *Roman Catholics* | 62,500 | 0.2% | 937,000 | 0.9% | 6.20% |
| *Orthodox* | 11,077,000 | 39.0% | 39,001,000 | 39.2% | 2.84% |
| *Independents* | 134,000 | 0.5% | 2,383,000 | 2.4% | 6.60% |
| *Protestants* | 717,000 | 2.5% | 16,714,000 | 16.8% | 7.25% |
| *Anglicans* | 3,000 | 0.0% | 690 | 0.0% | −3.21% |
| Pentecostals | 213,000 | 0.8% | 10,889,000 | 11.0% | 9.13% |
| Evangelicals | 809,000 | 2.8% | 14,159,000 | 14.2% | 6.57% |
| **Total population** | **28,415,000** | **100.0%** | **99,391,000** | **100.0%** | **2.82%** |

Source: Todd M. Johnson and Gina A. Zurlo (eds), *World Christian Database* (Leiden/Boston: Brill), accessed March 2016.

expanded empire. Most of the Western missionaries who came to Ethiopia in the nineteenth and twentieth centuries, whether they acknowledged it or not, capitalised on the spiritual seed the national church had sown. In certain cases, the missionaries filled the gaps where the presence of the EOC was weak.

Emperor Haile Selassie I, who came to the throne in 1930, attempted to modernise the EOC. He took a number of initiatives, especially following the restoration of independence after the brief Italian occupation. The Emperor sought to give the EOC a modern face at both the national and the local levels. At the national level, he adopted a more enlightened approach towards religion in general, as exemplified by his slogan 'the nation is for all; religion is for the individual'. The national church, both the lower-level priests and its upper-echelon hierarchy, was resistant to change and was one of those countervailing powers with which the forces of modernisation had to contend.

The Emperor's position vis-à-vis the national church, for most of his reign, was ambivalent. It appears that he sought to introduce reforms by imperial authority rather than allowing the EOC to cultivate a sense of autonomy to initiate them. The Emperor's initial steps involved introducing institutional reforms. For that purpose, he made securing the national autonomy of the church his top priority. It was imperative for Haile Selassie's scheme of modernisation to have a revitalised and nationalised church under his control. The struggle for the church's independence from Egypt, which started in the immediate post-war period, culminated in its full independence in 1959. The Emperor also played a pivotal role in setting up the Department of Mission and Evangelism in 1963. The Department was created basically to engage the church in gaining new adherents and helping the existing members to stay strong in their faith as the country was gradually going through social and economic transformations.

The establishment of the Theological College in 1961 was another crucial step taken by the Emperor to revive the EOC. He aimed to give a boost to the Orthodox Church so that it could keep pace with his modernising agenda. The intention of having the College was to train and raise clergymen, religious teachers and missionaries as part of their preparation to become effective workers in their church assignments. The Emperor seems to have keenly realised that the understanding formed by modern education had outstripped knowledge of religious faith as the nation was undergoing a major transition. This was a time when inbuilt cultural consensuses were losing ground among the youth and the rising intelligentsia.

Above all, a radical move made by the Emperor was the instrumental role he played in the publication in 1961 of the Bible in Amharic, the local language. This had huge unintended consequences, as it shifted the knowledge centre of the source of the Christian faith from a special priestly elite to the ordinary people – a factor that inadvertently undermined the historic church. The availability of the translation of the message into the national language is one of the crucial factors that facilitated the spread of the Evangelical faith in Ethiopia.

The EOC, which had been a bulwark of the state and the Emperor, was radically altered in status with the Ethiopian Revolution of 1974. The Derg, the military regime that ruled Ethiopia after the Emperor had been deposed, disestablished the church by political fiat. Consequently, the church lost both its landholdings and its political influence.

The elemental role played by the EOC in shaping Ethiopian culture and the identity of its people, though diminished, is still influential. Even today, most of the national holidays observed in Ethiopia are in keeping with the tradition of the EOC. In contemporary Ethiopia, it seems that the EOC is undergoing a redefinition of itself as an autonomous institution battered with new political winds from a home front that allows liberty to all religions. It also faces stiff competition from an expansive Christian movement unfolding in the form of evangelicalism, which it sees not only as a rival but also as a foreign import that lacks Ethiopian-ness. Among other factors prompting the church to redefine itself is the surge of renewed interest in the national church among the youth and the intelligentsia, at home and among its diasporic constituencies.

Ethiopia offers a somewhat peculiar situation for the study of evangelical Christianity in Africa because of the absence of the colonial factor and the existence of a national church strongly connected with the state. Unlike other African countries in which evangelical Christianity has encountered African traditional religions, in Ethiopia the encounter was mainly between the established forms of Christianity and those introduced by Western missionaries. Consequently, the type of religion with which the Western variant of Christianity interfaced and interacted in other African societies is largely missing from the picture. This situation has considerably shaped the character of the evangelical movement in Ethiopia.

Before turning to the evangelical movement it is necessary to set the backdrop by bringing the missionary factor into focus. The Jesuits were pioneer missionaries in Ethiopia in the sixteenth and seventeenth centuries, but they did not leave an enduring legacy, because of misguided political involvement, which led to their expulsion. The modern Protestant missionary enterprise in Ethiopia dates back to the seventeenth century, with the coming of a German Lutheran missionary by the name of Peter Heyling. His legacy is equally limited. He tried to do his mission work through the EOC. The only thing to his credit is the translation of a portion of the New Testament into Amharic.

Various missionaries found their way to Ethiopia during the eighteenth and nineteenth centuries. One memorable experience of the missionary enterprise in Ethiopia is closely tied to the tumultuous period of Emperor Tewodros (1855–68). This ruler, who had new ideas to reform both the nation and the EOC, gave serious attention to the affairs of the church. His radical initiative, however, was greeted with some resistance. He wanted the church to be more self-sufficient in terms of running its affairs, both institutionally and financially. A pivotal aspect of his policy was to foster friendly relations with European missionaries. He envisaged that through their assistance and instrumentality he might build connections with the West. His move was largely informed by the need to address local and external challenges, namely overcoming local opposition and neutralising the Egyptian menace. The romance with the missionaries came to a dramatic end in 1868, following an armed confrontation with a British expedition, in which the Emperor took his own life rather than surrender.

A legacy of the Protestant missionary enterprise during the time of Tewodros was the formation of a small congregation of Evangelical Christians from the Ethiopian Jewish community known locally as *Felashas* (also known as *Beta Israel),* much to the credit of the Pilgrimage Mission.

Western missionaries did not have much success after Tewodros. Emperor Yohannes IV, who came to the throne in 1872, was a fervent Orthodox Christian. Unwilling to host missionaries in his nation, he ordered them to leave at short notice. An interesting by-product of the withdrawal of the missionaries was their imaginative approach to doing evangelism in Ethiopia by other means. They set up mission stations along the Red Sea coast, far from the reach of the Emperor. They began to recruit ex-slave converts and train and equip them so that they could be sent as local missionaries to their respective villages. The success of their new endeavour was registered mostly in the Oromo-inhabited regions of Wollega, where the evangelical faith has flourished ever since.

The Church Missionary Society (CMS) also made heroic efforts to evangelise Ethiopia in the nineteenth century. Among the various missionary agents sent by the CMS, Johann Ludwig Krapf stands out as a prominent figure. The CMS's approach was to work within the EOC parameters by strategically focusing on the translation of the Bible into Amharic in order to expand knowledge of the Scriptures. Their ultimate objective was to invigorate the giant church and prompt it to engage in mission work. The combined challenges that missionaries faced from the EOC and local officials frustrated their work and consequently put a halt to their missionising vision. Krapf, whose desire was to reach the Oromo, one of the largest ethnic groups in Ethiopia, succeeded in translating portions of the New Testament into the Oromo language.

Although Emperor Menelik II allowed in Lutheran missionaries from Sweden such as Karl Cederqvist, the missionary enterprise saw its heyday during the reign of Haile Selassie. He opened the door for missionaries to work in Ethiopia to promote his project of modernisation and nation-building, subsequent to his exile in Britain. In 1944 his government passed a mission decree, which made the missionary factor in Ethiopia remarkably different to what it had been under his predecessors. The 1944 decree not only legalised the missionary enterprise in Ethiopia but also gave new opportunities for numerous mission organisations to enter and operate in Ethiopia. Haile Selassie was able to appreciate and garner the skills and resources of Western missionaries, particularly in the areas of modern education and medicine.

Several mission organisations that came to Ethiopia during his reign have significantly shaped the religious and demographic landscape of Ethiopia. The Sudan Interior Mission (SIM), whose daughter Kale Hiwot Church claims a membership of 8 million, can be cited as a good example. The Lutherans from the USA, albeit preceded by the Swedish Evangelical Lutherans, are another group worth mentioning. The history of the Mekane Yesu Church, currently boasting more than 4 million members, is associated with Lutherans. Others with noteworthy accomplishments include the Mennonites, the Baptists and the Seventh-day Adventists.

It has to be noted, however, that though Protestant missionaries have introduced evangelical Christianity to Ethiopia from the West, its exponential growth has resulted mainly from the contributions of native agencies. This is because of the legal and cultural restrictions under which the missionaries operated. Nonetheless, there was a remarkable expansion of the Evangelical movement during the times of the Ethiopian Revolution in the absence of the external agencies. It is important to recognise the indigenous dimension of the missionary enterprise. Thus, while the advent of Western Protestant missionaries in Ethiopia gave a strong impetus to the rise of the Evangelical movement in Ethiopia, that missionary enterprise in Ethiopia tapped into the fund of spiritual resources that were already there. Evangelical Christians, who constituted less than 1% of the Ethiopian population in the early 1960s, have grown rapidly over the last five decades. The 1994 government census recorded the number of Evangelical Christians at close to 6 million, and the census collected in 2007 put the figure close to 14 million, roughly 19% of the population. Enjoying relative respite from the challenge of persecution, particularly under the communist regime of 1974–90, the Evangelical movement has continued to experience explosive expansion.

In the Ethiopian situation, the term 'Evangelical' is an inclusive expression that embraces a myriad of denominations. It stands as a convenient umbrella to designate the various strands of Christianity outside the Catholic and Orthodox churches. Uniquely, the movement has also received the standard tag of *Pente* (a shortened reference to Pentecostalism), a folk conception not found elsewhere. The Evangelical movement made a significant inroad in Ethiopia in a relatively short period of time. Having its base originally in the rural areas of Ethiopia, it penetrated the cities and gradually captured the youth and the urban sectors of the population.

It could safely be argued that the rise of the Pentecostal movement in the 1960s and the 1974 Ethiopian Revolution provided the contexts for the growth of the Evangelical movement. The Pentecostal movement in Ethiopia stems from scattered beginnings in the early 1960s. It was an autonomous initiative pioneered by young Ethiopians. Although a small number of missionaries from Europe nurtured Pentecostal doctrines, they were confined to a few areas like Addis Ababa and Awasa. Forerunners of the Pentecostal movement were members of a promising elite who were able to use their skills and resources to establish a vibrant independent Pentecostal church called Mulu Wengel. It was one of the most powerful agents in the diffusion of Pentecostalism and the spread of the Evangelical faith across other countries. The name Mulu Wengel, literally 'Full Gospel', is noteworthy because it reveals the theology of Pentecostals concerning the promises of the Bible to provide full salvation, embracing a person's physical as well as spiritual needs. Pentecostals encouraged practices such as speaking in tongues, healing the sick through prayer, the laying on of hands, exorcism and the holding of prayer vigils. Some of these elements clearly resonate with some aspects of traditional religious practice in Ethiopia.

Pentecostalism in the Ethiopian context tends to exhibit a type of creative culture. It is a homegrown brand of adaptive religious initiative that sought to negotiate both modernity and established forms of religion, occasioned by social and cultural changes. The movement, whose followers came mainly from an Ethiopian Orthodox background, provided a strong impetus for the rise of an indigenous missionary enterprise. This was encapsulated in their slogan 'the gospel for Ethiopia by Ethiopians'. Pentecostals have reshaped religious narratives in Ethiopia. They considerably advanced the expansion of the Evangelical movement using networks of friendly associations, chapels and revival meetings. The manner in which Pentecostals produced a creative culture is particularly well expressed in new gospel songs, which incorporate traditional as well as modern musical instruments and which attract interest from diverse constituencies; such songs combine meditative and oral theology and appeal to a wide cross-section of Ethiopian society.

Their simple liturgical practices, their spirit-filled style of worship and their fast growth have alarmed both mission-based churches and the established church. The movement was seen as countercultural and their members were subjected to repeated persecutions. The persecution experience lent Pentecostals a new sense of identity, a messianic zeal and a commitment to redouble their efforts to evangelise.

The Pentecostals' persecution, their organising skills and their prior encounters and contestations with radical Marxist groups of their generation, constituted significant transferable experiences on which the Evangelical churches at large were able to capitalise when they came under fire throughout the period of the Ethiopian Revolution. A notable factor that, ironically, hastened the spread of the Evangelical faith in Ethiopia was the presence of a dictatorial power under the guise of Marxism between 1974 and 1990. The military elite that ruled Ethiopia for 17 years evinced extreme hostility towards the Evangelical faith, due to a misperception of its nature and the ill-conceived idea they held that it posed a serious threat to the nation because of its association with the West. Thus, the rulers engaged in a massive persecution project to wipe out Evangelicalism by expelling foreign missionaries, closing down churches, arresting key leaders and on occasion even executing them, as in the case of the Reverend Gudina Tumsa. Paradoxically, the persecution experience had a boomerang effect. For one thing, it provided the moment for the intensification of commitments on the part of Evangelical Christians to hold on to their faith and enthusiastically share it with others. For another, it created the context in which Ethiopians who were going through bleak years of despair and existential perplexities were predisposed to embrace the faith.

For most Evangelicals, the Revolution drove Christianity into the heart of the people, where faith was not just observed by going to the church but existentially claimed, lived and manifested. The gospel songs that came from the pit of suffering not only provided solace and comfort but became the chief avenues by which the Evangelical Church assumed its indigenous identity. Following the collapse of the Marxist regime, Evangelical Christianity kept the momentum of its growth as it entered a new phase, shaped by the ramifications of another de-centring political development, relative freedom and increasing global influence.

## Eritrea

Eritrea is located in the northern tip of the Horn of Africa. Over 40% of the population adhere to the Orthodox faith. Evangelicals constitute less than 1%. The picture of Christianity in Eritrea strongly parallels that of Ethiopia: the two countries share a long-running common Christian heritage and, until Eritrea's official separation from Ethiopia in 1993, there were multiple intersecting events impinging across the board. The issues examined above with regard to the development of Christianity in Ethiopia bear strong parallels to that in Eritrea. Consequently, this section focuses on those aspects unique to Eritrea.

Eritrea came under Italian colonial rule in 1890, which lasted until a brief period of British rule during World War II. Eritrea was then federated to Ethiopia in 1950 before its ultimate integration in 1962. The Catholic Church consequently has a longstanding presence in Eritrea. The Jesuits had had a presence in Eritrea since the sixteenth century, but serious engagements in mission work date from 1839 and the coming of the Lazarists under Giustino de Jacobis. Another Catholic order, the Capuchins, arrived in Eritrea in 1846 and benefited from the support of the Italian colonial governors. Catholicism assumed an instrumental role in solidifying Italian colonialism in Eritrea. Enjoying state support, the church also had the upper hand in shaping the spiritual contours of Eritrean society. It ran orphanages and schools, including Santa Famila, renamed Asmara University, founded in 1958.

Protestant missionaries started to make headway in the second half of the nineteenth century. The Swedish Evangelical Mission (SEM) arrived in Eritrea in 1863. It translated the New Testament and the Psalms, along with other portions of the Old Testament, into local languages like Tigre and Tigrinya. Overall, the impact of the SEM in spreading the Evangelical movement in Eritrea is limited, however. In the modern era, several missions linked to the SEM and the American Faith Mission operated in Eritrea. Nonetheless, the Evangelical faith gained both momentum and currency in the 1960s, mainly due to analogous developments mentioned above in connection with Ethiopia. A unique feature of the Eritrean situation is that Pentecostalism took a twist as it penetrated the established Orthodox Church from the inside. With a small beginning of stirrings of revivals at Enda Gabriel Orthodox Church in Asmara, the movement soon spread to other Orthodox churches, like Enda Medhanelm and Endermariam. The initial wave sprang from a Sunday school Bible study group known as Finote Berhran, but it then advanced rapidly into other areas where similar

*Christianity in Eritrea, 1970 and 2015*

| | 1970 | | 2015 | | Average annual growth rate (%), 1970–2015 |
|---|---|---|---|---|---|
| Tradition | Population | % | Population | % | |
| Christians | 857,000 | 47.5% | 2,433,000 | 46.5% | 2.35% |
| *Roman Catholics* | 75,000 | 4.2% | 165,000 | 3.2% | 1.77% |
| *Orthodox* | 761,000 | 42.1% | 2,203,000 | 42.1% | 2.39% |
| *Independents* | 3,100 | 0.2% | 24,000 | 0.5% | 4.65% |
| *Protestants* | 10,100 | 0.6% | 56,300 | 1.1% | 3.90% |
| Pentecostals | 700 | 0.0% | 140,000 | 2.7% | 12.50% |
| Evangelicals | 6,400 | 0.4% | 34,400 | 0.7% | 3.81% |
| **Total population** | **1,805,000** | **100.0%** | **5,228,000** | **100.0%** | **2.39%** |

Source: Todd M. Johnson and Gina A. Zurlo (eds), *World Christian Database* (Leiden/Boston: Brill), accessed March 2016.

groups existed. Attempts to put a check on the movement by the clergy rebounded, as these further alienated their followers. Young enthusiasts who were questing for new faith expressions soon found their way by joining the newly established Mulu Wengel Pentecostal Church. The influx of such enthusiastic elements from an EOC background proved to be vital assets to the Mulu Wengel Church. It is interesting to note that this group birthed new breeds of evangelists and pastors, with influential roles among Evangelical churches in Eritrea and the diaspora.

The story of Christianity in Eritrea is not complete without reference to the current persecution and the paradoxical expansion of the Evangelical faith. Although there was an expectation of better prospects, Evangelical Christians were beset by new challenges in the post-independence era. The new Eritrean leadership saw the movement, particularly its Pentecostal strain, as a nuisance. Evangelical Christians were viewed as inimical to a totalitarian regime. Eritrea does not have an official state religion. The rulers recognise only four religions, namely the Eritrean Orthodox Church, Islam, the Eritrean Catholic Church and the Eritrean Evangelical Church (*Kenisha*). The relationship between the state and religion has been particularly problematic since the government introduced a new policy in 2002 ordering the closure of all other religions except the four officially recognised ones. This move severely affected Christians branded as *Pentes*. The *Pentes* present a counter-hegemonic narrative by their very nature, like the situation during the Derg in Ethiopia. The sudden surge in the Evangelical movement, when it attracted not only the youth but also members of the middle class and professionals, was a crucial factor behind the hostility of the regime to the Evangelicals. The closure of churches, the arrest of prominent leaders and the dispersal of Evangelical Christians across neighbouring countries and to the West should be seen against this backdrop.

## Somalia

Somalia is located in the Horn of Africa. There were two separate colonies, ruled by the Italians and the British, before Somalia became independent in 1960. The discussion that follows is an overview of the situation of Christianity without making distinction between the two Somalias that existed prior to independence.

More than 98% of the Somalis adhere to Sunni Islam. The estimated proportion of the population that is Christian – Catholic and Protestant combined – is about 0.3%. Thus, Christianity is a minority religion in Somalia, with likely just over 3,000 practitioners in a population of nearly 11 million. Most Christian adherents come from minority ethnic groups and belong to the Church of the Nazarene. No Evangelical church is known to exist in Somalia. The translation of the Bible into Somali was completed in 1979. However, it is dangerous to carry the Bible in Somalia since it makes one an obvious target for attack.

There is one Catholic diocese for the entire country, the Diocese of Mogadishu. The presence of the Catholic Church in Somalia dates back to the colonial period. The Catholic Church made significant efforts to establish its presence, at least in the area of Mogadishu, from 1928. The Church established a cathedral by order of the colonial governor, who sought to promote Christianity. The operations of the Catholic Church were interrupted during World War II, a situation that severely affected a fledgling community of local converts.

Christian missions, mostly Catholic, ran schools, orphanages and medical centres before they were expelled during the Marxist rule of the 1970s. The Red Sea Mission Team that operated in Somalia for a while was also expelled, in 1977. The efforts of Christian mission have met with little success. The Somali are a very proud people and regard Christianity as a sign of inferiority.

A missionary group that has made strenuous efforts to reach Somalia are the Mennonites, who arrived in 1952. Keeping a low profile, they mainly used the establishment of bookstores and schools as evangelistic tools to accomplish their mission objectives. Some converts, who even achieved scholarly prominence, later seemed to remain aloof or revert to their Islamic faith.

Somalia has become a safe haven for Islamic radicalism. Al-Shabaab, the militant Islamist group, is active within a large part of Somalia. Al-Shabaab has declared that it wants Somalia free of Christianity. The group monitors suspected Christians, including spying on their mobile phone communications. It has been merciless in publicly beheading local Somali converts after accusing them of being spies of foreign agents and deserters. There

*Christianity in Somalia, 1970 and 2015*

| | 1970 | | 2015 | | Average annual growth rate (%), 1970–2015 |
|---|---|---|---|---|---|
| Tradition | Population | % | Population | % | |
| Christians | 4,900 | 0.1% | 3,200 | 0.0% | −0.95% |
| *Roman Catholics* | 3,800 | 0.1% | 90 | 0.0% | −7.98% |
| *Orthodox* | 250 | 0.0% | 1,000 | 0.0% | 3.13% |
| *Independents* | 80 | 0.0% | 400 | 0.0% | 3.64% |
| *Protestants* | 550 | 0.0% | 1,300 | 0.0% | 1.93% |
| *Anglicans* | 200 | 0.0% | 220 | 0.0% | 0.21% |
| Pentecostals | 16 | 0.0% | 350 | 0.0% | 7.08% |
| Evangelicals | 610 | 0.0% | 460 | 0.0% | −0.64% |
| **Total population** | **3,445,000** | **100.0%** | **10,787,000** | **100.0%** | **2.57%** |

Source: Todd M. Johnson and Gina A. Zurlo (eds), *World Christian Database* (Leiden/Boston: Brill), accessed March 2016.

are Christians operating in Somalia to provide compassionate humanitarian services, but they work in an extremely hostile environment. It is hard to gauge their success. Ethiopian Evangelical Christians are operating clandestinely in northern Somaliland, where the level of hostility is not as great as in the south. There might not be churches legally or publicly operating, but there are growing numbers of Somali Christians meeting informally in houses. Al-Shabaab has publicly declared that those who are suspected of being Christian will be subject to death on the spot, and so Christians keep their faith completely secret.

## Djibouti

Djibouti is a barren strip of desert between Ethiopia, Somalia and Eritrea. It was a French colony until its independence in 1977. The situation of Christianity more or less resembles that in Somalia. The inhabitants of the two countries profess the same religion. French rule in Djibouti was accompanied by the advent of Catholic missionaries, who were the first to introduce Christianity, in the year 1885. Muslims comprise roughly 97% of the population. Although religious freedom is guaranteed in the constitution, the majority of inhabitants who practise Christianity in Djibouti are expatriates and immigrants from various countries. Catholics, Orthodox and Evangelicals together constitute less than 2% of the population. The proportion of Christians in Djibouti is higher than in Somalia because of the existence of a sizeable community of Ethiopians who reside in the capital, either permanently or transitionally en route to Western counties. Although it is not permitted to evangelise the local people, the government has recognised the presence of the churches. As such, there is no restriction on following other religions in Djibouti. The Église Protestante de Djibouti, established in 1960 mainly for French troops, opens its door to house various immigrant Christian groups in the city.

*Christianity in Djibouti, 1970 and 2015*

| | 1970 | | 2015 | | Average annual growth rate (%), 1970–2015 |
|---|---|---|---|---|---|
| Tradition | Population | % | Population | % | |
| Christians | 12,000 | 7.5% | 11,100 | 1.2% | −0.17% |
| *Roman Catholics* | 11,000 | 6.9% | 7,300 | 0.8% | −0.91% |
| *Orthodox* | 800 | 0.5% | 2,300 | 0.3% | 2.32% |
| *Independents* | 0 | 0.0% | 340 | 0.0% | 8.12% |
| *Protestants* | 200 | 0.1% | 720 | 0.1% | 2.89% |
| Pentecostals | 0 | 0.0% | 440 | 0.0% | 8.75% |
| Evangelicals | 40 | 0.0% | 350 | 0.0% | 4.94% |
| **Total population** | **160,000** | **100.0%** | **888,000** | **100.0%** | **3.89%** |

Source: Todd M. Johnson and Gina A. Zurlo (eds), *World Christian Database* (Leiden/Boston: Brill), accessed March 2016.

## Bibliography

Eshete, Tibebe, *The Evangelical Movement in Ethiopia: Resistance and Resilience* (Waco, TX: Baylor University Press, 2009).

Haustein, Jörg, *Writing Religious History: The Historiography of Ethiopian Pentecostalism* (Wiesbaden: Harrassowitz, 2011).

Kaplan, Steven, *The Monastic Holy Man and the Christianization of Early Solomonic Ethiopia* (Wiesbaden: Steiner, 1984).

Tamrat, Tadesse, *Church and State in Ethiopia* (Oxford: Oxford University Press, 1972).

Yesehaq, Abune, *The Ethiopian Orthodox Tewahedo Church* (New York: Vantage, 1989).

# Angola and São Tomé and Príncipe

## Luciano Chanhelela Chianeque

### Angola

Prior to Portuguese colonial rule, the area known today as Angola was governed by tribal kingdoms such as Mbakongo, Ndongo, Mbundu, Kwanyama, Nganguela and Cokwe. Among the tribes of Angola the largest today is the Mbundu, who represent almost half the total population. The arrival of the first Portuguese explorers in 1482 heralded the beginning of a period of great suffering for the people of Angola, particularly through the Atlantic slave trade, under which vast numbers of black African slaves were traded to Portuguese merchants, who bought them to sell as cheap labour for use on Brazilian agricultural plantations. Famines and epidemics compounded the hardship. When Portuguese colonial rule became more firmly established in the eighteenth and nineteenth centuries, the authorities implemented a policy of assimilation. The aim was that Africans would abandon their traditional lives and cultures and adopt a Portuguese identity and way of life. In practice, it was the coloured (mulatto) people who assimilated rather than the majority black population.

After a bitter war of liberation Angola gained its independence from Portugal on 11 November 1975. Unfortunately, the three main liberation movements were also at war with one another, and each proclaimed the independence in a different city: the MPLA (the People's Movement for the Liberation of Angola) in Luanda; the FNLA (the National Front for the Liberation of Angola) in Uíge; and UNITA (the National Union for the Total Independence of Angola) in Huambo. Since there was no proper handover from the Portuguese colonial regime to an independent government, the different liberation movements were left to fight for control of the country. Independence therefore ushered in a protracted period of warfare that was not resolved until 2002. Following the death of UNITA leader Jonas Savimbi in Moxico Province in that year, a lasting ceasefire agreement was reached. The country has since been rebuilt and a new constitution was adopted by parliament in 2010.

#### *The Coming of Christianity*

The people of Angola were strongly influenced by their traditional religion, characterised by belief in an Almighty Creator to whom the human community is related through spirits and ancestors. Religious observance was woven into every aspect of communal life and found expression particularly in rites of passage associated with puberty, marriage, pregnancy, childbirth and death. Their religious view of the world made them receptive to the Christian message first brought by Portuguese Roman Catholics. In 1491 a Catholic mission station was built in the São Salvador area (Zaire Province) and soon local people were baptised in large numbers. The early sixteenth century saw the establishment of a Christian kingdom when King João I of the powerful Kongo kingdom was converted and later was succeeded by his son, Afonso I, who also became a Christian.

Protestant missions did not get underway until 1878, when a British Baptist missionary arrived. This was followed in 1880 by the arrival of American Congregationalists, who established mission stations in the central part of Angola – in Bailundo, Camundongo, Chilesso, Chissamba, Elende, Dondi, Galangui, Lobito, Huambo and Kuito. In 1885 Methodist missionaries arrived from America and set up their missions in Luanda and Quessua, Malanje. In 1897 the Angola Evangelical Mission was established in Cabinda, and the North Angola Mission started in 1925, in Uíge.

Religious affiliation in Angola was difficult to define because many who claimed membership of a specific Christian denomination also shared perceptions of the natural and supernatural order characteristic of indigenous religious systems. Sometimes the Christian sphere of the life of a community was institutionally separate from the indigenous sphere. In other cases, the local meaning and practice of Christianity were modified by indigenous patterns of belief and practice.

Although Roman Catholic missions were staffed largely by non-Portuguese people during the colonial era, the relevant statutes and accords provided that foreign missionaries could be admitted only with the approval of the Portuguese government and the Vatican, and on condition that they be integrated with the Portuguese missionary organisations. Foreign Roman Catholic missionaries were required to renounce the laws

*Christianity in Angola, 1970 and 2015*

| | 1970 | | 2015 | | Average annual growth rate (%), 1970–2015 |
|---|---|---|---|---|---|
| Tradition | Population | % | Population | % | |
| Christians | 4,700,000 | 74.6% | 23,223,000 | 92.8% | 3.61% |
| *Roman Catholics* | 2,667,000 | 42.3% | 14,558,000 | 58.2% | 3.84% |
| *Independents* | 62,300 | 1.0% | 1,027,000 | 4.1% | 6.43% |
| *Protestants* | 415,000 | 6.6% | 6,195,000 | 24.8% | 6.19% |
| *Anglicans* | 2,000 | 0.0% | 42,100 | 0.2% | 7.01% |
| Pentecostals | 66,100 | 1.0% | 5,216,000 | 20.8% | 10.19% |
| Evangelicals | 199,000 | 3.2% | 4,523,000 | 18.1% | 7.19% |
| **Total population** | **6,301,000** | **100.0%** | **25,022,000** | **100.0%** | **3.11%** |

Source: Todd M. Johnson and Gina A. Zurlo (eds), *World Christian Database* (Leiden/Boston: Brill), accessed March 2016.

of their own countries, submit to Portuguese law and furnish proof of their ability to speak and write the Portuguese language correctly. Missionary activity was placed under the authority of Portuguese priests. All of this was consistent with the Colonial Act of 1930, which determined that Portuguese Catholic missions overseas were 'instruments of civilisation and Portuguese national influence'. In 1940, the education of Africans was declared the exclusive responsibility of missionary personnel. All church activities, education included, were to be subsidised by the state. Protestant missions were permitted to engage in educational activity, but without subsidy and on condition that Portuguese was the language of instruction.

The main Protestant missions had arrived in Angola in the late nineteenth century and had been at work before the Portuguese managed to establish control over the entire territory. Their early years, therefore, were little affected by Portuguese policy and practice. Before the establishment of the New State (*Estado Novo*) in Portugal in 1926, the authorities kept an eye on the Protestant missions but were not particularly hostile to them; they were tolerated. Settlers and local administrators often were hostile, however, because Protestant missionaries tended to be protective of what they considered their charges. In those early years and later, Protestant missionaries were not only evangelists but also teachers, healers (medical doctors) and counsellors – all perhaps paternalistically, but in ways that involved contact with Africans in a more sustained fashion than was characteristic of Roman Catholic missionaries and local administrators.

Protestant missionaries worked at learning the local languages, in part to communicate better with those in their mission field but above all in order to translate the Old Testament and the New Testament into African languages. Protestant missionaries were much more likely than administrators and settlers to know a local language. Roman Catholic missionaries did not similarly emphasise the translation of the Bible and, with some exceptions, did not make a point of learning a Bantu language. In so doing, the Protestant missionaries contributed to the preservation of local languages, literature and culture.

### *Patterns of Evangelisation*

Because specific Protestant denominations were associated with particular ethnic communities, the structures of religious organisations were linked to the structures of these communities. This connection was brought about in part by the tendency of entire communities to turn to the variety of Protestantism offered locally. The conversion of isolated individuals was rare. Those individuals who did not become Christians remained to a greater or lesser extent adherents to the indigenous system. Unless they migrated to one of the larger towns, persons of a specific locality did not have the option of another kind of Christianity. Members of a community who had not yet become Christians were tied by kinship and propinquity to those individuals who had. On the one hand, indigenous patterns of social relations affected church organisation; on the other hand, the presence of Christians in the community affected the local culture to varying degrees. Christians who could quote Scripture in the local tongue contributed phrases to the culture that others picked up, and the attributes of the Christian God as interpreted by the specific denomination sometimes became attached to the high god of the indigenous religious system and typically made that deity more prominent than previously.

Their involvement in the languages of their mission areas, their medical and other welfare activity, and their ability to adapt to local structures gave Protestants much more influence than their numbers would suggest. For example, the leaders of the three major nationalist movements in the 1960s – the MPLA, UNITA and the FNLA – had been raised as Protestants, and many others in these movements were also Protestants, even if their commitment may have diminished over time.

The Portuguese settlers used forced labour in order to develop their estates without paying the local people. Therefore they brought people from the Bailundo, Katchiungo, Cahala, Ucuma, Huambo, Bie and Kwanza Sul areas – evangelised already by the Congregational Church – to Saurimo and Lucapa in Lundas Province. Despite the ill-treatment they suffered, these Christian converts carried with them the newly translated New Testaments and sang the songs they had learnt at their mission stations. Although forced to work under conditions close to slavery, through their worship and way of life they offered a powerful witness. When Protestant missionaries finally arrived, they found that Congregationalist worship and preaching were already established. Forced labour turned out to be a platform for effective mission.

### *Contemporary Christianity*

During the colonial period, notwithstanding the ill-treatment suffered by local people at the hands of Portuguese settlers and the contempt they showed towards Protestant churches, stability and discipline characterised church life in Angola. The situation has changed markedly since the first democratic elections in 1992 and particularly since the ceasefire in 2002 that followed the death of Savimbi. The country has become a battlefield for new religious movements, some of which are employing highly questionable methods. The government is gravely concerned about the activities of 'fringe' Christian groups, which use their churches as a base for criminal activity. For example, in March 2016 José Julino Kalupeteka, the leader of the Luz do Mundo (Light of the World) Church, appeared in court accused of the attempted killing of eight people, resisting state authority and damaging property at Sumi Hill, Caála municipality, Huambo Province. Kalupeteka was convicted and sentenced to 28 years in prison.

Such an extreme case highlights the challenge facing the churches in Angola today, as religion is being used as a vehicle for attaining material ends. People struggling with poverty can easily be attracted by movements that promise well-being and wealth, based on a blend of Western 'prosperity gospel' and African traditional religion. A plethora of new movements offer instant solutions to life's problems with little or no attention to the need for repentance and the discipline of Christian life. The currency of Christianity is becoming debased and its influence on popular culture and national life appears to be diminishing. The question for the churches is whether they can promote authentic spirituality and cultivate genuine discipleship among their members so as to commend Christianity to an increasingly sceptical public.

## São Tomé and Príncipe

Many parallels exist between Angola's story and that of São Tomé and Príncipe, a small nation off the west coast of Africa in the Gulf of Guinea that comprises two large islands, each with an archipelago of smaller ones. In the fifteenth century the islands were colonised by the Portuguese, who developed sugar plantations based on slave labour and who also used them as a staging post in the Atlantic slave trade. Through Portuguese influence the majority of the ethnically mixed population became Roman Catholic. Traditional African religion still, though, exercises pervasive influence. The Democratic Republic of São Tomé and Príncipe attained independence in 1975.

The roots of Protestant Christianity in the islands can be traced to two slaves, Silivondela and Chanja, who had come to faith through the work of the Camundongo mission station at Kuito, in Angola's Bié Province, in the early 1920s. They asked John T. Tucker, a missionary of the United Church

*Christianity in São Tomé and Príncipe, 1970 and 2015*

| | 1970 | | 2015 | | Average annual growth rate (%), 1970–2015 |
|---|---|---|---|---|---|
| Tradition | Population | % | Population | % | |
| Christians | 72,200 | 97.2% | 183,000 | 96.0% | 2.09% |
| *Roman Catholics* | 62,700 | 84.5% | 151,000 | 79.3% | 1.97% |
| *Independents* | 2,000 | 2.7% | 16,400 | 8.6% | 4.79% |
| *Protestants* | 1,000 | 1.3% | 15,800 | 8.3% | 6.33% |
| Pentecostals | 900 | 1.2% | 26,800 | 14.1% | 7.83% |
| Evangelicals | 820 | 1.1% | 10,200 | 5.4% | 5.78% |
| **Total population** | **74,300** | **100.0%** | **190,000** | **100.0%** | **2.11%** |

Source: Todd M. Johnson and Gina A. Zurlo (eds), *World Christian Database* (Leiden/Boston: Brill), accessed March 2016.

of Canada based at the Dondi mission in Angola, to send them literature, including Bibles and hymn books. This led to Angolan missionaries being sent to the island, an arrangement that continued until 1975. After that, there was no further involvement of Angolan missionaries in São Tomé and Príncipe; however, help was sought from Portugal and this resulted in Pentecostal pastors coming to serve on the islands, leading to growth in Pentecostalism. The Seventh-day Adventists have also established a significant presence. Many of the issues with which Christians in Angola are struggling are replicated in São Tomé and Príncipe.

## Future Challenges

Key to the future will be the authenticity of Christianity. Those who announce it need to be themselves transformed by the word they preach. Only then will their witness be relevant to society. Only then will they be able to address issues related to the exercise of power and the conduct of government. It is through the power of their example that Christians will be able to exercise positive influence in both countries.

The renewal of theological education will be of particular importance. There is a need for pedagogy that is proactive, preventive and curative, reflecting the perspective of the Kingdom of God. There is a need for theological education that better empowers the gifts and ministries of ordinary Christians so that they may serve as agents for the Kingdom of God, as seen in their daily lives, and in the propagation and teaching of the Word of God. There is a need for the churches to commit to achieving high quality in the theological education they offer. In this regard, denominational divisions inhibit progress. Much could be gained by coming together to pool resources and create institutions that offer a higher quality of theological education. As a popular Angolan proverb states: 'If you want to go quickly, go alone; if you want to go further, go with others'.

Everyday life has manifestly changed since the majority of people accepted Christianity as their way of life. The challenge, however, is for the day-to-day life of Christian people to be in accordance with the faith that they proclaim, demonstrating that the love of Jesus of Nazareth compels them to love, care, nurture and be responsible for one another.

## Bibliography

Chianeque, Luciano, 'A Comparison of the Angolan Diaspora with Their Biblical Counterparts in the Post Exilic Period' (Masters Thesis, University of Durban, Westville, 2000).

Chianeque, Luciano, 'Theological Education in Angola and Mozambique', in Isabel Phiri and Dietrich Werner (eds), *Handbook of Theological Education in Africa* (Oxford: Regnum Books International, 2013), pp. 218–22.

Henderson,Lawrence W., *The Church in Angola: A River of Many Currents* (Cleveland, OH: Pilgrim Press, 1992).

# Gabon, Equatorial Guinea, Republic of the Congo and Democratic Republic of the Congo

Jean-Gottfried Mutombo

While making up a majority of the population, Christians in Gabon, Equatorial Guinea, the Republic of the Congo (ROC) and the Democratic Republic of the Congo (DRC, formerly known as Belgian Congo and Zaire) live and work in a context of corruption, poverty, unemployment, insecurity of medical care, wars and armed conflicts, theft, looting of natural resources, raping of women and children, child soldiers, street children, violence, bad governance and failing infrastructure. These problems demand the establishment of liberating discourse as well as the development of appropriate prophetic and pastoral attitudes. The churches' potential is found essentially in their capacity for mobilisation; the commitment and devotion of their clergy, laymen and laywomen; and especially in the vitality of their youth. Their participation in social development and intervention, particularly in times of crisis, reflects this potential for mobilisation.

The Catholic Church and traditional Protestant churches make up the trunks of Christianity in these countries, while Independent and Charismatic churches are the branches. By combining tradition and modernity, integrating African and Western cultures, and being attentive to contextual failures, this Christianity is the result of diverse local and foreign influences. At the beginning of the twenty-first century, this Christianity fits in just as well in Africa as on the continents from which it came.

## The Catholic Church

In each country, the Catholic Church is organised on the basis of an episcopal conference comprising several dioceses in which congregations of various backgrounds work together. The episcopal conferences of ROC, Gabon and Equatorial Guinea are grouped together in the Association of Episcopal Conferences of Central Africa Region (ACERAC) whereas the National Episcopal Conference of Congo (DRC) is part of the Association of Episcopal Conferences of Central Africa (ACEAC).

The Catholic Church's first attempt at evangelisation, in the fifteenth century, was, in the end, unsuccessful, since the gospel did not take root in the cultures of the people who were evangelised. The foreign character of the church and its involvement in the slave trade became the root of Kimpa Vita's religious movement, for which she paid with her life in 1706. A second Catholic attempt at evangelisation began in the nineteenth century, at the same time and almost in the same area as the Protestant evangelisation. Introduced by the French Spiritan fathers in Gabon, the ROC and the DOC, and by the Spanish Claretian Brothers in Equatorial Guinea, this second wave of evangelisation was woven into the context of the slave trade and colonisation.

Réné Bessieux and Grégoire Sey arrived at Baraka, Gabon, in 1844, where Protestant Americans had already settled. In 1880 Carrie and Jean-Baptiste Visseq established themselves at Boma (DRC), near the Protestant station of Palaba, founded in 1878. Carrie and Prosper Augouard headed out from Boma in 1883 to build the first church, St Joseph of Linzolo (ROC). In Equatorial Guinea, the Claretian Brothers began their mission in 1882, while the Protestant mission had been active there since 1858. Up until decolonisation in the 1960s, missionaries of different nationalities, confessions and congregations shared in this pioneer work.

The Catholic Church became the dominant religious power. This was due mainly to the support of the colonial powers, defined in the agreements or concordats they signed with the Holy See. These took the form of aid in the establishment of a mission, the acquisition of land and the subsidy of schools and hospitals. In return, missionaries were utilised to help with the acceptance of colonisation.

For political reasons, politicians today still favour the Catholic Church. This is seen in signed agreements (such as that between the Holy See and Equatorial Guinea on 13 October 2012) as well as the financing or donation of church buildings by heads of state. Examples include Notre Dame Cathedral in Mongomo, Equatorial Guinea, in 2011, by President Teodoro Obiang Nguema Mbasogo; Notre Dame de Lourdes in Libreville, Gabon, in 2015, by President Ali Bongo; and headquarters for the ACERAC at Brazzaville, ROC, in 2015, by President Denis Sassou Nguesso.

*Christianity in Gabon, 1970 and 2015*

| | 1970 | | 2015 | | Average annual growth rate (%), 1970–2015 |
|---|---|---|---|---|---|
| Tradition | Population | % | Population | % | |
| Christians | 518,000 | 87.8% | 1,461,000 | 84.7% | 2.33% |
| *Roman Catholics* | 290,000 | 49.2% | 949,000 | 55.0% | 2.67% |
| *Independents* | 63,000 | 10.7% | 283,000 | 16.4% | 3.39% |
| *Protestants* | 92,000 | 15.6% | 197,000 | 11.4% | 1.70% |
| Pentecostals | 3,500 | 0.6% | 163,000 | 9.5% | 8.91% |
| Evangelicals | 20,200 | 3.4% | 47,800 | 2.8% | 1.94% |
| **Total population** | **590,000** | **100.0%** | **1,725,000** | **100.0%** | **2.41%** |

Source: Todd M. Johnson and Gina A. Zurlo (eds), *World Christian Database* (Leiden/Boston: Brill), accessed March 2016.

Such favouritism lends itself to competition with, even discrimination against and tension towards, Protestant missions. This rivalry is further explained by the Catholics' use of the same missionary strategies as the Protestants. Thanks to subsidies, the Catholic missions have contributed much to society, especially by forming a native framework for their educational institutions – schools, seminaries, institutes and universities. At the dawn of independence in the 1960s, the majority of high-level political leaders were products of these institutions. Among them were Presidents Joseph Kasa-Vubu and Mobutu Sese Seko (DRC), Fulbert Youlou (ROC), Leon M'ba (Gabon) and Teodoro Obiang Nguema Mbasogo (Equatorial Guinea). In the DRC, for example, almost all of the prime ministers or government officials from independence until the fall of Mobutu in 1997 were Catholics. This situation has been at times a source of frustration and competition. Monsignor Ifoko Bokambanza Bokeleale, then National President of the Church of Christ in Congo (an association of Protestant churches), complained of it in a pastoral letter of 1995.

The visits of Pope John Paul II in the 1980s increased the influence of the Catholic Church. He visited the ROC and DRC in 1980, Gabon and Equatorial Guinea in 1982, and the DRC again in 1985. Various heads of state visited the Vatican as well, including Equatorial Guinea's Obiang (2010 and 2013), ROC's Denis Sassou (2010 and 2013), the DRC's Joseph Kabila (2008) and his wife Olive Lembe (2013), and Gabon's Ali Bongo (2009 and 2013).

The charismatic appeal of certain ecclesiastical personalities as well as the socio-political engagement of others allowed the Catholic Church to win society's trust and an appreciation for its political role. Evidence of this is seen in the direction of national conferences and transitional parliaments in the early 1990s, with significant roles being played by Monsignor Basile Mvé in Gabon, Monsignor Ernest Kombo in ROC and Monsignor Laurent Monsengwo in the DRC.

The question of what ramifications might result from religious involvement in politics was already being asked at the time these countries

*Christianity in Equatorial Guinea, 1970 and 2015*

| | 1970 | | 2015 | | Average annual growth rate (%), 1970–2015 |
|---|---|---|---|---|---|
| Tradition | Population | % | Population | % | |
| Christians | 257,000 | 88.3% | 746,000 | 88.3% | 2.40% |
| *Roman Catholics* | 231,000 | 79.3% | 684,000 | 80.9% | 2.44% |
| *Independents* | 6,400 | 2.2% | 33,200 | 3.9% | 3.74% |
| *Protestants* | 14,800 | 5.1% | 28,700 | 3.4% | 1.49% |
| Pentecostals | 440 | 0.2% | 45,600 | 5.4% | 10.84% |
| Evangelicals | 7,400 | 2.6% | 18,100 | 2.1% | 2.00% |
| **Total population** | **291,000** | **100.0%** | **845,000** | **100.0%** | **2.40%** |

Source: Todd M. Johnson and Gina A. Zurlo (eds), *World Christian Database* (Leiden/Boston: Brill), accessed March 2016.

attained independence. Yet it does not appear to have found a practical, satisfactory solution in spite of the existence of legal support within the Catholic Church. A case in point is that of Fulbert Youlou, an ordained priest who, in 1960, became the first President of the ROC against the wishes of the ecclesiastical hierarchy. This created confusion in the management of both the political world and that of the church. Thus, constitutions and laws, while at the same time guaranteeing religious liberty, also make reference to the secularity of the state and the separation between state and religion. In addition, those of the ROC and Equatorial Guinea forbade the use of religion for political ends.

The relationship of the Catholic Church to political power is varied – at times harmonious, at times conflictual. If the colonial period was generally characterised by harmonious relationships, the modern period of independence shifts between harmony and conflict. Against the prophetic mission of the church, political power often resorts to intimidation or exclusion, defamation, verbal and physical violence, the closing of church media outlets, persecution and assassination, exile, torture and manipulation, and also setting churches and religious movements against each other.

Upheld by the colonial powers, the Catholic Church maintained a competitive and discriminatory stance towards Protestant churches. The end of colonisation and the attainment of independence brought a change of attitude, not only to Protestant churches but also to Independent churches. A certain solidarity between the churches was established, similar to that discovered by churches when facing political dictatorships.

The different socio-political crises that these countries experienced led to the progressive development of an 'ecumenism for peace'. This was particularly visible during important religious and political ceremonies and found expression in different peace initiatives and programmes that have combated such scourges as malaria, HIV/AIDS and violence. The visits of Pope John Paul II to Kinshasa, Brazzaville, Libreville and Malabo provided

*Christianity in Republic of the Congo, 1970 and 2015*

| | 1970 | | 2015 | | Average annual growth rate (%), 1970–2015 |
|---|---|---|---|---|---|
| Tradition | Population | % | Population | % | |
| Christians | 1,224,000 | 91.7% | 4,127,000 | 89.3% | 2.74% |
| *Roman Catholics* | 399,000 | 29.9% | 3,190,000 | 69.0% | 4.73% |
| *Orthodox* | 300 | 0.0% | 440 | 0.0% | 0.85% |
| *Independents* | 126,000 | 9.4% | 574,000 | 12.4% | 3.43% |
| *Protestants* | 177,000 | 13.3% | 489,000 | 10.6% | 2.28% |
| Pentecostals | 89,000 | 6.7% | 945,000 | 20.5% | 5.39% |
| Evangelicals | 118,000 | 8.9% | 225,000 | 4.9% | 1.44% |
| **Total population** | **1,335,000** | **100.0%** | **4,620,000** | **100.0%** | **2.80%** |

Source: Todd M. Johnson and Gina A. Zurlo (eds), *World Christian Database* (Leiden/Boston: Brill), accessed March 2016.

a kick-start for inter-church connections. It also reinforced Christian witness when other churches took part in welcome ceremonies.

During the crisis that led to Mobutu's downfall in 1997, religious denominations initiated talks for the purpose of avoiding war in Kinshasa. Up until his death, Cardinal Frédéric Etsou managed these negotiations. The leaders of religious denominations also played an important role in the peace negotiations at Sun City (South Africa), having overseen the development of transitional institutions and lending support for the democratic process. The inter-ethnic rivalries that resurged with the opposing militias during ROC's civil war (1993–2002) allowed the Catholic Church to play a major role in peace initiatives, along with the ecumenical Council of Churches in Congo.

The confirmation of religious liberty in each country's constitution during the 1990s brought new breath to ecumenism and inter-religious relationships. In spite of certain successes, these relations suffer at times of mistrust due to doctrinal differences and the political tendencies of certain religious leaders.

### *The Catholic Church and Africanisation*

As countries gained independence, the Catholic Church had to change its approach to mission. One of the consequences was progressive Africanisation of the leadership and inculturation of the gospel.

François Ndong was ordained in 1961 as the first Bishop of Gabon and the first African bishop in the Central African region. In 1959 Joseph Malula was named Auxiliary Bishop and in 1964 became the first Congolese Archbishop of Kinshasa. During that same year, ROC officially became the first communist state in Africa. This was the beginning of a long period of trials for the churches, such as bans on Christian youth movements and a reversal of values. In this context Théophile Mbemba, consecrated in 1961

*Christianity in Democratic Republic of the Congo, 1970 and 2015*

| | 1970 | | 2015 | | Average annual growth rate (%), 1970–2015 |
|---|---|---|---|---|---|
| Tradition | Population | % | Population | % | |
| Christians | 17,960,000 | 89.8% | 73,384,000 | 95.0% | 3.18% |
| *Roman Catholics* | 9,908,000 | 49.5% | 41,565,000 | 53.8% | 3.24% |
| *Orthodox* | 7,000 | 0.0% | 13,600 | 0.0% | 1.49% |
| *Independents* | 4,711,000 | 23.5% | 20,612,000 | 26.7% | 3.33% |
| *Protestants* | 3,921,000 | 19.6% | 13,561,000 | 17.6% | 2.80% |
| *Anglicans* | 100,000 | 0.5% | 581,000 | 0.8% | 3.99% |
| Pentecostals | 4,818,000 | 24.1% | 23,769,000 | 30.8% | 3.61% |
| Evangelicals | 1,349,000 | 6.7% | 5,230,000 | 6.8% | 3.06% |
| **Total population** | **20,010,000** | **100.0%** | **77,267,000** | **100.0%** | **3.05%** |

Source: Todd M. Johnson and Gina A. Zurlo (eds), *World Christian Database* (Leiden/Boston: Brill), accessed March 2016.

as the first Congolese Bishop, became the first Congolese Archbishop of Brazzaville. He would be replaced by Émile Biayenda, who was appointed Cardinal in 1973 and assassinated in 1977.

After Equatorial Guinea gained independence in 1968, the Catholic Church was faced with the dictatorial regime headed by the first President, Francisco Macias Nguema. Described as the bloodiest dictator of Africa, he established a reign of terror resulting in the expulsion of missionaries, the imprisonment of priests, assassinations and forced exiles. Calling himself 'Son of God', Macias demanded that his name be invoked at the start of any religious service. He was executed in 1979 following a coup by Teodoro Obiang Nguema Mbasogo, who established a new dictatorship. Despite an initial effort to be accommodating to the Catholic Church and the small Protestant community in the country, Obiang attempted to control the churches and their services by demanding to know the content of sermons.

One result of the winds of change following World War II was growing awareness of the need for inculturation of the gospel. In 1948, far from such centres as Kinshasa, Brazzaville, Libreville and Malabo, in the province of Katanga (in the south-east of the DRC), Father Placide Tempels (a Belgian Franciscan) published his book *Bantu Philosophy*. He was the first to recognise among the Africans of the Luba tribe (North Katanga), who participated in his study, the existence of a system of thinking capable of establishing philosophy and wisdom. He stressed the necessity of adapting 'the teaching of true religion to that which shows a respect for the ontology' of the Bantu. This work caused mixed reactions within the Catholic Church of the Belgian Congo. However, it seems to have inspired Bishop Barthélemy Batanta of Brazzaville in his liturgical reforms of 1957, 10 years after the spiritual awakening of the Evangelical Church in Congo.

Bishop Batanta was the first to adapt the Catholic liturgy of his diocese to the culture of the Kongo people. He integrated hymnody, music, rhythm and dance into the celebration in order to give a Congolese face to the church through the promotion of African art and rhythm. This liturgy won the sympathy of people and caused a large growth in the churches of Brazzaville and Pointe-Noire, especially in the villages. Funerary culture picked up this religious character, with singing, dancing, eating and drinking, reminiscent of a party. The organisation of the parish followed the model of *Dibundu* (the Lari word for community). The integration of Kongo matrilineal system into the organisation of the church paved the way for the Legion of Mary to be adopted and ritualised. Thus it became a factor in the use of spiritual energy during visits to the sick and in the restoration of trust within community life.

Political independence along with the creative ideas of the Second Vatican Council opened up new chapters for the church in Francophone

Africa. Following Batanta, Malula created the Zairean rite in 1973. It involved the faithful in the liturgy by recognising and taking into account local culture. It organised a ministry of lay people. It allowed the active participation of the congregation in the Mass through singing and dancing.

This has worked as an instrument for evangelisation. Art and music which are inspired by biblical texts and reflect elements of local culture have contributed to the growth of the church. However, these are also mingled with Western elements, as can be seen from the liturgical clothes or the ornaments of the churches. The image of Jesus as a black man, developed by Kimpa Vita in the eighteenth century, resurfaced as a theological recovery but was banished by the Capuchin monks. The Congolese theologian Leon Kabasele contributed to African Christology by putting forward Jesus as the Chief (*Ntita* and *Luaba*), an image arising out of the Luba (Kasai) culture.

The inculturation of the gospel and the liturgical reforms became the Catholic Church's response to the threat represented by Independent churches, whose success in the eyes of the population rests on the integration of African cultural elements with expressions of Christian faith.

The Catholic Church has experienced spiritual awakenings within itself. In ROC, Ta Malanda, a faithful Catholic, fought by use of a cross against the Bakongo's ancestor worship, magic and sorcery. For this reason his movement was called Croix-Koma (literally Cross-Koma): the Kikongo verb *kukoma* means 'sink' or 'nail', the implication being that 'I renounce witchcraft, otherwise the cross of Jesus will nail me'. The movement continued to evolve within the Catholic Church until the death of its founder in 1971. The Catholic Charismatic renewal that emerged during the 1970s was framed by the Catholic Church as a counterweight to the emergence of invasive Revival churches.

## Protestant Churches

The Protestant churches in question here are the Church of Christ of Congo (ECC) of the DRC, the Evangelical Church of Congo (ROC), the Salvation Army, the Evangelical Church of Gabon, the Christian Alliance of the Evangelical Council of Gabon and the Council of Evangelical Churches in Equatorial Guinea. To this are added Independent churches and the Revival movements of Protestant churches.

Protestant evangelisation owed much to the sensitisation by David Livingstone of Western Christian opinion regarding the state of Africans who were lacking the gospel and facing the slave trade. Motivated by this call and drawing upon the lessons of earlier attempts at evangelisation, missionaries linked preaching the gospel with improving the conditions of the natives and seeking their freedom from slavery. Among the first converts were many who benefited from this plan of evangelisation. This explains the choice of Baraka, a former slave centre, by American missionaries John Wilson and Benjamin Leighton Griswold for the starting point of their mission to Gabon in 1842. The Evangelical Church of Gabon grew out of this mission. In Equatorial Guinea, Presbyterian mission work began in 1858 at Corisco, where the Methodists also began work in 1870. The World Evangelical Crusade eventually merged with the Presbyterians and the Methodists to form the Reformed Church of Equatorial Guinea, which in turn developed into the Council of Evangelical Churches of Equatorial Guinea.

The Church of Christ in Congo (ECC) arose from the work begun in 1878 by George Grenfell and Thomas Comber (of the Baptist Missionary Society) and Henry Craven and M. J. Strom (of the Livingstone Inland Mission) at Palabala in lower Congo. Thanks to his talent as an explorer, Grenfell counselled missionary societies from various denominations to go where they could by starting from lower Congo and following the Congo River up into the country's interior. Today, the ECC counts more than 60 communities representing different Baptist, Reformed/Presbyterian, Evangelical, Pentecostal, Methodist, Mennonite, Disciples of Christ, Darbyist and other denominations. The Evangelical Church of Congo was founded at Brazzaville in 1909 by Svenska Missions Forbundet (SMF), which had been active in Manyanga (lower Congo) since 1881.

The Protestant churches represent a second religious dimension because of their geographical reach, which extends into remote areas, as well as their demographic importance, social programmes and socio-political interventions. This occurred despite the fact that most Protestant missions, because of their origins, were viewed as 'strangers' and 'outside the colonial order'. It is also despite the fact that they critiqued the abuses and human rights violations of colonial agents. The influence of Protestant churches is held together by three factors.

The first is their missionary strategy: preach the gospel; call for repentance and baptism; build church buildings, schools, universities, hospitals and clinics; create stations or missionary centres; use catechists, evangelists and native pastors in the Bible schools which they created; learn the local languages and cultures; develop Bible societies for the translation of the Bible, songs and other Christian literature; and initiate development projects with the goal of fighting poverty.

The second factor is the collaboration between Protestant churches at the national, African and international levels, which is visible in the exchange of personnel, the transfer of mission fields and missionary programmes, and the replacement of missionaries.

Thirdly, Protestants used unity as a strategy for survival. Developed in a context of discrimination, the missions and the resultant Protestant churches minimised their denominational differences in order to develop a Protestant brotherhood by initiating common projects such as printing houses, guest houses, universities and hospitals. An example from the DRC is the creation of the Church of Christ in Congo (ECC) in 1970. This was the result of a unification process begun by the General Conference of 1902 and inspired by the Edinburgh World Missionary Conference (1910) and its Continuation Committee (1911) until to led to the creation of the Protestant Council of Congo (1924). The influence of the ECC has increased in recent years due, on the one hand, to the impact of the Protestant University of Congo (Kinshasa) and the Free University of the Great Lakes Countries (Goma) and, on the other, to the Centenary Protestant Cathedral, which stands as a symbol of Protestant unity in the DRC. Inaugurated in 1994 by Monsignor Bokeleale, this building, with a capacity of 7,600, finds itself at the crossroads of official meetings, both national and international.

Like the Catholic Church, Protestant churches and other religious movements are partners with the state in social domains such as education and health. However, because of their impact on society, churches are often solicited by politicians to aid their political aspirations. Some of their directors become arms of power or opposition, while others opt for political activism, combining the political mandate with the religious mandate. In most cases, it is either the 'politics of the belly' or the 'pastoral ministry of the belly' which takes precedence. Herein lies the question of loyalty with regard to the role of church leaders in promoting human dignity and democracy, as well as fighting against social injustice.

The region is burgeoning with Independent religious movements – churches of healing and revival that for the most part draw their origins from Protestant churches but are now reacting against them. Among the Independent churches, Kimbanguism is the most influential among a list that also includes Mpeve a Nlongo (Church of the Holy Spirit), Bima, Church of Bonzie, Kitawala and the Black Church (Mpadi).

Ecumenical peace is the basis for collaboration between Protestants and other denominations and religions, in particular Islam, which has partnered with them in religious ceremonies, such as the service organised by the Centenary Protestant Cathedral in 2000 during the National Consultation that sought to bring peace to the DRC.

### *Protestant Churches and Africanisation*

At the dawn of independence certain Protestant missions were aware of some dissent among native Christians. At Katanga (DRC), a group of faithful Christians under the direction of Monsignor Kabwe-ka-Leza left the mission of Garenganze and created the Protestant Baptist Church in Africa (EPROBRA) in 1956. This spirit of autonomy became widespread within all the churches of the countries that attained independence. In Protestant language, the term 'mother church' was replaced by 'sister church' in order to distinguish churches of overseas founders from local churches. In 1960 the Salvation Army within the two Congos was the first to become autonomous. In 1961 the Evangelical Church of Congo (ROC) and the Evangelical Community of Congo (DRC) acquired autonomy from the Swedish Mission; the Evangelical Church of Gabon became autonomous that year as well. This autonomy was accompanied by the Africanisation of church leaders. Ndongo Amvame was the first indigenous leader to be elected President of the Evangelical Churches of Gabon. In the DRC, Joel Bulaya became the first President of the Protestant Council of Congo (1960–1).

Protestant churches have known various spiritual revivals. Some of them led to the creation of Independent churches, while others contributed to the enrichment of churches. Still others were harmful, by provoking divisions and weakening some churches. The first revival in 1921 was launched by the preaching and healing ministry of Simon Kimbangu, former catechist of the Baptist Missionary Society (BMS). The colonial authorities considered him to be subversive, and thus the movement was repressed and stifled, with the blessing of the Catholic Church. Kimbangu was imprisoned until his death in 1951 and his followers were persecuted. With the influence of his third son, Joseph Diangenda, the movement was officially recognised in 1959 by the Belgian colonial authorities and has carried the name Church of Jesus Christ on Earth by His Special Envoy Simon Kimbangu (EJCSK) since 1987. By the recommendation of Protestants in the DRC, in 1969 the Kimbanguist Church was admitted to the World Council of Churches (Geneva) and in 1974 to the All Africa Conference of Churches (Nairobi). In 1978 the Church was recognised by ROC; it then also organised in Angola, Gabon, some European countries, North America and other places. The third component regarding the growth of its membership is related to such social engagements as schools, hospitals, universities and development projects. Thus it became the most important Independent church in Africa. There has been a degree of unease between Kimbanguism and its ecclesiastical partners ever since the Kimbanguist Church started celebrating Christmas on 25 May, the birthdate of Samuel Dialungana Kiangani, deceased spiritual leader and father of the current spiritual leader.

During the 1930s the Evangelical Church of Gabon experienced religious revival under the influence of British Pentecostalism, leading to the creation of the Evangelical Pentecostal Church of Gabon in 1939. In 1956 its name was changed to the Assemblies of God of Gabon. It is one of the most important churches in the region, with influence extending into ROC, Cameroon and Equatorial Guinea.

The spiritual awakening that the region experienced and that was inspired by the local culture is a factor in the liberation. The Evangelical Church of Congo experienced spiritual revival in 1947 under the ministry of Daniel Ndoundou. Learning from the consequences of the persecution of Kimbangu and his followers and in order to avoid a church split, the Swedish missionaries integrated this revival, which was strongly marked by traditional Kongo culture. In this way they created a hybrid church. Among the various manifestations were gifts of prophecy and healing, songs revealed in local languages (in dreams or visions), called *Kilombo*, and treatment of illnesses by plants.

The great awakening that influenced several countries in French-speaking Africa seems to have been the launching point for Pentecostalism introduced to Kinshasa in 1969 by the evangelisation crusade and healing miracles of the American evangelist T. L. Osborn. Like him, many other evangelists of international renown visited the DRC under the auspices of the Assemblies of God community, a Protestant church. However, the outcome of the revivals slipped out of their control. Thus many revival churches or awakened churches became established outside the Protestant framework, all the while claiming to be Protestant. The proliferation of these churches was widespread thanks to the political and socio-economic crises of the 1980s and 1990s, the restoration of trust between peoples following the fall of the Berlin Wall in 1989, and the demographic mobility and liberalisation of political life in the 1990s. As urban phenomena, these churches exercised their influence in cities. Most do not invest in social work, but some of their leaders – who behave like gurus or self-proclaimed (arch)bishops, apostles or prophets – benefit from the poverty and naivety of their members in order to live lives of opulence and preach the prosperity gospel.

By their missionary strategy and lifestyles, these church leaders establish aggressive competition with traditional churches, which they label as 'cold', and try to lay waste to their membership by preaching against them. However, when considered positively, they can offer possibilities to traditional churches of seizing on the secret of their growth, enhancing their identity and finding explanations for the changing allegiance of their members. Certain attentive Protestant churches, instead of trying to control or stifle them, end up integrating elements that are their strengths: evangelistic campaigns in public places, intercessory groups and services geared towards praise and worship.

Some revival churches, such as the Bethany Evangelical Center in Gabon, have been established through the initiative of local people. Others have resulted from immigration from neighbouring countries. This is the case with the Celestial Church of Christ, the Holy Spirit Church of

Unity, Deeper Life Bible Church as well as the Full Gospel Business Men's Fellowship.

## Faith in an Age of Migration

During the 1980s, the gospel that had been received and enriched by more than a century of experience was then taken from ROC, the DRC, Gabon and Equatorial Guinea to other African countries and also to the continents from which it initially came. This evangelisation is peculiar in that it opens up the connections from South to South and South to North. Thus it reverses the original order of North to South. This evangelisation can be characterised in three ways. Certain churches that are conscious of their global mission send missionaries at their own expense to other countries. Others work with their students or immigrants to begin a church in another country; this is the case with the Kimbanguist Church. At the other end of this trend are those Christians or pastors who plant churches on their own initiative. They do not depend on a structure or country of origin. In certain countries, churches are integrated while in others they battle for integration. Finally, there are pastors or priests who are sent by their African churches at the request of partner churches in order to serve in bringing their spiritual experience in the different partner churches in Africa and the rest of the world. These exchanges are always enriching from either side. The liturgy, the Bible teaching and the evangelisation carry African imprints with them into other parishes.

## Faith in an Age of Violence

Since the early 1990s, ongoing violence and conflict in the DRC have led to political instability and a weakening of the state's authority. At the same time it has increased the population's suffering. Among the causes are poor relations with neighbours, the abusive exploitation of natural resources, and inter-ethnic and political conflicts. The churches are meeting new challenges: displaced persons and refugees, atrocities and trauma, humiliation, rape, family instability, insecurity, famine, suffering, destruction of infrastructure and human lives, and the depopulation of parishes as a result of members fleeing war and violence. In a country where more than 90% of the population are Christians, both perpetrators and victims are church members. For example, self-proclaimed Bishop Jean-Marie Runiga of the Charismatic Church Église, Jesus seul Sauveur (Church, Jesus Only Saviour), was chief of the 'M23 rebellion' in 2012–13.

Even where public power has failed, the churches witness by prophetic creativity, both pastoral and diaconal, in order to bring hope, perspective and light to these dark times. Churches are often limited in terms of their resources, and the solidarity of overseas churches and partnering organisations has always been appreciated. It allows them to strengthen their capacity to intervene, especially in local and regional peace initiatives. It also allows for the care and social reintegration of refugees and displaced persons, especially women and children who are victims of rape, as well as the weak and needy. For example, under the widely recognised leadership of Dr Denis Mukwege, the Protestant hospital at Panzi in South Kivu offers care to women and young girls who have been raped. Its fight against sexual violence helps to restore hope in a country where rape has become a weapon of war.

## Conclusion

There is a sense of consistency in the Christianity of this region from the fifteenth century until today. The desire of African Christians to see Christianity take root in their cultures, to express themselves through their values, to find the church within the framework of a true community life and to be a factor for human progress remains very strong. Their opposition to all forms of servitude and contempt on the basis of Christianity serves as a lesson even now, as it gives a new identity and vitality to the diversity of churches.

Despite weaknesses tied to the actions of men and women who laboured through complex working conditions, these churches have carried and still carry a great contribution in the strengthening of faith in Christ, socio-spiritual transformation, the promotion of Christian values and the integral development of society. In the Republic of Congo, the Democratic Republic of Congo, Gabon and Equatorial Guinea, the churches are active in countering corruption, theft, violence and poverty, so as to promote justice and peace, building a family of God in which it is good to live.

## Bibliography

Asch, Susan, *L'Église du Prophète Simon Kimbangu: de ses origines à son rôle actuel au Zaïre* (Paris: Karthala, 1983).

Baur, John, *2000 Years of Christianity in Africa: An African Church History*, 2nd edn (Nairobi: Paulines Publications Africa, 1994).

Falk, Peter, *The Growth of the Church in Africa* (Grand Rapids, MI: Zondervan, 1979).

Mezui, Hervé Essono, 'Église catholique, vie politique et démocratisation au Gabon (1945–1995)' (Thèse soutenue à l'Université Lumière-Lyon, 2006).

Sundkler, Bengt and Christopher Steed, *A History of the Church in Africa* (Cambridge: Cambridge University Press, 2004).

# Central African Republic, Togo, Côte d'Ivoire, Benin and Cameroon

Elias Kifon Bongmba

The countries considered in this chapter are all former French colonies. In the case of Cameroon, France and Britain divided the territory between themselves after the departure of Germany from colonial rule in Africa. Christianity in the region did not inhabit a vacuum because there were indigenous religions in each place, such as Vodun in Benin. This chapter provides a broad overview, with a focus on missionisation, the growth of local churches, local initiatives and evangelists, social services and church–state relations in the region.

## Overview of Christianity in the Region

The modern history of Christianity in these Francophone countries features European and American Evangelical and Roman Catholic penetration of the region. It is a story that reveals Christianity's beginnings and growth to its present diversity of institutions, ministries, social services and leadership; a complementary and sometimes conflictual and violent relationship with the state; and diverse pastoral and theological perspectives. These categories serve as the organising motifs for the interpretative perspective offered in this chapter. Missionary activity in the region has declined, but there are still strong ties with churches in the West that consider African churches no longer as branches of their overseas work but as partners. However, such partnerships are not as strong as they could be, because of the heavy dependence of some African churches on the Northern countries.

Early Christian missions in Togo were started in the Peki area (now in Ghana) by the North German Missionary Society (the Bremen Mission) in 1847. These early attempts did not succeed. In 1853 Christian Hornberger arrived in Keta and set up a station from where the mission work spread to other parts of the region. The Bremen Mission expanded its work to Waya in 1857 and to Wegbe Ho in 1859. Missionaries in the region also encouraged the company F. M. Victor and Sons to establish trading ties with the region. The region experienced a conflict that was detrimental to the advance of mission when the Ashanti started fighting a war against the Wegbe Ho and Waya. Mission engagement in the region expanded after peace was restored. When slavery was brought under control, the church grew in Togo and the Bremen Mission started schools.

Christian missionaries reached the Central African Republic through Gabon and the Republic of the Congo. The early missionaries were the Holy Ghost Fathers, and the Catholic Church established vicariates in Loango (in the Republic of the Congo) in 1886 and in Ubangi (in the Democratic Republic of the Congo) in 1890. In 1894 Monsignor Prosper Augouard started the Saint Paul Mission in Bangui, which would serve as the hub of most of the missionary work well into the twentieth century. The work expanded to Fort Lamy (in Chad), where the Missionary Oblates of Mary Immaculate established their ministry. Missionary work expanded after World War II and by 1965 there were five Catholic dioceses in the country.

On the Protestant side, the Brethren Church started missionary work in the Central African Republic in 1919 and established several centres for its work in the country, including Bangui. One of the largest churches that resulted was the Église Évangéliques des Frères. It opened Bible schools, started a theological seminary in 1970, published and distributed Christian literature and translated the Bible into local languages. It opened its first hospital in 1957. Baptist missionaries arrived in Central Africa in 1912 but left shortly afterwards, for medical reasons. Their work included the planting of local churches throughout the country, stations in present-day Chad, Bible translation and the establishment of dispensaries, a Bible school and a theological seminary to train pastors. Mission work in the two countries was separated at the time of independence. The Églises Baptistes de la RCA went through some internal divisions and in 1977 the Union Fraternelle des Églises Baptistes and the Association des Églises Baptistes Contrafricaines were formed. Mission work in the country continues under the Baptist Mid-Missions. The Swedish Baptist Church was started by Swedish Baptists, who in addition to local churches built schools, an orphanage and medical facilities. The African Inland Mission started its work in the country in 1924, and from these beginnings grew the Église Evangélique Centrafricaine. The Swedish Pentecostal Church began its work in the country in 1927.

*Christianity in Central African Republic, 1970 and 2015*

| | 1970 | | 2015 | | Average annual growth rate (%), 1970–2015 |
|---|---|---|---|---|---|
| Tradition | Population | % | Population | % | |
| Christians | 1,162,000 | 63.6% | 3,578,000 | 73.0% | 2.53% |
| *Roman Catholics* | 278,000 | 15.2% | 1,590,000 | 32.4% | 3.95% |
| *Independents* | 217,000 | 11.9% | 884,000 | 18.0% | 3.17% |
| *Protestants* | 223,000 | 12.2% | 819,000 | 16.7% | 2.93% |
| Pentecostals | 101,000 | 5.5% | 935,000 | 19.1% | 5.07% |
| Evangelicals | 484,000 | 26.5% | 1,359,000 | 27.7% | 2.32% |
| **Total population** | **1,829,000** | **100.0%** | **4,900,000** | **100.0%** | **2.21%** |

Source: Todd M. Johnson and Gina A. Zurlo (eds), *World Christian Database* (Leiden/Boston: Brill), accessed March 2016.

The Presbyterian Church (USA) started work in Gabon in 1861. When it faced restrictions from the French colonial administration it relinquished its Gabon operations to the Societé des Missions Evangéliques de Paris. Missionary work started in Cameroon on 16 April 1879, when members of the Presbyterian Church in Benito went to the town of Batanga in Cameroon and started a church. Adolphus C. Good completed important pioneering work in Cameroon, setting up mission stations. World War I disrupted the work; church property was damaged extensively and the German government eventually paid the Presbyterian Mission for those damages. At all of these stations, mission work promoted evangelisation, education and medical work. Dager Biblical Seminary was opened in 1922 and the Presbyterians opened the Institute des Missions Evangélique (Cameroon Christian College) in 1944. The Hope School for Missionary Children was started at Elat in 1922. The Presbyterians collaborated with the French colonial government on education policies and curriculum, including the eradication of vernacular education, and received grants from the government to run schools. As part of the educational outreach, the missionaries learned local languages and translated the New Testament into Bulu in 1926 and into Basa in 1941. They also promoted publication of literature in local languages.

Catholic mission began in Cameroon in 1890 with the work of the Pallottine Mission at Edea and the Mill Hill Fathers of London in the English-speaking part of the country. Today, the Catholic Church is the largest Christian denomination, with 26 dioceses. The Catholic Church operates schools and health services throughout the country. The most prominent Catholic leaders in the country are Christian Cardinal Tumi, former Metropolitan Archbishop of Douala, and the late Archbishop Jean Zoa of Yaoundé. The church operates l'Université Catholique d'Afrique Centrale (UCAC), located in Yaoundé. Other ecclesiastical provinces also have universities and operate major seminaries at Bambui in the North-west Region and Nkolbessong near Yaoundé. Late in the twentieth century, in a move to

*Christianity in Togo, 1970 and 2015*

| | 1970 | | 2015 | | Average annual growth rate (%), 1970–2015 |
|---|---|---|---|---|---|
| Tradition | Population | % | Population | % | |
| Christians | 584,000 | 27.6% | 3,495,000 | 47.8% | 4.06% |
| *Roman Catholics* | 428,000 | 20.2% | 1,934,000 | 26.5% | 3.41% |
| *Independents* | 36,300 | 1.7% | 238,000 | 3.3% | 4.27% |
| *Protestants* | 66,500 | 3.1% | 1,121,000 | 15.3% | 6.48% |
| Pentecostals | 38,300 | 1.8% | 981,000 | 13.4% | 7.48% |
| Evangelicals | 14,200 | 0.7% | 671,000 | 9.2% | 8.94% |
| **Total population** | **2,116,000** | **100.0%** | **7,305,000** | **100.0%** | **2.79%** |

Source: Todd M. Johnson and Gina A. Zurlo (eds), *World Christian Database* (Leiden/Boston: Brill), accessed March 2016.

indigenise the church, Thomas Nkuissi, the former Bishop of Nkongsamba, promoted Africanisation of the church through programmes of inculturation and indigenisation, and local clerical orders and ordained priests. However, he was accused of lacking stability and was suspended from the priesthood. During the early twenty-first century, the Catholic Church has faced ethnic challenges focused on the replacement of the Archbishop of Yaoundé and also the Archbishop of Douala. In both cities, the indigenes resisted the appointment of bishops who were members of the Bamileke ethnic group. The Catholic Church has also faced challenges because some priests have been killed, notably the theologian and artist Engelbert Mveng. Catholic missionaries still serve in Cameroon, and the Catholic community maintains good relations with Rome. Both Pope John Paul II and Pope Benedict XVI visited Cameroon on their maiden tours of Africa.

## Local Evangelists

Locals who embraced Christianity were central to the spread of the Christian faith to their own people and to other parts of their country. Two examples illustrate a scenario that can be detected in many countries in the region. In Togo, Joseph Tawai was baptised into one of the churches founded by the Bremen Mission Society (a consortium of Lutheran and Reformed Churches) at Maiera but later returned to his own region to preach. Local evangelist Rudolph Mallet worked with missionary Joseph Spieth on translation and was a dedicated individual whom the missionaries wanted to ordain, but the home office in Bremen opposed such a move. Louis Birkmeister, a missionary of the Bremen Mission in Togo, later ordained Mallet.

In the western part of Cameroon (today the Anglophone region of the country), Joseph Mamdu Dom (also called Mamadu), Daniel Hangu, Robert Nteff, Robert Jam and Johannes Tonto travelled from the Grassfields to the coastal regions. While there, they were converted to Christ through the work of Pastor Joseph Burnley, who also trained them to preach and share the gospel, eventually sending them back to their home regions to serve

*Christianity in Cote d'Ivoire, 1970 and 2015*

| | 1970 | | 2015 | | Average annual growth rate (%), 1970–2015 |
|---|---|---|---|---|---|
| Tradition | Population | % | Population | % | |
| Christians | 1,348,000 | 25.7% | 7,920,000 | 34.9% | 4.01% |
| *Roman Catholics* | 627,000 | 12.0% | 4,404,000 | 19.4% | 4.43% |
| *Orthodox* | 3,000 | 0.1% | 67,300 | 0.3% | 7.16% |
| *Independents* | 309,000 | 5.9% | 1,564,000 | 6.9% | 3.67% |
| *Protestants* | 149,000 | 2.8% | 2,214,000 | 9.8% | 6.18% |
| Pentecostals | 59,100 | 1.1% | 2,407,000 | 10.6% | 8.59% |
| Evangelicals | 63,000 | 1.2% | 2,064,000 | 9.1% | 8.06% |
| **Total population** | **5,242,000** | **100.0%** | **22,702,000** | **100.0%** | **3.31%** |

Source: Todd M. Johnson and Gina A. Zurlo (eds), *World Christian Database* (Leiden/Boston: Brill), accessed March 2016.

as evangelists. Beginning with the Bum area in 1922 and preaching first to the chief of the area, Mamadu went round the region planting churches. He exhorted people to abandon traditional beliefs and the practice of witchcraft. He organised churches in Songka, Wum and Aghen before moving in 1927 to the Wimbum area in Donga Mantung Division, where he established churches at Mbonsankfu, Ngulu, Ntumbaw, Sehn and Ngu. The prayer group at Mbonsankfu was relocated to the town of Ndu to become Ndu Baptist Church in 1928. In 1940, Mamadu planted churches in Ande, in the Mbembe Missaje, before moving back closer to his hometown to start a church at Su-Bum, which he served as its pastor. He lived to see the churches of the Cameroon Baptist Convention achieve autonomy in 1954, and he spoke to the delegates attending the general session of the newly formed Cameroon Baptist Convention at Mbem. Mamadu died in February 1968.

## Christian Independence

African Christians who felt left out of church leadership and also thought that many of their spiritual needs were not met in mission churches established African Initiated (Independent) Churches in the region. The most spectacular example is the Harrist Church in Côte d'Ivoire, which traces its origins to the remarkable work of William Wadé Harris. Harris was born around 1860 in the village of Half Garaway in Liberia. He became a member of the African Methodist Episcopal Church. Later in life, he worked on ships and travelled in the region. In 1909 Harris, along with Edward Blyden, was involved in a plot to have Britain annex Liberia. His involvement in the plot was an anti-colonial stance against the Americans, who controlled Liberia at the time. Harris paid a fine of $500 and served two years in prison, where he received a call to preach. On release he went around preaching, admonishing his followers to abandon traditional beliefs, particularly the use of sasswood poison to determine guilt in witchcraft accusations. Harris moved to Côte d'Ivoire after the death of

*Christianity in Benin, 1970 and 2015*

| | 1970 | | 2015 | | Average annual growth rate (%), 1970–2015 |
|---|---|---|---|---|---|
| Tradition | Population | % | Population | % | |
| Christians | 515,000 | 17.7% | 4,818,000 | 44.3% | 5.09% |
| *Roman Catholics* | 394,000 | 13.5% | 2,480,000 | 22.8% | 4.17% |
| *Independents* | 41,400 | 1.4% | 1,344,000 | 12.4% | 8.04% |
| *Protestants* | 52,600 | 1.8% | 1,074,000 | 9.9% | 6.94% |
| Pentecostals | 44,500 | 1.5% | 2,090,000 | 19.2% | 8.93% |
| Evangelicals | 52,700 | 1.8% | 993,000 | 9.1% | 6.74% |
| **Total population** | **2,908,000** | **100.0%** | **10,880,000** | **100.0%** | **2.98%** |

Source: Todd M. Johnson and Gina A. Zurlo (eds), *World Christian Database* (Leiden/Boston: Brill), accessed March 2016.

his wife and preached to record crowds, converting between 100,000 and 200,000 people to Christianity. His initial goal was not to set up a separate church. He promoted modernisation and education but ran into trouble with the law in Côte d'Ivoire and was sent to jail. On his release he was deported to Liberia and was never given permission to return to Côte d'Ivoire. He died in 1929 but many of his followers continued the work he had begun, with the result that the teachings of Harris spread widely. Structurally, the church resembled the social structure of the village. Elders, apostles and ministers served as leaders but were not on a salary from the church. The new church leaders also followed the tradition of Harris in promoting hymns and music, and they put together a new hymnbook, the *Dida Harrist Hymnody*. In Cameroon, the Native Baptist Church grew out of the work of Jamaican missionaries, but when the Germans colonised Cameroon Baptist work was shifted to the Basel Mission. However, Joshua Dibundu Dibue of the Native Baptist Church insisted on a congregational polity and continued to lead the church on his own terms. He composed numerous hymns. In 1949 the Native Church became an independent church, l'Église Baptiste du Cameroun.

## Social Services

Churches in region from the beginning of missionary work have established services in education, health, and economic and social development. In addition to national churches, providers of social services today include faith-based organisations, such as World Vision, Catholic Relief and Heifer International. In Cameroon, the Roman Catholic Church and nearly all Protestant denominations make some such provision as part of their service to their members and the public. The Cameroon Baptist Convention operates 115 elementary and 10 secondary schools, one teacher-training centre and the Cameroon Baptist Theological Seminary. The Presbyterian Church in Cameroon, started by the Basel Mission, is now an independent

*Christianity in Cameroon, 1970 and 2015*

| | 1970 | | 2015 | | Average annual growth rate (%), 1970–2015 |
|---|---|---|---|---|---|
| Tradition | Population | % | Population | % | |
| Christians | 3,152,000 | 46.6% | 13,781,000 | 59.0% | 3.33% |
| *Roman Catholics* | 1,529,000 | 22.6% | 5,679,000 | 24.3% | 2.96% |
| *Orthodox* | 1,000 | 0.0% | 1,200 | 0.0% | 0.41% |
| *Independents* | 105,000 | 1.5% | 1,808,000 | 7.7% | 6.53% |
| *Protestants* | 753,000 | 11.1% | 4,706,000 | 20.2% | 4.16% |
| *Anglicans* | 0 | 0.0% | 2,100 | 0.0% | 12.62% |
| Pentecostals | 97,100 | 1.4% | 2,678,000 | 11.5% | 7.65% |
| Evangelicals | 235,000 | 3.5% | 1,431,000 | 6.1% | 4.10% |
| **Total population** | **6,771,000** | **100.0%** | **23,344,000** | **100.0%** | **2.79%** |

Source: Todd M. Johnson and Gina A. Zurlo (eds), *World Christian Database* (Leiden/Boston: Brill), accessed March 2016.

denomination running 64 primary schools, 19 secondary schools and one theological seminary in addition to its health work in many areas of the country. In the Francophone zone, the Église Presbytérienne du Cameroun runs eight hospitals, 32 primary schools and 11 secondary schools. The Église Evangélique du Cameroun operates 14 secondary schools and one university. The Evangelical Lutheran Church operates educational and health care institutions, mainly in northern Cameroon.

Medical work was promoted to take care of the health of missionaries and locals. The Presbyterian Mission established a central hospital at Elat that supported other hospitals and dispensaries in the region. Although in competition with local therapeutic beliefs and institutions, modern biomedical approaches to health were used effectively in treating infections. This brought many people to the hospitals and led to many conversions. Other medical services included leprosy clinics, care of orphans and a centre for the training of African staff. The government bestowed honours on two missionary doctors, Dr Hyman Weber and Dr George Thorne. The government also gave subsidies to the mission hospitals.

The Cameroon Baptist Convention Health Services (CBCHS) was established in 1938, as part of a growing trend in mission work to provide social services to the people. Today, Cameroonian leaders manage the health services and physicians, and staff are mostly Cameroonians. In addition to providing health care and doing extensive work on HIV/AIDS, the Baptist health board also operates the Baptist Training School for Health Personnel (BTSHP) at Banso, home of the Banso Baptist Hospital. This hospital is also a site for the Christian Internal Medicine Specialisation (CIMS) residency programme and a former site for the Pan-African Academy of Christian Surgeons (PAACS), which now has a residency programme at Mbingo Baptist Hospital in Bamenda. CBCHS also operates the Center for Clinical Pastoral Education and Social Services (CECPES) to train counsellors to minister in the hospitals. CBCHS also runs a rehabilitation centre to serve persons living with disabilities and operates the Mutual Guarantee Financing Company (MUGFIC) to encourage savings and investments as part of a broad project of poverty alleviation. The work of the CBCHS and other denominations in Cameroon in combatting HIV/AIDS has been exemplary, providing treatment and relief services, partnering with international organisations and supporting researchers who address the HIV crisis. Through its AIDS Care and Prevention (ACP) programme, the CBCHS has encouraged people to be tested and has provided counselling and treatment. As part of its programme to combat stigmatisation, the CBCHS decided to call AIDS orphans 'chosen ones'. The HIV/AIDS services of the CBCHS are based at the Baptist Hospital in Mutengene. Its work as a partner in developing the pilot project Prevention of Mother to Child

Transmission of HIV (PMTCT) earned the accolade 'best and promising practice' from the US Agency for International Development.

## Church and State

Since 2013, the Central African Republic has gone through political crises that have degenerated into sectarian violence due to rapid politicisation of religion, manifested in conflicts that have pitted Christians against the Muslim Séléka rebel forces that toppled President François Bozizé. Hundreds of people have been killed, although the Séléka forces have also victimised Muslims. The Séléka fighters have carried out brutal attacks against civilians and looted property. They have attacked hospitals and killed patients, and attacked the Church of Our Lady of Africa in Bangui, wounding several people and looting the rectory. The conflict spread beyond the capital city and involved a wide area in which opposing militias have not only fought each other but also targeted civilians. The United Nations High Commissioner for Refugees reported that nearly 100,000 people have been forced to leave their homes in Bangui alone. The fighting forces have unfortunately engaged children as young as 13 years, with the United Nations estimating that around 3,500 children were involved in the fighting. Churches in the Central African Republic have condemned the fighting and criticised the use of religion to justify violent acts. Many people fleeing the violence have also taken shelter in church buildings.

Two broad trends can be detected in the relationship between church and state in the other Francophone countries of this region. The first is the use of religion for political and personal goals in Togo, Benin and Côte d'Ivoire, and the second is illustrated by the long antagonistic relation between Cardinal Tumi and the political leaders of Cameroon. In Benin, Matthew Kérékou took power in a military coup in 1972 and installed a Marxist regime promising to free the country from foreign ideology. He ruled until 1991, when he was defeated in the presidential elections by Nicéphore Soglo. It was ironic that, later, Kérékou, who ruled as a dictator, became one of Africa's pro-democracy leaders when he agreed to hold a national sovereignty conference attended by different political leaders to discuss and implement reforms and work for the democratisation of the country. Catholic clergy in Benin and other parts of Africa took the lead in organising similar conferences, which prepared the way for a transition to democracy. Kérékou, originally a Catholic Christian, reportedly spoke with Isidore de Souza, the Catholic Archbishop of Cotonou, and confessed the failures of his government and asked for forgiveness. He claimed that he had been born again and from then on took on a religious Pentecostal discourse that saw everything from a dualistic perspective of light and darkness, to contrast himself with politicians who promoted Vodun, the traditional religion in Benin. He cast himself as a democrat and Christian who acknowledged God as the Creator of the world, to whom he prayed for all the people of Benin to be blessed with His power and grace. He promised to serve according to a constitution that would be respected and look like a sacred text. In embracing Christianity, Kérékou castigated fetishism and wanted to free the country from all evil forces, including the forces of the clan, a promise that propelled him to electoral victory. However, Kérékou used both Christian and traditional religious symbols to promote his political power.

In Côte d'Ivoire, former President Laurent Gbagbo also turned to Pentecostalism in order to stay in power. Gbagbo constructed a narrative claiming his country was a nation chosen by God and the people were to make a new covenant with God as God's people. Following the death of President Felix Houphouët-Boigny in 1993, Henri Konan Bédié (President of the National Assembly) competed with Prime Minister Alassane Ouattara for the presidency. In this struggle Bédié used the notion of *ivoirité* to argue that Ouattara was not Ivorian. He went on to push the philosophy of *Refondation,* a term which refers to bringing change and introducing a reforming attitude that would affect all areas of the life of the individual and the nation. The violence that followed the elections emboldened Gbagbo and his supporters to march forward with a nationalist agenda, accusing all who had a different perspective of interfering with Ivorian national affairs. In the ensuing struggle Gbagbo's forces were overrun and he was replaced by Ouattara, who would soon face charges at the international court in The Hague. When Gbagbo later came to power, he continued to promote his Christian ideology with the support of Christian leaders who helped him promote *Refondation.* In public manifestations his supporters have used Jewish symbols like the Star of David, prayed in Hebrew and carried the Israeli flag. Supporters of Gbagbo continue to use Hebrew symbols and coordinate the national calendar with celebrations and motifs from ancient Israel. Gbagbo the born-again President was seen as the chosen redeemer of the people who would bring freedom.

The second perspective on church–state relations in the region is reflected in the confrontation between Christian Cardinal Tumi and government leaders in Cameroon. Cardinal Tumi fought the authorities in Cameroon from the time he led the Christian Study Group (CSG), a Bible study group in Bamenda formed at the behest of the Bishop of Bamenda, Monsignor Paul Verdzekov, to address the social crisis of the country from a Christian perspective. When this ecumenical group discussed a pastoral letter in Bamenda in 1977, the governor of the province, David Abouem, a Tchoyi, interrogated them and warned them to stop what they were doing to avoid arrest. In 1979 Tumi was appointed Bishop of Yagoua in the north of Cameroon and, while there, state authorities challenged his pastoral letter in which he encouraged Christians to be strong in their faith. The governor of North Province (now Region), Ousmane Mey, accused Tumi of subversive activities. Tumi wrote to President Ahmadou Ahidjo and complained that there were no religious freedoms in North Province. Tumi was later accused by the next governor of North Province, Fon Fosi Yakum Ntaw, of subversive activities because Tumi was constructing church buildings without permits.

During Tumi's tenure as President of the National Episcopal Conference, the bishops issued a pastoral letter on the state of the economy of Cameroon in which they argued that the economic crisis was caused in part by the actions of state leaders. The state responded by attacking Tumi, and instructed state radio and television not to cover him. When Tumi was appointed to the College of Cardinals in 1988, President Paul Biya congratulated him and gave him a vehicle, but tensions remained between Tumi and the Biya regime, with Tumi being accused of disliking the President. When Tumi was transferred to Douala as Metropolitan Archbishop, his critics claimed he had been transferred to the hotbed of political opposition to work against President Biya and to support the Social Democratic Front.

From his new position in Douala, Tumi continued to criticise political corruption, charging that the government's anti-gang unit was itself complicit in criminal activities and abusing its powers by torturing civilians. Forces of law and order also provided military-style weapons to criminals to terrorise people and were engaged in extrajudicial killings and unlawful detention of citizens. Tumi called on the state to solve the problem of crime without violating public liberties. In an open letter, Tumi also appealed to the armed robbers to stop their activities. Tumi called for democratic reforms as a path and framework to ease conflicts and tensions. Some members of the regime attempted to implicate Tumi in an alleged coup plot. This was leaked to the press by Robert Tonye, one of the participants who was supposed to plant arms in Tumi's official residence in Douala. Tumi worked with bishops of neighboring countries to get Tonye and his family out of Cameroon and into exile in Canada. Tumi has charged that the public administration in Cameroon is corrupt, the judiciary is weak and helpless, people live in poverty and human rights are abused constantly. He dreams of a country where individuals assume responsibility, hold convictions and express personal autonomy in pursuing personal goals. This will happen when the rule of law is restored in Cameroon and people practise virtue.

## Pentecostalism

Pentecostalism and Charismatic movements have influenced church growth in the region. Both classical Pentecostal and neo-Pentecostal-type churches in the region have shaped ecclesial and public discourse in very distinct ways. Nigerian Pentecostal preacher Benson Idahosa held a crusade in Douala in 1993, proclaiming a gospel of prosperity. While working at the Pan-African Institute for Development in Buea, Cameroon, Billy Lubansa from the Democratic Republic of the Congo also conducted a crusade and invited speakers from different parts of Africa, often funding their visits with his own money. Pentecostalism has grown in Cameroon during the early twenty-first century from humble beginnings with the ministry of Dr Zacharias Fomum, which initially disrupted the Anglophone-dominated Presbyterian Church in Cameroon, which traces its roots to the Basel Mission. Ironically, the mainline Protestant churches in Cameroon gave Fomum a large platform for his crusades in the 1980s, where he called on people to be born again. The physics professor, who is seen by some as the 'Adeboye of Cameroon', left the Presbyterian Church to run his own ministry until his death in 2009.

Pentecostalism has been resisted in Cameroon by both ecclesial and state authorities. Pentecostal-leaning practices that emerged within the Catholic diocese of Buea, in South-west Region, were banned by the bishop. He in turn was accused of playing an ethnic card, since he came from North-west Region and the banned practices were initiated by a priest from South-west Region. A similar charge was made when Bishop Pius Awah, who also hailed from North-west Region, disciplined Father Etienne Khumbah, who had started a Pentecostal-leaning ministry in the Bojongo area of South-west Region. The Cameroon government has condemned some Pentecostal activities and charged that some pastors exploit the population with promises of healing and wealth that will not materialise.

Despite the conflict, Pentecostalism has also infiltrated the Presbyterian Church in Cameroon. At the Molyko congregation, young people have demonstrated in favour of Pentecostal-type music. They have also encouraged evangelistic campaigns and the practice of members testifying to the miracles and healing that God is doing in their lives. This development in the Presbyterian Church has benefited greatly from Nigerian ministry and gospel music, especially music by Agatha Moses. It has also been influenced by Nigerian films that portray conflict between the forces of good and evil, in which the Christian God always wins and is presented as the one who protects believers.

An influential figure in the growth of Pentecostal practices was Michael Bame Bame. Initially he stemmed the exodus from the English-speaking parish of the Presbyterian Church in Cameroon in Djoungolo, which was triggered by massive conversions to the preaching and ministry of Fomum in Yaoundé, where Bame Bame served as Dean of the Faculty of Protestant Theology. Bame Bame later started his own Pentecostal-leaning ministry called Pilot Revival Prayer Group, following a spiritual experience that he and his wife had in the Democratic Republic of the Congo. He called for members to seek the baptism of the Holy Spirit and gradually incorporated speaking in tongues and spiritual healing. These initiatives attracted many people to follow him. Eventually a split over these teachings emerged between Dean Bame and the newly appointed pastor of the congregation in Djoungolo, the Reverend Isaac Sakwe Elangwe. There was an ethnic dimension to this division since Elangwe came from South-west Province, while Bame Bame hailed from North-west Province. When attempts to mediate the dispute failed, Bame Bame and his followers started the Church of Patmos in Bastos, Yaoundé, in 1999.

Pentecostals have struggled in Cameroon because state officials intrude into their activities, arguing that this is necessary to protect the population from exploitation. In 2013, Cameroon's President ordered that some Pentecostal churches be closed. While many might not agree with Pentecostal teachings, banning their churches is just as questionable as embracing Pentecostalism and using it for one's political goals. The greatest challenge churches in the region face continues to be social issues. They have worked very hard to respond to the scourge of HIV/AIDS, but the challenge of poverty remains and African churches have to come up with creative ways of responding to poverty today.

## Christianity as a Lived Religion

Christianity in the region is a lived religion, confounding any expectations that secularisation represents the current direction of history. Christianity is lived since it has become a central religious perspective for many people. First, people seek healing through the Christian churches. Many flock to churches in search of healing in the wake of the disease burden created by the HIV/AIDS pandemic and the economic decline through which the region has gone. Church medical services in the region continue to serve people through their clinics, but there is a hunger for divine healing, expressing an existential angst that churches are working to address through various healing ministries.

Secondly, churches have become social centres and venues for the arts. People flock to the churches for entertainment. Gospel music is a major attraction in the region and one hears the music played on the radio, in taxicabs and at major transport hubs where people take buses for long journeys within the country. Cameroon has given permits to many Christian radio stations, and some of these are operated by Pentecostal-leaning Christians who play gospel music and broadcast testimonies throughout the day. In Cameroon, Nigerian gospel music has flooded the market and local artists like Grace Takeh have also recorded well received albums. Gospel music is now sung and danced to at wakes and funerals. Local artists use indigenous motifs to portray Christianity. A notable public and artistic display of Christianity is the Basilica of Our Lady of Peace in Yamoussoukro, in Côte d'Ivoire, built by Former President Félix Houphouët-Boigny. This highly criticised but impressive structure remains an artistic marvel.

Thirdly, Christianity has touched public life in different ways. Politicians in Côte d'Ivoire and Benin have openly embraced Christianity, especially the Pentecostal tradition. Christian symbols such as crosses, holy water from Israel, devotional literature and online versions of the Bible accessible on a mobile device demonstrate some of the many ways in which Christianity is playing a central role in the public sphere.

Fourthly, Christianity as a lived religion is now such a dominant force that some clergy and the faithful openly condemn traditional religions. The condemnation of traditional religious practices by Pentecostals is taking its toll, and many fear that, in addition to losing traditional religions, some communities might lose their cultures. Finally, in many places in Cameroon, English and French are replacing local languages in church services. Some consider this an unfortunate development, and it might be an indication that some of the gains of the Second Vatican Council are being rolled away.

## Bibliography

Bongmba, Elias K., *Facing a Pandemic: The African Church and Crisis of AIDS* (Waco, TX: Baylor University Press, 2007).

Claffey, Patrick, *Christian Churches in Dahomey-Benin: A Study of their Socio-Political Role* (Leiden: Brill, 2007).

Mokosso, Henry Efesoa, *American Evangelical Enterprise in Africa: The Case of the United Presbyterian Mission in Cameroun 1879–1957* (New York: Peter Lang, 2007).

Tumi, Christian, *My Faith: A Cameroon to be Renewed* (Douala: Éditions Veritas, 2001).

Walker, Sheila S., *The Religious Revolution in the Ivory Coast: The Prophet Harris and the Harrist Church* (Chapel Hill, NC: University of North Carolina Press, 1983).

I am indebted to the many other sources I have consulted, including the work of Konstanze n'Guessan, Patrick Claffey, Camilla Strandsbjerg, Sheila Walker, Ken Priebe, Robert Mbe Akoko, Henry Efeoa Mokosso and Côme Kinata.

# Nigeria

## Elijah Obinna

Nigeria is the most populous country in Africa and the seventh most populous country in the world. It is situated in the Western Africa region and has an area of 923,768 $km^2$. It shares land borders with the republics of Benin in the west, Chad and Cameroon in the east, and Niger in the north. As a nation of more than 180 million people, Nigeria has evolved in a cultural setting that is a study in contrasts, with much complexity and many dimensions. It is a vast country characterised by a multiplicity of cultural and religious loyalties, ethnic plurality and linguistic differences as well as diverse historical experiences.

Nigeria's social boundaries are often described as artificial, in the sense that certain ethnic groups and communities were split and located within colonial state territories of different European powers following the Berlin Conference of 1884–5. Thus, although Nigeria formally became one entity in 1914 after the amalgamation of the then Northern and Southern Protectorates, along with Lagos, many members of the different ethnic groups found their kinsfolk and neighbours just outside the new nation's political boundaries. Nigeria became an independent nation within the British Commonwealth on 1 October 1960. Today, there are estimated to be more than 250 ethnic groups and 300 dialects in Nigeria. Although several religions exist in Nigeria, religious affiliation is closely aligned with distinct regional divisions, thus helping to accentuate regional and ethnic distinctions. Additionally, all the ethnic groups have distinctive cultures, which together constitute the variety of culture and religion in the country, often expressed in terms of 'unity in diversity'.

Christianity is not only the second-largest but also the fastest-growing religion in Nigeria. In many cities it is not hard to see shops and offices named with such slogans as 'Jesus is Lord', 'Grace and Mercy', 'In God we trust', 'Jesus is my Saviour' and 'Jesus is coming again', and cars and lorries with stickers like 'I am a winner', 'I shall be fruitful', 'My year of advancement and total recovery', 'I shall not die', 'I am favoured' and 'I am blessed'. Many Nigerian Christians candidly exhibit their beliefs in this way. This scenario appears to be the case especially in the southern and western parts of the country. In the north, where Islam is stronger, such public expressions of Christian faith are much less common.

The earliest attempts to establish Christianity in Nigeria were undertaken by the Spanish and Italian Capuchins who arrived at Benin in August 1515 and the Portuguese Augustinian monks from São Tomé who entered Warri in the 1570s. However, by the dawn of the eighteenth century there was little to show for these earlier missionary endeavours, only a few relics like a huge cross in the centre of Warri, a few church decorations surviving among the indigenous ritual spaces and a few memories still preserved in oral tradition today.

During the nineteenth century, influenced by the Industrial Revolution, the missionary awakening in Europe and the abolition of the slave trade, several freed slaves and some Europeans attempted to establish Christianity in Nigeria. Christian mission was closely linked with European commerce and colonialism, and chaplains accompanied traders not just to provide services for the traders, but also to seek to convert indigenous Africans. Some of those chaplains established mission stations at trading posts and even beyond. Due to increased interest in Africa generated by the 'scramble' for the continent, the number of missionaries and mission agencies grew exponentially through the last part of the nineteenth and early part of the twentieth centuries.

In 1842, Thomas Freeman, a freed slave who arrived in Badagry, led a party of Wesleyan Methodists from the Gold Coast as far inland as Abeokuta. The next missionary effort was led by Henry Townsend of the Church Missionary Society (CMS) in Sierra Leone and extended the organisation's missionary effort to Badagry. On 10 April 1846, the Scottish Presbyterians, through the Scottish Missionary Society (SMS) from Jamaica, established themselves in Calabar and beyond. In the 1850s more Methodist missionaries arrived in southern Nigeria and in the 1880s began to move north. In 1893 another Methodist group, the Primitive Methodists, joined the mission in Nigeria. This group had been working on the island of

*Christianity in Nigeria, 1970 and 2015*

| | 1970 | | 2015 | | Average annual growth rate (%), 1970–2015 |
|---|---|---|---|---|---|
| Tradition | Population | % | Population | % | |
| Christians | 21,469,000 | 38.2% | 84,133,000 | 46.2% | 3.08% |
| *Roman Catholics* | 3,890,000 | 6.9% | 22,938,000 | 12.6% | 4.02% |
| *Orthodox* | 2,500 | 0.0% | 49,500 | 0.0% | 6.86% |
| *Independents* | 3,234,000 | 5.8% | 32,156,000 | 17.6% | 5.24% |
| *Protestants* | 3,959,000 | 7.1% | 31,106,000 | 17.1% | 4.69% |
| *Anglicans* | 2,941,000 | 5.2% | 22,000,000 | 12.1% | 4.57% |
| Pentecostals | 3,768,000 | 6.7% | 54,198,000 | 29.7% | 6.10% |
| Evangelicals | 5,416,000 | 9.6% | 36,712,000 | 20.1% | 4.34% |
| **Total population** | **56,132,000** | **100.0%** | **182,202,000** | **100.0%** | **2.65%** |

Source: Todd M. Johnson and Gina A. Zurlo (eds), *World Christian Database* (Leiden/Boston: Brill), accessed March 2016.

Fernando Po but had to relocate, as they faced opposition from the Roman Catholics. The Primitive Methodists worked mostly in the eastern part of Nigeria, particularly among the Efik-speaking people.

In 1850 Thomas Brown, pioneer missionary of the American Southern Baptist Convention (known in Nigeria as the American Baptist Mission), began work in Nigeria. Most of the Baptist missionary work was focused on the Yoruba and had its headquarters in Ogbomosho. In 1853 some Brazilian emigrants, who were mostly Portuguese-speaking Roman Catholics, gathered together and acquired a piece of land for a church in Lagos. By 1863, when a Roman Catholic priest first visited Lagos, a church had already been established, but it was not until 1867 that the first resident priest arrived to take charge of it.

In the southern part of Nigeria, where missionary work was most concentrated, the Protestant missions (especially the Anglican Church Missionary Society – CMS) maintained an unchallenged influence. However, in 1885, Roman Catholic missionaries began work in the Lower Niger. The establishment of the French Roman Catholic Church challenged what was perceived as the 'unquestionable spheres of English national life'. The CMS saw Roman Catholic penetration into the Niger as a continuation of the French drive to challenge British interests. The Irish Protestant Qua Ibo Mission was established in 1890 by S. B. Bill. This concentrated much of its efforts on the Niger Delta and among the Igbo. By 1905 the Qua Ibo Mission had reached many major Igbo cities.

The establishment of Christianity in the northern part of Nigeria was undertaken largely by the Sudan Interior Mission (SIM), which began its missionary work in 1893 and established its first mission station at Pategi in 1901. In 1954, SIM churches were incorporated as the Evangelical Church of West Africa (ECWA); today the ECWA is known as the Evangelical Church Winning All, to reflect its global efforts.

Next was the Sudan Pioneer Mission (SPM), which was established in 1895 through missionary work led by Karl Kumm. The name of the mission was changed to Sudan United Mission (SUM) in 1904. SUM established different churches and founded an association that served as an umbrella for ecclesiastical fellowship for the churches called Tarayar Ekklesiyoyin Kristi a Nigeria (the Fellowship of the Churches of Christ in Nigeria), or TEKAN.

In Nigeria, the initial spread of Pentecostalism is linked to the Revival movement of the early twentieth century, identified with such leaders as Garrick Sokari Braide, founder of the Christ Army Church (1918); Moses Orimolade, founder of the Eternal Sacred Order of the Cherubim and Seraphim (1925); Josiah Olunowo Oshitelu, founder of the Church of the Lord, Aladura (1930); and Joseph Ayodele Babalola, founder of the Christ

Apostolic Church (1941). In 1918 J. B. Shadare and Eshinshinade founded a praying band called Precious Stone or Diamond Stone. In 1923 the Diamond Stone became affiliated with Faith Tabernacle Congregation in the USA and Pastor D. O. Odubanjo became its presiding pastor in Nigeria. In 1931 the Faith Tabernacle Congregation in Nigeria became officially affiliated with the Apostolic Church, Great Britain, and took the name the Apostolic Church, Nigeria. Between the years 1931 and 1935 a group of young men and women who were living at Old Umuahia, Abia State, Nigeria, established a number of churches under the name Church of Jesus Christ. In June 1939 they became affiliated with the Assemblies of God in Springfield, Missouri, USA, and were officially renamed Assemblies of God.

Nigeria has witnessed an increasing proliferation of Pentecostal and Charismatic churches, especially since the 1950s and 1960s. Bishop Benson Idahosa has the reputation of taking the Pentecostal movement in Nigeria to its highest point while also unknowingly initiating its negative association with the 'prosperity gospel'. We can therefore say that Bishop Idahosa constitutes an interval between the golden age of Pentecostalism in Nigeria, represented by Joseph Ayo Babalola, and its resurgence with the emergence of the Redeemed Christian Church of God (RCCG), an indigenous manifestation of Pentecostalism, under J. O. Akindayomi in 1952.

When Pastor Enoch Adeboye took over as the General Overseer of RCCG, warning bells were already ringing with regard to the tradition of Pentecostalism and its increasing alignment with the prosperity message. The Nigerian masses in the 1980s were already groaning under the burden of the Structural Adjustment Programmes (SAPs) and the austerity measures put in place by the Nigerian government of that time. It is therefore no wonder that they caught on quickly to the prosperity message of Bishop Idahosa as the message of hope for a better tomorrow.

In pursuance of global evangelisation, some of the Nigerian churches engage in what is often termed 'reverse mission', aimed at re-evangelising what they perceive as the 'secularised' or 'pagan' West. Thus some of these churches define themselves as 'global' or 'international' churches with a 'global mission'. Some of these churches have continued to maximise mass media and Internet websites as conscious strategies of self-insertion and identification within the global religious landscape. The mission-related churches have also acted in ways that put them on the global map. The anti-gay stance of the (Anglican) Church of Nigeria on the ordination of homosexual bishops by Western Anglican churches has attracted both local and global attention.

The official establishment of the Christian Association of Nigeria (CAN) in 1976 marked a turning point in the Nigerian religious landscape. CAN has five subsidiary bodies: the Pentecostal Fellowship of Nigeria (PFN), the

Catholic Secretariat of Nigeria (CSN), Christian Council of Nigeria (CCN), the Organisation of African Instituted Churches (OAIC) and the TEKAN and ECWA Fellowships. The Association serves as Christians' rallying point in reaction to Islamic politics in Nigeria. Some of CAN's objectives include a continued insistence on Nigeria's status as a secular state, the prevention of Islamisation and the acquisition of power and resources for Christian constituencies. CAN has often berated Christians for their complacency and charges them not only to be politically informed but also to participate actively in partisan politics. CAN seeks to serve as a watchdog against a fundamentalist Islamic resurgence and as an unregistered opposition party to the government, especially with regard to those policies that it considers to be undermining Christian freedom.

### Bible Translation and the Role of Vernacular Languages

When the Church Missionary Society (CMS) first began work among the Igbo of southern Nigeria in 1841, its members were eager to use translation of the Bible and other materials as a central part of their missionary strategy. The missionaries J. F. Schon, a German, and Archbishop Samuel Ajai Crowther, a Yoruba, had already been working with many Igbo among the freed slaves in Sierra Leone and had carried out some preliminary study of the language and translated various materials into Igbo. By the 1870s interest in translating the Bible into Igbo was being renewed, possibly due to the influence of a number of skilled mother-tongue speakers. Much of the credit goes to CMS missionary Thomas John Dennis, who worked on the Igbo translation project from the late 1890s. By 1906 Dennis and his co-workers had completed the Bible translation in the Onitsha dialect, but for some years he had been feeling that a 'Union' version (which combined several different Igbo dialects) was needed for effective mission work to continue throughout the whole area. The Union Igbo Bible, translated and made available for use between 1906 and 1912, was expected to serve as the Bible for the Igbo people of southern Nigeria. This expectation, however, has not been fulfilled, as the Bible translation has rather become a source of ongoing controversy.

The mid-nineteenth century witnessed the establishment of Christianity in Nigeria as well as the translation of the Bible into local languages. A. W. Banfield of the Mennonite Brethren in Christ (MBC) lived among the Nupe people and within 18 months made the first draft translation of John's gospel. By 1908 he had translated the four gospels into Nupe. By 1912 he had translated Acts, and in 1914 Banfield completed the entire Nupe New Testament. He also produced a 200-page book of Old Testament stories.

Translation of the Bible into local dialects has continued to increase. Nigeria was among the first countries in Africa to form a national Bible translating organisation. In 1962 the University of Nigeria signed a cooperative agreement with Wycliffe Bible Translators, SIL International, to carry out language development work. Out of that partnership, the Nigeria Bible Translation Trust (NBTT) was established. In 1976 NBTT assumed responsibility for Bible translation for the minority language groups in Nigeria. Currently, NBTT has at least 107 projects running across the country and is conducting surveys of 42 further language communities, with the possibility of starting translation work.

The Bible Society of Nigeria (BSN) is another major stakeholder in Bible translation in Nigeria. The BSN was founded on 8 February 1966 through the pioneering efforts of the late Ezeogo Elder Dr Francis Akanu Ibiam, the first indigenous governor of the defunct Eastern Region of Nigeria. Earlier, in February 1965, Ibiam had organised a consultation with representatives of most of the churches in Nigeria on the need to form a national Bible society in Nigeria. Following the consultation, the Bible Society of Nigeria was inaugurated and subsequently took over the activities of the British and Foreign Bible Society (BFBS), which had operated in Nigeria as far back as 1807. Currently the BSN has 39 areas (districts) across the country and six Bible depots. So far, the BSN has translated the entire Bible into 24 Nigerian languages and the New Testament into 60 further local languages. It has ongoing work on translating the Bible into 16 more languages.

## Theology and Worship

In Nigeria most churches have theological colleges, including Bigard Memorial Seminary, Trinity Theological College, Methodist Theological Institute, Hugh Goldie Lay/Theological Training Institute, School of Divinity, SS Peter and Paul Major Seminary, Seat of Wisdom Seminary, Theological College of Northern Nigeria, Esien Ukpabio Presbyterian Theological College, Word of Faith Bible Institute, Missionary Seminary of St Paul's, and School of Ministry of Mountain of Fire and Miracles. These schools are devoted to the training of pastors, evangelists and catechists and other categories of church workers. Although most of the schools recognise systematic theology, symbolic theology, practical or applied theology, historical theology and other disciplines as specific areas of theology, their primary focus is the adaptation of Christian theology to the existential needs of the country. There is an over-riding concern among students and theological tutors for the application of theological truths to specific life situations.

Leading Nigerian theologians such as Ogbu Kalu, Matthews Ojo, Donatus Ukpong, Afe Adogame, Benebo Fubara-Manuel and Udobata Onunwa have explored Christianity from a wide range of traditions. Each has identified the phenomenon of Pentecostalisation and Charismatisation of Christianity in Nigeria as of particular significance today. During the early part of the twentieth century, many indigenous Christians saw the spiritualities of the historic mission denominations as being overly cerebral. In particular, their neglect of African worldviews of mystical causality and their inability to integrate Charismatic renewal phenomena into worship distanced historic mission Christians from many ordinary Nigerians. Tying into popular narratives about the devil as the head of all the demons who were once cast out from heaven and settled in Africa, many Pentecostal and Charismatic churches devote much time to deliverance from the satanic forces that are believed to oppose Christians and are held to cause material and psychic problems in the sphere of health and wealth.

The attraction of Charismatic Pentecostalism in Nigeria is not confined to Pentecostal and Charismatic churches but also materialises in prayer groups under the auspices of established Protestant churches, the Charismatic renewal in the Roman Catholic Church and non-denominational fellowships that 'born again' Christians attend without leaving their churches. Many mainline churches feature Pentecostal and Charismatic elements, including: monthly or weekly healing, deliverance and anointing services; 'prophetic prayers'; warfare prayers; family deliverance and tarry nights. Common at such services are prophecies, revelations, speaking in tongues, spiritual songs and loud shouts of 'Hallelujah' and 'Amen'. Other features include spiritual healing involving laying on of hands, anointing oil, 'Holy Ghost Stone', 'blessing of water', 'Holy Ghost Koboko' and prophetic prayers. Slogans such as 'Warfare equals welfare', 'This witch must die', 'Holy Ghost fire against my enemies', 'My enemies die! Die! Die! Die!', 'The louder your Amen the nearer your miracle' and 'The higher your jump the nearer your miracle' are becoming recurrent within mainline congregations. Prayers are often considered effectual when rendered between midnight and 3 am, as this period is considered to be the peak time at which the demons are at work. These forces are declared to be the enemies of human beings and communities, hindering them from achieving their life goals and accessing the good things in life. The crux of the matter is that although they are Christians, members of the mainline and Charismatic and Pentecostal churches are not exempted from the harsh realities of life and, as such, solutions are often sought from multiple sources. This 'window shopping' in the spiritual marketplace is often described as attempting to 'go where it works'.

### Socio-economic and Political Engagement

The explicit involvement of Nigeria's churches in the public sphere is most remarkable. The social-political involvement of churches at both the local and international levels has shaped contemporary Christianity in Nigeria.

Many of the churches constitute ministries that offer social services that state and local governments fail to provide, including schools, hospitals and other welfare-related services for both their members and wider communities. Following Nigeria's independence and the civil war, it was thought that Christianity in Nigeria would become less significant or fizzle out because it was closely associated with colonialism and depended so much on its school systems. The federal government took over primary and post-primary schools at the end of the civil war. It banned all denominational religious activities, including prayers. Additionally, participation in religious activities was made optional for teachers and pupils. The predictions of the end of Christianity have proved to be premature, however, given the enormous increase in Christianity within Nigeria. There has been, rather, a shift from churches being docile to churches being active agents of socio-political, economic and democratic liberation.

In the Nigerian context, Christianity and public life are intimately intertwined. Public ethics, value systems and political and economic structures combine as national concerns and are rationalised and viewed with the same urgency as religious faith. Many Nigerian Christians use the Scriptures as a resource for constructing a theology that can guide them in their day-to-day life, encompassing the construction of ritual practices and sacred narratives as well as moral and ethical ideologies.

Mobility is a major attribute of life in contemporary Nigeria. This involves more than a geographical shift from villages to the cities or vice versa. Social mobility occurs as individuals change their positions in society and as a result develop new networks of friends and acquaintances. There is also a psychological mobility – the personality changes that individuals experience as they imbibe new ideas and values. Such individuals are freed from the constraints that bound them to life in the traditional rural village, with its customs and expected social relationships. Churches provide their members and adherents with a 'place to feel at home' within a small sub-group. Many churches, especially in the cities of Nigeria, provide their members with space where they find guaranteed sociability, status, security and welfare at times of personal or family crisis. Conversely, this often involves 'incapsulation' in the religious group: the process of social control by which the religious community exercises totalitarian regulations over the social and religious lives of its members.

The capacity of churches in Nigeria to act as a social force can be assessed with reference to three dimensions: the social impact on the wider society of their missionary and civic activities; the social impact on their members' lives; and the extent to which they contribute to the 'de-privatisation' of religion and its visibility in the public sphere. Many churches are involved in the campaign against HIV/AIDS. As part of its corporate social responsibility to the Lagos state government, the Deeper Christian Life Ministry has recently begun the construction of a flyover bridge in the Gbagada area of the city of Lagos. Some of the churches are gradually becoming training grounds for national football players. For instance, Joshua's Football Academy provided two players for the Nigerian Under-17 World Championships in 2009; similarly, Mike Okinawa's football team is helping to recruit talented Nigerian football players.

Contemporary Christianity in Nigeria is a major contributor in the development and provision of quality education. Some of the churches are not only proprietors of nursery, primary and secondary schools but also of private universities, where they have scholarship programmes for indigent students. Currently, the church-owned universities in Nigeria include: Covenant University, established by the Living Faith Church; Babcock University, established by the Seventh-day Adventist Church; Bowen University, established by the Baptist Church; Benson Idahosa University, established by the Church of God Mission; Bingham University, established by ECWA; Redeemed University, established by the Redeemed Christian Church of God; Ajayi Crowther University, established by the Anglican Church; Crawford University, established by the Apostolic Faith Church; Caritas University, established by the Catholic Church; and Wesley University of Technology, established by the Methodist Church.

These institutions have provided many Nigerians with educational opportunities, given that the government universities can hardly provide for the increasing number of university applicants. Additionally, these universities provide uninterrupted academic sessions, unlike the government universities, which are characterised by incessant industrial action. They also offer employment opportunities to Nigerian youths. Nonetheless, many of these institutions are unaffordable for poor church members, who might have contributed their 'widow's mite' towards their establishment.

Despite its broad appeal, Christianity in Nigeria remains fragile. It is faced with the challenge of applying Christian morality and ethics, the promotion of biblically based social values such as honesty, accountability, fairness and equality in everyday life. Thousands of new members might join the church each day, but it can still be argued that Christianity in Nigeria is a giant standing on clay legs. This is accentuated by the increasing prevalence of vices such as corruption, greed, selfishness, dishonesty, callousness among both the holders of public office and ordinary citizens, the spread of diseases (especially HIV/AIDS) and inter-religious and intra-religious conflicts and violence. Many churches and their leaders lack the moral competence to challenge the status quo.

## Christianity and Religious Violence in Nigeria

Nigeria is a multi-religious, multi-ethnic and multi-cultural society with enormous potential for socio-economic and democratic development. However, intense conflicts and violence have characterised national life over the past decade. These scenarios have continued to shape and reshape Nigeria's international relations, as no one can be sure when the next outbreak of violence might erupt. Nigeria is usually characterised as being deeply divided, as major political or socio-economic issues are often vigorously contested along the lines of complex ethnic, religious and regional boundaries. While religious identification and membership remain fashionable among Nigerians, the ways in which they are appropriated have often increased violence in the country.

For instance, some members of the Izala movement and the Muslim Students Society rejected the 1979 constitution and advocated the establishment of an Islamic state. This gave room for an alliance of conservative Muslim groups, which drew huge support from the Jama'atu Nasril Islam, a political-religious body established in 1962. Most of the emirs and their councils belong to the traditional conservative establishments of Islam, whereas the newer groups like Izala (a movement against innovations and for orthodoxy) and Maitatsine ('he who curses others') see violence as a means of achieving their desired purity of Islam and the establishment of an Islamic state.

The Izala movement was founded in Jos by Sheikh Ismaila Idris in 1978. The movement's principal concern is for the cleansing of Islam and the abolition of practices that are not 'original' to the Qur'an and Sunnah. The Maitatsine group was founded by Alhaji Marwa Maitatsine in the late 1970s and was in operation throughout the 1980s. The group is driven by the socio-economic disadvantages suffered by the marginalised and poor in the interests of the rich members of the society. Its members exhibit intense hatred for agents of the state, including the police and members of the armed forces, perhaps because of their own repeated violent encounters with them. The group inspired the horrific uprisings in Kano in 1980, Bauchi in 1982 and Yola in 1984.

Religiously based violence continues to break out all too frequently. For instance, in February 2002 the members of a youth choir in a Methodist church in Plateau State were hacked to death and burnt in the church. In July 2002, 88 villages belonging to Christians were destroyed in the same state, leaving at least 100,000 people homeless, with approximately 5,000 killed. December 2002 witnessed another attack in Kano State, where six Christians in a single family were burnt to death as Muslim militants took vengeance on Pastor Sunday Madumere, in reaction to the role he played in the conversion to Christianity of many Muslims in the city of Kano. In

July 2003, the Kano State Environmental Planning and Protection Agency (KASEPA) demolished about 20 church buildings, claiming that it was removing illegal structures that had no certificate of occupancy.

No matter what the remote or immediate causes are of a violent incident, many end up becoming religious. In 2002, for instance, a reporter for a popular Nigerian newspaper, *This Day*, published an article arguing that Muslims should refrain from protesting against Nigeria's hosting of the Miss World contest in Kaduna. The report suggested that perhaps if Muhammad were alive he might take a wife from among the contestants. The statement was a comment from a reporter, not representing a Christian view, and was contained in a newspaper that is not identified in any way with Christianity. Yet it ignited a wave of violence between Christians and Muslims, leading to the loss of over 200 lives.

Furthermore, the local–global import of violence in Nigeria is demonstrated by the case of the Danish cartoons, which included one showing Muhammad with a bomb-shaped turban and an ignited fuse. After the Danish newspaper *Jyllands-Posten* printed the caricatures on 30 September 2005, other Western newspapers (mostly in Europe) followed suit, asserting their values and the right to freedom of expression. Demonstrations against the cartoon went global, and in Nigeria these developed into anti-Christian riots, leading to violence and the loss of lives and property. Muslims in Kano State burnt Danish and Norwegian flags and barred Danish companies from bidding for major construction contracts. Kano lawmakers called on people of their state to boycott Danish goods. In Maiduguri, protesters against the cartoons attacked Christians and burnt down churches, killing at least 15 people.

Violence has been taken to a new level by the Boko Haram group ('Western or non-Islamic education is sin'). The group was founded in 2002 in Maiduguri by Ustaz Mohammed Yusuf, with the aim of imposing Sharia law throughout all 36 states of Nigeria. Despite the reported death of Yusuf in 2009, the group has continued to extend its influence. The abduction of the Chibok girls from their school on 14 April 2014 in Borno State and the increasing violence against women and girls has captured the world's attention. These uprisings and conflicts are affecting the mission of churches, especially in the north-east.

While it could be argued that there has not been a Christian group like the Izala, Maitatsine and Boko Haram movements, since the 1960s Christians have always come out on mass to defend their faith whenever there is violence. Many Christians, especially those in the volatile northern states, appear to have forgotten the biblical teaching of turning the other cheek to an enemy and have re-appropriated the Old Testament code of 'an eye for an eye and a tooth for a tooth'.

For instance, on 21 February 2000, the Christian Association of Nigeria's Kaduna chapter staged a peaceful procession with leaves and Bibles in their hands at the Governor's House and the State House of Assembly to protest against the forceful move by the state government to impose Sharia as state law. On their way back from the Governor's House to their various destinations they were attacked and several of them were killed, and properties and houses belonging to Christians were destroyed.

Nonetheless, Christianity in Nigeria is a phenomenon of major scope and persistence. It continues to spread across the different regions of the country. Many Nigerian churches are also taking up extra-religious functions, such as social welfare programmes, to meet various personal and social needs of the people amid the uncertainties and difficulties within the country. Thus their focus is not only the spiritual well-being of their members but also the interface of religion with social and economic life. The future of Christianity in Nigeria will therefore be shaped not only by internal dynamics but by political and economic forces at work at a global level.

## Bibliography

Ajayi, Jacob Festus Ade, *Christian Missions in Nigeria, 1841–1891: the Making of a New Elite* (London: Longmans, Green and Co., 1965).

Iwuchukwu, Marinus, *Muslim-Christian Dialogue in Post-Colonial Northern Nigeria: The Challenges of Inclusive Cultural and Religious Pluralism* (Basingstoke: Palgrave Macmillan, 2013).

Kalu,Ogbu U., *Embattled Gods: Christianization of Igboland, 1841–1991* (Trenton, NJ: Africa World Press, 2003).

Korieh, Chima J. and G. Ugo Nwokeji (eds), *Religion, History and Politics in Nigeria: Essays in Honour of Ogbu U. Kalu* (New York: University Press of America. 2005).

Ojo, Matthews A., *The End-Time Army: Charismatic Movements in Modern Nigeria* (Trenton, NJ: Africa World Press, 2006).

# Ghana, Liberia and Sierra Leone

## Cephas N. Omenyo

The Church in Ghana, Liberia and Sierra Leone is broadly made up of three major traditions: Roman Catholic, Protestant (historic Western mission-founded churches) and Pentecostal, generally in this chronological order. Christians are in the majority in the first two countries. Liberia, for instance, is sometimes referred to as a 'Christian state'. More importantly, the enormous influence of Christianity in these three states – historically, socially and politically rather than simply in terms of the number of adherents – explains why it is generally believed that Christians are in the majority.

The various Roman Catholic dioceses are united under the respective National Catholic Secretariats and the Catholic Bishops' Conferences. The main Protestant churches are the Presbyterians, the Methodists, the Anglicans and the Baptists. These are organised ecumenically under their respective National Christian Councils. They are usually referred to as the historic mission-founded churches. The Pentecostal/Charismatic churches are organised under separate national bodies. The churches in these states are growing at a most remarkable rate. A number of churches are playing major roles in the process of transformation of their respective nations.

### Traditional Social Structure

The Portuguese (in search of gold) were among the first European visitors to the west coast of Africa, around the fifteenth century. They discovered enormous deposits (earning present-day Ghana the name Gold Coast). As a result, many European nations, including the Danish, French, Dutch and English, built several forts that served as trading posts along the west coast, some of which still survive. Trade later developed into the slave trade, which continued until it was abolished in the nineteenth century. From the fifteenth century onwards, a number of independent states of varying size, power and wealth emerged in West Africa, notably Ghana. For most of the older states, their traditional governance and religion have always been inseparable.

These pre-colonial West African states had their own religious institutions at the advent of the Western missions. On the whole, citizens were open to God. For them, the spiritual was the inner reality of the material world, and this was given religious expression in their daily activities. They shared a common worldview that held that God is immanent and real, and He was accordingly acknowledged in their primal religions as the creator, the sustainer of the world and the dependable one. They believed that they were surrounded by a host of spirit beings, both malevolent and benevolent, whose actions impinged on their lives. They had a strong belief in ancestors, who were considered to possess the power to assist family members. They had their own idea of salvation that ensured the holistic well-being of their societies. The states had their own traditional non-formal educational, economic and marriage institutions, which ensured harmonious living and continuity of society.

## Major Guest Religions

Generally, African cultures had, and still have, a spirituality that is open and all embracing. Consequently, these West African countries have played host to both Islam and Christianity. Islam was established and made, and continues to make, an impact through the trading activities of the Fulani and Hausa traders. Long before the advent of Christianity in these states, Muslims had exploited most parts of traditional West Africa. This posed a major challenge to Christian missions, since citizens of these nations were threatened with death if they converted to Christianity. Furthermore, Islam was attractive to many because it was perceived as a non-Western religion and, unlike Christianity, it does not insist on a sudden break with the African past regarding some traditional social practices such as polygamy. Islamic beliefs, religious practices and culture were introduced generally to West Africa, making a major impact on the region.

## Early Catholic Enterprise

Christianity in Ghana, Liberia and Sierra Leone dates back to the fifteenth century, when various European countries embarked on exploratory

*Christianity in Ghana, 1970 and 2015*

| | 1970 | | 2015 | | Average annual growth rate (%), 1970–2015 |
|---|---|---|---|---|---|
| Tradition | Population | % | Population | % | |
| Christians | 4,344,000 | 50.5% | 17,625,000 | 64.3% | 3.16% |
| *Roman Catholics* | 1,167,000 | 13.6% | 3,401,000 | 12.4% | 2.40% |
| *Orthodox* | 1,000 | 0.0% | 4,600 | 0.0% | 3.45% |
| *Independents* | 1,306,000 | 15.2% | 5,811,000 | 21.2% | 3.37% |
| *Protestants* | 944,000 | 11.0% | 7,044,000 | 25.7% | 4.57% |
| *Anglicans* | 100,000 | 1.2% | 289,000 | 1.1% | 2.39% |
| Pentecostals | 1,409,000 | 16.4% | 10,237,000 | 37.3% | 4.51% |
| Evangelicals | 420,000 | 4.9% | 5,564,000 | 20.3% | 5.91% |
| **Total population** | **8,597,000** | **100.0%** | **27,410,000** | **100.0%** | **2.61%** |

Source: Todd M. Johnson and Gina A. Zurlo (eds), *World Christian Database* (Leiden/Boston: Brill), accessed March 2016.

enterprises in the region. Ghanaian Christianity is usually dated to January 1482, when the first Roman Catholic Mass was held on the shores of Elmina. This enterprise was a result of both Henry the Navigator's evangelistic zeal and the activities of merchants who discovered gold. A number of chaplains were appointed to serve in the forts and castles built by the Europeans along the coast, and some of them ventured beyond the walls of the castles to preach to the indigenous people. The mission of the Catholics suffered a jolt in the 1770s, however, following the Portuguese defeat at the hands of the Protestant Dutch. The Catholic mission was renewed in Elmina in 1880 following the arrival of Father Auguste Moreau and Father Eugene Murat. On the whole, the Christian missionary enterprise during this early period did not yield any direct fruits; conversions were not recorded, there is no evidence of surviving churches and the missionary activities suffered demise.

## Major Developments in the Eighteenth and Nineteenth Centuries

The eighteenth century witnessed two major developments in West Africa. While Africans were treated as sub-humans and sold in their millions as slaves, particularly to British parts of America and Brazil, the period also saw a vigorous evangelistic outreach to indigenous Africans by European missionaries and their African counterparts.

The church in Sierra Leone was the result of the anti-slavery movement. Between 1771 and 1774, the amateur botanist Henry Smeathman spent three years collecting species in Sierra Leone. It was on Smeathman's advice that the English decided to resettle freed slaves in Sierra Leone. The first batch of about 400 came from England in 1787, meeting with some climatic problems and strong antagonism from the indigenous people. In 1792 the second batch arrived from Nova Scotia. These were 1,200 ex-slaves who fought on the side of England during the American War of Independence. The third batch of settlers came from Maroon communities in the mountains of Jamaica. They had been exiled earlier

*Christianity in Liberia, 1970 and 2015*

| | 1970 | | 2015 | | Average annual growth rate (%), 1970–2015 |
|---|---|---|---|---|---|
| Tradition | Population | % | Population | % | |
| Christians | 395,000 | 27.9% | 1,857,000 | 41.2% | 3.50% |
| *Roman Catholics* | 23,700 | 1.7% | 349,000 | 7.7% | 6.16% |
| *Independents* | 137,000 | 9.7% | 719,000 | 16.0% | 3.75% |
| *Protestants* | 120,000 | 8.5% | 577,000 | 12.8% | 3.55% |
| *Anglicans* | 11,000 | 0.8% | 43,200 | 1.0% | 3.09% |
| Pentecostals | 99,800 | 7.0% | 691,000 | 15.3% | 4.39% |
| Evangelicals | 75,300 | 5.3% | 369,000 | 8.2% | 3.60% |
| **Total population** | **1,420,000** | **100.0%** | **4,503,000** | **100.0%** | **2.60%** |

Source: Todd M. Johnson and Gina A. Zurlo (eds), *World Christian Database* (Leiden/Boston: Brill), accessed March 2016.

to Nova Scotia but were later permitted to join the other settlers in Sierra Leone. Most of these settlers were Christians who belonged to a variety of denominations – Baptist, Wesleyan and Anabaptist. These returnees were later overtaken numerically by large numbers of Africans from the Lower Guinea Coast, freed by British men-of-war from ships transporting them to plantation slavery.

Before the Church Missionary Society started its work among them, the returnee Africans, especially the Methodists, had moved to preach among their fellow Africans. It is significant to note that some of these settlers had been church leaders in the diaspora. Examples of these were Mary Perth, who had formed her own congregation while a slave in Norfolk, Virginia, and David George, the Baptist leader.

The Church Missionary Society chose Sierra Leone as a mission field because its leaders hoped that Christianity might eventually be carried to the rest of Africa, from Sierra Leone as the radiating centre. With time, the resistance of Islam was overcome and the Anglican Church emerged. The development of the church in Sierra Leone followed distinctive strategies. These were education, the development of the local language and devolution. As a result, the Christian faith spread to other West African countries, such as Nigeria and the Gambia.

Following William Carey's missionary advocacy in 1792, Sierra Leone played host to Protestant missionaries in 1795. Unfortunately, this enterprise had to be abandoned in 1797 due to health considerations. However, in 1804 German Protestant missionaries ventured to Sierra Leone. The earliest sustained missionary society that worked in Ghana was established by Moravians under the auspices of the Basel Mission in 1828. They were followed by the Wesleyan Missionary Society in 1835. Other missionaries came from the North German Missionary Society, which arrived in 1847, as well as the Roman Catholic Mission, which resumed

*Christianity in Sierra Leone, 1970 and 2015*

| | 1970 | | 2015 | | Average annual growth rate (%), 1970–2015 |
|---|---|---|---|---|---|
| Tradition | Population | % | Population | % | |
| Christians | 218,000 | 8.7% | 856,000 | 13.3% | 3.09% |
| *Roman Catholics* | 47,500 | 1.9% | 354,000 | 5.5% | 4.57% |
| *Orthodox* | 500 | 0.0% | 520 | 0.0% | 0.09% |
| *Independents* | 21,000 | 0.8% | 178,000 | 2.8% | 4.88% |
| *Protestants* | 97,800 | 3.9% | 323,000 | 5.0% | 2.69% |
| *Anglicans* | 25,000 | 1.0% | 21,800 | 0.3% | −0.30% |
| Pentecostals | 19,700 | 0.8% | 238,000 | 3.7% | 5.69% |
| Evangelicals | 32,200 | 1.3% | 167,000 | 2.6% | 3.72% |
| **Total population** | **2,514,000** | **100.0%** | **6,453,000** | **100.0%** | **2.12%** |

Source: Todd M. Johnson and Gina A. Zurlo (eds), *World Christian Database* (Leiden/Boston: Brill), accessed March 2016.

work in Ghana in 1880, and the Society for the Propagation of the Gospel (SPG), which resumed work in Ghana in 1904. Later missionary bodies included the Seventh-day Adventists and the Baptist Mission (both 1898) and the Salvation Army (1911).

The Republic of Liberia received its African settlers from the United States. The American Colonization Society proposed to solve the awkward social problems faced by the large number of freed Africans among the slave owning-communities in southern states by sponsoring an emigration scheme to Africa similar to that of Britain. By 1838 the total population of American origin approached 2,300. The early settlers, similar to the Sierra Leone example, faced harsh climatic conditions and deep hostility from the local population. The American missionary societies that managed to survive the difficulties of the climate and establish themselves on the coast included the American Protestant Episcopal Church, the Presbyterians and the African Methodist Episcopal Zion Church.

Some Liberians hold a strong view that Liberia is a Christian nation because all 11 men who signed the Declaration of Independence in 1847 were Christians and the Declaration was signed in a Baptist church. The American Protestant Episcopal Church played a significant role in propelling the growth of Christianity in Liberia. By 1914, the church had about 11,000 members and was involved in a number of literary projects spearheaded by Bishops John Payne and Johannes Gottlieb Auer, the latter a former Basel missionary from the Gold Coast. These leaders laid the foundations for a substantial literature in the Grebo language. The first black bishop of the church, S. D. Ferguson, confirmed a young Grebo nationalist, William Wadé Harris, who emerged in the early 1910s as the 'black Elijah' of West African Christianity.

Of all those who emigrated to Liberia, none was as influential as Edward W. Blyden, who arrived in Liberia in 1851 and became deeply involved in the educational direction of the country. When Liberia College was founded, he was appointed Professor of Greek and Latin and Literature. His magnum opus, *Christianity, Islam and the Negro Race* (1887), had an immediate and profound impact on issues of African identity.

The Western missionaries who worked in the region executed a well planned Christian education programme aimed at equipping indigenous Africans, particularly in Sierra Leone and Ghana during the nineteenth century. This largely explains the gains the various missionaries made in their respective mission fields. The policy led to the establishment of the Fourah Bay College in Sierra Leone in 1827, with Samuel Adjai Crowther as its first student. His training enabled him to provide good leadership as African Bishop with the Church Missionary Society (CMS) in the Niger River region.

In Ghana, the Basel Mission established a comprehensive school system with rich educational content from the basic school, culminating in the establishment of the Theological Seminary at Akropong, in July 1848. The Seminary was modelled on the Missionshaus at Basel, where missionaries were trained, and offered high-quality training for church leaders, including training in the English, Greek and Hebrew languages in addition to specific conventional theological subjects. The vernacular was the main language in which subjects were taught, laying a deep foundation for meaningful dialogue to take place between the gospel and culture. The high quality of education provided by the missionaries – particularly the Basel Mission, the Wesleyan Missionary Society, the Catholics and the Anglican missions – produced the early nationalists who fought for the independence of the country and offered leadership in governance in all three countries.

Another significant development that explains the success of the Western missionary movement in West Africa in general was the enactment of the policy of intentionally and willingly ending mission activities in those West African states, through the influence of the visionary leader of the CMS, Henry Venn, in 1841. This policy sought to equip and position indigenous churches to be self-financing, self-propagating and self-governing. The implementation of the policy helped give confidence to indigenous leaders to take up leadership and to prepare local churches to be autonomous in the post-independence era.

It is noteworthy that black preachers and indigenous Africans were deeply involved in the Christian missionary enterprise during the eighteenth and nineteenth centuries. For instance, some of the freed slaves were involved in itinerant preaching in Ghana and Liberia. African ex-slaves from the West Indies served as missionaries, indigenous church leaders and teachers in West African countries.

On the whole, by the end of the nineteenth century, Christian mission in Ghana, Liberia and Sierra Leone had introduced the indigenous people to the gospel, with its transforming effects. The missions also introduced important social services such as scientific/orthodox medicine, agriculture, Western classroom education and the beginnings of literature in local vernacular languages. The nineteenth century ended with much success in the Christian missionary enterprise in the three West African states. However, the young churches faced equally major challenges that threatened the future of Christianity in the region.

Generally speaking, Western missionaries had a rather derogatory and poor image of Africans. For instance, although indigenous Africans were deeply involved in the missionary enterprises of the various Western missionary societies, as pastors, teachers, catechists, interpreters and church elders, they were not treated as partners. The best-trained African pastors (some from the best institutions in Europe or America), for instance, were treated as 'mission assistants' and not as colleagues of the Western missionaries. One of the major consequences of this was agitation by African church leaders for self-rule, which created tension between Western and indigenous church leaders.

Another challenge that emerged in the churches was the lack of a critical engagement of the gospel with African cultures. Christianity as it was transmitted failed to engage with the traditional religious worldview of the African. Indigenous Christians were unable to reconcile traditional African values with Christian ones. This deficit in the work of the Christian mission led to the gospel and African culture being on parallel lines. Indigenous converts were alienated from their own culture and people. In some cases they had to establish their families in *salems* (Christian quarters). Christianity was thus seen as disruptive and divisive of society.

Furthermore, African Christians were unable to relate to their deep-felt needs. This resulted in apparent religious infidelity by some African converts. Some lived double-standard lives, having more confidence in traditional priests than in Western missionaries to solve their pressing problems. This was a regular complaint found in the records of most Western missionaries. This tendency was to result in the emergence of churches founded by indigenous Africans for Africans in the ensuing century.

## Developments during the Twentieth Century

The turn of the twentieth century witnessed significant changes in the Christian landscape in Africa, including Ghana, Liberia and Sierra Leone. The period saw Western missionaries transferring leadership to Africans. Under indigenous African leadership the churches continued to expand. The number of Christians and churches increased remarkably. The churches continued pursuing social services such as building and running schools and hospitals, agricultural extension services and rehabilitation services for the disabled. On the whole, African leaders continued almost all the mission projects they inherited from the Western missionaries.

Christianity in these West African states experienced a major paradigm shift with the emergence of 'African prophets' such as the Liberian William Wadé Harris and two Ghanaians, Sampson Oppong and John Swatson. These prophets claimed they received divine revelations through which they were called to preach the gospel independent of Western missionaries and were not constrained by Western forms of ministry. They made converts in torrents at places where Western missionaries made converts in trickles. Their success is attributed mainly to the fact that they scratched where the African itched most – their messages resonated with African spiritual realities. They sought to provide answers to the strongly felt needs of African followers. In spite of their claim to independent calls through revelations to ministry, they worked closely with the Western missionaries. They were very charismatic, but they readily admitted their incompetence as far as teaching the Bible was concerned. They therefore baptised their converts and encouraged them to sit at the feet of the Western missionaries, who would nurture them with the Word of God.

The African prophets did not establish their own independent churches. Nevertheless, after their deaths, some of their followers established churches independent of Western mission-founded churches. Their churches are variously called African Independent Churches, African Indigenous Churches and African Initiated Churches (AICs). In Ghana, these churches are popularly referred to as *Sunsum Sore* or 'spiritual churches' because of the emphasis they put on spiritual things. These churches include the Church of the Twelve Apostles, the Musama Disco Christo Church, the Church of the Lord and the African Faith Tabernacle. In the mid-twentieth century, many scholars predicted that the AICs would be the distinctive face of African Christianity. Indeed, they have innovated with new forms like the Pentecostal groups or the Charismatic churches, while a minority of the Pentecostal-type churches have largely maintained features of the AICs. Although these churches can be differentiated on the basis of theology, practices and spirituality, they can nevertheless be grouped together as AICs. The Pentecostal-type movement has also managed to influence the historic churches to the extent that all the mainline Western mission-founded churches have Charismatic groups within them.

## Developments in the Twenty-first Century

Against the backdrop of long Western European missionary influence, the churches established in most parts of Africa were replicas of Western Christian traditions, theologies and expressions. Consequently, despite the fact that Western mission-founded churches in the three African states were led by indigenous people, they followed inherited practices and at the same time tried to make way for some African expressions. Henry Venn's policy of self-propagation, self-financing and self-governing has made a tremendous impact. But what is found wanting among churches in these states has been self-theologising. Contextualisation of Christian theology, worship and practices remains a challenge.

Nevertheless, theologians from these three states have made concerted efforts to engage the gospel with African cultures. One of the earliest, from Sierra Leone, was Harry Sawyer, who helped to educate generations of West Africans. He is acknowledged as a pioneer in the development of

African theology. Sawyer was followed by others from Ghana, particularly Christian Baeta, Kwesi Dickson, John Pobee and Kwame Bediako. Bediako is noted for his approach, of a hermeneutic of identity, of conversion, transformation and salvation of cultures beyond the classical paradigm of continuity and discontinuity. His major research was on the second-century church fathers in the context of the gospel crossing from a Semitic to a Hellenistic cultural environment as a paradigm for the gospel and culture encounter in African contexts in the recent past. His understanding of the crucial role of language in the appropriation of the gospel and in local agency in the history of African Christianity, and his commitment to mother-tongue hermeneutics, advanced the idea of the translatability of the gospel. His Christocentric theology, notably his understanding of the uniqueness of Jesus Christ as the Servant Lord, and his ancestor Christology challenged the divinity and sacredness of the ancestors but acknowledged their positive role in the community. His contribution as a world Christian with particular reference to primal religion as the substructure of Christianity was unique. Many younger theologians, who are making efforts to contextualise African theology, have also emerged from these three countries in recent times.

Ghanaian Christianity has, over time, seen different forms of worship and spirituality. In the nineteenth and early twentieth centuries, historic mission-founded churches followed the spirituality of the mother churches in Europe. Attempts to contextualise were met with great opposition, and in one classic case, Ephraim Amu, a teacher at the Presbyterian Training College, was dismissed, firstly for insisting on preaching in a native garment in the pulpit and secondly for introducing African drums and horns into the College and teaching students how to drum and dance.

In recent times, however, the Pentecostal/Charismatic movement has greatly influenced the worship and spirituality of Christian churches in Ghana. One finds that in both historic mission-founded churches as well as in the Pentecostal and Charismatic churches, there is emphasis on healing and deliverance and anointing with oil. The worship services, which are well attended by young people, are very vibrant, with spontaneous singing and dancing accompanied by music, predominantly from American jazz instruments.

The evangelistic scene in Ghana is an active one. Various mission models are in use to reach out to people. There are expansionist activities, which include crusades, conventions and conferences. Open-air preaching, which was a significant part of mission Christianity, has been modified and given a Pentecostal touch. Both historic mission churches and Pentecostal/Charismatic churches are involved in major evangelistic and church growth programmes. It is noteworthy that from the inception of Western missionary activities in these countries, indigenous Africans have been involved in all the stages of mission work, from the pre-Western missionary days through the Western missionary era to the post-Western missionary era. African initiatives have consistently characterised mission work in these countries. The most recent development is Africans embarking on trans-national mission enterprises. Both the Pentecostal-type churches and the older Western mission-founded churches have established branches in other African countries as well as on other continents, particularly Europe and North America. The Church of Pentecost of Ghana, for instance, has over 4,400 well established congregations and a membership of more than 400,000 across the world. It appears this trend will be on the ascendency in coming years among all the churches from these states.

Mission in these states is not limited to expansionist activity but also includes *diakonia,* which is seen in the provision of formal education, health service delivery and relief services, as well as agricultural extension services. The historic churches, especially the Catholic Church, Presbyterian Church and Methodist Church, are key players in the ministry of *diakonia*. These services have gone far in supporting the work of the governments in poverty alleviation and social development. The churches together offer more than 40% of the medical services in Ghana, particularly in remote areas where most medical professionals do not wish to serve. In the past, the Pentecostal-type churches did not feel the need to commit resources to social services. However, in recent times there has been an increasing awareness and effort to offer services to a few less well endowed citizens and to remote areas.

The HIV/AIDS pandemic has been a major health concern in all three countries but particularly Liberia and Sierra Leone. The churches in these states have acted positively to combat the pandemic and have offered support to people who suffer from this disease. The churches have been offering advocacy by way of issuing communiqués and organising educational programmes. They are actively involved in providing services such as running voluntary counselling and testing (VCT) centres and offering clinical management and pastoral care, as well as training HIV/AIDS counsellors.

The Ebola pandemic that recently affected Sierra Leone and Liberia has threatened development and has attracted attention globally. The virus killed so many so quickly. The churches in these states were deeply involved in the control, cure and eradication of the pandemic. They mounted educational programmes to enlighten their members on how to avoid being infected. They also helped to dispel the belief that Ebola either was a punishment from God or was caused by evil spirits and witchcraft. There were two notable reactions to the Ebola pandemic, particularly on the part of Christians in Sierra Leone. Firstly, some claimed to receive revelations from God that if they washed themselves with salt water they would be cured and/or protected. Secondly, some preachers claimed that if all believers would in unison (nationwide) shout 'Jesus' the nation would be saved from the outbreak. Christian leaders educated their members to understand that the only way to fight the disease was to follow the practical steps outlined by the Ministry of Health and the National Ebola Response Committee. The Ebola outbreak severely challenged long-held and valued cultural traditions. The churches therefore engaged in community sensitisation activities related to prevention and containment of Ebola. Ironically, the pandemic made Christianity in Liberia and Sierra Leone more prominent than ever. In Liberia, the government formally honoured the Liberia Council of Churches (LCC) for the fight against the disease. President Ellen Johnson Sirleaf, who personally presented the award, referred to the LCC as 'Champions of Peace' and Grand Commander, 'Order of the Star of Africa'.

Generally, relations between people of different faiths are cordial in these countries. For instance, there is a remarkable tolerance between Christians and Muslims. In Ghana and Sierra Leone, many Muslims were educated in Christian schools; both Christians and Muslims celebrate each other's religious holidays; in some cases they know each other's prayers and they inter-marry. Thus Christians have Muslims in their families and vice versa. At national gatherings, prayers are usually said by Christians, Muslims and traditionalists to demonstrate the peaceful coexistence of the various religions. In both Liberia and Sierra Leone there was collaboration between Muslim and Christian leaders during their respective civil wars, a development that helped to bring peace to these countries.

There are efforts by church leaders to control zealous preachers who preach inflammatory sermons that have the potential to spark crises. For instance, in 2008 the Presbyterian Church of Ghana set up an Inter-faith Research and Resource Centre (PIRRC) in the capital city, Accra. This centre is aimed at informing, equipping and training the Christian church in Ghana and other West African states in inter-faith issues through research, seminars, short courses and academic studies and at providing resources through a library. It has convened and facilitated national, regional and international Christian–Muslim conversations on mutually relevant issues.

However, it is important to note that from time to time there are isolated tense undercurrents between Christians and Muslims in some communities. A case in point is the raging debate that emerged in Ghana in 2015 on whether non-Christian students in government-assisted mission schools could be forced to participate in worship. This debate was initiated by some Muslim scholars who saw the compulsory participation of their children in worship services in the school as a violation of their human rights. The leaders of the mission churches insisted that all students in their schools have to participate in the worship service as part of the school discipline. The situation in most of these schools has remained the same.

The flood of Pentecostal revivalism, the fastest-growing segment of Christianity in all three states over the last three decades, has captured the attention of both theologians and social scientists. The impact of Pentecostalism is strongly felt in all spheres of life, including politics, educational institutions, local communities, public institutions and even in older/mainline Western-founded churches that hitherto were opposed to the Pentecostal phenomenon.

The success of the Pentecostal movement in these states can be explained by their attempt to sink the roots of Christianity into African culture and life. Their religious practices, such as healing and deliverance, and the emphasis they put on prosperity reflect the African circumstances and address the felt needs of their adherents. Their mass followers think Pentecostalism is answering the deep questions Africans are asking because it takes the African worldview seriously. Pentecostalism in Ghana, Sierra Leone and Liberia has emerged to give hope in states plagued by war, poverty and catastrophic diseases. The promise that Pentecostalism in these countries holds transcends denominational barriers by impacting the older/mainline Western mission-founded churches to a large extent.

## Conclusion

Christianity has had a tremendous impact on Ghana, Liberia and Sierra Leone. The growth of Christianity in these three West African countries is indicative of the fact that over the years local Christians have owned it and discovered that the faith has resources to help them face specific African challenges, hence the numbers it attracts. Individual Africans have served as key agents/missionaries in the spread of Christianity from its arrival until today. The growing number of missions, particularly from Ghana, in Western countries points to the fact that Africans are mature enough not just to be self-sufficient but also to actively spread the gospel message to countries that were in the past labelled Christian, which shows that African Christians from Ghana, Liberia and Sierra Leone are of age. Indications are that Pentecostalism, which is reshaping Christianity in Africa, is going to be the future of Christianity in these countries.

## Bibliography

Agbeti, John Kofi, *West African Church History – Christian Missions and Church Foundations, 1482–1919* (Leiden: Brill, 1986).

Omenyo, Cephas N., *Pentecost Outside Pentecostalism: A Study of the Development of Charismatic Renewal in the Mainline Churches in Ghana* (Zoetermeer: Uitgeverij Boekencentrum, 2002).

Sanneh, Lamin, *West African Christianity* (Maryknoll, NY: Orbis Books, 1992).
Sundkler, Bengt and Christopher Steed, *A History of the Church in Africa* (Cambridge: Cambridge University Press, 2004).
Walls, Andrew F., *The Missionary Movement in Christian History: Studies in the Transmission of Faith* (Maryknoll, NY; Orbis Books, 2004).

# Senegal, the Gambia, Guinea, Guinea-Bissau and Cape Verde

## Simon Kossi Dossou

Given that Christianity is the faith of the majority in much of Sub-Saharan Africa, something of an exception is represented by the Christians of Senegal, the Gambia and Guinea (sometimes called Guinea-Conakry to make a distinction to Guinea-Bissau and Equatorial Guinea). In these three West African nations Christians form a minority in largely Muslim populations. Similarly, the peoples of Guinea-Bissau and Cape Verde are for the most part Christian, but as Portuguese-speakers they are an exception in a region of West Africa dominated by Francophone and Anglophone populations. In this chapter, therefore, consideration will be given to Christians in minority situations – a challenging exercise in terms of attaining an appropriate balance. In addition, as is true for much of the Southern Hemisphere, these five countries are passing through a time of rapid religious change, marked especially by an expansion of Christianity, so the picture painted here is likely to date quickly.

### Senegal

Senegal was 'discovered' by the Portuguese in 1445. Since these Portuguese explorers were Catholic Christians, they planted the religion in towns such as Gorée, Saint-Louis and Rufisque. It was only later, in the seventeenth century, that the Vatican would assume leadership of this mission initiative. Although some native Senegalese were converted to Christianity, for many years Christianity remained the religion of foreign settlers, and the missionaries failed to make the impact anticipated.

By contrast, Islam, which came into the country through the camel trains, found a positive welcome, mainly because of two influential Tukulor kings – El Hadj Omar Tall in the north and Samory Touré in the south. In addition, the competition between Muslims and Christians to win adherents swung in favour of Islam because the Muslim religious leaders (*marabouts*) were Senegalese rather than Arab, while the Christian leaders were nearly all European, which gave the Senegalese the feeling that Christianity was a foreign religion.

The Christian faith in Senegal is sustained by certain churches that are more or less mirror images of their mother denominations. The main churches or religious communities are discussed below.

The Catholic Church in Senegal came under the aegis of the Vatican in the seventeenth century. But beginning in 1819 a sharp rise in the number of converts to Catholicism resulted through the work of the Sisters of St Joseph of Cluny (France). They settled in Saint-Louis, where they opened a church and a girls' school. This was followed by the construction of the Saint-Louis Cathedral, which was inaugurated in 1828. Later the Gorée Church was built. The first priests who were native to Saint-Louis were ordained in 1840. In 1943 the first Catholic secondary school in the country was founded in the same town.

Little by little, Catholicism took hold throughout the country, facilitated in part by the fact that the governors were almost exclusively Catholic. Several monastic communities, including the Benedictines and the Franciscans, arrived from Europe to practise their lives of piety and to engage in various socio-economic activities. Today, the Catholic clergy in Senegal consists mainly of native Senegalese and there is no lack of vocations to the priesthood. As will be seen with other churches in the country, coexistence between Muslims, Christians and followers of other religions is generally very peaceful.

It was in 1863 that Eugène Casalis, Director of the Société des Missions Evangéliques de Paris (SMEP), sent a young Swiss man named Louis Jacques to Senegal to learn the language and customs. He was based in Casamance, where a mission station (including a school) was quickly established. As early as 1867, three Senegalese, including a woman named Salimata Ndiaye, were sent to a Protestant school in France. The two men died of yellow fever so it was Salimata alone who returned in 1876, complete with a school diploma, to become a teacher at the girls' school in Saint-Louis.

In a period of heightened foreign missionary activity, several missionaries came to Senegal to serve the church, but their efforts failed to find fertile

*Christianity in Senegal, 1970 and 2015*

| | 1970 | | 2015 | | Average annual growth rate (%), 1970–2015 |
|---|---|---|---|---|---|
| Tradition | Population | % | Population | % | |
| Christians | 229,000 | 5.4% | 805,000 | 5.3% | 2.83% |
| *Roman Catholics* | 183,000 | 4.3% | 761,000 | 5.0% | 3.22% |
| *Independents* | 5,500 | 0.1% | 28,200 | 0.2% | 3.70% |
| *Protestants* | 4,100 | 0.1% | 16,000 | 0.1% | 3.08% |
| *Anglicans* | 100 | 0.0% | 250 | 0.0% | 2.06% |
| Pentecostals | 6,500 | 0.2% | 60,200 | 0.4% | 5.07% |
| Evangelicals | 2,700 | 0.1% | 11,600 | 0.1% | 3.31% |
| **Total population** | **4,218,000** | **100.0%** | **15,129,000** | **100.0%** | **2.88%** |

Source: Todd M. Johnson and Gina A. Zurlo (eds), *World Christian Database* (Leiden/Boston: Brill), accessed March 2016.

ground among the native population. From 1924 to 1960, the Protestant Church of Senegal (PCS) faltered as the colonial authorities did not allow it to grow, and so it became the church of foreigners from all over Africa and the wider world. Through thick and thin, the PCS continued to survive, despite much internal misunderstanding, until the ordination of its first Senegalese minister – Samuel Vauvert Dansoko, of Bambara descent – on 5 December 1982. He left to pursue further studies, and settled in the USA.

The PCS underwent a major crisis in 1996, which resulted in its temporary closure by the administrative authorities. After several mediation attempts led by the All Africa Conference of Churches and by CEVAA (Communauté d'Églises en Mission – a network of French-speaking churches collaborating in mission), the Côte d'Ivoire minister Jonas Adou was sent to Senegal in 2003 with the task of reviving the PCS. Adou embarked on the work of an internal restructuring of the Church and trained leaders to work with women and young people, equipping them to become church deacons, preachers and elders. The life of the Church resumed on a serious footing, resulting in the training of three Senegalese ministers in the Protestant universities of Cameroon and Benin. These ministers are now in post. Two additional places of worship were opened: Dieuppeul in Dakar and Khor in Saint-Louis. A further parish is in the process of being established in Casamance. A centre for social projects, named Centre Liberté, has been built, with an adjoining nursery school and a primary school. Philippe Jean-Baptiste Mendy is the present moderator of the church.

The Lutheran Church of Senegal is one of the most recent churches to emerge as part of Senegal's Christian landscape. Its history began in 1974 and is recognised as a not-for-profit and non-political Evangelical association by the national authorities, through an official document dated 14 February 1987. Emerging into the context of the existing Senegal Protestant churches, the Lutheran Church grew quite quickly and now comprises 13 parishes, along with further areas of mission outreach. It is represented in six regions of the country: Thiès, Fatick, Dakar, Louga, Saint-Louis and Kaolack. Three departments have been formed: theological training, community development and social action. The church has 6,500 members under the pastoral care of 21 ordained ministers, six trainee ministers, two female theologians and nine Finnish missionaries (including two ministers and one female theologian). It also has 19 catechists and 27 assistant or lay catechists. The main distinctive feature of the Lutheran Church is the emphasis it places on combining evangelisation with social witness expressed through various projects. In this way, many young men and women are supported and guided through their studies and apprenticeships towards employment. Likewise, the very young and the very old are looked after, depending on the church's means.

Despite the dominance of Islam in Senegal, a large number of Protestant churches are engaging in spiritual activities in and around Dakar. Expatriate Christians founded these churches while stationed in Senegal, often as international civil servants. Once their congregations became established, the members continued to keep the flame alive after the original founder had left the country. Some managed to establish themselves in towns such as Thiès, Mbour and Ziguinchor. Examples include the Baptist Church of Dakar, Evangelical Foursquare Mission in Senegal, International Life Mission, Evangelical Church of Dakar, Methodist Church of Grand Yoff, United Methodist Church of Grand Yoff et Nord-Foire, Dakar, and Church of International Grace.

The New Apostolic Church has occupied a large space in the Christian landscape of Senegal in recent years. It was founded in 1863 and developed from the Apostolic Catholic Church, which professes the imminent return of Jesus Christ. The church recognises and practises three sacraments: Holy Sealing, Holy Baptism and Holy Communion. Holy Sealing is the gift of the Holy Spirit, received by the laying on of hands and the prayer of an apostle of the church. Holy Baptism with water is performed by the sprinkling of consecrated water and the laying on of hands. Holy Communion is the distribution of consecrated bread by the minister. The New Apostolic Church was authorised by ministerial decree on 30 May 2003, although it had been in Senegal since 1965, through the work of Amadou and Claire Lise Sow. For many years the faithful have worshipped in a house in Dakar, but since 2000 the church has taken root in some villages. Given that all proselytising is forbidden in Senegal, the faithful were few in number in the beginning but grew more and more and are becoming a considerable community. There are some 16,000 members in Senegal and around 8,000 faithful in the rest of West Africa. They are particularly active and are growing in number, including in Gambia.

Although Senegalese Islam is tolerant and has accepted the principle of religious coexistence, conflicts have been known to flare up between Christians and Muslim groups aggrieved at seeing churches proselytising among their adherents. While the Evangelical churches have been most affected by such conflicts, the Catholic Church has also experienced them in recent years.

## The Gambia

The Gambia covers an area of 10,689 km$^2$ and is almost totally surrounded by Senegal. In 2015 its population was just under 2 million. Its capital is Banjul and the next two cities of significance are Serekunda and Brikama.

As a result of the historic slave trade, the Gambia came under the authority of first the Portuguese and then the British. The latter were the real colonial power, from which the country gained its independence in 1965. Since independence, the Gambia has been led successively by President Dawda Jawara and, from 1994, by Yahya Jammeh. The country's economy is based mainly on agriculture, fishing and tourism.

As is true in many West African countries, Christianity is a minority faith in the Gambia. However, just as is the case in other principally Muslim countries in the region, Christians in the Gambia are free to express their faith without undue worry. Article 25 of the national constitution confirms the principle of protecting the rights of every citizen to practise the faith of their choice.

Arab traders came into contact with the Gambia in the ninth or tenth century, with Islam consequently being introduced into the country. European contact did not occur until 1455, when the Portuguese arrived and set up trading posts along the Gambia River to organise the black slave trade. This marked the beginning of Roman Catholic influence in the country. In 1894 the Gambia became a British protectorate and from that point the Christian faith, in all its diversity, began to take root.

Roman Catholics are to be found particularly in the west and south. Among the most visible of the Protestant denominations in the country are Anglicans, Methodists, Baptists, Seventh-day Adventists, Jehovah's Witnesses and Evangelical Lutherans, together with numerous other Evangelical groupings. In 1963, the Gambian Christian Council was created, which acts as an ecumenical association comprising the Roman Catholic Church, the Anglican Church and the Methodist Church.

The Catholic Church was to gain its first Apostolic Prefecture in 1931, while the Anglican Church established the Diocese of the Gambia in 1935. The first Gambian national to become an Anglican bishop was Bishop Solomon Tilewa Johnson, born in 1954. He was consecrated Bishop of Gambia and the Rio Pongas in 1990; and elected Primate and Archbishop of the Province of West Africa in 2012. He died suddenly in 2014.

*Christianity in the Gambia, 1970 and 2015*

| | 1970 | | 2015 | | Average annual growth rate (%), 1970–2015 |
|---|---|---|---|---|---|
| Tradition | Population | % | Population | % | |
| Christians | 14,500 | 3.2% | 91,200 | 4.6% | 4.17% |
| *Roman Catholics* | 9,300 | 2.1% | 58,500 | 2.9% | 4.16% |
| *Orthodox* | 100 | 0.0% | 600 | 0.0% | 4.06% |
| *Independents* | 820 | 0.2% | 15,000 | 0.8% | 6.67% |
| *Protestants* | 1,600 | 0.4% | 10,900 | 0.5% | 4.39% |
| *Anglicans* | 2,000 | 0.4% | 3,000 | 0.2% | 0.91% |
| Pentecostals | 510 | 0.1% | 19,400 | 1.0% | 8.44% |
| Evangelicals | 720 | 0.2% | 5,500 | 0.3% | 4.64% |
| **Total population** | **447,000** | **100.0%** | **1,991,000** | **100.0%** | **3.37%** |

Source: Todd M. Johnson and Gina A. Zurlo (eds), *World Christian Database* (Leiden/Boston: Brill), accessed March 2016.

As a general rule, Christians are free to practise their religion in the Gambia, but they must avoid all acts of proselytism. It is equally worthy of note that the Muslims of the Gambia are a peace-loving people, moderate in the expression of their faith and respectful of the activities of the Christians. Christians must, however, recognise that certain limits exist that should not be exceeded. For example, if young Muslim children attending Christian schools were to be baptised, they would usually renounce the Christian faith once they returned to their families for the school holidays. According to Catholic Bishop Robert Ellison:

> one must respect the religious values of Islam, try to encourage Muslims to be faithful to their particular values, and to make these values seen in our life and in our faith. The values of love, of compassion, of forgiveness, of understanding and of mutual respect. Leave the rest in the hands of God and the Holy Spirit.

As is the case in other primarily Muslim countries in West Africa, there have usually been Christian leaders who played significant roles in state and society. They are particularly sought after to preside over peace councils, as well as other social activities such as aid to refugees. They are involved in the aftermath of natural disasters such as floods. Christians generally tend to be involved in community projects – activities greatly valued by state leaders, who are usually Muslim.

In conclusion, despite its largely Muslim nature, the Gambia is a country in which religious freedom is respected – each religious persuasion being free to express itself. Christian congregations practise their faith without undue constraint, but equally they must respect the faith of others.

## Guinea

Guinea is a country in West Africa of 245,857 km2, with a population of approximately 12 million. Historically it was colonised by France, as were several other countries in the region; it gained its independence in 1958, having refused to comply with the trend of most African countries at the time to stay in a close relationship with the colonising power. Guinea's progress from September 1958 was not without problems. Nevertheless its population – made up of men and women of faith – continued to forge courageously ahead with social and political development, in no way compromising their early move towards independence.

Christianity in Guinea is generally considered to be a minority religion in a largely Muslim country. The majority of Guinean Muslims are Sunni, with a minority of Shiites. The Christian presence, however, is greatly respected since the political context shows much tolerance in matters of religious belief. Thus a Guinean, whether Muslim or Christian, can as a rule assume any function in the country provided he or she is suitably qualified.

The Christian population includes Roman Catholics, Anglicans, Baptists, Jehovah's Witnesses, Seventh-day Adventists and some Evangelical or Pentecostal communities. Baha'is and Hindus are found in small numbers, as are expatriate Buddhists practising traditional Chinese beliefs. It is quite possible that there are also some self-confessed atheists, particularly in view of the fact that the country had adopted an ideology akin to Marxism/Leninism during the early years of independence.

Despite the overall climate of tolerance in the country, in July 2013 some Muslims rose up against some Christian groups. For three days the town of Nzérékore suffered an ethnic/religious confrontation resulting in approximately 50 deaths (some sources say 54), with several people wounded.

The government of Guinea coordinates the country's religious activities through its Inter-Faith Council. The Council includes members of the Anglican, Catholic and Protestant churches, as well as of the General Secretariat of Religious Affairs, which comprises the offices of Christian affairs, Islamic affairs, pilgrimages, places of worship and economic affairs and trusts, as well as the office of the Inspector General. The Inter-Faith Council attempts to pre-empt inter-faith conflicts before they actually occur or to intervene quickly if they do.

The Christian churches make every effort to live peaceably together. This is a commendable witness in a nation where they are a minority faith group. For this reason, many Christian leaders – particularly Anglicans and Catholics – have been elected to high-ranking posts in government to help promote peace in the country. The churches' social involvement is valued by the whole population of Guinea. It was the churches that spearheaded the campaign against the recent Ebola epidemic. In addition, their ecumenical and bilateral partners cooperate sensitively with them for the welfare of the country as a whole.

In conclusion, Christians in Guinea-Conakry – despite their minority status – play a significant role in society. The politico-administrative

*Christianity in Guinea, 1970 and 2015*

| | 1970 | | 2015 | | Average annual growth rate (%), 1970–2015 |
|---|---|---|---|---|---|
| Tradition | Population | % | Population | % | |
| Christians | 55,400 | 1.3% | 490,000 | 3.9% | 4.96% |
| *Roman Catholics* | 48,400 | 1.1% | 304,000 | 2.4% | 4.17% |
| *Independents* | 1,800 | 0.0% | 38,500 | 0.3% | 7.04% |
| *Protestants* | 3,100 | 0.1% | 109,000 | 0.9% | 8.24% |
| *Anglicans* | 2,000 | 0.0% | 1,400 | 0.0% | −0.79% |
| Pentecostals | 1,200 | 0.0% | 74,200 | 0.6% | 9.68% |
| Evangelicals | 3,600 | 0.1% | 107,000 | 0.9% | 7.82% |
| **Total population** | **4,215,000** | **100.0%** | **12,609,000** | **100.0%** | **2.46%** |

Source: Todd M. Johnson and Gina A. Zurlo (eds), *World Christian Database* (Leiden/Boston: Brill), accessed March 2016.

authorities recognise the church's important contribution to the country's development and have undertaken to protect its interests from any form of persecution at the hands of extremist groups, whatever their origin.

## Guinea-Bissau

Guinea-Bissau is in a minority among West African countries, on two counts: first, it is Portuguese-speaking, along with Cape Verde; and secondly, it is a small country. It has a mainland area of 28,000 km$^2$ and a marine area of 8,120 km$^2$, with 60 or so islands in the Atlantic Ocean. The population is made up primarily of young people. Population density is 42 inhabitants per square mile. Infant mortality is still relatively high.

Contact with Europeans goes back as far as 1446, but it was only in 1879 that the country became a Portuguese colony. After a war lasting 12 years, Guinea-Bissau became a republic recognised by the United Nations in 1973. However, the country remains politically unstable because of the interests of various drug traffickers who create and destroy governments depending on their personal interests. Sadly, it is well known that Guinea-Bissau has become a hub of the cocaine trade.

As is the case throughout most of Africa, religion plays a significant role in the lives of the people of Guinea-Bissau. As regards religious identity, studies reveal the following approximate statistics: Islam, 50%; traditional religions, 40%; and Christianity, 10%. Christians are concentrated in the major cities, particularly the capital, Bissau. The Christian community includes Roman Catholics and a variety of Protestant denominations.

The national constitution guarantees religious freedom and it is recognised that different governments have respected the citizen's right to worship as he or she may choose. Moreover, it would appear that there has been no notable discrimination or abuse in the country in recent years on the grounds of religious adherence. This is seen as a positive aspect in the achievements of the different national leaders.

*Christianity in Guinea-Bissau, 1970 and 2015*

| | 1970 | | 2015 | | Average annual growth rate (%), 1970–2015 |
|---|---|---|---|---|---|
| Tradition | Population | % | Population | % | |
| Christians | 66,800 | 9.4% | 225,000 | 12.2% | 2.73% |
| *Roman Catholics* | 59,600 | 8.4% | 191,000 | 10.4% | 2.62% |
| *Independents* | 0 | 0.0% | 45,400 | 2.5% | 20.58% |
| *Protestants* | 2,500 | 0.4% | 29,100 | 1.6% | 5.57% |
| *Anglicans* | 200 | 0.0% | 290 | 0.0% | 0.83% |
| Pentecostals | 0 | 0.0% | 56,000 | 3.0% | 21.14% |
| Evangelicals | 2,500 | 0.4% | 26,300 | 1.4% | 5.34% |
| **Total population** | **712,000** | **100.0%** | **1,844,000** | **100.0%** | **2.14%** |

Source: Todd M. Johnson and Gina A. Zurlo (eds), *World Christian Database* (Leiden/Boston: Brill), accessed March 2016.

Western observers consider that the Bissau Guineans practise syncretism, mixing Christian or Muslim beliefs with practices from traditional religion. However, African experts in religious phenomena feel that the West exaggerates its criticism of syncretistic tendencies.

Very little information is available regarding the prominent personalities of faith groups in Guinea-Bissau. Church leaders devote themselves to the preaching of the gospel, to practical community activities and to being a presence in society. High on their agenda are matters of peace promotion and the war against scourges linked to the trade in drugs and the consequent proliferation of small arms and petty crime.

In conclusion, Guinea-Bissau is working towards political stability and a harmonious society. Moreover, religious freedom for all is a guarantee that an authentic Christian faith can be practised and can exercise a corrective influence on some of the less wholesome aspects of national life.

## Cape Verde

Cape Verde is an island nation in the Atlantic Ocean off the coast of West Africa. It comprises an archipelago of small islands, uninhabited until the arrival of Portuguese settlers in 1456. Once they had become established, they began to populate the country with Portuguese and with slaves imported from various parts of Africa, particularly West Africa. A small number of other Europeans as well as a community of Spanish and Portuguese Jews fleeing the Inquisition came and settled in the archipelago. The cohabitation between these Europeans and the slaves originating from West Africa resulted in the mixed-race population that we find today.

With its half-million inhabitants, Cape Verde would appear to be the least-populated West African country. However, its density of 129.8 inhabitants per km$^2$ could be regarded as considerable, in view of the fact that the land is harsh and barren. The population is relatively young. It has been calculated that the Cape Verdeans who live in the USA, in Portugal, elsewhere in Europe and in many other African countries – Senegal in

*Christianity in Cape Verde, 1970 and 2015*

| | 1970 | | 2015 | | Average annual growth rate (%), 1970–2015 |
|---|---|---|---|---|---|
| Tradition | Population | % | Population | % | |
| Christians | 269,000 | 99.5% | 494,000 | 94.9% | 1.36% |
| *Roman Catholics* | 259,000 | 95.7% | 468,000 | 89.9% | 1.33% |
| *Independents* | 250 | 0.1% | 38,500 | 7.4% | 11.84% |
| *Protestants* | 8,200 | 3.0% | 19,000 | 3.7% | 1.88% |
| Pentecostals | 10 | 0.0% | 39,200 | 7.5% | 20.18% |
| Evangelicals | 7,800 | 2.9% | 10,100 | 1.9% | 0.57% |
| **Total population** | **270,000** | **100.0%** | **521,000** | **100.0%** | **1.47%** |

Source: Todd M. Johnson and Gina A. Zurlo (eds), *World Christian Database* (Leiden/Boston: Brill), accessed March 2016.

particular – exceed the total number of those who live in Cape Verde itself: their total is estimated at 700,000.

It was only in 1975 that Cape Verde gained independence and became a republic. It is a member of the African Union and adheres to several institutions of that organisation. The Cape Verde economy is based primarily on commerce, transportation, tourism and the public service sector. The country possesses few natural resources apart from salt, pozzolan (a mineral used in the fabrication of cement) and fisheries. International aid represents an important proportion of the state budget. It should also be remembered that the sizeable number of Cape Verdeans resident outside the country contribute in different ways to the country's economy.

The Portuguese colonial settlers of Cape Verde naturally brought their Christian faith with them, and this remains the country's principal religion. Roman Catholicism is practised by 90% of the population, over whom the clergy exercise a strong influence. Despite this entrenched Catholicism, during the colonial period most of the priests, living in close proximity to the local people, had wives, children and even mistresses. This situation appears not to have changed to any great degree over the course of the country's religious history. Hence it is alleged that the grandfather of Amílcar Cabral, a leader at the time of national independence, was in fact a curate.

Protestantism, mainly represented by the Methodists, became established as the second largest faith group and is scattered throughout the whole country. Apart from Methodism, the Seventh-day Adventist Church is represented, as also are the Assemblies of God. Judaism also took root from the very start of the country becoming populated. In addition, Jehovah's Witnesses, Mormons and Pentecostal churches are present. Islam slowly began to infiltrate the country with the passage of African traders, particularly from Senegal. However, the presence and influence of Islam remain very small, despite the close proximity of Mauritania and Senegal.

To conclude, Cape Verde, composed of 10 principal islands, is the smallest country in West Africa, and Christianity (especially Catholicism) features as the main religion. Its population, with a larger proportion living outside the country than within, constitutes its greatest resource, although it has yet to achieve its full potential. Despite the small population and its weak economy, the good husbandry exercised by the political classes in recent years has been worthy of recognition nationally and internationally. The Catholic Church's practice of permitting the clergy to marry presents a challenge to Christianity as a whole over the nature of clergy required by the church in Africa today.

## Conclusion

These are five countries where the experience of being a minority looms large in the life of Christian communities. For the most part, this is a matter of being Christian in predominantly Islamic societies but, even where Christians form a majority of the population, in Guinea-Bissau and Cape Verde, their Lusophone character makes them a minority in a predominantly Francophone and Anglophone region. Nonetheless, churches have been established and continue to consolidate and grow, despite setbacks. In a generally tolerant environment, Christians contribute to the social and political welfare of their nations. Constructive relationships with the Muslim community are key in this regard.

## Bibliography

Alokpo, Michel, *Va et raconte-leur! Histoire des Églises Protestantes et Evangéliques du Bénin: Annuaire Evangélique* (Cotonou: Nouvelle Presse Industries Graphiques, 2003).

Dossou, Simon K. (ed.), *Église et pouvoir politique en Afrique: Perspectives théologiques et historiques* (Yaoundé: Clé, 2013).

Phiri, Isabel Apawo and Dietrich Werner (eds), *Handbook of Theological Education in Africa* (Pietermaritzburg: Cluster Publications, 2013).

Sanneh, Lamin, *West African Christianity: The Religious Impact* (Maryknoll, NY: Orbis Books, 1990).

Université Protestante au Congo, *Revue Congolaise de théologie Protestante, églises de réveil: Défis messianiques et eschatologiques? Actes de la Conférence Internationale Organisée par l'Université Protestante au Congo et Protestant Theological University/Utrecht (Pays-Bas) de 12 au 16 Mai 2011, no. 21 Spécial 2012.*

# Niger, Mauritania, Mali, Chad and Burkina Faso

## Emmanuel Foro SJ

### Niger

The Niger Republic gained its independence from France in 1960. It remained politically unstable, however, until 2011, when a military coup brought the current President, Mahamadou Issoufou, to power, with renewed confirmation in 2016. The landlocked country is 1,267,000 km$^2$ in size, surrounded by Algeria, Benin, Burkina Faso, Chad, Libya, Mali and Nigeria. It is among the poorest countries in the world. The effects of the current economic crisis are apparent not only in rural areas but also in the capital city, Niamey, with its population of more than a million. A recent study by sociologist Ouassa Tiékoura has highlighted the effects of poverty on women forced into sex work as the only option for survival.

The peoples of Niger include Hausa, Zarma or Songhai, Tuareg, Fulani, Kanuri, Gurma, Arab and Tubu. Islam and African religion are strong within these ethnic groups and therefore it is not surprising that the population of Niger is predominantly Muslim. Christians form a small minority. The largest group among Christians is the Catholic Church, divided into two dioceses, Maradi and Niamey, the latter as Archdiocese. A large majority of the Christian population is from neighbouring countries like Burkina Faso, Nigeria and Benin, as well as expatriates from different backgrounds on mission in the country. In many ways, Niger is a 'new land' in terms of development, democracy and faith.

The Catholic Church traces its origins in Niger to 1931, when the Society of African Missions (SMA) began its work in the country. Niger

*Christianity in Niger, 1970 and 2015*

| | 1970 | | 2015 | | Average annual growth rate (%), 1970–2015 |
|---|---|---|---|---|---|
| Tradition | Population | % | Population | % | |
| Christians | 16,900 | 0.4% | 66,600 | 0.3% | 3.10% |
| *Roman Catholics* | 13,400 | 0.3% | 22,400 | 0.1% | 1.16% |
| *Independents* | 1,100 | 0.0% | 19,900 | 0.1% | 6.69% |
| *Protestants* | 2,500 | 0.1% | 23,900 | 0.1% | 5.19% |
| Pentecostals | 510 | 0.0% | 31,800 | 0.2% | 9.62% |
| Evangelicals | 2,400 | 0.1% | 22,100 | 0.1% | 5.02% |
| **Total population** | **4,497,000** | **100.0%** | **19,899,000** | **100.0%** | **3.36%** |

Source: Todd M. Johnson and Gina A. Zurlo (eds), *World Christian Database* (Leiden/Boston: Brill), accessed March 2016.

belongs to the Bishops' Conference of Burkina-Niger. The fourth and current Archbishop of Niamey is Laurent Lompo, who was consecrated in June 2015, the first indigenous citizen to hold this office. That same year, churches were vandalised in Niger because of an alleged offence to the image of the Prophet Mohammed. The second diocese is Maradi, located in the south of the country and headed since 2001 by Bishop Ambroise Ouédraogo. Despite the small number of faithful, Niger counts about 400 baptisms per year, spread around the 26 parishes, and several institutions run by the church. Some 10 schools and 20 health centres add to other forms of social assistance through the diocesan development offices and Caritas, the Catholic Church's development wing.

Cultural complexity can be identified as one of the main issues facing the church besides common challenges to human flourishing. Giving traditional beliefs a place in the life and worship of the church can lead to fears of syncretism. Yet either genuine inculturation or 'baptising heathen practices' is essential if the church is to find a future among the peoples of Niger. This necessary dialogue with local realities is of great relevance for the whole church. It also bears on the question of peaceful coexistence with Islam. Tensions between Muslims and Christians led to incidents of violence in January 2015 but, since then, leaders from both faiths have worked hard to achieve inter-communal harmony.

## Mauritania

The Islamic Republic of Mauritania (formerly known as Shenguet) – so self-proclaimed since 1958 – is a vast but thinly populated country covering 1,030,700 km$^2$. The country borders the Atlantic Ocean on its western side; Nouakchott is the capital city. Ethnic groups in Mauritania fall into three broad categories: Moors (Berbers and Arabs), Black Moors and African Blacks. The Almorabitoun, or people of the ribat, were founded in 1048 by the Sanhadja Berber Abdallah ibn Yassin in order to fight a religious war

*Christianity in Mauritania, 1970 and 2015*

| | 1970 | | 2015 | | Average annual growth rate (%), 1970–2015 |
|---|---|---|---|---|---|
| Tradition | Population | % | Population | % | |
| Christians | 6,200 | 0.5% | 10,000 | 0.2% | 1.08% |
| *Roman Catholics* | 6,200 | 0.5% | 5,000 | 0.1% | −0.46% |
| *Independents* | 0 | 0.0% | 2,300 | 0.1% | 12.90% |
| *Protestants* | 40 | 0.0% | 1,200 | 0.0% | 7.75% |
| *Anglicans* | 0 | 0.0% | 1,200 | 0.0% | 11.23% |
| Pentecostals | 0 | 0.0% | 2,600 | 0.1% | 13.16% |
| Evangelicals | 40 | 0.0% | 1,300 | 0.0% | 8.02% |
| **Total population** | **1,149,000** | **100.0%** | **4,068,000** | **100.0%** | **2.85%** |

Source: Todd M. Johnson and Gina A. Zurlo (eds), *World Christian Database* (Leiden/Boston: Brill), accessed March 2016.

(*jihad*) against the animist Wagadou, called by the name of their capital city in Ghana kingdom (also known as Kumbi Saleh) of the black Soninke people. The Berbers conquered Kumbi Saleh in 1076 and ruled only 11 years but achieved astounding success in the Islamisation of the whole region through their rulers. Successive struggles and conquests filled local history until the twentieth-century Western occupation. The area has known a very rich political and cultural history, partly because of its geographical location between the southern (darker skin) and the northern (lighter skin) sides of the continent.

Despite European contact as early as 1443, it was not until 1912 that French colonial rule began in Oualata, the capital city at that time. The habitual political struggles with this alien domination continued until national independence in 1960. In that sense, Mauritania was only ever superficially colonised. The Catholic population – in existence since 1965 and gathered in the single diocese of Nouakchott – forms a tiny minority of the population. Mauritania has fewer than 20 priests, some 40 religious and a few seminarians, all under Bishop A. Martin Happe of Nouakchott, a missionary of the White Fathers. The Protestant population is even smaller, with churches dispersed across the desert and mostly constituted by international workers and immigrants.

Islam dominates the religious life of the country and, indeed, it is often assumed that the entire population is Muslim; official figures indicate that the population is 100% Muslim.

Mauritanian Islam is almost entirely of the Sunni type, with the shari'a regulating all areas of domestic and public life in the country. The little church can express itself only through works of charity that revolve in large part around refugees. The local community recognises Caritas as a leading non-governmental organisation in the country. Because of the criminalisation of apostasy, recruitment of Mauritanian citizens to the Christian faith is not at all safe or legal, despite a general perception of acceptance by the Muslims. Currently, the churches tend to restrict their efforts to quietly influencing the cultural and intellectual life of the country and cultivating peaceful coexistence with their Muslim neighbours.

## Mali

All historical sources refer to the great classic on Mali, Abderhaman Es-Sâdi's *Tarikh es-Soudan* ('History of the Sudan' – Sudan was the name of the country before it became Mali in 1947). Mali is an ancient civilisation, going back to the legendary wisdom and riches of Mansa Kankan Moussa of Timbuktu (the cultural city of the Middle Ages), who made a pilgrimage to Mecca in 1325, impressing all on the way by his immense generosity with gold. Before Catholic missionaries arrived in 1895 through Ségou, the culture was already rich and diverse, with distinctive musical traditions and oral historians called *griots*. The Malian church, however, considers the foundation of Kita in 1888 as the beginning of Christianity in this area.

The modern state of Mali is vast, covering 1,240,000 km$^2$, sharing borders with Burkina Faso and Niger. Islam dominates, with Christians forming a small minority. The population comprises a variety of ethnic groups (with complex ramifications), including the Bambara, Malinke, Dioula, Senoufo, Sarakole, Songhaï, Dogon, Bobo and Tukulor. A substantial part of the country is in the Sahara Desert, while the south-western region is arable and irrigated by the River Niger, known locally as the Djoliba.

At the end of the nineteenth century, Christianity came to Mali through the work of the Missionaries of Africa (White Fathers) in Ségou and Timbuktu. Today, around two-thirds of the Christians in the country are Catholics, distributed among six dioceses gathered under a single ecclesiastical province and with Bamako the only archdiocese. The church is served by about 200 priests and more than 1,200 catechists, expecting about 4,000 baptisms per year. Self-sustenance and authentic Christian identity are works in progress.

Islam is not only the largest religion in Mali; it also directs the culture of the people. The admixture with traditional cultures gives the impression that massive syncretism rules the day within a context of general apathy concerning deep spiritual realities. Occasional consultation with a diviner or the wearing of a talisman is current practice. The traditional practice of polygamy, also accepted by Islam, orients men and women's relationships. Religious coexistence is generally peaceful outside of specific moments of tension, although there has been an escalation of Islamic extremism since 2013. Outright persecution is a recent phenomenon linked with Islamic radicalism coming from the north. The historical peaceful coexistence is now considered fragile.

Nonetheless, the church continues to grow, through a natural increase in the number of Christian families and inward migration of Christians from

*Christianity in Mali, 1970 and 2015*

| | 1970 | | 2015 | | Average annual growth rate (%), 1970–2015 |
|---|---|---|---|---|---|
| Tradition | Population | % | Population | % | |
| Christians | 85,200 | 1.4% | 527,000 | 3.0% | 4.13% |
| *Roman Catholics* | 60,700 | 1.0% | 411,000 | 2.3% | 4.34% |
| *Independents* | 320 | 0.0% | 17,400 | 0.1% | 9.31% |
| *Protestants* | 20,100 | 0.3% | 102,000 | 0.6% | 3.68% |
| Pentecostals | 45 | 0.0% | 31,600 | 0.2% | 15.68% |
| Evangelicals | 20,400 | 0.3% | 112,000 | 0.6% | 3.85% |
| **Total population** | **5,949,000** | **100.0%** | **17,600,000** | **100.0%** | **2.44%** |

Source: Todd M. Johnson and Gina A. Zurlo (eds), *World Christian Database* (Leiden/Boston: Brill), accessed March 2016.

elsewhere. Internally, the Malian church is vibrant, with beautiful rituals and devotional practices. It also boasts significant institutional strength, with various training centres, schools, health centres, pilgrimage centres, seminaries and developmental projects beneficial to all.

## Chad

Chad has a land area of 1,284,000 km$^2$ and is surrounded by the Central African Republic, Libya, Cameroon, Nigeria, Niger and Sudan. It is a landlocked country with Lake Chad as its main water resource. More than 120 languages are spoken among numerous ethnic groups, such as the Sara, Mayo-Kebbi, Kanem-Bornou, Ouaddai, Hadjarai, Tanjile, Gorane and Fitri-Batha. While the majority of the population are Muslim there is also a substantial and growing Christian presence. Reliable and universally agreed statistics are hard to come by and there is always controversy over any attempts to provide a precise breakdown of the religious affiliation of the population. N'Djamena, the capital city – known in colonial times as Fort Lamy – has a population of 1.26 million. Historically, it was a meeting point for Muslim pilgrims going to Mecca. The Fayçal Mosque stands today as a prestigious building in the city.

The political history of Chad was one of instability and civil wars until 1990, when the military installed the current President, Idriss Déby Itno, who has been recurrently confirmed in office since. Apart from the new extractive industries based in the south, Chad is essentially agricultural, with some pastoralists located in the north. Some 13 languages have been given official status and they are spoken across the 22 administrative regions. Chadian Arabic is the most common language, the language of trade and even, since 1982, the second national language alongside French.

In 1885 the Berlin Conference allocated Chad to France. The actual conquest, however, occurred only in 1920, although the records of the military *prouesses* of Colonel Étienne Largeau pre-date World War I. Chad remained a French colony until independence in 1960, with Fort-Lamy

*Christianity in Chad, 1970 and 2015*

| | 1970 | | 2015 | | Average annual growth rate (%), 1970–2015 |
|---|---|---|---|---|---|
| Tradition | Population | % | Population | % | |
| Christians | 843,000 | 23.1% | 4,939,000 | 35.2% | 4.01% |
| *Roman Catholics* | 231,000 | 6.3% | 2,154,000 | 15.3% | 5.09% |
| *Independents* | 36,900 | 1.0% | 667,000 | 4.8% | 6.64% |
| *Protestants* | 211,000 | 5.8% | 1,450,000 | 10.3% | 4.38% |
| Pentecostals | 12,100 | 0.3% | 896,000 | 6.4% | 10.05% |
| Evangelicals | 263,000 | 7.2% | 1,630,000 | 11.6% | 4.14% |
| **Total population** | **3,645,000** | **100.0%** | **14,037,000** | **100.0%** | **3.04%** |

Source: Todd M. Johnson and Gina A. Zurlo (eds), *World Christian Database* (Leiden/Boston: Brill), accessed March 2016.

in the west and Fort-Archambault (Sarh) in the south as its main cities. The French rulers contributed very little in terms of investment and development but churches did, and still do, contribute much to human flourishing in Chad.

Chad's first encounter with Christianity was in 1663, when a Franciscan group arrived in the country. However, they did not make any lasting impact. It was on the back of colonial power that the Roman Catholic Church established itself through the Holy Ghost Fathers in 1929. Two years earlier, in 1927, Protestant work had begun with the arrival of American Baptists.

Islam, the main religion, was introduced in the eleventh century and reached the status of state religion during the seventeenth century. The dominant type is Sunni (as in most West African countries). The whole northern region is basically Muslim, while the south has a more mixed religious complexion, including a significant Christian presence. The Baha'i faith and the Jehovah's Witnesses are minority religious communities. Traditional African religion is in evidence, particularly in the well structured life of the Sara people and also among many of the 200 ethnic groups in the country. The *yondo*, or initiation, of the Sara people is safeguarded by the Mbang of Bédaya. The first President of the country, François (N'Garta) Tombalbaye (in office from 1960 to 1975), was a fierce defender of this cultural heritage, of which many Chadians are proud today. He was also from the southern region favoured by the French and his rule was marked by French influence.

Many Protestant denominations, such as Lutheran, Evangelical, Baptist and United, have emerged since the first American Baptist mission started in 1927. On the Catholic side, the Jesuits have contributed immensely to the Chadian church since their first priest, Frédéric de Bélinay, arrived in Fort-Lamy in 1935. Catholics form the largest Christian group and are organised around seven dioceses and one apostolic vicariate (Mongo in the south-central region of Guéra). Under the eight bishops are 122 parishes, 265 priests (150 of whom are citizens), 385 religious (male and female) and around 7,000 committed lay ministers or catechists. The church runs two major seminaries for the training of priests, with about 100 seminarians. Philosophy is taught at Sarh and theology at Bakara in N'Djamena.

The contribution of churches to education is well known and highly appreciated in Chad. The Catholic Church alone runs more than 100 primary schools and 16 secondary schools countrywide. Church-sponsored schools rank high in terms of performance. For example, the Lycée du Sacré Coeur of N'Djamena and the Collège Charles-Lwanga of Sarh achieved outstanding results in 2015.

The Catholic Church holds great moral authority, although it is not highly engaged politically. In addition to its highly regarded schools, the church is a significant player in provision of health care. Christian churches provide around 20% of the health care nationwide through around 150 clinical centres, including at least eight hospitals and 10 homes for the needy, such as the elderly and orphaned children. Faith-based non-governmental organisations (NGOs) continue to introduce special educational projects, developmental initiatives, cultural and communication centres, and diverse services to refugees and displaced people, particularly in the most abandoned zones like the Guéra region. The university training and health centre Le Bon Samaritain in southern N'Djamena stands high among the various social works of the church in Chad. Géraud Magrin rightly argues that Christianity could be considered a parallel structure of governance and development of the country after presenting figures of church involvement in social progress in the educational, health and economic fields. These social initiatives express the vibrancy of the outworking of Catholic social teaching in Chad, an integral part of the mission entrusted by Christ, without eclipsing the spiritual dimension of evangelisation. No fewer than 20,000 baptisms are administered annually. Despite the above-mentioned ecclesial self-sufficiency, peaceful cooperation with political and administrative leaders is the hallmark of the Christian community in Chad.

The recent growth in material resources occasioned some mild and short-lived confrontation between church and state. Indeed, the cost of living increased because of the discovery of oil in the south, which affected all institutions, including schools. Salary increment is mandatory for teachers and new values creep in. The general issues of just distribution of proceeds from the oil business in Doba (southern Chad) caused some tension between the then-local bishop, Michele Russo, a Comboni missionary, and the Deby government. The prelate, Italian by birth, was expelled from the country in October 2012; he was readmitted some months later but resigned in 2014.

One of the most laudable initiatives of the churches has been the inter-religious and ecumenical dialogue spearheaded by the Christians but supported and animated by all religious communities. Protestants, Muslims and Catholics meet together on a rotational basis, thus creating a safer religious environment for all. Two centres for dialogue are functional in Chad. Bishop Henri Coudray, leader of the Catholic Church in Mongo and expert on Islamo-Christian dialogue, has played a leading role in developing this dialogue among Christians and between Christians and Muslims. It is a significant initiative, fostering hope for lasting peace.

## Burkina Faso

Located between Mali, Niger, Benin, Togo, Ghana and Côte d'Ivoire in West Africa, Burkina Faso is a predominantly agricultural society, with more than 60% of the population depending for their livelihood on subsistence agriculture and cattle. Known as Upper Volta until 1984, the country's first encounter with Christianity came in 1895, when a White Father missionary, Father Augustin Hacquard, came through Ségou and Timbuktu for a quick exploration. Father Guillaume Templier was the first to reside in Ouagadougou, followed by Father Johany Thévenoud, who became the first Bishop of Ouagadougou, in 1921.

The Catholic Church celebrated its local centenary in the year 2000. Christianity in the country is therefore relatively young. But it is vibrant. Catholicism leads the way in numbers and presence, although other churches, particularly the Assemblies of God, are having considerable success in evangelism in rural areas. The total number of priests is about 1,500 and of baptised Catholics approaching 3 million. Living side by side with Islam, African traditional religion and other confessional communities, Christians oscillate between syncretism and fundamentalist rejection of traditional cultures. Given that modern education has still not reached all parts of the country, ecumenism and dialogue with others is an enormous challenge. Good traditional social structures constitute the main guarantor of the apparent harmony that the churches of Burkina Faso enjoy among themselves and with other religious and philosophical groups. For this to be consolidated, however, will require more intentionality and deeper training in the faith. The Catholic bishops join with those of the dioceses in neighbouring Niger to constitute the Conference of Bishops of Burkina Faso and of Niger.

The early encounters of the missionaries with black Africans to the north had aroused suspicions that they lacked any real sense of religion and simply practised superstition without any deeper structure of belief. Gradually, however, the missionaries came to realise that the Africans among whom they were living were profoundly religious and guided by a tradition of faith in their journey through life. Burkina Faso (then with a mosaic of peoples) had first contact with Islam in 1458, when Timbuktu fell

*Christianity in Burkina Faso, 1970 and 2015*

| Tradition | 1970 Population | 1970 % | 2015 Population | 2015 % | Average annual growth rate (%), 1970–2015 |
|---|---|---|---|---|---|
| Christians | 523,000 | 9.3% | 4,223,000 | 23.3% | 4.75% |
| *Roman Catholics* | 416,000 | 7.4% | 2,576,000 | 14.2% | 4.13% |
| *Independents* | 7,100 | 0.1% | 88,800 | 0.5% | 5.79% |
| *Protestants* | 97,000 | 1.7% | 1,980,000 | 10.9% | 6.93% |
| Pentecostals | 89,100 | 1.6% | 2,033,000 | 11.2% | 7.20% |
| Evangelicals | 95,800 | 1.7% | 1,907,000 | 10.5% | 6.87% |
| **Total population** | **5,625,000** | **100.0%** | **18,106,000** | **100.0%** | **2.63%** |

Source: Todd M. Johnson and Gina A. Zurlo (eds), *World Christian Database* (Leiden/Boston: Brill), accessed March 2016.

to the Songhai Kingdom and people migrated through Yatenga Province in the north. However, the first mosque, in Ouahigouya, was not built until the nineteenth century.

The Mossi people make up around 40% of the population of Burkina Faso, with the remaining 60% comprising approximately 60 other ethnic groups. Most of the population, including the Mossi, migrated from Ghana, Mali or one of the fallen kingdoms of preceding eras. It is probably the peoples of the western part of the country, mainly the Bobo, who have the longest history in Burkina Faso.

Islam dominates the country numerically, although this is not always apparent, since the Christian community has benefited in the past from modern education and alignment with the colonial regime. Society, however, is marked by a symbiosis among confessional communities because of the great significance of the family in social relations. This allows space for the adherents of Christianity and African traditional religion to play a full part in the social life of the Burkinabè.

Burkina Faso has a land size of about 274,000 km$^2$. Its economy has been among the weakest of the world due to its geographical position and the situation of being landlocked between six neighbouring countries. Politically, the country has been very unstable since its independence from France in 1960. There have since been seven overthrows of government, with only two taking place through popular uprising, the rest being military and often leaving many citizens dead. Although analysts acclaim the Burkinabè rigour in managing their meagre resources, the country is not untroubled by corruption. Regional unrest has also affected Burkina Faso, most particularly the prolonged Ivorian disturbance in the early 2000s. More recently, the country has suffered the effects of terrorism, which infiltrated through neighbouring Mali and culminated in the January 2016 attack on Splendid Hotel in the capital city of Ouagadougou.

In terms of globalisation, Burkina Faso is dancing to the tune of the technological world, with its benefits and losses. Social structures are more fragile than hitherto and individual liberties and pursuits are gaining in acceptance. Most historical studies emphasise marriage customs and family structures that confer identity and role on individuals. Among the various ethnic groups, ancestral regulations allowed smooth collaboration while arbitrating free expression and exhibition of cultural differences. With Dubai, Beijing and Washington, DC, adding to the traditional European travel destinations, new initiatives are seen across the country, beginning with Ouagadougou, where business flourishes in various directions, and this has led to an increase in self-employment on the part of young graduates and merchants (both local and international). Technology and development may not be able to replace religion, but they contribute a good deal to people's self-perception and their perception of the surrounding world. In that sense, religion serves more and more personal purposes and this-worldly needs.

In Burkina Faso's 15 Catholic dioceses a great number of baptisms are performed every Easter. A city parish like the Cathedral of Ouagadougou presents well over 250 candidates for baptismal initiation every year. Most city parishes have added two or three Masses or enlarged their church building capacity to accommodate the faithful flocking to worship every weekend. Since 2010, around 90,000 catechumens have been selected for baptism nationwide. The rapidly growing population provides the context for such growth in membership of the church. Caritas, also known in Burkina Faso as Organisation Catholique pour le Développement et la Solidarité (OCADES), represents the social dimension of Catholic witness. Other churches offer education, health, communication, cultural or developmental support to the people alongside direct evangelisation.

Great piety and devotion in believers is evident all year round. Besides the Sunday liturgies, various groups meet according to their specific spiritualities: Marian, Social Action, Charismatic, friends of a particular saint or devotees of the souls in purgatory. Chapels and churches receive such groups on a daily basis. Islam contributed very positively to Catholic rediscovery and joy of praying publicly and regularly in Ouagadougou: Angelus is significantly observed with other public witnessing practices, also encouraged by Evangelical Christians, Pentecostals and the Revival Churches. Catholics hope to have Di Alfred Diban Ki-Zerbo, first catechist of the country, recognised one day among the blessed of God in heaven.

Local communities are increasingly financially self-sustaining – a positive sign of maturity of the Burkinabè church. Halls, shrines and places for pilgrimage are found in every diocese, meeting people's needs. There is also an increasing number of well trained laity demonstrating effective leadership and mature collaboration with clergy and religious in all fields of church life (among them more than 3,000 catechists distributed in the 160 parishes). About 90 priests from Burkina Faso currently serve various parishes in France. Neighbouring African countries, such as Mali, Chad and Niger, have also benefited from the *fidei donum* priests.

Notwithstanding many signs of vitality within Burkinabè Christianity, some significant challenges can be identified. The first comes from secretive and esoteric movements such as Freemasonry and Rosicrucianism, which are increasingly coming into the open and wielding influence in society. Much is said about the lobbying capacities and financial support that these exclusive groups offer to their members. These can easily become de facto religions for people concerned with achieving economic success and admission to circles of influence.

The second is that with the increase in awareness of religious identity have come pressures to adopt more radical forms of religion that could easily eclipse the cohesion enjoyed until now (with the exception of isolated occasional tensions related to public order). Missionaries from east and west nowadays introduce their adepts to new ideologies and proselytising rhetoric that is more grounded in political power and economic security than any spiritual concerns.

Thirdly, with the rise of egocentrism and the fragmentation of families, there is a risk that the ancestral value of great caution and slowness to reach irreversible decisions about fighting 'enemies' might be eroded. The warm and humorous relationships that have traditionally prevailed among the Burkinabè have made for a peaceful society and are well worth maintaining in the face of divisive forces that threaten social cohesion.

## Bibliography

Boulaga, Fabien Eboussi, *A contretemps: l'enjeu de Dieu en Afrique* (Paris: Karthala, 1991).

Compaoré, André Roch, *Politiques de Thomas Sankara et de Blaise Compaoré et enseignements de l'Église Catholique* (Paris: L'Harmattan, 2015).

Marie, Alain (ed), *L'Afrique des individus: itinéraire citadins dans l'Afrique contemporaine Abidjan, Bamako, Dakar, Niamey* (Paris: Karthala, 1997).

Vandame, Charles, *Cinquante ans de vie de l'Église Catholique au Tchad: Épreuves et espérance* (Paris: L'Harmattan, 2012).

Yanogo, Bernard-Désiré, *Église famille de Dieu au Burkina Faso: contribution théologique et perspectives pastorales* (Abidjan: Imprimob, 2005).

# Major Christian Traditions

# Anglicans

## James Tengatenga

It has been observed that the average Anglican today is a 30-year-old woman in Central Africa. The demographic centre of global Anglicanism has shifted to Africa. Of the 38 member churches (provinces) of the Anglican Communion, 12 are in Africa, including the provinces with the most members. It is estimated that about half of all Anglicans are in Africa. Anglicanism is, however, notably absent from some African countries, including most of the Sahara, although the Diocese of Egypt does serve some of the countries in the Maghreb.

Although 'African Anglicans' is an oxymoron, Christian Africans of the Anglican persuasion do not see it as such. They have transcended that image. Like most things in modern Africa (and indeed in Christianity over the ages) there has been appropriation and redemption of terms and concepts. Only in the Sudan and South Sudan is the denomination officially known with a different title: the Episcopal Church of Sudan and South Sudan. Linguistically, African Anglicanism, in addition to the plethora of local languages and dialects, speaks four international languages: Mozambique and Angola are Lusophone; the Great Lakes Region, Mauritius, Seychelles, and Madagascar are Francophone; Cameroon and some of West Africa are bilingual (Anglophone and Francophone); Egypt and the Maghreb use Arabic; the rest are Anglophone. South Africa has Afrikaans as well as English, while the Indian Ocean also uses Mauritian Creole. As is evident, this linguistic picture is in direct relationship with the colonial powers that once occupied the various parts of the continent. The church has become indigenous and is led by indigenes. Like other churches, it is growing, engaged ecumenically and coming to terms with the multi-faith context within which it works.

Africa has about 400 Anglican dioceses. In Anglican ecclesiology, the diocese, led by its bishop, is the basic unit of the church. The Anglican Communion, however, is organised in units called provinces, generally comprising at least four dioceses and led by a primate (who is also an archbishop). The intention is that a province corresponds to a single country, thus being the Anglican Church of that country. Seven current African provinces fulfil this criterion: Kenya, Tanzania, Uganda (each of which was formed in 1970), Nigeria (1979), Burundi, Congo and Rwanda (each formed in 1992). The rest are multinational provinces, including Southern Africa (Angola, Lesotho, Mozambique, Namibia, South Africa and Swaziland), formed in 1870; Central Africa (Botswana, Malawi, Zambia and Zimbabwe), 1955; the Indian Ocean (Madagascar, Mauritius, and Seychelles), 1973; the Sudan (Sudan and South Sudan), 1976; and West Africa (Cameroon, Gambia, Ghana, Liberia and Sierra Leone), 1979. With the gaining of national independence by many countries, a sense of a united African identity emerged in the provinces. This self-understanding was heralded at the inauguration of the Province of East Africa in 1960 in Uganda and actually became a reality in the formation of the Council of Anglican Provinces in Africa (CAPA) at Chilema Ecumenical Conference Centre in Malawi in 1979. Egypt has been part of the province that includes the Middle East and Cyprus but has always been considered part of Africa and hence has a place in the CAPA. With its responsibilities over Ethiopia and the Maghreb region, the Diocese of Egypt might become a province on its own and more identified with pan-African Anglicanism.

## History

African Anglicanism is a product of the missionary activities of the Church of England in the nineteenth century. It spread through the agency of the Society for the Propagation of the Gospel (SPG), the Church Missionary Society (CMS) and the Universities' Mission to Central Africa (UMCA), in cooperation with local evangelists and some collaboration with the Congregationalist London Missionary Society (LMS). The established status of the Church of England tended to be replicated in some form in the mission field. The British Empire went together with mission, even though the two were distinct and were quite often in conflict. As in many parts of the Empire, the leadership of the church was by bishops of English stock, who tended to be alumni of the Oxbridge universities. In most of Southern Africa, Anglican mission followed the trailblazing work of David Livingstone. In West Africa it followed the traders and was augmented by the establishment of Sierra Leone and Liberia as states for freed American slaves.

*Anglicans in Sub-Saharan Africa, 1970*

| Region | Total population | Christian population | Anglican population | % of region Anglican | % of Christians Anglican |
|---|---|---|---|---|---|
| *Eastern Africa* | 110,428,000 | 54,913,000 | 3,102,000 | 2.8% | 5.7% |
| *Middle Africa* | 40,846,000 | 29,888,000 | 102,000 | 0.3% | 0.3% |
| *Southern Africa* | 25,454,000 | 19,291,000 | 1,347,000 | 5.3% | 7.0% |
| *Western Africa* | 106,015,000 | 30,143,000 | 3,085,000 | 2.9% | 10.2% |
| Sub-Saharan Africa | 282,743,000 | 134,235,000 | 7,635,000 | 2.7% | 5.7% |
| Globe | 3,682,488,000 | 1,230,688,000 | 47,408,000 | 1.3% | 3.9% |

Source: Todd M. Johnson and Gina A. Zurlo (eds), *World Christian Database* (Leiden/Boston: Brill), accessed March 2016.

Generally speaking, this missionary activity was based on the mission theory called manifest destiny. Developments in Europe in the immediate post-Enlightenment and Industrial Revolution period led Europeans to believe that they had a mission to save the world and that cultural and industrial development would help in the Christianising enterprise. Although the LMS was ecumenical rather than Anglican, it was instrumental in the spread of Anglicanism in Sub-Saharan Africa. It was David Livingstone, the noted Congregationalist LMS missionary, who made the famous call to the British church to bring 'Christianity, Commerce and Civilisation' to Southern Africa. In response to this call, the UMCA was formed, and it evangelised Tanzania and Malawi and parts of the Indian Ocean, which in turn influenced the CMS to come to East Africa and the Indian Ocean. The Province of Nigeria was the product of the CMS and the Province of West Africa that of the SPG. The UMCA and the SPG were of the Anglo-Catholic tradition, while the CMS was of the Evangelical tradition in the Church of England. The UMCA and SPG later joined to become the United Society for the Propagation of the Gospel (USPG), which has since morphed into the United Society (US). Much of the growth of the church, however, came through local agency, the most famous example being the East African Revival, which spawned indigenous evangelists who took the gospel all over East Africa and the Congo.

## Intra-Church

### *Women*

Women in Africa make up the majority of churchgoers. It is estimated that 75% of any congregation is made up of women. They organise themselves in many guilds. The most famous women's organisation (and very often the most powerful at a local level) is the Mothers' Union. It provides the iconic picture of the sea of blue-and-white-clad women (black and white for those from Southern Africa) seen at Anglican gatherings. Begun in the UK in 1876 by Mary Sumner, its initial mission was to minister to young married women with children. It has now grown into a ministry of and for women, focusing on the family. In recent years African Anglican

*Anglicans in Sub-Saharan Africa, 2015*

| Region | Total population | Christian population | Anglican population | % of region Anglican | % of Christians Anglican |
|---|---|---|---|---|---|
| *Eastern Africa* | 394,477,000 | 259,865,000 | 29,915,000 | 7.6% | 11.5% |
| *Middle Africa* | 151,952,000 | 125,422,000 | 625,000 | 0.4% | 0.5% |
| *Southern Africa* | 62,634,000 | 51,611,000 | 3,078,000 | 4.9% | 6.0% |
| *Western Africa* | 353,224,000 | 127,638,000 | 22,363,000 | 6.3% | 17.5% |
| Sub-Saharan Africa | 962,287,000 | 564,536,000 | 55,982,000 | 5.8% | 9.9% |
| Globe | 7,349,472,000 | 2,416,268,000 | 90,697,000 | 1.2% | 3.8% |

Source: Todd M. Johnson and Gina A. Zurlo (eds), *World Christian Database* (Leiden/Boston: Brill), accessed March 2016.

women in the diaspora are reinvigorating the movement in the UK, and some are beginning branches in the USA. In its own way it has become an empowerment movement for women. Other uniformed groups also exist; most recently the Daughters of the King (an American-founded organisation, 1885) has taken root. In addition to groups for adult women, there are various organisations for girls, such as the St Agnes Guild in Central Africa. Most of the church's work in the empowerment of women and literacy is carried out through these organisations. Their basic tenets relate to spirituality, evangelism and service, albeit approached and emphasised differently by each guild.

Anglican understanding in Africa (as everywhere) is that all the baptised are ministers by virtue of their baptism. As such, there are lay women leaders in the councils of the church and in other pastoral and liturgical ministries. Given the shortage of clergy in many dioceses, it is not uncommon for the lay leadership (and thus non-sacramental liturgical leadership) to be by women. This prevalence of women in the church, however, has not always translated into female leadership in the sacramental (ordained) ministry. Like most of the Anglican Communion, the churches in Africa have been challenged over the ordination of women. Each province has had to deal with the matter as it arose and one by one they have been accepting it. Some, like West Africa and Tanzania, have resolved to let individual dioceses that are ready to ordain women do so. Others, notably Nigeria and Central Africa, do not yet permit the ordination of women.

The Anglican Church of Southern Africa has taken the lead in Africa by ordaining the first and second women into the episcopate, namely Bishops Ellinah Wamukoya of Swaziland and Margaret Vertue of False Bay (South Africa). There has been some robust discussion of women in the episcopate in Kenya but no agreement has yet been reached. Whether this development and the recent ordination of the first female bishop in the Church of England will have a domino effect remains to be seen. Although the church in Africa is autonomous, what happens in the Church of England does have both a direct and an indirect influence on it.

*Changes in Anglicans in Sub-Saharan Africa, 1970–2015, growth rate, % per year*

| Region | Total population | Christian population | Anglican population |
|---|---|---|---|
| *Eastern Africa* | 2.87% | 3.52% | 5.17% |
| *Middle Africa* | 2.96% | 3.24% | 4.11% |
| *Southern Africa* | 2.02% | 2.21% | 1.85% |
| *Western Africa* | 2.71% | 3.26% | 4.50% |
| Sub-Saharan Africa | 2.76% | 3.24% | 4.53% |
| Globe | 1.55% | 1.51% | 1.45% |

Source: Todd M. Johnson and Gina A. Zurlo (eds), *World Christian Database* (Leiden/Boston: Brill), accessed March 2016.

Disagreement about women in the ordained ministry, and especially the episcopate, can play havoc with church partnership relationships. Although many dioceses and provinces that do not ordain women have links with dioceses that do, it seems not to have affected those relationships. Generally, the women are permitted to wear clerical vestments, process and preach but not to celebrate the sacraments. It does, however, raise a theological anomaly as it calls into question the validity and transitivity of ministry as understood in the Anglican Communion. It makes for a theological conundrum begging resolution.

### *Youth*

Africa has a young population. It is estimated that over 65% of the population is under 35 years of age. The challenge is that the church is still organised primarily for adults. The Anglican Church is learning to respond to the needs of the younger group, however. 'Praise groups' who sing rousing contemporary tunes during worship have been widely introduced. Young people carry out much of the evangelistic outreach, with their choirs and market preaching. Nevertheless, older responses to the needs of the young are still being employed to good effect. By and large, the Boy Scout movement has moved out of the church, but the Boys' Brigade and Girls' Brigade are growing in many parts of the African church. In addition, traditional youth gatherings and residential conferences continue to thrive. Yet although the church is full of young people, there are still many who are unchurched or leaving the mainline churches for the new Evangelical and Pentecostal movements and a few to secularism. The Anglican Church will need to find a way of stemming this movement before the age demographic changes.

### *Men*

Generally, men have seen themselves as the ones who run the church. They are the clergy, elders and church councillors even though they are few in number in relation to women, children and youth. The Brotherhood of St Andrew was established to help men participate in evangelising fellow men. In some places this movement has taken root, but in many places it has not. In South Africa, Mozambique and Zimbabwe, the Order of Bernard Mizeki is a growing movement. Iviyo is another South African movement, similar to the Balokole of the East African Revival; the Balokole have been key players in the evangelisation of East Africa and the Great Lakes Region. In some countries there are no specific names for men's fellowships but they are a growing phenomenon. In Zimbabwe, Anglicans borrowed from the Methodists the Wabvuwi movement. This is a movement of men committed to evangelism and service. It has now spread to Malawi.

Following the model of the Mothers' Union, some parts of Africa have established the Fathers' Union. These are lay-led initiatives of revival and renewal, and service to the church and community, which are helping in churching the unchurched and reviving lukewarm and lapsed men.

### *Religious Orders*

Beyond the faithful pilgrimage of the laity and the clergy, there is a thriving male and female religious life. Found mainly in Anglo-Catholic provinces, there are both home-grown orders and those originating in the USA and the UK. Tanzania, Malawi and Zambia have only female orders, while elsewhere there are both male and female. The order in Zambia is an extension of the Tanzanian Chama cha Mariam Mtakatifu (Community of St Mary). They were founded under the Community of the Sacred Passion (UK based) but later became an independent order. The Community of St Mary in Malawi is part of the Community of St Mary (Eastern Province) based in the USA. The Order of the Holy Paraclete is found in Ghana, Swaziland and the UK. Swaziland, Lesotho and South Africa also have the Community of the Holy Name, which is part of the community of the same name in the UK. Lesotho, in addition, has two other orders: the Society of the Precious Blood (also found in South Africa) and the Society of the Sacred Mission (also in South Africa, the UK and Australia). The other orders found in South Africa are the Community of Jesus' Compassion, the Community of the Resurrection of Our Lord, the Community of St Michael and All Angels, the Society of St John the Divine, the Order of the Holy Cross (which is also found in the USA and Canada) and the Oratory of the Good Shepherd. Zimbabwe has Chita Chezita Rinoyera (Community of the Holy Name), the Community of the Blessed Lady Mary, Chita Che Zvipo Zve Moto (Community of the Gifts of Fire) and the Community of the Holy Transfiguration. In Madagascar there is Fikambaban'ny Mpanompovavin I Jesus Kristy (Society of the Servants of Jesus Christ). There is a growing membership of the tertiary Order of the Society of St Francis.

### *Renewal and Revival*

Following the Decade of Evangelism in the 1990s there has been a renewal of faith and desire to evangelise. A key African figure in this was Cyril Okorocha, who headed the Anglican Communion Office department for the Decade. His current successor in that office is another African, John Kafwanka. One of the by-products of the Decade is the renewal and charismatic movement called Sharing of Ministries Abroad (SOMA). This movement uses parish and diocesan links in Africa and in the UK and the USA. It has mobilised the faithful into living into the baptismal covenant and experiencing and using the gifts of the Spirit. Many of these teams regularly work in East, Central and Southern Africa. Southern Africa has taken the lead in some aspects of this ministry in organising international renewal and training conferences.

Yet another evangelism body is the Church Army, a uniformed organisation of both male and female officers commissioned for evangelism that grew out of the ministry in the UK. It is a major movement in East Africa but is less known in other parts of the continent. Through a training school (Carlile College) in Nairobi, Kenya, they train lay evangelists and urban lay ministers for today's African cities.

Chaplaincies are also part of the ministry of the church. Strictly speaking, they are pastoral rather than evangelistic. As is only logical, the church has chaplains in the many schools, colleges and hospitals that it runs. In addition, it has chaplains in secular and state institutions such as the police services, prisons and the armed forces.

### *Contextualisation/Inculturation*

Another challenge to Anglicanism is that of inculturation. In a real sense, African Anglicans are the Church of England in Africa. Shaking off the Englishness of its traditions and rituals has been a long process and is still in progress. Many attempts have been made to work out what this might look like beyond vesture and music. The church still has Western-style vestments, albeit increasingly depicting African theological symbols. The Provinces of West Africa and Southern Africa have given a lead. Music has also come a long way but there is more to be done to move beyond translations of the *Church Hymnal* and *Hymns Ancient and Modern*. African tunes and locally composed lyrics are slowly gaining pride of place in the regular church repertoire. More inculturation is found in the informal services, funerals, outdoor services and events than in the regular church services. There is also a tentative movement towards adapting theological language and idiom. Theological education has yet to catch up with all these trends but is taking tentative steps.

Liturgical revision is proceeding only slowly. Apart from the fact that the service is in local languages and whatever colonial language was present, liturgy does not reflect much of the local cultures. Kenya attempted the exercise once and now includes local cultural idiom, but the inculturation is only partial. Southern Africa has tried, but its liturgy still sounds very Western. Anglicanism needs to work further on this frontier for it to reflect its African-ness in the light of its principle of *lex orandi, lex credendi* ('the law of praying is the law of believing' – that is, what the church does in worship reflects its true beliefs). It seems that Western missionaries understood this need more than post-colonial Anglicans. Some, like Bishop Colenso of Zululand in the nineteenth century, risked being misconstrued. This appropriation and adaptation of African cultures needs to go further for African Anglicanism to influence and benefit global Anglicanism.

Despite this slow progress on inculturation, Anglican theologians have made significant contributions to the pan-African theological discourse on Christianity and African-ness. There is no bigger name in this than John Mbiti of Kenya. Ghanaian John Pobee and Kenyan Jesse Mugambi have also made significant contributions to this discourse and have led the discussion on what an African Christian theology would be like. Desmond Tutu of South Africa and David Gitari of Kenya have made contributions not only to the African-ness question but also to issues of church and state, and faith and society, in Africa. These contributions are significant not only within Anglicanism but also for the African *oecumene*.

### *The Sexuality Question*

The ordination of homosexual people and the blessing of their unions in some parts of the Anglican Communion have caused some anxiety. The multiplicity of provinces and contexts leads to a diversity of responses. Statements have been made about the so-called African position. Does such a position exist? Some have simplistically divided the African positions on this matter between the CMS- and SPG-founded churches. There is some truth in this division, but it is not entirely accurate. It is not true, as some have wanted to claim, that there is no homosexuality in Africa. What is true is that it receives different responses in different places. Generally speaking, the historic attitude has been 'don't ask, don't tell, but we know, and it's okay'. As long as homosexuality was in the closet it was fine – or, more accurately, a non-issue. Secular political pressure from the West rubbing against national self-determination and sovereignty created an explosive situation. This pressure, coupled with strident Western individualism, elicited a post-colonial backlash. African societies have generally found ways of dealing with out-of-the-ordinary behaviours and tendencies, and these are markedly different from the Western ways. Undeniably, there is a conservative evangelical outlook to African Anglican responses. The fact that there is a turf war and religious struggle between Christians and Muslims does not make matters any easier and invariably leads to categorical positions being espoused and pronounced.

Uganda is a microcosm of this situation. In addition, Ugandans find themselves faced with the dilemma of being generous to an attitude to homosexuality that would make nonsense of their venerated martyrs. Southern Africa, on the other hand, with its multiple voices and recent history of human rights battles, presents a different attitude – there is toleration more than there is agreement. Most of the provinces fall between these two scenarios. One cannot be oblivious to the muddying of the waters (if not a hijacking of the process) by an American coalition, which has inevitably raised the age-old question of Christ and culture as well as the role of the Bible, which has to be faced rationally. Even though, in answering that question, there may be some commonalities between some Americans and Africans, there is definitely a distinctly African answer (perhaps more correctly 'answers'), which is yet to be heard. A significant voice in the more evangelical and conservative stance in response to this situation is that of the Global Anglican Future Conference (GAFCON), which has a significant African contingent.

Although a pan-African answer has been attempted, to date it has proved elusive. Primates have issued statements that have not always been representative of their provinces and have masked the real dilemmas therein. The Council of Anglican Provinces in Africa has been used in trying to formulate a position, but that has not worked well. The South-to-South relations encouraged in the wake of the Partnership in Mission era of the 1980s morphed into the Global South agglomeration. An attempt has been made to use it to formulate a bigger-than-pan-African position. This, too, has been fraught with the difficulty of opening up a theological question that needs a post-colonial theological response. A good and appropriate possibility has been created through the *Indaba,* a process that has been adopted by the Anglican Communion from a Zulu concept (*baraza* in KiSwahili and *padare* in chiShona). It is an intense and honest (no-holds-barred) discourse, discussion and debate leading to denouement. It has the potential to spawn new theological language and solutions to this conundrum. This is not a uniquely Anglican question. It is a question for the *oecumene*. One would (presumptuously, perhaps) wonder whether there is a vicariousness in this development and if so whether African Anglicans will rise to the occasion.

Mutual coexistence seems to be prevailing. This development in many ways belies the strident separatist diatribes that appear in the news. Part of the reason is that there is a soul to the Anglican Communion that binds Anglicans of all persuasions together. The common name for it is 'bonds of affection', and it incorporates the African 'I am because we are and we are because I am'. This is why the situation is so fraught. Even when parts of the Communion differ in their positions there is a tendency not to break Communion. *Koinonia* is important to Anglicans – almost to a fault. The web of relationships makes it nonsense to claim broken Communion with one or the other. Space does not allow for a detailed discussion of this point, but suffice it to say that within Anglicanism it seems that the more one wants out, the more one wants in! African Anglicanism needs to move beyond simplistic post-colonial diatribe and pride in numbers to informed and robust theological discourse that goes beyond adapted

African cultural clichés. One challenge facing African Anglicans in this respect is that of coming to terms with a positive outlook to African-ness, beyond the negative caricature of the social Darwinism of yesteryear into which they were socialised. Theological discourse is not the monopoly of the West. African Anglican theological colleges and universities would serve the Communion more if this discourse were to be taken up without undue interference from the church hierarchy.

### Inter-church

The Anglican Church is engaged in ecumenical life on the continent. It has been a founding member of most, if not all, of the national councils of churches. All provinces are members of the All Africa Conference of Churches (AACC) and the World Council of Churches (WCC). One of the weaknesses in the African Anglican churches' engagement in ecumenism is that there are very few local dialogues towards unity. African Anglicans tend to be involved only in the international Anglican dialogues with others, which has led to interesting international relationships like the one that obtains in the wake of the Porvoo (Europe), Canadian and US Anglican–Lutheran agreements. African Anglicans find themselves both united with and alienated from their Lutheran friends. When members of both traditions arrive in the Nordic countries and North America they live within the local concordats, but once back home they are strangers, working together only in the councils of churches and the Good Friday *Via Dolorosa*. There is a diversity of how Anglicans and other denominations work together. More local dialogues need to take place. This lack is not unique to Anglicans. This vestige of the mission scramble for Africa needs attention in post-colonial Africa. Given the bridging role local Anglican churches tend to play in the various countries, this should not be a tall order. Since African Initiated Churches (AICs) do not exist in other parts of the Communion, the African churches will need to take the initiative in this dialogue. Africans will do well to initiate and engage in dialogues towards full organic and visible unity. It is hoped that increased participation in the Inter-Anglican Standing Commission on Unity, Faith and Order will translate into local African dialogues. The current chair of this body is the Archbishop of Burundi.

### Inter-faith

Another challenge for the Anglican Church in Africa is that of inter-faith dialogue, which has three trajectories. The first is that with Islam. Many countries long maintained a 'live and let live' stance, a kind of mutual respect and acceptance. In countries like Malawi, Mozambique and Tanzania, relations were very good (albeit a little competitive), to the extent that Anglican leadership, during colonial times, would be called upon to interpret Islam to the colonial powers. However, the rise of the 'petrodollar' from the Middle East since the mid-1970s and an evangelistic, radical and militarised Islam has turned the tables. Tensions and violence are found in Tanzania, Kenya, the Sudan, Egypt and Nigeria. The militarisation of Islam has meant that dialogue is nearly impossible in some parts. This development has not stopped Anglicans engaging with Islam. From the very beginning of the Programme for Christian and Muslim Relations in Africa (PROCMURA), Anglicans have been involved and continue to be engaged. Unfortunately, the current troubles in the Sudan, Nigeria and lately Kenya, which are mirrored in smaller ways in other parts of Africa, are increasing the tension and threatening the possibility of dialogue.

The second trajectory is that between Christianity and African traditional religions, which has been a challenge from the beginning of missions. By and large, Anglican attitudes were shaped by missionary attitudes, which were generally negative or at best ambivalent. Like other Christian traditions with roots in the West, Anglicans continue the struggle of taking local cultures seriously, building on them and, where need be, challenging the evils therein.

The third and least apparent one is the challenge of a growing secularism leading to atheism. Growing affluence (and Westernisation) and cynicism over the growing pentecostal/prophetic/signs-and-wonders manifestations of Christianity is threatening the Christian landscape. It is not yet clear how Anglicans are responding here. The work of Sharing of Ministries Abroad and similar organisations is part of the response, but whether it will stem that tide is yet to be seen.

## Church, Society and State

The relationship of the Anglican Church on the continent to slavery is conflicted but, by and large, positive. The establishment of Liberia and Sierra Leone was a sign of new existence in the aftermath of slavery. Some freed slaves from the West Indian plantations came over to minister to fellow freed slaves. It is from among these that some of the early leadership of the church came (e.g. Philip Quaque and Samuel Ajayi Crowther). The imposing slave castles of Ghana continue as a reminder of this history. Luanda was the western exit for the trade by the Portuguese in the central part of Africa between Mozambique and Angola. At David Livingstone's invitation the UMCA was established to respond to the slave trade in Malawi and Mozambique and later in Tanzania. When the mission was aborted to regroup in Zanzibar, some of the slaves under their care were left in Malawi, others they took with them to Zanzibar and yet others they took to Cape Town. Thus the Diocese of Cape Town was brought into the service of the freed slaves. The diocesan orphanage and school at Woodstock became home to them.

Bishop Tozer built the cathedral in Zanzibar on top of the slave market. Many rescued slaves were trained as teachers and evangelists and formed the first cohort of indigenous clergy. Leonard Kamungu, who later helped evangelise eastern Zambia with Bishop Hornby, was one such slave from Malawi. The story of Bagamoyo on the Tanzanian shore speaks volumes, in the same way that the story of the Ghanaian castles speaks in relation to the Americas. Some of these former slaves became the core teams that helped not only the UMCA in Malawi, Mozambique and Tanzania but also the CMS missionaries in Kenya and Uganda. The missionaries in East and Central Africa were thus part of the on-the-ground forces for the abolition of slavery that was being championed by William Wilberforce and others in the British Parliament. Not knowing what to do with the slaves they intercepted in the Indian Ocean, the British Navy settled them in Madagascar, Mauritius and the Seychelles. In the Seychelles, a school and village named after Henry Venn, the CMS General Secretary, were established for them. This antislavery stance continues to inspire later generations of indigenous Anglicans in their involvement in today's struggle against slavery, human trafficking and violations of human rights.

In addition to work in education, health and development, the Anglican Church is also involved in disaster relief and refugee work. Its leadership is involved in peace and reconciliation work. Bishop Dinis Sengulane has championed the cause of peace in Mozambique; among his many initiatives is the 'swords into ploughshares' scheme, in which he was disarming the militarised population. Janani Luwum was martyred for standing up to the dictator Idi Amin in Uganda. Archbishop David Gitari and Bishop Henry Okullu have borne witness to human rights and good governance in Kenya. Archbishop Desmond Tutu and his successors have stood with the people under all sorts of oppression and led South Africa to freedom, reconciliation and peace. Archbishop Daniel Deng Bul Yak of the church in the two Sudans has been involved in brokering peace in those countries. Archbishop Bernard Ntahoturi is deputy leader of the National Peace and Reconciliation initiative in Burundi. Not a few leaders have suffered for their witness in troubled countries. The Bishops of Kano and Jos have suffered under the situation in northern Nigeria. Justice, peace, truth and ministry to the whole person are ways in which Anglican witness is carried out in obedience to, and participation in, the *missio Dei*.

## Conclusion

Anglicans in Africa are a growing and indigenous church in leadership, worship and witness as much as they are part of a world communion.

Theological articulation in African idiom continues to be a frontier they strive to cross as they contribute to international theological discourse in the one, holy catholic and apostolic church. Engagement in society and state, and ecumenical and inter-faith initiatives are integral to the witness of the Anglican Church across Sub-Saharan Africa today.

## Bibliography

Gish, Steven D., *Desmond Tutu: A Biography* (Westport, CT: Greenwood Biographies, 2004).

Gitari, David, *Anglican Liturgical Inculturation in Africa: The Kanamai Statement 'African Culture and Anglican Liturgy'* (Piscataway, NJ: Gorgias Liturgical Studies, 2010).

Lindsay, Ross, *Out of Africa: The Breakaway Anglican Churches* (Maitland, FL: Xulon Press, 2011).

Pobee, John S., *Invitation to be an African Anglican* (Accra: Asempa Publishers, 2000).

Ward, Kevin, *A History of Global Anglicanism* (Cambridge: Cambridge University Press, 2006).

# Independents

## Nicta Lubaale

The African Independent Churches (AICs) are a heterogeneous community of churches, widely spread across Sub-Saharan Africa. The late nineteenth century and early twentieth century was the founding period of the AICs. This was a time when Africa was going through social, political and economic change. Colonialism was taking root across the continent. The mission-founded churches were spreading and in many cases were interlinked with the political interests of the countries of origin of the missionaries. The AICs attempted to bring a different mode of doing mission. Using the resourcefulness of Africa, they emerged onto the landscape with clarity regarding the *imago Dei*. Their understanding of the self-actualisation of God in the African changed the perception of the Christian message. This was shaped by the development by the original AIC communities of 'founding visions' – a term used by AIC scholars today for how the AIC founders believed themselves called to live and act in a world caught between traditional values and culture and those of the colonising society, and the result of a process of profound reflection on these realities interpreted through the light of the Christian Scriptures. In this chapter I focus on three AICs and how they have continuously engaged with the founding visions of their churches as they interact with the contemporary mission environment – Christ Holy Church International in Nigeria, West Africa; the Holy Spirit Church of East Africa in Kenya, East Africa; and the Zion Christian Church in Zimbabwe, Southern Africa. These are all 'Spiritual' churches, representing the largest and most numerous group of AICs founded during the first part of the twentieth century.

### Common Traits

AICs in general affirm the place and value of African culture in the mission of God and build the confidence of Africans as a people whose culture can contribute to the extension of the Kingdom of God. The type of AICs called Spiritual churches are sometimes referred to as prophet(ic) churches. They emphasise the gifts of the Holy Spirit, reflected in prophecy, healing ministries and lengthy prayer services. The Spiritual churches:

- responded to cultural domination by defending the integrity of African values

- responded to colonial domination by means of prayer and prophecy – an approach different from that of another kind of AICs, the Nationalist churches
- emphasised the role of the Holy Spirit in the church and wider society – evaluating changes from a spiritual perspective and offering spiritual responses
- emphasised their shared priesthood in Christ.

In West Africa they are known as the Aladura churches, in East Africa they are referred to as Roho or Akorinu churches, while in Southern Africa they are known as Zionist and Apostolic churches.

The Spiritual churches' approach to mission is based on a deep sense of social consciousness that developed during the founding era of AICs and that has enabled them to work from a holistic understanding of the mission of God. This included confronting the difficult issues around cultural, political and economic domination during the colonial era. Prophecy was used in the founding era and is still used in the twenty-first century as a major means of galvanising the AICs, especially of the Spiritual tradition, to respond to issues within the church and wider society.

These churches redefined priesthood in the church and community as Africans came into leadership of the church and as the empowerment the Holy Spirit gives to the church for the priesthood of all was recognised and brought to the surface. Common people – peasant farmers, factory workers and labourers in commercial agricultural – moved into leadership. Some became the heads of churches. These characteristics continue today. The other key trait of AICs is the participation of women in the priesthood. This is done both through ordained women leaders, who comprise a small part of the priesthood, and also through the much larger numbers who exercise their influence through prayer, prophecy and visions and in this way play a major role in directing the affairs of the churches.

The AICs read the Bible and engage with it from within the thought patterns and presuppositions of their local settings rather than through thought patterns imposed from the West. From the Scriptures they

*Independents in Sub-Saharan Africa, 1970*

| Region | Total population | Christian population | Independent population | % of region Independent | % of Christians Independent |
|---|---|---|---|---|---|
| *Eastern Africa* | 110,428,000 | 54,913,000 | 4,377,000 | 4.0% | 8.0% |
| *Middle Africa* | 40,846,000 | 29,888,000 | 5,330,000 | 13.1% | 17.8% |
| *Southern Africa* | 25,454,000 | 19,291,000 | 4,958,000 | 19.5% | 25.7% |
| *Western Africa* | 106,015,000 | 30,143,000 | 5,102,000 | 4.8% | 16.9% |
| Sub-Saharan Africa | 282,743,000 | 134,235,000 | 19,767,000 | 7.0% | 14.7% |
| Globe | 3,682,488,000 | 1,230,688,000 | 96,373,000 | 2.6% | 7.8% |

Source: Todd M. Johnson and Gina A. Zurlo (eds), *World Christian Database* (Leiden/Boston: Brill), accessed March 2016.

developed a narrative hermeneutic and an oral theology that related to the realities that affected their communities. After realising that hymns and other liturgical forms from the Western context (even after translation into local languages) imposed alien cultural or philosophical frameworks, AICs went ahead to compose hymns that told the gospel story from their own perspective and also introduced local rhythms as they brought the African drum and other instruments into church worship. This opened space for Africans to compose songs freely, contributing to the shared priesthood. Participants in the worship service bring a song relating to the issues that emerge in a worship service as people share their testimonies, dreams, Scriptures and prophecy.

AICs bring people at the outskirts of society into the mission of God. They have developed competencies in building communities of missioners in what are sometimes referred to as difficult contexts. Serving in the informal urban settlements, for example, is not a sacrifice to the AICs. It is a way of life lived by the missioners in appreciation of the resourcefulness God has given to them to serve in such environments. Migrant workers still continue to play a major role in starting churches within and across countries. The effect of practising mission in this way is the presence of Christian communities who care for each other and celebrate life together in difficult circumstances. In similar ways, members of AICs are continuing to plant churches in Europe and the USA. The initiative is usually taken by members who are in these regions as students and migrant workers.

## Christ Holy Church International: The Founding Vision and Social Consciousness

Christ Holy Church International (CHCI), a large AIC in Nigeria, was founded by a woman, Prophetess Agnes Okoh, who received the calling in 1943 but started her ministry in 1947 at Onitsha in the Anambra State in south-east Nigeria. Agnes Okoh was a rural woman who could not read or write and had been widowed at an early age. In distress she found comfort in prayer and in listening to the Scriptures as the Bible was read to her.

*Independents in Sub-Saharan Africa, 2015*

| Region | Total population | Christian population | Independent population | % of region Independent | % of Christians Independent |
|---|---|---|---|---|---|
| *Eastern Africa* | 394,477,000 | 259,865,000 | 30,641,000 | 7.8% | 11.8% |
| *Middle Africa* | 151,952,000 | 125,422,000 | 25,904,000 | 17.1% | 20.7% |
| *Southern Africa* | 62,634,000 | 51,611,000 | 24,352,000 | 38.9% | 47.2% |
| *Western Africa* | 353,224,000 | 127,638,000 | 42,306,000 | 12.0% | 33.2% |
| Sub-Saharan Africa | 962,287,000 | 564,536,000 | 123,202,000 | 12.8% | 21.8% |
| Globe | 7,349,472,000 | 2,416,268,000 | 419,897,000 | 5.7% | 17.4% |

Source: Todd M. Johnson and Gina A. Zurlo (eds), *World Christian Database* (Leiden/Boston: Brill), accessed March 2016.

The church she founded focused on proclaiming the gospel, emphasising holiness, healing and enabling people to overcome the powers of evil. Prophetess Agnes Okoh ministered as an itinerant evangelist in various states of Nigeria, preaching publicly, 'Come to Jesus Christ all of you who are struggling and you will find a good life'. The actions of Prophetess Okoh indicate that she combined preaching repentance with enabling people to access basic services. This is reflected in the way that early in her ministry the church trained traditional birth attendants to provide maternity services which integrated spiritual support to the mothers.

In the 1970s, the Prophetess settled at Ndoni, her place of birth. This is considered to be the church's most important site, where major spiritual events are held, such as the ordination ceremonies for seminary students after completion of their studies. The church and its followers, like many other AICs, experienced marginalisation because of the attitudes of the people in mission-founded churches who considered AICs to be deviants from Christian teaching. The fact that the church was founded by a rural woman who was a widow and considered to be illiterate compounded the marginal place of her followers during the founding period. In the narrative of the members of CHCI, phrases like 'we were not considered to be a church', 'we were looked at as small things' and 'we were despised and laughed at because of our choice to become members of an AIC' are common even today as the followers reflect on the church's early history, especially the first 30 years. In this narrative the phrase 'Mama Odozi Obodo's concern for the poor' is used repeatedly when the church leadership is speaking of the needs of people in economic difficulty. Odozi Obodo, which means 'nation builder', remains today the catchphrase of Christ Holy Church International.

In the founding values of Christ Holy Church International, women were supposed to give birth with the help of church-trained traditional birth attendants. This was one of the defining beliefs of the church, as pregnant mothers preferred the services of the traditional birth attendants to the services provided by hospitals. This was an issue of belief but also

*Changes in Independents in Sub-Saharan Africa, 1970–2015, growth rate, % per year*

| Region | Total population | Christian population | Independent population |
|---|---|---|---|
| *Eastern Africa* | 2.87% | 3.52% | 4.42% |
| *Middle Africa* | 2.96% | 3.24% | 3.58% |
| *Southern Africa* | 2.02% | 2.21% | 3.60% |
| *Western Africa* | 2.71% | 3.26% | 4.81% |
| Sub-Saharan Africa | 2.76% | 3.24% | 4.15% |
| Globe | 1.55% | 1.51% | 3.33% |

Source: Todd M. Johnson and Gina A. Zurlo (eds), *World Christian Database* (Leiden/Boston: Brill), accessed March 2016.

it indicates the marginality of the mothers who did not have access to hospital maternity services – still a major issue in many African countries. The church has moved on to the establishment of professional maternity homes that meet government standards. The services are provided to the wider society as part of the church's witness.

The church has built what it terms a youth development centre at Asaba, opened in April 2015. In the narrative of the leadership and members, this was built by the command of the Holy Spirit to establish a place for training young people in skills for employment after completing their secondary education. The resources were raised by the women's fellowship of the church over a period of six years. In a thanksgiving service at the official opening of the centre, a woman leader rose up and said, 'We have finished with Asaba. The Holy Spirit is telling us that Port Harcourt is the next place for us to construct a youth centre.' The affirmation was 'Hallelujah, praise be to God'. The action they took to build the centre was a direct response to the voice of the Holy Spirit in relation to the enormous needs of young people on the African continent, where the transition from primary and secondary education to tertiary institutions is infrequent, due to the lack of resources. Listening to the voice of the Holy Spirit either in private or in public, discerning the intentions of the message and consequently mobilising the church community to act are significant parts of the process of theological reflection that leads to action on specific issues in AICs. One other development in Christ Holy Church International is the establishment of the administrative offices in Abuja, the political capital of Nigeria, where the church has located part of the headquarters function to enable the church to engage at the national level with political and social-economic realities. The church's headquarters were long in Onitsha, while Ndoni, the founding place of the church, remains the centre for major spiritual gatherings such as the ordination of ministers.

## The Holy Spirit Church of East Africa: What Changes and What May Not Change

The Holy Spirit Church of East Africa (HSCEA) is one of the AICs of the Roho (Holy Spirit) tradition founded in the 1920s in the Western Region of Kenya. In this region the founding period was tumultuous, as the new AICs were in deep disagreement with the mission-founded churches and attempted to practise the Christian faith in a radically different way. The birth of this movement was linked to a period of disagreement in the Friends Church, when a group of people who claimed to have been filled with the Holy Spirit either moved out or were expelled. Subsequently, those who had left went beyond the initial cause of disagreement over the understanding of how the Holy Spirit operates in the church and community.

The church rejected modern medicine, disapproved of the ordination of women, regarded money as unclean, rejected the use of the pulpit in places of worship, affirmed the use of the local languages and introduced the African drum and other instruments, hence changing the mode of worship. The founders and the subsequent generation of followers believed in simplicity as essential to holiness. Their expectation of Christ's imminent return required them to live holy lives and to separate themselves from what is 'of the flesh' and from worldly things, including riches. This was a major part of the narrative that is still found in their songs.

Over a period of time the church members started reviewing their beliefs as they interacted with the challenging realities of their mission environment. I will exemplify two particular areas. As already noted, the church from its founding days had rejected the use of modern medicine. This belief was based on a vow made by the founders during the colonial period, the lack of knowledge about the source of drugs, and a sense of loss of local control over the healing process due to pressure from the invading culture. Seventy years later, a challenge came when church members became involved in the mobilisation of the local community around Bukoyani, the church's headquarters in western Kenya, to respond to the social needs around them. In the process of analysis, the church members and the rest of the community zeroed in on operating a dispensary as a response to the health challenges they faced. The complexity of the situation was not whether church members were going to hospital or not. It was the fact that the founders had made a vow never to use modern medicine, yet there was a demand to build a dispensary in the compound of the church where the founders preached. After months of discussion, the church reached a decision. Finally, the leadership of the church held a service in which the vows were 'undone' (a way of seeking permission from God, with consent given by the oldest survivor of the founding period). This was, in effect, a public declaration that the church was no longer against modern medicine. Consequently, it started building the dispensary. The project was later turned into a youth resource, but the declaration that modern medicine was acceptable was in itself a transformation of the church's theology. The other ceremony that communicated the major change in the church was the ordination of the first woman priest in the year 2012. This was also done at the headquarters of the church at Bukoyani, in Vihiga County in western Kenya.

Other changes have taken place through different processes. Two young pastors leading a congregation in Kibera, a large informal settlement in Nairobi, requested the leadership of the HSCEA to allow them to start using a pulpit in the church. A consecration service for the installation of the pulpit was held after the approval of the senior leadership of the denomination. The demand for the use of the pulpit has not gone beyond the Kibera congregation. The reality is that the pulpit is left in a certain corner of the church, with little use. According to Pastor Ambani, one of the initiators of the proposal to install the pulpit, the change does not mean much, as he asserts that his fellow pastor who initiated the conversations 'simply wanted to be like the new churches'. This was perhaps a personal initiative without a clear theological basis, unlikely to result in major changes. However, as will be seen later, it could have had major implications for the church's understanding of the hermeneutical process.

The processes that lead to changes in beliefs are motivated by both formal and informal discussions in leaders' meetings and in the day-to-day conversation of the members. The announcement of the major changes taking place is done in major events like the services and is preceded by lengthy periods of reflection. In many AICs, this involves prayer, prophecy, visions, dreams, the reading of Scriptures, reading the signs of the times and listening to the voices of the congregants and other people in the community. What is surprising about this church is that the lengthy processes of reflection are mediated by the unwritten narratives of this church community, who continuously relate the changes to the founding era of the church. This practice reflects the centrality of oral theology, even in the midst of major theological changes.

## The Zion Christian Church: From the Sidelines to Self-assertion

The Zion Christian Church (ZCC) in Zimbabwe was founded by Bishop Samuel Mutendi, who was a migrant worker in South Africa. The church was historically linked to the Zion Christian Church of South Africa, of which Mutendi was a member during his working life there. From the beginning, the ZCC in Zimbabwe had the vision of the Kingdom of God as a good life, which included education through the establishment of schools in the 1930s. The founder preached, prayed for people's healing and confronted the colonial government. The founder's stand against colonialism led to the expulsion of the church from urban centres. The narrative of the church members includes how the colonial government drove its founder to the rural areas, some of which were infested with tsetse flies, and how they were imprisoned several times and suffered other forms of persecution. The fact that the church established several schools in the early 1980s, immediately after the political changes that ended the colonial era, reflects the church's vision of the gospel of abundance of life seen in the founders' fight against sickness and poverty. This part of the church's mission, suppressed for more than three decades, was brought into the public space as the ZCC started establishing schools and became involved in agricultural development as well as tree-planting campaigns.

The ZCC in Zimbabwe has built a large structure named Mbungo conference centre, located in rural Masvingo. This is a place of pilgrimage for the thousands of followers who travel from all over Southern Africa for periodic major gatherings. The former simple, mostly traditional, structures have been replaced by modern buildings. The ZCC has a presence in Europe and North America through the church's missionaries, who are in these countries as students or migrant workers. One of the recent highlights in the mission of the ZCC is a building in Wellingborough, UK, named ZCC Wellingborough Wellness Centre. The changes seem to reflect a major shift from the older image of the ZCC and other AICs as communities of churches that worship under trees or in temporary structures to the establishment of modern infrastructure. The founding vision of Bishop Samuel Mutendi, who lived until 1976, continues nevertheless as a major part of the narrative of the church. The current leader, Bishop Nehemiah Mutendi, and the church members continue to refer to the founding vision of the first Bishop Mutendi and the followers, and they continue to narrate the suffering that the founder and his generation went through as they worked to preach the gospel of Jesus Christ that liberates people from sickness and poverty. This understanding of the founding vision seems to underpin the church's future development.

### Tension between Oral Theology and the Written Text

It is not easy to engage with churches on doctrines and practices that are not documented, which can be given various interpretations in different contexts. This has hindered the use of AIC resources for theological education. The interaction between the written text and the lived, oral, text remains a challenge to the AICs, as the written text remains dominant in the wider society of which they are also a part. This tension is evident in the way AIC ministers themselves handle written and unwritten sermons. Pastor Kenneth Ambani (who is in his early 40s), an emerging theological scholar from the HSCEA, keeps working with this tension. Ambani says that using the pulpit and a written text helps him to remain structured while preaching. In response to my enquiry whether there is a difference between preaching from a prepared text and preaching an unwritten text, Ambani's response is that preparing a sermon without writing calls for more prayer and openness to what the Holy Spirit is saying when you are in the worship service together with all the other congregants. The Roho churches work from the concept that the Holy Spirit will give you the sermon while in the worship service. This provides an opportunity for the minister to listen to the testimonies, songs, visions and prophecy in the service as well as to the experiences of the community during the previous week. This communal way of sermon preparation among AICs of the Roho tradition is now under pressure to conform to the assertion that a minister must have the sermon ready for the congregation before the worship day. There seems to be a correlation between the removal of the pulpit and the written text, and the free flow and work of the Holy Spirit through the congregation. The pulpit and the written sermon take the power to shape the sermon from the community of worshippers and transfer it to an individual minister – the preacher. The pulpit also implies the surrender of ministerial authority to an individual who stands at one point in the church, and it invites all the other worshippers to focus on the preacher. In contrast, the open space relates to shared priesthood, where all worshippers have a place in shaping the sermon of the day. This could be the reason why the leadership of the church is unlikely to call for the formalisation of the pulpit in the church – as it deeply contradicts the way priesthood is understood and practised.

## Movement, Institutionalisation and Infrastructure

The gradual shift towards modern infrastructure for buildings and the strengthening of governance and administrative structures are among the major developments of these AICs in the contemporary world. All three churches still operate as movements and still value the place of the Holy Spirit in prophecy, healing, dreams and visions. The challenge for the future is how these developments will impact on one of the major resources in the mission of AICs: the engagement of people on the outskirts of society in the churches' mission. The interaction between the founding values and modern institutional and infrastructural development will be critical in the life of the churches as they progress. The challenge that remains is whether the flow of the Spirit, which the HSCEA has guarded through leaving the worship space open for communal priesthood, will be protected in the modern infrastructural developments. Will the AICs continue to listen to the voice of the Holy Spirit, which can come from any person, irrespective of their social status?

The present leader of the ZCC is committed to getting prophets to London, in the UK, to carry out their ministry. These ministers have been repeatedly denied visas because of what is perceived by the British High Commission in Harare to be the lack of a credible financial base. This struggle reflects the continuing value of the participation of people who are not of high economic status in the mission of the church, wherever it is. The church's ministry in Britain seems not to be complete without the prophets, and the continuing struggle by the church to make sure that they travel is a reminder of the importance of recognising the work of the Holy Spirit through what the rest of society could refer to as common people.

## Interaction of the Rural and Urban

The character of AICs as communities built on communal family values provides a strong social protection framework in rural settings. Such structures are the bedrock of African society, where state institutions do not adequately respond to the needs of people and can even be completely absent. The teaching of the Scriptures contributes to the affirming of communal values, but the visible structures of community have for a long time been based on traditional structures. This subtly underlies the AICs' attempts to impose these values on what they consider to be the individualistic urban settings, where isolation is on the rise. Gerrie ter Haar observes that:

> one of the main strengths of African Independent Churches lies in their capacity for community building. In general, it can be said that at times of radical social change these churches have proved able to build new (moral) communities, and as such are capable of fulfilling an important role both in the new urbanised context of Africa as well as in the rural areas. (Gerrie ter Haar, 'World Religions and Community Religions: Where Does Africa Fit?', Occasional Paper, Centre of African Studies, Copenhagen: University of Copenhagen, 2000, 9)

Archbishop Daniel Okoh, the present leader of CHCI, mentions that at the founding of the church the farmers were the main contributors to the resources that sustained the mission of the church but over time this reality has changed. Now, in his view, it is the mainly urban-based business people who are the main contributors to the work of the church. More of Africa's population is rural than urban, but the depressed prices of agricultural produce has undermined rural economies and led to the dominance of the urban economy. This social change is going to affect AICs across the continent as it continues to urbanise and also as the urban values are brought to rural areas through the media and the increased mobility of populations. What remains to be seen is whether the waning influence of the rural economy will gradually lead to the dominance of urban values because of the rising urban economy, or whether the AICs will continue to affirm their founding values, in which community is a key aspect of the gospel that transcends the rural–urban divide and confronts the values of the emerging African middle-class elite. In this context, it is interesting that CHCI has maintained Ndoni as the place where spiritual functions like the ordination of ministers who have completed seminary education are carried out. This reflects the differentiation between the location of the administrative and the spiritual bases of the church. The rural still holds the spiritual base, while the administrative base is shifting to Abuja, the capital city.

In contrast, the ZCC's construction of a mega-structure in Mbungo is in itself a statement that the rural is the base for both the administrative and the spiritual functions of the church. The ZCC seems to work from the margins to reclaim the space in Zimbabwe's urban centres that it had been were denied or pushed out of. Yet even here, the new building concretises the dynamic of the modern, which will continue to interact with the traditional.

## Conclusion

The actions of the CHCI reflect a continuation of the founding values at the same time that the current generation is moving forwards to do mission in a way that relates to current realities. The establishment of the administrative centre in the capital city is a clear statement that the church will not stay at the sidelines. This is important in the African context, where the capital cities regard everywhere else, including the smaller up-country cities, as rural. Yet the church has decided also to retain the sacred spaces of the rural and to honour these spaces as locations of functions and processes that even affect what is carried out in the administrative office in the capital.

The ZCC in Zimbabwe is clearly moving back to the spaces from which its members expelled during the rule of the minority white government that ruled Zimbabwe with values and actions close to those practised by apartheid South Africa. Its mode of doing mission is an assertion that it did not choose to be at the sidelines of society and that it was actively asserting its place in contemporary society.

The process the HSCEA has been using to transform its beliefs around medicine, the ordination of women and the way the worship space is treated reflects a unique way in which an AIC negotiates into the future. This communal discernment process enables this AIC to isolate what it considers changeable from the unchangeable. The way the worship space is treated or controlled is linked to the value and practice of shared priesthood that this space visibly provides. It is clear for now that there is an overwhelming, silent yet firm refusal to alter this space, even with the liberty provided by the denomination to introduce a pulpit.

The trends in these three churches show that the future of the mission of AICs lies in their continuing ability to engage with their founding visions. In many AICs, the founding period is regarded as sacred, and the practices and doctrines derived from this period are considered to be sacred. It is in this period that AIC founders read the Scriptures in a different way from that of the dominant churches. Although these founding visions continue to provide resources for the churches' faith and life, it is clear that there are tensions between the past and present and that these tensions will continue to challenge the AICs to a continuous reformation.

The three churches seem to be working through the process of articulating the founding vision while at the same time updating it. What seems to be the mediating factor is the narrative that transmits the shared values and demands for accountability to subsequent generations of followers. The question that remains is whether the transmission of the founding values of these churches will continue to be largely oral, a factor that democratises access to the founding vision, or whether the churches will move towards more documentation, so that the values are passed on to present and coming generations who are oriented to written texts. It is in the hands of the AICs to look at the future through their resourcefulness and developing institutions and to develop processes that will expand access to this resourcefulness, both within the AIC family and in the wider church.

## Bibliography

Chitando, Ezra, Masiiwa Ragies Gunda and Joachim Kügler (eds), *Multiplying in the Spirit: African Independent Churches in Zimbabwe* (Bamberg: University of Bamberg Press, 2014).

Daneel, Inus, *Quest for Belonging: Introduction to a Study of African Independent Churches* (Gweru: Mambo Press, 1987).

Oduro, Thomas, *Christ Holy Church International: The Story of an African Independent Church* (Minneapolis, MN: Lutheran University Press, 2007).

Padwick, Timothy John, 'Spirit, Desire and the World: Roho Churches of Western Kenya in the Era of Globalisation' (PhD Thesis, University of Birmingham, 2003).

Peel, J. D. Y., *Aladura: A Religious Movement Among the Yoruba* (Oxford: Oxford University Press, 1968).

# Orthodox


## Ralph Lee and Daniel Seifemichael


Orthodox Christianity has several strongholds in Sub-Saharan Africa, but by far the largest, most enduring and most vibrant expression is that found in Ethiopia and its related church in Eritrea. Projections suggest that Ethiopia will have the largest Orthodox church in the world by 2050. Gaining autocephalous status, and so independence from the (Egyptian) Coptic Orthodox Church, in 1959, the Ethiopian Orthodox Tewahedo Church has a membership of 40–45 million, with churches spread across the country, but with a particularly high concentration in the northern and central Amhara and Tigray Regions, which were parts of the ancient Aksumite Kingdom, and in parts of Oromia Region and the Southern Nations, Nationalities, and Peoples' Region. A significant diaspora community is found in the USA, Europe (especially the UK), the Middle East and Australia, and these boost the total membership to as high as 50 million. Trinidad and Tobago is home to an important branch of the church, established by African missionaries in the 1950s and originally under the auspices of the Coptic Orthodox Church, but soon connected with the Ethiopian Church through the endeavours of Emperor Haile Selassie. It has a large non-Ethiopian membership, including many converts from Rastafarianism.

Within Ethiopia are 35,000 parish churches and more than 500,000 clergy, divided among 44 dioceses; outside the country are a further 11 dioceses. A total of 56 bishops comprise the Synod, led since 2013 by His Holiness Abuna Matthias I, Sixth Patriarch of the Ethiopian Orthodox Tewahedo Church, Archbishop of Aksum and Ichege (abbot) of the See of Saint Teklehaimanot. The approximately 3 million members of the Eritrean Orthodox Tewahedo Church have essentially an identical tradition, being a part of the Ethiopian Church until Eritrean autocephaly was recognised by Egypt after Eritrea gained independence in 1993.

### The Ethiopian Church: History and Connections

The Church's name, Tewahedo, is the Classical Ethiopic (Ge'ez) for 'united' or 'fused' and expresses the church's staunch miaphysite standpoint, articulating the union of divinity and humanity in Christ in a single nature rather than the formula developed at the Council of Chalcedon in 451 CE (preferred by Western churches) that refers to two natures. The miaphysite interpretation was mistakenly associated with Eutyches's view that Christ's humanity ceased to exist after the ascension. In fact, it expresses the full humanity and divinity of Christ but without allowing the separation of these natures that, in the view of the miaphysites, the Chalcedonian view allows. In fact, the writings of the Ethiopian Church reflect more a pre-Chalcedonian than a strictly miaphysite Christology.

Typical of the Orthodox expression, the roots of Ethiopian Christianity are central in its contemporary expression. Evidence points to the conversion of the first Christian emperors of Ethiopia, Ezana and Sayzana, in around 330 CE. Christianity was adopted as the state religion in 334 CE, making Ethiopia one of the earliest Christian nations. An even earlier presence of Christians is likely, particularly at the important port of Adulis on the Red Sea. Ethiopian Church tradition asserts the introduction of Christianity at the time of the Apostles, and the church vigorously affirms the Ethiopian Eunuch of Acts 8 as its first convert.

The strong claims of Jewish heritage in Ethiopia are affirmed in important ancient texts. Ethiopians trace their Christian heritage to King Solomon's time, when, as the national epic *Kebra Nagast* (*Kəbrä Nägäśt*) recounts, the Ark of the Covenant (*Tabot*) was brought to Aksum from Jerusalem by Menelik, the son of Solomon and the Queen of Sheba. The account has the Ark accompanied by cohorts of Levites and the nation converting to Judaism from the worship of the sun and moon. Moreover, in the *Kebra Nagast* Solomon sees a vision of the sun setting on Israel and rising on Ethiopia, which then appropriates the special status of God's chosen people.

The historicity of this account is irrelevant, as it lies at the heart of the Ethiopian Orthodox Tewahedo Church's, and even of aspects of the nation's, identity, influencing many contemporary areas, including theology, church architecture and popular devotion. The theological influence is pervasive, as the incarnation is understood through Mary as *Tabot* or synonymously 'dwelling place of divinity'; churches are divided into three parts, mimicking Solomon's Temple, and house a replica of the Ark or *Tabot* in the central 'holy of holies'; and in popular devotion,

*Orthodox in Sub-Saharan Africa, 1970*

| Region | Total population | Christian population | Orthodox population | % of region Orthodox | % of Christians Orthodox |
|---|---|---|---|---|---|
| *Eastern Africa* | 110,428,000 | 54,913,000 | 12,126,000 | 11.0% | 22.1% |
| *Middle Africa* | 40,846,000 | 29,888,000 | 8,300 | 0.0% | 0.0% |
| *Southern Africa* | 25,454,000 | 19,291,000 | 30,100 | 0.1% | 0.2% |
| *Western Africa* | 106,015,000 | 30,143,000 | 7,100 | 0.0% | 0.0% |
| Sub-Saharan Africa | 282,743,000 | 134,235,000 | 12,172,000 | 4.3% | 9.1% |
| Globe | 3,682,488,000 | 1,230,688,000 | 143,967,000 | 3.9% | 11.7% |

Source: Todd M. Johnson and Gina A. Zurlo (eds), *World Christian Database* (Leiden/Boston: Brill), accessed March 2016.

celebrations of major feasts centre around the procession of the Ark, the most dramatic being Epiphany (*Ṭəmqət*, meaning 'baptism'), the celebration of the baptism of Christ. At Epiphany, *Tabots* from many churches are brought to a field, where they and the clergy spend the night, in a festival that resembles the Feast of Tabernacles. When the Empress Taytu took the Ark of the Covenant to support the routing of the Italian invaders at Adwa in 1896, the Ethiopian victory was attributed to the power of the Ark. The church is not only a religious institution but was for many centuries the repository of the cultural, political and social life of the Ethiopian people, and it retains today an integral role in all aspects of national life.

The focus on the Ark and on Old Testament practices – such as circumcision, keeping Saturday as well as Sunday as a Sabbath, and Levitical food regulations – has led to a superficial labelling of the Ethiopian Church as syncretistic with Judaism. This is mistaken, and a close examination shows the Ark to symbolise a profoundly Christian understanding of the Incarnation and of divine indwelling in believers. Ethiopians would affirm the confession from the *Kebra Nagast* of their Emperor Gelawdewos (1521/2–1559 CE) justifying the 'Judaic' nature of Ethiopian Christianity because of what is believed to be the nation's Jewish heritage, but not because Ethiopians abide by the Law of Moses.

## The Heritage of the Ethiopian Church: Intellectual, Literary and Physical

Autocephalous status, gained in 1959, should not be seen as the start of an independent church, as the institution has a long and diverse tradition of its own. The Ethiopian Church has its own strong expression of Christianity, with Ge'ez being the language of the authoritative text of the Bible (probably translated in the fourth century CE) and all sacred texts, the lingua franca before Christ and in the early centuries CE. Saint Yared (512–83 CE) is considered the founder of Ethiopian Orthodox music and poetry. His musical-poetical compositions in Ge'ez are still used liturgically and have a distinctive style, with strong theological symbolism in the poetry and the movements accompanying chants. Only three musical instruments are

*Orthodox in Sub-Saharan Africa, 2015*

| Region | Total population | Christian population | Orthodox population | % of region Orthodox | % of Christians Orthodox |
|---|---|---|---|---|---|
| *Eastern Africa* | 394,477,000 | 259,865,000 | 42,002,000 | 10.7% | 16.2% |
| *Middle Africa* | 151,952,000 | 125,422,000 | 15,200 | 0.0% | 0.0% |
| *Southern Africa* | 62,634,000 | 51,611,000 | 30,200 | 0.1% | 0.1% |
| *Western Africa* | 353,224,000 | 127,638,000 | 123,000 | 0.0% | 0.1% |
| Sub-Saharan Africa | 962,287,000 | 564,536,000 | 42,170,000 | 4.4% | 7.5% |
| Globe | 7,349,472,000 | 2,416,268,000 | 283,073,000 | 3.9% | 11.7% |

Source: Todd M. Johnson and Gina A. Zurlo (eds), *World Christian Database* (Leiden/Boston: Brill), accessed March 2016.

used during the liturgy to this day: the *kebero* (a double-headed drum), the *senasel* (a sistrum or type of rattle), and the *mequamia* (prayer staff used for rhythmic beating of the ground and movement in the air).

The church also has distinctive Bible commentaries, called *andemta*, deriving their name from the repeated use of *andem* (an abbreviation meaning 'another one says') to introduce successive interpretations of a verse. These evolved from Ge'ez commentary known as *tergwame*, but *andemta* are written mostly in Amharic, probably because this predominantly oral tradition was committed to writing in the late seventeenth century in monasteries around the then capital, Gondar. Although Ge'ez remains authoritative, there is a strong trend towards Bible reading and non-sung parts of the liturgy being in the vernacular.

Ethiopia's church buildings are unique, and its important ancient churches are tourist attractions, but most importantly they are spiritual centres of pilgrimage where the devout can find places for prayer, penitential washing and spiritual counsel. The notable pre-thirteenth-century rock-hewn churches of Lalibela in Amhara Region, which are UNESCO (United Nations Educational, Scientific and Cultural Organisation) World Heritage sites, are particularly important, but pilgrimage is common to numerous other rock-hewn churches centred in Tigray Region, and to many other sites. A further centre of pilgrimage is the monastery at Debre Libanos, founded by Saint Teklehaimanot, to whom is attributed the evangelistic efforts of the thirteenth and fourteenth centuries, when the church was extended to the south, into his native Shewa Province and beyond. The saint's cave is now a church, containing a celebrated healing spring of holy water, and the site also has a modern church (built in the 1960s by order of Emperor Haile Selassie), with contemporary stained-glass windows designed by the famous Ethiopian artist Afewerk Tekle. Aksum remains one of the most important centres of pilgrimage, with the foundations of the first Christian church building in Ethiopia, Maryam Seyon (St Mary of Zion), built in 340 CE. A smaller seventeenth-century church with the same name was built next to this site by Emperor Fasil (1603–67) and the modern cathedral of Our Lady St Mary of Zion, built in

*Changes in Orthodox in Sub-Saharan Africa, 1970–2015, growth rate, % per year*

| Annual growth rate, 1970–2015 | Total population | Christian population | Orthodox population |
|---|---|---|---|
| *Eastern Africa* | 2.87% | 3.52% | 2.80% |
| *Middle Africa* | 2.96% | 3.24% | 1.36% |
| *Southern Africa* | 2.02% | 2.21% | 0.01% |
| *Western Africa* | 2.71% | 3.26% | 6.54% |
| Sub-Saharan Africa | 2.76% | 3.24% | 2.80% |
| Globe | 1.55% | 1.51% | 1.51% |

Source: Todd M. Johnson and Gina A. Zurlo (eds), *World Christian Database* (Leiden/Boston: Brill), accessed March 2016.

the 1950s, also stands on the same site. The prestige of this site is greatly enhanced by the presence of the Chapel of the Tablet, containing what all devout Ethiopian Orthodox affirm to be the Ark of the Covenant. Important too is the Ethiopian monastery in Jerusalem, representing a centuries-long tradition of Ethiopian Christian presence in Jerusalem as well as in Lebanon and Syria. Many less famous buildings are also important spiritual centres and places of pilgrimage, and many growing cities are seeing large new churches built.

## The Ethiopian Church in the Late Twentieth Century: Communism and Post-communism

Autocephaly in 1959 marks the beginning of the contemporary era in the Ethiopian Church in many ways. Independence allowed the church to form its own structure, centred on the parish council, comprising clergy and laity, that serves as the centre of spiritual service, education, evangelism and social programmes of the church. The General Parish Council Department oversees the organisation of local parish councils and the parish and diocesan development and charitable activities, Sunday schools, voluntary service, heritage preservation, legal matters, foreign relations and ecumenical affairs, as well as the Ecclesiastical Court responsible for theological, sacramental and ecclesiastical affairs. The Council of Scholars (Liqawənt Guba'e) was established to revise translations of Ge'ez books and to oversee doctrine, edit church books, and promote the social and religious teaching of the church.

The church is involved in practical social and development projects throughout the country, with connected organisations including the Ethiopian Orthodox Tewahedo Church Development and Inter-Church Aid Commission (EOTC-DICAC), which is engaged in various development programmes, including environmental rehabilitation, rural water supply, hygiene and sanitation, the construction of access roads, small-scale irrigation development, education, health and nutrition, immunisation, food security, livelihood improvement, infant and child feeding, prevention and control of HIV/AIDS and support of those with the infection, support of refugees and returnees, emergency relief and rehabilitation, gender mainstreaming, mitigating harmful practices (such as early marriage and female genital mutilation), the development of monastic institutions, and building the capacities of communities, clergy and Sunday-school members. Clergy have often been role models for community-based development endeavours. Important donors – including UNHCR, the EU, UNICEF, UNDP, Christian Aid, Dan Church Aid, ACT-Forum, Water Aid, Intermon-Oxfam, USAID and World Vision – have understood the church's potential to deliver at the local level.

Another agency is the Ethiopian Orthodox Tewahedo Church Child and Family Affairs Organisation (EOTC-CFAO), a faith-based local non-governmental organisation (NGO) caring for orphaned and destitute children and working on community development programmes in partnership with local and international donors. Ethiopia has at least 5 million children in difficult circumstances, including street children, orphans, children who have been traumatised, displaced, disabled, abused or neglected, delinquent children and those with insufficient family support. EOTC-CFAO aims to cater for basic needs and promote the physical, mental, emotional and spiritual growth and development of unaccompanied children, enabling communities to take care of poor, orphaned and other vulnerable children and empowering families to provide for the physical, mental and psychological needs of children. The agency currently serves more than 6,000 children and youth in its 23 child-care centres.

The Ethiopian Church has also participated in important ecumenical dialogues since autocephaly. In 1948 it was part of the foundation of the World Council of Churches and later was a founding member of the All Africa Conference of Churches (AACC). In 1965 the Council of Oriental Orthodox Churches was held in Addis Ababa, the first joint meeting of the oriental churches since the Council of Ephesus (431). Ecumenical and foreign relations ceased under communism but were revived significantly under the leadership of the fifth Patriarch, Abuna Paulos (1992–2012), who chaired several national church conferences organised by the Bible Society of Ethiopia, and EOTC-DICAC, and a national institute for peace and development, with particular efforts to promote a peaceful resolution of the recent Ethio-Eritrean war. His efforts also promoted inter-faith peace and development initiatives within the country that led ultimately to the foundation of the Inter-Religious Council of Ethiopia (IRCE).

One of the greatest challenges to the Ethiopian Church was the communist revolution in 1974. This resulted in the de facto disestablishment of the church, the confiscation of much of its land and the wrenching of the church from its central place in the running of the country. The execution in 1979 of the second Patriarch, Abuna Tewofilos (1971–9), was a warning to the church, but despite this and other pressure new bishops and new churches were consecrated and attendance was robust. His successor, Abuna Teklehaimanot (1976–88), was a noble figure widely liked by the laity, and he promoted participation in the church. The failure of communist attempts to quash the influence of the church was evident in large turnouts at midnight vigils throughout the imposition of an 18-year night-time curfew in Addis Ababa, and perhaps more clearly by the declaration of a day of prayer and fasting for peace by the communist deputy after the flight of the President only days before the overthrow of this regime.

The fall of communism in 1991 brought new freedoms to Ethiopia. The church was allowed to reclaim some land and to conduct its activities without intrusion. A new challenge came for the Orthodox Church because its traditional homelands, previously inaccessible to Protestant missionary activity due to the civil war, were now peaceful, and there was a rush for the north by many mission agencies. This, for the first time in history, brought laity in the Orthodox strongholds of the north of Ethiopia face to face with Protestant Christianity. Protestant Christianity had developed strongly in the south, away from the powerful influence of Orthodoxy, with the unfortunate outcome being a devastating lack of understanding between Protestant and Orthodox Christians. While mutual understanding is still poor, a small number of Protestants and Orthodox are interested in pursuing deeper mutual understanding, with Orthodox scholars developing considered critiques of Protestant thought and a notable handful of Protestant scholars committing themselves to the study of the traditional literature of the Orthodox Church.

The active participation of laity, particularly youth, in the mission of the church is a significant feature that developed vigorously in the twentieth century. Once the church was administratively independent from the Coptic Orthodox Church, new movements developed based on the Coptic Church's Sunday-school movements were quickly reorganised along Ethiopian lines. Important urban church youth groups started weekly assemblies at churches in Addis Ababa and Asmara that later developed into more formal Sunday schools. Simultaneously, university students in Addis Ababa started gathering, forming the Haymanote Abaw ('Faith of the Fathers') association aimed at deepening religious knowledge through discussion of new scientific and philosophical ideas and the preservation of religious tradition, advised by leading intellectuals, scholars, courtiers and ministers, with the Patriarch Abuna Tewofilos and Emperor Haile Selassie as its patrons. The primary activity of this association was evening classes taught by traditional scholars, but it extended also to social projects. This association, with its strong Christian ethos and imperial connection, was closed with the advent of communism. From 1985, the then Archbishop of Shewa Province, Abune Gorgorios, started to develop limited educational programmes for students in higher education, seeking to increase understanding of the Orthodox faith while avoiding the scrutiny of the communists. In 1990, as communism was crumbling, the military government sent university students for military training at Blate, in the south of Ethiopia, a mobilisation that developed a closer bond between independent youth groups; ultimately they united in the

Mahabere Kidusan ('Association of Saints'), which is now very popular among Orthodox university students. After the fall of communism, Abuna Paulos promoted youth participation in religious life and revived many associations that had been banned or persecuted by the communists.

## Monasticism, Education and the Arts

For centuries the church served as the centre of education in Ethiopia and, even with the introduction of Western-style education, this endured until the advent of communism. Indeed, the traditional system of education may be one of the longest continually serving systems of education in the world. Its origin in its current form is uncertain, but it certainly dates from the seventeenth century, and possibly earlier, to the evolution of scholarly systems in the fifteenth and sixteenth centuries CE. Traditionally, it is connected with the sixth-century CE 'Nine Saints', who came from Constantinople, Antioch and Armenia and contributed to the strengthening of the church, and the establishment of Ethiopia's still-thriving distinct expression of monasticism. They also catalysed the strong development of Ethiopian literature, the study of which is primarily the task of monks.

The strongly ascetic process of monastic studies may take decades. From early stages of learning to chant important liturgical texts, it passes to study of the Ge'ez language that culminates in learning to compose the extempore symbolic poems called *qene* that are used in liturgy and other contexts, and then to the study of the extensive corpus of biblical commentary known as *andemta*, which covers the four fields of Old Testament, New Testament, Patristic literature and monastic literature. Most traditional scholars are male, but there are notable female teachers, particularly of *qene*. The extraordinary Ethiopian monks serve in the remotest parts of the country and along with their learning and asceticism are characterised by their devotion to their spiritual flock, which includes not only religious service but also extensive involvement in social, agricultural and technological development projects.

Contemporary state education is free from church influence, but the church has also developed a more modern system of clergy-training seminaries in all dioceses and higher-level training at the Holy Trinity Theological College in Addis Ababa, reopened in 1992. The latter has bachelor's and master's programmes in theology, including a thriving evening class programme that is open to men and women, with the regular programme being only for clergy. Holy Trinity Theological College's programme is in English and includes both Ethiopian traditional material and broader material. There are also centres of higher learning at the Abba Selama Kesate Birhan Theological College in Mekelle, and at the Sewaswe Birhan St Paul Theological Seminary in Addis Ababa.

The church has been the leading patron of Ethiopian national art, sponsoring painting and book production, and both of these remain an important part of monastic culture. Ethiopian art, until the twentieth century, was essentially Christian art, and the church still enjoys a thriving artistic tradition that draws on the traditional approach. The church has also been a major producer of books, with a strong culture of producing goatskin books written with vegetable inks that is still alive today, only partly superseded by modern book production.

Historically, literary tradition was confined to the church and Ethiopia is today the repository of one of the world's largest collections of ancient manuscripts. Among the most important of these are the illustrated gospels known as the Garima Gospels, which are dated to the sixth century CE. In addition to biblical texts and translated texts, the Ethiopian Church has its own rich literary heritage, with arguably the most important contributors being the sixth-century hymn writer and theologian-poet Saint Yared and the notable fourteenth- and fifteenth-century theologian Abba Giyorgis of Gascha (also known as Giyorgis of Sagla), whose works are still used liturgically, in theological applications and in popular piety. In recent years, the production of manuscripts has declined and the tradition is under threat, as is the traditional production of icons and artistic crosses used in churches and in lay devotion.

## Contemporary Challenges

With the lack of mutual understanding between Orthodox and Protestant expressions of Christianity and the newfound confidence of Islam in Ethiopia, the church's main challenge is working in what has become a multi-faith society. There are positive signs, with leaders from the church engaging in ecumenical dialogues such as the Lausanne Orthodox Initiative, but these attitudes have largely not permeated to the laity. Also, secular influences have incorrectly blamed the Orthodox Church for significant problems in the country, such as low agricultural productivity arising from the rigorous fasting regime of the church, or for the problems of early marriage, which originated out of a desire to protect young girls after their parents' death.

The church would benefit from finding allies within the broader faith communities to define the place for faith in modern Ethiopia. Economic hardship also presents the church with significant challenges. Economic growth has picked up in recent decades, but raging inflation and growing youth unemployment present the country with significant trials, particularly in urban areas, and the church needs to reach out to youth who are disillusioned. Unfortunately, in modern Ethiopia the religious, cultural and physical heritage of the church is probably not sufficient to engage the country's growing population of youth.

An important debate within the church is over language. The desire of many to keep the traditional language and its exceptional poetry is in tension with the need to engage youth, who struggle to understand Ge'ez and would like to hear the liturgy in their own language. There have been creative approaches, not appreciated by some, using local languages for prayers and Bible readings, and this debate will continue. Economic difficulties have also caused difficulty in recruiting clergy, again requiring innovative approaches.

### Newer Expressions of Orthodoxy in Sub-Saharan Africa

Contemporary expressions of Orthodoxy in sub-Saharan Africa are much broader than the remarkable autocephalous Ethiopian and Eritrean Orthodox Tewahedo Churches and their ancient historical connection with the Coptic Orthodox Church of Egypt. A parallel Greek-speaking Alexandrian Orthodox Church affirming the Christology of the 451 CE Council of Chalcedon has maintained an unbroken, if at times fraught, presence in Alexandria, despite both internecine conflict and the unrelenting pressure of being a tiny Christian minority in a Muslim-ruled land. Nineteenth-century European explorers opened the African interior to both missionaries and merchants. As new administrative and economic centres arose, economic migrants arrived in droves, taking advantage of the relative security provided by the colonial powers. Each of these immigrant populations brought their culture, their foods and their religion with them as they took root in cities across the continent. The Greeks were no exception to this trend.

Orthodoxy thus grew in Sub-Saharan Africa outside Ethiopia and Eritrea as an immigrant church. In coordination with the Greek Patriarch of Alexandria, priests would visit Greek communities and ensure that the faithful had access to the sacraments, with services in Greek. Eventually, when the community grew large enough to support it, a church would be built, usually in the capital city. Priests eventually became resident. Greek bishops were appointed with jurisdiction over entire colonies and countries. The structure seemed impressive, but the churches were small and the Orthodox were limited essentially to members of the Greek community or expatriates from other Orthodox countries. This initial spread of Orthodoxy across the cities of Africa was African in name only. Local populations had little interest in what was essentially Greek Orthodoxy.

This began to change dramatically in the 1920s in both Uganda and Kenya, where frustration with both British missionary religion and heavy-handed colonial policy provoked some to leave mission churches. African Christian leaders were attracted to Christianity but felt that the colonial authorities, in cooperation with missionaries, were using religion as a means to control 'native' populations. Breaking away from these restraints, these African Christians sought a form of Christianity that was true to what the Bible revealed about the early church but which was free from colonial manipulation. One of the earliest manifestations of these movements were the churches led by black Africans formed in South Africa early in the twentieth century. They identified themselves as Ethiopian churches, probably because of the expression of African independence crystallised at the Battle of Adwa in 1896, when the Ethiopians drove out their potential colonisers, the Italians. What they heard about Orthodox Christianity was immediately attractive to them, both because of the church's historical connections to earliest Christianity, but also because the Orthodox Church was not allied with any of the colonial powers. Indeed, some of the 'Ethiopian churches' later became part of the Ethiopian Orthodox Tewahedo Church, where today they have indigenous, non-Ethiopian-born priests and deacons and prayer books in the Xhosa, Tswana and Zulu languages.

These movements in Kenya and Uganda were part of a more general reaction across the continent during the twentieth century against missionary Christianity and its perceived compromises with European agendas. What made the churches in British East Africa unique was their desire to identify with the earliest form of institutional Christianity, the Orthodox Church. This desire was derailed, however, when the church leader with whom they connected, whom they thought was Orthodox, turned out to be a schismatic South African archbishop of the so-called African Orthodox Church, with connections to Marcus Garvey's Universal Negro Improvement Association and African Communities League. It was a tiny movement with several American and Caribbean congregations, with Archbishop Daniel Williams providing leadership in South Africa. When Archbishop Williams received invitations from the churches in Uganda and Kenya to come and help them, he immediately travelled to Uganda and spent many months there instructing leaders, baptising Christians and ordaining four priests, including Reuben Spartas, who had emerged as the leader of the Ugandan Orthodox churches. Before his departure, the Archbishop was asked by a Greek merchant in Kampala if he would baptise his daughter. After the service, the merchant informed Father Spartas that, whatever else the baptism service was, it was not an Orthodox service. This, of course, provoked a crisis in the new church. The merchant offered to contact an Orthodox monk in Tanzania to see if he could come and help. The monk agreed and spent some months working with the Ugandan priests and acquainting them with Orthodox liturgies and practices. The Kenyan Orthodox Church went through a similar experience, of being trained by the South African Archbishop only to discover that he was not actually Orthodox and having to learn from scratch the Orthodox liturgies and traditions.

Suspicious of these initial schismatic associations, the Patriarchate of Alexandria did not accept the Ugandan and Kenyan churches as fully Orthodox until after World War II. The Kenyan church in particular continued to be associated with resistance to British rule. When the British authorities cracked down on the Mau Mau armed resistance to their policies, the Kenyan Orthodox Church was banned and its leaders arrested. The ban was in place for more than a decade and had devastating results on the church. With Kenyan independence in 1963, the Orthodox Church of Kenya began to rebuild its leadership and infrastructure as well as fend off continuing tendencies to internal schism.

Crucial in the development of not just the Kenyan church but African Orthodoxy in general was the establishment of a theological seminary in Nairobi in 1982 under the leadership of Dr Andreas Tillyrides. Tillyrides, now Archbishop Makarios of Kenya and Irinoupolis, has overseen the training of not only hundreds of clergy for the Kenyan church but, gradually, the leadership for all Sub-Saharan Orthodoxy as well. As a result of increasingly well trained indigenous priests and bishops, the church in Kenya has grown to nearly 250 parishes and nearly 350,000 members. The Orthodox Church in Uganda has experienced similar growth, as has the church in northern Tanzania. There are still Orthodox churches across the continent that have held on to an ethnocentric practice of Orthodoxy, but Orthodox leaders, including the current Patriarch Theodros II, increasingly are committed to indigenising leadership and allowing Orthodoxy to take root in local populations rather than remain the preserve of tiny ethnic minorities. Where this is happening today, such as in Rwanda and Burundi, the number of Orthodox churches and members is exploding.

Although the trend of African Orthodoxy to move from ethnic enclave to indigenous church is clear, a number of factors continue to make this transition challenging. Even among its best examples, the Orthodox churches of Africa are poorly resourced. The pressure to fall in with the ever-present corrupt practices of the surrounding politics seems overwhelming. The temptation to grab power for oneself makes the threat of schism very real. The lack of stewardship on the part of members threatens to make the churches dependent upon foreign money and thus unwilling to own the faith for themselves. These challenges are daunting, and any one of them could derail Orthodoxy in any of the dozens of African countries where Orthodox churches are present and growing.

Orthodoxy in Africa is messy and complicated. But it is growing, and it will continue to do so for the foreseeable future. Just as global Roman Catholic and Protestant Christianity has seen a shift in terms of numbers and leadership from the Northern to the Southern hemisphere, it is no longer far-fetched to think that the same might be happening with global Orthodoxy.

## Bibliography

Bausi, Alessandro (ed.), *Languages and Cultures of Eastern Christianity: Ethiopia*, Vol. 4 of the Worlds of Eastern Christianity, 300–1500 (Ashgate: Variorum, 2012).

Chaillot, Christine, *The Ethiopian Orthodox Tewahedo Church Tradition* (Paris: Inter-Orthodox Dialogue, 2002).

Tillyrides, Makarios, *Yearbook and Review* (Harare: Greek Orthodox Archdiocese of Zimbabwe and Southern Africa, 2001).

Uhlig, Siegbert and Alessandro Bausi (eds), *Encyclopaedia Aethiopica*, 5 vols (Wiesbaden: Harrassowitz Verlag, 2003–14).

Ullendorff, Edward, *Ethiopia and the Bible*: *The Schweich Lectures of the British Academy 1967* (London: Oxford University Press, 1968).

# Protestants

## Setri Nyomi

Christianity has been in Africa for longer than most people think. According to the biblical narratives, Jesus, the Christ, lived in Africa in his infancy when King Herod was pursuing him (Matthew 2). The story of the Ethiopian eunuch in the eighth chapter of the Acts of the Apostles provides another entry point of Christianity in Africa. The beginning of the Coptic Orthodox Church in Egypt constitutes yet another entry of Christianity into Africa in the early centuries. Africans are among some of the noted early patriarchs of the Christian church. Some well known examples of African early Christian leaders are Clement, Tertullian, Origen, Athanasius, Cyril, Cyprian and Augustine.

It may puzzle readers that an essay on Protestants in Sub-Saharan Africa begins with references to the history of Christianity in Africa that deals mostly with Northern Africa. It is our conviction that this linkage, however brief, is important to establish the point that the appearance of Protestants on the scene in Africa is not in a vacuum. Neither is the Protestant expression of Christianity in Africa an introduction of a foreign phenomenon. The linkage is to demonstrate that the arrival of Protestant Christianity in Africa marks a 'coming home' of the Christian faith in Africa. The chapter therefore begins its discussion with Africa's Protestant beginnings.

African Protestants, like other Protestants around the world, hold very dear the key principles of Protestantism – *Solus Christus, Sola Fide, Sola Gratia, Sola Scriptura, Soli Deo Gloria*. However, one also finds some signs of specificity among African Christians. We live our Christianity in context. There is a healthy interaction between gospel and culture that is often experienced as both a challenge and an opportunity. Even within Sub-Saharan Africa, one finds noticeable differences in culture from community to community and country to country. Therefore one can talk only in general terms about how this impacts Christian life in context. This chapter points to only a few of the many areas in which African Protestant Christians live in their contexts.

### Protestant Beginnings and Mission-Instituted Churches

The global Protestant Reformation is normally traced to 31 October 1517 in Wittenberg, Germany. When Martin Luther nailed his 95 theses to the front door of the castle church there, a renewal movement (which would come to be known as Protestantism) began in the Christian church. It is important to note that there are precursors to this particular event that share affinity with its aims. Examples include the Waldensian movement, which began as a result of the ministry of Pierre Valdes in France in the twelfth century, and the movement begun by Jan Hus in Bohemia in the fourteenth century.

As a renewal movement, the Protestant Reformation is rooted in the coming of the Lord Jesus Christ into the world in flesh and the events of the Cross and the Resurrection. Therefore Protestants do not trace their full history merely to the sixteenth century. The sixteenth century is important as the point of the renewal of a much older reality. Thus any part of the church that is a result of the Protestant Reformation or identifies with it has that dual sense of history – rootedness in the beginnings of the Christian church and identification with the sixteenth-century Protestant renewal. When did this Protestant movement begin to impact Sub-Saharan Africa, and how is the impact currently felt in the twenty-first century?

Around 1652, when the Dutch East Indian Company began settling in the Cape of Good Hope, in what is now South Africa, most of those who came were members of the Dutch Reformed Church. This marked the arrival of Protestant Christianity in Africa. Thus the Dutch Reformed presence in Africa is more than 350 years old. Churches that sprang out of this reality are of different races, especially in Southern Africa. While it has spread to other countries, such as Namibia, Swaziland, Botswana, Zimbabwe and Zambia, the Dutch Reformed Church and some of its offshoots have a chequered history. In the twentieth century, they became notorious because of their support of apartheid. Today, the Dutch Reformed churches are working hard to put behind them the apartheid past and forge a new identity together with other Protestant churches.

Most Sub-Saharan African Protestant churches arose as a result of missionary activities. The main Protestant missions to Africa were formed in the eighteenth and nineteenth centuries. Before that, there had been some Christian entries that could be described as chaplaincies to the trade

*Protestants in Sub-Saharan Africa, 1970*

| Region | Total population | Christian population | Protestant population | % of region Protestant | % of Christians Protestant |
|---|---|---|---|---|---|
| *Eastern Africa* | 110,428,000 | 54,913,000 | 7,747,000 | 7.0% | 14.1% |
| *Middle Africa* | 40,846,000 | 29,888,000 | 5,807,000 | 14.2% | 19.4% |
| *Southern Africa* | 25,454,000 | 19,291,000 | 7,257,000 | 28.5% | 37.6% |
| *Western Africa* | 106,015,000 | 30,143,000 | 5,529,000 | 5.2% | 18.3% |
| Sub-Saharan Africa | 282,743,000 | 134,235,000 | 26,339,000 | 9.3% | 19.6% |
| Globe | 3,682,488,000 | 1,230,688,000 | 207,470,000 | 5.6% | 16.9% |

Source: Todd M. Johnson and Gina A. Zurlo (eds), *World Christian Database* (Leiden/Boston: Brill), accessed March 2016.

missions or later to the colonial powers. For the most part, however, the chaplains had little interaction with indigenous peoples.

European Protestant missionary bodies that came with the specific goal of reaching out to Africans included the London Missionary Society, the Paris Evangelical Mission, the Wesleyan Mission, the Basel Mission and the Bremen Mission. Mission arms of churches in the USA as well as Canada also participated in evangelisation in Africa that led to the establishment of Protestant churches. Thanks to the work of the foreign missionaries, Protestant churches can be found in Benin, Burkina Faso, Burundi, Cameroon, the Democratic Republic of the Congo, the Republic of the Congo, Côte d'Ivoire, Ethiopia, Ghana, Liberia, Kenya, Malawi, Namibia, Nigeria, Rwanda, Senegal, Sierra Leone, South Africa, Tanzania, Togo, Uganda, Zambia, Zimbabwe and others.

It is true, however, that while the mission bodies can take credit for this work, many indigenous Africans and persons of African descent were also instrumental in the success of churches that flourished after humble beginnings. For example, in the nineteenth century, during the missionary activities of the Basel Mission in Ghana, Moravians were invited from Jamaica to come and strengthen the work.

Today, the churches founded by these missions continue in close cooperation with one another through ecumenical mission bodies such as the Council for World Mission, CEVAA (Evangelical Community for Apostolic Action), Mission 21 and the Norddeutsche Mission. These bodies have worked hard to turn their past relationships (in which the 'parent body', usually found in Western Europe or North America, holds power over the churches they have founded) to new paradigms, in which all the churches are making real efforts to engage in mission as equal partners and to share the resources with which they engage in mission.

The Protestant Church in many African countries struggled with the question of gospel and culture. How could it be faithful to the gospel and, at the same time, express the faith in a way that was true to the African cultural context? It took until the middle of the twentieth century for

*Protestants in Sub-Saharan Africa, 2015*

| Region | Total population | Christian population | Protestant population | % of region Protestant | % of Christians Protestant |
|---|---|---|---|---|---|
| *Eastern Africa* | 394,477,000 | 259,865,000 | 73,626,000 | 18.7% | 28.3% |
| *Middle Africa* | 151,952,000 | 125,422,000 | 27,460,000 | 18.1% | 21.9% |
| *Southern Africa* | 62,634,000 | 51,611,000 | 12,743,000 | 20.4% | 24.7% |
| *Western Africa* | 353,224,000 | 127,638,000 | 45,752,000 | 13.0% | 35.9% |
| Sub-Saharan Africa | 962,287,000 | 564,536,000 | 159,582,000 | 16.6% | 28.3% |
| Globe | 7,349,472,000 | 2,416,268,000 | 453,790,000 | 6.2% | 18.8% |

Source: Todd M. Johnson and Gina A. Zurlo (eds), *World Christian Database* (Leiden/Boston: Brill), accessed March 2016.

this struggle to begin yielding results. In the second half of the twentieth century, youth movements in most of the Protestant churches were instrumental in moving them towards worship that reflects African rhythm and African culture.

Today, Protestant churches are found across the continent. Countries with Protestant majorities include Botswana, Cameroon, Ghana, Kenya, Malawi, Nigeria, South Africa, Tanzania and Zambia. Major Protestant denominations in Sub-Saharan Africa include Baptists, Congregationalists, Methodists, Presbyterians and Reformed. Their impact on Sub-Saharan Africa includes the establishment of schools, hospitals, agriculture stations and other social institutions. Many are at the forefront of prophetic ministries seeking justice and advocating for good governance.

One of the unintended consequences of the manner in which ministry took place in the eighteenth, nineteenth and twentieth centuries is that many mainline Protestant churches have become identified with specific ethnicities. This is because, for effectiveness, the missionaries focused on specific geographical areas in the countries they found themselves in. Thus the Presbyterian Church of Nigeria comprises ethnicities from the south-eastern part of Nigeria, while Baptists are mainly Yoruba. In Kenya, Presbyterians are mainly Kikuyu while Methodists are mainly Meru. This is mirrored in many other parts of Africa. Today, the churches are making gallant efforts to overcome this legacy.

In the process of the struggle for more indigenous content in worship, some active persons led movements out of the mission-instituted churches to form African Instituted Churches, which can, therefore, be seen as offshoots of the Protestant movement in Africa. Some of them arose because they did not see the mission-initiated Protestant churches as indigenising enough, or they were reacting to what they saw as the Western trappings of the mainline Protestant churches. Whatever the reasons for their formation, many of the Independent churches initially drew their membership from the Protestant churches. It is sufficient to note these linkages here without further comment, since churches in these categories are dealt with in other chapters in this volume.

*Changes in Protestants in Sub-Saharan Africa, 1970–2015, growth rate, % per year*

| Region | Total population | Christian population | Protestant population |
|---|---|---|---|
| *Eastern Africa* | 2.87% | 3.52% | 5.13% |
| *Middle Africa* | 2.96% | 3.24% | 3.51% |
| *Southern Africa* | 2.02% | 2.21% | 1.26% |
| *Western Africa* | 2.71% | 3.26% | 4.81% |
| Sub-Saharan Africa | 2.76% | 3.24% | 4.09% |
| Globe | 1.55% | 1.51% | 1.75% |

Source: Todd M. Johnson and Gina A. Zurlo (eds), *World Christian Database* (Leiden/Boston: Brill), accessed March 2016.

## Worship

Being an African Protestant Christian might show itself in the joyfulness of our worship in spite of the challenging or difficult circumstances in which we find ourselves. Dancing in joy in the presence of God is not a retreat into opium to soothe people from their difficult realities. It is indeed a recognition that we are in the presence of God, who stands with us in the difficulties, and a defiance of the forces of evil. With God, the evil forces will not have the last word. Thus the more the difficulties come, the more people find solace in commitment to God and expression of this in joyful community worship. This characteristic is a part of African spirituality that goes beyond being Christian. In African spirituality, the contemplative is important but usually serves to strengthen joyful expression. During the early missionary activities, the use of traditional African musical instruments (such as drums and other percussion instruments) was frowned upon. In the last few decades, Africans have found new meaning in using them to make our worship even more joyful.

Worship is intertwined with the daily experiences of people. There is continuity between people's experiences, difficulties, joys and challenges and what is done in worship. There is no separation between the secular and the spiritual. Thus a farmer sees the land as God's gift, of which she or he is a steward, called upon to respect the land, to utilise it effectively for feeding people, and to leave it in good condition for generations yet to come. This is not just an economic activity, but part of worship life. Many Protestant communities incorporate harvest time in worship.

## Theological Reflection and Relevance to African Socio-cultural Realities

In the heat of their suffering, many Africans find solace and strength in reflecting on the Scriptures. It has been said that colonialists thought they would 'tame' the Africans by giving them Bibles, but Africans read the Bible and found in it reason to claim their rights to freedom and independence. This sense of the God who identifies with the oppressed was further developed among some Africans as Black Theology. The former President of the World Alliance of Reformed Churches, Allan Boesak (a South African theologian), has made some contributions in this area from a South African perspective. His book *Farewell to Innocence – A Socio-ethical Study on Black Theology and Power* (Orbis Books, 1977) gives ample evidence of this.

In recent years, the theology of reconstruction has been gaining ground as a meaningful theological expression of African Christians. As Africa experiences broken walls, broken institutions, broken systems and various other effects of injustice, slavery, colonialism, conflicts and other evils, African Christians feel called by God to engage in reconstruction, as did the people of Judah in the time of Nehemiah. Like Nehemiah and the people of his time, this reconstruction involves the recognition of the problem, the taking of responsibilities, an efficient analytical survey of how we got where we are today, and the resolve of the people to rise up and rebuild. The reconstruction process is not easy and will have many detractors. It involves new affirmations of elements of African culture which have been discounted by foreign missionaries as well as being prophetic in rebuilding systems and institutions torn down by selfish governments, conflicts and legacies of economic injustice. The All Africa Conference of Churches, which unites most African Protestant churches, has been a leader in this venture since the 1990s.

Theological reflection is very important for Protestant churches in Africa. This is reflected in the value placed on well trained clergy, who will in turn lead their churches to value good theological reflections that make the Christian faith relevant to the people in the churches. Such theological reflections constantly take place through theological formation centres, church worship settings, governance meetings, seminars, confirmation classes and other settings. One major challenge is that many Protestants in Africa, including scholars, have yielded to the belief that Africans are mainly persons of oral tradition. As a result, not as many African theological works have been published as could have been.

Living as Christians in context means mediating how people see the wonderful deeds of God in contexts in which people are suffering as a result of the injustices inherent in our world. African Protestant Christians understand themselves as called upon to live and testify that life will replace the forces of death. This led many of the Protestant churches in Africa to be at the forefront of the fight against apartheid. Protestant churches played a significant role in the South Africa Council of Churches, working with other Christian leaders such as Desmond Tutu to unmask and dismantle apartheid. One such leader in the struggle against apartheid is Allan Boesak. It is significant that the worldwide Protestant family joined hands with colleagues in South Africa in making a clear stand for justice. Apartheid is evil and no church that tolerates it will be tolerated as an authentic member of the fellowship. This struggle was supported by worldwide ecumenical bodies such as the World Council of Churches, the then World Alliance of Reformed Churches and the Lutheran World Federation.

Today, Africans face other realities. Many of these are linked with globalisation and the results of economic injustice. African Christians are asking 'Why?' As Protestant Christians, many of the church leaders make efforts to address these issues. While there are some African Protestant churches which avoid addressing these issues, thinking they need to leave this to social activists so that they can focus on what they see as spiritual matters, many African Protestant voices in fact feel that the evil that causes so many to be impoverished and so many to die should be renounced as part of our Christian calling. Thus, being instrumental in combating economic injustice and climate injustice has become a very important element on the agenda of some Protestant churches. It is to be noted that it was African churches that called on the then World Alliance of Reformed Churches to take strong action on global economic injustice. This eventually led to the adoption of the Accra Confession, when the World Alliance of Reformed Churches met in its twenty-fourth General Council in Accra, Ghana, in 2004. That this confession bears an African stamp is an important contribution of African Protestants to the global Christian family.

African Protestants dare to be prophetic, challenging the forces of evil in every form because they see the proclaiming of God's wonderful deeds in their different contexts as having liberative implications that are relevant to every context. Thus, if in Africa both internal and external forces are oppressive to people, impoverishing them and denying them health, educational and other resources, being Protestant in the African context calls us to address these issues in relevant ways. These are some of the reasons why many Protestant Christian leaders, through their national councils of churches and other means, are at the forefront of prophetic ministries seeking justice, advocating for good governance and unmasking all forms of evil and modern-day expressions of injustice (economic, climate, gender, racial and other).

The negative ways in which some cultural tendencies seep into the lives of Protestant Christians have also been challenged – for example, the ways in which some cul‘ural practices devalue women. This is increasingly challenged by African Protestant Christians.

Historically, Protestant churches have made many contributions to national and social life in many Sub-Saharan Africa countries. These contributions are in the health, education, agriculture, economic and political sectors. Their impact on Sub-Saharan Africa includes the establishment of schools, hospitals, agriculture stations and other social enterprises. Some of the best-known schools and hospitals have been established by Protestant churches. In addition, Protestant churches have been at the forefront of prophetically challenging African governments whenever their countries face national crises. In Togo, Liberia, Ghana, South Africa, Kenya, Cameroon and Nigeria, Protestant churches have been effective forces in addressing national crises that threatened to destabilise. Constant statements from their highest gatherings as well as engagement with political leaders have often helped bring about peace or pointed the way to better governance.

As Africa deals with many challenges, including conflicts, wars, displacement of peoples, diseases such as malaria, HIV/AIDS, cholera and

Ebola, poverty and many others, the Protestant churches have sought to stand by people in their communities and to engage in actions that bring life in the place of death.

## Ecumenical Engagement, Mission and Theological Education

Many Protestant churches in Sub-Saharan Africa are ecumenically engaged, while some are suspicious of the ecumenical movement. Some of that suspicion is based on what they see as agendas foreign to their core calling as African Christians, whereas those ecumenically engaged understand the Christian calling necessarily to include responding to the need for Christian unity that our Lord Jesus Christ expressed in the High Priestly Prayer of John 17.

Ecumenical commitment is expressed in many ways in Africa. For example, it has led to organic church unions in a number of places. The United Church of Zambia; the Church of Central Africa – Presbyterian in Malawi, Zambia and Zimbabwe; the Uniting Reformed Church of Southern Africa; and the Uniting Presbyterian Church of Southern Africa are just a few examples.

Most Protestant churches do understand that every church is called to pray for as well as to further the course of Christian unity. Protestants are not called to exclusionist isolation. This is one main motivation behind their active engagement in ecumenical activities. Many mainline Protestant churches are members of the national councils of churches as well as the continental ecumenical organ, the All Africa Conference of Churches. They are also members of the World Council of Churches and Christian World Communions such as the World Communion of Reformed Churches, Lutheran World Federation, Disciples Ecumenical Consultative Council, World Methodist Council, Baptist World Alliance and World Mennonite Conference. Membership of these bodies constitutes a signal of the commitment of African Protestant churches to ecumenical engagement.

African Protestants have also contributed in significant ways to the governance and leadership of global ecumenical organs. Many have served in the governing bodies of major ecumenical organisations and have distinguished themselves as leaders of the modern ecumenical movement, especially in the twentieth and twenty-first centuries. Such African Protestant ecumenical leaders include Sir Akanu Ibiam of Nigeria (Reformed), Josiah Kibira of Tanzania (Lutheran), C. G. Baeta of Ghana (Reformed), Allan Boesak of South Africa (Reformed), Justice Annie Jiagge of Ghana (Reformed), John Henry Okullu of Kenya (Anglican), John Gatu of Kenya (Reformed), Aaron Tolen of Cameroon (Reformed), Mercy Amba Oduyoye of Ghana (Methodist), Ishmael Noko of Zimbabwe (Lutheran), Musimbi Kanyoro of Kenya (Lutheran), Jerry Pillay of South

Africa (Reformed), Setri Nyomi of Ghana (Reformed), Samuel Kobia of Kenya (Methodist) and Isabel Phiri of Malawi (Reformed). This is not an exhaustive list. It serves to give a glimpse of Sub-Saharan Protestant leaders who have contributed to Christianity worldwide.

Protestant Christians in Africa take mission very seriously. This is traditionally understood to be the calling to evangelise and to bring people who are not Christians into the Christian faith. Annual general assemblies, synods and church conferences normally evaluate the health of their churches by examining the extent to which they are evangelising and growing in numbers. This is important to African Protestant Christians.

Equally important is the understanding that the mission of the church in Africa is broader than evangelism. Africa is the continent on which suffering is abundant. The task of addressing the suffering is also part of the understanding of mission. So when African Protestants engage in relief work, challenge the forces of evil and become agents in God's transformation of their societies, they understand themselves to be doing God's mission. With this understanding, many churches, councils, pastors and leaders see their mission as including being the voices of the voiceless, engagement in the messy business of being prophetic, with all the risks it carries for the church, and confronting the forces of evil in every form.

In this twenty-first century, Protestant Christians in Africa are seeking to be more effective in mission. Sometimes the temptation among Protestant Africans is to do mission in disunited or even in competitive ways. Thus, whether in evangelism or in other forms of mission, the competition has led to each church or denomination wanting to be seen as better than the others and more attractive. The Protestant Church in Africa is taking struggling steps to move beyond that, so that their commitment to mission in unity is stronger.

Mission relationships are also part of the lives of Protestant churches in Africa. For many decades, some African churches had relationships with foreign mission bodies that fostered a mode of operation that could be described as very dependent. This dependency usually came with displays of power on the side of the mission bodies that were unhealthy for the mission of God. The last couple of decades in the twentieth century began seeing paradigm shifts in this area and now, as observed above, there are increasingly more healthy relationships. Since that time, many African Protestant churches have also evangelised and established congregations and churches in areas that had not been reached by Christianity. These new churches depend on their African 'mother' churches. Churches are learning to ensure that these relationships are healthy.

Protestant churches value a high level of education for their clergy and other agents. Theological education takes place both in both church-related theological seminaries and in government- and private-church-instituted universities all over Africa. These institutions have highly qualified indigenous faculties. In addition to the theological institutions initiated by individual Protestant churches for the formation of their clergy and other agents, many also train their clergy in ecumenically organised institutions. For example, for more than 50 years Protestants from the different denominations in Ghana have been training clergy in Trinity Theological Seminary in Legon. Similar examples include what is now St Paul's University in Limuru, Kenya, and the United Theological College in Harare, Zimbabwe. They work hand in hand with the Protestant churches to equip the churches with competent leaders of the next generation.

Africa has produced many Protestant theologians, who have greatly contributed to theological education on the continent and beyond. Although any attempt to provide names risks leaving out some important contributors, a very partial list of African theologians who made great contributions to theological education includes Christian Baeta, Kwesi Dickson, John Mbiti, Lamin Sanneh, John de Gruchy, Steve de Gruchy, Kwame Bediako, Allan Boesak, John Pobee, Russel Botman, Isabel Phiri, Tinyiko Maluleke, Nyambura Njoroge, Jesse Mugambi and Priscille Djomhoue. Christian Baeta, for example, devoted himself to promoting Christian unity. Steve de Gruchy led the movement for a paradigm shift in mission to a more holistic approach. Isabel Phiri combined her in-depth reflections on mission thinking today with a passion for ecumenical engagement. In their groundbreaking roles, each faced the challenge of going against the dominant assumptions of the day, which often devalued original African theological contributions.

Theological education in Africa is strengthened by the formation of associations of theological institutions. The Conference of African Theological Institutions (CATI) has been an important association in this regard. There are also regional associations such as the West African Association of Theological Institutions (WAATI), ASTHEOL for Francophone Africa, the Association of Theological Institutions in Eastern Africa (ATIEA) and the Association of Theological Institutions in Southern and Central Africa (ATISCA). In addition, the Association for Christian Theological Education in Africa (ACTEA) mainly links the Evangelical theological institutions.

## Gender and Youth

The Protestant movement in Africa was for a long time found wanting in the gender justice area. Women's ordination started for most in the middle of the twentieth century but a good percentage of Protestant churches still do not ordain women. However, the numbers of churches that do ordain women have been on the increase.

Women constitute the majority of members in most Protestant churches. All over Africa, groups such as the Women's Fellowship, the Women's Guild, the Women's Bible Class and Women in Fellowship have been important platforms for gathering, mutual learning, inspiration, empowerment and contribution to the life of the Protestant churches. Through these groups and others, women have made significant contributions to the life and growth of Protestant churches in Africa.

However, when it comes to decision-making structures, men dominate unfairly. There are efforts to change this in some places so that the Protestant churches can become more gender sensitive. For example, in response to the Programme to Affirm, Challenge and Transform of the then World Alliance of Reformed Churches in the early 1990s, many Reformed churches in Africa took a critical look at ways in which their structures perpetrated gender injustice and they began taking steps towards a more inclusive view of women and men in the mission of God. A key stimulator of change in this direction is the Circle of Concerned African Women Theologians, initiated by Mercy Amba Oduyoye of Ghana. The Circle has made great strides and continues to make an impact on the continent in many areas.

In Protestant churches in Africa, young people constitute a fairly high percentage of membership. Persons who are under 35 years old constitute 25–40% of the membership. They have contributed to the shift to joyful worship as well as to ideas that make the Protestant Church in Africa relevant in the twenty-first century. This move has not always been easy. Often, traditionalists tend to kick against what is seen as youthful exuberance. Sometimes this has led to young people moving from the mainline Protestant churches to the Charismatic churches.

## Divisions, Proliferation of Churches and the Inter-faith Context

A particular blind spot for Protestant churches is the tendency to divide over doctrinal worship practice or leadership issues. While this phenomenon is by no means the overwhelming reality, it is nevertheless a worrisome feature of Protestant churches in Africa. Thus, in some countries, disagreements do lead to divisions in a church and new churches come into being.

In recent decades, new churches are emerging as a result of individual leaders indicating that they feel called to start churches. These often start as one-congregation churches. Some of these churches, commonly called Charismatic churches, have become mega-churches, and some have developed national structures and are well distributed in the nations in which they exist. Others remain one-sanctuary churches, with the founder fully in charge of all administration. These Charismatic churches are often attractive to young people who grew up in mainline Protestant churches.

For most African countries there are literally thousands of churches as a result of this proliferation.

Most African countries have multi-religious communities. The three main religions on the continent are Christianity, Islam and traditional African religions. As indicated above, Protestant churches in Africa are very evangelistic. Therefore, for a long time, little attention was paid to dialogue with other religions. In recent decades, many African Protestant churches have come to see that the value of dialogue and the value of evangelism are not necessarily mutually exclusive. Therefore churches have quite vibrant dialogues in many countries. This has been especially helpful in addressing national issues (including crises) and building communities in which people of different religions live in peace and harmony.

## Conclusion

Protestants in Sub-Saharan Africa are a strong force with a long history of making significant contributions to life in Africa. As part of the Christian church in the world, their impact is felt both on the continent and beyond the continent. They have faced many challenges and yet continue to grow. Together with other expressions of Christianity on the continent of Africa, the Protestant churches are alive and well in the twenty-first century.

## Bibliography

Bauswein, Jean-Jacques and Lukas Vischer, *Reformed Churches in the World* (Cambridge: Eerdmans, 1999).

Bediako, Kwame, *Christianity in Africa: The Renewal of Non-Western Religion* (Maryknoll, NY: Orbis Books, 1995).

Boesak, Allan, *Farewell to Innocence – A Socio-ethical Study on Black Theology and Power* (Maryknoll, NY: Orbis Books, 1977).

Hastings, Adrian, *The Church in Africa 1450–1950* (Oxford: Clarendon Press, 1994).

Maluleke, Tinyiko S., 'Christianity in a Distressed Africa: A Time to Own and Own Up', *Missionalia*, 26:3 (December 1998), 324–40.

# Roman Catholics

## Anthony Egan SJ

Roman Catholicism is the largest single Christian church in Africa. Africa is also the fastest- and most consistently growing part of the Catholic Church in the twenty-first century. According to October 2015 statistics released by the Vatican, there were 206,224,000 Catholics in Africa, constituting 18.92% of the continent's population and served by 705 bishops, 41,826 priests, 427 permanent deacons, 8,427 religious brothers, 69,883 women religious, and 79 male and 917 women members of secular institutes. Seminarians in training for the priesthood, at both high-school and college level, number 80,744. In addition, 7,226 lay missionaries work on the continent, together with 409,994 lay catechists. Apart from parishes and mission stations, the church runs 1,167 hospitals, 5,252 dispensaries, 201 leprosy centres, 630 homes for the elderly, chronically ill or disabled, 1,292 orphanages, 2,641 nursery schools, 1,774 marriage counselling centres, 264 schools and 2,339 other institutes, including a number of universities, the latter serving 132,990 students. About 25 million alumni of Catholic schools currently live in Africa.

These statistics, impressive by any standard, highlight the size and scope of Catholicism's African footprint. Recent Popes have marvelled at this achievement, made largely in the late nineteenth and twentieth centuries. Pope Benedict XVI has called the African Church Catholicism's 'lung'. But this achievement must be carefully read against a set of defining features that made this growth happen and against a number of challenges and tensions within the church.

The two key defining features for contemporary African Catholicism were the Second Vatican Council (1962–5) and the decolonisation of Africa from the late 1950s, peaking in the 1960s and culminating in the end of apartheid in South Africa in 1994. Both serve as contextualisation for the present and thus need a brief historical examination.

The Second Vatican Council, called by Pope John XXIII and completed under his successor, Paul VI, radically renewed the inner and outer face of global Catholicism. In successive constitutions and decrees, an inward-looking and essentially European institution was globalised, to a limited degree democratised, and set on an outward-looking and more open engagement with the world. The Council decentralised somewhat its hierarchical structure, paving the way for more collegial governance and generating national, regional and continental conferences of bishops. It emphasised the role of laity in the church, stressing collaborative ministry between them, the clergy and religious congregations in catechising, evangelising and social outreach. Similarly, clergy and laity alike were encouraged to promote justice in all its forms, renew its efforts in media, education and health care, and encourage family life. By downplaying Catholic religious exclusivism, it opened up ecumenical and inter-faith dialogue and cooperation. The Council also promoted liturgy in the vernacular, embraced a renewal of liturgical music and endorsed inculturation – the (albeit careful) expression of Christian faith through local cultural practices.

Although the presence of local and foreign-born African bishops at the Second Vatican Council was relatively small, and had fairly little direct impact, the impact of the Council on the African church was considerable. The empowerment of the laity revitalised Catholic organisations on the continent in every area of life, above all regenerating and deepening the role of lay catechists in transmitting the faith. The most apparent reform, however, was the introduction of vernacular liturgy. It is perhaps a result of liturgical reform that African Catholicism, then and now, is characterised by vibrant and joyous liturgical celebration. Whether celebrated according to Roman or African rites (the latter with Vatican approval), the exuberance of worship can frequently be mistaken by an outsider for a Charismatic or Pentecostal service. In this, African Catholic liturgy was and is often ahead of the rest of the church: when asked in the late 1960s by a few Irish bishops how they might help him implement the Council in Africa, a missionary told them that they in fact already had the Mass in English and local languages. Would they like to borrow the East African texts to use in Ireland?

Similarly, the African church swept through other inculturated changes. This ranged from the use of drums during worship, through hymns, to, in the case of Zaire (now the Democratic Republic of the Congo), a whole new

*Roman Catholics in Sub-Saharan Africa, 1970*

| Region | Total population | Christian population | Roman Catholic population | % of region Roman Catholic | % of Christians Roman Catholic |
|---|---|---|---|---|---|
| *Eastern Africa* | 110,428,000 | 54,913,000 | 19,085,000 | 17.3% | 34.8% |
| *Middle Africa* | 40,846,000 | 29,888,000 | 15,596,000 | 38.2% | 52.2% |
| *Southern Africa* | 25,454,000 | 19,291,000 | 2,171,000 | 8.5% | 11.3% |
| *Western Africa* | 106,015,000 | 30,143,000 | 7,632,000 | 7.2% | 25.3% |
| Sub-Saharan Africa | 282,743,000 | 134,235,000 | 44,483,000 | 15.7% | 33.1% |
| Globe | 3,682,488,000 | 1,230,688,000 | 666,779,000 | 18.1% | 54.2% |

Source: Todd M. Johnson and Gina A. Zurlo (eds), *World Christian Database* (Leiden/Boston: Brill), accessed March 2016.

Mass, the Missa Luba, which combined the established rite with imagery drawn from African tradition. A new generation of local theologians, encouraged by missionary professors in seminaries, developed new African theologies and philosophies, often in dialogue with their Protestant counterparts. By the early 1970s, a number of African bishops' conferences had already called for the abolition of compulsory clerical celibacy for diocesan priests. This was seen as an impediment to vocations, culturally and pastorally a problem in a society where a man was not considered adult until he was himself a parent. Rome rejected these requests and also set about limiting the autonomy of local bishops' conferences.

As elsewhere in the Catholic Church, the experimentation and enthusiasm for change were curtailed first by Paul VI and later by John Paul II, through a series of encyclicals that reaffirmed clerical celibacy (1967) and the prohibition on artificial birth control (1968) and by reining in the authority of local ordinaries and bishops' conferences. During the 1970s, a new generation of more traditionally minded African bishops were appointed (most of them local clergy, many of them with postgraduate training in Rome). The drive for reform had faded and conservative forces were in the ascendant. Although this did not (as elsewhere) create a crisis for the church and a decline in membership, many of the challenges and ambiguities in African Catholicism did not abate; if anything, they would evolve in new directions.

Decolonisation, the end of European rule in Africa, is the second historical force important for understanding contemporary African Catholicism. The church played an ambivalent role in colonial times: as a European institution it often relied heavily on its ties to colonial authorities, sometimes (as in Portuguese-ruled Africa) enjoying special privileges in return for its services to the state – in short, becoming an agent of colonialism. At one extreme, it has been claimed (by Catholic and secular scholars alike) that the church in Rwanda and Burundi actively supported 'divide and rule' colonial policies emphasising differences between Hutus and Tutsis that would lead to cycles of massacre and genocide in the post-colonial era.

*Roman Catholics in Sub-Saharan Africa, 2015*

| Region | Total population | Christian population | Roman Catholic population | % of region Roman Catholic | % of Christians Roman Catholic |
|---|---|---|---|---|---|
| *Eastern Africa* | 394,477,000 | 259,865,000 | 88,281,000 | 22.4% | 34.0% |
| *Middle Africa* | 151,952,000 | 125,422,000 | 70,520,000 | 46.4% | 56.2% |
| *Southern Africa* | 62,634,000 | 51,611,000 | 5,490,000 | 8.8% | 10.6% |
| *Western Africa* | 353,224,000 | 127,638,000 | 40,655,000 | 11.5% | 31.9% |
| Sub-Saharan Africa | 962,287,000 | 564,536,000 | 204,946,000 | 21.3% | 36.3% |
| Globe | 7,349,472,000 | 2,416,268,000 | 1,230,563,000 | 16.7% | 50.9% |

Source: Todd M. Johnson and Gina A. Zurlo (eds), *World Christian Database* (Leiden/Boston: Brill), accessed March 2016.

Contrarily, the church through schools and hospitals often met the needs of Africans not provided for (or inadequately so) by the colonial state, earning grassroots sympathy for its work. Many African nationalists were products of church schools: some, like Julius Nyerere of Tanzania (currently under scrutiny for sainthood), were devout Catholics as well as nationalists; others, like Robert Mugabe of Zimbabwe, would develop more ambivalent views; while some would show hostility after independence.

In areas where wars of national liberation were fought (such as Kenya, Zimbabwe, Angola, Mozambique and South Africa), the degree to which the Catholic Church identified with the struggle became a key factor in its post-liberation acceptance by the new states. The church in Angola and Mozambique suffered for its support for colonial authority. Property was expropriated, foreign clergy sometimes expelled and much of its educational and health infrastructure nationalised. It has taken decades for the church to regain lost ground in both countries. In contrast, the Catholic Church in South Africa's principled opposition to apartheid since the 1950s, and its considerable (and under-researched) role in non-violent resistance, earned it respect and even some political leverage after 1994.

Another marked effect of decolonisation was the role of the new ruling elites. Though many were products of church schools, some embraced secularist ideas like *laicité* in French Africa, often informed by liberalism and Marxism, like Sékou Touré of Guinea (originally a Muslim by background). Where the Catholic Church found ways to dialogue with these ideologies after independence, a more equable relationship was struck. Whether the relationship was good or bad, however, a common pattern emerged that furthered tension with the Catholic Church: the emergence of corrupt, autocratic post-colonial governments in Africa. If the church was too close to such leaders, it was tainted by their corruption and discredited after their fall; if it opposed such tyrants, it was likely to be persecuted.

In many places, too, African clergy – themselves de facto part of this new mission-educated African elite – became anti-colonial political leaders. In Congo Brazzaville, for example, Fulbert Youlou – a priest laicised by the

*Changes in Roman Catholics in Sub-Saharan Africa, 1970–2015, growth rate, % per year*

| Region | Total population | Christian population | Roman Catholic population |
|---|---|---|---|
| *Eastern Africa* | 2.87% | 3.52% | 3.46% |
| *Middle Africa* | 2.96% | 3.24% | 3.41% |
| *Southern Africa* | 2.02% | 2.21% | 2.08% |
| *Western Africa* | 2.71% | 3.26% | 3.79% |
| Sub-Saharan Africa | 2.76% | 3.24% | 3.45% |
| Globe | 1.55% | 1.51% | 1.37% |

Source: Todd M. Johnson and Gina A. Zurlo (eds), *World Christian Database* (Leiden/Boston: Brill), accessed March 2016.

church for his nationalist politics – became the country's first President. (Decades later a Jesuit priest and bishop, Ernest Kombo, would be elected President of the High Council of the Republic, to guide the Congo back to democracy).

The two defining features noted above – the Second Vatican Council and decolonisation – are significant in that they set two broad agendas for the Catholic Church in Africa. The first, the changes brought to Catholicism by the Council and the subsequent recentralisation of ecclesial authority under Rome, gives context to the internal difficulties (often overlooked in the light of the church's rapid growth and apparent vibrancy on the continent) that the church faces regarding its mission in Africa. These include tensions over theological inculturation, relations with other religious traditions (Protestantism, Islam, African traditional religion), attitudes to celibacy, gender, sexuality and the HIV/AIDS crisis. Decolonisation and its legacy pose ongoing challenges for the public role of Catholicism in Africa: the extent to which the church (as one of the few highly functioning institutions on the continent with a vast network of services) must provide an alternative to often dysfunctional and corrupt governments and become a voice for democracy and human rights. This is read against a background in which the church itself might not always live up to the values it espouses for the state. The two features merge when one asks, to what degree is the Catholic Church in Africa itself a 'decolonised' institution?

As noted at the beginning of this essay, the Catholic Church in Africa is an enormous, growing and influential institution. There have been interesting developments: the migration of African priests and religious to the churches of Europe and North America, and the development of local missionary religious congregations (notably in countries like Nigeria, Ghana, Kenya and Uganda, where vocations are numerous) who serve both overseas and within other African countries. Many African bishops and clergy have served and serve in papal commissions and departments in the Vatican under the pontificates of John Paul II, Benedict XVI and Francis. A small but growing number of African cardinals belong to the College of Cardinals that elects the Pope. Numerous posts at Roman universities, like the Gregorian, are filled by African scholars. Many African professors are tenured in North American and European university faculties of Catholic theology and philosophy. This is a reflection of the proliferation of seminaries (including the world's largest Catholic seminary, located in Nigeria), the concern for higher education, and the sheer numbers of Africa's Catholics.

The church has built upon its foundations, developing the infrastructure created by generations of European missionaries who raised funds mainly in Europe to create schools, clinics, hospitals and even universities.

The result is reflected in the impressive statistics and examples noted above. However, with all this infrastructure – some of it battered, misused or simply expropriated by anti-clerical post-colonial states – there has emerged a challenge: maintenance in a post-missionary era. As the church contracts in Europe, the number of missionaries has declined rapidly and with them the overseas funding of the institutions they built. These resources, sometimes the only functional services in districts where civil government delivery is either poor or nonexistent, are highly stretched. Local church donors, especially in poor regions, are few. Some rely on aid from secular international non-governmental organisations (INGOs), though this sometimes generates tensions, such as when the INGOs' policies on issues like birth control or condom provision for HIV/AIDS prevention clash with Catholic sensibilities and African cultural practices. Many struggle to meet their service goals.

One of the desires of bishops' conferences around the continent has become the creation of a self-sustaining church. This has been most notably achieved through greater lay participation at various levels. At base levels, Small Christian Communities have become expressions of the local church. Lay led, they are the 'out-stations' of urban and rural parishes that attend to the day-to-day functioning of the community, catechesis and prayer services in the absence of the priest, who might visit weekly, monthly or in some cases every few months to provide the sacraments of Initiation, Penance and Eucharist. Justice and peace groups at the parish and diocesan levels link into national conference structures, often serving as important voices for democracy and human rights. The higher one moves in church structures, however, the more clericalised the institutions become. Few, if any, examples of paid lay parish ministers or chaplains exist, as has become common in the Catholic Church in North America and Western Europe. Nor do many lay theologians teach in Catholic universities or seminaries, apart from a handful of women religious (who are technically laity under canon law).

The latter highlights the complex role of the priest in African Catholicism. It might be suggested that, contrary to the vision of theologians and bishops of the era of the Second Vatican Council (missionary and local alike), the Catholic Church in Africa today is more clericalised than ever before. There are reasons for this. First, the post-Council restoration of a more traditionalist understanding of priesthood and the appointment of Vatican-minded bishops in the African hierarchy has re-emphasised a model of the priesthood that is uneasy with lay leadership in the church as a whole and in Africa in particular. This segues into a hierarchical cultural understanding in many areas, including a patriarchal view of women. Second, as in many poorer countries in Europe's past, ordination has become a means of social mobility. Seminarians receive higher education (including for the most talented graduate studies overseas), stable employment (in a continent still marked by poverty and inequality) and an enhanced social status upon ordination often perceived as culturally akin to minor chieftainship. In parts of West Africa, upon ordination priests receive substantial gifts from relatives and parishioners: money, vestments and increasingly a better-than-average motorcar. Such incentives offset the disadvantages of ordination, such as not being allowed to marry and raise a family. Even here, the power of clerical culture allows many who might reject the Roman discipline of celibacy to quietly ignore the restriction. So long as they are discreet and avoid anything that might be deemed criminal, there is little sign within many African dioceses (as indeed in some dioceses outside Africa too, it should be noted) that Rome's restrictions will be enforced. When such issues are occasionally raised, based upon comprehensive but almost entirely anecdotal evidence, they are dismissed as at best hearsay and at worst as an attempt to bring the church into disrepute – or to advance the forbidden agenda of changing the rules of celibacy. Critics of the church's refusal to face the problem – most of them from within, including theologians and priests – call this denial.

Catholic relations with other religious traditions have historically generated tensions. Relations with non-Catholic Christians are varied. On the ground, among lay Catholic intellectuals and some theologians, there has been a growing uneasiness about the limitedness of ecumenism, particularly in the post-colonial era. For many believers across denominations, the Reformation was a European dispute that had nothing to do with Africa. Theologians who desired to create a truly African theology, though well informed about the terms of the dispute, sometimes felt that the Reformation was a distraction from inculturation. In some places where different churches had evangelised different tribes and communities, tensions between Christian communities could take on dimensions of ethnic conflict that needed to be eased in the post-colonial era. A general view of the current situation would suggest that African Catholics are caught between two poles: on the one side, a more exclusive 'Roman' theology that has returned to dominate seminaries (and thus become the discourse of most clergy), downplaying ecumenism and inculturation while preaching religious tolerance and dialogue; and on the other, a distinctive blurring of Christian identities, including drawing on African traditional religious practices and the new Pentecostal traditions that are also growing dramatically on the continent. While moving away from past condemnation, African bishops' conferences struggle with achieving a balance between embracing African culture, including aspects of African religion, and (with one eye fixed on Rome) preserving the doctrines and practices of the universal church. It is not easy: at what point, for example, does the continent-wide veneration of one's ancestors (which the church often equates with honouring the saints) or recourse to traditional spiritual healers become worship of other 'gods' – or witchcraft? Many Catholics (including priests, some formed in highly 'Roman' seminaries) believe in both Christ and the ancestors, Western science and traditional healing.

The Catholic Charismatic Renewal enjoys some influence on the continent, notably in countries like South Africa, Cameroon, Nigeria and Kenya. This movement draws on 'Catholicised' elements of Pentecostalism (and in some cases aspects of African traditional religion) – speaking in tongues, spiritual healing, being 'slain in the spirit' and so on – without leading to a schism from the religious mainstream. What gives the Charismatic Renewal in many parts of Africa its distinctiveness is its preoccupation with healing. Healing might be the single greatest element in both African Pentecostalism and African traditional religion (perhaps not surprising on a continent with high levels of contagious diseases and limited public health infrastructure), and the Renewal's embrace of it makes sense: it is the church's way to meet an existing spiritual need that is often not explicitly expressed in its spiritual mainstream. This occurs not without tensions, however: Charismatic healing frequently embraces a worldview of witchcraft and demons that the Westernised hierarchies would prefer to downplay. Some Charismatic groups and individual leaders have become so obsessed by this that conflicts have arisen between them and local bishops. Tensions, too, arise between Catholics who see diseases like HIV/AIDS as a spiritual malaise and the majority, particularly those in health care, who see it biomedically, albeit with multifaceted social dimensions.

The Catholic Church's relationship with Islam, which in parts of West Africa, the Sahel and the east coast of the continent has been established longer than Christianity, is even more complex. Adequately categorising African Islam theologically is difficult. It varies between theologically progressive and open to pluralism, including liberal democracy, and militant, as epitomised by rigid Sharia law, anti-Christian persecution and practices like female genital mutilation, which many Muslims see as owing more to local cultural accretions than to the Qur'an. In many parts of Africa, competition between Muslims and Christians (including Catholics) for converts is fierce. In parts of northern Nigeria and East Africa, this has led to low-intensity civil war between government forces (many of them Muslim) and groups like Boko Haram (Nigeria) and Al-Shabaab (East Africa). Such conflict is arguably less about theology than about the state of post-colonial politics, particularly the failures of many decolonised African states to deliver to citizens. In failed, failing or weak states, strong religions like Islam and Catholicism create social infrastructures as well as communal spiritual identities. A key factor here is numerical balances between religious groups: the more religiously diverse the communities, the more Christians and Muslims alike support and promote religious tolerance and liberal democratic values.

It is primarily from the twin features of the positive signs of a growing, vibrant church in Africa and the less salubrious signs of clericalism and denial that one might analyse the most important ecclesiastical development in the contemporary African church: the African Synods of 1994 and 2009. As with most regional, continental and international synods held since the early 1970s (an exception perhaps being the Extraordinary Synod on the Family in 2015), they reflect the uneasy tension between collegiality and centralism in Catholic governance. While both were African synods, they were held in Rome. Although the synods employed African theologians as consultors, some of whom helped to draft the preparatory documents and the final statements, everything was carefully vetted by authorities in Rome, including the prepared statements made by bishops at the meetings. The findings of these synods reflect not only these tensions but also the ambivalence with which theology in Africa has become an inculturated African theology.

The 1994 Synod, and John Paul II's 1995 post-synodal Apostolic Exhortation *Ecclesia in Africa*, described the church as the Family of God in Africa and embraced the work of inculturation, directly linking it to the doctrine of Incarnation: inculturation 'incarnating' Christ on the continent. On inculturation, the Pope indicated two essential criteria to be followed in practice: compatibility with the Christian message and Communion with the universal Church. Many observers noted that while sounding good, the positive imagery underplayed or glossed over significant issues. The image of family insufficiently interrogated the complexity of forms of family life on the continent – the 'Christian' nuclear family, the extended family, and polygamy, and in some areas the reality of single-parent families. Similarly, it failed to grapple with the complexities of African culture and the persistence of African traditional religious practices among many Catholics.

In contrast to the *ad intra* focus of 1994, the second Synod (2009) and Benedict's post-synodal exhortation highlighted the ways in which the church could be at the service of justice and peace in Africa. While reaffirming the image of the African church as the Family of God and acknowledging its importance to the well-being of global Catholicism (the 'lung' image), the Synod raised the important issue of the social role of the church, not only in terms of its service to the continent in areas like health and education but also in the promotion of justice and peace. Here the tone was both realistic and challenging: realistic in the sense that it recognised the church's limitations and challenging in the sense that the church had to do more. Particularly important to the Synod was the church's role in promoting human life, economic justice, greater social equality, opposition to corruption and building democratic states. In short, it was both an acknowledgment that decolonisation had not delivered all the social goods its leaders had promised and a pledge to Africa that the Catholic Church was on the side of positive social change.

Why did the 2009 Synod take this stance? First, despite the 're-Romanisation' of the church, it must be acknowledged that African Catholicism has to a significant degree the features of a post-colonial church, no longer tied up with foreign-born missionaries and their home churches but, for better and worse, with local societies and cultures. Second, the African church now saw its social and spiritual challenges rooted in the decolonised states in which it operated: fears of a hostile new state ready to punish the church for its colonial sins had abated; its decolonised African identity (however influenced by Rome) was no longer in question; its ongoing social importance to new African states had been affirmed, even if part of that was now to challenge the failures of these new states. The question was no longer one of adjustment, but of how to make Catholicism's considerable and growing presence felt in the 'post-colony'.

Decolonisation, as has been noted, has had a mixed impact in Africa. Although no longer ruled by Europe, Africa's journey has been pockmarked by corrupt new ruling elites, often in alliance with multinationals, who have extracted the continent's resources to their mutual benefit at the expense of Africa's citizens. Elsewhere poorly-thought-out socialist strategies have created economic failure and increased poverty. Although progress has been made through the African Union in promoting democracy and good governance, cronyism between heads of state and an often knee-jerk anti-West response to outside criticism remain major problems. The Catholic Church's response to this ongoing struggle for good governance and social justice has taken a number of often interlinked forms: prophetic denunciation, diplomacy and education. Informed by Catholic social thought and tempered by more than a century of grassroots experience, the Catholic Church in Africa combines these modalities in socio-political situations as varied as election monitoring, service to refugees displaced by wars, civic education of laity in public life, and public statements denouncing corruption, atrocities and election-rigging, as well as quiet negotiation and mediation between parties.

That the church had a role, for example, in ending the civil war in Sudan that led to the creation of Africa's newest nation-state, South Sudan, is indisputable; the story that is yet to be told is how extensive this was. What is known is that Catholic leaders denounced human rights abuses and promoted a negotiated ceasefire between the Muslim north and non-Muslim south. As the new country develops, the church continues to pour resources – particularly education – into South Sudan, while trying to mediate the end to factional violence that has marred its independence.

Education for justice and the training of new leaders committed to democracy and clean governance continue to feature across the continent. Hekima College in Nairobi, Kenya, offers workshops, short courses and a master's degree in peace studies and conflict resolution. Other Catholic social justice centres train many people (including non-Catholics) in similar areas and do valuable social research that informs the wider public. A notable example of the latter is the 'food basket' – a survey of basic foodstuff costs – that was initiated in Zambia by the Lusaka-based Jesuit Centre for Theological Reflection and is currently being introduced in other African countries.

An innovation in Catholic political advocacy has been the creation in some countries of Parliamentary Liaison Offices. First introduced in 1999, the South African Office has built up good cross-party relations in Parliament and has made interventions promoting and sometimes challenging proposed legislation. Such work, combined with the quiet presence of papal nunciatures (Vatican State embassies), adds a diplomatic dimension to the church's social mission.

Beyond the overtly political, the church's presence in post-colonial Africa extends widely and deeply into areas like education and health care. As noted above, many of the rulers of newly independent Africa failed to provide these services, whether because the state itself was too poor or because new elites neglected citizens, distracted by their pursuit of personal gain. The result is that, today, some of the best hospitals and clinics, schools and universities are church-run. (Parallels exist within other Christian churches and Islam.) Such a situation is not without its challenges. The perennial question for schools, for example, is the extent to which they should admit non-Catholics (which most do). Although since the Second Vatican Council the mentality of Catholic exclusivity has largely faded away (apart from the obvious exception – minor seminaries), there remains the problem of maintaining a school's Catholic identity or ethos. Beyond this dilemma is the debate over whether the focus of schools should be on educating an elite – with the hope that a social justice ethos might have an impact on the next generation – or educating the poor. It is not easy to resolve, particularly when considering the great disparity of resources these schools have, which mirrors the gaps between rich and poor on the continent. Although it cannot deal directly with income gaps between private fee-paying elite schools and state-funded township and rural schools, the Catholic Institute of Education in South Africa, for example, has tried to bridge this gap by providing ongoing teacher formation across the rich–poor divide.

Catholic health care is another challenging area. Although the presence of Catholic-founded and Catholic-run hospitals and clinics across Africa is considerable, providing wide-ranging care in areas underserved or simply overlooked by the state, the decline of religious orders of men and women dedicated to health care presents a problem. The decline in priest, brother or sister doctors and nurses means (as in schools founded by teaching orders) having to foot the bill for lay staff in an era when foreign funding is drying up. The question of Catholic ethos resurges again, compounded by the moral dilemmas many Catholic hospitals face today with regard to HIV/AIDS. The Catholic Church is the single largest private HIV/AIDS care provider in Africa (in fact, as the World Health Organization has noted, in the world). Like other churches, the Catholic Church has been deeply involved in almost all aspects of dealing with the pandemic, particularly in Southern and Eastern Africa, which have still the highest HIV infection rate in the world. This has included human rights advocacy for persons living with HIV, lobbying governments and pharmaceutical companies to provide free or cheap antiretroviral drugs, AIDS awareness education and direct medical care. The challenge here has been the official Catholic rejection of condom use as a strategy to prevent the spread of HIV, the reasoning being that the condom is an artificial form of contraception (officially rejected by the church) and that ready access to and use of condoms might promote promiscuity. Although this teaching and argument are by no means accepted by all Catholics, Catholic hospitals are at least officially expected to abide by the rule. The result has been an uneasy engagement of Catholic health-care institutions in Africa in dealing with HIV/AIDS. Many hospitals and carers have condoms available 'under the counter' and remind their patients of the classic Catholic moral theology maxim: follow your formed and informed conscience. Theologians, priests and bishops, too, are by no means all of one mind with the church's teaching. Low-key debate continues throughout the African (and global) church.

Inevitably, perhaps, as one looks at the contemporary Catholic Church in Sub-Saharan Africa, the question must be asked: what about the future? Can the Church continue to grow? Apart from South Africa, which has seen a marked increase in secularism (from 1% to 10% over the last 20 years), there seems little sign of secularisation in Africa. The Catholic Church continues to enjoy considerable influence and prestige, largely through its social work. In many parts of the continent it might even be seen as performing the functions normally associated with the state. Although it might not have inculturated as extensively or quickly as the Second Vatican Council generation desired, it has developed roots in

African consciousness. Whether this will change, and the church decline in numbers and influence, as African states consolidate democracy, human rights and service delivery to citizens – reducing in the process the Catholic Church's social influence – is unclear.

## Bibliography

Baur, John, *2000 Years of Christianity in Africa: An African History 62–1992* (Nairobi: Paulines Publications Africa, 1994).

Dowd, Robert A., *Christianity, Islam and Liberal Democracy: Lessons from Sub-Saharan Africa* (New York: Oxford University Press, 2015).

Orobator, Agbonkhianmege E. (ed.), *Reconciliation, Justice and Peace: The Second African Synod* (Maryknoll, NY: Orbis Books, 2011).

Sundkler, Bengt and Christopher Steed, *A History of the Church in Africa* (Cambridge: Cambridge University Press, 2000).

Wall, Barbra Mann, *Into Africa: A Transnational History of Catholic Medical Missions and Social Change* (New Brunswick, NJ: Rutgers University Press, 2015).

# Evangelicals


## Anthony Balcomb


The presence of the Christian religion in Sub-Saharan Africa could now be described as ubiquitous. It has so insinuated itself into the African habitus in this region that if you live there it is quite likely that you have embraced it in some form or another. And, if we are to believe the statistics coming out of a 2010 study, the chances that you have embraced one of the Evangelical incarnations of the religion are about one in four. This ratio has probably increased since 2010. In Sub-Saharan Africa, Evangelicals are to be found throughout the social spectrum. What follows is an attempt to understand what Evangelicalism is, what it does for its followers and how it translates into the social structures of African society.

### What Evangelicalism Is

Evangelicals have a distinctive basic theology that can be traced back to various movements coming out of the Protestant Reformation: Anabaptism, Pietism and the eighteenth-century revivals under George Whitefield and John Wesley. The defining features of this theology are its focus on the individual and its emphasis on a personal relationship with God through Jesus Christ. This relationship must be cultivated through prayer, Bible study, worship and witness, under the guidance of the Holy Spirit. The intense awareness of a personal God who invites people into a loving, reciprocating relationship is the central theological motif of Evangelicalism and expresses itself in many different forms. It is a relationship that is described as 'walking with the Lord', which means cultivating a consciousness of God's presence and guidance through the Word of God (the Bible and the prompting of the Spirit), through prayer and public witness. Sometimes this relationship is accompanied by a strong sense of sin and of the need for forgiveness, and abstention from worldly pursuits, while at other times it is manifest more in the blessings of a generous and powerful God who wants your health and prosperity. The normative pattern of social behaviour for Evangelicals involves: abstention from alcohol, tobacco and premarital sex; modesty in dress; honesty, diligence and integrity in the workplace; discipline in lifestyle; and strict protocols of correct behaviour between the sexes. Where the so-called 'prosperity gospel' prevails, many of these characteristics are eclipsed, although not necessarily obliterated, by the belief that God's main concern for you is your prosperity, health and success in this life.

Evangelicals stand in the tradition of doctrinal orthodoxy as outlined in the Nicene Creed. However, they have no unifying magisterium that enforces orthodoxy with regard to doctrine and church polity and are instead guided by their denominations, local churches, charismatic leaders and Bible teachers, or simply their own understandings of how God is leading them. This makes for interesting, wide, diverse and sometimes creative understandings of the faith.

Evangelicalism exists throughout the Protestant and Anglican traditions and even has quasi-manifestations in Roman Catholicism. Unlike their Western counterparts, Protestants in Sub-Saharan Africa are highly likely also to be Evangelical. The typical Western Protestant division between Evangelicals and Ecumenicals has little validity in the African context. Evangelicalsim in this region also has its own denominational expressions, as well as numerous Independent churches that have spontaneously developed through the guidance of the Spirit. It has a wide spectrum of doctrinal emphases, from conservative Evangelical churches, such as the Baptist Church, the Church of England in South Africa and the African Evangelical Church, to the plethora of Pentecostal and Charismatic churches that are recognised by their emphasis on the Holy Spirit, the practice of the gifts of the Spirit, the baptism in the Spirit and so-called 'power encounters'. Evangelicalism also manifests in a wide variety of para-church organisations, such as the Association of Evangelicals in Africa, Scripture Union, International Federation of Evangelical Students, World Evangelical Alliance, Lausanne Committee for World Evangelization and African Enterprise. It is important to note that Pentecostals are the fastest growing and most numerous of the Evangelicals. It must also be noted, however, that while all Pentecostals are Evangelical, not all Evangelicals are Pentecostal.

Evangelicals have an intense interest in Scripture, take it very seriously and generally adopt the principle of *sola scriptura* (the Bible is the only guide

*Evangelicals in Sub-Saharan Africa, 1970*

| Region | Total population | Christian population | Evangelical population | % of region Evangelical | % of Christians Evangelical |
|---|---|---|---|---|---|
| *Eastern Africa* | 110,428,000 | 54,913,000 | 6,013,000 | 5.5% | 11.0% |
| *Middle Africa* | 40,846,000 | 29,888,000 | 2,676,000 | 6.6% | 9.0% |
| *Southern Africa* | 25,454,000 | 19,291,000 | 3,098,000 | 12.2% | 16.1% |
| *Western Africa* | 106,015,000 | 30,143,000 | 6,209,000 | 5.9% | 20.6% |
| Sub-Saharan Africa | 282,743,000 | 134,235,000 | 17,997,000 | 6.4% | 13.4% |
| Globe | 3,682,488,000 | 1,230,688,000 | 105,864,000 | 2.9% | 8.6% |

Source: Todd M. Johnson and Gina A. Zurlo (eds), *World Christian Database* (Leiden/Boston: Brill), accessed March 2016.

for faith). While there is an effort among some theologically literate Evangelicals to follow the basic Protestant principles of biblical interpretation (that is, Scripture 'interprets itself'), most often the individualist paradigm prevails. This makes for interesting and creative readings of the Bible. Both ordinary believers and the theologically educated undertake intense and lively discussion around the meaning of Scripture. If you believe that the Holy Spirit is guiding you, then Scripture is a resource with potentially endless itineraries of meaning. Some of these might be entirely new and important enough to attract other believers and even possibly to start a new church. Others might be totally outlandish but nevertheless influential for entire congregations (this occurs frequently among some of the prosperity preachers). Any of these, however, can be highly significant to those who hold them.

Evangelicalism has distinctive social manifestations. In its nonconformist, independent forms it is characteristically anti-clerical, anti-institutional and voluntarist. Although Evangelicals are strongly biased towards an individualistic understanding of society, they have little time for the concept of individual human rights, which they (and especially those who have entered into theological debate with Ecumenicals) associate with secular humanism, the *bête noire* of most Evangelicals. Evangelicals can be trusted to have a conservative stance towards all matters pertaining to human sexuality, including issues around gender and homosexuality, although, arguably, these positions are no different from those of the majority of Africans. They are usually intolerant of other religions and, indeed, of any points of view that differ from their own when it comes to what they believe to be the truth. Evangelicals are nothing if not certain about what they believe, and that theological certainty usually translates, for better or worse, into certainties in most other areas of human endeavour. They are, by definition, a proselytising, if not *the* proselytising, voice of contemporary Christianity in Africa and, as such, are likely to view other religions and their followers as candidates for conversion, rivals in the mission field or works of the devil.

*Evangelicals in Sub-Saharan Africa, 2015*

| Region | Total population | Christian population | Evangelical population | % of region Evangelical | % of Christians Evangelical |
|---|---|---|---|---|---|
| *Eastern Africa* | 394,477,000 | 259,865,000 | 60,851,000 | 15.4% | 23.4% |
| *Middle Africa* | 151,952,000 | 125,422,000 | 14,476,000 | 9.5% | 11.5% |
| *Southern Africa* | 62,634,000 | 51,611,000 | 6,110,000 | 9.8% | 11.8% |
| *Western Africa* | 353,224,000 | 127,638,000 | 48,743,000 | 13.8% | 38.2% |
| Sub-Saharan Africa | 962,287,000 | 564,536,000 | 130,179,000 | 13.5% | 23.1% |
| Globe | 7,349,472,000 | 2,416,268,000 | 320,405,000 | 4.4% | 13.3% |

Source: Todd M. Johnson and Gina A. Zurlo (eds), *World Christian Database* (Leiden/Boston: Brill), accessed March 2016.

Within global Evangelicalism, however, there is a significant voice that can be described as socio-politically progressive. These progressive Evangelicals like to point out that, historically, Evangelicals were on the cutting edge of the abolition of the slave trade and that their influence on democracy has been fundamental at the grassroots level. Some significant Evangelical voices in Sub-Saharan Africa echo these concerns. For example, Archbishop David Gitari of Kenya and Archbishop Luwum of Uganda, Anglicans of Evangelical persuasion (as most African Anglicans are), resisted the regimes of Daniel Arap Moi and Idi Amin, respectively. The Concerned Evangelicals group in South Africa spoke out against that country's apartheid regime. Luwum (who paid the ultimate price for his witness) was influenced by the East African Revival of the 1920s and 1930s, a non-Pentecostal revivalist movement that emphasised repentance, public confession of personal sin and intense personal piety. These prophetic voices within African Evangelicalism, however, are the exception rather than the rule. Evangelicals generally have little appreciation of the structural, systemic and socio-political dimensions of the gospel because these simply do not fit into their individualistic paradigm, even though such issues loom large in the Old Testament prophetic Scriptures as well as in the teachings of Jesus. To most Evangelicals, the antidote to sin in society is salvation of the individual: the more people who 'get saved', the better society will become; the more 'born again' Christians who enter politics, the greater the possibility of better government; the more 'saved' people there are in business, the more honest business will become; and so on.

Although Evangelicals prioritise individual salvation, they do not ignore social outreach programmes entirely. Many are involved in social uplift initiatives among the poor. Arguably, however, their most telling contribution among the poor and marginalised has been their positive message of self-worth and a keen sense of personal agency leading to what the church-growth school of mission calls 'redemption and lift'. That is, the experience of salvation enables upward mobility socially and economically in society. If poverty in Africa is one of the effects of globalisation,

*Changes in Evangelicals in Sub-Saharan Africa, 1970–2015, growth rate, % per year*

| Region | Total population | Christian population | Evangelical population |
|---|---|---|---|
| *Eastern Africa* | 2.87% | 3.52% | 5.28% |
| *Middle Africa* | 2.96% | 3.24% | 3.82% |
| *Southern Africa* | 2.02% | 2.21% | 1.52% |
| *Western Africa* | 2.71% | 3.26% | 4.69% |
| Sub-Saharan Africa | 2.76% | 3.24% | 4.50% |
| Globe | 1.55% | 1.51% | 2.49% |

Source: Todd M. Johnson and Gina A. Zurlo (eds), *World Christian Database* (Leiden/Boston: Brill), accessed March 2016.

then Evangelicalism meets the needs that globalisation creates on a more fundamental level, by providing people with some of the psychological and social capacities they need to cope with the profound socio-economic challenges that globalisation brings. This might be one of the reasons for Evangelicalism's remarkable growth in modern Africa.

## What Evangelicalism Does for its Followers in Africa

When Evangelicals experience and embrace the good news of the gospel, a process of transformation of the individual begins. Although there is such a thing as second- and third-generation Evangelicalism, the ideal scenario in Evangelical theology is the unique transaction that takes place between each individual believer and God through Jesus Christ. This is formulated in terms of rebirth. Old things pass away and all things become new. All things become new because the believer becomes new. This is not the adoption of a new religion or new code of behaviour; it is an existential transformation of the individual that brings salvation, and with it certainty, well-being, purpose, meaning and joy. There is no better description of this in the African context than that given in a novel by Chinua Achebe:

> It was the poetry of the new religion, something felt in the marrow. The hymn about brothers who sat in darkness and in fear seemed to answer a vague and persistent question that haunted his young soul … He felt relief within as the hymn poured into his parched soul. The words of the hymn were like the drops of frozen rain melting on the dry palate of the panting earth. Nwoye's callow mind was greatly puzzled. (Chinua Achebe, *Things Fall Apart*, Oxford: Heinemann, 1986, 105)

In Achebe's story people make many different responses to the gospel message. Indeed, the hero of the novel, Okwonkwo, made himself the arch enemy of the new religion. But Nwoye's response was a typically Evangelical one. The gospel is experienced at a profoundly existential level. It answers a deep yearning in the soul rather than appealing to the intellect. The following statement by a group of African Evangelicals is elucidating in this regard:

> Rightly presented and understood, the gospel of Jesus Christ is capable of meeting the primal man [sic] at the point(s) of his greatest need, providing him with ultimate answers to his longings and effective ways of coping with the persistent problems in his life. Sometimes this will happen suddenly, but, more often than not, it is a process or processes of 'power encounter' between Christian and the primal world-views in which the former transforms the latter's view of God, man, and the 'powers' through Jesus Christ. (Quoted in Howell, 1994: 1)

Two constructs are being used here, one ethnographic and one theological. The term 'primal' is probably a reference to Harold Turner's construct of an African worldview, which is used by some prominent African thinkers such as Kwame Bediako and Ogbu Kalu. It refers to the condition that existed first – that is, before the advent of modernity. A primal construction of reality is one in which animals and plants have their own spiritual place in the universe; where there is a strong sense that humankind is vulnerable and finite and in need of transcendent power; where humans are perceived to exist in a spiritual world of beings more powerful and ultimate than themselves, including ancestors, and with whom relationships can be entered into; and where there is no sharp dichotomy between sacred and profane. The theological construct of 'the powers' is based on a kind of re-enchantment of the universe that resonates with an African worldview and finds its scriptural legitimation in the sixth chapter of Paul's letter to the Ephesians, in which he asserts that believers 'wrestle not against flesh and blood but against principalities and powers'. It has been popularised by the 'spiritual warfare' theory of Charles Kraft and the Church Growth School in America and can reach phantasmagoric proportions among some of its more 'enchanted' interpreters in Africa, the Nigerian pastor Daniel Olukoya of the Mountain of Fire and Miracles Ministries being a good example.

The suggestion made by these scholars is that Evangelicalism transacts at the interface of the African and modern universes. It meets the needs that an African condition creates and opens the way to what a modern condition demands. It resonates both with the spirituality of Africa and with the materialism and individualism of modernity. Its individualism gives its adherents the sense of agency that in the African universe is opaque and complex due to the plethora of other agencies that have to be negotiated, including ancestors, spirits, a remote deity and a multiplicity of local deities. Such a cosmology has been called 'diffused monotheism' by the Nigerian scholar Bolaji Idowu. These entities have a direct impact on the material existence of the 'primal man', who finds himself profoundly vulnerable in the complex web of powers through which he must navigate. 'Primal women' in such a universe arguably find themselves even more vulnerable, as they are frequently accused of witchcraft (that is, of being an agent who is able to manipulate the powers in a destructive way). Although Evangelicals are not known for their concern about women's liberation, the empowerment and sense of agency that Evangelicalism brings is clearly not restricted to men. An Evangelical understanding of the gospel claims that the risen Christ has brought these 'principalities and powers' under His control. To receive Christ is therefore to bring the control that Christ has to the individual in a way that he or she was unable to enjoy under the previous regime. The liberation and subsequent empowerment that the believer experiences in this transaction give a new sense of agency in a world where individualism is paramount – that is, the modern world – and into which the Evangelical believer fits hand in glove, because Evangelicalism acts in concert with three essential forces in modernity: the centrality of the individual, the mastery of nature, and the disenchantment of the universe. It has already been argued that the first of these is a central characteristic of Evangelicalism. The second and third are implicit in the above definition. When conversion begins, sometimes but not always with a kind of 'Damascus road' crisis experience of encounter with the risen Christ, there begins also a process or processes of 'power encounter' between the Christian and primal universes 'in which the former transforms the latter's view of God, man, and the "powers" through Jesus Christ' (quoted in Allison Howell, *The Religious Itinerary of Ghanaian People: The Kasena and the Christian Gospel*, London: Peter Lang, 1994, 1).

African Evangelicalism, according to these scholars, is characterised by an uncompromising dualism between 'the powers' and Christianity. The rupture between these two regimes of power, for all intents and purposes, appears to be to do with forsaking African culture and adopting Western culture. Indeed, many aspects of African Evangelicalism make it an easy target for the post-colonial criticism that it is just another manifestation of the mimicry of the coloniser by the colonised; that they are just so many meek little 'Fridays' being 'civilised' by so many 'Robinson Crusoes'. African Evangelicals themselves, however, insist that the Christianity that they embrace has an African, not a European, identity, and some interesting examples support their claim. Three paradigmatic ones from South African history are Ntsikana ka Gaba, Tiyo Soga and Nicholas Bhengu.

Ntsikana was a Xhosa prophet who had an epiphany-like encounter with Christ through his favourite ox, Hulushe, in about 1815. He immediately washed the ochre from his skin, which symbolised the shedding of his traditional religion, and began to teach repentance from sin and conversion to Christ. He gathered a group of converts around him and composed a famous hymn that contained the first articulations of an indigenous Xhosa Christian theology; only towards the end of his life did he encourage his followers to consult with Western missionaries and learn further from them.

Tiyo Soga's father was one of Ntsikana's converts. Soga is representative of a conversion process that took him much further than Ntsikana down the road towards modernity. He was educated in mission schools and through further schooling in Scotland, in order that he might be better equipped to serve as an evangelist among his own people. He became a missionary, journalist and scholar, working to translate both the Bible and John Bunyan's *The Pilgrim's Progress* into Xhosa. He married a Scottish woman and was attacked by people on both sides of the racial divide for his apparent mimicry of the 'perfect English gentleman' of the day. His own position on the matter was that he was as proudly African as he was Christian. He became a vociferous and articulate exponent of both Christianity and African nationalism. Both he and Ntsikana have been held up by Africans as early forerunners of African nationalism, which is indicative of the profound influence that Evangelical Christianity had in its early formation.

Nicholas Bhengu was a Zulu-speaking court interpreter who converted to Christ through American missionaries in 1929. He joined the South African Assemblies of God and became the founder of an evangelistic mission known as the Back to God Crusade in 1959. Hundreds of thousands of people were converted, healed and transformed under his ministry and the Back to God Crusade arguably became the biggest self-propagating, self-governing and self-supporting indigenous Evangelical movement in Sub-Saharan Africa. Although the core of his message was salvation through repentance from sin and faith in Christ, his understanding of salvation included the restoration of self-confidence and dignity for African people in the face of apartheid. He taught that Christianity was African before it became European and his meetings brought about remarkable healing between the so-called 'red people' (because of the custom of covering their skin with red ochre) and 'school people' – in other words, the traditional rural Black and the urban educated Black. His was a form of Christianity that was clearly Evangelical, that indeed seemed to meet Africans at the point of their deepest need, and that acted as a bridge to modernity without sacrificing African dignity and pride.

These three case studies have been cited as exemplary of an African Evangelicalism that fulfils the very specific needs of those who embrace it. They also contradict the theory that Evangelicalism is about mimesis or the 'Robinson Crusoe syndrome'. Ntsikana's experience was apparently completely independent of missionary influence until near the end of his life. During the course of his lifetime, Soga very specifically distanced himself from the racism of most of the early missionaries in the Eastern Cape. Bhengu's operation was entirely self-sufficient and completely independent of white influence. In fact, in the Assemblies of God in South Africa Bhengu arguably had far more influence, a much higher profile and greater stature than any of his white counterparts. The case studies also reinforce the idea that Evangelicalism transacts at the interface between an African and modern way of being in the world and is experienced as empowering for the individual, specifically within a modern context. This is further interrogated when analysing how Evangelicalism translates into social structures.

## How Evangelicalism Translates Socially, Economically and Politically

That religious faith translates into feelings, values, attitudes, capacities, propensities and tendencies within social contexts has been deemed axiomatic ever since Max Weber wrote *The Protestant Ethic and the Spirit of Capitalism* (1905). An important piece of research that takes as its departure point Weber's hypothesis (and in which this author took part) has been done by a capitalist think-tank among Pentecostals in the South African context. Since it has been asserted in this discussion that Evangelicalism in Sub-Saharan Africa meets the needs that globalisation creates, it would be important to look more carefully at what this research uncovered.

The Centre for Development and Enterprise (CDE), based in Johannesburg, undertook research among Pentecostals (mainly in the Gauteng region, but also in Cape Town and Durban) between 2005 and 2007. This research consisted of: interviews with pastors, aimed at investigating their basic message; surveys investigating how their faith had penetrated the fabric of society in terms of values, attitudes and behaviour; and interviews with Pentecostal politicians and businesspeople in order to investigate the role their faith played in their respective work arenas. It should be borne in mind that the study was hardly 'objective' (in the sense that it was without an agenda). This was a capitalist organisation looking for signs that would benefit a capitalist economy. This should not detract from its importance, however.

In this research, the influence of Evangelical faith in the socio-economic sphere was discernible at three levels: the psychological and emotional; the impartation of skills; and the moral. According to the research, the faith induces a number of benefits on a psychological level: believers find meaning and identity and therefore can 'put up with the meaningless and dis-identifying world of the mega-structures'; the 'emotional rejection of worldly concerns relaxes them and releases energy for the same worldly concerns, precisely because these things mean so little for them'; and a buoyant and positive mood is promoted among the faithful that is often in sharp contrast to the pessimism and low morale that exists around them. This is besides the benefits that religious faith in general brings to the areas of hypertension, longevity, depression, suicide, alcohol and drug use, and youth delinquency. All of these contribute significantly to a kind of spiritual and social capital that in turn translates into a healthier and more productive citizenship.

On a skills level, many Evangelical churches provide numerous opportunities: to communicate a simple message; to organise promotional efforts; to make lists; to use telephones; to solve personality clashes; to set goals and reach them; to come to meetings on time, run them efficiently and implement the decisions made there; to do household budgeting, get training in marriage and sexual disciplines; and to meet life partners. Such opportunities for skills training are especially important in the African context, where the institutional infrastructure for such training in civil society is usually very weak.

On the moral level, the Evangelical faith elicits a condition that Weber famously described as 'this-worldly asceticism'. This refers to the Evangelical believer's attitude towards worldly pleasures that are deemed sinful and therefore forbidden, but at the same time it emphasises hard work, honesty and the deferral of gratification and instant consumption, all in the context of a worldview that is free of magic and superstition and therefore favours predictability and 'rational' planning – all of which adds up to sound economic habits such as frugality, saving, capital accumulation and economic advancement. Combined with stable relationships in the home and an emphasis on education, this makes for the dream upwardly mobile middle-class citizen bound only for success in a capitalist society. (See *Under the Radar: Pentecostalism in South Africa and Its Potential Social and Economic Role*, Johannesburg: Centre for Development and Enterprise, March 2008.)

It must be said that these attributes do not apply to the so-called 'prosperity gospel' in its more extreme forms. The glorification of rampant consumerism, the reinforcement of the 'big man' syndrome in Africa and exploitation of the religious beliefs of ordinary Africans by 'servants of God' who make millions through the apparent gullibility of their followers can hardly be associated with asceticism, rationalism or frugality. However, it must also be said that the association of Evangelicalism with capitalism in general lends credence to the theory that Evangelicalism is the 'watchdog' of neo-liberalism in Africa, just as the Christian mission was the 'watchdog' of imperialism in the early nineteenth century. Analysing religious practice in terms of its pragmatic usefulness in the context of a hegemonic economic system is one thing; to argue its veracity on the basis that it reinforces the values, practices and institutions of such a system is surely another thing altogether. Arguably the role of any true religion, including the Evangelical variety, is to express solidarity with those who have been marginalised by the values and practices of an economic system and not valorise how it acts in concert with them. Perhaps more rigorous thinking needs to be done by Evangelicals themselves concerning the meaning and integrity of the gospel of Jesus Christ and how it should manifest in a 'fallen' world.

Significant work has been done on the role of Evangelicals in politics in Africa. Although the Evangelical approach to politics is consistent with an individualistic understanding of salvation in general, this does not mean that Evangelicals do not play an important role in the political arena. They demonstrate a wide range of interventions into such an arena, from the belief that populating it with 'born again' people will ultimately change the face of politics, to blatant support of the political status quo on the basis of Paul's teaching that political powers are ordained by God, to opposing secularism in the belief that it is anti-Christian, to the 'can do' approach that one can do anything through Christ, Who strengthens you, including start and lead Christian political parties and even influence entire countries to become more Christian. Evangelicals do it all. President Daniel Arap Moi of Kenya, a member of an Evangelical church, believed that he could spread Christian love and unity among the Kenyan people. Frederick Chiluba, to the delight of the Evangelicals, declared Zambia a Christian nation. Unfortunately, both of them succumbed to the temptations that accompany positions of power and tarnished the image of Evangelicals in politics as a result. Indeed, conspicuous by its absence when it comes to the direct involvement of Evangelicals in the formal political arena is an understanding of the pitfalls involved, although such insight could have been gleaned from even a cursory examination of the 2,000 or so years of Christianity's attempts at involvement in that arena. In other words, the problems associated with the notion that God comes to you *de novum* are no better illustrated than in the political arena. In the South African context, for example, opposition to the apartheid regime by some Evangelicals translated into uncritical support for the forces of the democratic revolution which, on the other side of a changed status quo, translated into identification with the new government of the African National Congress (ANC) until this also compromised them. On the other hand, those whose political quietism translated into support for the apartheid government in the name of obedience to Scripture soon also found themselves thoroughly compromised with an evil regime. Evangelicals, in other words, have found it particularly difficult to navigate the tempestuous political waters of Sub-Saharan Africa.

This does not mean that Evangelicals have not had a positive influence on the development of democracy in the region. However, this influence has been mainly indirect, through the inculcation of individual agency and the provision of voluntary associations. These provide the space in which the basic principles of democratic practice can be worked out, in an atmosphere where self-worth is encouraged and relationships of equality, mutual acceptance, tolerance and respect emerge out of a common faith and sense of a common destiny. These communities also provide a moral and spiritual compass for their members, which enables them to participate in popular discontent with government, especially with respect to corruption. Moreover, their theology of the powers is not always restricted to the spiritual sphere. The 'wrestling' against wickedness in high places can translate into more institutional participation in politics. However, the divine authority that they believe they have can militate against notions of tolerance, diversity and pluralism.

## Conclusion – Interpreting Evangelicalism through Different Paradigms

Evangelicalism in Sub-Saharan Africa is too powerful, too popular and too pervasive to ignore. How it is understood depends on the paradigm one uses to interpret it. It has been understood by Africans themselves in two different ways – firstly as a function of the neo-liberal project of conquest, and secondly as a function of the liberating gospel. The truth is probably to be found in a combination of both of these perspectives. The existential reality of Africans is that they live in a world powerfully influenced by forces that are both modern and pre-modern. Evangelicalism enables them to transact between these forces in a way that many clearly find, at the least, helpful and, at the most, liberating. This might not fit easily with ideal conceptions of the gospel, from whatever theological perspective these are constructed. But this is probably of little concern to Evangelicals themselves.

## Bibliography


Bediako, Gillian Mary, Benhardt Y. Quarshie and J. Kwabena-Asamoah-Gyadu (eds), *Seeing New Facets of the Diamond – Christianity as a Universal Faith. Essays in Honour of Kwame Bediako* (Oxford: Regnum Africa, 2014).

Bediako, Kwame, *Christianity in Africa – The Renewal of a Non-Western Religion* (Edinburgh: Edinburgh University Press, 1995).

Kalu, Ogbu, *African Pentecostalism – An Introduction* (Oxford: Oxford University Press, 2008).

Meyer, Birgit, *Translating the Devil: Religion and Modernity Among the Ewe in Ghana* (Edinburgh: Edinburgh University Press, 1999).

Ranger, Terence (ed.), *Evangelical Christianity and Democracy in Africa* (Oxford: Oxford University Press, 2008).

# Pentecostals/Charismatics

## Michael Adeleke Ogunewu and Isaac Deji Ayegboyin

The rapid expansion of Pentecostalism as a distinctive Christian tradition is widely acknowledged by scholars interested in this burgeoning field of study. The early twenty-first century has seen numerous important studies on Pentecostalism being published by both local and international authors, a development that is indicative of how important this stream of Christianity has become in modern Africa. The authors on Pentecostal/Charismatic Christianity are unanimous in the view that its growth has been explosive, especially from the second half of the twentieth century. The developments in Africa constitute part of the worldwide story of Pentecostalism. Today, Pentecostalism is claimed to be the largest Protestant church movement in the world and a force in global Christianity rivalling Roman Catholicism in terms of numbers and spread. It might even be misleading to talk about Pentecostalism as a movement separate from Catholicism, because the Catholic Charismatic Renewal Movement is one of the most well known and best organised such groups in the world today.

The development of Pentecostalism has been so striking and impressive that, in the early 1950s, the World Council of Churches (WCC) began to recognise the movement as being a 'third force' in Christianity, after Roman Catholicism and mainline Protestantism. Arnold Bittlinger edited a volume entitled *The Church Is Charismatic* (1981) for the WCC in which the impact of Charismatic history and theology on world Christianity is extensively discussed. In other words, Pentecostal/Charismatic Christianity must be viewed as more than a church denomination. Pentecostalism is acknowledged as a distinctive wave of renewal that not only forms as distinct church groups but also emerges as a form of spirituality present within churches open to the experience of the Holy Spirit. The point is that even though Pentecostalism as a Christian movement is relatively young, it has affected millions of Christians and thousands of denominations throughout the world.

### Historical Development of Pentecostalism

Pentecostalism as a movement of renewal is inspired by events in the Acts of the Apostles when the Holy Spirit, descending upon the fearful apostles, transforms them into bold, ardent and convincing evangelists. In addition to the insistence that those who are baptised by the Holy Spirit must speak in tongues as initial evidence, Pentecostalism also emphasises the manifestations of spiritual gifts or charismata such as prophecy, visions and revelations, healing miracles and other signs and wonders. Scholars usually distinguish between the classical Pentecostals and the neo-Pentecostals or Charismatics. The classical Pentecostals are the historically older and doctrinally well established denominations like the Assemblies of God, the Church of the Foursquare Gospel, the Elim Pentecostal Church, the Church of God and many others that trace their roots to William J. Seymour's famous Azusa Street Revival of 1906. Although the list provided is mainly North American in origin, these classical Pentecostal denominations have established branches in various African countries that function under the leadership of indigenous pastors.

Neo-Pentecostalism, on the other hand, consists of three main types of movement: newer independent Charismatic churches, usually associated with the 'prosperity gospel'; trans-denominational Charismatic groups like the Full Gospel Businessmen's Fellowship International; and renewal movements within non-Pentecostal churches like the Catholic Charismatic groups. Thus, in Africa the combined expression Pentecostal/Charismatic may be used to describe all Christian movements – churches, para-church organisations, indigenous Charismatic communities, renewal movements in mainline denominations – that emphasise the experience of the Holy Spirit as definitive for spirituality and practice.

The origin of modern-day Pentecostalism is usually traced to the ministry of Charles Fox Parham at the Bethel Bible College in Topeka, Kansas, in the USA in 1901. Pentecostalism, however, became a global phenomenon from 1906 through Seymour's Azusa Street Revival (Seymour, incidentally, was a former student of Parham). In spite of these historical origins in the USA, scholars now generally accept that Pentecostalism must not be considered as exclusively North American in its origins. There is reason to believe that the American versions of the movement have had some influence

*Pentecostals/Charismatics in Sub-Saharan Africa, 1970*

| Region | Total population | Christian population | Pentecostal/ Charismatic population | % of region Pentecostal/ Charismatic | % of Christians Pentecostal/ Charismatic |
|---|---|---|---|---|---|
| *Eastern Africa* | 110,428,000 | 54,913,000 | 3,451,000 | 3.1% | 6.3% |
| *Middle Africa* | 40,846,000 | 29,888,000 | 5,188,000 | 12.7% | 17.4% |
| *Southern Africa* | 25,454,000 | 19,291,000 | 4,597,000 | 18.1% | 23.8% |
| *Western Africa* | 106,015,000 | 30,143,000 | 5,537,000 | 5.2% | 18.4% |
| Sub-Saharan Africa | 282,743,000 | 134,235,000 | 18,772,000 | 6.6% | 14.0% |
| Globe | 3,682,488,000 | 1,230,688,000 | 62,689,000 | 1.7% | 5.1% |

Source: Todd M. Johnson and Gina A. Zurlo (eds), *World Christian Database* (Leiden/Boston: Brill), accessed March 2016.

on its development in other places, including Africa. Nevertheless, many Pentecostal/Charismatic initiatives in Africa developed independently of the North American versions. In any case, long before Pentecostal movements came on the scene, the African Independent Churches (AICs), with their emphasis on Holy Spirit experiences, had already 'Charismaticised' Christianity in Africa. Indeed, it was the pressure that the AICs brought to bear on the historic mission denominations that led to the tolerance of renewal movements within these older denominations. The coming of the Pentecostals served only to heighten a form of renewal that had already been underway in Africa since the early decades of the twentieth century.

## Pentecostalism in Africa

In the period of its massive growth since the 1960s, Pentecostalism in Sub-Saharan Africa has been a predominantly indigenous movement led by dynamic African preachers and prophets. The precursors were indigenous prophet figures, many of whom were driven out of historic mission denominations. They suffered for pursuing Holy Spirit-inspired activities that were sometimes scandalously perceived by church authorities as 'occult'. Thus, although evangelists and missionaries from Europe and North America had established Pentecostal movements in Sub-Saharan Africa from the 1920s, it was the evangelising efforts of native Charismatic preachers, many of them displaying prophetic graces, that accounted for Pentecostalism's great success and expansion within the region.

In most of Africa, as we have noted, the precursors of modern-day Pentecostalism were the early-twentieth-century AICs. In Nigeria they were known as *Aladura* (praying churches), in Ghana as Spiritual churches and in Southern Africa as Zionist churches. Their main aspiration was to restore to the African church the vitality of the presence of the Holy Spirit that they felt had been neglected by the historic mission denominations. In worship, they laid emphasis on the experience of the Holy Spirit in response to the 'dry denominationalism' of the mission churches. A number of the larger AICs came into contact with overseas Pentecostal churches through the

*Pentecostals/Charismatics in Sub-Saharan Africa, 2015*

| Region | Total population | Christian population | Pentecostal/ Charismatic population | % of region Pentecostal/ Charismatic | % of Christians Pentecostal/ Charismatic |
|---|---|---|---|---|---|
| *Eastern Africa* | 394,477,000 | 259,865,000 | 65,478,000 | 16.6% | 25.2% |
| *Middle Africa* | 151,952,000 | 125,422,000 | 34,675,000 | 22.8% | 27.7% |
| *Southern Africa* | 62,634,000 | 51,611,000 | 28,786,000 | 46.0% | 55.8% |
| *Western Africa* | 353,224,000 | 127,638,000 | 73,190,000 | 20.7% | 57.3% |
| Sub-Saharan Africa | 962,287,000 | 564,536,000 | 202,128,000 | 21.0% | 35.8% |
| Globe | 7,349,472,000 | 2,416,268,000 | 640,307,000 | 8.7% | 26.5% |

Source: Todd M. Johnson and Gina A. Zurlo (eds), *World Christian Database* (Leiden/Boston: Brill), accessed March 2016.

medium of literature, beginning in the late 1920s. These included the Faith Tabernacle Church in the USA and later the Apostolic Church in Britain. On coming to Nigeria, the British Apostolic Church metamorphosed into what is today known as The Apostolic Church (TAC).

Following the emergence of early Pentecostal denominations, other waves of Pentecostal/Charismatic movements started through the evangelism activities of young high-school and university students across West Africa. Most of these belonged to the conservative Evangelical Scripture Union (SU) movement. Conservative Evangelical groups embraced a 'holiness' or 'righteousness' theology, which stresses moral perfection, strict personal ethics and biblical inerrancy. This holiness ethic, which is also present among the classical Pentecostals, emphasises repentance and restitution for past wrongs. Believers are expected not to lie, cheat, steal, quarrel, gossip, give or take bribes, smoke, fornicate, beat their spouses, lose their temper or deny assistance to other members in need. Only limited contact is allowed between members of the opposite sex and a strict dress code for everyone is enforced. Marital infidelity is severely denounced and divorce is not permitted.

The SU and the various Fellowships of Evangelical Students across Africa's universities took on a very Charismatic character, sometimes to the chagrin of world Evangelical leaders. To appreciate the transition between Evangelicalism and contemporary Pentecostalism in Africa, it is important to understand the 'responsible church membership' policy advocated by the Evangelical para-church movement. Each member was supposed to belong to a particular denomination, which at this time included the Roman Catholics, mainline Protestants and classical Pentecostals. A majority of the Evangelical students came from the first two; that is, they were either Catholics or Protestants. SU preaching was often very critical of these older denominations, describing them as morally permissive, spiritually dead and liturgically routine churches led by priests and pastors who were theologically trained but dead in their sins because they were not

*Changes in Pentecostals/Charismatics in Sub-Saharan Africa, 1970–2015, growth rate, % per year*

| Region | Total population | Christian population | Pentecostal/Charismatic population |
|---|---|---|---|
| *Eastern Africa* | 2.87% | 3.52% | 6.76% |
| *Middle Africa* | 2.96% | 3.24% | 4.31% |
| *Southern Africa* | 2.02% | 2.21% | 4.16% |
| *Western Africa* | 2.71% | 3.26% | 5.91% |
| Sub-Saharan Africa | 2.76% | 3.24% | 5.42% |
| Globe | 1.55% | 1.51% | 5.30% |

Source: Todd M. Johnson and Gina A. Zurlo (eds), *World Christian Database* (Leiden/Boston: Brill), accessed March 2016.

born again. Student members of historic mission denominations gradually became disenchanted as their 'spiritual pride' was vehemently opposed by church authorities. Many young people, with their Evangelical spirituality emphasising the born-again experience, Bible reading and study, a life of holiness, and active witnessing for Christ, gradually felt denominationally uprooted. By the 1970s, a host of town fellowships meeting in urban Africa had emerged, constituted by SU members seeking to supplement their faith outside their denominations.

A number of these Evangelical fellowships would in the 1970s develop into Charismatic churches. Thus, almost without exception, the very early leaders of Charismatic churches across Africa had come through the ranks of one of the conservative Evangelical groups in their region. Although local Evangelical leaders initiated the new Charismatic groups with roots in conservative Evangelicalism, they either developed links with American televangelists or learnt from their activities. The three areas in which these North American connections are most visible are the emphasis on a gospel of prosperity, the principle of sowing and reaping as a means of fund-raising and the extensive use of media for church activities. Prominent personalities within the new Pentecostal/Charismatic circles across Africa include Ray McCauley of South Africa, Nicholas Duncan-Williams of Ghana, and Enoch Adeboye, William Kumuyi, the late Benson Idahosa, David Oyedepo and Daniel Olukoya, all of Nigeria.

S. G. Elton and Benson Idahosa played significant roles in the expansion of the frontiers of Pentecostalism in Nigeria and neighbouring West African countries. Elton worked with The Apostolic Church but became an independent Pentecostal evangelist after his break with it. He joined forces with such American televangelists as Oral Roberts and Gordon Lindsay to start a church-planting programme across the nation. Elton subsequently met Benson Idahosa, who was to be a leading figure in the expansion of Pentecostalism across Africa.

Benson Idahosa's Christian experience started in January 1959 as a convert of the Assemblies of God. Claiming to have instructions from God, he left the church in October 1968. Shortly after that, he met Elton, who exerted much influence on him. Elton provided Idahosa with financial and moral support and facilitated his connection with an American Pentecostal organisation, Christ for the Nations, led by Gordon and Freda Lindsay of Dallas, Texas. In 1971, through the influence of Elton, Idahosa attended a Bible school in America. He returned to Nigeria in 1972 to embark on nation-wide church-planting activities, which added to the explosion of Pentecostalism in the country. Idahosa was the first African evangelist to popularise the gospel of prosperity. Today, he is acclaimed as the 'father of the prosperity gospel' in Nigeria.

Claiming to have a divine mandate to preach the gospel all over the world, Idahosa established Idahosa World Outreach and the All Nations for Christ Bible Institute in the mid-1970s. By the mid-1980s, he had travelled to nearly 70 countries and conducted crusades in many towns across West Africa. Furthermore, Idahosa provided educational and ministerial training opportunities for students from across the continent of Africa, by initiating a scholarship programme that enabled him to train many for the work of the ministry. That programme was at his All Nations for Christ Bible Institute and usually lasted nine months. In this way, Idahosa assisted in raising gospel ministers for countries in Africa other than Nigeria, which significantly aided the expansion of Pentecostalism. For example, among the graduates of his Bible Institute in 1988 were 15 people from Ghana, seven from Chad, four from Côte d'Ivoire, three from Kenya, two from Zimbabwe, two from Cameroon and one each from Sierra Leone and Togo.

At the end of the training, graduates usually returned to their home base and were initiated into the gospel ministry. Many of them later became pillars of Pentecostalism in their various countries. Among these was Duncan-Williams, who in 1979 established Action Chapel International, acclaimed as Ghana's first Charismatic church. James Saah, Duncan-Williams's associate bishop, and Charles Agyem-Asare, who founded the World Miracle Bible Church, were also trained at Idahosa's Bible Institute. Suleiman Umar returned to Niamey, Chad, after his training at the Institute and established the Église Vie Abondante (Abundant Life Church) in 1990. It is believed to be the first independent Charismatic church in the country. Thus, in later decades, many of Idahosa's disciples became pioneers of Pentecostalism in their various countries, and Idahosa played a significant role in the expansion of Pentecostal/Charismatic Christianity across Africa.

The Pentecostal/Charismatic churches and movements, initially on the fringes of Christian life, have now moved to the centre, crossing into every branch of the church on the continent of Africa. They have given a new face to Christianity in Africa, which is outwardly expressive, inwardly liberating and, like the older AICs, appropriately responsive to the existential needs of the African.

Contemporary Pentecostalism, with its message that focuses on experiencing the Spirit, physical and spiritual prosperity and articulating solutions to existential problems through all kinds of healing and deliverance ministries, has proved very attractive to the African public. Pentecostal/Charismatic churches are now found throughout Africa and their theological emphases demonstrate continuities with the older AICs. The dimension of prosperity teaching, combined with traditional themes of speaking in tongues, exorcism, healing, deliverance and miracles, has served as an added attraction, especially for young people, across Africa.

Thus, if we leave aside the AICs as belonging to a different type of Holy Spirit movement, a typology of Pentecostal/Charismatic Christianity in Africa would include the following:

1. *Classical Pentecostal denominations of foreign origin*, like the Assemblies of God, the Apostolic Faith and the International Church of the Foursquare Gospel.
2. *Indigenous Pentecostal denominations* – home-grown Pentecostal groups, dating from the 1950s and 1960s. These were not set up under the auspices of foreign Pentecostal missions. In Nigeria, the first in this group was the Ogo Oluwa Society, which blossomed into the Redeemed Christian Church of God in 1952. Others include the Gospel Pentecostal Assembly (1958) founded in Lagos by Pastor Badejo and the Gospel Faith Mission, which was a merger of Apostolic Faith Mission and the Gospel Mission (1962). In Ghana, they include the Christ Apostolic Church and the Church of Pentecost.
3. *Neo-Pentecostal churches and movements*, manifested in three main streams: born-again or Charismatic ministries; trans-denominational Charismatic fellowships like the Full Gospel Businessmen's Fellowship International; and renewal groups within historic mission denominations, like the Catholic Charismatic Renewal Movement.

Pentecostalism in Sub-Saharan Africa has not developed as a monolithic movement, and even the contemporary churches that receive the most attention in this chapter have manifested in different ways. Today, Pentecostalism has become the representative face of Christianity in Africa. The most significant of the types we have identified are the neo-Pentecostal churches and movements and the rest of this chapter therefore focuses on them. They have developed as local churches, but the contemporary Pentecostals are now best understood as international movements. Their general characteristics include large or mega-sized urban congregations, appeal to upwardly mobile youth, internationalism, extensive use of modern media, preaching of prosperity and active engagement in public life. Contemporary African Pentecostal churches are important not just in their home countries. A number of them have established branches in Europe and North America.

Contemporary Nigerian Pentecostal churches such as the Redeemed Christian Church of God led by Enoch A. Adeboye and the Living Faith Church Worldwide (also known as Winners Chapel) led by David O. Oyedepo, along with Ghana's Lighthouse Chapel International led by Dag Heward-Mills, are among the most popular contemporary Pentecostal churches of African origin that attract African immigrants in the Northern continents. In addition to the establishment of international branches, the leaders of these new African movements have developed powerful networks with popular North American versions of their movements. Their leaders are often invited to speak at Pentecostal conferences and conventions abroad. Similarly, North American Charismatic leaders regularly visit Africa, including T. D. Jakes, Creflo Dollar and Mike Murdock.

Other contemporary Pentecostal churches led by Africans abroad did not start in Africa. Two of the best-known are the Church of the Embassy of the Blessed Kingdom of God for all Nations (abbreviated to Embassy of God) in Ukraine and the Kingsway International Christian Center (KICC) in the UK. The Embassy of God in Ukraine is led by the Nigerian Charismatic pastor Sunday Adelaja and, at its height, had about 25,000 members. Adelaja's record as having led the single largest church in all of Europe says much about the sort of contemporary Pentecostal movement we are discussing here. Another Nigerian, Matthew Ashimolowo, pastors the KICC, which is said to be the largest congregation in the UK, with a membership of about 12,000 people from an estimated 48 nations. The difference between the two Nigerian-led churches is that, whereas most of the members of KICC are African immigrants, virtually all of the members of the Embassy of God are white Eastern Europeans.

Contemporary Pentecostalism is popular in Africa for other reasons, and one of them, as noted above, is the extensive use that churches make of media. They have been very creative in the use of modern media technology, with corporate worship in particular being very contemporary and media-driven. The appropriation of media technologies has become part of the globalising options available to the African Charismatic movements.

### Prosperity Gospel

An important theological emphasis that has come to be associated with neo-Pentecostal or Charismatic churches is the gospel of prosperity. It is not preached the same way in every church, but its general orientation is that in Jesus Christ, God wills all believers to do well in both health and wealth. The historical roots of the prosperity teaching are to be found in the USA in the decades after the mid-1960s. The prominent American teachers of prosperity include Kenneth Hagin, Kenneth and Gloria Copeland, T. L. Osborn, Mike Murdock and others whose television ministries and literature circulate widely among African neo-Pentecostal preachers. In Africa, Nigeria has emerged as effectively the headquarters of prosperity theology. Building on the influence of Benson Idahosa in the 1980s, prosperity teaching has developed as a prominent feature of many of the neo-Pentecostal churches and is preached at large evangelistic rallies in Nigeria and across Sub-Saharan Africa.

The most notable emphasis of prosperity preaching lies in the area of financial prosperity. Prosperity preachers believe that God wills all

Christians to flourish in all areas of life, and they argue that when God is with you, you are bound to prosper. According to them, failure, poverty, unhappiness and all forms of difficulties and calamities should not be the lot of Christians.

Benson Idahosa, whom indigenous sources identify as the father of prosperity theology in Africa, taught that no one in God's family was ever destined to exist in sickness, fear, ignorance, poverty, loneliness or mediocrity. God's abundant goodness will be enjoyed and utilised by those who discipline themselves and become decisive, bold, adventurous, believing, daring, risk-taking and determined. One of the Bible texts commonly used to support this teaching is 3 John 2, 'Beloved, I wish above all things that thou mayest prosper and be in health, even as thy soul prospereth' (King James Version).

In the same vein, W. F. Kumuyi of the Deeper Life Bible Church in Lagos, though of the holiness tradition, is of the view that it is God's perfect will that believers should enjoy perfect health, spiritual and material blessings, victory, promotion, peace, joy and satisfaction throughout their sojourn on earth. The Word of God contains thousands of promises that should make believers remain blessed all the days of their lives. To the typical exponents of the prosperity gospel, material things and well-being constitute the only sure indicators of God's favour. Consequently, any form of misfortune is an indication of the presence of supernatural evil in one form or another in the life of the individual, and this surely is as a result of sin.

## Deliverance Ministries

A number of other themes have developed alongside prosperity in African Pentecostalism. One of these is 'healing and deliverance', with the two expressed together to refer to the restoration of health through prayer for people believed to be afflicted by demons. The underlying worldview that evil powers, including witchcraft, are often responsible for human problems is typical of African traditional thought and is present in all forms of Christianity. However, it is the Pentecostals who have continued the tradition of creating ritual contexts in which to deal with demons, in continuity with the practices of the AICs, which first introduced these forms of ministries into Christianity in Africa. Deliverance is generally understood to include exorcism and refers to practices in which individuals or communities are set free from bondage through the expulsion of demons or evil forces that have either afflicted the victims with infirmities or stagnated the community's social progress. Such bondage is manifest through persistent hardship in various forms, which may include, but are not restricted to, delay in marriage, joblessness, miscarriage, divorce, mysterious death and illnesses, and lack of progress in most communities where witchcraft and other traditional practices dominate people's lives. In other words, in situations where the effects of what comes under 'prosperity' are not felt, healing and deliverance must take place to free victims of spiritual oppression and bondage.

In a sense, deliverance in African Pentecostalism is the same as what is generally described as spiritual warfare in which the Christian exercises authority over the devil and his agents. In deliverance ministries, African traditional religious beliefs and practices are considered demonic doorways by which spiritual possessions and oppressions occur. Deliverance ministration is therefore characterised as breaking 'ancestral' curses and financial hardship, expelling demons, breaking satanic holds on individuals, dislodging stubborn problems, breaking evil or satanic covenants and setting people free from all sorts of calamities in the name of Jesus, with 'violent' prayers.

The rationale for deliverance ministries within Pentecostalism is that a believer cannot demonstrate the power of God unless he or she is ready to come into confrontation with the devil. The popular belief is that there is no victory without conflict and no conquest without warfare. Mountain of Fire and Miracles Ministries is a prominent deliverance ministry in Nigeria, with centres across the continent. Its General Overseer, Dr Daniel Olukoya, while explaining the evolution of the ministry, states that it was initiated to counter the attack of Satan in these last days. According to him, Satan is becoming so ferocious that there is the need to intensify aggressive and violent prayers against him so as to meet force with force. On this premise, the Mountain of Fire and Miracles Ministries started in 1989 and has since brought deliverance ministry to prominence within Pentecostalism in Nigeria.

Another leader within the deliverance circle, Reverend G. F. Oyor of the God-Will-Do-It Ministries, justifying the deliverance ministry, states that many Christians today are almost totally ignorant of the nature of evil spirits because they are fearful of things beyond human understanding. They choose to ignore this portion of God's ministry and as a result multitudes are needlessly living in torment. Much of the ministry of Christ was devoted to casting devils out of tormented people. Jesus states in Mark 16: 17 that if we are true believers these signs shall follow us: 'In my name shall they cast out devils'. This should be part of our ministry to believers and non-believers alike.

### Internationalist Pentecostalism

A prominent feature of contemporary African Pentecostalism is its international outlook. Many of the names of the churches and the symbols they adopt suggest that Pentecostals see their movement as one with a calling beyond local ministries. Thus not only do most contemporary Pentecostal churches have the expressions 'international', 'global' or 'worldwide' as part of their names, but the globe has also become an important part of church logos. These movements have a strong sense of having been called and mandated by God to evangelise the world. Their leaders travel widely as 'exporters' and 'importers' of spiritual capital, leading revival meetings and conferences abroad. It has become a matter of pride in mission to talk about branches of local contemporary Pentecostal churches abroad to which the leader is invited to speak from time to time. A number also organise annual homecoming summits for members able to visit Africa. African Pentecostalism has become a trans-national phenomenon justifying the self-definition as international, global or worldwide.

## Contemporary Pentecostalism and Public Life

Contemporary Pentecostals across Africa are now actively involved in the socio-economic and political lives of their countries. Many of them are engaged in the founding of economic and educational institutions, especially micro-finance concerns and universities and colleges. Virtually all the major churches have very heavy media presence either through tel-evangelism and radio ministries, or their leaders are recorded commenting on issues of public concern. The mere fact that the followings of contemporary Pentecostal churches are youthful has been enough to capture the attention of the political establishment of various countries. Early classical Pentecostals stayed away from active politics because they were concerned with other-worldly matters. In the last three decades of the twentieth century the new stream of revivalist movements that we have called contemporary Pentecostals chose a new path, including engagement with politics. The relationship between the new movements and politics has emerged in various ways. Politics, like religion, is a game of numbers, and therefore custodians of political power and those aspiring to occupy elected office cannot afford to be distant from these churches, which have become mass movements in African society. Africa's political leaders regularly show up at the revival meetings of Charismatic churches and the churches' very powerful leaders have in many cases become strong allies of presidents of West African countries.

The Nigerian scenario is a typical example of how Pentecostals are involved in the political life of the nation. Chris Okotie, a Pentecostal pastor, has twice been a presidential candidate, although without winning. In the 2011 elections, Tunde Bakare, another Pentecostal pastor, was picked as running mate to Muhammad Buhari, on the ticket of Congress for Progressive Change (CPC), but lost to the then incumbent President, Goodluck Jonathan. Today, however, the Vice President, Professor Yemi

Osinbajo, is a Pentecostal pastor from the Redeemed Christian Church of God.

The patronage between Charismatic Christianity and the political establishments in West Africa is mutual. Political leaders, several of whom are under pressure because of failed economic promises, stand in need of the tacit endorsements that the Charismatic leaders bring, and their prophetic prayers for God's protection are also coveted. One way to appreciate the significance of these Charismatic leaders is to look at the position of Prophet T. B. Joshua of Nigeria. He has built a religious empire and his television programmes are very popular because of his healing, exorcism and deliverance ministry. On a number of occasions, powerful public servants and leading politicians have been shown attending his meetings. In the closing months of his life in 2012, the late President of Ghana, John E. A. Mills, was a very familiar face in Joshua's Synagogue Church of All Nations. Indeed, Prophet Joshua was supposed to have predicted that President Mills was going to be the eventual winner of Ghana's 2008 elections, and when it happened the President publicly acknowledged the impact of the Prophet on his political life. Joshua has also been shown in the media alongside the current President of Tanzania. Still in Nigeria, there are pictures of former President Goodluck Jonathan kneeling publicly before the leader of the Redeemed Christian Church of God, Enoch A. Adeboye, for prayer. Ghana's Bishop Charles Agyinasare of the Perez Chapel International was a regular spiritual consultant to both President Mills of Ghana and President Laurent Gbagbo of Côte d'Ivoire. Archbishop Nicholas Duncan-Williams, pioneering founder of Charismatic churches in West Africa and leader of the Action Chapel International, loses no opportunity to talk about the 'spiritual' services he has provided for President Ellen Johnson Sirleaf of Liberia.

Some of the best institutions of higher learning in Africa today belong to Charismatic communities. In Ghana, the Central University is owned by Mensa Otabil's International Central Gospel Church, and the Dominion University Colleges are owned by Duncan-Williams's Action Chapel International. In Nigeria, David Oyedepo's Winners Chapel owns the highly regarded Covenant University, while the Apostolic Faith Mission, Foursquare Gospel Church and Mountain of Fire and Miracles Ministries also run their own private universities.

In Cameroon, the Full Gospel Church runs a technical college in Muyuka, a secondary grammar school in Bamenda, a teacher-training college in Mbengwi and three primary/nursery schools in the South-west Province. It also runs four health establishments (two in the South-west Province, one in Yaoundé and another in Garoua). The Apostolic Church runs a secondary school in Bamenda and a hospital in Banga. All of these establishments started during the period of the economic crisis and only 'believers' are employed in them.

There are certain qualitative differences between Africa's older Independent churches and the contemporary Pentecostals. However, it is important to note that when it comes to beliefs and practices, continuities in several areas between the two Holy Spirit-centred traditions show especially how much their interpretations of Scripture and the influence of the primal worldview cohere with each other. The most distinctive characteristic of Pentecostalism generally is its emphasis on miracles and on signs and wonders, including healing. In the African context, however, the ministries of healing and signs and wonders are undergirded by the worldview that misfortune and ill-health are caused by demons and witchcraft. The ministry to reverse these situations covers a wide range of areas, including (un)employment, protection, financial breakthroughs and personal and family preservation from evil. The ability of these churches to work within the African worldview of mystical causality and to provide the spiritual interventions needed to deal with it account in part for their popularity on the continent. The attention to evil and its effects on human life and society has led to the formation of many such contemporary Pentecostal ministries, whose leaders specialise in these areas of supernatural intervention.

## Conclusion

Today, Pentecostalism has come to stay at the heart of African Christianity. Its spread across the African continent is tremendous. This dramatic growth can be explained by its orientation to existential issues, including the creation of ritual contexts for dealing with evil and the offer of the hope of prosperity as an existential reality.

## Bibliography

Asamoah-Gyadu, J. Kwabena, *Contemporary Pentecostal Christianity: Interpretations from an African Context* (Oxford: Regnum Books International, 2013).

Burgess, Richard, *Nigeria's Christian Revolution: The Civil War Revival and Its Pentecostal Progeny (1967–2006)* (Carlisle: Paternoster, 2008).

Ojo, Matthews A., *The End-Time Army: Charismatic Movements in Modern Nigeria* (Trenton, NJ: Africa World Press, 2006).

Omenyo, Cephas N., *Pentecost Outside Pentecostalism: A Study of the Development of Charismatic Renewal in the Mainline Churches in Ghana* (Zoetermeer: Uitgeverij Boekencentrum, 2002).

Ukah, Asonzeh F. K., *A New Paradigm of Pentecostal Power: A Study of the Redeemed Christian Church of God in Nigeria* (Trenton, NJ: Africa World Press, 2008).

# Key Themes

# Faith and Culture

## Mary N. Getui

This chapter on faith and culture addresses the following headings. 'As It Was at the Beginning' provides an overview of the African cultural setting prior to the coming of Christianity. 'Things Fall Apart' is devoted to the encounter between African culture and Christianity as introduced into Africa by the missionaries who doubled up or were close allies of the colonial administrators and traders. 'A Place to Feel at Home' is a discussion of the ways in which the discomfort that came with the disruption and condemnation of African cultural practices and beliefs led to the emergence of the African Independent/Initiated/Indigenous Churches (AICs). 'Inculturation' examines an approach to the relationship between Christianity and African culture and the quest to strike a balance between gospel and culture. 'Mending the Boat' focuses on an alternative or substitute rite of passage, and suggests that since rites of passage, especially initiation that marks the transition from childhood to adulthood, were abandoned at the instigation of Christianity, the resultant vacuum has left many young people in Africa without direction and purpose in life; therefore, it is time to mend the boat through incorporation of a biblically based and relevant curriculum that is informed by and draws from some aspects of the indigenous initiation programme. 'Joyfully Christian and Truly African' examines the testimony of a leading African church leader that Christianity and African culture can go hand in hand. In this chapter the term 'Christianity' will be used interchangeably with 'faith'. Reference is made to selected authors to support and provide a basis for discussion of some key ideas.

### As it Was at the Beginning

One of the classic sources on indigenous African religion is John Mbiti's *African Religions and Philosophy* (London: Heinemann, 1969). Striding across the African continent with details and illustrations, Mbiti qualifies the statement 'Religion permeates into all the departments of life so fully that it is not easy or possible to isolate it', by addressing the following topics: the nature of God; the works of God; God and nature; the worship of God; spiritual beings; spirits and the living-dead; the creation and original state of man; ethnic groups, kinship and the individual; birth and childhood; initiation and puberty rites; marriage and procreation; death and the hereafter; specialists such as medicine men, rainmakers, kings and priests;

mystical power, magic, witchcraft and sorcery; the concept of evil, ethics and justice; Christianity, Islam and other religions in Africa; and the search for new values, identity and security. Further, Mbiti in another book, *Introduction to African Religion* (London: Heinemann, 1975), gives deeper insights into African religion by addressing the following: the African heritage; what African religion is; where African religion is found; African views on the universe; belief in God; how God is approached by people; the spirits; the origin and early state of humanity; birth and youth; marriage and family life; death and the hereafter; rituals and festivals; religious objects and places; religious leaders; magic and medicine; morals in African religion; the meeting of African religion and other religions; and the value of religion.

These two sources provide a good picture of how 'things were' in pre-colonial or pre-Christianity Africa. They provide a necessary foundation and background on which to base the discussion of faith and culture. While the discussion of this chapter is not quite a comparison of faith and culture, 'the beginnings' before the coming of other religions, especially Christianity, serve as an important reference point.

Jomo Kenyatta's book *Facing Mount Kenya* (London: Secker and Warburg, 1938) is a vivid source on the Gikuyu indigenous cultural set-up. While Kenyatta's focus is on a specific community, the principles and ideas he identifies apply to other communities in Africa. Such similarity is clear in Kwame Gyekye's book *African Cultural Values* (Philadelphia: Sankofa, 1996), which focuses on the Akan of Ghana. Some of the key African cultural values he highlights include religious values, humanity and brotherhood, communal and individualist values, moral values, the family, economic values, chieftaincy, political values, aesthetic values, knowledge and wisdom, human rights, ancestorship and tradition, and the place of traditional African cultural values in the modern context. He uses the term 'culture' in a comprehensive sense, to encompass the entire life of a people. Gyekye recognises that some of these cultural values are still substantially maintained. This makes the effort to address faith and culture worthwhile and relevant. While Gyekye's work is not focused on faith, he suggests that religion ought to be respected so as not to negate the efforts of science and technology. The African cultural values that Gyekye considers appropriate for contemporary society include humanity and brotherhood, communication and individualism, morality, the family, economic systems, chieftaincy and politics, human rights, knowledge and wisdom, as well as aesthetics. Some of these, for example humanity and brotherhood or morality, are clearly in line with the teachings of Christianity.

Mbiti's broad ideas on African religion, Gyekye's analysis of African cultural values that focuses on the Akan and Kenyatta's concentration on the Gikuyu are taken further in Hannah Wangeci Kinoti's book

*African Ethics: Gikuyu Traditional Morality* (Nairobi: CUEAA Press, 2013). Kinoti provides information on the cultural setting of Gikuyu society in the pre-colonial period with regard to, among others, social organisation and religious beliefs, and the changes that have occurred since the 1880s, when the missionaries, European traders and administrators first set foot in Gikuyuland. She highlights the political, economic and social, as well as the religious and cultural, changes that have taken place.

In the Foreword to Kinoti's book, J. G. Donders indicates that she has set out to analyse what happened to Gikuyu moral and social thought and practice under an oppressive colonial system and the influence of Christianity, which had been introduced by foreign missionaries. Donders further observes that the book goes a long way to establish the impact of colonialism as well as that of Christian missionaries, who frequently disregarded or misinterpreted the moral and religious values of the Gikuyu and other African peoples. Donders, a missionary, admits that at the initial stages of this work, of which he was the supervisor, he did not fully appreciate its value or importance. In the end, however, Donders affirms that the book is a confirmation that God was already at work in the world before Christ's coming and that God's moral law is to be found in all societies. At the beginning, before Christianity was introduced into Africa, there were systems and structures in place, including religious ones, which offered the solid anchor and pillar on which each community was pegged.

## Things Fall Apart

Many African sources, both oral and written, are awash with reference to the encounter between faith and culture and the consequent situation of 'things falling apart'. Two examples are used in this essay, namely Chinua Achebe's *Things Fall Apart* (London: Heinemann, 1958) and Ngugi wa Thiong'o's *The River Between* (Nairobi: Heinemann, 1965). In a captivating manner, Achebe narrates the arrival and impact of the British missionaries, administrators and traders in Nigeria. He quotes an elder describing Christianity as 'an abominable religion' and further 'a lunatic religion' with dire implications for the younger generation. Achebe's narrative illustrates that there is an uneasy relationship between, on one hand, the missionaries, converts, traders and administrators and, on the other hand, the people of Umuofia. This is attributed mainly to the fact that 'the white man' had not made the effort to understand the customs of the people: '"Does the white man understand our customs about land?" "How can he when he does not even speak our tongue? … He has put a knife on the things that held us together and we have fallen apart."'

Thiong'o, on the other hand, uses the symbolism of two ridges – Kameno, which is holding true to the Gikuyu traditions, and Makuyu, where the

Gikuyu converts to Christianity reside. Joshua, the leader of the Christians and a strict parent who protects his family from any cultural contamination, is shocked when his daughter Muthoni runs away to Kameno in order to undergo circumcision. Muthoni says that she wants to be a woman, a beautiful Gikuyu woman, and she can only achieve this 'in the manner' of the tribe – that is, by going through circumcision.

This move by Muthoni brought heartbreak and disappointment to Joshua. What Joshua did not know is that in this matter his faithful wife Miriam was more sympathetic to Muthoni than to him. Ngugi describes Miriam thus: 'one could still tell by her eyes that this was a religion learnt and accepted; inside the true Gikuyu woman was sleeping'. In essence Miriam was a Christian externally, but internally she was Gikuyu. This goes to show that the missionaries' approach of condemning and doing away with African cultural practices was not achieving its intended purpose.

This creates a scenario of 'things falling apart' in Joshua's family. Muthoni ceased to exist for him, for she had brought everlasting disgrace to him and to his house, which he had meant to be an example of what a Christian home should grow into. According to Joshua, Muthoni had gone back to Egypt. As for Joshua himself, he would travel on to the New Jerusalem, but obviously without Miriam.

When Ngugi wa Thiong'o addressed the Sixth General Assembly of the Presbyterian Church of East Africa in 1970, he offered the following assessment:

> [A]cceptance of the Christian church meant the outright rejection of all the African customs. It meant the rejection of those values and rituals that held us together: it meant adopting what in effect was a debased European middle-class mode of living and behavior. The European missionary attacked the primitive rites of our people, and condemned our beautiful dances, the images of our gods, recoiling from their suggestions of satanic sensuality. The early African convert did the same, often with greater zeal, for he had to prove how Christian he was through his rejection of his past roots. So that in Kenya, while European settlers robbed people of their land and products of their sweat, the missionary robbed people of their soul. Thus was the African body and soul bartered for thirty pieces of silver and the promise of European heaven.'

No doubt, the encounter between faith and culture contributed to cultural disruption in Africa at various levels – individual, family and wider society.

## A Place to Feel at Home

African Independent Churches are a good illustration of a cultural reaction or response to the disruption brought about in Africa by Christianity. There are other factors that have contributed to the rise of the AICs, such as political quest, nationalistic interests and leadership wrangles, but for the purpose of this chapter our interest is in the cultural factor. It is clear that these churches arose primarily in areas where there was intense and perhaps forceful contact between African traditional communities and culture and Euro-colonial and Christian missionary influence.

It is further noted that AICs have evolved a unique spirituality and ethos that meet the needs of their adherents. They have persisted and will continue to persist due to their cultural and social responsiveness and innovation. Their origins are distinctly African. They have also adapted to the needs, worldview and lifestyle of the African. This is what led Welborn and Ogot (London: Oxford University Press, 1966) to refer to these Churches as 'a place to feel at home'. As such, the AICs have made a great contribution in indigenising the Christian faith. Through them, a new African Christianity has come into play.

Some of the AICs have come together under the Organization of African Instituted Churches, which subscribes to the school of thought that the Christianity that came to Africa was blended with Western culture. The AICs are therefore an effort to have a Christianity that is blended with African culture. Some of the distinct African features that the AICs embrace include: African names; use of traditional singing and dancing styles, instruments and rhythms; understanding the Bible teachings within the context of African culture and using cultural symbols that are compatible with Christianity; governance structures that are in line with African tradition, such as the council of elders; social family practices such as polygamy; and healing rituals.

The AICs are found across the continent, and the views above, therefore, could apply to the Aladura Church in West Africa, the Kimbanguist Church in the Democratic Republic of the Congo and the Spirit, Messianic or Zionist churches in Southern Africa. These AICs are a manifestation or expression of Christianity that recognises and accommodates African cultural beliefs and practices.

## Inculturation

Inculturation has often been described as the 'Africanisation of Christianity'. Laurenti Magesa, in the introduction to his book *Anatomy of Inculturation: Transforming the Church in Africa* (Nairobi: Paulines Publications, 2004), raises pertinent issues that are relevant to faith and culture. These include what happens when the faith and the church are taken from one geographical and/or social situation to another. What happens when they are made to move across peoples and cultures? In other words, in its long history of evangelising peoples, how has the Christian faith inserted itself into different socio-cultural and economic-political situations? It is important to acknowledge that Christianity is an outward-looking and proselytising movement that demands an immediate change in both perception and action as people are 'converted'. Further, it ought also to be acknowledged that reception cannot occur except according to the perception of the receiver. These are pertinent concerns that determine the reception and even the practice of Christianity in a specific cultural milieu.

Inculturation is the process whereby the faith already embodied in one culture encounters another culture. In this encounter, the faith becomes part and parcel of this new culture. It fuses with the new culture and simultaneously transforms it into a novel religious-cultural reality. In practical terms, this process involves the interaction of mutual critiques and affirmation. It entails acceptance or rejection of thought forms, symbolic and linguistic expression and attitudes between the faith-cultures in question.

Magesa's contribution to the discussion of inculturation is based on field research in three East African countries (Kenya, Tanzania and Uganda), but he also indicates that the ideas could apply to other regions of Africa and the wider world. His book focuses on the question of how people in East Africa have appropriated and actually practised Christianity. It is an investigation of the religious habits, thoughts and actions of East African Christians – how they have incarnated the Christian message and made it part and parcel of their own human environment. Magesa's findings are based on extensive research, covering representative churches of mainline Christianity, the AICs and also Christians of the Pentecostal/Charismatic wave. Both urban and rural settings were included in his study and it covered a variety of ethnic groups.

Some of the key findings of the study that are relevant to our consideration of faith and culture include the recommendation by church leaders that a programmatic endeavour to engage with the 'meeting' of two cultural realities in time and space is essential. This would involve: integration of Christian doctrines with useful African traditional cultural values while paying attention to the modern way of life; the effort to bring together various aspects of indigenous culture into the Christian context so as to construct a more authentic Christian life; the fusion of African cultures with biblical teaching, without sacrificing the basic values or principles of either; and advancing and increasing African cultural pride and identity.

This is echoed by various authors in the essays collected in Paul Gifford's *Inculturation in the South African Context* (Nairobi: Paulines Publications, 2000). They address a variety of topics – God, evil, women, saints and ancestors, initiation, sacraments, spirituality, the Bible and AICs. Their thesis is that, in the past, the church has limited the Christ experience to Western beliefs, values and systems, but there is an urgent need for the reformation of Christianity within other cultures so as to enrich the church globally. Inculturation is thus an effort to strike a fresh integration of faith and culture.

## Mending the Boat

As already noted, Mbiti, Kenyatta, Ngugi and Kinoti have indicated that in Eastern Africa, circumcision is among the cultural practices that the missionaries condemned, especially female circumcision. J. Z. Skakhane indicates the same for Southern Africa. The painful procedure and the accompanying abhorrent rituals are among the reasons for condemning this rite of passage. Beneath these abhorrent features, however, lie deep cultural values, such as socialisation on marriage, family, age-group loyalty, community relationships, simple remedies, endurance of pain, relationship with the spouse and confidentiality.

The church, however, did not provide an alternative to or replacement for this rite. To this vacuum are attributed some of the challenges facing young people today, which include identity crisis and drug and substance abuse as well as sexual promiscuity. Indeed, it can be argued that the reason there are so many unstable families today is that marriage preparation has been ignored or compromised. It is in response to this realisation that concerned individuals and churches have come up with 'alternative rites of passage'.

One such initiative, within the Seventh-day Adventist Church in Kenya, has been spearheaded by Pastor Dr John Macharia Gichuiri since 2004. In his Doctor of Ministry dissertation entitled 'An Adventist Functional Substitute for Initiation Rites of Passage for Kikuyu Boys and Abagusii Girls in Kenya', he has recommended and outlined a contemporary Seventh-day Adventist approach. He has compiled a manual, 'Now That You Are Becoming', in which the following topics are covered: Now That You Are a Man; Christian Beliefs; Christian Education; Money Matters; Guidance and Counselling; The Role of a Woman; The Constitution of Kenya; Types of Government; Biblical Counselling; Health Issues; Self-Reliance Tips, Life Skills, Drugs and Substance Abuse; Nutrition, Patriotism, HIV and AIDS and Sexually Transmitted Infections; Study Habits; Integrity; Words of Wisdom; Christian History; Communication; Action Planning; Basics of Growing Up – Understanding Adolescence; Relationships and Self-esteem.

The substitute rite takes place in Nairobi for boys and girls, and in Nyamira County in western Kenya for girls. The main inhabitants of Nyamira County are Abagusii, whose culture includes circumcision of girls. Some traditional aspects of carrying out this rite are omitted; for example, the 'operation' for the boys is done in hospital and no 'operation' is carried out on the girls. Nonetheless, there are underlying traditional cultural principles that are incorporated into the programme. These include mentorship, age-set systems, group loyalty dynamics and a special name for the group. This name is dependent on a key occurrence that takes place in the particular year of initiation. For example, the initiates of 2014, when

Kenya celebrated the jubilee of its independence in 1964, took the name 'Golden Jubilee' and the theme 'God with Kenya This Far'. It is expected that this group will be especially patriotic and grateful to God for their country and will not be prone to vices such as ethnic bias or violence.

Parents of some of the children who have gone through this rite, as well as teachers and others who interact with the initiates, testify to a significant behaviour change after the programme. The children themselves indicate that they have been transformed. Each comes out as a new person with enhanced self-esteem, self-determination and a sense of maturity.

The programme is not exclusive to Seventh-day Adventists – children from other denominations also participate. Christian teachings as outlined in the manual are expected to assist the initiates in coping with life as Christians in contemporary Africa. To cover the costs of the programme, a modest fee is charged. This can be likened to the traditional set-up where the community constituted and gathered what the initiates would require for the initiation ceremony.

Another proponent of this school of thought is Skakhane, who examines the situation in Southern Africa, and in particular the initiation of boys among the Sotho and Xhosa, and compares this to the sacraments in the Christian tradition. His interest is to seek contributions that African initiation rites might offer to the celebration of the Christian sacraments. He highlights the following: involvement of the whole community; ample preparation for the rite; instructors and instructions for the new role in society; cultivation of acceptable behaviour; and incorporation into a community that is loving, accepting, supportive, strengthening, forgiving, reconciling and healing.

## Joyfully Christian and Truly African

John G. Gatu, a retired minister of the Presbyterian Church of East Africa, was one of the most prominent African ecumenists of the twentieth century. He is the author of *Joyfully Christian and Truly African* (Nairobi: Acton, 2006). In the Foreword to this book, J. N. K. Mugambi describes Gatu as a great leader, mediator, pastor, preacher, counsellor, speaker, poet, writer and ecumenist. The book comprises excerpts drawn from Gatu's writings and speeches from 1960 to 2005, the audience being teachers, pastors, students, missionaries and ecumenical partners in various local and international fora. Gatu is associated with the 'moratorium' on missionary funds and personnel, which he controversially proposed in 1971.

At the time, Gatu was concerned to address the constraints that hinder African Christians and churches from expressing themselves courageously as Africans and as Christians. In his view, selfhood of the churches in Africa had been inhibited by the dominance of missionary funds and personnel.

The moratorium was intended to help African Christians and churches to be self-reliant and find their own integrity without control, patronage, tutelage and sanctions from abroad. Gatu's proposal was not well received by some mission boards in Europe and North America, who regarded the moratorium as a move to restrict their generosity.

Gatu's proposal, however, is consonant with African cultural values that propose and promote self-reliance of the individual and of the community. He cautions that the church in Africa cannot be built on alms given by overseas churches. Africa needs to 'produce the five loaves and two fishes and let Christ do the multiplication'. Gatu also suggests that a time has come for the withdrawal of foreign missionaries from many parts of the 'Third World', that churches of the Third World must be allowed to find their own identity and that the continuation of the present missionary movement is a hindrance to the church in Africa. Indeed, selfhood, just like self-reliance, is a commendable attribute in the African indigenous set-up. Gatu acknowledges the challenges of shortage of staff and budgetary constraints but he terms these a 'happy' challenge that the churches in Africa could well meet in faith and trust.

Mugambi also attributes to Gatu the conviction that in Christ there should be unity of purpose, directed towards making the gospel relevant in specific contexts, particularly in tropical Africa. In Gatu's view, there is neither the need nor the necessity to apologise for one's racial, ethnic and cultural identity. The identity into which one is born is a divine endowment. At the same time, when one becomes a Christian, one must integrate the new faith into one's natural and cultural identity in such a way that one becomes a new creation.

Gatu is concerned that the missionaries marginalised African beliefs, demonstrating a lack of appreciation that God is the creator of all and that Christ came for the resurrection of all. He further indicates that God had been present in Africa even before the coming of the missionaries. On the missionary attempts to eradicate indigenous rituals, Gatu says that African rituals were consequently replaced by church rituals that never satisfied the needs fulfilled by traditional religious rites and concepts of life in Africa. Hence there is a need to review the rituals and uphold those that do not contradict the Christian faith.

Gatu also indicates that the African pastor cannot claim to be able to fill the gap created by Western theology, which talks only about God on high and the unseen God, as opposed to the idea of a God that Africans can see on their mountains, along the rivers and in the forests. This is a critical issue for the church ministers, priests and pastors who are the shepherds of the flock, with great influence on the beliefs and practices of the adherents. Gatu further indicates that for Holy Communion, utensils of local significance in a particular traditional setting should be preferred, because in that way the inner being of the participants is involved and more meaning is accrued.

Gatu is aware of and alert to the tension that his ideas are bound to raise and calls for dialogue on issues of faith and culture. This is what Magesa calls communication, as opposed to imposition. The former might not yield any fruit, for imposition has no cultural roots; communication, on the other hand, makes the message part of the culture.

## Conclusion

What is emerging from this discussion is that the gospel is essentially a cultural reality. But what too many Christian missionaries have done in Africa is to transmit to their listeners their own cultural understanding of the gospel. They have bequeathed to their converts the interpretation of Christ's message as it has developed in their own home communities and not as the message could apply in Africa, a context with a rich cultural heritage.

Magesa commends the advice offered by an elderly Christian from West Africa on the significance of the relationship between faith and culture. When asked why people in his area did not adhere strictly to the teachings given to them by the missionary church officials, he responded: 'We eat everything they give us, but we digest it in our own way'. This is to emphasise that the Christian faith cannot be assimilated by the people of a given culture unless it is 'digested' in that culture.

Key constituencies whose contribution and participation are called upon for a healthy balance between faith and culture include the entire church family, both leaders and members. Good will and open-mindedness are sought so that these key players understand what faith and culture entail and the need for dialogue and communication between them. The key players also need to acknowledge the 'happy' challenges that are involved and be courageous and bold enough to take the bull by the horns. Contemporary African missionaries have plenty of lessons on faith and culture from the African experience from which they can draw as they reach out to others with the gospel message. At a time when the base of Christianity is shifting to the global South, effective integration of faith and culture within the African milieu is more important than ever.

## Bibliography

Gatu, John G., *Joyfully Christianity and Truly African* (Nairobi: Acton, 2006).

Gichuiri, John Macharia, 'An Adventist Functional Substitute for Initiation Rites of Passage for Kikuyu Boys and Abagusii Girls in Kenya' (DMin Dissertation, Andrews University, 2014).

Gyekye, Kwame, *African Cultural Values* (Philadelphia, PA: Sankofa, 1996).

Kinoti, Hannah Wangeci, *African Ethics: Gikuyu Traditional Morality* (Nairobi: CUEAA Press, 2013).

Magesa, Laurenti, *Anatomy of Incultration: Transforming the Church in Africa* (Nairobi: Paulines Publications Africa, 2004).

# Worship and Spirituality

John S. Pobee

The early history of Christianity in much of Sub-Saharan Africa was shaped by the strategy of adventurers like the fifteenth-century Portuguese explorer Vasco da Gama, who sought to outflank the Islamic territory to the south and east of Europe. Thus, among other things, missionary Christianity came to Sub-Saharan Africa in a spirit of fear of the Muslim crusade and thus was neither attentive enough nor amenable to the history of Judaism, Christianity and Islam as *ahl-al-kitab*, People of Scripture, Abrahamic religions and siblings. The Christian missionary practice of the *tabula rasa* reflected the foregoing Crusader mentality.

The uneasy and even violent current relationships between Christians and Muslims in parts of Africa (e.g. Boko Haram in Nigeria, Al-Shabaab in Kenya and Somalia, the violence between the largely Muslim Seleka and largely Christian Anti-Baleka in the Central African Republic) are not just acts of violence but also shortchange human dignity, which stands at the core of Christian religion and spirituality. The nationalist independence movement, among other things, made for Africa-wide rearrangements by which North Africa has become present in Sub-Saharan Africa. Thus, alongside North Atlantic Christian missionary initiatives, the Oriental Orthodox (Coptic) Church of Egypt and Ethiopian Orthodox Church now also have a presence in Sub-Sahara, with implications for worship and spirituality. Sub-Saharan Africa today is a supermarket of religions, types of worship and spiritualities, with people shopping around and sometimes patronising more than one religion, type of worship and spirituality.

## Religious Pluralism and Sundered Christianity

In spite of evidence of growing unbelief (i.e. ignorance, bewilderment regarding belief and some straight rejection), religion – principally African traditional religions, Christianity, Islam and some Buddhism and Hinduism – is significant, important, vital and influential. Christianity, beginning as a guest missionary religion, has established such a presence that Africa has become a heartland of world Christianity and a paradigm of non-Western Christianity, signalling that Christian faith is lived and makes a difference to the lives of people. Alongside the North Atlantic-initiated Christianity, there are today vibrant African initiatives in Christianity, which scholars have characterised variously as syncretistic, prophetic, witchcraft eradication movements, separatist churches, nativistic churches, messianic movements, and spiritual and/or Pentecostal churches. The varieties of designations signal they are varieties in a genre, implying different and diverse emphases in worship and spirituality. Their African-ness is most clearly demonstrated in their style of worship and their spiritualities.

The foregoing facts have led to a range of African Christian worship styles and spiritualities, for the aforementioned descriptions signal contours of African spirituality. Religion that is an experience of the Holy Spirit of God manifests in acts of power; religion that is power against evil forces of darkness such as witchcraft, which appears to be a preoccupation of African lives. In such emphases, dissatisfaction is expressed with the received missionary worship and spirituality. Worship and spirituality in Sub-Saharan Africa are at the interface of three religions, each claiming a following from the same Africans.

Sub-Saharan Africa thus presents a supermarket of religions and therefore requires religions to make themselves attractive, whatever may be said of the prevenient grace of God. Worship and spirituality must be consistent with the epistemology and ontology of Africans in their pluriformity. Further, missionary Christianity was minted with the ideology of Christendom, with implications for worship and spirituality. Such a construct has been out of joint with a region marked by the poor (i.e. the marginalised and excluded). The African Christian initiatives represent unarticulated efforts at modelling the ideology of God's preferential option for the poor.

While pluralism may sometimes, if not often, be managed and structured in negative ways, such as conflicts and hostility, it also makes it possible to build Christian institutions in continuity with diverse other constructs. Thus African Christianity, worship and spirituality became an engagement between Scripture and African cultures and challenges. The apparent love of revelation through dreams and visions, complex and long rituals, separation of clean and unclean animals, the practice of polygamy in spite of the norm of monogamy and the descent of the Spirit of God on prophets and other church functionaries are points at which the engagement is seen. The heritage of African religions is manifest in the penchant for absolutely personal and public prayer. Thus there is spiritual continuity between traditional African and Christian prayer. Religions in Africa share a love for meditation and wrestling of the soul with Divinity in which (spiritual) secret strength is found even in the face of political challenges. Thus Simon Kimbangu of the Congo was cheerfully in a Belgian prison for 30 years. Archbishop Janani Luwum of the Anglican Church of Uganda through prayer remained calm in the face of General Idi Amin Dada. Luwum is commemorated with a tomb outside Namirembe Cathedral, Kampala, Uganda, thus making a statement and call for spirituality nourished by fervent prayer and martyrdom. A significant aspect of the East Africa Revival is Africa's yearning to continue in the traditional African penchant for fervent prayer.

## An Incarnational Faith

Worship and spirituality are modes and vehicles of the three cornerstones of religion, namely ecstatic experience, belief and ritual. The continuing agenda, then, is *appropriately* culturing those cornerstones in the African context, recontextualising the North Atlantic legacies from the missionaries so as to have African worship and spirituality at the heart of culture to take its place there. That character of the Incarnation vis-à-vis worship is expressed in public, communal and/or private acts that recognise the sacred as the Ground of Being. It includes such acts as praise, petition, repentance, thanksgiving, adoration and sacrifice. Whatever the human involvement, Christian worship and spirituality insist on God as Creator, Redeemer and Sanctifier, with all that undergirded by Scripture, the Word of God.

Christianity defines itself by the Incarnation (John 1: 1–18; Galatians 4: 3). The Pentecost experience confirmed that various people heard the Word of God in their own languages and vernacular (Acts 2: 6). The eschatological vision of Revelation 7 also paints a picture of people of every tribe and tongue at worship around the altar and throne of the Lamb. Accordingly, gospel, worship and spirituality have taken the hue and colour of the locale – Semitic, Greek, Latin, Celtic, English, Slavic, Coptic Ethiopic and so on. There is no special pleading for African Christian gospel, worship and spiritualities, to signal African identities around the one altar and throne of Christ.

Consequently, North Atlantic missions cultivated native agents of missions, called evangelists and catechists, such as Bernard Mizeki (Anglican) of South Rhodesia and Molimile Molele (Methodist), also of Rhodesia. The Basel Mission in the Gold Coast used David Asante (1830–93), Theophilus Opoku (1842–1913) and Carl Christian Reindorf (1834–1917) as foot soldiers of mission and worship in the vernaculars of Twi and Ga-Adangbe. Thus the vernacular was crucial for consolidating mission, forming indigenous persons as agents of mission as well as reaching and engaging Africans in worship and spirituality. African mission agents like the catechists and the evangelists and even African priests have been described as unsung heroes of African church history. For though African church history has often been written from the perspective of mission societies and missionaries, the African catechist is the one who stayed in the most outlandish places to nurture, with patience and commitment, Christian identity, worship and spirituality in people. Like the translation of Scripture and liturgical texts and like indigenous African music such as the lyrics of the Methodist Church of Ghana or the enervating music of the AICs, which sustain African rhythm and idiom, they are indicative of the concern to live the Incarnation self-understanding of the Christian faith and church, worship and spirituality in Africa.

The Incarnation self-definition is held *in tandem with* mission self-understanding (Matthew 28: 16–20). Mission is concerned to lead souls to the divine heights of Evangelical realisation and sanctification of human lives with a view to life eternal. Mission, like worship, thus has everything to do with spirituality: teaching people the demands of Christ and *doing* them (1 John 2: 1–3).

The North Atlantic provenance of Christian missions in Sub-Saharan Africa reflects the theology, organisation, polity, worship, spirituality and spiritual readings, disciplines and music of their origins. Thus African Anglicans continue to use the Book of Common Prayer, with its English idiom. African Roman Catholics use the Latin rite as a resource for worship and spirituality. African Lutherans not only hold on to the *Confessio Augustana* but also discuss political theology in terms of Luther's theology of the Two Kingdoms. All these mean African Christians start with an assumed definition of Christianity, rather than their own particular African encounter with Divinity, 'to see', 'hear', 'follow' and 'obey' Christ as Africans. Even when the resources are translated into the vernacular, they still are captive to the English, French, Portuguese, German or Latin idiom. Thus authentic African worship and spirituality are interfered with, if not hijacked and shortchanged.

The North Atlantic inheritance has meant that African worship and spirituality have been excessively rational and cerebral and do not appropriately respond to the simple voices of Africans, thus shortchanging viable worship and spirituality. Thus at African rites of passage (i.e. at birth, puberty, marriage and death), the inherited Christian practices, in spite of the missionary practice of the *tabula rasa*, are unashamedly mixed up with traditional African practices which verge on worship and spirituality which have sometimes been castigated as superstition. Such stances have not been helpful, because superstition through the history of Christianity has been part of the stock-in-trade.

However, alongside the foregoing cerebral style stands the use of art by Africans to capture ideas of worship and spirituality. The east wall behind the altar in the sanctuary of the Church of Cyrene, Bulawayo, Zimbabwe, carries an art piece with a black African Jesus, high and lifted up and glorified, in Eucharistic vestments at the centre and holding the host. His feet still have the nails of the crucifixion. Thus Jesus Christ is depicted and proclaimed as the great high priest as well as sacrifice for atonement for sin. The art then proclaims Christ would be an African too. He is martyr and priest, offering atonement for humankind.

To the left of Christ is Simon Wase Cyrere (Simon of Cyrene) carrying a cross. This is the biblical story of Simon who was compelled by the soldiers to carry the cross of Christ (Mark 15: 21). Thus African worship and spirituality have a tendency to be biblical and even biblicist. Simon is depicted as barefooted and wearing shorts, thus portraying the simple and poor of Africa who have faith and courage to follow Christ. Sacrifice, martyrdom and courage are characteristic notes of African Christian spirituality.

To the right of Christ stands Bernard Mizeki in sartorial wear, the interpreter and catechist who followed Bishop G. W. H. Knight-Bruce to develop the Anglican Church in Shonaland. He was murdered in 1896 in the Shona uprising. Mizeki carries a spear, a reminder of how he was murdered for his faith. The sartorial wear is a hint at worship and spirituality with a sacerdotal character and focus. Thus his ministry attempted to capture the vernacular paradigm of the Incarnation and Anglicanism (cf. number 24 of the Thirty-Nine Articles). The painting thus portrays worship and spirituality which stress the high-priesthood of Christ, the call to all, the poor included, to costly discipleship, to be active followers even in suffering and death – martyrdom and loneliness in praise of God.

Five days after Mizeki's martyrdom, Shona Methodist evangelist Molimile Molele was murdered. Anglicans in Zimbabwe today have a shrine to Mizeki. The shrine commemorates 'a gentle man … always making peace, in whom the Holy Spirit of God dwelt, and worthy of imitation', the testimony of Kapuya, a brother catechist. But there is not a similar veneration of Molele in the Methodist Church because, beholden to an ideological-theological dislike of saints in the Methodist Church, the Methodists are unable to honour such an exemplary ancestor, as African traditional society would interpret him. Thus there is continuity and change in spirituality. The difference was between High Church Anglicanism and a more reformed Christian tradition.

The Zimbabwean art piece focusing on the Crucifixion narrative may be a hint at a fundamental emphasis of African spirituality and worship. In a continent in the grip of poverty, violence and threats to human dignity, the narrative of the crucifixion and resurrection of Jesus becomes a meaningful exegesis of their circumstances, which equips them to be able not to lose heart (2 Corinthians 4: 16–18).

The crucifixion–resurrection motif of African spirituality receives further confirmation from the devoted patronage by the faithful of Good Friday services from noon to 3 pm, to travel with Jesus on the cross. The focus is further underlined by the choice of the colours of red (*kobene*, i.e. deep red) and black (*biisii*), which are the colours for deep sorrow and mourning. The patronage and colours worn on the occasion are indices of the crucial importance in the motif of the crucifixion–resurrection of Christ for the worship and spirituality of Sub-Saharan African Christians.

The normative demands of the Incarnation and mission make worship and spirituality a hermeneutic process retrieving tradition in the present to create and construct it, *appropriately*, in the African context. It is a 'Passover of language' – that is, 'beginning with the ecclesial furrow where language of faith germinates, we restore the gospel's power to speak to Africans through the primordial symbol of their existence' (J. M. Ela, *My Faith as an African*, Maryknoll: Orbis, 1989, 44). North Atlantic Christian cultural presuppositions are replaced and supplemented with African symbolism.

### Factional Spirituality and Worship

The pluriformity of African worship and spirituality arises not only because of the vernacular paradigm of the Incarnation but also because of the Una Sancta is sundered into Roman Catholic, Orthodox, Anglican, Protestant and African Christian initiatives. Thus African Christians have been nurtured in 'factional' worship and spirituality, thereby obfuscating a holistic vision of church, mission, worship, spirituality and denomination, sometimes with no love lost between the groupings, even in the same denomination. For example, in Tanganyika, church members evangelised by the Church Missionary Society (Anglican) would rather attend worship of the Lutheran Church than that of the High Church Anglicans evangelised by the Society for the Propagation of the Gospel.

### Revival Movements

Especially in Eastern Africa, there have arisen revival movements, such as the Balokole of Uganda and Rwanda, the Jamaa of the Congo, movements that showed dissatisfaction with a 'dead' church and therefore resorted to such expressions and emphases as 'awake', 'sin', 'repentance', 'coming out of Egypt', 'separation' and 'Holy Spirit' as their stock-in-trade. Also there was emphasis on 'confession of sin', 'saving blood of Christ' and 'saved ones'. That the phenomenon represented a quest for renewal of worship and spirituality is supported by their designation *abomwoyo* (people of the Spirit) or *abarabukiinwe* (people who have received a revelation). Whatever else they did, they were also protests against un-Christian practices such as bride-wealth and customary food taboos. In all this, there was a sub-plot, a desire to appropriate Christianity not through the hierarchy or school but through a typically African construct, a decentralised association unified by singing and some basic forms of behaviour. The mass movements of the Christian story of Uganda were in part spawned by the individual conversions, martyrdom and civil wars of the 1890s. So revival is not necessarily independent of experience of martyrdom and the will to confess.

## Double Missionary Vision

The mission vocation of the Church sometimes shaded off into 'double missionary vision'. Christian missions, worship and spirituality stood alongside colonialism, racism and the slave trade. They failed to rise up to true spirituality and 'worship in the market-place' (St John Chrysostom). Thus the Dutch Reformed Church in apartheid South Africa was an accomplice in the system which dehumanised people of colour, short-changing Christian spirituality as conforming to the image of God and full stature of Christ (Genesis 1: 27, Matthew 5: 17–20, 48; Matthew 6: 33; Romans 12: 1–2; Philippians 2: 5–11). Spirituality is defined in terms of the values of the Kingdom of God, namely justice and righteousness, truth and truthfulness (John 8: 31–2), peace and reconciliation (2 Corinthians 5: 15–17), love, mercy, compassion. These values, which are spiritual, also take social, economic and political forms. Thus bread-and-butter issues are spiritual challenges as well. That is the significance of the involvement of the African churches' programmes in alleviating hunger, poverty and ignorance. The use of education and health as agents of mission is to live spirituality in the sanctuary as in the marketplace, to shore up the prerogative dignity of Africans as also created in the image and likeness of God-Christ. Unfortunately, such endeavours are often interpreted primarily as acts of social welfare and not seen much as a living Christian vocation of worship and spirituality. Clear and focused interpretation of acts can underline worship and spirituality.

The shortchanging of Christian spirituality has been a recurring theme in Africa. In the Vasco da Gama era, Christians – individuals and institutions – had been accomplices in the slave trade, which was a violation of spirituality as shoring up human dignity, even though Christian groups were also in the vanguard of the anti-slavery campaign. Such involvement in the slave trade was an illustration of the Reformers' quaint phrase *simul justus atque peccator* (at once justified [and saved] and yet sinner [sinful]). Thus spirituality is essentially a journey of spiritual quest with high points and low points, a process rather than a realised, once-and-for-all event.

That failure of spirituality by Christian churches and institutions has been a recurring theme of Christian history. Roman Catholic missionaries were accomplices in the massacre of 400 Africans in Wiriyamu, Chawola and Juwau in Mozambique on 16 December 1971. This was part of the attempt of the Portuguese colonial administration to destroy the freedom fighters of the Frente de Libertação de Moçambique ('Frelimo'; the Mozambique Liberation Front). The subsequent investigation and protest by the Catholic hierarchy looked tame in the face of the overriding declared high missionary and civilising purpose, thus shortchanging the spiritual ingredient of affirming human life and dignity.

The triangle of the Belgian colonial administration, mining and agricultural firms like l'Union Minière du Haut Katanga, and Roman Catholic missionaries in the Congo joined hands in implementing an unjust system. Christians, including bishops, were accomplices in the horrendous massacres of fellow Christians in Rwanda in the 1990s. Such double missionary vision shortchanged authentic Christian worship and spirituality for the renewal and transformation of peoples and society. For the dismissal (the *Ite, Missa est*) at the end of Eucharistic worship is a commission for spirituality to flow from worship to renew secular life (spirituality outside the sanctuary).

In signalling the double missionary vision, the relation between worship and spirituality is highlighted. From the very beginning, worship was integral to Christian faith and practice. Jesus was regularly in places of worship, namely the synagogue and the temple (Mark 1: 16–17; Luke 2: 46; John 8: 20), which represented different types of worship, such as learning the Word of God and sacrificial religion/spirituality. But not all acts of worship are spiritually sound. Jesus not only articulated that 'not everyone who says Lord, Lord, shall enter the Kingdom of God' but also, like the Old Testament prophets, he denounced empty and hypocritical religiosity (Matthew 23; Jeremiah 7; Amos 5: 15, 21; Hosea 6: 6). In order to attain authentic spirituality and true worship there must be also obedience to the will of God expressed in the values of the Kingdom of God. Spirituality is fundamentally sensitive and focused obedience to the will of God in particular contexts and situations, nurtured by the Word of God (cf. Matthew 28: 20). It is deception and jaundiced spirituality to have religion without justice. Worship without heart and mind is empty (Jeremiah 1: 16–28).

The double missionary vision is in its own way a judgement on failed Christian spirituality. Conversely, to describe Christian missions as guardian angels of African nationalism, in its own way, signals a Christian spirituality that shored up the dignity of Africans as also created in God's image and likeness. The stories of martyrs and confessors in African church history are indicative of expended life, a supreme act of spirituality. In this regard, Bernard Mizeki, Molele of Shonaland and Ugandan martyrs led by Charles Lwanga, chief of royal pages, in 1886 are examples of and for Christian spirituality. The Ugandan martyrs are commemorated on 3 June with the theme 'Living the Christian Faith'. In Uganda, again, there was the murder of the Anglican Archbishop Janani Luwum by General Idi Amin Dada. Elsewhere in Africa, there have been such confessors as Anglican Archbishop Ambrose Reeves, Anglican Archbishop Trevor Huddleston, Colin Winter, Roman Catholic Archbishop Denys Hurley and the Anglican Archbishop Desmond Mpilo Tutu, who stood up to challenge Afrikaner nationalism and inhuman apartheid in their pursuit of obedience to the will of God. Being a martyr or a confessor is an act of living Christian faith and spirituality, 'sanctification of the holy Name', and presenting one's very self as a 'living sacrifice, holy and acceptable to God' (Romans 12: 1).

## African Christian Initiatives

The description of this genre of Christian church as a church founded by Africans in Africa for Africans is a signal that even if they are protest movements against North Atlantic captivity of church worship and spirituality, they are also authentic indigenous responses to the gospel and a quest for African 'havens of belonging' and 'places to feel at home'. Worship and spirituality are informed by the foregoing as responses to African consciousness. As such, African Independent Churches (AICs) have developed holistic spirituality, characterised by notions of: wholeness of creation; humans in community nourished by a spiritual view of life, nourishing a sense of family and community; communion of saints by which memory of our predecessors is nurtured; faith as not a private act but a life-giving organ of society; the renewal of the Holy Spirit in continuity with and greater than spirits around us; and a focus on spiritual healing. As such AICs represent 'the primal imagination' entailing commitment to a vernacular paradigm of being a church for the transportation of people to spiritual realms. Today, however, non-Africans also subscribe to the genre and institutions of AICs.

The AICs have taken a cue from African traditional religions in offering ritual and spiritual remedies to questions and problems arising out of Africans' sense of vulnerability, physical and spiritual. They find their succour in the God of the Christian gospel. Alongside the foregoing is the fact that AICs, eschewing heavy intellectualism, focus on prayer and worship as the heart and dynamic of their vibrant religious life. The AICs focus on culture, identity and social change as factors for communicating the catholicity of the church.

The emphasis of AICs on spirit and spirituality may be further developed along three lines. First, AICs stress the conscious experience of receiving the Holy Spirit. It is in this line that baptism in the Holy Spirit is stressed. In other words, baptism by water and regeneration of the Holy Spirit are deemed inadequate. Second, such receipt of the Holy Spirit is accompanied by glossolalia, implying that human language is inadequate for the currents of the Holy Spirit. Third is the stress on healing and exorcism effected through prayer, laying on of hands and invocation of the Holy Spirit. This is, however, a leaf from Scripture, the life and ministry of Jesus and the early church. Of course, in the historic churches moral and spiritual healing is provided for sacramentally, while miraculous cures are consigned to shrines and saints. But the sacramental life of the historic churches appears to have little apparent reference to the multidimensional needs of Christians vis-à-vis suffering and relief from suffering. Ministry of the Christian church will be adjudged deficient if healing is not treated as a normal act of spirituality (Mark 1: 21–8, 32–4).

We dare not suggest that the thinking and practices of AICs vis-à-vis the Spirit leave us no worry. Some leaders have claimed to be filled with the Holy Spirit while focusing attention on themselves rather than on God. They give the impression that the Holy Spirit will work automatically at their bidding. A spirituality of waiting on God to do things in God's own time is shortchanged. It appears that the leader is invoking a kind of magic by which the divinity may be compelled to yield to the supplicant's will. At worst, this can result in empty showmanship and hypocrisy in the name of spirituality.

The focus on the power of the Spirit answers well the cosmology and soteriology of the all-pervasive primal tradition of Africans vis-à-vis reality and salvation. In the process, the biblical material is run through the prism of the regenerative capacity of Africans' perception. Herein is the unique contribution of the AICs to world Christianity.

Worship and spirituality have been the measure and test of the long-standing Niceno-Constantinopolitan self-definition of the church as one, holy, catholic and apostolic, the Una Sancta, the imperial model from the Roman Empire. AICs are the reminder of new times calling for a revisiting of the traditional marks of the church. The received tradition informed by one empire, one ruler (emperor) and one religion is irrelevant in contemporary Africa, in which there could be no accommodation between Christian church and empire. Such understanding reminds us of how the oneness of the church has been questioned in practice, for instance with the 'Great Schism' between the Latin and Greek churches in 1054 or the division between Roman Catholics and Protestants in the sixteenth and seventeenth centuries.

The vision of the holy church was already questioned by the Donatist schism of the early church, in which the incidence of martyrdom as the seed of the church slanted holiness towards zeal for the Lord. Similarly, catholicity is understood not only in terms of the church being 'worldwide'. Issues of communication such as culture, identity and social change have become the critical indices of catholicity. As the Manifesto of the

Organization of African Instituted Churches puts it, 'most of us are stable, growing churches with a Christian doctrine based on the Bible as sole authority, as a special dispensation of the Holy Spirit, faith in the God of the Bible and its promises'. Those are the elements of the claim to belong to the church. For the same reason, the Manifesto insists that while the AICs may not express theology in written form, their faith is expressed 'in liturgy, worship and structures. Our services are alive with warm expressions of joy and in new spiritual and indigenous songs.'

In earlier times Christian missions aimed at the three-self principle of mission growing into self-governing, self-supporting and self-propagating churches. AICs have exposed the limitations of the formula. In organisation, worship and spirituality AICs attempt to be at once self-governing and self-critical, self-supporting and self-motivating, self-propagating and self-contextualising.

## The Ethiopian Orthodox Church

Thus far, our subject has been ventilated through the Latin church of the West and native African mintings, albeit against the backdrop of Latin Christianity. But Sub-Saharan Africa has a third tradition, Eastern Christianity (represented by Ethiopian Orthodox Church), which is also ancient, going back to the Church of Alexandria founded by St Mark, which represented Monophysite, non-Chalcedonian Christianity. It is that church that gave birth to the Ethiopian Orthodox Church, preserving the creed, liturgy and monastic spirituality of the Orthodox tradition and developing its own unique ecclesiological liturgical and artistic tradition.

That tradition had a Hebraic sub-structure, and thus Coptic Orthodox Christianity is at once Old Testament and New Testament. For example, church buildings follow the Judaic model of the Temple. Church members observe Pentateuchal dietary laws regarding clean and unclean, practise circumcision on the eighth day and hold the Sabbath equal to Sunday. The Kingdom of Ethiopia and the church have been treated as equal to the Judaic kingdom. The holy city of Aksum was regarded as the renewed and realised Jerusalem of Scripture on African soil and home of the Ark of the Covenant. There was profound identification of religion and natural and national identity, making them 'God's holy people' adhering to the essentials of Christian belief and sacramental practice.

Worship and spirituality are woven around festivals such as Hosanna, the Palm festival; Tamket, Feast of our Lady of Zion; and Epiphany, the Baptismal Feast at which the faithful are rebaptised annually. A particular difficulty since the nineteenth century has been the adoption of Amharic as official language of the Ethiopian Church, in contrast to the more popular Ge'ez. Thus Scripture and the liturgy became unintelligible to the masses, making these tools of worship and spirituality exclusive to the learned monks.

In 1830, the Church Missionary Society came to Ethiopia with the assignment not so much to establish a mission as to purify and strengthen the Ethiopian Church, which was beholden to praying to Mary and the saints, veneration of images, kissing the cross, keeping fasts and cherishing monasteries. The agenda was to be undergirded by circulation of the Scriptures in Amharic.

## Conclusion

Worship, like spirituality, in Sub-Saharan Africa has been and will continue to be a work in progress, attempting to respond to and obey the self-disclosure of the God who 'in times past, spoke in partial and various ways to our ancestors' (Hebrews 1: 1). At the heart of that call is the challenge to reflect 'the refulgence of (the Divine) glory on this earth, our habitation'. The response is informed by Scripture and tradition and the particular African needs with a search for *appropriate* worship and spirituality in the varied and diverse African contexts, although Africans have a tendency to stress the reality of what is not yet seen as the object of hope. In a society not rich in literacy and not beholden to intellectualism, music and song, art and other forms of symbolism are critical modes of living worship and spirituality. In a continent almost synonymous with poverty and injustice, seeking the human face of God in the concrete challenges of African societies has been a way of expressing spirituality as a supreme act of obedience to the Creator, Redeemer and Enabler. Confessors and martyrs in Sub-Saharan Africa have been examples of supreme obedience to the will of God and sanctification of the Holy Name. What is not often articulated is that such acts of obedience to the will of God rather than the will of society and Caesar are in fact expressions of worship in the public square, committed and sensitive spirituality, done in the joy of the Holy Spirit, who is continuous with and yet different from the traditional African yearning for the Spirit.

## Bibliography

Asamoah-Gyadu, J. Kwabena, *Sighs and Signs of the Spirit: Ghanaian Perspectives on Pentecostalism and Renewal in Africa* (Akropong Akuapem: Regnum Africa, 2015).

Ela, Jean-Marc, *My Faith as an African* (Maryknoll, NY: Orbis Books, 1989).

Larbi, E. Kingsley, *Pentecostalism: The Eddies of Ghanaian Christianity* (Accra: Centre for Pentecostal and Charismatic Studies, 2001).

Shorter, Aylward, *African Christian Spirituality* (London: Chapman, 1978).

Taylor, John V., *The Primal Vision* (London: SCM, 1963).

# Theology

## Francis Anekwe Oborji

From the middle of the twentieth century, African authors have produced an abundance of works on Christian theology from an African perspective. Before this period, African theology existed largely in oral form and was not expressed systematically. Discussion of African theology usually considers the modern scene in Sub-Saharan Africa, leaving aside the African origins of the Coptic tradition in Egypt and Ethiopia as well as the Church of Carthage of North Africa. The writings of African theologians in the modern period deal with two main topics: inculturation and liberation theology. The two trends are not contradictory but rather complement each other. They represent two sides of the same process. However, African theologians today present a more unitary perception of inculturation and liberation with the emergent new trend of African theology of reconstruction. The three trends – inculturation, liberation and reconstruction – are attempts by African theologians to relate the Christian message to the socio-religious, cultural, political and economic reality of Africa. African theology evolved in the context of giving a theological response to the changing African reality and as a search in African culture and religious traditions for the inculturation of the gospel on the continent.

This chapter will offer an overview of the three principal trends of African theology as we know it today:

- inculturation
- liberation
- reconstruction.

### African Inculturation Theology

In the inculturation stream of African theology, one major area stands out for appraisal: African Christology. It is a credit to the fertility of contemporary African theologians that Christology is perhaps the aspect of theology that has received the greatest attention. Thus, many Christological models have recently sprung from the pens of African theologians. Christ has been designated as the liberator, the ancestor, the first-born son, the master of initiation, the healer, the African king, the African chief, mediator, saviour, redeemer with power and so forth. All these concepts and images are very familiar to most African people and they can serve to illustrate the figure of Jesus Christ. Of these, the model of Christ as our ancestor has received much attention, especially in East and Central Africa but also in West Africa. For some, it is the most distinctively African and the most profound. In fact, the notion of the ancestor is so deeply embedded in African religious consciousness that the idea of Christ as ancestor seems to have arisen independently in the minds of different theologians in different parts of the continent.

Championed by such theologians as Bénézet Bujo (Congo) and Charles Nyamiti (Tanzania), it is one of the motifs that can quite easily fit into most of Africa. Nyamiti's work *Christ as Our Ancestor: Christology from an African Perspective* (1984) is perhaps the most elaborate presentation of the new Christology, demonstrating both similarities and differences between African ancestral beliefs and Christ's ancestorship. According to him, the five characteristics valid for both are natural relationship, supernatural status, mediation, being a model of behaviour, and having title to regular, sacred Communion. But there are also important differences. Nyamiti recognises that Christ's relationship to humanity transcends family and clan or racial boundaries. Christ is God-man and Son of God. He is a more perfect model of behaviour and has, being God, a supernatural model of communication. Still, there is a basic sameness in structure, with a difference of level and mode. Nyamiti thus defines brother-ancestor as a relative of a person with whom he has a common parent and of whom he is mediator to God, archetype of behaviour, and with whom – thanks to his supernatural status acquired through death – he is entitled to have regular, sacred Communion. On account of Christ's relationship in the Trinity and his relationship with humanity, his ancestorship is divine, immanent and at the same time mediative, prophetic, royal and sacerdotal. Hence, for Nyamiti, the traditional titles of Christ are incorporated in his ancestorship: from an African perspective, Christ could be called our 'Brother-Ancestor' because through him and in the divine Spirit, we have been reconciled with God and made partakers of the Trinitarian life. This has consequences for Christians, who are now invited to live a life of sharing and Communion in the pattern of the Trinitarian life.

With slightly different nuances and in what may be a more acceptable approach, Bénézet Bujo in his book *African Theology in Its Social Context* (1992) attributes to Christ the title of 'Ancestor par excellence' – that is, 'Proto-Ancestor' – in whom the whole life of the African Christian can be rooted. To arrive at this title, Bujo does not place Christ the Ancestor at the level of biological lineage (as Nyamiti does), as if Christ is just one of the ordinary human ancestors, that is, at the level of consanguinity. Rather, Christ the Ancestor is of the transcendental level. Christ is the 'Unique Ancestor', the source of life and the highest model of all ancestorship. Bujo proposes Christological-Eucharistic ecclesiology, oriented towards the African concept of life. He examines the significance of Jesus as life-giver, a central theme in the New Testament, especially in Pauline theology. For example, Paul draws a parallel between the first and second Adam (cf. 1 Corinthians 15: 45–9; Romans 5: 12–21), and speaks of Christ as the first-born from the dead, as the head of the body, the church (Colossians 1: 15–20). In him resides the fullness of God, who has chosen to use him to reconcile all things (Colossians 1: 19–20). In John's gospel, Jesus is presented as one who has come so that his followers may have life and have it in abundance (John 10: 10). He gives his life for the sheep (John 10: 11–15). Jesus is the true vine and we can bear fruit only when we remain attached to him (John 15: 1–6). Even more, Jesus is the resurrection and the one who lives in him and believes in him will never die (John 11: 25–6). This implies that the exalted Jesus is the means through which God imparts his divine life to the world; he is, as it were, the bread of life, the source of eternal life (John 6: 32–58) and, therefore, the proto-life source.

In African theology, Christ is seen as the life-giving ancestor and the one who presides over the new family of God, the new extended universal family. The same Jesus Christ can be considered as the Great Healer, the Liberator and the Great Master of Initiation. Throughout Africa one finds processes of initiation viewed as rites of passage at every stage of human existence, but more markedly at the passage from adolescence to adulthood. According to Anselme T. Sanon of Burkina Faso, Christ was initiated in the customs of his Jewish people. He was also initiated into God's plan, which was the route to his perfection through obedience in his death and resurrection. Christ's initiation into a new existence is the *raîson d'être* of our being initiated into a new existence, and he himself leads us into the fullness of life. Thus he comes to be master of initiation, the elder brother in his father's foyer, initiating others into the same household. Christ is also designated as the African king, who, like the traditional African potentates, is very much concerned about the spiritual and physical well-being of the people. The African kings fulfilled significant sacramental roles for their communities, and through their annual festivals maintained harmony between their societies and their Ultimate Reality. Through an equally detailed examination of Christ's designation as king in the Scriptures, Chris Manus, the author of this model of African Christology, argues that the visions and the conceptions of African kingship cultures can enrich the same concept in the New Testament, at least for the African mind.

John Pobee, in his seminal book *Towards an African Theology* (1979), attributes to Christ the title of 'the Great and Greatest Ancestor – in Akan language *Nana*'. He seeks to answer the question, 'Why should an Akan relate to Jesus of Nazareth, who does not belong to his clan, family, tribe or nation?' The reason can be located, first, in the 'functional' or existential activity of Jesus (as the New Testament itself expresses), which focuses on the deeds of Jesus in relation to the individual believer. In this way, Jesus's divinity is described essentially in functional terms and, in a certain sense, is displayed through his humanity. This agrees with the Akan outlook, which prefers concreteness to abstraction. Secondly, as Ancestor (*Nana*) the God-man is characterised by the power and authority to judge, reward and punish people. However, Pobee emphasises the superiority of the Ancestorship of Christ to that of other ancestors by virtue of being closest to God and, indeed, God. As *Nana*, Pobee argues, Christ has authority over not only humanity but also all spirit beings, the cosmic powers and the ancestors. The practical relevance of this Christology includes letting his standards reign supreme in personal orientation, in the structures of society, in the economic processes and in political forces. In practical terms this means personal and social justice and re-creation. For some critics, Pobee's Christology does not touch the crucial issue of how Christ is not a tribal ancestor (*Nana*). Obviously, people from other tribes may not accept Christ the *Nana* of the Akan as their own ancestor. It follows, therefore, that Christ transcends the *Nana* of Akan people.

Nonetheless, in the view of African theologians, it is meaningful for the African to speak of Jesus as Ancestor par excellence, for in him are fulfilled all the qualities and virtues that Africans ascribe to their ancestors. In other words, the historical Jesus fulfils the highest ideals ascribed to the ancestors in African thought – he heals, he cures, he raises the dead and so on. In short, he imparts life force in all its fullness. This love and power he bequeaths, after death, to his disciples. It is precisely in his death and resurrection, with its soteriological meaning, that Jesus transcends the ancestors. This is Christology from below and provides a point of departure for a Christology in the African context. Consequently, theologians describe the church as the focal point from which the life of the proto-ancestor flows and spreads to all humanity. Thus, they see the Eucharist as the 'ancestral meal' instituted by the proto-ancestor and as that which should stand at the heart of African ecclesiology. The Eucharist is not simply an object of contemplation. Rather, it is the very life of the church and the source of its growth, life that is not merely biological generation, but rather mystical and spiritual. The purpose of the Eucharist (as with some African death–life rituals) is to impart life in all its fullness for the welfare of the whole community. This life is the Spirit. For African theologians, the ancestral model is Trinitarian, in that the Father, Son and Spirit are the source, imparter and substance, respectively, of the divine life in the community. An ecclesiology based on such an ancestral model presents a number of challenges to the life of the church. In traditional African society, each member is expected to make his or her contributions to the vital force of the whole community. The meeting point of Christianity and African traditional religion could be found in this concept of communitarian life, sharing and relationality.

African critics of ancestral Christology raise some basic questions about its relevance theologically and socio-culturally. Theologically, can the ancestor Christological paradigm really serve to reveal the whole person of Jesus Christ? How do we exploit this concept to capture all the richness of traditional Christology within the context of the theology of the Trinity? What about non-African Christian believers in Jesus Christ? It is not clear how the life of Christ is imparted to these biological ancestors, whether it is on the basis of a common grace (as Nyamiti seems to say) or by a kind of universalism derived from the efficacy of the resurrection (as Bujo argues). If Christ is the mystical and spiritual Brother-Ancestor, how can he be related to biological ancestors who are not strictly within the community bound together by faith? Socio-culturally, if this ancestor model is to be valid today, how long will it have relevance in Africa, given the momentum of the processes of modernisation, urbanisation and universalism of education? As a result, the ancestor paradigm might have to be re-examined and evaluated by emerging African theologians.

## African Liberation Theology

African liberation theology has a broader perspective and exhibits a variety of methods. This theology endeavours to integrate the theme of liberation into the rest of the African cultural background and socio-political and economic spheres. It discusses the oppressive socio-cultural structures inherited from traditional society, modern socio-political and economic systems, and emancipation from other forms of oppression such as disease, poverty, hunger, ignorance and the subjugation of women. Advocates of the African theology of liberation include Jean-Marc Éla, Engelbert Mveng, Mercy Amba Oduyoye, Elochukwu Uzukwu and Kwame Bediako. For lack of space, the analysis in this essay is limited to Éla's theology, since he could be regarded as the most representative of liberation theologians. A Catholic priest and theologian from Cameroon, among his most important works on this theme are *African Cry* (1986) and *My Faith as an African* (1995).

The starting point of Éla's theology is the relationship that should exist between inculturation and liberation in African theology. He is critical of an African theology that bases its concern mainly on anthropological and cultural problems, as if African society and churches can achieve their identity by considering only anthropological and cultural problems. In his view, such pre-occupation with cultural identity could be a dangerous alibi, so as to ignore the more burning issues in contemporary Africa. What is needed instead, according to Éla, is an inculturation that is relevant to the culture being born out of Africans' daily struggles for survival. In a sense, Éla is advocating a middle way between inculturation and liberation theologies in Africa. In this context, he refers to the tensions that mark the life of ordinary African Christians. This is because the Christianity of missioners supplies no answers to the difficulties of daily life. Christians continue to follow the traditions of their villages or districts. This ambivalence, Éla contends, is the source of many tensions that mark the people. Such situations have consequences, including the proliferation and strong influence of sects among young people confused about the future, and the polite indifference of African intellectuals who view Christianity as an out-of-date religion in a world that has come of age. For Éla, these factors call the church to re-examine its witness, 'or else Christianity will be seen as a religion only for women and children'.

In the opinion of Éla, the African situation as it is today requires that we pay a double 'regard' or take a hard look at our history as a people. Such a double 'view' of the past and the future requires fidelity to the past, to our 'dangerous' memories (J. B. Metz) and our pathetic and heroic memories. It also involves creativity to make new paths into the future with hope and optimism. This creativity is what he calls the 'ethics of transgression' for the sake of epistemological rupture. Such creativity led him to articulate theologically his pastoral experience with the Kirdi people of Tokombèrè village in northern Cameroon and turn it into a theological paradigm. He extrapolated from it a theology of revelation that takes seriously God's self-communication in history and a theology of salvation as liberation in the name of God's kingdom of peace and justice. For Éla, this is the scenario the local church in Africa is called upon to address today in its missionary endeavours. The urgent need to rethink the local church's social role for Africa's regeneration arises not so much out of a ready-made solution or theories, but from what Éla himself calls the 'shock' of the gospel in Africa: the 'coexistence of the gospel in Africa with the Veritable Empire of injustice and hunger'.

For Éla, the shock that the local church might have experienced through its pastoral experience was the realisation that even though a greater part of Africa is a deeply and massively Christian region, it tends to remain a veritable empire of hunger. He asks the question: how could the local church coexist with such a situation without 'shocking' it with the gospel?

In his writings, Éla captures various angles of this 'shock' as he describes the frustration, the apparently meaningless existence, the extreme and paralysing poverty, the violation of basic human rights, the colonial and neo-colonial violence, the multinational exploitation, as well as the hunger experienced by the people. It is this 'rough ground' that, according to Éla, provides the unique context and challenge for Christianity and theology in Africa today: our practice of Christian faith faces a major challenge from African men and women who agonise over where their next meal is coming from.

Furthermore, as Éla notes, the problem does not arise out of lack of commitment by rural populations, which can be easily addressed through moral and spiritual motivation. Rather, the problem has to do with a social system that is not geared to respond to the social needs of the majority. Elsewhere he notes that food shortages result not so much from natural calamities as from the imposition of an economic model that is much more oriented to the outside world than to the needs of the local community. Similarly, the health, medical and educational systems are set up in such a way that only an elite minority benefit. As a result, a gulf grows between the living standard of the comfortable minority of the 'haves' and that of the disinherited majority of the 'have-nots'.

One might have expected Éla to have developed a political system that could address the political scene he describes in his writings. Unfortunately, this is not the case. Africa is tired of a liberation theology that begins with and ends only in lamentations and criticism without showing a way of getting out of the jungle. A new challenge to African theology is to develop constructive theological thinking on the rebuilding of African socio-political reality. This was the challenge addressed by Ugandan theologian Emmanuel Katongole in his book *The Sacrifice of Africa: A Political Theology for Africa* (2010). The issues discussed by Katongole have also dominated the debate among the proponents of an African theology of reconstruction.

## African Theology of Reconstruction

The theology of reconstruction as a new trend (still in its infancy) in African theology is an attempt to unify the two early trends of inculturation and liberation theologies in Africa. The African theology of reconstruction has continued with the old themes of cultural identity and social liberation, but with a renewed emphasis on the role of the church and Christians in the social transformation of Africa.

The beginning of the 1990s was characterised by positive changes at both the African and the international levels. It was the end of the Cold War, in which African countries had been caught up for decades. The end of the Cold War marked the end of communism. Before that, Africa had been a battlefield where the capitalist bloc and the communist bloc were fighting for geopolitical strategies and control of African natural and mineral resources. The beginning of the 1990s also saw the end of apartheid in South Africa and the independence of Namibia and Zimbabwe, as well as of Mozambique and Angola. The fall of communism and the beginning of democracies in Africa was welcomed as a time for African renaissance. This international political situation called for a new theological response in Africa. Prior to 1990, African theology was motivated mainly by a struggle for African cultural identity and liberation from Western colonial and neo-colonial exploitation. With the new wind of change, the African church felt the call to respond positively to this new situation, which was for many a sign of hope. Also, the release of Nelson Mandela from prison in South Africa in 1990 was an important event for Africa.

In November 1991, the All Africa Conference of Churches (AACC) met in Mombasa (Kenya) to reflect on the response of the church in the post-apartheid era. The Anglican Archbishop Desmond Tutu, then President of the AACC, asked the Kenyan theologian Jesse Mugambi to reflect on the theological implications of Africa's changing situation for Southern Africa and Africa as a whole. The Mombasa meeting issued a document: *The Church of Africa: Towards a Theology of Reconstruction*. Mugambi became the architect of this shift to reconstruction in African theology. Mugambi's theology of reconstruction was first articulated in his book *From Liberation to Reconstruction: African Christian Theology After the Cold War* (1995). The constructive feedback he received prompted him to publish another volume on reconstruction, under the title *Christian Theology and Social Reconstruction* (2003).

As Innocent H. Maganya has noted, whether one should speak in terms of a shift from previous theological emphases to the reconstruction paradigm is open to question. The themes of inculturation and liberation come back often in the writings of the proponents of the theology of reconstruction. It might be better to speak of a 'new liberation theology' or a new awareness of the role of theologians in the transformation of society. Charles Villa-Vicencio of South Africa proposed a theology of reconstruction based on respect for laws and human rights. He called on the church to take part in the building of a new South Africa. Villa-Vicencio later published these proposals in his book *A Theology of Reconstruction: Nation-Building and Human Rights* (1992).

Among the guests at the Mombasa conference was Kä Mana, from the Democratic Republic of the Congo, who also has written extensively on the theme of reconstruction. Of particular note is his book *L'Afrique va-t-elle mourir: Bousculer l'imaginaire africain. Essai d'éthique politique*

(1991). Kä Mana proposes a model of reconstruction of Africa based on the theology of resurrection and salvation in Christ. He appeals to the Egyptian mythology of Isis and Osiris – their struggles for life and rebuilding existence – and to the model of the life–death–resurrection of Christ event. From these two distinct backgrounds, Kä Mana proposes a new society that passes from political ethics to Christological ethics and politics. Christians of today are called to articulate in the public domain Jesus Christ as the horizon of our existence or as him before whom one is to reconstruct humanity. The theology of reconstruction comes with the challenge of what to do between the logic of the market economy and the logic of love, as manifested by Christ. In this regard, the reconstruction of Africa must begin with the principles of the structuring of our social consciousness. The dictatorships of the belly, of alienation and powerlessness, are the arena from which the struggle for the future must begin. At stake is changing these realities and introducing a new way of thinking, to promote an Africa that is responsible for its own destiny. It is neither optimism nor pessimism, but a desire for hope in the building of a new society.

With the Mombasa meeting, a new orientation in African theology among Protestants was launched: theology that emphasises the social transformation of the continent. Advocates of the African theology of reconstruction have called for an end to the theology of identity and cultural consciousness among African authors. Time has come to shift from liberation to reconstructive transformation of Africa. Incarnation and liberation are seen as not sufficient to address the new social and political situation in Africa. In the view of the theologians of reconstruction, both inculturation and liberation responded to a situation of ecclesiastical and colonial bondage that no longer obtains. In place of the inculturation–liberation paradigm, which was mainly reactive, we should install a proactive theology of reconstruction. Instead of preoccupation with the ascendancy of liberation over inculturation or vice versa – a matter that is still much debated in African theology – advocates of the theology of reconstruction call for an innovative transcendence of both. It is interesting that Catholic theologians have written nothing on the theme, except the last work of Jean-Marc Éla: *Repenser la théologie Africaine* (2003). His work is not dealing directly with the theme of reconstruction, but he joins Mugambi in arguing that there was a crisis in the hermeneutics of African theology that was calling for a new way of doing theology in Africa.

Mugambi, Villa-Vicencio and Kä Mana are so far the leading theologians in the field of reconstruction. People have studied their works and have brought constructive remarks to the development of this new paradigm. Among these figures is Tinyiko Maluleke of South Africa. He questions the wisdom of advocates of reconstruction theology when they ask Africans to forget their history and culture in order to face the new challenges. For Maluleke, advocates of the theology of reconstruction appear to jump too quickly from Egypt to Canaan, from exile to post-exile, skipping the meandering and the long journey in the wilderness. The African continent and peoples have spent a long time in the wilderness since the beginning of the modern era. Any African theology that skips this experience or that asks the African people to forget their past and their historical experience in the rush to reconstruct and rebuild in the emerging realities misses an essential point in the contextual reality of Africans, as well as a key methodological issue.

Valentin Dedji from Cameroon has also made some constructive remarks in his study of the works of leading proponents of the African theology of reconstruction. In his work titled *Reconstruction and Renewal in African Theology* (2003), Dedji is critical of the contribution of reconstructionists Mugambi, Kä Mana, Éla and Kwame Bediako. These four African theologians have a common interest. Dedji, however, argues that the crucial issue today in Africa is that of gospel and justice rather than gospel and culture. Dedji calls for a theology of reconstruction that gives priority to biblical motifs such as reconstruction, forgiveness and repentance. Although Dedji does not develop these themes in relation to reconstruction theology as such, nonetheless he has brought out important themes for today's Africa that are lacking in the works of Mugambi, Kä Mana and Villa-Vicencio.

The themes of reconciliation, justice and peace received some attention in two volumes recently edited by Nigerian Jesuit theologian A. E. Orobator: *Reconciliation, Justice and Peace: The Second African Synod* (2011) and *Theological Re-imagination: Conversations on Church, Religion, and Society in Africa* (2014). In these two volumes, references are often made to the conversational and communicative styles in African cultures, which have been recently captured in the writings of some African scholars with the word *palaver*. The palaver model has been and is still the medium and process by which individual and community life issues are discussed, researched, cultivated, nurtured and actuated in many African communities.

Palaver is not led by the chief but by a council of elders, people who are well known, respected and knowledgeable about issues of communal life. In the palaver discourse the chief participates actively like every other community member and gives his views as any other active community member. The chief's power comes into force when the elders and the whole assembly have agreed on the way forward over an issue in the palaver assembly. The chief uses his authority to confirm the common position on the issue at hand to safeguard and implement the deliberations. He does this with the assistance from all the community members, who are the primary custodians of the community values. According to Laurenti Magesa, palaver could be described as a constant fellowship of African sages, leading the community towards the realisation of harmonious relationships and ethical norms that protect and promote life in all its complexity.

For Orobator, African palaver seems the most theologically fertile concept for the theological re-imagination already underway on the continent. This is because the African theological enterprise has shed its self-imposed innocence and naivety that once reduced it to merely aping theological models and answers fabricated for overseas contexts and consumption. However, with the emerging theological palaver conversation among African theologians, the era of doing theology in Africa by proxy seems to be coming to an end. Today, the works of African authors demonstrate the creativity of theological imagination in Africa, with theologians themselves asking their own questions and discovering their own answers. This is the African palaver style of theologising, which has started characterising the journey of theological reflection on the continent today.

African theology draws on Christian Scripture and tradition but equally from African religious traditions, cultures, histories and contexts as valuable and valid sources of theologising. African Independent Churches and Pentecostals have much to contribute in this regard. African theologians pursue their scholarship not as ivory-tower academicians but as believing and practising Christians who have the experience to substantiate their claims. They have appropriated the scholastic definition of theology as 'faith seeking understanding', but with the fundamental difference that while *fides quaerens intellectum* hinges on a Cartesian *Cogito ergo sum* ('I think, therefore I am'), the quest of African authors pivots on the African epistemological axiom *Cognatus ergo sumus, ergo sum* ('We are in relation, therefore, I am'). In fact, in the African context, theology is inseparable from the theologian's personal faith narrative, quest and journey as these unfold within and are fed by concerns of and from his or her Christian community. Shared faith narrative, quest and journey are grist to the theological mill among African theologians.

## Conclusion

Today, African theologians are urged to minimise the conflict that has existed between the proponents of the three dominant trends: inculturation, liberation and reconstruction. This is in keeping with the theologians' idea of an integrative African theology. It is a theology that pays attention to issues of social transformation of Africa as it grapples with the question of faith commitment throughout the continent. Viewed from that perspective, the strength of African theology lies in the fact that it seeks to match theoretical and academic elaboration with social and practical commitment. This is what will make the difference in the future.

## Bibliography

Bujo, Bénézet and Juvénal Ilunga Muya (eds), *African Theology: The Contribution of the Pioneers* (3 vols) (Nairobi: Paulines Publications Africa, 2003, 2006, 2013).

Kä Mana, *Christians and Churches of Africa: Salvation in Christ and Building a New African Society* (Maryknoll, NY: Orbis Books, 2004).

Mugambi, Jesse N. K., *From Liberation to Reconstruction: African Christian Theology After the Cold War* (Nairobi: East African Educational Publishers, 1995).

Oborji, Francis Anekwe, *Trends in African Theology Since Vatican II: A Missiological Orientation* (2nd edition) (Rome: Leberit Press, 2005).

Orobator, Agbonkhianmeghe E. (ed.), *Theological Reimagination: Conversations on Church, Religion, and Society in Africa* (Nairobi: Paulines Publications Africa, 2014).

# Social and Political Context

## Musa Dube and Malebogo Kgalemang

The contemporary social and political context of the African continent is shaped by its multi-layered histories. Most African countries' histories are framed by the following eras: pre-colonial, colonial, struggles for independence, post-independence and contemporary globalisation within a neo-liberal economic framework. These historical stages have not run in a linear form but rather with constant flashbacks and intertwined plots. The colonial history, as post-colonial studies underline, remains alive in shaping the social and political contexts of the continent. These contexts mean that African social and political contexts have been a rocking boat grafted in international waves that are beyond Africa's immediate control. The church was participating in all the stages, both shaping and being shaped by African and political social contexts.

Linguistically, the continent is divided into four categories, according to the languages of their colonial past: English-speaking, French-speaking, Portuguese-speaking and Spanish-speaking. The number of indigenous languages of Africa is in the range 700–3,000 and are divided into four families: Niger-Congo, Afro-Asiatic, Nilo-Saharan and Khoisan. Africa is thus a vast continent with a variety of socio-political structures that cannot be easily generalised. It goes without saying that African social and political structures and contexts, as well as Africa's people, are inevitably hybrid. This chapter will manage only to sketch broad strokes about the political and social contexts of Africa, which are not representative of all countries, given the immense diversities of the continent. The broad strokes will be under the following subheadings:

- Pre-colonial Social and Political Contexts
- Modern Colonialism and the African Social and Political Contexts
- Struggle for Independence: The Cold War and the Post-independence Crisis
- African Social and Political Contexts in the Globalisation Era

### Pre-colonial Social and Political Contexts

Prior to colonisation, most African communities were arranged as kingdoms that were ruled by kings through a council of elders and communal consultation and consensus building. The identity of the community was not necessarily tribal, although it is commonly identified as such (a 'tribe' describes people who are descendants of one ancestor, whose identity remains constant). Although an ethnic group could be named after a founding ancestor, African kingdoms included several ethnic groups, foreigners, traders, asylum seekers, sojourners and war captives. The Zulus of South Africa, for example, are an ethnic group named after their king, Shaka Zulu, but he was notorious for conquering other ethnic groups and integrating them into his kingdom. Long before modern colonisation, African kingdoms had elaborate trade routes from and to the sea, into the interior and back, and they interacted with people from other kingdoms and continents. A good example is the East African interaction with Arabic-speaking traders that resulted in one of the widely spoken indigenous languages, Swahili. The latter is spoken in Kenya, Tanzania, Uganda, Rwanda, Burundi and the Democratic Republic of the Congo. Similarly, in West Africa Hausa developed into a lingua franca, through trade interaction. Thus, people who speak one language are not always from one tribe, as illustrated by Swahili and Hausa.

The African continent also had several empires internally before Western colonisation. These include Buganda, Munamutapa, Dahomey, Oyo and Zululand. Empires always include people of different geographical, cultural and social structures. In sum, 'tribal identity and tribalism' of the African continent, which are often presented as examples of monolithic groups that are unable to accommodate difference, is a colonial and Western creation of African identities. African ethnic groups such as the Akan, Igbo, Tutsi, Hutus, Kikuyu, Hausa, Tswana, Zulu and Ndebele are ethnic groups that are diverse within themselves, yet used to live together within a particular geographical area, and to identify themselves with a particular name and culture. The Hutu and Tutsi genocide in Rwanda is often presented as a case of tribalism, yet study of these groups indicates that in pre-colonial times they were ethnic names that had shifted to indicate class; hence someone who moved to the upper class could become a Tutsi and a Tutsi who lost social status could become a Hutu. Being a Hutu or Tutsi did not depend on a blood ancestor: it was fluid. Understanding this pre-colonial history is central to understanding the contemporary political and social context of the African continent and how the interaction with Western colonial powers reconstructed the indigenous structures.

African kingdoms were located in large and small villages that were subdivided into wards and clans led by communally appointed chiefs and headmen. The leaders administered social order and economic resources for the community. The resources that were administered included land, minerals, crafts and spiritual resources. Most African communities were agrarian, pastoralists, large-scale nomadic pastoralists (Maasai), nomadic hunter gatherers (Khoisan) and a small class of artisans, who were miners, ironsmiths, craft makers, musicians, storytellers and dancers. Land was a central resource, hosting the living and the dead (ancestors) and providing sustenance for people and their domestic animals as well as sustaining forests and wild animals, which were central to the well-being of society. Land was thus held to be almost sacred, since most African communities realised that the land was central to the sustenance of life. There was no concept of buying and selling land, nor did individuals desire to hold large chunks of land beyond their sustenance needs. Kings held large chunks of land within their kingdoms for the community.

The political structures administered the land for the community. This included distributing residential, pastoral and ploughing land to different wards, clans and individuals. Sojourners who wished to settle could request and be allocated land. Some sites were also designated as holy areas. The latter could be particular mountains, rivers, valleys or desert areas. Most political leaders were also spiritual leaders. They administered spiritual rituals for and on behalf of the well-being of the community either in times of crisis, such as severe drought, or during particular seasons of the year, such as marking the beginning of the rainy season or at harvest time. In ethnic groups where political leaders did not administer communal rituals and prayers, they worked with spiritual leaders who carried out rituals and prayers for the community, on the advice of the king.

While the empire-oriented kingdoms of Shaka Zulu and Dahomey were absolute monarchies, in general the kings, chiefs and headmen were not dictators, as their administration was through the council of elders and community consultation that involved consensus building on issues affecting the well-being of the kingdom. The Swati King also ruled through a council of representatives that included the queen mother, members of the royal family and commoners. The queen mother was, and still is, the high priest in the Swati Reed Dance, a ritual that seeks to cleanse and prepare the land for rain and fertility, which culminates with the King being given the privilege of choosing one of the young dancers as his wife. Among the Tswana-speaking people, several proverbs and sayings underline the political role of the King and community participation. Examples are as follows: *Kgosi ke kgosi ka batho* (a king is only a king through people); *Kgosi thotobolo o olela matlakala otle* (a king is a dumping ground that receives all people and their concerns); *mafoko a kgotla amantle otle* (all people are free to express their opinion at the public meeting); *mmualebe o bua la gagwe* (everyone has the right to express their thoughts). Among the Tswana-speakers, as well as many Bantu-speakers, who range from Southern Africa to West Africa, these indigenous political structures remain operative in the rural areas, existing and working hand with national governments. The indigenous political structures remain administrators of justice, land and rituals for their communities, although within the given national structures. People in Westernised urban areas, where land has become commercialised and sold, can still be allocated free residential and agricultural land in rural areas; where justice involves lawyers with high legal fees, people of all classes in rural areas have access to justice through their indigenous leaders, who arbitrate all cases without any charge.

It is important to touch on gender and age in the pre-colonial political and social structures. Age was an important social category. Ageing was associated with wisdom and power, while youthfulness was also associated with intelligence. Thus, the Tswana-speakers held that *bothale jwa phala botswa phalaneng* (the wisdom of elders comes from the youth) and that *susu a ilele suswana gore suswana atle a moilele* (elders must respect the young ones so that they can also respect the elders). Initiation schools for teenagers were held regularly for age mates to be prepared to cross over to adulthood. The age regiments were prepared for both girls and boys and given names. The initiation schools instilled into the initiates what is expected from them as adult women and men. In some communities, graduation into adulthood was marked by circumcision of all boys; without circumcision one could never qualify as an adult man, regardless of age. Graduation from initiation endowed the youth with adult rights and responsibilities. They included the right to attend the public consultation meeting at the court, to marry, to have residential and agricultural land, to drink alcoholic drinks and the responsibility to defend the nation, whenever the need arose.

Respect for all elders in the family and old people was imperative, since it was closely woven into structure of the living dead (ancestors). The older a person became, the closer they came to the status of ancestors, hence deserving all respect, honour and care. It was believed that failure to respect, honour and care for elders and very old people within families and the community annoyed the ancestors and they could withdraw their role of interceding before God for the living and the community. So important was the age of elders and 'very old people' that their authority within the family could surpass the social category of gender. Part of this philosophy remains evident as elders and 'very old people' continue to be cared for by family members, rather than being moved to an old people's home. In the HIV/AIDS context, when young adult parents were dying en masse and leaving behind young children, grandmothers were able to step in and raise the children, although with physical and economic challenges.

## Modern Colonialism and the African Social and Political Contexts

African contact with European countries goes as far back as Greco-Roman times, as attested in several ancient Greek texts. Modern African contact with Europeans began in the fifteenth century with explorers from Spain, Portugal and Holland, who tended to be trade-oriented and limited to the coastal shores, without necessarily being interested in settling. In the eighteenth and nineteenth centuries the number of explorers increased, sponsored by associations, societies and governments. They were coming from various other countries, such as Belgium, Britain, France and Germany. They consisted of traders, military groups, explorers and religious travellers such as missionaries. Among the classic explorers who advocated the colonisation of the African continent were David Livingstone, the famed Scottish medical missionary, who called for three Cs – Christianity, Commerce and Colonisation – and Cecil John Rhodes, whose dream was to build a railway from Cape to Cairo. With the rapid growth of European industrialisation, there was demand for raw materials such as minerals, cotton, beans and labour, which intensified the exploration and claim of the African lands, characterised initially by the signing treaties, soon followed by the use of military might where there was resistance. Competition among European powers led to the so-called 'Scramble for Africa' and the 1884–5 Berlin Conference that sought to coordinate a peaceful partitioning of the African countries among the colonising powers. Modern colonialism left very few African countries untouched. Ethiopia is notable for having successfully resisted Italian colonisation. Most countries were colonised by Britain, France, Germany, Italy, Belgium, Portugal or Spain, forming about 40 political units. The boundaries that were drawn by the European powers disregarded the pre-existing boundaries of various kingdoms, villages and ethnic groups. Consequently, one ethnic group could be found in three different colonies. Sometimes the colonial boundaries separated families and, at other times, they separated residents from their fields, pastures and hunting grounds.

The colonial powers reconstituted the political and social structures of African communities. To start with, colonisation was an imposition of foreign rule for the economic interests of the coloniser. At first, colonial rulers sought to undermine the political role of kings, chiefs and headmen, but they faced several challenges. The latter included insufficient personnel, travel constraints and lack of immunity against indigenous diseases, as well as lack of legitimacy among the colonised and the challenge of lack of understanding cultural structures. The colonial powers then resorted to indirect rule, and sought to co-opt existing leaders to rule their own people on behalf of the coloniser, using their own indigenous structures. This approach was complicated by several factors, including some resisting leaders and the assumption that African communities consisted of monolithic tribes that share one ancestor. To start with the former, in places where indigenous leaders were too powerful to be co-opted for the needs of colonisers, they were often deposed, by abolishing hereditary rights of succession, so the colonisers could assume the right to appoint new puppet leaders (divide and rule approach). At times, new collaborative individuals from smaller ethnic groups were imposed on larger ethnic groups to minimise rebellion, by disabling powerful kings and ethnic groups. In the process, certain ethnic groups were chosen and given authority to rule others and 'tribal identity' was created as an unchangeable category. In the case of the Hutu and Tutsi, for example, members were forced to carry identity cards that identified them as Hutu or Tutsi, with the pre-existing fluidity cancelled and power given to the Tutsi. Many decades later, the colonial construction exploded into one of the worst genocides among communities that lived together, spoke one language, but carried colonially established 'tribal' identity. With the creation of colonial institutions such as Western schools, churches, hospitals, trade centres, army and administrators, there was a need to train some Africans for the needs and interests of the colony.

In the colonial context, economic flourishing was not intended for the colonised, but for the interests of the colonising powers and their people. Land was the first resource to be grabbed, since a colony is the taking of foreign lands for the interests of the coloniser. So the 'Scramble for Africa' describes the taking of African land by European powers, to exploit its resources for the industries and needs of the colonisers. Large chunks of land were turned into fields for cash crops for exporting, rather than for the needs of native populations. In such countries as Zimbabwe and South Africa, where there were white settler coloniser populations, large chunks of fertile land were taken from native populations and given to minority settlers. Indigenous Zimbabweans were moved to crowded, infertile places or could remain in their original settlements as servants on the farms of white people and with limited rights to the agricultural use of the land. The colonial political and social contexts were hostile to African people; they were created to exploit and subjugate them rather than to empower them.

Elaborate ideologies had to be constructed to legitimise and sanctify the conscience of the coloniser and 'opiumise' the colonised. As post-colonial studies analysis of the writings of colonial explorers, traders, missionaries, administrators, sailors and so on has shown, it was a construction of the Other as unworthy infants, savages, uncivilised, primitive, lazy and evil pagans, who did not know or deserve to use their resources and thus needed civilising missions from the duty-bound colonial powers that would teach, train, convert, civilise and rule them. The continent and the land itself were described as empty, dark and hostile. The colonial archive is consistent in the negative construction of African people, their cultures, and economic, political, social, religious and cultural institutions as worthy only of dismissal. Such a presentation of the Other served a purpose of justifying the creation of colonial political and social contexts that allowed the exploitation and subjugation of African people.

It was within these social and political contexts of the eighteenth- and nineteenth century colonial project that the Sub-Saharan region began to be Christianised. Missionary associations and their workers hardly maintained a critical stance towards the imperial projects of their mother countries. Colonialism was not named as an unacceptable evil. As attested by missionary letters, diaries, reports and books, they were convinced, together with their mother countries, that African structures and belief systems needed to be overhauled and replaced by Western ones. Missionaries were participants in the 'Scramble for Africa' Berlin Conference without offering a word of objection. Such a luminary as David Livingstone carried on his project of opening Africa for the three Cs without any ethical conflict. The Christianisation of Sub-Saharan Africa was carried out in the imperial political and economic context that legitimised the exploitation and suppression of the Other, for the sake of Western countries. Repeatedly, African church historians have shown that missionaries were, more often than not, forerunners of the colonial projects of their mother countries. Within this political context of colonising the Other, missionaries often built hospitals and schools as institutions that served to suppress the available African social and cultural institutions, rather than working within them.

### Struggle for Independence: The Cold War and the Post-independence Crisis

The colonial social and political contexts could only create resistance from the dispossessed. The struggle for autonomy was always there from the first colonial contact, although it escalated during the second half of the twentieth century. Among the earliest recorded instances of resistance against colonial oppression and its structures of exclusion and exploitation is the case of Kimpa Vita, a Congolese woman who was baptised Dona Beatrice in the Catholic Church. Claiming to be possessed by the spirit of St Patrick, Kimpa Vita insisted that Jesus and his disciples were black and they came to São Salvador, the capital of her country. Kimpa Vita insisted that all the white images of biblical characters that hung in the cathedral should be removed since they were idols. Kimpa Vita's prophetic words found wide support and she had a massive following, thus threatening the colonial authorities, which had her crucified in 1706.

Kimpa Vita's resistance marked the beginning of a continent-wide Christian resistance movement widely known as African Independent Churches (AICs). These were Africans who accepted Christianity but did not accept the colonial ideology, which called for the erasure of indigenous social and political structures, in favour of Western ones. AICs were thus founded by Africans and they practised a Christianity that affirmed African leadership, political structures and cultures. The AIC movement grew continent wide and fed into national political movements that began to agitate for the independence of African countries.

The spirit of resistance on the continent is attested by the fact that the colonial project moved from forming treaties to the use of military force. Such countries as Ethiopia successfully resisted military powers of the coloniser. At the beginning of the twentieth century, several resistance movements started, nationally, regionally and internationally connected. Ghana became the first independent country in 1957, sparking further energies from/to/for other countries. By the end of the 1970s only a handful of countries remained under colonial rule, including the settler colonies of South Africa and Rhodesia (later to become Zimbabwe). In these countries, the social and political contexts were designed to dehumanise black people. South Africa with its apartheid regime basically constructed black people as low-class labour, for the service of white people, since they not only were denied land but were also denied quality education. The South African and Zimbabwean liberation wars were bitterly fought with international and regional networks, all seeking the creation of justice-oriented structures that embrace and empower all citizens. Zimbabwe gained its independence in 1980 and South Africa had its first democratically elected government in 1994. The tradition of African Christianity was mired between resistance and collaboration during this time in South Africa, as attested by those churches that were proponents of apartheid ideology, the exponential growth AICs and the rise neo-Pentecostal churches as well as the collective production of the Kairos Document by some churches, which sought to prophetically denounce apartheid.

With independence, African governments faced huge challenges to create social and political contexts that are empowering to their citizens. Some of the challenges were inherited, others internal, while others were external, and still others were related to natural resources. The inherited challenges included the fact that African governments occupied boundaries that were created by colonisers, which put together ethnic groups that did not necessarily regard themselves as belonging to one nation or kingdom. Further, during colonial times, some puppets kings, chiefs and ethnic groups had been used against others and there were scores to settle. Land that was taken during colonial times, sometimes forcibly taken, at other times given by indigenous leaders who did not have the concept of selling land, was now individually owned by former colonisers with legal papers to prove it: title deeds! Huge indigenous populations remained landless, thus making their independence futile. Internally, African governments had insufficient infrastructure and insufficient qualified personnel, and the new leaders were themselves products of the colonial ideologies that they had overthrown. Their governments were further caught in the Cold War and later in Western-imposed structural adjustment economic policies of the World Bank and International Monetary Fund (IMF), whose recommended economic frameworks did not work and left many governments with huge debts. The indebted African governments could not service their own citizens, since they had huge loans to pay to the World Bank and the IMF. Some countries' main challenges pertained to lack of resources to finance national projects.

Given the above challenges, the post-independence African context was marked by: coups (especially in West Africa); ethnic-based civil wars and violence, for instance in Mozambique and Zimbabwe; and explosive genocide, such as that experienced in Rwanda between the Tutsi and the Hutus. Zimbabwe has been engaged in a protracted struggle to regain land from the settler colonisers. The East African region has faced persistent conflict that is both ethnically and religiously driven, as in the case of South and North Sudan, Rwanda and Burundi. Some corrupt and violent leaders such as Mobutu Sese Seko of Zaire (now Democratic Republic of the Congo) and Jonas Savimbi of Angola found support from Western countries, who kept them in power, just because they served as conduits in the struggle against communism during the Cold War. Such leaders were ousted only when communism lost its world influence. Other political and social challenges consisted of natural disasters such as drought, famine, HIV/AIDS and, recently, Ebola. In the past 30 years, the HIV/AIDS epidemic has created major social challenges and has affected all sectors of society. Concerted efforts nationally, regionally and internationally have, though, now brought HIV/AIDS to the stage of being a manageable epidemic.

One of the challenging political contexts in the post-independence stage is that many sitting presidents, who first led their countries to independence, also veered towards single-party political structures that enabled them to be lifetime leaders. These tendencies were influenced by both domestic and international political philosophies. Internal and external advocacy has pushed countries towards multi-party systems and limited terms for serving presidents (usually to two terms). Advocacy was mounted by national and regional trade unions, rising numbers of middle-class people, fellow leaders through regional organisations such as the African Union and the Southern African Development Community (SADC), non-governmental organisations, faith-based organisations, the Economic Community of West African States and the international community. Civil organisations are also actively involved in standing in the gap to provide, where they can, educational, health and economic services to citizens who fall between the cracks. Churches have been central to the provision of schools and hospitals. Faith-based organisations have also been instrumental in midwifing peace in regions and countries that are haunted by persistent conflict and violence, such as East Africa. While in recent decades most countries have responded positively and embraced multi-party systems, some argue that multi-party systems are not necessarily the solution, nor do they constitute democracy, given the persistent ethnic and party-based post-election violence witnessed in countries such as Kenya (2007) and Zimbabwe (2008).

Yet there are some countries, such as Botswana, that have maintained peace and practised multi-party democracy since independence. Countries such as Namibia emerged from colonial regimes with democratically oriented constitutions that already limited the terms for sitting presidents to a maximum of two. Some countries have managed to have a peaceful transition from oppressive settler regimes to democratic government, such as South Africa through such programmes as the Truth and Reconciliation Commission, which was chaired by Archbishop Desmond M. Tutu. South Africa is credited with one of the most democratic constitutions in the world, which protects the rights of all. Be that as it may, some argue that the black masses of South Africa remain landless and powerless, since land was never redistributed to the dispossessed. Rwanda is also noted for engineering itself away from violence and creating enabling social and political contexts for its citizens.

African Christianity has been actively involved in midwifing reconciliation. Other social indicators highlight that the African continent as a whole is not caught in a rut. With 65% of the growing population being below 35 years of age, it is currently the continent with the fastest economic growth in the world. Consequently, Africa is an international investment destination. Currently, Africa also has the highest percentage of women political leaders and representatives, higher than in 'First World' countries such as the USA.

## African Social and Political Contexts in the Globalisation Era

In conclusion, African social and political contexts have been a rocking boat and an experiment, given that it is widely acknowledged that nations can be understood as 'imagined communities'. Since the foundation and boundaries of contemporary African nations were not even initiated by those who found themselves within the particular borders, owning such a collective identity has been a process, an experiment. The struggle for independence was the first stage of building a shared vision of living together. But such a vision was rudely challenged for daring to proceed without healing the colonial wounds and sufficiently struggling with ways of living peacefully with ethnic, religious, racial and gender differences. Those countries that have taken to truth and reconciliation seem to have created a helpful bridge for crossing, although the process has recognised that it does not necessarily address structural inequalities established by decades (even centuries) of dispossession of indigenous populations, especially dispossession of their lands.

The vision of being independent African countries has also been challenged by the realisation that Western countries' programmes, policies and interventions have not always been midwives to positive social and political contexts. As much as African countries are, and will always remain, part and parcel of the international community, they will also need to guard against imposed developmental policies, programmes, aid and partnerships that are manufactured in Western contexts and assumed to be a one-size-fits-all garment. National, regional and continental civil societies, regional and collective economic bodies, unions and associations have already become crucial partners on the road to creating empowering social and political contexts on the African continent. The collaboration of Christianity with oppressive social and political structures has been a humbling lesson to the worldwide church, just as those African Christianities that raised voices of resistance are a ray of hope for how Christian institutions might occupy a prophetic role in their political and social contexts.

Crucially, the African social and political contexts have entered a new era of neo-liberal globalisation. Neo-liberalism is an economic ideology which promotes deregulation and privatisation of markets and services; it thus encourages a handing over from governments to private companies of key national welfare services, such as the supply of water, electricity, education, health, communication and communal pastures. Private companies are interested in profit rather than creating social and political contexts that allow all members of the community to have access to affordable services and goods. The contemporary neo-Pentecostal movements, with their emphasis on the gospel of prosperity and victorious living, are associated with this neo-liberal context. Neo-Pentecostal Christianity is a global movement that uses social media to spread its message across all borders, emphasising individual competence, a global and competent African church, and a theology of deliverance and healing from all material and spiritual forces of limitation. It is unclear whether the neo-Pentecostal movements have a prophetic voice towards globalisation. Rather, they seem to enable individual members to function within its ethics. Their gospel seeks to construct a globally competent African. The neo-liberal economic approach is increasing the gap between the poor and the rich as well as allowing First World countries to buy government-based service companies. Many young African governments are being pressurised by the IMF, World Bank and donors to privatise and they have begun to cut down on employees and to sell service departments to corporate firms. The social and political context of Africa is, therefore, best described as *a luta continua* – the struggle continues amidst a thousand other challenging forces.

## Bibliography


Appiah, Kwame A. and Henry Louis Gates (eds), *Africana: The Encyclopaedia of the African and African American Experience* (New York: Basic Civitas Books, 1999).

Asamoah-Gyadu, Kwabena J., *African Charismatics: Current Developments Within Independent Indigenous Pentecostalism in Ghana* (Leiden: Brill, 2005).

Oduyoye, Mercy A., *Hearing and Knowing: Theological Reflections on Christianity in Africa* (Maryknoll, NY: Orbis Books, 1986).

Tutu, Desmond M., *No Future without Forgiveness* (New York: Doubleday, 2000).

Wamue, Grace and Matthew M. Theuri (eds), *Quests for Integrity in Africa* (Nairobi: Acton, 2003).

# Mission and Evangelism

## Esther Mombo

The rapid growth of Christianity evident in Africa today is the result, to a great extent, of mission and evangelism conceived and implemented during the nineteenth and twentieth centuries. Founded and established by missionaries from Europe and North America, the church has grown by leaps and bounds. While each missionary and agency had a distinctive emphasis, in general the methodology used was a fourfold format in which evangelism, education, health care and industrial services were used in establishing mission centres out of which whole communities were evangelised. In some places, those who became Christians were identified as 'readers' because Christianity was identified with literacy. The fourfold format of mission and evangelism was meant to liberate the people from what was viewed as a degraded state of life compared with that which obtained in the missionaries' countries of origin. Salvation and liberation meant accepting and accommodating the teaching of the gospel as presented by the missionary in his or her cultural terms. The endeavours of the missionaries and their early converts led to the establishment of churches, schools, hospitals and other institutions that sought to meet the needs of people in society.

The growth of Christianity in modern times is undeniable, both statistically and in its youthful vigour. The visibility of Christianity is seen in the use of names and symbols from the Bible in public spaces such as transport, shops and apartments, such as the Shalom Saloon, Ebenezer Holdings, Amazing Grace Apartments, Victory General Shop, Trinity Hospital, Bethsaida Hospital, Glorious Boutique, Goshen Workshop, Elijah Hair Salon, Goshen Fashion Shop, Jericho Metal Workshop, Tumaini (Faith) Bar, Blessed Shelter Hardware, Unity Welding Shop, Provident General Store, Exodus Paints, Glory Paints, God's Blessed Shop, Rehoboth General, Glory Milk Bar, Eden Supermarket, Genesis Flats, Heavenly Hair Products, Anointed Fashions or Lazaro Apartments. The list could go on endlessly. The pervasive presence of the Christian faith is thus literally inscribed on the landscape.

The role of education in the growth of the church in Africa has been central, as literacy was identified with Christianity. At the beginning, literacy was introduced to help people read the Bible. The translation of the Bible was key for evangelism and it was usually the first text that was translated into the local languages and it was used as a textbook when people were learning to read. It remains today one of the texts that is readily available in many homes and institutions and is used in discussion of social and political matters.

As well as reading the Bible, the 'readers' were also taught writing and arithmetic. Together with the rudimentary or 'bush' schools, the mission work extended to found schools for men and women, colleges for teacher training, medical schools and universities. Education, as a form of evangelism, helped the mission churches to prepare leaders in different sectors of society. The pioneer leaders and the second- and third-generation leaders were products of mission schools. The introduction of formal education became a basis of establishing new communities. These communities became a channel though which Western ideas were entrenched in society. By receiving an education, one had a chance to enhance one's social mobility.

The uptake of education among men was higher than among women. It was structured along patriarchal lines, making it harder for women to receive the same education. This meant that women came into the field of education later than the men and thus were not able to be fully engaged in the public life of their communities. After independence, however, the few pioneer women began to work for more space for women in all sectors. The situation for women is better today than a decade ago.

Education continues to be key in all sectors of society, including the church. The growing churches are those that have embraced different forms of education and especially technology. These churches have become spaces where members are encouraged to do their best in the expectation that God has ordained the best for all. While the introduction of formal education by the mission agencies is not without complications in the impact it had on society, these are much outweighed by the benefits in terms of development brought by the introduction of modern education.

## The Social Context of Evangelism

The public display of Christianity is in a context of complex realities and challenges with which people are faced on a daily basis. There seems to be a disconnect between the visible marks of Christianity and the challenges that people are facing in Africa. These challenges can be broadly described at the levels of economics, politics, society and culture. There are threats to the lives of children, women, young people and the elderly. The issues around environmental and ecological degradation are real, so that the land on which people depend is facing the challenges of prolonged droughts or excessive rains leading to floods. Economic issues include corruption in some countries, economic stagnation and the concentration of wealth in the hands of the few. In the political sphere, the integrity of Christianity can be undermined by leaders who profess the Christian faith but seek to remain in office indefinitely. Another pressing reality today is religious intolerance, which has resulted in terrorist attacks in different countries. Health issues also arouse much concern, with diseases such as HIV/AIDS and Ebola having devastating effects. These can increase Africa's marginalisation in terms of exclusion and discrimination by the wider world.

Mission can be understood as participating in Jesus's mission of liberating love and doing this as part of the community. African Christians have indeed been engaged in this mission – hence the explosion of Christianity. However, the numerical growth of Christianity does not necessarily mean that it is shaping the life of African societies. The issues of authentic Christian conversion that preoccupied the early European missionaries have returned in new forms. Thus there is a call for a focus on 'holistic' mission.

The fact that the ministry of Jesus was based on a liberation manifesto and a promise of life in abundance to his followers alerts us to the reality that Christianity is intended to challenge destructive, life-denying systems of power. Life in abundance means witnessing to Christ by working towards the values of the Kingdom, including justice and peace. The mission of the church is the mission of God to the whole world, manifested in the life and teaching of Jesus Christ. The task of the church is to proclaim the gospel of Christ and by so doing to generate among people a fellowship that provides the blueprint for the society of God. The works of God are the works of justice and compassion whereby people are liberated here and now from the immediate physical hardships or injustices pressing upon them.

The message of God is the gospel of ultimate deliverance, and this cannot be lived in abstract terms but only within the life of the community. The church's long record of community service is as indisputable as the record of preaching the Word, even if the theology behind it has not been well articulated. What appears to haunt Christianity today is the disconnect between the things of the spirit and what is seen as material or secular. The question that one perhaps faces is, how does one do mission in a context that is already pervasively religious? What seems to be happening is that many are using the 'spiritual' to enrich themselves in material terms. So the spiritual dimension has not been omitted, but it is used to increase prosperity in the world. What appears to be lacking in this kind of mission is active and transformative engagement with injustices in society.

### The Plural Context of Evangelism

Christianity in Sub-Saharan Africa was founded in the context of religious plurality. Different traditions have sometimes been in bitter rivalry and at other times at peace with each other. But in recent times the tensions between the different religious traditions have increased with the emergence of such groups as Boko Haram in Nigeria, Ansar al-Din in Mali, Seleka Rebels in the Central Africa Republic, Al-Shabaab in Kenya and the Lord's Resistance Army in Uganda. The presence of such groups reflects a global context that promotes radicalisation and privileges violence. It would seem that African Christians and their counterpart African Muslims bear the brunt of conflicts that have their origins outside the continent. The challenge for Christians and Muslims is how they live with each other and how they share the resources available to them. It is often in regard to access to scarce resources that historical injustices arise and tensions increase as either party feels denied. As well as sharing resources, both religions are missionary, and seeking an increase in number is part and parcel of their mission. The question of how they effectively actualise their missionary imperative without creating dangerous tensions is one that is unlikely to disappear in the near future.

In broad terms, Christians have related to Muslims on the continent in two ways: dialogue and evangelism. Both have positive and negative aspects, depending on how they are implemented and which groups are engaged in the encounter. In theological educational institutions, courses on other faiths are offered in order to provide the tools for dialogue. In some schools, the aim is to prepare students to convert members of the other faiths or non-believers through such initiatives as open-air meetings.

The schools that take the dialogue perspective take cognisance of the other religious traditions and live as witnesses rather than aggressively promoting conversion to their faith. Yet, while this may be their public position, often the underlying interest or goal is the hope that conversion will take place. Dialogue becomes one way of being a witness, and the results of witnessing include not only understanding each other but also the possibility of conversion. The other aim of dialogue is peaceful co-existence. Africa bears the brunt of conflicts that appear to be religious but may have other underlying causes. In this context, ecumenical and inter-religious dialogue is not a luxury. In a world wounded by conflict and division, such dialogue is not something extra or optional, but essential. It represents a way of relating, even if the openness and vulnerability might not be fully reciprocated. Ideally, mutuality in dialogue is present in communication, trust, understanding, challenge, growth and even spiritual development. Dialogue is not an apology for one's faith but rather living alongside each other, struggling with issues that are more than religious.

As well as dialogue, evangelism has been an imperative for Christians who are commanded to share the good news of salvation with all people. In evangelism, Christians share their experience of Jesus Christ so that people accept him and follow his ways. Different forms of evangelism conducted by Christians include open-air meetings known as crusades, sharing tracts and offering Bible correspondence courses. Those who convert and follow are mentored to grow into the Christian faith in order to become evangelists themselves. Sometimes those who have converted to the Christian faith are in danger and churches provide protection for them. In some instances, evangelism has led to open confrontation, leaving people in bitter rivalry and tensions.

Living in a diverse community is a reality in Africa and perhaps what is needed is a way of thinking in terms of diversity and of the religious rights of one another. While both Christianity and Islam are missionary religions, the issue of numbers raises rivalry and conflict. Both have to come to terms with the challenge of being open and accepting of each other while, at the same time, remaining faithful to the teaching of their foundational texts.

## Evangelism in the Context of Injustice

An important part of the context of the growing Christianity in Africa is the presence of poverty. In both the UN Millennium Development Goals and the current Sustainable Development Goals, poverty reduction has remained key. Africa continues to be described as a paragon of poverty, as was the case when Christianity was introduced in the eighteenth and nineteenth centuries. The mission agencies worked on their fourfold mission strategy so that the Christians would be self-sufficient both in terms of faith and in terms of economic management. The theme of poverty reduction has been key in the Christian mission in Africa. Yet the stubborn reality of poverty still defines the life of many African communities.

Poverty is at the heart of all the important problems in Africa, be they social, spiritual or moral. Poverty among Africans has both internal and external international causes, and it is difficult to distinguish clearly between the problems, symptoms and causes. Africa's poverty is manifested in different ways including hunger, low income, disease, dehumanisation and injustice. It has different causes and dimensions depending on whether the poor live in urban or rural areas and whether they live within extended family structures, in nuclear families or alone. Those who experience poverty can be divided into two categories – the marginalised and the exploited. The marginalised are those who are outside the prevailing economic system, such as the unemployed, the homeless, abandoned children, outcasts, the handicapped and the aged. The exploited are those who are treated unjustly by the social economic system.

The challenge for Christian evangelism is how to develop the kind of holistic mission that will eradicate poverty, so that people can live life in abundance. Central to the mission of the church is the advocacy dimension, so that the Christian community not only becomes the conscience of society but also becomes a testimony and witness to the values and ethics of the Kingdom of God. Justice, for instance, is central to poverty eradication. The church in some parts of Africa has been involved in civic education during elections and this has shown positive results. But civic education should go beyond enlightening people on elections. There is the need for a 'civic theology' to help communities demand accountability on all fronts, including the economic front.

The growth of Christianity in Africa appears to encourage people to want material wealth to be achieved through prayer but not to question the reasons for the poverty and conflict all around them. Among the forms of Christianity that are growing fast in Africa is the 'faith gospel', popularly known as the 'prosperity gospel'. One of the messages preached is that God wants the best for his children materially, be it food, clothing or cars. Every Christian therefore should now share in the victory of Christ over sin, sickness and poverty. Believers have the right to the blessing of health and wealth won by Christ and can obtain these blessings merely by joining a prosperity gospel church. The publicity for this teaching is done both through media and the fact that giving becomes part of the teaching. It is as though God can be persuaded by people 'planting a seed'.

To those who are struggling with poverty the gospel of prosperity is very appealing, because the material prosperity granted by a 'miracle-working God' appears not to require much effort on their part. For those who have acquired material wealth, the prosperity gospel validates their position. To both groups, the prosperity gospel functions by diverting all attention from the economic and social reasons for poverty. The reasons for poverty are given as lack of faith or curses from ancestors. Those who advocate the prosperity gospel capitalise on people's desire for material gain. In their preaching they give a cheap 'hope' to people who are in hopeless situations. Christianity appears to be a means of production and, like other such means, it can be misused. The challenge for the church is how to develop an evangelism that does more than merely use religion as a means to material gain or as a quick-fix solution to poverty and illness.

The influence of prosperity gospel theology cannot be underestimated in Sub-Saharan Africa. A Christianity that will make a difference in the lives of the people is one that will be rooted in the community's engagement with the social realities of the context and will not be divorced from justice and peace issues within society. There is a need to cultivate a renewed spirituality around a disciplined obedience to the will of God, a profound commitment to living out the values of the Kingdom and a vocation to promote human flourishing.

## Christianity and Leadership

The issues around leadership both in the church and in society are perennial and have often been identified as an impediment to the growth and development of church and society. There is a distinct lack of the kind of leadership that opens up democratic space and allows the creativity and energy of citizens to flourish. While there are some outstanding examples of effective leadership, these are the exceptions that prove the rule, and it appears as though the mechanisms for choosing leaders have loopholes that favour the election of unworthy leaders. Factors like tribalism and nepotism affect the choice of leaders in both the religious and the political spheres. This is happening at a time when there are many opportunities for leadership training at all levels of society.

A disconnect seems to exist, though, between the training of leaders and the realities in which they work, and this poses a challenge to church and society. There is need for a fresh discovery of leadership, understood and practised as service to the people. Leadership that will grow a community that is not fragmented is able to conceive and articulate the kind of vision that will motivate those whom they lead to move beyond the politics of conflict and strife. Such leadership will be ready to move on when a prescribed term is completed rather than attempt to change the constitution to allow them to continue in office.

This is possible if the social imagination of the people is changed through a democratic space that allows them to question, analyse, suggest and participate, without fear or intimidation. This is possible when leaders are able to change and shape people's social imagination in a way that opens up new possibilities. Those in leadership fear the critique of an educated public, since they lack a clear process to step down gracefully after their term in office. While some countries have managed to have leaders retire and take a back seat, in others this is yet to be realised. The religious scene is no different, as the leaders of some churches remain in position until death. With a growing mass of people able to advocate the need for proper processes, this is a challenge that urgently needs to be tackled.

## Evangelism among a Youthful Population

It has been noted that in Sub-Saharan Africa almost 45% of the population is aged 0–15 years, which means that more than 50% of the population comprises children under 18 years of age. This is reflected in both church and society. The youth of the church and the continent is a blessing but also a challenge. The blessing is that the youth bring into the church growth, imagination and vision. The challenge is the lack of space to accommodate the youthful spirit within the leadership challenges discussed above. The questions include what is to be done for the youth and how to engage the youth in the changes that they require. There is a growing phenomenon of artists singing the gospel in new ways that are contextual. It is assumed that with this new wave of music young people will be retained in the church. This remains an illusion because music is one way of expressing the challenging realities of social stress, crime, drugs, ethnic tensions, political violence, and high rates of unemployment and scarcity of resources. These energetic and vibrant young people are tired of waiting to be involved in the destinies of their lives. Most of the young people on the continent are cut off from traditional family, community and spiritual roots. They are absorbed by a search for values and opportunities that are not available.

Young people are vulnerable to the whims of political and religious leaders who take advantage of their youthfulness and use them in conflict. Young people are vulnerable to the ills in society, notably diseases such as HIV/AIDS. Research has shown that while major advances have been made in almost every area of the response to the epidemic, progress for adolescents is falling behind. In fact, HIV/AIDS has become the leading cause of death for adolescents in Africa. The reasons for this are many, including the teaching of the churches that is divorced from the realities of the youth. It was Franklin Roosevelt who said that 'we cannot always build the future for our youth, but we can build our youth for the future'. The challenge for Africa is to build the youth for the future, and this is possible only when the gospel is preached and acted upon to challenge institutionalised forms that destroy young people instead of preparing them for the future.

### Evangelism and Women

The overwhelming presence of women in the churches in Africa attests to the fact that the church in Africa is largely composed of, and sustained by, women of unceasing devotion. Work among women was an integral part of mission for two reasons. First, it was one way of liberating women from what the missionaries then saw as women's oppressions within the traditional African cultural practices of food taboos and initiation, marriage and funeral rites. One result of mission work among women was the creation of organisations through which women could find spiritual and moral support from each other. They would also exercise their freedom to minister to each other, to explore Scripture together and to speak to their family lives as a whole. These organisations, which are found in all church denominations and different traditions, are a source of financial support for the churches through fund-raising and self-generating financial projects for the growth of the church. These groups are engaged in mission and evangelism for the churches in the ministry of caring for the young, the aged, the disabled and others. They provide support for those affected and infected by HIV and have borne the brunt of all health challenges on the continent.

A common feature of the different traditions in the churches is the ideology of patriarchy, which has influenced the teaching of the churches on the role and place of women. The women's organisations themselves have served the interest of patriarchal ideology to contribute to their isolation and exclusion from leadership roles. It is the men who take up the paid and officially recognised leadership. Officially, most churches observed the Ecumenical Decade of the Churches in Solidarity with Women (1988–98). Some churches widened their scope in relation to the liberation of women, but the reality is that women remain on the margins.

The Circle of Concerned African Women Theologians, established in 1989, has been key to examining the plight of women from a holistic perspective. The themes under which the Circle has done its work, both in writing and in engaging the churches, have included reading and interpreting the Bible, an objective critique of African culture, violence against women, health and healing, and dialogue and diapraxis on inter-faith matters. In writing about the plight of women in Africa, the Circle recognises that the total well-being of African people depends on a holistic approach to liberation. It does not dichotomise the spiritual and the material or the public and the private. Women have been engaged in holistic mission and evangelism from the margins, both at the level of the practical action of women's organisations and at the level of writing theology.

## African Christianity as Missionary Agent in Today's World

Another aspect of the growth of African Christianity is visible in the way different churches or groups are sending missionaries to Europe and North America. While the missionaries to the global North are not the same as the missionaries who came to Africa in the eighteenth and nineteenth centuries, they have a vision of bringing God's word to Europe, which is assumed to have lost its erstwhile zeal for the gospel. Paul in Acts 16 received a call from a man of Macedonia requesting him to come and help them. When Paul responded to the call in the course of his second missionary journey, his first convert was Lydia, a businesswoman dealing in purple cloth. The Christian faith grew in Europe until, many years later, it became the base for a worldwide missionary movement that included the establishment of missions in Africa. Today, however, it is apparent that Christianity in Europe is declining, and this has prompted African Christians to identify Europe as a mission field.

Today, Africa, once regarded the 'dark continent', is able to send missionaries to Europe. In some cases, African missionaries are brought to Europe by churches that formerly sent missionaries to Africa and are in partnership with the churches that arose from their missions. These missionaries work within the structures of the church. They serve within the church and it is expected that through their presence and work, those who have lapsed can find their way back into church and those who have been outside the church can be evangelised. The idea here is that there is no fixed place for mission to begin but mission is from everywhere to everywhere. In other cases, African missionaries are creating churches alongside the churches in Europe to cater for the needs of migrants who feel at home worshipping in their own space. Both forms have benefits and also challenges. The benefits include the introduction of new forms of church in a different context and also providing space for people to worship the way they know best. This 'reverse mission' reveals how difficult it is for the church in Europe to welcome African expressions of Christianity.

## Conclusion

The realities of Sub-Saharan Africa are complex and they need a complex approach to evangelism. The need for a holistic approach to mission and evangelism is one that calls for a deeper engagement with the issues rather than being satisfied merely with the numbers narratives. Africa is not an island but part of the 'global village' made possible with the communication revolution. The complex situation calls for the development of a theology and spirituality to meet the needs of African communities navigating the age of globalisation.

## Bibliography

Bosch, David J., *Transforming Mission: Paradigm Shifts in Theology of Mission* (Maryknoll, NY: Orbis Books, 1993).

Gifford, Paul, *African Christianity: Its Public Role* (London: Hurst, 1998).

Kalu, Ogbu U. (ed.), *African Christianity: An African Story* (Pretoria: Department of Church History, University of Pretoria, 2005).

Katongole, Emmanuel, *The Sacrifice of Africa: A Political Theology for Africa* (Grand Rapids, MI: Eerdmans, 2011).

von Sicard, Sigvard, David Bone and Johnson Mbillah, *Programme for Christian–Muslim Relations in Africa 1959–2009* (Nairobi: PROCMURA, 2010).

# Gender

**Isabel A. Phiri and Chammah J. Kaunda**

Often when people talk about gender, they think it is a synonym for women. In this essay we understand gender to mean differentiating the role or function of male and female human beings in society based on their sex. From the beginning we also need to differentiate between gender and sex. Our sex is determined at birth. We are born either male or female human beings. Science has now shown us that there are others who are born with both male and female sexual organs. Others are born male but have more female hormones and yet others are born female and have more male hormones. The decisions on what we do as male or female are made by our culture and religious beliefs and practices. Our interactions and the ways we use power between women and men are influenced by our culture and religious beliefs and practices. In this essay we shall focus on the Christian and cultural construction of gender roles as a very significant factor. We internalise the social, cultural and religious constructions of our roles and pass them on from one generation to the other. We are cognisant that even within one culture and in the various expressions of African Christianity, gender roles do not remain static. They sometimes change out of necessity or through the influence of other cultures and the coming of new understandings of our Christian beliefs in the light of scientific facts.

A gendered approach to African Christianity refers to exposing the injustices that exist in the church, culture and interpretation of the Bible in the relationship between men and women. It acknowledges that human beings construct culture; therefore, cultural practices in the Bible and in our own cultures should not be confused with the will of God. It highlights the importance of acknowledging that both men and women are created in the image of God and are gifted by God to serve humanity and creation. It acknowledges that there are many interpretations of the relationships between men and women and the gendered interpretation is one of them. In this essay we have chosen to include the experiences of women in addition to focusing on the relationship between women and men because women's experiences have been ignored for a very long time and this has contributed to the imbalance between the two genders. We understand gender justice as promoting the humanity of both women and men in the church and using their gifts as revealed by God. Any form of discrimination and oppression mars the image of God in creation and humanity, for God is a God of justice and the practice of Christianity is supposed to reflect the justice of God.

Our central aim in this essay is to analyse trends in the ways in which African churches and scholars are discussing the concepts of gender in African Christianity. We have chosen to outline reflections on three decades of engagement in church discussions, actions and academic research and teaching in the area of gender in African Christianity. In order to concretise our analysis, our entry point is the response of African churches to the Ecumenical Decade of the Churches in Solidarity with Women (1988-98; hereafter 'the Decade'). Secondly, we shall draw from the research projects and publications of the Circle of Concerned African Women Theologians (hereafter 'the Circle') from 1989 to the present. Thirdly, we aim to demonstrate that while the initial conversation on gender in African Christianity took the global trend of focusing on creating a just community of women and men in the church, through equal leadership opportunities, ordination and mainstreaming gender in theological education, the prevalence of HIV/AIDS ,which is predominantly a heterosexual issue on the African continent, forced the churches in Africa to engage in dialogue about gender in relation to different aspects of human sexuality.

## The Ecumenical Decade of the Churches in Solidarity with Women

Ghanaian theologian Mercy A. Oduyoye reports that the person who proposed in 1987 that the World Council of Churches should initiate the Ecumenical Decade of the Churches in Solidarity with Women was an African Methodist bishop who felt that many churches in Africa were not aware that the United Nations had declared a Decade for Women 1976–85. Therefore they did not engage with patriarchy and discrimination against women in the churches. Thus, when the Decade was launched in 1988, the churches in Africa agreed to its purposes, which were:

- empowering women to challenge oppressive structures in the global community, their country and their church
- affirming, through shared leadership and decision-making, theology and spirituality, the decisive contributions of women in the churches and communities
- giving visibility to women's perspectives and actions in the work and struggle for justice, peace and the integrity of creation
- enabling the churches to free themselves from racism, sexism and classism, and from teachings and practices that discriminate against women
- encouraging the churches to take actions in solidarity with women.

In response to the call for this Decade, the All Africa Conference of Churches (AACC) established a women's desk, which mobilised church women's organisations and held a series of conferences to reflect on a number of themes, including the participation of women in the life of the church, women and economic justice, and violence against women in the church and in wider society. Some churches and national councils of churches in Africa followed up by establishing their own women's desks to carry the themes of the Decade further. In addition, the Circle was inaugurated in Ghana in 1989 to focus on research and publications on the themes of the Decade.

## Theological Education

The Circle has been successful in introducing consideration of gender in African Christianity to significant theological institutions. It has also been successful in its mission to publish on gender issues in African Christianity. In the first phase of its work, the Circle theologians intensified their efforts to make the voices of women heard in the churches in Africa through biblical and theological reflections. They addressed the issue of women's ordination, as most of the churches in Africa opposed this, especially the mission churches, even though the churches in their places of origin in the global North were ordaining women. Within Africa, cultures were used as the basis for rejecting the ordination of women. Thus, the Circle focused on interrogating cultures as a site of struggle to unravel the spiritual role of women within African traditional heritage. Various empirical studies done by the Circle demonstrated that African cultures have space for women's leadership in socio-political, economic and religious matters. The Circle developed a theological method of sifting culture on the premise that anything that does not affirm the humanity of women and men in the community must be rejected, no matter how much authority it might have in the culture. Only those aspects of culture that promote life were affirmed. The same methodology has been used as a hermeneutical point of departure in re-reading the Bible for the empowerment of women.

Linked to the ordination of women is theological education of women. The Circle argued that theological education should not be limited to the ordained ministry but must be accessible to the whole people of God, including lay people. In this way, the emphasis was on strengthening the voices and the participation of the laity, of whom the majority are women. As a result, the Circle directed much of its research energy on theological reflection towards the lay ministry of women in the churches in Africa. This opened doors to critical analysis of church women's organisations, the role of pastors' wives, the participation of women in theological education and transformation of theological curricula.

First, the Circle acknowledged the significance of church women's organisations in Africa. They brought to the fore the fact that the church in Africa has grown to what it is because of the enormous contribution of church women's organisations. Many people have come to faith and stayed in the churches because of the evangelistic and diaconal ministry of the church women's organisations. The research of the Circle reveals that the leaders of most of these organisations have not received adequate theological education, despite the work they are doing. In addition, the research discovered that many of these organisations opposed the ordination of women while simultaneously raising financial support for theological education for women; the church women's organisation of the Nkhoma Synod of the Church of Central Africa Presbyterian in Malawi is a notable example. The Circle, therefore, has emphasised the need for gender-sensitive theological education for women in these organisations.

Secondly, the Circle highlighted issues of gender-based violence (GBV) or violence against women (VAW) from the onset. They identified GBV as being rooted in religious and cultural expectations of the roles ascribed to each gender and the power imbalance between men and women. Although men and boys also suffer from GBV for various reasons, the research of the Circle focused on women and girls because they are the most common victims. The Circle has highlighted the ideals of Christianity to promote values of unconditional love, respect, justice, compassion and non-violence towards women and children. They have shown that women and girls suffer abuse by perpetrators who use Scripture to justify it and therefore feel no remorse. Circle members have conducted research to identify specific Scriptures, cultural beliefs and practices, and traditional teachings and to delineate the different forms of violence, such as physical, psychological/emotional, economic, sexual and spiritual. They have shown the link between GBV and HIV/AIDS. They have also classified violence as it is found in supposedly safe domestic contexts and in such social contexts as churches, schools, seminaries, universities, hospitals, prisons, police stations and workplaces. They have identified alternative readings of Scripture, culture and traditions to promote life-affirming African Christian theologies.

Thirdly, there have been some conversations on the role of ministers' wives, who take enormous responsibilities but are not recognised by the churches. For example, Molly Longwe, a Baptist minister's wife in Malawi, wrote a doctoral thesis entitled 'The Experiences of Pastors' Wives (Amayi Busa) in the Baptist Convention of Malawi (BACOMA)'. She demonstrated how these women play a crucial role in African Christianity and do enormous amounts of unpaid work. Pastors' wives, like the women's organisations, provide diaconal and evangelistic services without adequate theological education.

Fourthly, the research of the Circle has shown that some theological institutions still exclude or control enrolment of women and employment of female staff. Most churches in Africa are still struggling with the issue of limiting theological education to the ordained ministry.

Fifthly, the Circle saw the theological institutions where ministers are trained as unequipped to deal with gender issues and thus a source of problems in that area. Consequently, most African Christian ministers are not adequately equipped to deal with issues of gender in their societies. The Circle therefore called for the transformation of the theological curriculum through the mainstreaming of gender across theological disciplines. In addition to this mainstreaming, the Circle has worked on establishing programmes on gender studies within various theological institutions in Africa, such as the Programme on Gender and Theology at St Paul's University, Limuru, Kenya, and the Programme on Gender and Religion of the School of Religion, Philosophy and Classics of the University of Kwa-Zulu-Natal in South Africa.

## HIV/AIDS as a Gendered Issue

HIV/AIDS as a major theological theme came on the agenda of the Circle in the early 2000s, in the second phase of its work, as a result of exposure to international statistics from UNAIDS. A 2015 report from UNAIDS showed that Sub-Saharan Africa was the most affected region in the world and that women account for more than half the total number of people living with HIV. The report also stressed that the predominant mode of transmission was and remains heterosexual intercourse. This raised issues of power relations between men and women. It also raised the issue of the role of religion and culture in disempowering women and therefore putting them at risk of HIV infection. It also raised the importance of awareness among women of their vulnerability to HIV infection and the need to conscientise men on their role in the spread of HIV/AIDS. The Circle became aware that there was no way of winning without engaging men. This resulted in the need to deal with masculinities. It became imperative to deal with the role of religious leaders in raising HIV/AIDS as a priority on the churches' missional agenda. It also became inevitable to engage in discussion of human sexuality. In what follows we deal with some of these themes.

### *Raising Awareness*

The initial response of the Circle to HIV/AIDS was to begin to raise awareness among women. The Circle called for an emergency continental conference in order to search for ways in which African women can give a systematic response to HIV/AIDS in solidarity with the Church in Africa. In August 2002, a third Pan-African Conference in Addis Ababa, Ethiopia, was convened under the theme 'Sex, Stigma and HIV and AIDS: African Women Challenging Religion, Culture and Social Practices'. Through this theme, the Circle sought to demonstrate the ways in which religious texts, faith communities and African cultures fuelled HIV/AIDS as it affects African women. In addition, the Circle also sought to show how these beliefs and practices can function as preventive measures. The Circle defines HIV/AIDS as a gender issue because more women than men were and are either infected or affected in Africa. Circle members called on African churches to read the Bible and to enact a spiritual and social ministry that is attuned to gender differences and that promotes the emancipation of women. Through research, the Circle demonstrated how religion disempowers women by promoting theologies of uncritical obedience and submission. Scholars in the Circle became critical about the meaning of these concepts in the context of HIV/AIDS. African women biblical scholars took on the issue of submission and re-read the Bible for women empowerment. They offered a critical reading of the key scriptural references that had been used to subordinate women. They interrogated texts such as the creation stories in Genesis 1 and 2, the story of Ruth, Gospel stories such as the woman at the well, and the Pauline household rules. In addition, women began to critique African cultures to expose the different cultural practices linked to the sexuality of women and men in Africa, to show where the danger points are and to call for transformation of such cultural beliefs. For example, Lois Moyo from Zimbabwe and Lilian Siwila from Zambia have critiqued rituals of widowhood practised by various churches as the weakest points in the spread of HIV/AIDS. It can be argued that African women scholars have demonstrated and have helped to bring to the fore the fact that African cultural history has never been static nor monolithic but dynamic and open to transformation whenever life is threatened.

### *HIV/AIDS and Masculinities*

In 2007 Circle members became convinced that gender justice can be achieved only when women and men come to the roundtable of dialogue in partnership. Thus, the fourth Pan-African Conference was summoned in Yaoundé, Cameroon, in September 2007 under the theme 'The Girl Child, Women, Religion and HIV and AIDS in Africa: A Gendered Perspective'. For the first time, male theologians were invited to the Circle conference, in recognition that women alone cannot stop the spread of HIV/AIDS in Africa. The emphasis was placed on the significance of a community approach to HIV/AIDS prevention. One of the key highlights was the Circle's focus on identifying liberating masculinities as means for responding to HIV/AIDS. These developments marked the beginning of African male theologians engaging with issues of masculinities from cultural, health, religious and theological perspectives. Dangerous masculinities were identified by re-looking at the Scriptures and African culture in two ways. The first included exposing dangerous interpretations of the Scriptures on masculinities that have promoted a lifestyle that contributes to the spread of HIV/AIDS and also interrogating African cultures in order to expose beliefs and practices supported by proverbs that encourage male promiscuity. Secondly, the Circle also reflected on both Scriptures and cultures to identify positive masculinities that are life-affirming and that should be promoted in African Christianity. This resulted in publications and the establishment of programmes in theological institutions that focus on issues of masculinities in the context of HIV/AIDS in Africa.

Some African male scholars have since engaged in reflection on what it means to be a man in the context of HIV/AIDS. A more sustained response to the call of the Circle for dialogue between women and men came from Ezra Chitando, a Zimbabwean theologian, who is a theological consultant for WCC-EHAIA and who has been a sustained voice in the quest for a transformation of masculinities in the face of HIV/AIDS in Africa. Through his numerous works, Chitando has demonstrated how the epidemic intersects with issues of masculinities, religion and culture in Africa.

A more recent example relating to masculinities in African Christianity is a study by a Kenyan theologian, Kennedy Owino. In his University of KwaZulu-Natal PhD thesis, Owino analysed a prominent group within South African Evangelical Christianity, the Mighty Men's Conference (MMC), to demonstrate how Evangelical discourses shape contemporary constructions of masculinities in post-apartheid South Africa. He notes, on the one hand, that the MMC through calling for men to return to 'godly manhood' reinforces a traditional construction of masculinities, which is based on male domination over women. On the other hand, he argues that the space also has potential for promoting positive masculinities. In these ways, African male theologians have continued to employ the concept of masculinity to investigate the social construction of male gender identity and of men's position in gender relations, as a response and means to promote gender justice and equality. The research on HIV/AIDS brought a paradigm shift from discussing gender as exclusively focused on women to gender as both masculinities and femininities. In this way, the transformation of African cultures is seen as crucial for resisting the surge of HIV/AIDS.

### *HIV/AIDS, Sex and Sexualities*

Thirdly, the research on HIV/AIDS also highlighted the issue of human sexuality, which was almost a taboo topic in many churches in Africa. It became inevitable for the churches to begin conversations about human sexuality with a focus on the diverse nature of human sexualities. Young people in the churches began to challenge the leaders with their views that some people are born with a sexual orientation other than heterosexual. The churches have responded to the question of homosexuality in diverse ways. This has been a difficult issue and the situation remains volatile in most churches in Africa.

Many churches have made statements on homosexuality that have strong biblical underpinnings. For example, in a statement on same-sex marriage, the Presbyterian Church of Ghana stated that homosexuality is 'not just … a moral problem but also … a spiritual problem. Any help for Christians involved to come out of the practice must require a spiritual warfare exercise; and we believe the spiritual authority at the disposal of the Christian Church can deal with this problem as churches in Ghana are helping practitioners of witchcraft come out of their practice.' The statement continued to state that, for the church in Ghana, 'One cannot be a Christian and also be gay and vice versa'.

The Evangelical Association of Malawi (EAM) has published a similar position to the church in Ghana, 'that same sex marriages are acts against the express will of God as revealed in the Holy Scriptures (Leviticus 18: 22; 1 Corinthians 6: 9; Romans 1: 26–27)'. It therefore 'strongly condemn[s] the promotion and practice of same sex marriages'. It also obliges people to 'keep vigilant and resist any move to introduce such deviant cultural behaviour and practice in [Malawian] society'.

Similarly, the Anglican Church of Uganda stresses and reaffirms the 1998 Lambeth Conference resolution that 'homosexual practice has no place in God's design of creation, the continuation of the human race through procreation, or His plan of redemption. Even natural law reveals that the very act of sexual intercourse is an experience of embracing the sexual "other".' The Church of Uganda still affirms Resolution 1.10 of the Lambeth Conference which stated that 'Homosexual practice is incompatible with Scripture'. This church has called on the government to ensure that homosexual practice or the promotion of homosexual relations is not adopted as a human right.

The above positions could be said to represent the general standpoint of most churches in Sub-Saharan Africa. Many of the churches in different parts of Africa do not see the issue of homosexuality as open to debate. In fact, most African countries hold same-sex sexual activity to be illegal. This is in contrast to the position of many churches in South Africa. As stated by the KwaZulu-Natal Council of Churches (KZNCC), while they do not actively promote homosexuality, they believe that it is 'sinful to actively discriminate and persecute homosexual people. Therefore churches are absolutely clear that they reject homophobia and support the protection of the rights of gay and lesbian people in civil law and any bill of human rights.' Yet there are issues of contestation among churches in South Africa as well. Some churches on the right, such as Roman Catholics, Lutherans, Seventh-day Adventists, Baptists and Moravians, see same-sex marriages as unacceptable and even undebatable. Those on the left, such as the Anglicans, Methodists, Congregationalists and Dutch Reformed, have taken a more open approach to the debate.

Among African theologians there is no unanimous agreement on the theological basis for responding to homosexuality. It has been argued that African theologians are heterosexual-centric and taking a strategic silence approach to homosexuality in their analysis of HIV/AIDS and gender issues. This is attributed to an assumption that most African theologians have taken the heterosexist approach that HIV/AIDS is essentially a heterosexual epidemic in Africa and consequently neglect homosexual transmission of the virus. In most debates on homosexuality in Africa, by either theologians or church leaders, the Bible and African cultures remain central, with contested interpretation of both traditions.

Within African theology, three approaches to homosexuality have emerged. Over time, as scholars have continued to reflect on the topic, these positions have proved to be fluid rather than fixed. The first, which is essentially reactive, is the puritan moralist approach. In this paradigm homosexuality is seen as either sin or un-African, or both. The puritan moralists believe that homosexuality has the potential to pollute both the Church and African cultures. Theologians such Bénézet Bujo of Congo and Emmanuel Martey of Ghana, and most right-wing theologians from conservative traditions, have based their responses on a religiously based moralist control that appeals to the Bible, African culture or both as a justification for exclusion. The rejection of homosexuality on the basis of the Bible and African cultures is widespread in African Christianity and can be seen in a special issue of the Catholic theological journal *African Ecclesial Review* from 2006, which was dedicated to demonstrating how homosexuality is both un-African and anti-Scriptural. It is argued there that 'In Africa, homosexuality is a taboo discussed in hushed tones. It is a distortion and a betrayal of marriage worldwide. Homosexual unions do not in any way contribute to the common good of humanity, as they are anti-life, anti-social and anti-Scriptural.'

The second position is the moderate and pastoral mediationist approach. It was the initial position taken by most Circle members. While proponents of this approach mention justice and human rights, they try as much as possible to tread softly. For example, this approach is found in the early writings of scholars such as Isabel Phiri, Nyambura Njoroge and Esther Mombo. These scholars have utilised an approach to homosexuality that is based on seeking ways of mediating between diverging positions within the churches themselves and between churches by calling for an open debate rather than forcing the churches to merely accept the issue or reject it outright. For instance, Njoroge argues that HIV/AIDS has forced the Circle to make a U-turn and put on its agenda some of the most controversial issues, such as homosexuality. But she does not argue explicitly for acceptance of homosexuality in the church; rather, she takes a mediation- and dialogue-promoting stance.

The third mode, which is also proactive, is prophetic. Scholars who have taken a sustained prophetic stance on homosexuality in African theologies include Musa Dube, Kaoma Kapya and Masiiwa Gunda. They have sought to go beyond merely questioning and challenging the appeal to African cultures and the Bible, by calling for shocking actions and alternative responses. For instance Dube included in guidelines on HIV/AIDS-sensitive liturgies in churches a service on homosexuals in a way that some churches found shocking. The concern of these prophetic scholars is to move the debate away from the puritan moralist approach, to focus on justice in a bold way. In this way, they are able to challenge the nature of justice in the churches in Africa with regard to homosexuality. They have called for a redefinition of gender in African Christianity by critiquing the normative gender lines that have defined and divided humanity into opposition female and male and by calling for gender multiplicity. Homosexuality is seen not just as a human rights issue but a justice issue, which is language that the churches understand. They have challenged both African cultures and biblical interpretation in the context of justice. This seems to be a viable approach in charting new directions in the debate on homosexuality in African Christianity.

Similarly, the work of the International Network of Religious Leaders Living with or Personally Affected by HIV/AIDS (INERELA+) and the SAVE (Safer practice, Access to treatment, Voluntary testing and Empowerment) campaign is another example of churches responding to HIV/AIDS through gender perspectives. INERELA+ started as an African organisation to help faith communities on issues of sex, sexuality, sexual orientation, gender and advocacy on HIV/AIDS. Although it has become international, its leadership remains on the African continent.

## Conclusion

What have African women theologians achieved over the decades of theological reflection on gender? First, they have recognised that gender is a global issue but have given the concept an African emphasis. The issues of inclusivity in the participation of women in the church and society, as initiated by the Ecumenical Decade of the Churches in Solidarity with Women, were given an African flavour. Secondly, they have grounded

African existential challenges such as ecological degradation, economic exploitation and social power struggles in gender. This has involved exposing cultural practices, violence against women and an inability to deal with human sexuality as challenges that the churches in Africa need to address. Thirdly, they have underlined gender as one of the key concepts of theological reflection in African Christianity, as can be deduced from current debates, which have strong gender implications. In this way, they have helped the churches to reflect on what it means to be the church in Africa and respond to gender challenges as they find expression in the continent. Fourthly, they have raised awareness of the intersectionality of religion, gender and development in Africa.

Finally, we have three observations. Firstly, the number of women theologians, including those involved in postgraduate studies and those in ordained ministry, remains small. Secondly, the deeply entrenched sexism in theological institutions and churches in Africa continues to shape African Christian life. Thirdly, there is a positive sign that might lead to gender transformation, as currently there are many male students interested in programmes with a focus on the issues of gender and religion. However, much still remains to be done to overcome deeply ingrained sexist attitudes within African societies and churches. This will involve expanding theological methods and frameworks of doing theology beyond the current ones in order to attend to emerging social trends that are helping reinforce sexist attitudes, thereby impeding the current search for gender transformation in African Christianity and in wider society.

## Bibliography

Dube, Musa W. (ed.), *Other Ways of Reading: African Women and the Bible* (Atlanta, GA: SBL; and Geneva: WCC, 2001).

Njoroge, Nyambura and Musa W. Dube (eds), *Talitha Cum: Theologies of African Women* (Pietermaritzburg: Cluster Publications, 2001).

Oduyoye, Mercy Amba, *Introducing African Women's Theology* (Sheffield: Sheffield Academic Press, 2001).

Pemberton, Carrie, *Circle Thinking: African Women Theologians in Dialogue with the West* (Leiden: Brill, 2003).

Phiri, Isabel Apawo and Sarojini Nadar (eds), *African Women, Religion and Health: Essays in Honour of Mercy Amba Oduyoye* (Maryknoll, NY: Orbis Books, 2006).

# Religious Freedom

## Frans Veerman and Christof Sauer

Freedom of religion or belief is a well established principle under international law. International organisations like the United Nations, as well as regional organisations, have long adopted treaties or resolutions that comprehensively address this fundamental right. Yet, there have been considerable violations of religious freedom in recent history. In this regard, the situation of Christians is illustrative. Religious freedom of Christians has been under serious pressure in different parts of the world for many years. Data from World Watch Research, the research department of the Christian aid agency Open Doors International that presents the annual World Watch List (WWL), indicate that in recent years levels of infringements on religious freedom have risen worldwide. The most rapid growth of such infringements on religious freedom has been in the countries of Africa, especially Sub-Saharan Africa.

### What is Freedom of Religion or Belief?

Religious freedom is multidimensional and can be assessed by distinguishing between pressure and violence in different spheres of life. The legal conception of its multidimensionality can be derived directly from Article 18 of the United Nations Universal Declaration of Human Rights (UDHR), which was later incorporated under Article 18 of the International Covenant on Civil and Political Rights (ICCPR):

> Everyone has the right to freedom of thought, conscience and religion; this right includes freedom to change his religion or belief, and freedom, either alone or in community with others and in public or private, to manifest his religion or belief in teaching, practice, worship and observance.

It is important to bear in mind that this presentation of freedom of religion or belief is much broader than is commonly perceived, in that it encompasses: (1) freedom to have, choose, change or leave a religion or belief; (2) freedom to manifest a religion or belief; (3) freedom from coercion; (4) freedom from discrimination; (5) the right of parents to give their children religious and moral education in accordance with their own beliefs; (6) the right to conscientious objection; (7) freedom to practise one's religious belief in the workplace.

The manifestation of religion or belief has several dimensions: (1) to worship or assemble in connection with a religion or belief, and to establish and maintain premises for these purposes; (2) to establish religious, humanitarian and charitable institutions; (3) to make, acquire and use articles and materials related to the rites or customs of a religion or belief, including to follow a particular diet; (4) to write, issue and disseminate relevant publications; (5) to teach a religion or belief in places suitable for the purposes and to establish theological seminaries or schools; (6) to solicit and receive voluntary financial and other contributions; (7) to train, appoint or elect leaders, priests and teachers; (8) to celebrate religious festivals and observe days of rest; (9) to communicate with individuals and communities on faith issues at national and international levels; (10) to display religious symbols, including the wearing of religious clothing. All these freedoms might be jeopardised by restrictions and different forms of hostility.

## Assessing Infringements on Religious Freedom

To assess the infringements on religious freedom of Christians worldwide, the WWL employs a helpful methodology that incorporates a number of key concepts and definitions. A Christian is defined as 'anyone who self-identifies as a Christian and/or someone belonging to a Christian community as defined by the church's historic creeds'. Persecution is considered as 'any hostility experienced as a result of one's identification with Christ. This can include hostile attitudes, words and actions towards Christians.' Two main expressions of persecution can be distinguished. While it might seem that attempts at 'smashing' Christians through violence is the most prevalent and invasive expression, it is, rather, pressure that robs Christians of space to survive in the long term. Pressure can be experienced in all spheres of life (private, family, community, national), as well as church life, and violence potentially cuts across all of these.

Various distinctive power dynamics frequently come into visible collision with the church. This chapter presents the concept of 'persecution dynamic' as the phase when a specific power dynamic has come into visible collision with a Christian community, leading to infringements on religious freedom. The WWL methodology distinguishes eight different persecution dynamics, grouped in three sets. The first set is driven by an exclusivist impulse. (1) Islamic extremism tries to bring a country or the world under the 'House of Islam' through violent or non-violent actions. (2) Different forms of religious nationalism (e.g. the Hindu, Buddhist and Orthodox Jewish variants) equally try to monopolise religion in a nation. (3) Tribal antagonism tries to enforce the continuing influence of age-old norms and values shaped in a tribal context, often in the form of traditional religion. (4) Denominational protectionism tries to maintain its own (usually majority) Christian denomination as the only legitimate or dominant expression of Christianity in a country.

The second set is driven by a secularist impulse. (1) Communist and post-communist oppression tries to maintain communism as the prescriptive ideology and/or controls the church through a system of registration and oversight that has come from communism. (2) Secularist intolerance tries to eradicate religion from the public domain, if possible even out of the hearts of people, and imposes an atheistic form of secularism as a new governing ideology.

The third set is primarily driven by an exploitative impulse. (1) Dictatorial paranoia does everything to maintain power but is not focused on realising a specific vision. (2) Organised corruption and crime lead to a climate of impunity, anarchy and corruption as a means for self-enrichment.

In many countries, more than one of the above dynamics are at play. But essentially all involve a claim for absolute power. The actual culprits effecting infringements of religious freedom or persecution are government officials at any level (from local to national), or actors from civil society, such as ethnic group leaders, non-Christian religious leaders, church leaders, fanatical movements, ordinary citizens (including mobs), the extended family, political parties, revolutionaries or paramilitary groups, organised crime cartels or networks, or multilateral organisations. Often more than one actor is active around a particular persecution dynamic.

## Varying Degrees of Religious Freedom

Among the countries in Sub-Saharan Africa, some display high levels of infringements of religious freedom, while others have just arrived at the point where the usual power play of different social and governmental forces turns into such infringements on religious minorities. While some of the countries require more detailed research, it can be said without any reservation that infringements on religious freedom or persecution are very complex in Sub-Saharan Africa, as they are intrinsically related to culture, identity, religion and, above all, political power. The complexity is further enhanced by the nearly complete symbiosis of radical forms of religion with the quest for political power. The table overleaf identifies the persecution dynamics at play, as well as the scores on the 2016 WWL of those countries that have been examined in more detail because they are considered the worst offenders.

In 10 countries, three or more persecution dynamics are identifiable. A combination of two showed in 12 countries, while a further 12 countries were suffering from one of those dynamics. If one compares the sub-scores on pressure and violence of those top 12 Sub-Saharan countries with the average of the global top 50, it becomes evident that infringements

| Country | Persecution dynamics | | | | | | | | Points awarded by the World Watch List 2016 |
|---|---|---|---|---|---|---|---|---|---|
| | Islamic extremism | Religious nationalism | Tribal antagonism | Denominational protectionism | Communist and post-communist oppression | Secularist intolerance | Dictatorial paranoia | Organised corruption and crime | |
| Angola | | | | | ✓ | | ✓ | | |
| Benin | | | ✓ | | | | | | |
| Botswana | | | | | | | | | |
| Burkina Faso | ✓ | | | | | | | | |
| Burundi | | | | | | | ✓ | | |
| Cameroon | ✓ | | | | | | ✓ | | 45 |
| Cape Verde | | | | | | | | | |
| Central African Republic | ✓ | | | | | | | ✓ | 59 |
| Chad | ✓ | | | | | | ✓ | | 51 |
| Comoros | ✓ | | | | | | ✓ | | 56 |
| Congo (Brazzaville) | ✓ | | | | | | ✓ | | |
| Congo (DRC) | ✓ | | | | | | ✓ | | 53 |
| Côte d'Ivoire | ✓ | | ✓ | | | | | | 41 |
| Djibouti | ✓ | | ✓ | | | | ✓ | | 58 |
| Equatorial Guinea | | | | | | | ✓ | | |
| Eritrea | ✓ | | | ✓ | ✓ | | ✓ | | 89 |
| Ethiopia | ✓ | | ✓ | ✓ | | ✓ | ✓ | | 67 |
| Gabon | | | | | | | | | |
| Gambia | ✓ | | | | | | ✓ | | 41 |
| Ghana | | | | | | | | | |
| Guinea (Conakry) | ✓ | | | | | | | | |
| Guinea-Bissau | ✓ | | ✓ | | | | ✓ | ✓ | |
| Kenya | ✓ | | ✓ | | | ✓ | | ✓ | 68 |
| Lesotho | | | | | | | | | |

| | | | | | | | | | |
|---|---|---|---|---|---|---|---|---|---|
| Liberia | | | | | | | | | |
| Madagascar | | | | | | | | | |
| Malawi | ✓ | | | | | ✓ | ✓ | | |
| Mali | ✓ | | | | | | | | 55 |
| Mauritania | ✓ | | | | | | | | 50 |
| Mauritius | | | | | | | | | |
| Mozambique | | | | | | | | | |
| Namibia | | | | | | | | | |
| Niger | ✓ | | | | | | | | 53 |
| Nigeria | ✓ | | ✓ | | | | | ✓ | 78 |
| Réunion | ✓ | | | | | | | | |
| Rwanda | | | | | | | ✓ | | |
| São Tomé and Príncipe | | | | | | | | | |
| Senegal | ✓ | | | | | | | | 42 |
| Seychelles | | | | | | | | | |
| Sierra Leone | | | | | | | | | |
| Somalia | ✓ | | ✓ | | | | | ✓ | 87 |
| South Africa | ✓ | | | | | ✓ | | ✓ | |
| South Sudan | ✓ | | | | | | ✓ | | |
| Sudan | ✓ | | | | | | ✓ | | 84 |
| Swaziland | | | | | | | | | |
| Tanzania | ✓ | | | | | ✓ | | | 57 |
| Togo | ✓ | | | | | | | | |
| Uganda | ✓ | | ✓ | | | | ✓ | | 45 |
| Zambia | | | | | | | | | |
| Zimbabwe | | | | | | | ✓ | | |
| Total | 28 | 0 | 9 | 2 | 2 | 5 | 19 | 6 | |

on religious freedom in Sub-Saharan Africa are more associated with violence. This is in addition to the pressure which is also quite high in these countries. The highest levels of pressure are exerted in Eritrea (89 points), Somalia (87) and Sudan (84), the lowest (within the top 12) in the Central African Republic (44.1) and Niger (43.6). The highest levels of violence are found in Nigeria (17), the Central African Republic (15) and Sudan (14), while the lowest are recorded in Djibouti (1) and Comoros (0).

Islamic extremism is a predominant source of infringements on religious freedom in 28 countries in Sub-Saharan Africa. This does not necessarily imply the prevalence of very robust manifestations of radical Islam in those countries or strong Islamisation of their societies. Sometimes it mainly signals that those who want to leave Islam face problems. Leaving Islam is regarded as apostasy, which is a very problematic issue, even for many Muslims who do not consider themselves radical. If one were to scrutinise the situation of converts in majority-Muslim areas in all countries in Sub-Saharan Africa that have substantial Muslim populations, it is quite likely that this persecution dynamic would be identified in even more countries, due to the generality and the severity of the issue.

Many Muslims in Sub-Saharan African countries are clustered together in majority-Muslim areas, or at least areas with substantial Muslim minorities. This corresponds with advice given to Muslims by the Muslim Brotherhood writer Yusuf al-Qaradawi to live in ghettos, in his vision document 'Priorities of the Islamic Movement in the Coming Phase'. Such ghettos facilitate the fight for the 'soul of Islam', which is a struggle to get Muslims to move from 'cultural' to 'devout' or from 'moderate' to 'radical'. The ghettos provide very limited possibilities for Christians to live there, even less as converts to Christianity from a Muslim background. The ghettos also offer a suitable base for a gradual Islamisation of surrounding areas.

Nigeria mirrors this situation. Currently, infringements on the religious freedom of Christians occur through different streams. Firstly, the rule of Sharia was unconstitutionally declared in 12 northern states. Local governments and social groups leave hardly any space for Christians to live their lives. This is exacerbated by Boko Haram atrocities in northern Nigeria, especially the six north-eastern states, carrying out an anti-Christian agenda that could qualify as ethnic cleansing, if not genocide. In addition, Hausa-Fulani Muslim herdsmen, often assisted by like-minded settlers, try to cleanse the Middle Belt of their original majority-Christian or African traditionalist inhabitants. This situation is a clear example of ethnic cleansing. Furthermore, mob violence all over northern Nigeria makes Christians vulnerable at any place and any time. While many analysts classify this issue simply as 'social unrest', it can be argued that it demonstrates a 'persecution eclipse', explaining why religious agendas are not recognised by external observers. Finally, a gradual expansion of political Islam over majority-Christian southern Nigeria with the intention to Islamise the south can be observed. Muslim leaders and their constituents pressure adherents of other religions via banking, business, symbolism, mosque-building, schools and non-governmental organisations (NGOs), to the extent that the Christians (and adherents of other religions) must either leave or gradually adopt Islamic mores and, in some cases, convert to Islam or resist this attempt to impose an Islamic identity on their land. Nigeria could be seen as a test case concerning the persecution dynamics of Islamic extremism in Sub-Saharan Africa and beyond. Similar dynamics can be observed elsewhere at various levels and with different intensities.

Combinations of Islamic extremism and dictatorial paranoia are manifested in 14 countries as sources of infringements on religious freedom. In some countries there is a rather close link between the actual agents of the two persecution dynamics. In other countries they are essentially different. In still other countries the relationship is ambiguous. This distinguishes the situation in some Sub-Saharan African countries from countries in North Africa and the Arabian Peninsula, where Islamic extremism and dictatorial paranoia as persecution dynamics are very often closely related.

Eritrea is an example of a country in which the relationship between the agents of Islamic extremism and dictatorial paranoia is ambiguous. Eritrea is suffering under the absolute dictatorial regime of Isaias Afewerki, geared towards exercising extensive influence over the life of its citizens, already for more than two decades. Eritrean Christians face great pressure and experience violence from the government due to the repressive nature of the Eritrean regime. The government intensified its crackdown on Christians in 2013/14, leading to more than 138 arrests of believers and church leaders without due process of law. The Commission of Inquiry established by the United Nations Human Rights Commission to investigate human rights abuses in Eritrea declares there are gross violations of human rights in Eritrea and says the country 'is ruled by fear, not rule of law'. A mass exodus of young people, many of them Christians, out of Eritrea continues. Many of the Eritrean refugees have become victims of Islamic State militants in Libya and of human traffickers in the Sinai Desert. At the same time, Eritrea is one of the countries that support radicals across the globe. The UN Security Council imposed sanctions on the country because it is helping Al-Shabaab. Radical Islam within Eritrea is also rising, and the rule of the regime is creating favourable conditions for that. In the coastal areas of the country and the lowlands, where Muslims constitute the majority, Christians face many challenges in the community. As the country is located very strategically and bordered by countries where radicalism is growing, Christians in the country are also facing serious challenges.

Secularist intolerance is leading to infringements on religious freedom in at least five countries. In Sub-Saharan Africa, UN institutions and international NGOs exert strong pressure on governments to adopt the sexual and reproductive health and rights (SRHR) agenda, often through 'package deals' in which evidently positive health outcomes are combined with ethically controversial health and sexuality issues. The offers to African governments are 'all or nothing', with strong pressure for 'all', even if the SRHR agenda is primarily alien to their societies. If churches object to ethically sensitive parts of the 'package deal', they are ridiculed and sometimes even subjected to hate campaigns.

In many Sub-Saharan African countries secularist intolerance still has a low profile. That is why it currently seems much less of a threat to religious freedom of Christians than some other persecution dynamics. The problem is that the battle is fought with passionate external assistance in the 'schoolrooms', by influencing children and youth through national education programmes, and in the 'courtrooms', by pushing for national legislation that creates the framework for further spread of the SRHR agenda. As evident in some 'forerunner' countries in Africa, implementation of such legislation makes the associational space for churches and other Christian institutions increasingly fade away, while the freedom for individual Christians to shape their professional and personal lives is reduced.

In South Africa secularist intolerance plays out in two different ways, namely through government policy and through activists who want to undermine the values of religion in society. The government, including the judiciary, is pushing to limit the role of Christianity, the role of any religion for that matter, to the private sphere. In this regard, for example, Christian broadcasting has become very challenging as the government either slowly responds to issues of the broadcasting licence or just simply rejects an application without good cause. On the activist side, there has been a smear campaign. Evangelicals in the country have been accused of having intolerant fundamentalist views on matters such as abortion, gay rights and theocracy. The country's policy to push for many reforms without considering the rights of religious groups or the values of a broad segment of society makes life more difficult for Christians.

The combination of Islamic extremism and secularist intolerance as persecution dynamics in majority-Christian countries has the potential to speed up Islamisation, which usually would signify serious infringements on religious freedom. Proponents of secularist intolerance aim to weaken the influence of the churches on public morals that are contrary to their radical secularist agenda. Agents of Islamic extremism adhere to the expansionist principle of *darul Islam* (House of Islam) and the obligation to bring non-Muslims under its rule, and are greatly helped by weakened and publicly ridiculed churches leaving a gap that they can fill.

In Kenya, secularist intolerance is growing as a source of infringement on religious freedom and favours further development of Islamic extremism as a source of religious intolerance. Since the 2010 constitution was endorsed by a popular referendum, Kenya has been busy implementing some of the principles enshrined in it. Among others, the country is trying to force religion out of the public domain. This can be discerned by looking at the government's approach to push for an unbalanced secularist agenda, which contradicts the values and principles of Christianity. Furthermore, as a regional hub in many ways as well as a host to many international organisations, Kenya has been under pressure to implement some policies that contradict the values of society and the church. In this atmosphere every scandal in the church is laid long under a magnifying glass by media houses that are largely owned by Muslims. Political Islam is well served by this battle of secularist activists that is weakening Kenyan churches. This becomes more evident when one realises that home-grown radical Muslims and militants crossing the border from Somalia are already severely persecuting Christians in the north-east and coastal regions and thus trying to weaken the church from the other end.

African traditionalism often leads to infringements on religious freedom of Christians, especially when people convert from tribal religion to Christianity or when Christians try to evangelise African traditionalists. In several African countries there is a certain degree of revival of African traditionalism that is sometimes facilitated by the government.

In Uganda, one of the means to which President Museveni resorted in order to consolidate his power is restoring the old Ugandan system based on clans, under the guise of respecting the culture and history of his people. As seen in history, this does not necessarily create favourable conditions for the church. Looking back to the end of the nineteenth century, one can see that Christians were persecuted (even killed) under those traditional systems. The current approach by the Ugandan President is likely to have an adverse effect on the churches, especially on Evangelicals who are trying to reach out to all Ugandans.

Organised corruption and crime as a persecution dynamic is reported for six countries. It can take different shapes. It can find its origin in autocratic government behaviour, in the activities of criminal gangs or in a combination of both. The cases mentioned are illustrations. They do not, however, include one of the most worrying forms of organised corruption, namely criminal groups preying upon internally displaced persons (IDPs) and refugees. Sub-Saharan Africa is home to several countries with many IDPs and/or refugees. Many of these people are Christians who have fled their homes or countries for reasons related to heavy infringements on religious freedom. More research into this phenomenon is needed.

Guinea-Bissau is considered a transit route for drugs from Latin America. This has created an environment of corruption, anarchy and the absence of rule of law. Judicial independence is missing. Even though the constitution was re-established in 2014, the country has made no positive strides towards eliminating narco-trafficking and corruption. This has created an environment in which Christians cannot speak freely about the values and precepts of the Bible and against social injustice.

Nigeria is a country where corruption is rampant. This cripples state institutions in responding to challenges that Christians face in their daily lives due to their faith. A corrupt army and judiciary have led many Christians to lose hope that any meaningful protection might come from the state.

In South Africa, there are tensions at all levels. Churches get brushed off by the ruling party when they criticise government and party corruption and maladministration. There are also tensions in all townships where gangsterism reigns. Priests and pastors are among those who have become victims of murder.

## Future Trends for Religious Freedom

This section summarises several key trends in Sub-Saharan African countries regarding infringements on the religious freedom of Christians. High levels of both violence against Christians and pressure on Christians in everyday life normally indicate a downward spiral. Comparison of data across time from the WWL and the Pew Forum confirms this trend.

'Ethnic cleansing' is an increasing source of infringements on religious freedom in a growing number of Sub-Saharan African countries. This aptly describes the dynamics created by agents of political Islam against the presence of Christians in what they consider their territory within countries. 'Ethnic cleansing', one of the most recent concepts punishable under international criminal law, means forcing out a competitor or those who differ in race, ethnicity or religion from a given area by employing unlawful means such as murder, destruction of property, torture, arbitrary arrest and detention, confinement of civilians in ghetto areas, displacement and deportation of the civilian population, extra-judicial executions, rape, military or other organised attacks or threats of attacks on civilians, or even genocide. What is happening in north-east Kenya, Nigeria, Somalia and Sudan can be considered typical examples, in some cases even touching genocide.

The typical set-up of political Islam is characterised by voluntary ghettoisation that helps to radicalise the Muslim community and purify it from non-Muslims – especially by putting enormous pressure on Muslims not to leave their religion – and to 'invade' surrounding non-Muslim territories. While not all Muslims adhere to this concept, the resistance of Muslim communities that would see this differently is often limited or ineffective. That explains why this process of stratification between Islam and Christianity, sometimes at a very local level, seems to develop so easily nowadays.

The situation has become very worrying for the future of religious freedom in the Sub-Saharan Africa. Many majority-Christian countries have become stratified between Islam and Christianity as a result of the strategy of political Islam. Sometimes this stratification exists at a very local level; at other times it covers large areas. This Islamic stratification movement is twofold. Majority-Muslim areas within those countries seek to consolidate and to side-step national legislation, and at the same time these areas continue to try to expand into majority-Christian areas. This expansion may be combined with serious violence, but many governments are not able to create stable states that could protect their citizens. This easily leads to a vicious circle in which governments are sidelined or co-opted, giving in to perpetrators of persecution for the sake of 'peace'. By doing so, they surrender their Christian populations to practices of ethnic cleansing, if not genocide.

Converts to Christianity are usually the first victims of infringements on religious freedom. It is useful to distinguish three different profiles of Christians: nominal Christians, active Christians and converts to Christianity. Nominal Christians means those with a Christian identity or who are considered Christians by antagonistic groups. This can include people who live a 'passive' Christian lifestyle within the boundaries of regular church life. It can also include people who have been considered Christians for ages but who hardly know what the Christian faith entails. Active Christians by contrast are those who are active in the public domain through evangelism or through social or political activities. A specific group requiring attention are converts to Christianity. This includes both people who leave their former religion or ideological background to become Christians and those who change their affiliation from one type of Christianity – often the majority type – to another. 'Defectors' who leave the ranks of a criminal organisation after conversion to Christianity are also part of this profile.

Converts normally are the first victims of infringements on religious freedom. For instance, converts to Christianity from a Muslim background are very vulnerable in their private, family and community spheres of life, even when society is not yet Islamised and government has not yet adopted Sharia law. The same applies to converts from African traditional religious backgrounds, from another Christian tradition (for instance, from an Orthodox Church background in Eritrea or Ethiopia), or for 'defectors' from the ranks of criminal organisations after conversion to Christianity.

Next in line after the converts are Christians who are actively missionary in the public domain. When a persecution situation develops further, nominal Christians are affected too, usually culminating in reduced visibility of Christianity in the public domain.

The strong signalling of Islamic extremism as a persecution dynamic in Sub-Saharan African countries in the above survey is partly due to the very strong and passionate resistance against conversion away from Islam within Muslim communities. The antagonism often includes a very negative view of Christian missionary activity in Muslim-majority areas. It means that wherever there is a 'fault-line' between Islam and Christianity, Christian life in and around Muslim-majority areas – or even areas with substantial Muslim minorities dominating local government – might come under serious pressure, potentially leading to ethnic cleansing based on religious affiliation. It seems this process has only just begun in Sub-Saharan Africa, but is endowed with an enormous potential for further escalation, particularly if externally funded Islamic NGOs continue to exert their influence.

Muslim civil society organisations pose a threat to religious freedom. Sub-Saharan African countries have a significant presence of Islamic NGOs, many of which were, or still are, paid by countries with strong political Islamic agendas, such as Saudi Arabia, Qatar and Iran. West Africa provides a clear example. The political liberalisation that swept through West Africa in the 1990s was an opportunity for Arab states, with Saudi Arabia in the lead, to pour money into the new Islamic associations and NGOs that emerged from the ashes of the military or single-party dictatorships that once held sway in the region. These associations and NGOs bypassed traditional mosques to become focal points for proselytising and disseminating fundamentalist Islamic ideology.

A concrete example is Niger, where, up until the 1990s, numerous military regimes clamped down on real and potential sources of dissent or threat. To this end, religious leaders were kept at arm's length and monitored. Before 1990, the Islamic Association of Niger (IAN) was the sole legal representative of the Muslim community and served as an auxiliary to the military. However, after the liberalisation of Niger's associational space in 1991, dozens of Islamic associations emerged. These organisations have been mostly concerned with the perceived erosion of Niger's religious identity by a secular democratic state. For example, in 2011 they successfully scuttled plans to adopt a new family law that gave more rights to women. These associations also fight against the supposedly pagan practices of the brotherhoods.

In other regions of Sub-Saharan Africa, comparable processes have taken place, although different in their details. Nowadays the presence of Islamic NGOs with a political Islamic agenda is pervasive in several Sub-Saharan countries, partly fed by the abundance of international oil money. Their presence has a 'flywheel effect' on the trends indicated earlier (passionate resistance against conversion and missionary activity in Muslim-majority areas, and the increase of ethnic cleansing based on religious affiliation in those areas).

Multilateral organisations and international NGOs are increasingly promoting secularist intolerance. The expansion of the humanist-secularist movement promoting the SRHR agenda through UN institutions and international NGOs has taken place over decades. While Western societies are almost at the point of saturation, non-Western societies are now increasingly being exposed to advocacy of the SRHR agenda. Humanist secularism has the potential to become a real source of infringements on the religious freedom of Christians. Its advocates have prepared societies for not tolerating Christian opinions on the SRHR agenda in the public domain, while national education programmes are increasingly invested with it. National legislation in a number of Sub-Saharan African countries tries to set the framework for further expansion of the agenda. It will be increasingly difficult for the church to contest the impact of the humanist-secularist movement in spreading its new, radical ethics that take families and societies away from Christian norms and values. At the same time, the church itself will likely be increasingly divided by the SRHR agenda.

## Conclusion

Sub-Saharan African countries are under a serious threat of further escalation of infringements on religious freedom. Several power dynamics have manifestly turned against Christians, churches and their institutions. Political Islam and humanist secularism are the most dynamic ones, though not equally visible in the region, giving rise to Islamic extremism and secularist intolerance as persecution dynamics. The interplay of Islamic extremism and secularist intolerance is of particular concern. However, the escalating effect seems stronger for Islam than for humanist secularism, especially in majority-Christian societies with tribal undertones.

In some countries, African traditionalism leads to tribal antagonism as a persecution dynamic, but in most cases its actions and effects are limited compared with the effects of Islamic extremism and dictatorial paranoia. Organised corruption worsens the dynamics in various settings, and in a few instances denominational protectionism adds its damaging effects. The churches in Sub-Saharan Africa must urgently find an answer to these threats to religious freedom.

## Bibliography

Boyd-McMillan, Ronald, *Faith That Endures* (Grand Rapids, MI: Revell, 2006).

Peeters, Marguerite, *Twenty Years of 'Sexual and Reproductive Health and Rights' in Africa* (Brussels: Institute for Intercultural Dialogue Dynamics, 2014).
Rotberg, Robert I., *Battling Terrorism in the Horn of Africa* (Cambridge, MA: World Peace Foundation, 2005).
Smit, Johannes A. and P. Pratap Kumar (eds), *Study of Religion in Southern Africa* (Leiden: Brill, 2005).
Soares, Benjamin F. and René Otayek (eds), *Islam and Muslim Politics in Africa* (New York: Palgrave, 2007).

## Acknowledgement

The authors are grateful to the staff of the World Watch Research Unit of Open Doors who researched much of the source material for this chapter, particularly Yonas Dembele, who supplied a country-level analysis on African countries not included in the World Watch List 2015, and who critically reviewed the text.

# Inter-religious Relations

## Evaristi Magoti Cornelli

This chapter concerns the question of inter-religious relations in Sub-Saharan Africa, which can also be described as 'Black Africa'. Understood as the way of life of a particular people as determined by their commitment to the Transcendent Reality, there are three main religions in Black Africa: African traditional religion (ATR), Islam and Christianity. Here, it is the relation between Christianity and the other two religious traditions that will be examined. Though important, this chapter will not explore relations between different strands within Christianity, Islam and ATR.

Relations between Christianity, ATR and Islam in Sub-Saharan Africa can be described in terms of tolerance, tension and violence. Even in countries like Tanzania, Kenya and Uganda, where adherents of these faith traditions have managed to live together for a long time without too much friction and violence among them, relations have at times been tense, leading to a failure of tolerance and giving way to the rise of violence on account of the different perceptions each holds about the others, as well as because of different belief systems and practices. Healthy relations among believers of ATR, Islam and Christianity will require changes in the way they view one another but also a better understanding of the practices and beliefs underpinning each of these religious traditions.

### Relations between Christianity and African Traditional Religion

The indigenous peoples of Africa south of the Sahara have their own heritage, including their religion. ATR is a way of life or life itself, a force or power or energy that sustains humans into being. The term 'African traditional religion', then, refers to the real life of black people. ATR provides black people with the capacity to face death and its agents. It is the principle to which they have recourse in understanding and actualising their existence. Data about believers in ATR are not readily available because some of those who believe in ATR also believe in either Christianity or Islam. Nevertheless, it can be estimated that 25% of people in black Africa are adherents of ATR.

Christianity is not an indigenous African religion even though it has been in the continent long enough to acquire some African spiritual elements. In many parts of Sub-Saharan Africa, Christianity was introduced through

European Roman Catholic and Protestant missionaries during the colonial period of the nineteenth and twentieth centuries, which involved German, British, French, Belgian, Italian and Portuguese colonisers. Since then, it has spread throughout Sub-Saharan Africa and currently forms one of the main features of its religious landscape. Unlike North Africa, which is predominantly Muslim, Africa south of the Sahara is predominantly Christian.

Adherents of ATR and Christianity in Black Africa have been in contact with each other ever since, and on the whole the two religions have experienced peaceful coexistence. Followers of ATR and Christians live together in the same families and communities; they inter-marry, participate in each other's burial ceremonies and cooperate together in a number of social, political and economic activities. Adherents of ATR attend schools, colleges and universities set up by Christians; receive treatment from Christian hospitals; and use infrastructures established by Christians. This does not mean, however, that relations between ATR and Christianity are completely healthy. They are affected significantly by existing, varying perceptions of each other.

From the beginning of Christianity's encounter with ATR, there have been some perceptions and attitudes that have not helped in this regard. One attitude concerns the mistrust of ATR by Christianity, on account of the assumed superiority of the latter. Christianity was introduced in Sub-Saharan Africa as a superior, modern and civilising religion. Closely associated with the colonial enterprise, early Christian missionaries did not believe that Africans were sufficiently developed rationally to have a religion. They did not perceive ATR to have any founder or founders; they did not find any written material resembling the Bible or the Qur'an; they did not notice Africans proselytising or seeking converts to their own way of life; and, above all, they did not see any visible structure of central governance and authority there. They therefore concluded that Africans had no religion.

The religious beliefs and practices observed among Africans in general were described by the pioneers of Christianity in Africa as superstitious, pagan, animistic, magic and/or fetishistic. It was believed that Africans did not worship God but their ancestors. The assumption behind these derogatory perceptions was that ATR, if it existed at all, was inferior to Christianity because it was less developed and uncivilised. Thus, from the very beginning, the relation between ATR and Christianity can best be described as one between inferior and superior, uncivilised and civilised, barbaric or outdated and modern religion.

Over the years, this consideration of ATR has not changed very much. The development of science, technology and globalisation might have changed the way we work and communicate, but it has not altered significantly the negative attitude of official Christianity to ATR. Moreover, after so many years of negative depiction, even some Africans themselves have been led to believe that ATR does, indeed, belong to a different age, that it has no answers to contemporary problems. As such, it has to be either discarded completely or 'modernised' to suit the needs of the present time and people.

Further, from the very beginning of the encounter between ATR and Christianity, Christianity has viewed adherents of ATR as legitimate targets for conversion. Being a proselytising religion, Christianity has aggressively sought to achieve conversion. This is because the mission of Christians is to make all peoples disciples of Jesus. It is not the intention here to delve into what this commission means or how mission is done versus how it should be done. It is important to bear in mind, however, that there have been different ways of doing Christian mission, one emphasising the need for dialogue with indigenous spiritualities and the other stressing planting Christian churches, in their European forms, in mission countries. The latter approach has dominated in Africa south of the Sahara.

The consequence of this continues to be the abandonment of African values and ways of life. Africans converting to Christianity have to adopt European customs. More specifically, for Africans, the process has almost always involved such things as rejecting African names and taking on European ones, abandoning traditional rituals and ceremonies like polygamy and embracing monogamy, and forsaking initiation rites.

Africans have in turn reacted to this 'non-indigenising' in two main ways. At the theological level, African intellectuals have argued for liberation and inculturation. The process of inculturation in Africa has emphasised the need to make the gospel relevant by taking African culture seriously. The model here is the Christ event: just as the Word became flesh and dwelt among us, Christianity, too, is invited to take the 'flesh' of African culture and dwell among Africans. Taking a cue from African political movements of liberation such as Negritude and Ujamaa socialism, but founded on the Christian Scriptures, proponents of liberation have argued for social, political and economic emancipation of Africans from the yoke of neo-colonialism – in Christian terms, from the domination of European Christian structures, doctrines and practices.

Pursued to its logical conclusion, the inculturation and liberation approach to evangelisation would have improved the quality of relationships between Christians and adherents of ATR. But in Sub-Saharan Africa, the two processes have stalled, in spite of the many calls from high Christian church authorities asking local leaders to engage in them. In some mainline Christian churches, it is the status quo of Christian dominance, superiority and 'modernisation' that still prevails, even though many Africans continue to pay lip service to Christianity.

A more radical response by Africans to this domination of European Christianity has been to break away from Christian traditions and establish what are variously known as African 'Independent', 'Indigenous', 'Initiated' or 'Instituted' Churches (AICs). Common to these churches is the fact that, originating in Africa, they do not depend on financial aid from outside and are, therefore, ecclesiastically free from the practical domination of mainline churches, with a theology and ethos that are distinctly African.

Adherents of ATR view Christianity in a number of ways. First, they see Christianity as an arrogant religion, bent on imposing its faith and practices on others. Adherents of ATR find it difficult to believe the Christian doctrine that for one to be saved it is necessary to be a Christian. What about those who died before the arrival of Christianity in Africa, they ask?

Secondly, adherents of ATR view Christianity as insensitive to their culture. They do not understand why they have to abandon their traditional customs in order to be Christians. More specifically, they do not understand why they have to abandon their names, their family structures, the marriage practices of polygamy, their languages, their traditional medicines, their naming ceremonies, their burial rites and their veneration of ancestors in order to become Christians.

Further, adherents of ATR view Christianity as an elitist religion in terms of its organisation, structure and beliefs. The teaching of the Christian faith is seen to be difficult to understand without the assistance of educated people with the knowledge and the expertise to explain its doctrines and practices. Unlike their Christian counterparts, African religionists do not find it necessary to describe God, as God is in God's own self. In ATR, God is God and cannot be known in his essence or substance.

Finally, for many adherents of ATR, Christianity is narrow and conservative, in that it has a fixed understanding of reality that does not change according to time or place. God's revelation in Christianity is not dynamic; it is seen as rather static and final, so much so that after Jesus Christ there can be no further revelation. This denies any continuing revelation in nature and in natural phenomena.

These negative perceptions of Christianity by Africans have not, however, prevented them from converting to Christianity, attending Christian schools, receiving health services from Christian hospitals or using infrastructure established and maintained by Christians. If anything, Africans have been the main consumers of social services provided by Christians. This might explain why, since its introduction to the region, Christianity has consistently experienced growth. Some scholars have warned, nevertheless, that the conversion of Africans to Christianity is superficial. When it comes to matters of life and death, African converts easily revert to their traditional ways of addressing the challenges of life.

In the consideration of many, Christianity (and Islam for that matter) is for Africans something like a veneer or ornament: it exists only on the surface. Beneath the veneer of 'civilisation' or 'Islamisation', black people remain always ready to break out and return to their own selves. This is because the roots of African thought do not change when people embrace these religions. The point is that, for black people, the European-Christian and Arabic civilisations are additions, in that they do not provide the controlling sensibilities that are fundamentally offered by their African heritage. Thus, under the light coating of imitation, the majority of black people remain African at the core.

It has already been noted that since the introduction of Christianity in Africa south of the Sahara, adherents of ATR and Christianity have been living together in relative peace, although there have been tensions involving some practices. But there have also been some real and substantial theological issues to deal with, including the virgin conception and birth of Jesus. Most adherents of ATR do not understand what this means and what it is supposed to achieve.

In addition, there is the question of the humanity and divinity of Jesus Christ. The idea of an individual who was man and God at the same time is for many Africans difficult to comprehend. Equally challenging are issues related to the Christian doctrines of the Trinity and consubstantiation. Also serious are issues related to the social, political and economic liberation of Africa and the place of African culture in Christianity. African culture is still marginalised, and until it is appreciated and finds a place in Christianity, relations between Christianity and adherents of ATR will remain tense.

The issue of poverty is also controversial. In Christianity, poverty plays a very significant role and is seen as an important quality for salvation. As the Scriptures say, 'Blessed are you who are poor, for yours is the kingdom of God'. The idea of extolling poverty, the condition of lacking material goods, does not augur well with African spirituality, which is always ready to summon all forces necessary to overcome the powers of death, including poverty.

The question is, must Africans abandon their identity in order to become Christians? Can mission be seen more in terms of dialogue and witness than in terms of conversion of Africans, who then abandon their own heritage and culture? Resolution of such issues as these could improve relations between adherents of ATR and Christians in the future.

### Relations between Christians and Muslims

The discussion about ATR and Christianity has shown that although they interact and cooperate in many social, political and economic activities, relations between them are strained in how they perceive each other. These differences have to be addressed in order to have a healthy relationship and sustainable peaceful coexistence between them. What about relations between Christians and Muslims?

Like Christianity, Islam is not an African indigenous religion. Having arrived in Sub-Saharan Africa from North Africa long before the arrival of Christianity, however, Islam has acquired more African traits. Founded by Mohammed in Mecca, Saudi Arabia, in AD 622, Islam quickly spread to different parts of Sub-Saharan Africa, where it came into contact with black people between the seventh and eighth centuries. Facilitated by trade between Arabs in the north and Africans in the south, Islam spread to different parts of Africa south of the desert. Today, Islam is found everywhere in Black Africa. When the population of North Africa is taken into account, the number of adherents of the two religions on the continent is almost equal.

Christians and Muslims do hold some things in common. Both Islam and Christianity are proselytising religions. Both believe that they have a divine mandate to go all over the world converting people. Christians and Muslims justify this by using their scriptures. Both Islam and Christianity have founders, Jesus and Mohammed respectively. Both claim to be 'revealed' religions, in that they came into existence as a result of God's direct intervention, correspondingly through the Bible and the Qur'an.

Relations between Christians and Muslims in Africa south of the Sahara fluctuate from tolerance to tension to violence. In some countries, like Tanzania, relations between Christians and Muslims are on the whole good. The main Christian organisations – the Christian Council of Tanzania (CCT), the umbrella organisation for the Protestant churches; the Evangelical Lutheran Church of Tanzania (ELCT); the Anglican Church of Tanzania (ACT); the Union of Pentecostal Churches in Tanzania (UPCT); and the Tanzania Episcopal Conference (TEC), the body of Catholic bishops – have have very good relations with Muslim organisations, including BAKWATA (Baraza Kuu la Waislamu wa Tanzania, or the Supreme Council of Muslims in Tanzania), the Supreme Council of Shia Ithnasheri of Tanzania (SCSIT) and Khidmat Islamic Propagation Society (KIPS). Usually the leaders of these organisations take a common stand on issues that affect religions in the country. For instance, on 4 May 2013, when a bomb exploded in a Catholic church in Arusha where the papal nuncio, Archbishop Franscisco Montecillo Padilla, was about to celebrate Mass, the leaders of these organisations came out very strongly to condemn the incident. Similarly, when on Sunday, 17 February 2013, Father Evaristi Mushi, a Catholic priest, was shot dead in Zanzibar, a predominantly Muslim region of the country, the condemnation from both Christian and Muslim organisations was swift. Furthermore, when on 11 February 2013 tensions developed between Muslims and Christians in Buselesele village, Chato District, in Geita Region, over who should slaughter animals for meat for the general public, leaders from organisations on both sides were highly instrumental in calming the situation.

Good relations between Christian and Muslim organisations are not unique to Tanzania. In Kenya, Christian organisations such as the Kenya Conference of Catholic Bishops (KCCB), the National Council of Churches in Kenya (NCCK), the Evangelical Alliance of Kenya (EAK) and the Organization of African Instituted Churches in Kenya (OAICK) have very good relations with Muslim organisations, including the Supreme Council of Kenyan Muslims, the National Muslim Leaders Forum and the Shia Ithna-Asheri Muslim Association. They all come together under the umbrella of Inter-Religious Council of Kenya (IRCK) so as to deepen inter-faith dialogue and to promote tolerance and better understanding of one another's faith. When, for instance, Al-Shabaab, a youth and militant movement based in Somalia, ambushed a bus at Garissa and selected only Christians to be killed, the condemnation of the incident came from both Christian and Muslim organisations in the country.

But not all organisations have taken a conciliatory approach to promote good relations between the two religions. In Tanzania, for example, the Al Milad and Khidmat Islamic propagation societies were in the early 1990s responsible for public seminars and preaching, the contents of which were considered by Christians to be derogatory and derisive towards their faith. In 1993, some members of BALUKTA (Baraza la Uendelezaji Koran in Tanzania, or the Council for the Development of the Qur'an in Tanzania), attacked and demolished several pork butcheries in Dar es Salaam, an incident that led to violence and forceful intervention by the government to stop the carnage.

In Nigeria, the militant Islamic organisation known as Boko Haram or Islamic State West Africa Province (ISWAP), based in north-eastern Nigeria but also active in some parts of Western Africa such as Chad, Niger and Cameroon, has been attacking, killing, maiming and displacing thousands of people either because of their religious beliefs or because of their acceptance of Western education and civilisation. Not so long ago in Uganda, a Christian movement known as the Lord's Resistance Army (or Movement) harboured similar ambitions to those of Boko Haram. Founded in 1987–8 by Alice Lakwena and Joseph Kony in northern Uganda, but operating also in South Sudan, the Central African Republic and in the Democratic Republic of the Congo, the movement sought to overthrow the secular government of President Yoweri Museveni and replace it with a theocratic state directed by the Ten Commandments. Like Boko Haram, it also abducted, killed, maimed and displaced thousands of people, mainly because of its goal to rule according to God's commands. Thus, although at the institutional level relations between some Christian and Muslim organisations are good, in that they try to work together to promote tolerance and better understanding of each other's faith and practices and to create peaceful coexistence, other Christian and Muslim organisations have lost patience with tolerance and have resorted to violence.

Underpinning tolerance, tension and violence between Christians and Muslims in Sub-Saharan Africa are a number of fundamental perceptions or attitudes that Christians and Muslims harbour against each other. Generally, Christians tend to see Muslims as fellows, comrades, neighbours, brothers and sisters, but beyond these labels, which suggest harmony and goodwill, a number of fundamental issues sometimes strain the apparently good relationship. One is that Christians tend to see Islam as an inferior religion because, unlike Christianity, which was founded by Jesus Christ, the Son of God, Mohammed, a human being, founded Islam. Muslims on their part believe that Jesus is only a messenger or prophet, not God incarnate.

Christians, furthermore, are inclined to view Muslims with suspicion and mistrust, as illustrated in cases of inter-religious marriages. Although Muslims and Christians inter-marry, these marriages usually have a hidden agenda. When a Christian marries a Muslim, attempts are usually made to convert the Muslim partner to Christianity. The argument that a husband and wife cannot live well together if they belong to different faith traditions is usually a camouflage for deep-seated Christian mistrust of Muslims. There is always an unspoken fear that Muslims are out to convert Christians and introduce Islamic law (Sharia) in the community. In matters related to practical living, Christians tend to see Muslims as ruthless and violent. They point to some Sharia law practices, which permit the stoning of sinners to death or cutting off the limbs of those who steal or do wrong.

Muslims, too, see Christians as friends, relatives, comrades, fellow brothers and sisters. Yet they also view them as infidels or *kafirun*, people who do not do the will of God or who have not surrendered to God. Thus, in a sense, Muslims do not believe that Christianity is a religion, so that to be a Christian is like living without faith or belief in God. Seen from this point of view, Christians become for Muslims legitimate targets of conversion. Muslims view Christians with suspicion. They believe that Christians intend to turn all of them into Christians. What is true about Christians' views of marriage between a Christian and a Muslim also applies to Muslims. A Muslim who marries a Christian is encouraged to convert the partner to Islam, before or after marriage.

Furthermore, Muslims tend to see Christianity as a religion that has enjoyed unfair social, political and economic privileges. The argument is that although Muslims are part and parcel of the societies of Africa south of the Sahara, they have been marginalised in the running of national affairs. The perception that history has always favoured Westernisation and Christian civilisation over against Islamic civilisation exists everywhere in Sub-Saharan Africa. In Côte d'Ivoire, people have fought two recent wars, the first from 2002 to 2007 and the second from 2010 to 2011. The causes of these civil wars are many and involve social, political and economic factors. Although they have not been characterised as religious wars, the religious element was very much present. Northern Côte d'Ivoire, which is predominantly Muslim and dominated by poor migrants from Mali and Burkina Faso, felt that it was politically marginalised and economically exploited by the Christian south, which is wealthier. The south had dominated national politics for more than 50 years, since the time of Félix Houphouët-Boigny, the founding father of the nation. To address its experience of political marginalisation and exploitation, the predominantly Muslim north, under the leadership of Alassane Ouattara, fought against the Christian south, which supported the then President, Laurent Gbagbo.

The situation in the Central African Republic has been similar to that of Côte d'Ivoire just described. The violence that erupted there in 2012 and 2013 started as a political conflict, but it slowly assumed a religious character when Seleka, an armed rebel movement representing Muslims in the north, started killing Christians in the south. Then the 'anti-balaka' militia forces in the Christian south also started killing Muslim civilians. Although the situation has calmed down and violence has diminished, the two communities still do not trust each other. Relations between them are tense and likely to remain so until the religious issues are resolved.

Most matters affecting Christian–Muslim relations are theological. As already mentioned, for Muslims, the founder of Christianity, Jesus Christ, is not God but just a great prophet. Muslims believe that God cannot beget children and it is improper to honour as divine anyone other than God. In addition, Muslims cannot accept the Christian doctrine of the Trinity because it sounds like polytheism. For Muslims, there is only one God. What is even more worrying for Muslims is the Christian teaching about the death and the resurrection of Jesus Christ. In their estimation, there was no resurrection, the pillar of Christian faith. A proper understanding of these issues and integration of Muslim communities in political leadership is necessary for better relations between Muslims and Christians in Sub-Saharan Africa.

## Conclusion

Focusing on relations between the three main religions in Sub-Saharan Africa – namely African traditional religions, Christianity and Islam – this chapter has shown that relations between and among them are, in general, good and that their adherents have, on the whole, been living together in relative peace and harmony. However, in different countries in Sub-Saharan Africa some affiliate groups have abandoned the virtue of tolerance. This chapter has illustrated that sustainable and healthy relations among the three faiths require better mutual understanding through a clear commitment to dialogue with a view to resolving doctrinal and practical issues that threaten peaceful coexistence.

## Bibliography

Erlich, Haggai, *Islam and Christianity in the Horn of Africa: Somalia, Ethiopia and Sudan* (Boulder, CO: Lynne Rienner Publishers, 2010).

Magesa, Laurenti, *African Religion in Dialogue Debate: From Intolerance to Coexistence* (Zurich: Lit Verlag, 2010).

Mbogoni, Lawrence E. Y., *The Cross Versus the Crescent: Religion and Politics in Tanzania from the 1880s to the 1990s* (Dar es Salaam: Mkuki na Nyota Publishers, 2004).

Ndaluka, Thomas Joseph, *Religious Discourse, Social Cohesion and Conflict: Muslim–Christian Relations in Tanzania* (Zurich: Lit Verlag, 2012).

Wijsen, Frans, *Religious Discourse, Social Cohesion and Conflict: Studying Muslim–Christian Relations* (Bern: Peter Lang, 2013).

# The Bible in African Christianity

## Ukachukwu Chris Manus

This chapter aims to describe and explain the esteem the Bible enjoys in today's burgeoning African Christianity. The Bible has become ubiquitous in Sub-Saharan Africa. In its various versions, it has estimated annual sales of 54 million copies in all the official languages spoken in Africa, namely English, French and Portuguese, as well as in many of Africa's vernacular languages. A corpus of sacred literature that had its origin in Judaism and the earliest Christianity can now be said to have become an African book. Evidence abounds that Africans have received the Bible as a holy book. Although the initial reception of the Bible in much of Africa may have been compromised by the colonial context in which it arrived, and despite it being used as a source of legitimation for colonial regimes, Africans now hold the Bible to be their 'God-sent' Book.

Throughout the continent, Pentecostals bellow out their calls in imitation of John the Baptist's proclamation of 'a baptism of repentance and forgiveness of sins'. Echoing the prophet Isaiah, they declare: 'Prepare the way of the Lord, make straight his paths' (Mark 1: 3b). From there they go on to challenge their audience to accept Jesus as Lord. Charismatics negotiate diverse meanings from the same Bible. All those 'holy noises' that rend the air of Africa at crusade grounds, revival centres and redemption camps are aimed at planting 'Holy Ghost Fire' time-bombs to blast and shatter both seen and unseen enemies. The vociferous cries of 'hallelujah' from innumerable churches are shouted as prayerful incantations being made to heaven to rain down blessings. Africans take the Bible very seriously, and biblical phrases are extracted from the text and reformulated to become potent forces to rout generational curses and to divert the 'evil eye' from the body of believers.

### The Impact of Bible Translations

It would be hard to overestimate the significance of the translation of the Bible into African vernacular languages. Translations into the languages of such peoples as the Igbo, the Yoruba, the Akan and the Hausa-Fulani in Western Africa; into Swahili in Eastern Africa; and into the isiZulu, the Shona and the Nguni languages of Southern Africa have rendered the Word of God accessible to a new audience that had long been using translations provided in the colonial period by mission-founded churches. The vernacular versions of the Bible have come to assist various ethnic peoples to meaningfully engage the biblical text in their own idioms and thought forms. Bible study sessions provide ordinary readers with the opportunity to re-create the Word of God in new horizons as they hear the texts read in their own mother tongues. In Base Christian Communities, there are Bible-sharing meetings structured as follows: Bible reading taken twice, sharing and teaching on the text, intercessory prayers based on the text, and testimonies given thereof by people with experience relevant to the text. Here, oftentimes, the sharers relive the Emmaus experience of the Lukan community: 'Were not our hearts burning within us while he spoke to us on the way and opened the scriptures to us' (Luke 24: 32). Translations in vernacular languages help the sharers assimilate the meanings of the shared texts. The versions enable them to allow the lessons to permeate into their lives and be taken into their workplaces. Lamin Sanneh has argued convincingly that the emphasis on vernacular translation helped to bring into being the prophet movements found in Sub-Saharan Africa. This demonstrates the significance and power of the availability of Bible translations for African Christianity.

A critical evaluation of some of the translations reveals how they succeed in enabling ordinary readers to comprehend the target text. Excellent vernacular translations have been successfully crafted in such languages as Sesotho, isiZulu, Luo, Kikuyu, Igbo, Yoruba, Edo, Efik, Akan and Asante to address the source and receptor languages. It is noticeable that in their handling of the sacred languages, translators have exhibited the skills of biblical scholarship in their use of literary theories such as narratives, fixed formulary discourses, direct and indirect discourses, techniques of redaction, chiasms, model portraits, use of fulfilment motifs, figures of speech such as irony and satire, linguistic theories and communications skills that exhibit cultural anthropological competence. Competences like these have made the translations easily accessible to today's vociferous preachers, pastors and even prophet-healers and 'men of God' in different regions of Africa.

While the trained African Bible scholar acknowledges the structural unity of the texts and probes the source text's sociological and historical backgrounds as well as the linguistic subtleties as necessary steps towards decoding the meanings embedded in the texts, the ordinary readers, especially the untrained pastors and evangelists, many of whom have taken the one-year Bible college programmes now found almost everywhere in Africa, thumb through the Bible, and read and interpret the texts through the light shed from Africa's indigenous languages and underlying cosmologies. This phenomenon, albeit a vernacular hermeneutics, is distinguishing the

African form of Christianity and promoting the development of specific genres of African proclamation. It is this interaction between the African and biblical social worlds and cultures, mediated through language, that has brought to birth the contemporary vibrant Christianity on the continent.

## African Popular Biblical Hermeneutics

The ubiquitous availability of the Bible as *textus receptus* within Africa's expanding Christianity has led to quite a diversity of interpretation. Generally, ordinary readers are the receptors of the pronouncements of trained readers. But as ordinary readers hear and listen, they ruminate over what they have heard from the experts or from the preaching of their pastors, and through their own reflections they bring to the meanings of the passages their own perceptions and understandings of how the text touches their lives and challenges the community ethos. Such simple readers of the Bible constitute the large majority of any congregation in the African churches. They usually initiate special interpretative models for understanding the texts in their own contexts. In Bible-sharing meetings, as well as in their homes, farms, trading posts, kiosks and shops, in unions, religious associations and workplaces, especially those of the womenfolk, they re-create and re-configure what they have heard, replay the central themes and reformulate the ideas in order to assimilate the spirit of the texts they have so digested in order to affect their lives.

The times the texts describe, although remote, these folks reshape to suit their living experiences here and now. In their teaching and testimonies, the observer can see their situations mirrored in the experiences of the people who wrote the Bible and of those for whom the Bible originally was written. By so doing, they broker unique insights into the application of the biblical text to contemporary issues of life, faith and morality in Africa. In this light, they constrain mainline biblical scholars to submit their findings to examination in light of their prospects for actualisation, application, inculturation and contextualisation. Ordinary readers thus bring forth new perspectives on what a passage meant in its original 'setting in life' (*Sitz im Leben*) and what it now means for members of their communities, the receptor setting (*Sitz im Leben Momento*).

In the small Christian Bible-sharing groups, these ordinary readers make critical and insightful comments on portions of the Bible read out, including remarks the experts might not recognise but which touch lives. The ordinary readers do so because their socio-economic, political and religious situations induce them to compare the equivalent situations of the earliest readers with their own. They evoke the experiences of the people of faith whose faces lie behind the texts of the Bible in light of their own contemporary contexts in modern Africa, where bad governance, corruption, terrorism and insurgencies, refugees, human trafficking, squalor, disease and malnutrition often prevail. In this way they complement the conventional critical tools of biblical exegesis with resources that they bring from their own cultural and historical experience. This sort of joint effort, no matter how simplistic or jejune it may look, advances African Christians' interpretation of the biblical texts in ways that promote integration of faith and life and engender commitment to personal and social transformation.

## The Role of the Bible in the Life of the Churches

John S. Mbiti, widely regarded as Africa's foremost biblical scholar and theologian, has long maintained that African Christianity is Bible-based. Many denominations in contemporary African Christianity take the Bible as their workbook. In their liturgical services, the 'established' churches read a number of passages of the Bible as prescribed in their lectionaries. The priests preach on these passages and deliver sermons that often vibrate through microphones and amplifiers to spread the good news of Jesus Christ, the Lord of the church. In Nigeria's Igboland, for example, people treasure the Bible as the Word of God (*Uka-Chukwu*) and the Word of Life (*Uka-Ndu*). In the Roman Catholic churches, usually four readings are taken from the Bible: an Old Testament passage; a responsorial hymn from the Psalter; a reading from the Epistles or Revelation; and the grounding text, a gospel passage. All the texts are provided in the missal. The same pattern is evident during morning Masses held every day of the week.

Churches with a less formal liturgy also give great prominence to the Bible in their worship. It is in the forefront as the purveyor of the history of salvation that God has planned and executed in Jesus Christ. For this reason, Pentecostals, Charismatics and Evangelicals accord great respect to the Bible-based preaching of their 'men of God', the prophets, prophet-healers and evangelists. There is a multitude of ebullient clerics, pastors and anointed 'men of God' and faith activists within the congregations. These men and women draw inspiration from the Scriptures to challenge from their pulpits the misdeeds of people in the society in the interest of *KingdomNomics*.

The African continent has many modern 'pharaohs', namely those despotic, tyrannical and autocratic heads of state who refuse to 'relinquish power after their terms in office are over', as US President Barack Obama recently noted. Many of the church activists and pastors see themselves clothed in the garb of Moses of the Book of Exodus to lead the struggle against such oppressors. The Bible has influenced many African prelates to preach against human trafficking and the purposeless migrations that have made the Mediterranean Sea become the black man's graveyard. The programmatic address of Jesus at Nazareth (Luke 4: 16–20) inspires some of the anointed pastors of the African Independent Churches to vigorously engage in the search for liberation and respect for human dignity. Peter's vision before going to Cornelius's house, 'Get up, Peter, slaughter and eat' (Acts 10: 13), constitutes a power-packed preaching text in the churches and Christian assemblies from which presiding pastors preach that since God does not show special preferences or partiality to any nation, race or ethnic group, it is normative for all Christians to combat xenophobia, nepotism and ethnic hatred in Africa.

Instead of the negative conception of the Bible as the 'white man's magical Book' widely held during the colonial era, today the Bible is held by its users to be a 'Letter' God has written to everyone who believes in him. The users invite all to hear and listen to the message of the 'Letter' and to make haste to change for good. As such, most African churches place no restrictions on biblical interpretation. The churches acknowledge the importance for Christians of reading the Word of God in local languages so that the eternal message of the 'Letter of God' may become inculturated in Africa, as had occurred in other places during earlier eras of Christian history. Cultures are ever-evolving and changing. Africa is no exception, and the Bible is one factor that has promoted positive cultural transformation. Where African cultures are found to be negative towards or contradictory to biblical teaching, the churches allow inter-religious dialogue to address the differences in opinion. In this way the Bible has enabled African traditional religion (ATR) and culture to be purged of non-positive elements and the limitations these had imposed on life. The churches continue to practise acculturation of biblical teaching in order to promote catechesis that can take root in African cultures. Bible-believing communities and their leaders are practising inculturation as they enable the Bible's message to become a significant transformative force within their society and culture.

## The Role of the Bible at Different Levels of African Society

African societies do not have a strict class hierarchy but, for the purposes of this chapter, some categories of class can be identified. First, there are the elites, who, though small in number, often see themselves as intellectually, professionally and socially superior to others. The political class are found in this group, including retired and serving army generals, bank executives or finance professionals, senior academics and the big-time business tycoons – all of whom regard themselves as the 'movers and shakers' in society. Secondly, there are the middle class, composed largely of lower-level business people who carry on their businesses in Africa's shantytowns and city markets. They include intermediate professionals like artisans, nurses and secondary-school teachers. Thirdly, there is the lower class in Africa, a group who are often unable to eke out a living. Among this class are the Wananchi in Kenya and the Talakawa or the Ogbenye in many parts of Nigeria. This class bears the brunt of the economic depredations created by the powerful. Among them are the youths, a bubbling, vibrant and restive group who roam Africa's villages, townships and cities in search of ever-elusive jobs. They take advantage of their youthful exuberance to initiate activities of various sorts, negative as well as positive. Many of them engage in militancy, while others establish new prayer houses and Christian Crusade Camps that look forward to becoming full-blown churches in the near future, as long as the Bible is available in the vernacular and church ownership is a tax-free venture in Africa.

There is no doubt that the Bible is understood differently among these social groups in Africa. The elites find in the Word of God wealth and divine blessings. They see the Bible as a source of 'blessings' and encouragement for them to 'take possession of their possessions'. They endear themselves to the makers of 'holy noises' – the 'hallelujah' praises of joy and the thunderous shouts that rend the quiet of African neighbourhoods. They form alliances with the pastors of 'mega' Pentecostal and Charismatic churches, especially those who preach wealth and the prosperity gospel, advocating that they should not be poor because they are children of God. The highly placed clerics of the 'established' churches often belong here. They uphold the Bible as the source of their empowerment to submit their authority to the leaders of the state because it has so been enjoined in Romans 13: 1–7. The Bible inspires the more critically minded of them to launch critiques of the leaders and chiefs who succour themselves in unholy alliances with the political class to perpetuate injustice. They see them from the perspective of the prophet Amos, as rulers who 'oppress the just, accept bribes and repel the needy at the gates' and reprimand them to 'seek good and not evil, that they may live' (Amos 5: 12b, 14). Many of the pastors among the Charismatics employ 1 Samuel 2: 12–17 to rebuke members of this class when the activities of their privileged children become a cause for concern in the community.

The middle class draw inspiration from the Bible to forge ahead and to influence the society to agree with them that 'no weapons fashioned against them would prosper' and that 'every kind of malevolent spiritual forces' sent by enemies shall be 'returned to sender'. For the common people – the Wananchi, the Talakawa and the Ogbenye – the Bible is God's Word of Life. They join many of the Bible churches and pray together with evangelists and prophet-healers so that 'Holy Ghost Fire' will 'scatter' and 'burn' the evildoers who vitiate (*dabaru*) their chances to move out of poverty and squalor. They readily agree with the prosperity gospellers that 'if one is poor, then such a person is not a friend of God'. Within this class, the youths interact seriously with the Bible. Where they are members of the mainline churches, they often join a choir and sing Bible-derived hymns for praise and worship. Others join Pentecostal, Charismatic and Evangelical churches where *sola scriptura* (Scripture alone) remains the source of Christian faith and morals. Many of the youths find themselves involved in different youth societies and associations like the Young Men's Christian Societies, the Students' Christian Movement, the Catholic Youth Organisations, Catholic Charismatic Renewal Movements and the National Federation of Catholic Students, who consistently dig through the Bible during conventions and crusades to seek answers for all their questions, worries and problems at school and beyond.

In African families, the Bible is held to be the 'fountain of life'. Family Bible-sharing sessions occupy significant places in family morning and evening devotions. From the Old Testament, the books of Samuel has powerful messages for Africans. In polygamous homes, 1 Samuel 1: 2 is read with great interest. In 1 Samuel 1: 5–11, the problem of barrenness and the family's strong desire for the birth of a male child described as Hannah's predicament resonates with African cultures of hate for barrenness and of deep desire for the birth of a male child. The story in 2 Samuel 13: 1–39, the incestuous rape of Tamar by her half-brother Amnon, gives inspiration to feminist activists to fight the recurring violence against women in African societies. In the New Testament, the story of the return of the young Jesus and his obedient submission to his parents (Luke 2: 41–52) are exemplary texts that parents cherish in their family catechesis. Jesus's attitude to children according to Mark 10: 13–16 inspires parents to cherish their children as mirroring the Kingdom of God in their simplicity and humility. The Synoptic narratives on the teaching of monogamy and faithfulness in marriage (Mark 10: 2–12) are employed to fortify family unity against the rising phenomenon of divorce in contemporary society. Ephesians 5: 21 – 6:19 is used to consolidate a family ethos of submission of wife to husband and vice versa, as well as a call for moral responsibility in parenting, obedience from children and even care for house-helps on the part of Christians in modern Africa.

In the public life of many African nations, the Bible is authoritative in civil religion. All Christian heads of state are sworn into office with the Bible in hand. Many political candidates quote from the Bible to invoke God to help them fulfil and execute their election promises to the people. The figure of Moses as Messiah of Israel is re-cast to invite the people to welcome their coming into governance in messianic terms, even though some of them, before long, turn out to become pharaohs who enslave the masses and exploit the poor in their own countries. In Lesotho, for example, the Bible is accorded pride of place in national life. The Sesotho

Bible, Bibele Photolelo E Ncha Le Libaka Tse Lenane La Bobeli, is proudly read in all the people's religious devotions. When they recite the Lord's Prayer, Ntat'a Rona Ea Maholimong, the people aver that since their nation is already high up (being a mountainous country), it is at the doorstep of God in heaven above, so their prayers ascend faster to God than those of other peoples who live on flat land below. In this way a biblical text is interwoven with the national geographical features to form a distinctive sense of identity.

## The Bible in Contemporary Culture

Since the advent of literacy through missionary educational programmes and activities in many parts of Sub-Saharan Africa, Bible stories have been appropriated into the plots of literary works by African creative writers. In this way, besides its religious function, the Bible as literature has exercised enormous influence on African culture. Its various literary genres of poetry, prose, prophecy, history, gospel, epistle and apocalypse have attracted many African writers. African literary artists retell Bible stories in such ways that both Old Testament and New Testament episodes and characters appear as if they were stories born in Africa itself. Today, many African literary luminaries embellish their works with Bible stories, perhaps knowing that these will lend them acceptance with the reading public. By incorporating biblical material in their literature, African writers recover the performative and communal character of the original texts.

The Ugandan Okot p'Bitek stands out as a representative figure in this regard. His *Song of Lawino* (1970) is a poem of dissent and resistance. Lawino, the wife of Ocali, disapproves of her husband's Westernised lifestyle. Her chastisement of him could not but have been inspired by the Bible and Christian education of the time. For Lawino, Ocali's mannerisms indicated an irreparable loss of his traditional Acholi cultural heritage and values. The idea of the 'good word in the Clean Book' reflects nothing else but the catechesis derived from the Bible – the 'Clean Book'. The Hunchback and Rubanga – the name of the Christian God in the Acholi language – draw attention to the Christianisation of the African gods and spirits. In other words, the Bible's presence among the Acholi hastened the giving of the attributes of the Christian God to local deities. Okot p'Bitek has skilfully used this literary piece to recreate religious experience. The Bible was known to have promoted mass conversions to the Christian faith by that time. Such reference to the Bible in literature has helped to provide enduring truths, values and morals that sustain African Christianity.

As the Bible originated from an oral culture, African Christians find in its narratives ideological parallels with their own folktales and, as such, take pride in the oral presentation of biblical texts on various occasions.

On festival days and celebrations like the November–December annual harvests and bazaars, women's associations, youths and men's fraternities and sodalities give dramatised performances derived from biblical texts. The journey of Mary and Joseph to Jerusalem for the census during which time the birth of the infant Jesus took place in the manger at Bethlehem is usually graphically performed at Christmas. The arrest, trial and crucifixion of Jesus are passionately acted out at Easter. On such occasions, performance is allowed to interact with the African Christian audience in the form of song, dance and gesticulation, interspersed here and there with rhythmic beats that lend an aura and ambience that transform the spirit of the congregation as performers rehearse what occurred on the first Easter. It is notable how the Bible narratives are spread far and wide through the medium of song-fests, folktales, wise-sayings, sermons and testimonies that resonate with the versatility of African traditional lore and wisdom.

As regards music, many of the vast number of hymns, chants and songs used in contemporary African Christian churches, congregations, open-air rallies and crusade grounds have been drawn from the Bible, particularly the Psalter, prophetic texts and the gospels. Mainline churches, African Independent Churches, Pentecostals, Evangelicals and Charismatics have all been active in biblically inspired musical compositions. Two popular examples must suffice:

1. Jesus' Power, Power, Power (2×)
   Satan's power, powerless power (2×)
   Jesus' Power, Powerful Power. (2×)

This piece is inspired by Jesus's victory over Satan during his temptations (Mark 1: 12–13). Christians sing it to extol Jesus's divinity and to denounce Satan and his wiles.

2. The Most Excellency is Jesus (2×)
   Shout Alleluia, Amen (2×)
   Amen, Alleluia, Amen.

This is a Christological chorus predominantly sung in mixed communities where the English language or Pidgin English is generally used during worship services. With the hymn, the congregants magnify the honour of Jesus and cap it with a thunderous Alleluia chorus.

These and many other variants of Christian music are cleverly blended with sounds from such musical instruments as the stringed bows, *samba*, gong, *ogwe*, drums, guitars, *ogenes*, flutes and brass bands so that the music produced synchronises so melodiously that the walls of the churches appear to fall apart while church members wriggle and dance away their sorrows in the Household of God. The beat and vociferous singing that follow the jingling of bells combine to create a compelling cultic atmosphere. The emergence of these hymnologies derived from the Bible and Christian tradition has given a distinctive character to the worship of Christians south of the Sahara. In many of the African Independent Churches, these Bible-inspired melodious renditions dispose people to fall into trances and claim spirit possessions, often manifesting distinctively African religious experiences.

Reference to the Bible, however, is by no means confined to churches or formal religious settings. It is just as likely to be heard in barber shops, watch repairers' workshops, bicycle repairers' sheds and cobblers' sheds, at roadside mechanics' workshops, and in cafeterias and *bukaterias* (local eateries) – all the places where idlers, loafers, job-seekers, fishermen and street-hawkers are found. Even prison yards are not excluded. In these places, many a time, the Bible has become 'the oil with which words are eaten'. Itinerant pastors and prophets as well as evangelists have made the Bible their essential hand luggage. They go in and out to meet the people to drum the words of the Bible into their ears, especially those of the prophets. Others, like some self-proclaimed Bible interpreters, preach doomsday occurrences to their unwary and gullible hearers. They tell of impending Armageddons of the contemporary world. They employ hell-turned phrases to proclaim imminent apocalypses and the tsunamis hanging over Africa if people do not repent.

It is common to hear proverbs like 'Physician, cure yourself', or 'Do here in your native place the things that we heard were done in Capernaum' (Luke 4: 23b); or 'so also faith of itself, if it does not have works, is dead' (James 2: 17); or 'a labourer is worthy of his hire' (Matthew 10: 10b). In many popular discourses the use of the Bible can even turn into sour arguments when some hearers react against what they perceive as judgemental and irritating jargon from the out-of-context texts gabbled in their ears. Some of the notice-seeking preachers use the Bible in political circles to insult the ruling class for their failure to heed the Word of God. Recently, one such charlatan proclaimed that the advent of Boko Haram in the north-east of Nigeria, Cameroon, Chad and Niger had long been spoken of in the Bible and that he had been calling upon the governments to watch out for Nebuchadnezzars but no one had listened to him. He ended his rhapsody by asserting 'failure to heed prophecy ends in destruction'. Even if the use of the Bible is unsavoury at times, there is no denying its prevalence or its power.

Land is an issue that engenders emotional and passionate reactions in popular discourse in many parts of Africa. For many Christian leaders, the Bible has greatly illuminated the matter. As land was sacred to biblical

Israel, so is land considered wealth for Africans. Heated arguments usually ensue whenever African Christians see people engaged in discourses on how land has forcefully been parcelled out without respect for traditions and the honouring of ancestral bodies interred therein and people's rights. From the spirit and letter of the Bible on the sacrosanctity of *H'Arets Israel* (Land of Biblical Israel), Christians in Africa disapprove of land-grabbing by the rich and the powerful such as was rampant in Kenya in the recent past, South Africa by the Boers and the ancestral land desecration through land-use decrees enacted during the military regimes in Nigeria. For Christians, landowners have inalienable rights to use their lands to create wealth and to erect buildings, as did landowners in the Bible. Christians believe that the Creator God who called Abraham out from the land of Ur of the Chaldees, Moses out of the land of Egypt, and Joshua to settle in Canaan, the Promised Land is the same God who has given them the mandate to defend African lands from abuse, undue annexation and reclamation by oppressors. On the value of land to its owners, a Nigerian gospel musician, Sonny Okosun, sings:

> Papas Land, E, e; Who Owns Papas Land, E, e,
> We wanna know, who owns the Land;
> Africa is Papas Land, From Cape to Cairo,
> Africans must Rule the Land,
> Papas Land, Papas Land.

Contemporary African Christians believe that in the spirit of the Bible, 'Papa[']s Land' is an ancestral heritage that must be protected at all costs. Such passionate commitment to social and political causes is fuelled and inspired by engagement with the Bible.

## Conclusion

This chapter has demonstrated the profound influence of the Bible in Africa today, at both personal and social levels. This represents an epoch-making development, demonstrating the fact that the Christian faith is steadily finding a permanent home in the Southern hemisphere, and in Africa par excellence. What began as a mysterious Book, unreachable by and impenetrable to Africans, has become a bastion of hope, deliverance, succour and enlightenment for millions of contemporary Africans who daily turn to the Bible to give meaning and quality to life through their everyday encounter with the Word of God. Formal biblical scholarship is complemented by the hermeneutics of ordinary readers of the Bible, who develop contextual interpretations, particularly through Bible study groups at the grassroots level. The result is a richly textured understanding of the God of the Bible as the Father and Creator who has offered his Son Jesus to become Saviour and Liberator, King, Healer and Warrior – a faith to meet the challenges of life in Africa today. It would be hard to overestimate the influence of the Bible in shaping popular religion in Sub-Saharan Africa. It is on the wings of the Bible that Christianity has spread and has become an indispensable resource for everyday life in contemporary Africa.

## Bibliography


Loba-Mkole, J. C. and Ernst R. Wendland (eds), *Interacting with Scriptures in Africa* (Nairobi: Acton, 2005).

Manus, Ukachukwu Chris, *Intercultural Hermeneutics in Africa: Methods and Approaches* (Nairobi: Acton, 2003).

Mbiti, John S., *Bible and Theology in African Christianity* (Nairobi: Oxford University Press, 1986).

Waweru, Humphrey M., *The Bible and African Culture: Mapping Transactional Inroads* (Eldoret: Zapf Chancery, 2011).

West, Gerald O. and Musa W. Dube (eds), *The Bible in Africa: Transactions, Trajectories and Trends* (Leiden: Brill, 2000).

# The Anthropology of Evil

## Afe Adogame

Belief in the stark reality and existence of evil and witchcraft is rife among Africans, although it is hardly an African trademark, as some observers would imagine: the discourse on evil, demonology, witches and witchcraft is a global phenomenon that fascinates exotically. The idea of an evil entity – a witch – fondly evokes a sense of the mysterious, a malevolent spiritual agent and a malign person. In some contexts, the image of a witch usually signifies an old, ugly-looking woman, while in other contexts an extremely beautiful woman might evoke suspicion. Historically, too, we can recognise witch-hunting as a feature of pre-modern societies and of the Christian society of medieval Europe. Historical perspectives from the ancient world on contemporary paganism, Wicca and neo-witchcraft movements show how witchcraft has meant different things to different people, raising questions about the distinction between fantasy and reality, faith and proof, suspicion and confession.

One can observe the reinvention of witchcraft as history, religion, fiction, fantasy and metaphor. While conceptions of evil, witches and witchcraft might have fizzled out, becoming valorised and deconstructed as fairy tales and fiction in some contexts, they nevertheless continue to feature concretely within the consciousness and religious sensibilities of many Africans. In most African societies and the African diaspora, conceptions of evil and witchcraft remain a robust reality that confronts modernity, although the meanings, aetiologies and modalities of combating it are rather fluid, diverse and contested. But how do we comprehend the resilience of epistemologies of evil and witchcraft in African religious life today?

One main thrust of African Pentecostal religiosity is a belief in the stark reality and existence of evil and witchcraft and there is a preponderance of deliverance and healing rituals to combat them. Thus, the epistemology and negotiation of spiritual warfare makes ample sense in their ritual cosmos. There is an observable resilience in concrete belief in and ritual attitude towards incorporeal, superhuman entities that are perceived to be inherently evil. It is the rapprochement with indigenous cosmology and ritual praxis that distinguishes Africa within global Pentecostalism(s) and accounts largely for its horizontal and vertical expansion and relative success. In some academic circles, it is just this affinity that launches African Pentecostalism into competing discourses of synthesis or syncretism.

Drawing upon brief contrasting case studies of three African-led Pentecostal churches – the Living Faith Church (LFC), also known as Winners Chapel; the Redeemed Christian Church of God (RCCG); and the Mountain of Fire and Miracles Ministries (MFM) – this chapter explores their imagination and preoccupation with the epistemology of evil, witchcraft and demons and how, through their extensive appropriation of spiritual warfare rhetoric and deliverance rituals in Africa and the African diaspora, they have carved out a niche in African Pentecostal discourse in local–global contexts. First, these churches share some affinities, in that their epistemologies of evil and witchcraft are similar, although the emphases in the methodologies used in combating them vary. Second, these churches are founded and led by charismatic figures who hail from south-western Nigeria, thus emerging from a similar geo-cultural precinct, the Yoruba ethnic group. Third, these new indigenous brands of Christianity have their religious messages packaged and branded in such a way as to repudiate European mission Christianity as too dressed in Western cultures and thus failing to countenance or comprehend African worldviews and realities. At the same time, these churches also vehemently renounce any links with occultism and traditional religious cultures.

Pa Josiah Akindayomi founded RCCG in Lagos, Nigeria, in 1952 following a divine call to a special mission. He became popular for his charismatic qualities and healing activities, although the church he founded did not witness any large-scale spread under his tutelage. The succession to leadership of Enoch Adejare Adeboye, a former university professor of applied mathematics and hydrodynamics, as the General Overseer in 1980 transformed the stature of RCCG and launched it onto global religious maps. Through Adeboye's charismatic qualities, healing activities coupled with modernisation processes, the RCCG has sustained considerable organisational and numerical growth, along with geo-ethnic spread within Nigeria and beyond – to more than 100 countries, with over 5 million members scattered across Africa, America, Europe, Asia, Australia, the Middle East and other parts of the world.

David Oyedepo, a trained architect, founded the LFC in the early 1980s in Kaduna, the commercial nerve centre of northern Nigeria. In 1981, Oyedepo claimed to have received a divine mandate to start a church ministry: 'The hour has come to liberate the world from all oppressions of the Devil through the preaching of the word of faith, and I am sending you.' He started the LFC as a house fellowship with 48 members in Kaduna, and within six months the membership rose to 500. Today, the church has relocated its international headquarters from Kaduna to Ota, to a large expanse of land now called Canaanland. The church has more than 1,000 branches in Nigeria, over 36 missions in 28 African countries and several branches in Europe and the United States.

The MFM was founded by Daniel Olukoya in Lagos in 1989. From its new international headquarters in Lagos, the church oversees its branches spread within and outside Nigeria. While the MFM lays claim to more than 500 branches worldwide, 300 of these exist in Nigeria alone. The MFM, like the other two churches in these case studies, has expanded beyond Nigeria, with branches located in other African countries, Europe, North America and Asia.

## Imagining Evil, Engaging Spiritual Warfare

In December 2011, a controversial YouTube video clip went viral, evoking prolonged public discourse, outrage and vexed criticism. This resulted when Bishop Oyedepo, the General Overseer of Winners Chapel (LFC), publicly slapped a teenage female parishioner during the 'altar call' at a deliverance service in response to her claiming 'I am a Witch for Jesus.' Without allowing her any opportunity to explain exactly what she meant, Oyedepo slapped the girl and accompanied it with a brisk proclamation: 'Jesus has no witches. If you do not want to repent I will allow you to go to the bottom of hell.' Not even the verbal defence of this action by the Bishop during a subsequent worship service, claiming that the girl came privately to apologise to him later, could pacify an angry public who, through social media, accused him of humiliation and assault.

Human and child rights activists and a cross-section of the virtual public denounced Oyedepo's action and defence of it. He was accused of having committed a criminal act and there were demands for justice to be served. Social media and the press even reported litigation instituted against the Bishop by some human rights lawyers. Although none of these incidents was independently verified by the author, the raging controversy undoubtedly had a backlash and impacted adversely on the public image and reputation of Bishop Oyedepo. This singular incident provides some insight into contested discourses of evil, witchcraft and demonology and into Oyedepo's imagination of the dichotomy between good and evil, between benevolent and malevolent spiritual imaginaries. He disavows any compatibility between Jesus as a benevolent being and witchcraft personified as a malevolent spiritual entity. I contend that such religious imagination derives from both biblical and indigenous African worldviews and conveys African Pentecostal churches' spiritual maps of the cosmos and epistemologies of ambivalent, antagonistic spiritual agencies within it.

One basic feature that reveals an affinity and continuity between African Pentecostal and indigenous cosmologies is the belief in indiscernible spiritual forces. Linked to this is the tenacity with which ritual enactments take place. Members of these Pentecostal churches believe that the physical world is populated by a multiplicity of supra-mundane entities. However, a remarkable change is in the constitution of this spiritual repertoire, as well as the agencies and strategies through which ritual enactments are authenticated. Basically, most African Pentecostals share a similar mentality in their belief tradition, employing an indigenous hermeneutic of spiritual power but casting it within new conceptual frames of reference. The bedrock of the Pentecostal belief system is the pre-eminence of benevolent powers: God, Jesus Christ, the Holy Spirit and angels. Within the indigenous religious worldview, benevolent powers – the Supreme Being, divinities and ancestors – are propitiated through divination, ritual prayer and sacrifice to ward off malevolent forces. Through elaborate rituals, they seek benevolent power, favour, healing and prosperity.

This tendency has continued in the Pentecostal churches, although the medium and object have changed. The benevolent powers of the indigenous worldview are radically translated as malevolent forces in the new Pentecostal rhetoric and imagination. Pentecostals argue that the Bible clearly portrays human life as lived in a context of perpetual warfare between the kingdoms of God and Satan. The appropriation of metaphorical language and imagery of warfare is rife in the Bible, pointing to the expediency of warfare on the part of God's forces to defeat the enemy – evil, Satan and his demonic forces. Most African Pentecostals are very critical of European mission churches, which they claim have been blinded by a Western worldview that ignores this facet of biblical teaching and social concern.

The texture of spiritual terrorism ventilated in African Pentecostal churches demonstrates the adaptation of Christianity to the existential needs and challenges that many Africans confront. Rituals in the LFC are packaged to handle spiritual terrorist attacks against sickness, unemployment, social insecurity, death, emotional stress, hunger, poverty, singleness, barrenness and virtually all life's vicissitudes. As members frequently testify during church services, deliverance and healing rituals, most existential problems are linked to a sole actor, the Devil/Satan/the Evil One. It is these enigmatic circumstances, consciously located within Satan's portfolio, that serve as stimuli of attraction and conversion to these churches. People throng to these spaces of worship, imagining that the churches are capable of dealing with the Devil in the spiritual battle that they confront daily.

Thus, most African Pentecostals are preoccupied with waging war against the terror, Satan and his cohorts. This is achieved mostly through elaborate prayer rites, rituals of healing, deliverance, fasting, anointing, spiritual baptism and night vigil services. Bishop Oyedepo invokes the fact that life can feel like a battle and insists that victory is the gift of God. Being engaged in a struggle is a sign that one is living the Christian life. The Devil is constantly active and very crafty in his attempts to thwart the aspirations of the Christian believer. There is, therefore, a need to invoke the promised help of the Holy Spirit and to discover the immunity from pain that is the rightful experience of the people of God. Such a message illustrates what Oyedepo and the LFC have come to represent for its members and clientele. Similar rhetoric and mental imaginaries of evil are commonplace in most African Pentecostal churches. However, further examples can be drawn from the two case studies below.

### Witches Need No Visas to Travel to Europe: Deliverance Rituals beyond Borders

An informant's remark aptly summarised the ritual attitude of most African Pentecostals in the diaspora when he commented that witches do not require any visas to travel to Europe from Africa. They are able to come whenever they have nocturnal assignments to accomplish. Therefore, according to the informant, Christians need to be constantly on the alert in case they may be subject to the presence and activity of witches. He claims that witches, wizards and sorcerers shuttle nocturnally across geographical boundaries unrestrained. In other regards, many Africans find their sojourn in Europe rather more complicated than they had envisaged. High hopes of 'making it' on arrival in Europe, to use Nigerian parlance for 'material success and upward social mobility', are often dashed.

In fact, 'secularising' Europe becomes personified as Satan's stronghold, the axis of evil. As a consequence, Europe is further perceived as the 'Dark Continent', in dire need of spiritual regeneration. Life is particularly difficult for many African migrants in Europe, because of declining economies, retrenched welfare systems, cultural gaps, xenophobia at individual and institutional levels, acute unemployment, police harassment and brutality, dashed hopes, stress, loneliness, regimented upbringing of children, extended family expectations from home, and mounting unpaid bills and mortgages. Under these distressing conditions, many Africans find spiritual, psychological and material succour in the church. Through elaborate rituals, a sense of identity, security and protection is provided for members.

As opposed to divination and sacrifice in indigenous ritual praxis, RCCG, LFC and MFM members engage in deliverance rituals, healing rituals, night vigils, prayer and fasting rituals, and thanksgiving rituals (rites of passage) in order to counteract Satan's evil machinations. They claim that the warfare motif in the Bible provides humans with ample instruments with which to thwart the 'evil eye' and the enemy's plans.

Prayer, fasting, repentance, forgiveness, righteousness and every other human attitude and behaviour that stands in obedience to God can be seen as acts of war and a means of enabling God to accomplish his plans in the human realm. Their liturgical tradition is thus a highly expressive action characterised by a heavy dose of rituals enacted to resolve individual and collective existential problems.

In the new Christian dispensation, this spiritual engagement and warfare motif is legitimised with biblical credence, often with reference to Ephesians 6: 10–17. Another oft-cited reference that gives weight to the warfare motif is 2 Corinthians 10: 3–4. Several other biblical references tease out the rhetoric of the Evil One/Devil as enemy, thus highlighting the expediency of spiritual warfare (see 1 Peter 5: 8–9; John 10: 10; 2 Kings 6: 18; James 4: 7; Isaiah 54: 17; Psalm 27: 1–3; and Luke 10: 19). Enoch Adeboye, the RCCG General Overseer, isolates 10 ways in which God fights evil/the enemy on behalf of members. For these Pentecostal churches, this military-cum-spiritual offensive and strategy can be achieved only through total dependence on God by faith. It is a spiritual warfare that can be fought only spiritually and not through any mundane means. Adeboye recommends that Christians should be on the offensive, taking an aggressive stance toward the forces of evil.

Faith healing becomes a highly attractive, alternative source of health. The RCCG, LFC and MFM offer spiritual power to overcome and heal the maladies of poverty. Banners, personal testimonies, sermons, hymns and gifts of the Spirit give testament to the centrality of power in their spiritual discourse and praxis. This quest for spiritual fervour has led to the personification of certain illnesses as the outright manifestation of Satan, the Devil, the demons or in fact its replica. There are frequent references to the evil spirit or demon of disease, illness, barrenness, death, doubt, adultery, poverty, lying, drunkenness and so on. Adeboye points out that everyone faces enemies, such as sickness, sorrow, failure, poverty, death, other people or whatever is warring against you. In the face of such hostility, he insists that prosperity, not poverty, is the proper destiny of the Christian believer. God's intention for the lives of his people is that they be fruitful in every way. The life of obedience to God will invariably result in prosperity. Barrenness and deprivation of every kind are to be overcome through active spiritual warfare. The paraphernalia of the Devil has become enlarged to include just anything that poses a roadblock to the attainment of health and wealth. This lends credence to the multiple understandings and translations of poverty. It is also against this backdrop that the mechanics of the prosperity gospel can be better understood and interpreted. Thus, there is a remarkable difference between this conceptualisation and the understandings of the prosperity gospel within American and European Pentecostalism.

The terrorism motif and theology assume a more complicated dimension with the distinction made between two axes of spiritual warfare. The horizontal axis, referred to as 'ground-level warfare', involves dealing with the various spirits (demons) that inhabit people, while 'cosmic-level warfare' is the vertical axis, dealing with different shades of higher-level spirits. In every society, they argue, the horizontal warfare contends with the issue of ground-level demonisation; the indwelling spirits or demons may be of varying kinds, including family spirits, occult spirits and 'ordinary' spirits, such as those attached to fear, death or homosexuality. Demons are believed to work at ground level in ways appropriate to the society in which they operate. They adapt their approach to the problems and concerns most prominent in any given society.

The vertical warfare is with: territorial spirits, assigned to cities, regions and nations; institutional spirits, such as those assigned to churches, governments, educational institutions, occult organisations and non-Christian religions; and spirits assigned to oversee and encourage special functions, including vices such as prostitution, abortion, homosexuality, gay marriages, gambling, pornography and war. Other spirits are assigned to such things as objects, buildings and other spaces as well as to non-material entities such as rituals and music. It is believed that people regularly become demonised through contact with non-material, 'demonically' infested entities. Ancestral spirits are also assigned to work with specific families. The cosmic spirits are apparently in charge of ground-level spirits, although they are tightly interconnected.

In spiritual warfare, African Pentecostals engage the spiritual mapping technique in discerning cosmic-level spirits and the geographical areas, institutions, vices and objects that they are assigned to as a step towards developing strategies to oppose and defeat them. The 'power encounter' concept that is central to the spiritual warfare discourse is reminiscent of scriptural encounters such as those between Moses and Pharaoh (Exodus 7–12) and between Elijah and the prophets of Baal (1 Kings 18). Healing and deliverance from evil persons and demons are perceived as power encounters. Thus, these churches claim that any approach to pragmatic Christianity and to spiritual warfare that ignores the three-dimensional balance of allegiance, truth and power encounters is incomplete. While African Pentecostal/Charismatic Christians believe in the reality of these evil, enigmatic forces that constitute terror, most Western Christians would be sceptical about the reality of their existence and, more importantly, what to do about them.

I shall illustrate this with two remarkable incidents during my ethnographic research among African Pentecostal churches in Germany. An RCCG Pastor sent from the RCCG International headquarters in Lagos to head one of the parishes in Bonn became very excited about building ecumenical links with German host churches. Through existing networks he came across a number of local Pentecostal church leaders. At one of the ecumenical meetings, his suggestion to host German pastors at an event aimed at 'breaking strongholds of the Devil in Germany' was met with deep suspicion and doubt. He had suggested that they engage in vertical warfare against institutional evil spirits. One of the identified demonic strongholds was the famous Köln Dom, on the grounds that demonic invasion of the edifice has turned it from a sacred space into a historical museum. His German Pentecostal 'brothers' rebuffed this claim and perceived it as effrontery, a strange, syncretistic cultural belief from Africa. Of course, this experience shattered any consequent attempts at network-building and also blacklisted the pastor within local ecumenical circles.

The other striking incident occurred at a 'deliverance' (night-vigil) ritual at an RCCG parish in Germany, where I was present as a participant observer. It will help to illustrate the tenacity of ritual enactments against evil, malevolent spiritual forces by African Pentecostals in diaspora. While deliverance rites are not limited in time or space, the preference for late evenings/nights for such ritual enactments is based on the imagined potency of prayers, as malevolent forces, witches, wizards and spirits are most active, mobile and dangerous during this time. As a result, this time is mapped as the instance when the fiercest spiritual wars are fought in the spiritual battlefield. Members are encouraged to bring all their prayer petitions, supplications and existential problems to this ritual forum where 'prayer warriors' are on standby, fully equipped to terrorise the Devil and his cohorts. This is analogous to ritual time allocation in the indigenous African religious worldview. Witches, wizards and evil spirits are believed to commute freely and unrestrainedly at night. This is when they are believed to attend nocturnal meetings in covens, in caves, treetops or groves, at road junctions or at other strategic locations.

The deliverance service was attended by some 60–70 participants, comprising RCCG members and guests from the German host Evangelical church. The German pastor and his congregants were invited to participate in this ritual worship. The event commenced with 'praise and worship' accompanied by drumming, loud music and dancing. This was followed by the exhortation (sermon) given by the local RCCG pastor. The carefully chosen theme was 'How to fight and win spiritual warfare in our world today'. The ritual service climaxed with the 'altar call', in which the preacher gave an open invitation to all those who wished to surrender their lives to Jesus Christ, to be 'born again'. Systematically, volunteers signified their decision by raised hands while other congregants prayed with eyes firmly closed. They were again asked to take a 'bold step of faith' by standing on their feet and walking to the rostrum, towards the preacher. In a solemn state, this interregnum marked a liminal phase in the ritual lives of those congregants who intended to 'give their lives to Christ'. The preacher engaged in a sustained spate of extemporised prayers, facing congregants who had lined up at the bottom of the rostrum, while church elders and 'prayer warriors' stood behind like bodyguards waiting to protect or arrest any backsliders or potential escapees.

As the prayers intensified, the atmosphere became somewhat charged and tense, spiritually. Suddenly, some of those standing started sobbing, screaming, weeping uncontrollably, jerking and moving their bodies indiscriminately. Some became 'slain in the Spirit' and fell down backwards towards the floor, although the church elders were quick to provide support. One of the German female guests became 'slain in the Spirit' as well, falling flat to the ground and muttering unintelligible sounds to the chagrin and amazement of the German pastor and his fellow guests from the Evangelical church. In a very swift reaction, based on a misreading of the situation, the German pastor rushed straight to his office and made phone calls to invite the services of the Rettungsdienst (emergency doctors and an ambulance). This threw the church into pandemonium, as virtually all the guests were scared and sought emergency exits. The African congregants, on the other hand, were unperturbed, as this was a regular occurrence. All attempts by the church leaders and members to explain and persuade the guests fell largely on deaf ears. Although the programme continued late into the night, it did so with the abrupt exit of several of the German guests.

Several interesting narratives emerged following this singular traumatic spiritual experience. I interviewed a number of participants after the programme to ascertain their assessment of the event. All the German guests concluded that what occurred was not Christian but something to do with syncretic African religious culture. Their African counterparts expressed disgust about the ambiguity of their guests' religious profession. They retorted: 'What we are doing is not new, it is not African at all. It is in the Bible for all to see. Are these churchgoers or real Christians?'

The centrality of deliverance rituals in MFM in Africa and in diaspora is partly anchored in the resilience and affinity of an indigenous worldview in which the cosmos is polarised by benevolent and malevolent spiritual entities. The sustained belief in the reality of malevolent spiritual powers, witches and wizards is concomitant with the retention of traditional aetiologies of disease, illness and evil. A text message captioned 'Prayer Chain Required' forwarded to MFM Edinburgh members on 30 April 2008 captures this resilience. It read:

> Prayer chain required! About 10,000 witches from all over the world are meeting tonight in Edinburgh in an annual witches' festival called 'Baalton festival for

> witchcraft'. This is formed from the word 'Baal'. They are currently on Calton Hill in Edinburgh and by 9pm they will all go nude till 3am initiating new members and unleashing curses. All good Christians are enjoined in a prayer chain to destroy their power in the name of Jesus Christ.

This was, in actual fact, referring to Edinburgh's annual Beltane Fire Festival, a neo-pagan fertility ritual ceremony linked to pre-Christian Gaelic/Celtic spirituality. Ostensibly, while the MFM's interpretation of the Beltane ritual might be controversial, it unveils a resilient belief in evil, witchcraft and demonic forces, which appear personified.

The remainder of this chapter will focus on a peculiar ritual language dosed with a certain tone of verbal aggression and militarism, and how it is employed in collective and personal deliverance rituals.

## The Poetics of Spiritual Warfare in MFM

As the name suggests, MFM (Mountain of Fire and Miracles Ministries) has its epistemological thrust and doctrinal emphasis on deliverance, holiness, miracles and healing. The church emphasises that its is a ministry specialising in delivering people from the manifold evil forces that thwart well-being and success. MFM's self-recognition reveals the tendency of engaging in rituals as a 'military strategy' in which 'an army of aggressive prayer warriors are being prepared in this end time'. MFM is self-portrayed as follows:

> a full gospel ministry devoted to the revival of apostolic signs, Holy Ghost fireworks and the unlimited power of God to deliver to the uttermost … Absolute holiness within and without, as the greatest spiritual insecticide, and a condition for heaven is taught openly. MFM is a do-it-yourself gospel ministry where your hands are trained to wage war and your fingers to fight evil … The vision to bring back apostolic signs involves a more precise and aggressive mode of prayer.

This corporate affirmation of belief summarises why, how and to what extent the rhetoric of spiritual warfare pervades the church's ritual cosmology. Olukoya affirms a militant approach to spirituality: 'we are supposed to do all our things militantly'.

Existing church literature and sermon genres are replete with extensive appropriation of warfare rhetoric, such as 'warfare prayers', 'battle cry', 'bullets of fire', 'spiritual terrorists', 'deliverance by fire', 'prayer warriors', 'sword of deliverance' and 'divine revolution', as well as military strategy and militant prayers. Such phrases are suggestive of not only how their belief structure is shaped but also how this impacts their ritual system. This can be clearly exemplified within the context of their ritual space, written texts and oral prayer genres and in the various prayer ritual strategies. The import and performative power of prayer and members' ritual attitude suggests that MFM members do not rely on a faith that is abstract and recondite. Members pay immense attention to the techniques of prayer because it is regarded as an instrument or mechanism of spiritual power. Members are charged to enact intensive prayer rituals as a potent tool for deliverance from this 'spiritual warfare zone' and 'Satan's strongholds'. The discourse on spiritual warfare is therefore an integral aspect of the MFM theology of spiritual forces. Features such as belief in spiritual forces demonstrate how prayer texts become a source and reservoir of MFM theology.

In a sermon titled 'Prayer as a Military Strategy', Olukoya highlights 'militant prayer points' and claims that members 'must pray fervently, effectually and with spiritual violence'. A few lines illustrating this kind of invocatory ritual will suffice here:

> I paralyze every evil hand pointing at my blessing, in the name of Jesus. I withdraw every satanic instruction targeted against me … Every evil river dry up, every evil shrine working against me, be roasted … I refuse to be subdued by the forces of darkness … I nullify every night arrow fired against me … Devil, you are a liar, you cannot capture my destiny.

Thus there is considerable use of militaristic language and imagery in the battle against Satan and his troops. MFM's extensive prayer repertoire indicates the import of invoking God, the name of Jesus, the Holy Ghost and angels in order to demolish and claim victory over Satan and his cohort. Such phrases as 'Fire of God', 'the blood of Jesus', 'Holy Ghost Fire' and 'Angels of God' assume the status of spiritual weaponry. Members are therefore not strangers to the reality of evil, enemies, witches, wizards and demons to which Olukoya alludes in his prayers. Manifold existential problems such as joblessness, illness, barrenness, unstable marital relationships, valid immigration documents, residence permits and lack of accommodation are largely situated along the contours of 'explanation, prediction and control'. It is out of these predicaments that members seek deliverance. The bedrock of their belief system is the pre-eminence of benevolent powers – God, Jesus Christ, the Holy Spirit and the angels. The preponderance of prayer rituals among MFM members is thus a way out of the spiritual quagmire that is occasioned by the malevolent forces that are perpetually bent on inflicting havoc on humans.

## Conclusion

This chapter has demonstrated how the RCCG, LFC and MFM, representing Africa's fastest-growing Pentecostal churches, have made their significant mark in global Christian circles through their imaginaries of evil and witchcraft and their ritual emphasis on deliverance, healing and spiritual warfare. Our explication of demonology and deliverance rhetoric foregrounds the prevalence and continuity of local epistemologies of spiritual constitution and agency in African Pentecostal ritual cosmology, thus accounting for their popularity and swelling clientele, particularly within Africa's religious milieu, but also beyond, into the diaspora.

## Bibliography

Adeboye, Enoch A., *Arresting the Arrester – Catching the Enemy in His Own Trap* (Largo, MD: Christian Living Books, 2002).

Adogame, Afe (ed.), *'Who Is Afraid of the Holy Ghost?': Pentecostalism and Globalization in Africa and Beyond* (Trenton, NJ: Africa World Press, 2011).

Adogame, Afe, 'Dealing with Local Satanic Technology: Deliverance Rhetoric in the Mountain of Fire and Miracles Ministries', *Journal of World Christianity*, 5:1 (2012), 75–101.

Oyedepo, David, *Anointing for Breakthrough* (Lagos: Dominion Publishing House, 1992).

Oyedepo, David, *Anointing for Exploits* (Lagos: Dominion Publishing House, 2000).

# Migration

## Amélé Adamavi-Aho Ekué

People are constantly on the move. They change geographical locations and at the same time rearrange their worldviews. This phenomenon undoubtedly also marks the reality of the African continent. Against the background of a total estimated African population of 1.1 billion, approximately 18.6 million migrants, 3.5 million refugees and 7 million internally displaced persons are recorded. It is noteworthy that more than two-thirds of all migrants from Sub-Saharan Africa migrate to other countries within Sub-Saharan Africa, and only around 1.5% of all Sub-Saharan Africans living outside their countries of origin live within the European Union. Africa hosts around 20% of the world's refugee population, with Uganda, Tanzania, Kenya, Sudan, Chad and Cameroon being the most important refugee-hosting countries in Africa over the past decade. Intra-regional and international African migration are characterised by mixed migration flows, with all traits of contemporary global migration, including forced labour, internal and circular migration. 'Push' factors, such as violent conflicts, climate change-induced droughts and floods, poor governance structures and poverty, have contributed to multi-destination movements across the continent, which have transformed Eastern and Central Africa (Sudan, Chad, Cameroon and Congo) into one of the principal centres of the refugee movements, and countries in Western Africa (such as Mali and Niger) into primary transit countries for African migrants en route to other destinations inside and outside the continent. Another noteworthy trend is the increasing number of female migrants, estimated at 44%, and of undocumented minors under the age of 18 years, at around 20%.

Migration movements have been formative throughout African history and cannot be ignored for the understanding of present ethnic and national dynamics on the continent. They have also had a significant influence on the history of religions, as well as on the self-understanding and the relations of Africans inside and outside the continent. The transatlantic slave trade and slavery on the continent, colonisation, Christian missions and migration movements of Europeans and Africans inside and outside the continent, as salient phases in African history, can all be viewed in association with these global phenomena of migration. While current research has paid particular attention to the migratory movements of Christian migrants from Africa to other countries and within the continent without differentiating Christian affiliations, it will be crucial for the study of world Christianity to understand how African migration patterns influence the development of diverse and new versions of Christianity.

Migration has become one of the most controversial themes of our time. The controversy is located within a public discourse which is, on the one hand, centred around political and economic perspectives on migration, with a tendency to underline the detrimental effects on societal cohesion. On the other hand, public opinion is nourished by fears of losing cultural, national and religious identities, especially with regard to Muslim immigration. Media reports on the current refugee crisis in the Mediterranean, accompanied by political statements, portray migrants as a potential threat to European societies. Africans crossing the seas to reach safer and more prosperous lands are often perceived as strangers with illegitimate claims. This reductionist and one-dimensional perspective of the public discourse veils the dynamics of migration as a theme relevant for the study of global Christianity.

This chapter therefore intends to raise awareness of the significance of migration in relation to Christianity in Africa as a multifaceted theme. Migration is not only a socio-political phenomenon and cannot be linked exclusively to migration from the African continent to other parts of the world. It must be understood as a dynamic and multidimensional expression of intercultural encounters: among people from other regions of the world conquering, settling and interfering with local populations in Africa; among peoples within Africa; and between Africans and people outside the continent. This has a significant bearing on the understanding of Christianity as a symbolic religious system, which rests upon a narrative both particular – that is, translatable, able to migrate into different cultural contexts – and universal in outreach.

This chapter is organised with the epistemological interest to unveil the frequently underscored dynamics of migration and Christianity as it finds expression across and beyond the continent. The first part will be dedicated to an overview of the topic as part of a wider public discourse which has contributed to a reductionist perspective. Thereafter, migration and Christianity will be explored as a field of interdisciplinary analysis, which provides systematic categories for the understanding of Christian articulation on the African continent. The relevance of the topic will be shown by covering core trends in selected case vignettes, which in turn are related to analytical categories. In the concluding part, attention will be paid to how migration and Christianity in Africa can serve as a paradigm for the study of global Christianity.

## Migration as a Field of Public Discourse

Positioning migration as a topic of cross-cultural relevance for the study of Christianity in Africa demands a reflection on how it is embedded within the wider public discourse. In a historical perspective, migration seems to accentuate to various degrees and with differing emphases the public awareness of Christianity in Africa.

Northern Africa was once counted among the centres of Christianity. In the fourth and fifth centuries, Christianity moved south of Egypt to Nubia, Axum and Ethiopia, with a lasting influence even after the Muslim expansion in the seventh century. Furthermore, migration is key to understanding the nexus between the Western imperialistic expansion and simultaneous missionary endeavours, with the attempt to implant Christianity in Africa.

Protestant missions in the nineteenth century constituted another important phase, illustrating how diverse currents of migration instigated developments in the history of Christianity on the African continent. European missionary societies were motivated by a revivalist movement of the time to contribute to the spread of the gospel and the conversion of Africans. These endeavours resulted at the end of the nineteenth century in African-led missions in several regions, such as the Niger Mission of the Anglican Church Missionary Society, under the leadership of Samuel Ajayi Crowther (1809–91), the first African bishop of the Anglican Church. This initial approach to indigenise Christianity was disrupted by the beginning of the European colonial era in Africa, between 1880 and 1890. European missionary societies in West Africa pursued their activities alongside the trade-houses established on the coastline and often, although not in all cases, compromised with the colonial objective to gain economic advantages in Africa. Economic and social transformations in the twentieth century also led to larger numbers of conversions to Christianity among the indigenous population aspiring to social, economic and political status. At the same time, the emergence of African Instituted Churches, especially of the prophetic-healing type organised around charismatic leaders in Western and Southern Africa, constituted an important turning point for the appropriation of Christianity in Africa. It is noteworthy that these developments were sponsored not only by external influences, the importation of foreign worldviews, but also by internal movements. This is valid for the geographical relocations, for instance, apparent in the cross-ethnic encounters, but more importantly for the autonomous African initiatives of integrating Christianity by way of cognitive rearrangements.

In a continuation of this process of inculturation, one can observe significant cross-national migratory movements in the 1980s, which have led to the spread of neo-Pentecostal and new Charismatic churches across the continent, especially in West Africa. The diffusion of churches of this spectrum of Christianity was tied to internal African migration movements caused by economic and political crises in the sub-region in this phase and was more often than not viewed by dictatorial regimes as oppositional seedbeds. For their adherents, these churches played a crucial role in accompanying the societal transition by offering stability in an otherwise highly volatile situation and by providing plausible religious interpretations.

The emergence of migrant-led churches at the end of the twentieth and beginning of twenty-first centuries in Europe and North America represents another crucial turning point in the history of African Christianity, which shows itself as a Christian expression no longer exclusively tied to a geographical and cultural location, but as a cross-cultural and international movement with strong missionary initiatives among local populations, especially in Europe and North America, whose allegiance to Christianity African migrants often perceive as weak. These autonomous missionary initiatives from Africa to the Western world (reverse mission) not only upend prior missionary currents from the North to the global South but also are frequently accompanied by social aspirations, for instance with regard to integration in the receiving countries. The genesis and development of African-led church communities in Europe's and North America's urban centres constitute momentous historic milestones, not only for the study of Christianity and its missionary impact, but also with regard to the way religion can be used constructively as an integrating societal factor. In this regard, the second and third generations of African Christian migrants will undoubtedly determine the future shape of African Christianity outside the continent and further contribute to debates on the constructive role of religion in public space.

## Migration as an Analytical Field

We propose migration as an analytical field for the understanding of Christianity, in order to raise awareness of the dynamics global migration movements have generated and how the effects of these dynamics have transformed the religious landscape and led to scholarly attention being given to global Christianity. Three inter-related dimensions have to be considered in this regard. First, from a methodological standpoint, the research on African Christianity by African researchers needs to be taken into consideration, offering corrective insights for the assessment of intercultural encounters. Secondly, the systematic approach of researchers underlining migrant-led churches' international and cross-cultural role will have to be evaluated. And last but not least, the contribution of migration to an intercultural and ecumenical theology will have to be discussed.

Several scholars have, from different heuristic entry points, drawn attention to the significance of African agency in the spread of Christianity across the continent. Historiography has been key in this respect, securing and documenting the traces of indigenous African appropriation of Christianity. Lamin Sanneh undoubtedly has offered a pioneering contribution to research on Christianity on the African continent, by stressing that the European missionary enterprise in Africa is not a radical rupture of African identity and agency, but rather one causative factor for the visibility of Africans as autonomous agents of change. Sanneh also introduces *translatability* and *vernacularisation* of the gospel message as categories for the description of the processes of inculturation, which may be described as a form of linguistic and cultural migration in the missionary era. It is precisely by describing Christianity as a vernacular translation movement that he laid the foundation for comprehending mission as a migratory movement, which entails translation – rendition of words and meaning – and thereby opens the possibility of intercultural exchange.

The rationale of translatability can also be applied to the study of migrant-led churches, with regard to both their historical emergence and their theological enquiry. Afe Adogame, Roswith Gerloff, Gerrie ter Haar and Frieder Ludwig have shown that these churches are not to be portrayed as exceptional cases within the history of Christianity in Africa, but as an expression of how Africans have engaged with the gospel from within the concreteness of their cultural realities *and* with an openness to a debate on the universal validity of the Christian message. Researchers agree that it would be too simplistic to reduce the description of African migrant-led churches to inward-oriented communities focused on safeguarding cultural, linguistic and confessional identities. Rather, they have to be seen as international church communities operating changes in their worldviews from inside, as well as reaching out to people of different nations with the claim that their interpretation of the biblical narrative may be relevant for them too. In other words, the translatability of the gospel is tested not only within the African cultural context but also within a wider framework of plausibility and relations which global migration has provided. This framework gives evidence of profound changes in the ecclesial landscape, for instance with regard to the formation of churches and communities in the diaspora, which have no or relatively loose institutional relationships to their mother churches in Africa, although they do have relatively solid ties to international networks of migrant-led churches in other regions of the world.

This development in turn raises questions of ecumenical relevance afresh, such as how it might be possible to give witness to the one gospel without compromising the communication of the Christian message in diverse cultures. The presence of African Christians in Europe and in North America constitutes therefore a vital reminder to keep universality and particularity together as the common roots of Christianity, which enables an intercultural dialogue at eye level. Migration as an analytical field for the study of Christianity in Africa has widened the horizon of academic investigation by introducing the perspective of *inter-contextuality*. Research is no longer restricted to explorations of phenomena and developments within the continent, but pays much more attention to the ramifications of cultural and religious rearrangements instigated by movements inside and outside geographical and cultural confines.

Against this background, new methodological and heuristic instruments for the systematic analysis of migration and its implications for African Christianity need to be developed, which ultimately will help to further articulate an intercultural theology and history in an era of global Christianity. The following case vignettes are intended to represent initial explorations, without any claim of comprehensiveness, for such an innovative systematic approach.

The case vignettes are associated with different regions of the continent and aim to show the different forms of migratory dynamics in both diachronic and synchronic perspective. Therefore, immigration to Africa, internal migration movements in Africa and emigration from Africa to countries overseas will be considered. The analytic category of space is utilised to systematically structure the case vignettes according to prevailing patterns. The structure follows the rationale of contest, negotiation and creation of spaces in a cognitive more than in a spatial understanding. However, this analytical procedure does not aim to deny the restriction and limitation of access to spaces, manifested in territories, borders and settlements, as currently visible and controversially discussed in the context of national migration policies.

## Contesting Space: Migration and Mission

The example of indigenous African missionaries in the Anglican Communion is illustrative of a specific form of migrant missionary movement in the nineteenth century. It reposes on the initiatives of Creole Christians, of Yoruba descent, like Samuel Ajayi Crowther. Born in the Nigerian Oyo state, Crowther was captured at the age of 12 by slave raiders and deported to Freetown, Sierra Leone, where he was educated by the Anglican Church Missionary Society and converted to Christianity. After further studies, ministerial formation and ordination in Britain, Crowther returned to Africa in 1843, where he opened a missionary station and started translating the Bible into Yoruba. The double ethnic belonging of the Creole Christians was undoubtedly instrumental in bridging the culture clashes and conflicts of loyalty the European mission had introduced. The space of missionary encounters between peoples habitually viewed as historically and culturally disconnected was often marked by asymmetric relationships, but also by recurrent attempts on either side to surmount the conflicts. The contested space is epitomised in the fundamental question of whether it is possible to be both Yoruba and Christian. Crowther and other Creole Christians, both critically distant from and committed to the Yoruba culture, served in the process of bridging the two identities and contributed thereby to forging a positive interaction between ethnic and confessional belonging and to overcoming the limits of the contested space.

Another example of an inter-cultural encounter in the nineteenth-century missionary period in West Africa is related to the migration of European deaconesses, who came to live among Africans and to evangelise the local women in particular. Towards the end of the nineteenth century the Basel Missionary Society and the North German Missionary Society of Bremen both began to send female missionaries to the regions in which they had built missionary stations. The intention was to aid the missionary endeavour of their male counterparts and to advance the evangelisation of young girls and women. The deaconesses were not only transcending geographical borders but also challenging gender role models in both their own and the African contexts. The deaconesses of German and Swiss origin brought to their encounters with the local women in Ghana and Togo their nineteenth-century bourgeois perceptions of society, which reserved the private sphere exclusively to women and the public sphere to men. Interestingly, the deaconesses were recruited from among single women and thus constituted marginal role models both within their own society and for the African societies to which they migrated. They were professionally visible outside the private domain yet dependent on the male missionaries and – most remarkable in the West African context, where motherhood is highly valued – were not married and had no children. Both the European deaconesses and the local women contested the pre-defined gendered space. The deaconesses were able to expand the understanding of female roles in the public sphere by positioning themselves as mothers for all, and local women such as Mercy Baëta, the first African woman teacher of the local Ewe Church, promoted the visibility of African women in the public sphere also beyond their ascribed maternal role.

## Negotiating Space: Internal Migration and Belonging

A case vignette from the Southern African region will illustrate how migration can incite the negotiation and renegotiation of space in both a physical and a cognitive sense, with a significant bearing on the self-understanding of Christianity. Since 2005, many refugees, mainly from

Zimbabwe but also from other African countries such as Rwanda, Burundi and the Democratic Republic of the Congo, have come to South Africa. Several thousands of these refugees from Southern and Central Africa found a transitional home in the Central Methodist Church in Johannesburg between 2007 and 2015. The church leadership recurrently negotiated with the South African authorities the conditions for the safe space they decided to offer to the traumatised and desperate undocumented refugees, among whom were many vulnerable people, unaccompanied minors and children. Diaconal services, a school and health and educational initiatives were set up, while the worship life at the church continued. The shelter was the object of a state-led raid with arrests following the complaints of local residents and businesspeople. In 2015, the responsible clergy declared the closure of the sanctuary while refuting speculation that external pressures had provoked the decision. Although this example illustrates one, certainly extreme, form of how migrant-led Christian communities are negotiating space inside and outside the church, other examples of internal migrants in Africa, forming church communities in every metropolitan region on the continent, can complement the picture. Space is negotiated both in a real sense, by providing possibilities of at least temporary residence, and in a figurative sense, by reassessing the meaning of the Christian message in the context of uprootedness and the search for belonging.

Another region in which internal migration has had a significant impact on Christian landscapes is the frontier region of Sierra Leone and Guinea. After the civil war from 1991 to 2002, thousands of refugees fled from Sierra Leone to neighbouring countries. Guinea offered a home to these refugees, many of whom had lost family members in the war, who found a familiar environment as the same ethnic groups were located on either side of the border. Guinea provides an example of internal migration and the formation of Christian communities in a Muslim-majority country, with approximately 85% of the population being Muslim of Sunni orientation with an influence of Sufism. However, the constitution, as well as legal and executive provisions, protect religious freedom and favour a climate of religious tolerance. Recent isolated eruptions of inter-ethnic religious violence, also against Christians, indicate that the situation of inter-faith cohabitation in Guinea will demand further meticulous monitoring. Apart from the mainline churches, there have been several smaller Evangelical and Pentecostal church communities, like the Holy Fire Church in the country's capital, Conakry, that civil war refugees initiated over the past 15 years. In their initial stages of formation they primarily reached out to fellow refugees from neighbouring countries and forged a sense of belonging and community among the uprooted. The negotiation of space comes to the fore in such a context of forced migration into a predominantly Muslim society as a test of social cohesion – allowing space for everyone – across religious lines.

### Creating Space: Emigration and Integration

Other aspects of relevance to a consideration of migration as an analytical framework for African Christianity are visible in the following case vignettes on the African Christian presence in Europe. They exemplify one trend of migration from the African continent to other parts of the world, whereby Africans have found new homes mainly in Europe and spread versions of Christianity that might have been African at the origin but that have undergone considerable changes in self-understanding, ritual practice and ecumenical outreach.

The Redeemed Christian Church of God (RCCG), founded in Nigeria in 1952 by Josiah Olufemi Akindayomi (1909–80), is considered one of the largest African-led churches of neo-Pentecostal type, and has numerous overseas congregations. From an originally small ethnic church among the Yoruba, the RCCG transformed into a multi-ethnic church with branches in other West African countries like Benin, Ghana, Togo and Côte d'Ivoire but also in Burundi, Kenya, Tanzania, the Democratic Republic of the Congo, Uganda, Malawi, Zambia and South Africa. Under the leadership of Enoch A. Adeboye, a former university lecturer in mathematics and ordained pastor in the church, it has developed extended networks in Europe and the Americas, particularly in the USA and the UK, where large Nigerian communities reside, and in more recent times in Asia, the Pacific and the Middle East, where migrant workers of Nigerian descent have established congregations. Like other Pentecostal and Charismatic churches of African origin, the RCCG developed a strong international self-understanding, which began to evolve in the 1970s and can be denoted as a feature that contributed to the trans-national expansion and transmission mode of the church.

The expansion of the RCCG is connected with the strong missionary zeal of the church. Both local congregations and itinerant missionaries carry out evangelistic activities. The encounter with local host communities is experienced as an invitation to awaken the 'valley of dry bones' (Ezekiel 37), to save souls and to contribute to spiritual renewal in lands from which missionaries formerly were sent to Africa. This reverse mission, in association with assertive missionary outreach campaigns and expansionist church-planting strategies in Western countries, underlines the communicative and international character of these churches.

Another type of church community of African background deserving consideration are inter-denominational churches like the African Christian Church in Hamburg, in which members of African descent from different countries and confessions worship together in the Ghanaian Twi language and in English. This community has formed a partnership with a local, originally homogeneous German Lutheran parish, celebrating regular international gospel services with each other and holding prayer evenings, Bible studies and informal meetings. This church community has developed strong ties to the local neighbourhood and reaches out to the German population while upholding forms of liturgical practice, like night vigils, that are particularly attractive to African church members. The African Christian Church joined a humanitarian alliance in the municipality in support of refugees from the Mediterranean region and thereby undoubtedly contributed to further creating space and visibility for migrant-led Christian initiatives towards integration.

Contrary to expectation, churches founded by Africans in migrant-receiving countries have not accentuated an inward orientation around a reinterpretation of African inculturation but rather have favoured the creation of new spaces of inter-cultural encounters. The new churches seek to situate themselves in a new social setting and to find meaningful responses to questions arising out of the migration situation and which are evocative beyond the limits of kinship. These communities are able to create space for a transcultural Christian conversation, because they serve as bridge-builders, translators of the gospel message between their countries of origin and the countries in which many Africans have become more than merely transitional residents. This is particularly valid for young church members of African descent, who will shape the future understanding and practice of a migrant-initiated African Christianity.

The presence of African Christians in Europe and in North America has also led to the discovery of sharp antagonisms within a movement that is historically and theologically heterogeneous. Undoubtedly one can say that migration has fostered the exchange of different worldviews and spiritual practices, which in turn has led to a further accentuation of the theological and practical distinctions among the various communities. This holds true for issues of lifestyle, individual morality and worldview, which serve at the same time as vehicles of promoting the missionary agenda and as instruments of public visibility.

## Migration and Global Christianity

Migration's impact on the transformation of global Christianity cannot be underestimated. However, as it represents a dynamic societal factor, its ramifications for the study of Christianity demand further research. Three areas may be indicated as desirable for such complementary investigations. First, the impact of trans-national circular migration on the expression of Christianity needs more thorough analysis. How do trans-national ecclesial networks associated with such movements (for instance from Africa to Europe and back) influence the sociological, theological and ethical contours of what has hitherto been described as contextual African Christianity? This question can only be indicative for a meticulous reflection needed on the validity of concepts of inter-contextuality and transculturality. Undoubtedly, contextual expressions of Christianity have not become obsolete, but within the stream of globalisation into which Christianity is also embedded they have been complemented with counter-current articulations that transcend static geographical and cultural contexts. The debate around the plausibility of terms, ranging from migrant churches to African diaspora churches, migrant-led churches, new African churches and international churches, only insufficiently addresses this concern. An increased interaction with non-African migrant Christian communities of diverse origin will broaden the analytical perspective and help to identify concurrent and divergent trends in transculturality.

Migration also calls for attention to the way in which it contributes to the alteration of confessional identities and ecclesial self-understanding. A recurrent observation made in the context of migration is the relative fluidity that characterises confessional belonging. Believers' allegiances to their confessions of origin may loosen and lead them to join, temporarily or permanently, other denominations. Furthermore, the phenomenon of Charismatisation or Pentecostalisation of churches until recently described as 'mainline' calls for a re-examination of the classical confessional taxonomy. It seems that migration has to be identified as a driving force in two contrasting directions. On the one hand, it underlines nuances and sometimes even sharpens conflicts around divisive theological and ethical themes. On the other hand, it erases differences by accentuating, for instance, immediacy in worldview and in ritual practice. The innovation within religious traditions may here be identified with the capacity of charismatic personalities within migrant-led churches to interpret the migration experience in a plausible manner and to anchor these experiences within the biblical narrative. Therefore, what contributes to the formation of 'new African churches', and consequently also new ways of articulating Christianity by African migrants, might be more the coherence with a shared worldview across confessional divisions – for instance with regard to the interpretation of evil, the influence of spirits and the possibility of immediate empowerment – than the continuity of the confessional tradition.

Finally, questions regarding the consequences for ecumenical relations need to be posed and examined afresh. If African-led migrant churches represent an African reformatory movement, it might be worth exploring how they relate to central theological topics, among which the ecumenical vision – *that all may be one* – will deserve a particular attention. Migration not only serves as a catalyst for quantitative trends in global Christianity, for instance with regard to the statistical increase in the numbers of Christians inside and outside Africa over the decades, but will have to be taken seriously in qualitative terms. Attention will need to be given not only to the sociological factors of migration-induced transformations in global Christianity, but more so to their religious and theological content. Studies on the prospects of global Christianity have perhaps overemphasised the importance of statistics, to the detriment of a topical discussion. The scenario they portray reinforces images of clashes between religious communities rather than furthering the debate on the translatability of the different 'languages' used by Christians. This aspect will be critical for future studies in global Christianity: to identify and interpret the means by which Christians of diverse cultural backgrounds are capable of bridging the intrinsic tension between contextuality and universality that characterises Christianity. Migration can offer a new paradigmatic framework for examining global Christianity in this respect.

## Conclusion

Migration as an analytical field for the study of African Christianity cannot be separated from research into global Christianity. As much as migration is a global and dynamic societal process with multiple manifestations, the development of different versions and dialects of Christianity has to be recognised as dynamic and non-static. This essay proposes taking both strands seriously for an analysis of migration and African Christianity, as well as embedding them into a systematic framework of understanding. The categories of contesting, negotiating and creating space serve to illustrate how, alongside migration movements of divergent orientation, Christian articulation by Africans inside and outside the continent has both offered and received impulses. The resulting plethora of African versions of Christianity adds to the diversification of the global religious landscape, a development that cannot be fully understood without taking into consideration the phenomenon of migration.

Certainly, this approach does not exhaustively capture all migration-related trends in global Christianity. However, it is crucial to encourage research that creatively engages with the dynamism of inter-cultural Christian encounters in the context of migration as one of the major trends in global Christianity today.

## Bibliography

Adogame, Afe, *The African Christian Diaspora: New Currents and Emerging Trends in World Christianity* (London: Bloomsbury, 2013).

Adogame, Afe, Roswith Gerloff and Klaus Hock (eds), *Christianity in Africa and the African Diaspora: The Appropriation of a Scattered Heritage* (London: Continuum, 2008).

Olupona, Jacob K. and Regina Gemignani (eds), *African Immigrant Religions in America* (New York: New York University Press, 2007).
ter Haar, Gerrie, *Halfway to Paradise: African Christians in Europe* (Cardiff: Cardiff Academic Press, 1998).
Wild-Wood, Emma, *Migration and Christian Identity in Congo (DRC)* (Leiden: Brill, 2008).

# Conclusion

# The Future of Christianity in Sub-Saharan Africa

## Mercy Amba Oduyoye

It would be presumptuous of me to say I am telling the future. This attempt is only an educated guess arising out of my own experience of the evolution of Christianity in the space under review, my memory of the shifts as I involved myself in the study of global Christianity from the epoch of the early church through to the modern ecumenical movement. Through all this I made it my business to focus on the area of the world in which God had placed me. One's locus is critical for what one observes and what one hopes for. This concluding chapter is therefore anchored on what I have read in the preceding chapters as they illuminate my experience of Christianity in Sub-Saharan Africa since 1940, when I became aware of my being part of this development. In fact I am, by this contribution, making a wish-list, expressing what I pray for and hope will come to pass. Most germane of all, it represents what I would like to be involved in if I had the requisite talents, and therefore what I would encourage those who have the gifts to undertake. But before I launch into this dream or vision, let me say how I see the landscape before us.

Although this volume restricts its enquiry to Africa south of the Sahara, it is necessary to acknowledge the influence of North Africa as a cradle of Christianity and the source of the highly important Ethiopian Orthodoxy. This also reminds us that the story of African Christianity goes back to the conversion of the Ethiopian official recorded in the New Testament and must not be defined solely in relation to the Western Christianity that came with missionaries from the North Atlantic in the nineteenth and twentieth centuries. In surveying Christianity in Africa today and seeking to discern what might be significant for its future, this concluding chapter will consider its organisation, its social function, its interaction with the political arena, its spiritual services, developments in liturgy and spirituality, and continuing concerns.

### Organisation of Christianity in Africa

The scene as we have it at the beginning of the twenty-first century of the Christian era has developed mainly as a result of the denominationalism of North Atlantic Christianity that Africa has inherited. This has spread through the work of missionaries from the Western churches and Africans who came into contact with their preaching. The latter became independent evangelisers when they moved to new locations or were employed by Western missionary societies as catechists and evangelists. These are the people who spread Christianity in Africa by initiating and animating small cells of converts who pray, sing and listen to the Bible being read and its stories being told. These cells grow into societies and congregations and eventually into churches, either associated with existing denominations or new communities of Christians, new churches that have their own names.

Within congregations, interest groups serve the church's mission while they become home bases for the members of the church. Within congregations also are various singing groups, women's groups, men's groups and youth groups. There are groups dedicated to praying, called 'prayer warriors' in some churches. Others are constituted as visiting groups for various categories of sick, housebound or incarcerated persons. All these interest groups serve the church and Christianity and provide structures that counter the anonymity of large congregations. Africa's traditional way of organising society so that no one feels isolated has influenced this development.

Denominationalism persists and its historical causes are many. From the Coptic Church of Egypt, the Ethiopian Orthodox Church became autocephalous, and political developments resulted in the Eritrean Orthodox Church attaining autocephaly from the Coptic Orthodox Church. Thus Oriental Christianity is well represented in Africa. The Western churches in Africa multiplied following political independence in the 1960s as denominations that could not gain access to Africa for political reasons arrived. The idea of comity of missions proposed at the Edinburgh 1910 World Missionary Conference never really worked, so one finds many denominations in any one geographical location. There is no reason to assume that this trend will not continue. Like elsewhere in the world, the internal organisation of churches does get modified, but generally, national denominations are divided into 'parishes' that are under the jurisdiction of a single 'overseer'. This trend continues either from the practice of dividing existing ones or by constituting new ones from newly grown societies, but often it is to cope with the growing numbers of ordained persons with leadership skills. New parishes or dioceses create room for more bishops.

Christianity continues to grow in Africa as the number of churches increases. At the 2013 assembly of the World Council of Churches (WCC) at Busan, South Korea, almost 100 member churches from Africa were present. Beyond these are many more – Pentecostal, Charismatic and some traditional denominations that dissociate themselves from the Ecumenical movement. Many African Initiated Churches and of course the Roman Catholic Church do not belong to the WCC. Oriental Christianity in Africa has a growing diaspora, as does the Eastern Orthodox Church of Alexandria. Both have been spreading in Africa in the form of immigrant congregations but increasingly attracting nationals. This trend is bound to continue and affect the landscape of Christianity in Africa in its organisation and spirituality. As persons have acquired the tendency to do 'church shopping', in search of an amenable spiritual home where their well-being (*alafia*) will be guaranteed, forms of Christianity and church organisation will continue to multiply to serve these needs.

Churches in Africa organised according to the North Atlantic heritage of the nineteenth century are commonly known as 'mainline churches'. In my view, this designation glorifies the 'Scramble for Africa' and its parallel 'scramble' for mission fields. It is questionable whether they are 'mainline', as some of the newer African Initiated Churches outstrip them in numbers, visibility, buildings and media presence. Pentecostal/Charismatic Christianity is growing and all signs indicate that this trend will continue as they attract persons in transition, those seeking anonymity and those who are interested in their teachings and spirituality. The Christianity of 'mega' media presentations is also fast becoming the order of the day.

The African Initiated Churches have by and large avoided the ecumenical councils of the nineteenth-century denominations and have organised their own manifestations of ecclesial unity to demonstrate the oneness of Christ or have remained free-standing. Many of the mission-founded churches, following their 'mother churches', have been associated with the WCC since its formation in 1948. This form of ecumenism exists in Africa in the All Africa Conference of Churches and in various national councils of churches. Although these councils meet periodically, by and large the churches keep their own denominational counsels. They make joint statements on national issues and occasionally pray together. My hope is that they do not 'unchurch' one another in the current atmosphere of subtle and not-so-subtle competitiveness. From the mid-twentieth century, ecumenical vision fostered the establishment of joint theological education institutions, but today some of these are being discontinued in favour of denominational establishments. When churches in Africa got into tertiary education, ecumenism was thrown overboard, hence the proliferation of church-sponsored universities. This trend of denominationalism will continue as Bible schools and denominational theological institutions multiply. The saving grace is that persons from all denominations are welcome into these new church educational institutions.

There are manifestations of unity in the Christian faith community that I pray will continue to grow and increase. Such initiatives as Evangelical fellowships, ministers' fraternities, and non-denominational and inter-denominational youth fellowships are providing ecumenical relations to minimise inter-church conflicts and intra-Christian competitiveness. All these showcase Christianity as a reconciling, healing and caring faith community that has the possibility of uniting in the service of society. The risk of co-option by political entities cannot be minimised, as has been demonstrated by cases in Swaziland and Zimbabwe. On the other hand, they can serve to foster inter-religious relations, as we see in Ghana and Nigeria.

The organisation of Christianity into concert bodies of Christians is inevitable and indeed a *sine qua non* to the identity of the religion. A group that distinguishes itself by faith and practice is bound to be named and to stimulate expectations from those outside. Therefore monitoring the development of Christianity in terms of how it is organised is a worthwhile exercise. Doing it together might enable learning and developments that will promote the Christian presence in Africa.

## Christianity at Work

Christianity is a visible manifestation of God's mission on earth, the task of restoring creation and enabling human beings to reveal themselves as made in the image and likeness of the source Being, God. I have read these research pieces asking myself, 'What on earth is Christianity on earth for?' With this in mind, the attempt here is to indicate the socio-economic contribution of the church. Literacy, the symbolic representation of oral speech, has been one of the most attested contributions of Christianity to life in Africa. Ethiopian Orthodox manuscripts in Ge'ez are among the most ancient Christian literature. The nineteenth-century missions to Africa were known for their introduction of Western forms of education. Contemporary Christian churches are fully involved in education at all levels, with their doors open to all. Modern education has had an impact on political development of Africa as it has instilled the unity and dignity of humanity and hence democratic principles that one hopes will increasingly bring well-being to community life.

Christianity of the missionary period was associated with the opening of schools, at times in cooperation with the governments of the day. In this way Christianity provided a service of enabling people to acquire literary skills, first to read the Bible, but broadly to become educated. Translating the Bible meant a collaboration between foreign missionaries and local native speakers. The terminology 'reducing' spoken words into script might not be too palatable, but it is a service of Christianity that continues to serve Africa well and might develop into more lucid expressions of Christian belief in the mother tongues of Africa.

With schools also came health services, clinics and hospitals and the training of health-care providers of many types that have become the bedrock of medical services in Africa. Because Western medicine gained ascendancy over indigenous healing practices, the question is raised as to the role of Christianity in raising suspicions about them and thwarting their development. The early manifestation of Christianity in parts of Africa cast doubts upon traditional medicine, associating it with witchcraft and traditional religion, which missionaries saw as antithetical to the Christian gospel. Now that 'scientific research' has begun in the field of herbal medicine and Africans are falling over themselves to try Chinese traditional medical herbs and practices, I hope Christianity will join in rehabilitating African medical practices that are proving to be lifesaving for many. In the field of healing, too, we need to believe and work on the basis that the hand of the Divine works everywhere and among all peoples, including Africans.

Contemporary health challenges are revealing stigma as a human trait that needs to be countered and I can see Christian theology contributing positively to the creation of inclusive communities that care for all who are under the threat of exclusion. Several churches are already serving in the arena of the trauma of HIV/AIDS but are yet to face the current threat of Ebola. In the field of health care, prevention and eradication are undertaken in partnership with governments and non-governmental organisations (NGOs), but for me the change of attitudes of persons towards 'the other' is a specifically religious, and definitely a Christian, service. It is God's mission and therefore the church's duty. We do have evidence to the effect that health services have been used as a means of attracting people to a central place for the purpose of evangelising them. For Jesus, however, healing was not a means of attracting followers. Rather, it was part of his mission of turning the world right side up, part of the task of getting the world to how God wills it.

An aspect of health-care services promoted now mostly by NGOs is the campaign against harmful traditional cultural practices that impact negatively on the health of women. Some churches have tried to discourage these practices, saying they are contrary to Christian beliefs. This line of argument has sometimes backfired or been simply ignored by church members themselves. In general, little progress has been made towards minimising violence against women inherent in widowhood rites because people simply brush it off, saying 'It is our culture'. Maybe working with NGOs that approach the challenge from a human rights angle will yield positive results in the future. Pentecostal/Charismatic churches are addressing issues of witchcraft, spirit possession and curses with exorcism and other forms of deliverance ministries. An ecumenical approach to these religio-cultural challenges might yield a way forward for the mitigation of harmful practices like marriages for underage girls. The harm caused by tampering with female genitalia (commonly referred to as female genital mutilation, or FGM) for cultural reasons continues, benefiting a section of society to the detriment of others. The church must work assiduously to provide alternatives. On FGM we have the example of the Presbyterian Church in Kenya to show that Christianity can be at work in this field.

The nineteenth-century missions aimed to replace the trade in human beings with trade in other resources that abounded in Africa. This of course has resulted in the exploitation of Africa's natural resources for the benefit of the trading partners, many of whom were also the senders of Christian missionaries. This rape of Africa by North Atlantic countries is now increasingly becoming a free-for-all, thanks to the controversial principle of globalisation. There is evidence that at the beginning of this encounter some Christian missions promoted agriculture and skills in building and carpentry. Skills development and other forms of economic activity have not been the forte the churches, and yet we have the unemployment of young people as a constant issue in our sermons and prayers. The survey we have in hand shows that Christianity has not made much impact on the economy of Africa, except the negative factor of its association with those who came to exploit, to steal and to kill.

Voluntary services and charitable works by Christians and churches reach people in difficult situations throughout Africa. The changes in the traditional organisation of family life, mainly as a result of urbanisation, have impacted negatively on traditional safety nets. We have more destitute people, people living on the streets of our cities, people traumatised by conflicts of many kinds – displaced, homeless and neglected. These human conditions pose multiple and complicated challenges to Christianity in Africa and the churches face them not head-on but with lamentations and moralising rhetoric. Preaching and announcing the love of God goes some way to give hope but needs to be complemented with practical action.

'Family life' appears on the agenda of many churches, but the content stops at premarital counselling and how wives should make husbands comfortable in the marriage. The rampant increase in divorces should alert the churches that their format of family life education is defective. The child factor is often totally ignored or left to the very comfortable atmosphere of Sunday school. Families need to be empowered to mentor children. Periodic gifts to orphanages, incarcerated persons and the destitute is a Christian duty, but churches need to begin to research the causes and join in rooting out these situations that demean human dignity. After-care of formerly incarcerated persons and those rescued from forced military service, many of them children and women, is yet to attract the attention of churches and Christians in Africa.

Christianity has the potential to make a difference in these situations, as over the years Christian organisations and churches have convinced partners of their ability to deliver services at the local level. Churches are present in slums as well as in kraals and villages. People gather at least weekly and are reached with messages of hope and education for practical life. One hopes this continues and intensifies and diversifies to reach all who are in need. The research here presented gives me hope that this will happen because Christians realise that they are in God's mission and at work with God.

### Christianity in the Political Arena

In Christianity, the 'give to Caesar and to God' solution has become more and more complicated as the organisation of the community grows more and more complex. Separation of church and state served the Enlightenment process in Europe and enabled Christianity to escape from the clutches of kings and popes. It continues to be an issue in the secularisation of the North Atlantic nations. In Africa, however, the need for the church to be independent of the state does not spell secularisation. Constitutions of secular states are careful to note that although they are not aligned to any one faith community, the state is not against religion and follows the United Nations Universal Declaration of Human Rights (UDHR) to provide freedom of religion for the individual. The need for the church to be independent of the state does not necessarily spell the secularisation that leans towards atheism.

This has meant that although most states adhere to the practice of not espousing one particular religion, on occasions when heads of African states have shown signs of espousing one religion the moves have most often been nipped in the bud. Christianity is as free as all religions to develop and thrive unhindered by the state. States might or might not require the registration of religious bodies, but the tendency to give them privileges because of the services they render the people is almost universal. Although most of the nations we are surveying do not have state religions, it is our experience that, in Namibia for example, governments do consult religious leaders on major issues and in periods of crisis. This is evidence that Christianity is expected to provide effective leadership for citizens, especially for the management of crisis situations. During election years, all churches are on their knees praying for peace. Examples abound of Christianity's services in this area. Namibia, Zimbabwe, Nigeria and Ghana are obvious cases.

This contribution of Christianity to political development has been present from the beginning of missions, and schools became the locus for political debates as independence from colonial powers was being mooted.

Churches have had waves to ride when they sided with local ambitions for independence against the coloniser's struggle to stay in power. The case of churches in Malawi and their relations with white settlers is only one graphic example. Whatever the case, Christianity cannot stay out of politics, for as the Mfantse proverb goes, 'It is as the house stands that the shrine has a place to lodge'.

This places the onus on the churches of the future to present a profile of Christianity that calls for God's justice, righteousness and mercy for all humanity. The church's own integrity must be pristine. The tendency for politicians to seek theological legitimisation for their political positions cannot be pandered to by Christians. Most challenging, however, is how politicians can play one Christian community against another to get their way. This calls for vigorous ecumenical relations that enable the churches and their leaders to take their own counsel and not to be manipulated by politicians. Religious conflicts can be used to fuel political interests. This calls for churches to work together as well as to promote inter-religious dialogue so as to present a united voice from the communities of faith on controversial national issues.

The political arena is full of traps for the churches, not least being the registration of churches and the privileges that accompany being recognised and consulted. As the political landscape of Africa becomes more complex and churches continue to diversify, the practice of heads of state adopting particular churches widens and the danger of Christianity being drawn into the legitimisation of political moves becomes more and more real. Recent attempts by certain heads of state to pronounce Christianity as the national religion are worrisome, especially when taken together with the state of Christian–Muslim relations in parts of Africa and the moves of certain Muslims to gain control of politics in many parts of the world, including some African countries. This calls for both an ecumenical as well as an inter-religious approach if Africa is to be saved from more religious conflicts that aim at religious takeover of countries that make a mockery of the religious freedom entrenched in the UDHR and in national constitutions. For some years now, attention has been focused on the patterns of evangelisation because of clashes with people of other faiths arising from the language of their proclamations. We continue therefore with an examination of patterns of evangelism in Christianity.

## Spiritual Services of Christianity

To evangelise, at its roots, means to proclaim the good news of the love of God in Christ Jesus to all humanity. The proclamation is expected to elicit a response from the hearers. The Matthew 28 text on which the Church bases its mandate to evangelise specifically includes: covering the whole inhabited world (a geographical mandate), proclaiming the good news of the love of God in Jesus Christ, baptising those who believe this message and nurturing them to become followers of Jesus of Nazareth. Proclaiming the good news should be in both word and deed, as Jesus demonstrated. This means that effective evangelisation has to have both sides and I would expand 'deeds' to include attitudes, how we relate to others.

The pattern of evangelisation as discussed by African Christians focuses extensively on the preached word. Sermons are preached to the converted, who sit in church pews Sunday after Sunday, a captive audience who listen without responding unless occasionally prompted by preachers to clap for Jesus. Occasionally a call to the altar may prompt those who have been moved by the proceedings to go up front for special prayers. Many sit listening in vain for the 'word of God' for their lives. But they will come back next Sunday because of what fellowshipping with other Christians does for them.

Evangelistic outreach in the form of open-air preaching in stadia, in parks, on street corners, in marketplaces and on television has become the norm in Africa. Strategies for following up those 'touched' vary. The increase that this brings to the membership of individual congregations is a matter for research. The individual standing at the street corner or moving from village to village in Africa has been known to spawn churches, as seen in the Harris movement. Many of the city types are private entrepreneurs who expect donations from their hearers as a contribution to their 'ministry'. Teams from churches also go from door to door to share the good news. This has been the special mark of Jehovah's Witnesses, but now several youth groups of other churches are trying this 'personal encounter' format in their bid to proclaim the good news.

This form of evangelisation has become known as 'churching the unchurched'. Other forms might yield the same results. But what of the mandate to meet human needs, as we read from Matthew 25? As you have done to one human being, you have done it to God. In view of this, churches and Christians try to live out the gospel to demonstrate to the 'unchurched' what it means to be Christian.

Evangelisation that results in changing attitudes, having the mind of Christ, living lives of integrity and an ethic that can be called Christian is more difficult to evaluate. We observe this by its absence and by the fact that most preaching consists of listing 'all the evil people do' and then adding 'and yet they call themselves Christians'. The effects of evangelisation depend on how we recognise the lives of the baptised as an attempt to follow 'the Jesus way'. A prominent phenomenon since the 1960s has been the growth of African churches outside Africa, first as loosely organised gatherings of African Christians who missed the way things are done at home or do not feel welcome at local churches where they have relocated. Many of these then seek relations with their churches back in Africa and eventually get sent ministers from home and become branches of the home church. Others remain free-standing churches and many more of these are being added. Many of these diaspora African congregations attract nationals of the host countries and have become a way of showcasing African Christianity around the world. The evangelisation originally aimed at Africans who miss the home church has now become a way of drawing others to Christ.

Another development is the periodic revival events that often carry the unfortunate label of 'crusades'. Some are massive and are held in open-air neutral spaces like stadia so that all might feel invited, welcome and at home. However, they tend to become routinised in such a way that when held by single congregations they are no more than attempts at reawakening the enthusiasm of the flagging church members who might come but do not invite friends to come hear the good news being preached. The attraction of these revivals is the expectation of miraculous healing and testimonies of answered prayers. These are meant to induce faith as well as strengthen faith. People are invited to come and participate with the promise that their lives 'will never be the same'.

I do not see the churches changing any of these. What I see is that new forms will be added and contemporary ones intensified, especially in line with the development of modern communication technology. By this I am referring to disseminating the good news and building communities by such techniques. Sermons on tape, text messages and tracts might give way to these as more people come to own phones and tablets. Instead of featuring 'regular' worship services on television, maybe we shall see more religious drama carrying the good news. With each new development in media technology, the church will be challenged to disseminate the good news appropriately, but the one-on-one contact with the call 'come and see' will never fade away as coming to faith is, in the final analysis, a personal decision.

## Developments in Liturgy and Spirituality

Spirituality is an all-encompassing concept that includes what we do with our beliefs – how our faith moves us to live our lives. This is why we need to take spirituality and liturgy together. Liturgy is not only the way we worship in the church but also what the church does after the 'in-house' ritual is over. The formal services planned and mostly controlled by the church's rules and rulers are a tradition that will remain but will be shaped to respond to contemporary needs. The sacramental liturgies remain firmly in the hands of the ordained. You need ordained persons of the particular

Christian family to minister the prescribed sacraments, be they two or seven. You need ordained persons to baptise, confirm, marry and bury, although some of these may be performed *in extremis* by persons with the required dispensation from their official church. The non-sacramental liturgies are open to the leadership of the non-ordained, that is, the lay persons, and in many churches these outnumber the sacramental liturgies.

In Africa, liturgy has been freed from books. Few congregations go by liturgies read from books. By and large, Christian gatherings in Africa depend heavily on the oral and the spontaneous. Even the Eucharistic liturgies that are more formal get modified with the insertion of songs, although leaving the words of the institution intact. The vernacularisation of worship has promoted congregational participation, including much singing and dancing.

Spirituality is writ large in African Christianity. We remember how the activities of the Spirit-filled women of the early church caused 'and also the Holy Spirit' to become part of the creed of Nicea. In today's African Christianity, a church that does not exhibit 'the gifts of the Spirit', especially in the form of glossolalia and other forms of enthusiastic exhibition of one's possession of the Holy Spirit, is considered a failed church. It is, however, a source of contention as to the difference between 'possessing the Holy Spirit' and being 'possessed by the Holy Spirit'. This debate arises from interaction with African indigenous religious imagination, which can never be discounted.

One thing is certain: a person guided and counselled by the Holy Spirit lives a Christ-like life. It is this that for me is central to the concept of spirituality and its manifestation in the church and by Christians. I look for spirituality in people's will to enhance the quality of life of others as for themselves. I find spirituality where people are engaged in stamping out evil, in righting wrongs, in seeking justice and doing what is just, and where they sustain and empower those who are engaged in contending with hostile environments, both physical and psychological.

Churches and Christians feature strongly in this arena, with the care of the vulnerable in all aspects of life. Orthodox spirituality, for example, is seen in environmental rehabilitation; sanitation; hygiene; access-road construction; small-scale irrigation; care of refugees, returnees and displaced persons; infant and child feeding; and gender mainstreaming. These and many others feature in the tasks undertaken by churches in Africa. I have to observe, however, that the church's spirituality as manifested in its concern for the well-being of women falls short of the standard of Jesus Christ, as it is still ruled by the demands of traditional cultures in Africa. While Christian women are in solidarity with the church, the church tends to take this for granted and operate as if the status quo should be preserved.

My hope is that sensitivity to the welfare of women will become an agenda item for the future church in Africa.

As Jean-Marc Éla has pointed out, 'The shock of the gospel in Africa' is the 'coexistence of the gospel in Africa with the Veritable Empire of injustice and hunger'. It is this that the spirituality of the church needs to engage. Christian spirituality has the task of guarding and promoting human dignity. Spirituality as seen in the lives of Christians is expected to be holistic, as Christian life should manifest Kingdom values and communities should experience peace and reconciliation, compassion and justice. While ecstasy in worship abounds, one rightly expects enthusiasm in seeking the welfare of the vulnerable, all the vulnerable, whatever their religious faith.

## Continuing Concerns

As John Pobee reminds us, Christianity came to Africa in a spirit of fear of Islamic expansion, searching for Prester John to help halt the advance of Islam. Today, the saga deepens in Africa with Boko Haram ('all things Western are anathema', a home-grown Nigerian movement), Al-Shabaab and other so-called 'radical' Islamic groups teaming up with those who want to establish Islamic states around the world and specifically those aiming at Islamising Africa. This has generated Islamophobia, which is becoming a barrier to inter-religious relations that promote mutual respect among people of different faiths. In spite of the common boast that Christians and Muslims live side by side and take care of one another as members of the same social family, Christian–Muslim relations have not enjoyed smooth sailing in Africa, and the seeming détente of the colonial era has given way to turf wars in Uganda, Kenya, Somalia and the Central African Republic and to periodic skirmishes in Ghana and elsewhere. In all this there are Christians and Muslims who insist on an atmosphere of mutual respect and work for it. The future of Christianity depends on this fragile atmosphere of striving for dialogue as represented by the Programme for Christian–Muslim Relations in Africa (PROCMURA), based in Nairobi, Kenya. Nationally this trajectory is present in commissions set up and promoted by governments.

The challenge of living in a multi-faith environment is the lot of Africa. From the beginning, Christian missions to Africa took a stand of discontinuity vis-à-vis indigenous religions. We know that this continues but has not succeeded in eliminating beliefs and practices that are closely woven into traditional culture and appear to be simply 'social'. We are learning that the indigenous African beliefs are closely woven into the fabric of all that we call traditional African culture. Rarely do adherents of African traditional religion (ATR) present open challenges to Christians and Muslims. This appearance of acquiescence to the presence of these two 'guest religions' is deceptive. I do not know about Islam, but I can see a lot of ATR seeping into Christianity and Christianity adjusting to ATR by openly admitting to its tenets and combating some of them. The booming deliverance ministries in Christianity thrive on beliefs associated with traditional religion. The exuberance of dancing in African Christianity reflects traditional religious dances, stimulated by spirit possession known in Akan as *akom*. The fervent exhibitionism in praying, for example, is a direct legacy from ATR. But when, according to traditional beliefs, periods that demand silence and sober living are called for, then Christians who counsel abstinence during Lenten periods insist on flouting these religious exercises, calling them pagan. Yet my sense is that as Christian churches absorb erstwhile adherence to Africa's autochthonous religious imagination, so Christianity in Africa absorbs the spirituality of ATR in an unannounced way.

Awareness of the fragility of coexistence of people of diverse faiths is for me a key concern that is bound to continue into the future of the continent and the church in Africa. Socio-religious concerns arise also from the interaction between Christianity and African culture. As much of African social culture has a religious component or basis, there has been throughout the presence of Christianity on the continent a tension that has often developed into crisis. Churches have continued to encroach upon and even take over much of what was family responsibility and practice, such as naming that incorporates babies into their natural family units. Other rites of passage, especially marriage and death rites, have been Christianised or present uneasy compromises and double rites and meanings. 'Gospel and culture' issues remain with African Christianity, requiring the crafting of a theology of religion that will enable further deliberation on them.

Theological challenges have shifted from the traditional dogmatics that produced the classical Christian creeds, which we affirm without attempting to understand. For me, this is the reason for the inconsonance of words and deeds in the lives of Christians in Africa. Presently, the focus of theology in Africa seems to be on the reality and activity of Satan and a cohort of demons that thwart the well-being (*alafia*) of people and so necessitate a theology that emphasises the attributes of God or a 'demonology' that explains the machinations of Satan. What all this calls for in terms of ethics and spirituality needs spelling out, not only by experts but also by the whole community. Theology for the people crafted by the people remains a challenge. How we classify the required theology, whether moral or pastoral or any other, is for me not as crucial as what it does in terms of promoting our understanding of what we believe in order that we may live out the same.

The future of Christianity in Africa is bound to be influenced by the themes and issues of contemporary Christianity in Africa, many of which are discussed in this volume. Foremost among them is leadership formation. Leadership is a recurrent theme in all aspects of life in Africa, especially in politics. It stands to reason that it should be a challenge in Christianity too. Gender, for instance, has become and will remain a challenge not only with respect to leadership but also in all aspects of life. On this, Phiri and Kaunda in their contribution to this volume surmise that a gendered approach to African Christianity demands that we explore the injustices that exist in the church, in culture and in the appropriation of biblical text in regard to the relationship between women and men. The current fear that women's rereading of the Bible amounts to rewriting it is simply a sign that women's perspectives have not been factored into interpretation of biblical texts and that some are afraid that the hermeneutical approaches of women will undermine men's authority and power as currently experienced. I posit that since it is human beings who create culture, cultural practices in the Bible and in our own African contexts should not be construed as the will of God. Since both women and men are created in the image of God and given the responsibility to care for all creation, decisions should be a joint responsibility.

I join these scholars to advocate prioritising women's experience from now on as this has been a regularly ignored factor in decision-making. Subjugation of women has been the norm on this continent and few interrogate cultural masculinity. They add that we need not fear to enter the controversy around same-sex relations, as human sexuality is an aspect of the factor of gender, which currently is being interpreted as the power relations between women and men. They hope that we shall outgrow the homophobic stance, with its tendency to castigate its existence among women while pussy-footing around the occurrence among men. It is my hope that we can remain open to the possibility of developing a culture that protects difference in sexual orientation rather than let the current situation shift into gear to make same-sex relations a death sentence. The growth of pastoral theology might help face the challenge of human sexuality in Africa. It is my hope that gender sensitivity will become a task for the African church and all African Christians and that we shall overcome deeply ingrained sexist attitudes.

Church women's organisations are particularly vibrant on this continent and mostly in solidarity with the church, especially taking care of the needs of clergy. Mostly they are co-opted by the church and their energies directed to enhance its mission. I know of only one church that refuses to have a separate women's organisation. But I know of many that succeed in bringing the women to heel when suspected of too much independence. The core issue for the future is how to live in the church as a community of women and men, all called to be Christ to the world. It is my hope that the church will promote theological education for women so that its deficiency among women does not remain a reason for excluding them from the leadership of the entire church while at the same time curbing their leadership in their own women's organisations.

Where leadership is discussed, the participation of women and young people is bound to feature. Today we recognise that young people are not waiting in the wings to become leaders of tomorrow. They are leaders today, and their needs and deeds shape our life together where they do not actually take the lead or dictate the terms. The original role of Sunday schools was to promote literacy and they became a parallel institution for the Christian education of young people. This format will need remodelling and revitalising, as very little of the educational material used in these schools is created in Africa. Children in these schools are nurtured on Bible stories, compete in learning memory verses and once a year present themselves during a week set aside for them to lead the church service. This does not look like a dynamic way of Christianising young minds. The future of the church cannot hang on this. Hopefully the church will struggle to transform its ministry with children and children's ministry in the church.

There was a period in Africa when the ecumenical movement called attention to urban and rural ministry. This made sense then, but today many of the new churches are concentrated in urban areas. Ministry specific to the needs of rural Africa has fallen behind. Christianity is fast becoming an urban religion, albeit occasional forays into rural areas to donate much-needed clothing and occasional contributions towards building churches. Services to rural areas in terms of daily needs have been left to other organisations. Who is actually preaching the good news in rural Africa is not clear to me, so I have to ask a question here: Is the future of Christianity in Africa to depend on urban and peri-urban areas, where people crave deliverance and prosperity? Race, class and gender are all continuing challenges of the church in Africa. So are the constant socio-political conflicts that disrupt life – land rights, the drying up of groundwater and other environmental challenges that plague Africa. Who brings good news? Economic challenges and wars drive Africans through the desert into the Mediterranean. But who is reading and rereading the Bible? In all of this we depend on the Bible to guide us through.

With globalisation and the exploitative brainwashing strategies that accompany the practice of religion, one cannot discount the growth of scepticism and secularism in Africa. But whatever happens to Christianity in Africa, it is certain that the Bible will remain its Holy Book. Nobody will dare rewrite it, but many will find the need to reread it. I have listened to lessons drawn from biblical texts that turn the events on their heads.

Depending on the circumstances of preachers and hearers, the Bible can be made to dispense either life-giving or death-dealing verdicts. Being available to most in their mother tongue, and in various other languages and more and more revised and modernised versions, the Bible and quotes from it are available to all and are on the lips of all. Therefore we cannot ignore its presence in the future of Christianity and what it will mean for Christianity in Africa. The explosion of Christianity in Africa has been attributed in part to the vernacularisation of its Holy Book. The final issue to which I would like to call attention is therefore the contribution of Chris Manus.

From pulpits in churches, on radio and on television, in myriads of Bible study groups, through text messages and songs, insights from the Bible are transmitted in Africa. The challenge here, as Manus notes, is that wisdom is derived directly from the text without reference to the original context of the biblical narrative. Scholarship on the text is totally ignored. Added to this is the fact that few read the Bible in its original languages, and we all know that translations are never 'entirely innocent'. Scholarship in this area is waning in Africa. For me, the critical factor is that most of the African translations are made from modern European languages and few resort to the original biblical languages and the critical apparatus that went into the European translations. My hope is that the church and the theological academies will see fit to remedy this lapse. They cannot shirk this task if the future of Christianity in Africa is to remain authentically biblical.

Lyrics, theology in song and 'gospels' all derive directly from biblical texts and events. Thus the narrative theology in song that we experience in church keeps people mindful of biblical and Christian teaching. Contemporary Christianity is awash with a belief in the spirit world. Every event and happening to individuals and communities is believed to have a spiritual provenance. Pastors derive their interpretations and counselling related to them from the Bible. The manifestation of 'spirit possession' as experienced in the autochthonous religious imagination is now present in the church, especially during 'crusades', revivals and other special events like 'all-night' sessions of prayer and deliverance. The Bible is used to authenticate these exhibitions and 'prayer warriors' are always at hand to banish the spirits that war against the faith and the well-being of the faithful.

In Africa the Bible is everywhere and in all hands. People boast of the number of Bibles that they have placed strategically in their homes, offices and cars. The Bible has become for them a talisman. As more and more mother-tongue Bibles are on the way, and the Bible societies ensure that they are affordable, the prevalence and power of the Bible will remain a major aspect of the profile of Christianity in Africa. With Bible in hand and the Blood of Jesus as their weapon, African Christians will continue to demonstrate the hold that Christianity has on Africa. They constitute the content of Christian preaching and counselling and with the power of the Holy Spirit at work in the church and in the individuals all is brought to fruition to the Glory of God.

## Conclusion

I have tried to base my view of the future of Christianity in Africa on the content of this volume and my own experience of 80 years in the church. It has not been possible for me to touch every chapter, as I have tried to stay close to my own experience and what I see or wish for the future of Christianity in Africa. My concluding remark is also personal. I have learnt from the vagaries of church history that the church belongs to God and that it is that factor alone that keeps it in the world. For this reason the church and for that matter Christianity will remain a part of the African landscape for as long as God needs it to be. Today, Christianity should be accepted as one of the 'traditional religions' of Africa. Having existed on the continent for over two millennia, it deserves no less an accolade.

## Bibliography

Asamoah-Gyadu, J. Kwabena, *Contemporary Pentecostal Christianity: Interpretations from an African Context* (Oxford: Regnum Books International, 2013).

Gifford, Paul, *African Christianity: Its Public Role* (Bloomington, IN: Indiana University Press, 1998).

Hanciles, Jehu H., *Beyond Christendom: Globalization, African Migration, and the Transformation of the West* (Maryknoll, NY: Orbis Books, 2008).

Jenkins, Philip, *The Next Christendom: The Coming of Global Christianity*, 3rd edn (Oxford: Oxford University Press, 2011).

Phiri, Isabel A. and Sarojini Nadar (eds), *African Women, Religion and Health: Essays in Honor of Mercy Amba Ewudziwa Oduyoye* (Maryknoll, NY: Orbis Books, 2006).

# Appendices

# Christianity by Country

The table that begins overleaf provides a quick-reference, country-by-country listing for Christianity and its major traditions for all the countries that appear in this volume. These statistics are found in the *World Christian Database* (see Methodology and Sources) and all figures relate to 1970 and 2015. Small numbers are left unrounded to distinguish known small populations from zero but do not represent precise estimates.

The columns are as follows:

- Country (name of country in English)
- Region of Africa in which country is located
- Total population of country (United Nations estimate, 1970, 2015)
- Tradition – total number of Christians and percentage of national population that is Christian, 1970, 2015 (and then separately for each tradition, as ordered by size in 2015 – Anglicans, Independents, Orthodox, Protestants, Roman Catholics – and finally Christian movements found in all previous traditions – Evangelicals, Pentecostals/Charismatics, shortened to 'Pentecostal' for the table)
- Percentage mean annual growth rate, 1970–2015.

The last page of the table presents regional totals.

| Country | Region | Tradition | 1970 Population | 1970 % | 2015 Population | 2015 % | Growth rate (%), 1970–2015 |
|---|---|---|---|---|---|---|---|
| Angola | Middle Africa | Total population | 6,301,000 | 100.0% | 25,022,000 | 100.0% | 3.1% |
| | | Christians | 4,700,000 | 74.6% | 23,223,000 | 92.8% | 3.6% |
| | | Roman Catholics | 2,667,000 | 42.3% | 14,558,000 | 58.2% | 3.8% |
| | | Protestants | 415,000 | 6.6% | 6,195,000 | 24.8% | 6.2% |
| | | Independents | 62,300 | 1.0% | 1,027,000 | 4.1% | 6.4% |
| | | Anglicans | 2,000 | 0.0% | 42,100 | 0.2% | 7.0% |
| | | Pentecostals | 66,100 | 1.1% | 5,216,000 | 20.9% | 10.2% |
| | | Evangelicals | 199,000 | 3.2% | 4,523,000 | 18.1% | 7.2% |
| Benin | Western Africa | Total population | 2,908,000 | 100.0% | 10,880,000 | 100.0% | 3.0% |
| | | Christians | 515,000 | 17.7% | 4,818,000 | 44.3% | 5.1% |
| | | Roman Catholics | 394,000 | 13.5% | 2,480,000 | 22.8% | 4.2% |
| | | Independents | 41,400 | 1.4% | 1,344,000 | 12.4% | 8.0% |
| | | Protestants | 52,600 | 1.8% | 1,074,000 | 9.9% | 6.9% |
| | | Pentecostals | 44,500 | 1.5% | 2,090,000 | 19.2% | 8.9% |
| | | Evangelicals | 52,700 | 1.8% | 993,000 | 9.1% | 6.7% |
| Botswana | Southern Africa | Total population | 693,000 | 100.0% | 2,262,000 | 100.0% | 2.7% |
| | | Christians | 259,000 | 37.4% | 1,585,000 | 70.0% | 4.1% |
| | | Independents | 45,200 | 6.5% | 969,000 | 42.8% | 7.0% |
| | | Protestants | 102,000 | 14.7% | 231,000 | 10.2% | 1.8% |
| | | Roman Catholics | 21,200 | 3.1% | 88,200 | 3.9% | 3.2% |
| | | Anglicans | 7,000 | 1.0% | 10,000 | 0.4% | 0.8% |
| | | Orthodox | 50 | 0.0% | 80 | 0.0% | 1.1% |
| | | Pentecostals | 47,300 | 6.8% | 1,042,000 | 46.1% | 7.1% |
| | | Evangelicals | 22,700 | 3.3% | 119,000 | 5.3% | 3.8% |
| Burkina Faso | Western Africa | Total population | 5,625,000 | 100.0% | 18,106,000 | 100.0% | 2.6% |
| | | Christians | 523,000 | 9.3% | 4,223,000 | 23.3% | 4.8% |
| | | Roman Catholics | 416,000 | 7.4% | 2,576,000 | 14.2% | 4.1% |
| | | Protestants | 97,000 | 1.7% | 1,980,000 | 10.9% | 6.9% |
| | | Independents | 7,100 | 0.1% | 88,800 | 0.5% | 5.8% |
| | | Pentecostals | 89,100 | 1.6% | 2,033,000 | 11.2% | 7.2% |
| | | Evangelicals | 95,800 | 1.7% | 1,907,000 | 10.5% | 6.9% |
| Burundi | Eastern Africa | Total population | 3,457,000 | 100.0% | 11,179,000 | 100.0% | 2.6% |
| | | Christians | 2,579,000 | 74.6% | 10,438,000 | 93.4% | 3.2% |
| | | Roman Catholics | 2,108,000 | 61.0% | 6,543,000 | 58.5% | 2.6% |
| | | Protestants | 147,000 | 4.2% | 1,549,000 | 13.9% | 5.4% |
| | | Anglicans | 45,000 | 1.3% | 1,080,000 | 9.7% | 7.3% |
| | | Independents | 1,600 | 0.1% | 293,000 | 2.6% | 12.2% |
| | | Orthodox | 1,000 | 0.0% | 2,200 | 0.0% | 1.8% |
| | | Evangelicals | 124,000 | 3.6% | 1,854,000 | 16.6% | 6.2% |
| | | Pentecostals | 98,000 | 2.8% | 1,643,000 | 14.7% | 6.5% |

| Country | Region | Tradition | 1970 Population | 1970 % | 2015 Population | 2015 % | Growth rate (%), 1970–2015 |
|---|---|---|---|---|---|---|---|
| Cameroon | Middle Africa | Total population | 6,771,000 | 100.0% | 23,344,000 | 100.0% | 2.8% |
| | | Christians | 3,152,000 | 46.6% | 13,781,000 | 59.0% | 3.3% |
| | | Roman Catholics | 1,529,000 | 22.6% | 5,679,000 | 24.3% | 3.0% |
| | | Protestants | 753,000 | 11.1% | 4,706,000 | 20.2% | 4.2% |
| | | Independents | 105,000 | 1.6% | 1,808,000 | 7.7% | 6.5% |
| | | Anglicans | 0 | 0.0% | 2,100 | 0.0% | 12.6% |
| | | Orthodox | 1,000 | 0.0% | 1,200 | 0.0% | 0.4% |
| | | Pentecostals | 97,100 | 1.4% | 2,678,000 | 11.5% | 7.7% |
| | | Evangelicals | 235,000 | 3.5% | 1,431,000 | 6.1% | 4.1% |
| Cape Verde | Western Africa | Total population | 270,000 | 100.0% | 521,000 | 100.0% | 1.5% |
| | | Christians | 269,000 | 99.5% | 494,000 | 94.9% | 1.4% |
| | | Roman Catholics | 259,000 | 95.7% | 468,000 | 89.9% | 1.3% |
| | | Independents | 250 | 0.1% | 38,500 | 7.4% | 11.8% |
| | | Protestants | 8,200 | 3.0% | 19,000 | 3.7% | 1.9% |
| | | Pentecostals | 10 | 0.0% | 39,200 | 7.5% | 20.2% |
| | | Evangelicals | 7,800 | 2.9% | 10,100 | 1.9% | 0.6% |
| Central African Republic | Middle Africa | Total population | 1,829,000 | 100.0% | 4,900,000 | 100.0% | 2.2% |
| | | Christians | 1,162,000 | 63.6% | 3,578,000 | 73.0% | 2.5% |
| | | Roman Catholics | 278,000 | 15.2% | 1,590,000 | 32.5% | 4.0% |
| | | Independents | 217,000 | 11.9% | 884,000 | 18.0% | 3.2% |
| | | Protestants | 223,000 | 12.2% | 819,000 | 16.7% | 2.9% |
| | | Evangelicals | 484,000 | 26.5% | 1,359,000 | 27.7% | 2.3% |
| | | Pentecostals | 101,000 | 5.5% | 935,000 | 19.1% | 5.1% |
| Chad | Middle Africa | Total population | 3,645,000 | 100.0% | 14,037,000 | 100.0% | 3.0% |
| | | Christians | 843,000 | 23.1% | 4,939,000 | 35.2% | 4.0% |
| | | Roman Catholics | 231,000 | 6.3% | 2,154,000 | 15.4% | 5.1% |
| | | Protestants | 211,000 | 5.8% | 1,450,000 | 10.3% | 4.4% |
| | | Independents | 36,900 | 1.0% | 667,000 | 4.8% | 6.6% |
| | | Evangelicals | 263,000 | 7.2% | 1,630,000 | 11.6% | 4.1% |
| | | Pentecostals | 12,100 | 0.3% | 896,000 | 6.4% | 10.1% |
| Comoros | Eastern Africa | Total population | 228,000 | 100.0% | 788,000 | 100.0% | 2.8% |
| | | Christians | 1,500 | 0.7% | 4,000 | 0.5% | 2.2% |
| | | Roman Catholics | 1,100 | 0.5% | 2,400 | 0.3% | 1.8% |
| | | Protestants | 330 | 0.1% | 1,200 | 0.2% | 3.0% |
| | | Independents | 30 | 0.0% | 250 | 0.0% | 4.8% |
| | | Evangelicals | 23 | 0.0% | 430 | 0.1% | 6.8% |
| | | Pentecostals | 9 | 0.0% | 280 | 0.0% | 8.0% |
| Republic of the Congo | Middle Africa | Total population | 1,335,000 | 100.0% | 4,620,000 | 100.0% | 2.8% |
| | | Christians | 1,224,000 | 91.7% | 4,127,000 | 89.3% | 2.7% |
| | | Roman Catholics | 399,000 | 29.9% | 3,190,000 | 69.0% | 4.7% |
| | | Independents | 126,000 | 9.4% | 574,000 | 12.4% | 3.4% |
| | | Protestants | 177,000 | 13.3% | 489,000 | 10.6% | 2.3% |
| | | Orthodox | 300 | 0.0% | 440 | 0.0% | 0.9% |
| | | Pentecostals | 89,000 | 6.7% | 945,000 | 20.5% | 5.4% |
| | | Evangelicals | 118,000 | 8.9% | 225,000 | 4.9% | 1.4% |

| Country | Region | Tradition | 1970 Population | 1970 % | 2015 Population | 2015 % | Growth rate (%), 1970–2015 |
|---|---|---|---|---|---|---|---|
| Democratic Republic of the Congo | Middle Africa | Total population | 20,010,000 | 100.0% | 77,267,000 | 100.0% | 3.1% |
| | | Christians | 17,960,000 | 89.8% | 73,384,000 | 95.0% | 3.2% |
| | | Roman Catholics | 9,908,000 | 49.5% | 41,565,000 | 53.8% | 3.2% |
| | | Independents | 4,711,000 | 23.5% | 20,612,000 | 26.7% | 3.3% |
| | | Protestants | 3,921,000 | 19.6% | 13,561,000 | 17.6% | 2.8% |
| | | Anglicans | 100,000 | 0.5% | 581,000 | 0.8% | 4.0% |
| | | Orthodox | 7,000 | 0.0% | 13,600 | 0.0% | 1.5% |
| | | Pentecostals | 4,818,000 | 24.1% | 23,769,000 | 30.8% | 3.6% |
| | | Evangelicals | 1,349,000 | 6.7% | 5,230,000 | 6.8% | 3.1% |
| Côte d'Ivoire | Western Africa | Total population | 5,242,000 | 100.0% | 22,702,000 | 100.0% | 3.3% |
| | | Christians | 1,348,000 | 25.7% | 7,920,000 | 34.9% | 4.0% |
| | | Roman Catholics | 627,000 | 12.0% | 4,404,000 | 19.4% | 4.4% |
| | | Protestants | 149,000 | 2.8% | 2,214,000 | 9.8% | 6.2% |
| | | Independents | 309,000 | 5.9% | 1,564,000 | 6.9% | 3.7% |
| | | Orthodox | 3,000 | 0.1% | 67,300 | 0.3% | 7.2% |
| | | Pentecostals | 59,100 | 1.1% | 2,407,000 | 10.6% | 8.6% |
| | | Evangelicals | 63,000 | 1.2% | 2,064,000 | 9.1% | 8.1% |
| Djibouti | Eastern Africa | Total population | 160,000 | 100.0% | 888,000 | 100.0% | 3.9% |
| | | Christians | 12,000 | 7.5% | 11,100 | 1.3% | −0.2% |
| | | Roman Catholics | 11,000 | 6.9% | 7,300 | 0.8% | −0.9% |
| | | Orthodox | 800 | 0.5% | 2,300 | 0.3% | 2.3% |
| | | Protestants | 200 | 0.1% | 720 | 0.1% | 2.9% |
| | | Independents | 0 | 0.0% | 340 | 0.0% | 8.1% |
| | | Pentecostals | 0 | 0.0% | 440 | 0.1% | 8.8% |
| | | Evangelicals | 40 | 0.0% | 350 | 0.0% | 4.9% |
| Equatorial Guinea | Middle Africa | Total population | 291,000 | 100.0% | 845,000 | 100.0% | 2.4% |
| | | Christians | 257,000 | 88.3% | 746,000 | 88.3% | 2.4% |
| | | Roman Catholics | 231,000 | 79.3% | 684,000 | 80.9% | 2.4% |
| | | Independents | 6,400 | 2.2% | 33,200 | 3.9% | 3.7% |
| | | Protestants | 14,800 | 5.1% | 28,700 | 3.4% | 1.5% |
| | | Pentecostals | 440 | 0.2% | 45,600 | 5.4% | 10.8% |
| | | Evangelicals | 7,400 | 2.6% | 18,100 | 2.2% | 2.0% |
| Eritrea | Eastern Africa | Total population | 1,805,000 | 100.0% | 5,228,000 | 100.0% | 2.4% |
| | | Christians | 857,000 | 47.5% | 2,433,000 | 46.5% | 2.4% |
| | | Orthodox | 761,000 | 42.1% | 2,203,000 | 42.2% | 2.4% |
| | | Roman Catholics | 75,000 | 4.2% | 165,000 | 3.2% | 1.8% |
| | | Protestants | 10,100 | 0.6% | 56,300 | 1.1% | 3.9% |
| | | Independents | 3,100 | 0.2% | 24,000 | 0.5% | 4.7% |
| | | Pentecostals | 700 | 0.0% | 140,000 | 2.7% | 12.5% |
| | | Evangelicals | 6,400 | 0.4% | 34,400 | 0.7% | 3.8% |

| Country | Region | Tradition | 1970 Population | 1970 % | 2015 Population | 2015 % | Growth rate (%), 1970–2015 |
|---|---|---|---|---|---|---|---|
| Ethiopia | Eastern Africa | Total population | 28,415,000 | 100.0% | 99,391,000 | 100.0% | 2.8% |
| | | Christians | 15,005,000 | 52.8% | 58,574,000 | 58.9% | 3.1% |
| | | Orthodox | 11,077,000 | 39.0% | 39,001,000 | 39.2% | 2.8% |
| | | Protestants | 717,000 | 2.5% | 16,714,000 | 16.8% | 7.3% |
| | | Independents | 134,000 | 0.5% | 2,383,000 | 2.4% | 6.6% |
| | | Roman Catholics | 62,500 | 0.2% | 937,000 | 0.9% | 6.2% |
| | | Anglicans | 3,000 | 0.0% | 690 | 0.0% | −3.2% |
| | | Evangelicals | 809,000 | 2.9% | 14,159,000 | 14.3% | 6.6% |
| | | Pentecostals | 213,000 | 0.8% | 10,889,000 | 11.0% | 9.1% |
| Gabon | Middle Africa | Total population | 590,000 | 100.0% | 1,725,000 | 100.0% | 2.4% |
| | | Christians | 518,000 | 87.8% | 1,461,000 | 84.7% | 2.3% |
| | | Roman Catholics | 290,000 | 49.2% | 949,000 | 55.0% | 2.7% |
| | | Independents | 63,000 | 10.7% | 283,000 | 16.4% | 3.4% |
| | | Protestants | 92,000 | 15.6% | 197,000 | 11.4% | 1.7% |
| | | Pentecostals | 3,500 | 0.6% | 163,000 | 9.5% | 8.9% |
| | | Evangelicals | 20,200 | 3.4% | 47,800 | 2.8% | 1.9% |
| Gambia | Western Africa | Total population | 447,000 | 100.0% | 1,991,000 | 100.0% | 3.4% |
| | | Christians | 14,500 | 3.2% | 91,200 | 4.6% | 4.2% |
| | | Roman Catholics | 9,300 | 2.1% | 58,500 | 2.9% | 4.2% |
| | | Independents | 820 | 0.2% | 15,000 | 0.8% | 6.7% |
| | | Protestants | 1,600 | 0.4% | 10,900 | 0.6% | 4.4% |
| | | Anglicans | 2,000 | 0.5% | 3,000 | 0.2% | 0.9% |
| | | Orthodox | 100 | 0.0% | 600 | 0.0% | 4.1% |
| | | Pentecostals | 510 | 0.1% | 19,400 | 1.0% | 8.4% |
| | | Evangelicals | 720 | 0.2% | 5,500 | 0.3% | 4.6% |
| Ghana | Western Africa | Total population | 8,597,000 | 100.0% | 27,410,000 | 100.0% | 2.6% |
| | | Christians | 4,344,000 | 50.5% | 17,625,000 | 64.3% | 3.2% |
| | | Protestants | 944,000 | 11.0% | 7,044,000 | 25.7% | 4.6% |
| | | Independents | 1,306,000 | 15.2% | 5,811,000 | 21.2% | 3.4% |
| | | Roman Catholics | 1,167,000 | 13.6% | 3,401,000 | 12.4% | 2.4% |
| | | Anglicans | 100,000 | 1.2% | 289,000 | 1.1% | 2.4% |
| | | Orthodox | 1,000 | 0.0% | 4,600 | 0.0% | 3.5% |
| | | Pentecostals | 1,409,000 | 16.4% | 10,237,000 | 37.4% | 4.5% |
| | | Evangelicals | 420,000 | 4.9% | 5,564,000 | 20.3% | 5.9% |
| Guinea | Western Africa | Total population | 4,215,000 | 100.0% | 12,609,000 | 100.0% | 2.5% |
| | | Christians | 55,400 | 1.3% | 490,000 | 3.9% | 5.0% |
| | | Roman Catholics | 48,400 | 1.2% | 304,000 | 2.4% | 4.2% |
| | | Protestants | 3,100 | 0.1% | 109,000 | 0.9% | 8.2% |
| | | Independents | 1,800 | 0.0% | 38,500 | 0.3% | 7.0% |
| | | Anglicans | 2,000 | 0.1% | 1,400 | 0.0% | −0.8% |
| | | Evangelicals | 3,600 | 0.1% | 107,000 | 0.9% | 7.8% |
| | | Pentecostals | 1,200 | 0.0% | 74,200 | 0.6% | 9.7% |

| Country | Region | Tradition | 1970 Population | 1970 % | 2015 Population | 2015 % | Growth rate (%), 1970–2015 |
|---|---|---|---|---|---|---|---|
| Guinea-Bissau | Western Africa | Total population | 712,000 | 100.0% | 1,844,000 | 100.0% | 2.1% |
| | | Christians | 66,800 | 9.4% | 225,000 | 12.2% | 2.7% |
| | | Roman Catholics | 59,600 | 8.4% | 191,000 | 10.4% | 2.6% |
| | | Independents | 0 | 0.0% | 45,400 | 2.5% | 20.6% |
| | | Protestants | 2,500 | 0.4% | 29,100 | 1.6% | 5.6% |
| | | Anglicans | 200 | 0.0% | 290 | 0.0% | 0.8% |
| | | Pentecostals | 0 | 0.0% | 56,000 | 3.0% | 21.1% |
| | | Evangelicals | 2,500 | 0.4% | 26,300 | 1.4% | 5.3% |
| Kenya | Eastern Africa | Total population | 11,252,000 | 100.0% | 46,050,000 | 100.0% | 3.2% |
| | | Christians | 7,058,000 | 62.7% | 37,275,000 | 81.0% | 3.8% |
| | | Protestants | 1,631,000 | 14.5% | 13,249,000 | 28.8% | 4.8% |
| | | Roman Catholics | 1,936,000 | 17.2% | 10,625,000 | 23.1% | 3.9% |
| | | Independents | 1,670,000 | 14.8% | 7,548,000 | 16.4% | 3.4% |
| | | Anglicans | 583,000 | 5.2% | 6,000,000 | 13.0% | 5.3% |
| | | Orthodox | 248,000 | 2.2% | 695,000 | 1.5% | 2.3% |
| | | Pentecostals | 1,171,000 | 10.4% | 14,153,000 | 30.7% | 5.7% |
| | | Evangelicals | 1,855,000 | 16.5% | 13,048,000 | 28.3% | 4.4% |
| Lesotho | Southern Africa | Total population | 1,032,000 | 100.0% | 2,135,000 | 100.0% | 1.6% |
| | | Christians | 841,000 | 81.5% | 1,967,000 | 92.1% | 1.9% |
| | | Roman Catholics | 411,000 | 39.8% | 1,106,000 | 51.8% | 2.2% |
| | | Protestants | 224,000 | 21.7% | 425,000 | 19.9% | 1.4% |
| | | Independents | 63,100 | 6.1% | 227,000 | 10.7% | 2.9% |
| | | Anglicans | 80,000 | 7.8% | 115,000 | 5.4% | 0.8% |
| | | Pentecostals | 67,100 | 6.5% | 379,000 | 17.8% | 3.9% |
| | | Evangelicals | 49,500 | 4.8% | 172,000 | 8.1% | 2.8% |
| Liberia | Western Africa | Total population | 1,420,000 | 100.0% | 4,503,000 | 100.0% | 2.6% |
| | | Christians | 395,000 | 27.9% | 1,857,000 | 41.2% | 3.5% |
| | | Independents | 137,000 | 9.7% | 719,000 | 16.0% | 3.8% |
| | | Protestants | 120,000 | 8.5% | 577,000 | 12.8% | 3.6% |
| | | Roman Catholics | 23,700 | 1.7% | 349,000 | 7.8% | 6.2% |
| | | Anglicans | 11,000 | 0.8% | 43,200 | 1.0% | 3.1% |
| | | Pentecostals | 99,800 | 7.0% | 691,000 | 15.3% | 4.4% |
| | | Evangelicals | 75,300 | 5.3% | 369,000 | 8.2% | 3.6% |
| Madagascar | Eastern Africa | Total population | 6,576,000 | 100.0% | 24,235,000 | 100.0% | 2.9% |
| | | Christians | 3,326,000 | 50.6% | 14,079,000 | 58.1% | 3.3% |
| | | Protestants | 1,351,000 | 20.5% | 7,206,000 | 29.7% | 3.8% |
| | | Roman Catholics | 1,595,000 | 24.3% | 6,220,000 | 25.7% | 3.1% |
| | | Independents | 146,000 | 2.2% | 1,179,000 | 4.9% | 4.8% |
| | | Anglicans | 50,400 | 0.8% | 450,000 | 1.9% | 5.0% |
| | | Orthodox | 540 | 0.0% | 32,600 | 0.1% | 9.5% |
| | | Evangelicals | 318,000 | 4.8% | 1,868,000 | 7.7% | 4.0% |
| | | Pentecostals | 60,400 | 0.9% | 1,603,000 | 6.6% | 7.6% |

| Country | Region | Tradition | 1970 Population | 1970 % | 2015 Population | 2015 % | Growth rate (%), 1970–2015 |
|---|---|---|---|---|---|---|---|
| Malawi | Eastern Africa | Total population | 4,604,000 | 100.0% | 17,215,000 | 100.0% | 3.0% |
| | | Christians | 2,664,000 | 57.9% | 13,735,000 | 79.8% | 3.7% |
| | | Roman Catholics | 993,000 | 21.6% | 5,901,000 | 34.3% | 4.0% |
| | | Protestants | 960,000 | 20.9% | 4,972,000 | 28.9% | 3.7% |
| | | Independents | 249,000 | 5.4% | 2,406,000 | 14.0% | 5.2% |
| | | Anglicans | 76,500 | 1.7% | 331,000 | 1.9% | 3.3% |
| | | Orthodox | 1,000 | 0.0% | 3,600 | 0.0% | 2.9% |
| | | Pentecostals | 103,000 | 2.2% | 3,711,000 | 21.6% | 8.3% |
| | | Evangelicals | 304,000 | 6.6% | 3,045,000 | 17.7% | 5.3% |
| Mali | Western Africa | Total population | 5,949,000 | 100.0% | 17,600,000 | 100.0% | 2.4% |
| | | Christians | 85,200 | 1.4% | 527,000 | 3.0% | 4.1% |
| | | Roman Catholics | 60,700 | 1.0% | 411,000 | 2.3% | 4.3% |
| | | Protestants | 20,100 | 0.3% | 102,000 | 0.6% | 3.7% |
| | | Independents | 320 | 0.0% | 17,400 | 0.1% | 9.3% |
| | | Evangelicals | 20,400 | 0.3% | 112,000 | 0.6% | 3.9% |
| | | Pentecostals | 45 | 0.0% | 31,600 | 0.2% | 15.7% |
| Mauritania | Western Africa | Total population | 1,149,000 | 100.0% | 4,068,000 | 100.0% | 2.9% |
| | | Christians | 6,200 | 0.5% | 10,000 | 0.3% | 1.1% |
| | | Roman Catholics | 6,200 | 0.5% | 5,000 | 0.1% | −0.5% |
| | | Independents | 0 | 0.0% | 2,300 | 0.1% | 12.9% |
| | | Protestants | 40 | 0.0% | 1,200 | 0.0% | 7.8% |
| | | Anglicans | 0 | 0.0% | 1,200 | 0.0% | 11.2% |
| | | Pentecostals | 0 | 0.0% | 2,600 | 0.1% | 13.2% |
| | | Evangelicals | 40 | 0.0% | 1,300 | 0.0% | 8.0% |
| Mauritius | Eastern Africa | Total population | 826,000 | 100.0% | 1,273,000 | 100.0% | 1.0% |
| | | Christians | 296,000 | 35.9% | 422,000 | 33.2% | 0.8% |
| | | Roman Catholics | 280,000 | 33.9% | 267,000 | 21.0% | −0.1% |
| | | Protestants | 5,900 | 0.7% | 149,000 | 11.7% | 7.5% |
| | | Independents | 2,900 | 0.4% | 19,200 | 1.5% | 4.3% |
| | | Anglicans | 8,000 | 1.0% | 5,200 | 0.4% | −1.0% |
| | | Pentecostals | 1,600 | 0.2% | 312,000 | 24.5% | 12.5% |
| | | Evangelicals | 3,000 | 0.4% | 142,000 | 11.2% | 8.9% |
| Mayotte | Eastern Africa | Total population | 37,000 | 100.0% | 240,000 | 100.0% | 4.3% |
| | | Christians | 360 | 1.0% | 1,400 | 0.6% | 3.0% |
| | | Independents | 0 | 0.0% | 650 | 0.3% | 9.7% |
| | | Roman Catholics | 260 | 0.7% | 510 | 0.2% | 1.5% |
| | | Protestants | 100 | 0.3% | 180 | 0.1% | 1.3% |
| | | Pentecostals | 0 | 0.0% | 400 | 0.2% | 8.5% |
| | | Evangelicals | 25 | 0.1% | 150 | 0.1% | 4.0% |

| Country | Region | Tradition | 1970 Population | 1970 % | 2015 Population | 2015 % | Growth rate (%), 1970–2015 |
|---|---|---|---|---|---|---|---|
| Mozambique | Eastern Africa | Total population | 9,262,000 | 100.0% | 27,978,000 | 100.0% | 2.5% |
| | | Christians | 2,611,000 | 28.2% | 14,818,000 | 53.0% | 3.9% |
| | | Roman Catholics | 1,553,000 | 16.8% | 6,409,000 | 22.9% | 3.2% |
| | | Independents | 99,300 | 1.1% | 3,684,000 | 13.2% | 8.4% |
| | | Protestants | 378,000 | 4.1% | 3,567,000 | 12.8% | 5.1% |
| | | Anglicans | 45,000 | 0.5% | 149,000 | 0.5% | 2.7% |
| | | Orthodox | 2,000 | 0.0% | 710 | 0.0% | −2.3% |
| | | Pentecostals | 142,000 | 1.5% | 5,445,000 | 19.5% | 8.4% |
| | | Evangelicals | 285,000 | 3.1% | 2,826,000 | 10.1% | 5.2% |
| Namibia | Southern Africa | Total population | 780,000 | 100.0% | 2,459,000 | 100.0% | 2.6% |
| | | Christians | 709,000 | 90.9% | 2,232,000 | 90.8% | 2.6% |
| | | Protestants | 402,000 | 51.5% | 1,487,000 | 60.5% | 3.0% |
| | | Roman Catholics | 116,000 | 14.9% | 517,000 | 21.0% | 3.4% |
| | | Independents | 63,900 | 8.2% | 297,000 | 12.1% | 3.5% |
| | | Anglicans | 20,000 | 2.6% | 75,000 | 3.1% | 3.0% |
| | | Pentecostals | 37,300 | 4.8% | 384,000 | 15.6% | 5.3% |
| | | Evangelicals | 67,400 | 8.6% | 325,000 | 13.2% | 3.6% |
| Niger | Western Africa | Total population | 4,497,000 | 100.0% | 19,899,000 | 100.0% | 3.4% |
| | | Christians | 16,900 | 0.4% | 66,600 | 0.3% | 3.1% |
| | | Protestants | 2,500 | 0.1% | 23,900 | 0.1% | 5.2% |
| | | Roman Catholics | 13,400 | 0.3% | 22,400 | 0.1% | 1.2% |
| | | Independents | 1,100 | 0.0% | 19,900 | 0.1% | 6.7% |
| | | Pentecostals | 510 | 0.0% | 31,800 | 0.2% | 9.6% |
| | | Evangelicals | 2,400 | 0.1% | 22,100 | 0.1% | 5.0% |
| Nigeria | Western Africa | Total population | 56,132,000 | 100.0% | 182,202,000 | 100.0% | 2.7% |
| | | Christians | 21,469,000 | 38.3% | 84,133,000 | 46.2% | 3.1% |
| | | Independents | 3,234,000 | 5.8% | 32,156,000 | 17.7% | 5.2% |
| | | Protestants | 3,959,000 | 7.0% | 31,106,000 | 17.1% | 4.7% |
| | | Roman Catholics | 3,890,000 | 6.9% | 22,938,000 | 12.6% | 4.0% |
| | | Anglicans | 2,941,000 | 5.2% | 22,000,000 | 12.1% | 4.6% |
| | | Orthodox | 2,500 | 0.0% | 49,500 | 0.0% | 6.9% |
| | | Pentecostals | 3,768,000 | 6.7% | 54,198,000 | 29.8% | 6.1% |
| | | Evangelicals | 5,416,000 | 9.7% | 36,712,000 | 20.2% | 4.4% |
| Réunion | Eastern Africa | Total population | 462,000 | 100.0% | 861,000 | 100.0% | 1.4% |
| | | Christians | 446,000 | 96.6% | 754,000 | 87.5% | 1.2% |
| | | Roman Catholics | 428,000 | 92.7% | 684,000 | 79.4% | 1.1% |
| | | Protestants | 2,200 | 0.5% | 57,400 | 6.7% | 7.5% |
| | | Independents | 1,000 | 0.2% | 11,400 | 1.3% | 5.6% |
| | | Pentecostals | 800 | 0.2% | 88,000 | 10.2% | 11.0% |
| | | Evangelicals | 1,200 | 0.3% | 53,800 | 6.2% | 8.8% |

| Country | Region | Tradition | 1970 Population | 1970 % | 2015 Population | 2015 % | Growth rate (%), 1970–2015 |
|---|---|---|---|---|---|---|---|
| Rwanda | Eastern Africa | Total population | 3,755,000 | 100.0% | 11,610,000 | 100.0% | 2.5% |
| | | Christians | 2,298,000 | 61.2% | 10,624,000 | 91.5% | 3.5% |
| | | Roman Catholics | 1,684,000 | 44.9% | 5,402,000 | 46.5% | 2.6% |
| | | Protestants | 332,000 | 8.8% | 2,238,000 | 19.3% | 4.3% |
| | | Anglicans | 162,000 | 4.3% | 1,550,000 | 13.4% | 5.2% |
| | | Independents | 23,200 | 0.6% | 1,118,000 | 9.6% | 9.0% |
| | | Orthodox | 500 | 0.0% | 1,500 | 0.0% | 2.5% |
| | | Evangelicals | 226,000 | 6.0% | 2,344,000 | 20.2% | 5.3% |
| | | Pentecostals | 98,700 | 2.6% | 2,202,000 | 19.0% | 7.1% |
| Saint Helena | Western Africa | Total population | 4,900 | 100.0% | 4,000 | 100.0% | −0.5% |
| | | Christians | 4,900 | 99.4% | 3,800 | 95.8% | −0.6% |
| | | Anglicans | 4,000 | 81.9% | 3,200 | 80.8% | −0.5% |
| | | Independents | 100 | 2.1% | 660 | 16.7% | 4.3% |
| | | Protestants | 400 | 8.1% | 490 | 12.4% | 0.5% |
| | | Roman Catholics | 0 | 0.0% | 110 | 2.8% | 5.5% |
| | | Pentecostals | 0 | 0.0% | 1,000 | 25.8% | 10.8% |
| | | Evangelicals | 140 | 2.9% | 130 | 3.4% | −0.1% |
| São Tomé and Príncipe | Middle Africa | Total population | 74,300 | 100.0% | 190,000 | 100.0% | 2.1% |
| | | Christians | 72,200 | 97.2% | 183,000 | 96.0% | 2.1% |
| | | Roman Catholics | 62,700 | 84.5% | 151,000 | 79.3% | 2.0% |
| | | Independents | 2,000 | 2.7% | 16,400 | 8.6% | 4.8% |
| | | Protestants | 1,000 | 1.4% | 15,800 | 8.3% | 6.3% |
| | | Pentecostals | 900 | 1.2% | 26,800 | 14.1% | 7.8% |
| | | Evangelicals | 820 | 1.1% | 10,200 | 5.4% | 5.8% |
| Senegal | Western Africa | Total population | 4,218,000 | 100.0% | 15,129,000 | 100.0% | 2.9% |
| | | Christians | 229,000 | 5.4% | 805,000 | 5.3% | 2.8% |
| | | Roman Catholics | 183,000 | 4.3% | 761,000 | 5.0% | 3.2% |
| | | Independents | 5,500 | 0.1% | 28,200 | 0.2% | 3.7% |
| | | Protestants | 4,100 | 0.1% | 16,000 | 0.1% | 3.1% |
| | | Anglicans | 100 | 0.0% | 250 | 0.0% | 2.1% |
| | | Pentecostals | 6,500 | 0.2% | 60,200 | 0.4% | 5.1% |
| | | Evangelicals | 2,700 | 0.1% | 11,600 | 0.1% | 3.3% |
| Seychelles | Eastern Africa | Total population | 52,400 | 100.0% | 96,500 | 100.0% | 1.4% |
| | | Christians | 51,500 | 98.3% | 91,300 | 94.7% | 1.3% |
| | | Roman Catholics | 45,300 | 86.5% | 78,300 | 81.2% | 1.2% |
| | | Anglicans | 3,900 | 7.5% | 5,300 | 5.5% | 0.7% |
| | | Protestants | 250 | 0.5% | 4,400 | 4.5% | 6.6% |
| | | Independents | 100 | 0.2% | 860 | 0.9% | 4.9% |
| | | Pentecostals | 0 | 0.0% | 5,300 | 5.5% | 15.0% |
| | | Evangelicals | 840 | 1.6% | 4,200 | 4.4% | 3.7% |

| Country | Region | Tradition | 1970 Population | 1970 % | 2015 Population | 2015 % | Growth rate (%), 1970–2015 |
|---|---|---|---|---|---|---|---|
| Sierra Leone | Western Africa | Total population | 2,514,000 | 100.0% | 6,453,000 | 100.0% | 2.1% |
| | | Christians | 218,000 | 8.7% | 856,000 | 13.3% | 3.1% |
| | | Roman Catholics | 47,500 | 1.9% | 354,000 | 5.5% | 4.6% |
| | | Protestants | 97,800 | 3.9% | 323,000 | 5.0% | 2.7% |
| | | Independents | 21,000 | 0.8% | 178,000 | 2.8% | 4.9% |
| | | Anglicans | 25,000 | 1.0% | 21,800 | 0.3% | −0.3% |
| | | Orthodox | 500 | 0.0% | 520 | 0.0% | 0.1% |
| | | Pentecostals | 19,700 | 0.8% | 238,000 | 3.7% | 5.7% |
| | | Evangelicals | 32,200 | 1.3% | 167,000 | 2.6% | 3.7% |
| Somalia | Eastern Africa | Total population | 3,445,000 | 100.0% | 10,787,000 | 100.0% | 2.6% |
| | | Christians | 4,900 | 0.1% | 3,200 | 0.0% | −1.0% |
| | | Protestants | 550 | 0.0% | 1,300 | 0.0% | 1.9% |
| | | Orthodox | 250 | 0.0% | 1,000 | 0.0% | 3.1% |
| | | Independents | 80 | 0.0% | 400 | 0.0% | 3.6% |
| | | Anglicans | 200 | 0.0% | 220 | 0.0% | 0.2% |
| | | Roman Catholics | 3,800 | 0.1% | 90 | 0.0% | −8.0% |
| | | Evangelicals | 610 | 0.0% | 460 | 0.0% | −0.6% |
| | | Pentecostals | 16 | 0.0% | 350 | 0.0% | 7.1% |
| South Africa | Southern Africa | Total population | 22,503,000 | 100.0% | 54,490,000 | 100.0% | 2.0% |
| | | Christians | 17,181,000 | 76.4% | 44,690,000 | 82.0% | 2.2% |
| | | Independents | 4,698,000 | 20.9% | 22,240,000 | 40.8% | 3.5% |
| | | Protestants | 6,464,000 | 28.7% | 10,464,000 | 19.2% | 1.1% |
| | | Roman Catholics | 1,589,000 | 7.1% | 3,722,000 | 6.8% | 1.9% |
| | | Anglicans | 1,236,000 | 5.5% | 2,850,000 | 5.2% | 1.9% |
| | | Orthodox | 30,000 | 0.1% | 30,100 | 0.1% | 0.0% |
| | | Pentecostals | 4,358,000 | 19.4% | 26,330,000 | 48.3% | 4.1% |
| | | Evangelicals | 2,898,000 | 12.9% | 5,337,000 | 9.8% | 1.4% |
| South Sudan | Eastern Africa | Total population | 3,647,000 | 100.0% | 12,340,000 | 100.0% | 2.8% |
| | | Christians | 721,000 | 19.8% | 7,462,000 | 60.5% | 5.3% |
| | | Roman Catholics | 627,000 | 17.2% | 6,110,000 | 49.5% | 5.2% |
| | | Anglicans | 210,000 | 5.8% | 1,750,000 | 14.2% | 4.8% |
| | | Protestants | 6,300 | 0.2% | 1,493,000 | 12.1% | 12.9% |
| | | Independents | 3,800 | 0.1% | 71,400 | 0.6% | 6.7% |
| | | Orthodox | 1,000 | 0.0% | 3,000 | 0.0% | 2.5% |
| | | Evangelicals | 109,000 | 3.0% | 1,639,000 | 13.3% | 6.2% |
| | | Pentecostals | 3,100 | 0.1% | 778,000 | 6.3% | 13.1% |
| Swaziland | Southern Africa | Total population | 446,000 | 100.0% | 1,287,000 | 100.0% | 2.4% |
| | | Christians | 300,000 | 67.3% | 1,137,000 | 88.3% | 3.0% |
| | | Independents | 88,200 | 19.8% | 619,000 | 48.1% | 4.4% |
| | | Protestants | 65,300 | 14.6% | 137,000 | 10.6% | 1.7% |
| | | Roman Catholics | 34,000 | 7.6% | 58,000 | 4.5% | 1.2% |
| | | Anglicans | 3,600 | 0.8% | 28,000 | 2.2% | 4.6% |
| | | Pentecostals | 86,800 | 19.5% | 649,000 | 50.5% | 4.6% |
| | | Evangelicals | 60,700 | 13.6% | 157,000 | 12.2% | 2.1% |

| Country | Region | Tradition | 1970 Population | 1970 % | 2015 Population | 2015 % | Growth rate (%), 1970–2015 |
|---|---|---|---|---|---|---|---|
| Tanzania | Eastern Africa | Total population | 13,606,000 | 100.0% | 53,470,000 | 100.0% | 3.1% |
| | | Christians | 5,008,000 | 36.8% | 29,584,000 | 55.3% | 4.0% |
| | | Roman Catholics | 2,807,000 | 20.6% | 15,367,000 | 28.7% | 3.9% |
| | | Protestants | 1,068,000 | 7.9% | 11,870,000 | 22.2% | 5.5% |
| | | Anglicans | 386,000 | 2.8% | 3,630,000 | 6.8% | 5.1% |
| | | Independents | 234,000 | 1.7% | 1,138,000 | 2.1% | 3.6% |
| | | Orthodox | 9,000 | 0.1% | 13,300 | 0.0% | 0.9% |
| | | Evangelicals | 753,000 | 5.5% | 8,337,000 | 15.6% | 5.5% |
| | | Pentecostals | 336,000 | 2.5% | 5,491,000 | 10.3% | 6.4% |
| Togo | Western Africa | Total population | 2,116,000 | 100.0% | 7,305,000 | 100.0% | 2.8% |
| | | Christians | 584,000 | 27.6% | 3,495,000 | 47.8% | 4.1% |
| | | Roman Catholics | 428,000 | 20.2% | 1,934,000 | 26.5% | 3.4% |
| | | Protestants | 66,500 | 3.1% | 1,121,000 | 15.4% | 6.5% |
| | | Independents | 36,300 | 1.7% | 238,000 | 3.3% | 4.3% |
| | | Pentecostals | 38,300 | 1.8% | 981,000 | 13.4% | 7.5% |
| | | Evangelicals | 14,200 | 0.7% | 671,000 | 9.2% | 8.9% |
| Uganda | Eastern Africa | Total population | 9,446,000 | 100.0% | 39,032,000 | 100.0% | 3.2% |
| | | Christians | 6,429,000 | 68.1% | 32,958,000 | 84.4% | 3.7% |
| | | Roman Catholics | 3,395,000 | 35.9% | 16,242,000 | 41.6% | 3.5% |
| | | Anglicans | 1,291,000 | 13.7% | 14,250,000 | 36.5% | 5.5% |
| | | Protestants | 111,000 | 1.2% | 2,016,000 | 5.2% | 6.7% |
| | | Independents | 260,000 | 2.8% | 1,323,000 | 3.4% | 3.7% |
| | | Orthodox | 11,200 | 0.1% | 30,500 | 0.1% | 2.3% |
| | | Pentecostals | 326,000 | 3.5% | 8,396,000 | 21.5% | 7.5% |
| | | Evangelicals | 698,000 | 7.4% | 7,364,000 | 18.9% | 5.4% |
| Zambia | Eastern Africa | Total population | 4,185,000 | 100.0% | 16,212,000 | 100.0% | 3.1% |
| | | Christians | 2,825,000 | 67.5% | 13,858,000 | 85.5% | 3.6% |
| | | Roman Catholics | 923,000 | 22.1% | 5,339,000 | 32.9% | 4.0% |
| | | Protestants | 296,000 | 7.1% | 5,144,000 | 31.7% | 6.6% |
| | | Independents | 844,000 | 20.2% | 2,924,000 | 18.0% | 2.8% |
| | | Anglicans | 85,000 | 2.0% | 294,000 | 1.8% | 2.8% |
| | | Orthodox | 5,200 | 0.1% | 7,700 | 0.1% | 0.9% |
| | | Pentecostals | 293,000 | 7.0% | 3,676,000 | 22.7% | 5.8% |
| | | Evangelicals | 239,000 | 5.7% | 2,939,000 | 18.1% | 5.7% |
| Zimbabwe | Eastern Africa | Total population | 5,206,000 | 100.0% | 15,603,000 | 100.0% | 2.5% |
| | | Christians | 2,719,000 | 52.2% | 12,740,000 | 81.7% | 3.5% |
| | | Independents | 704,000 | 13.5% | 6,516,000 | 41.8% | 5.1% |
| | | Protestants | 730,000 | 14.0% | 3,338,000 | 21.4% | 3.4% |
| | | Roman Catholics | 557,000 | 10.7% | 1,983,000 | 12.7% | 2.9% |
| | | Anglicans | 153,000 | 2.9% | 420,000 | 2.7% | 2.3% |
| | | Orthodox | 8,000 | 0.2% | 5,400 | 0.0% | −0.9% |
| | | Pentecostals | 604,000 | 11.6% | 6,944,000 | 44.5% | 5.6% |
| | | Evangelicals | 282,000 | 5.4% | 1,191,000 | 7.6% | 3.3% |

| Region | Tradition | 1970 Population | 1970 % | 2015 Population | 2015 % | Growth rate (%), 1970–2015 |
|---|---|---|---|---|---|---|
| Eastern Africa | Total population | 110,428,000 | 100.0% | 394,477,000 | 100.0% | 2.9% |
| | Christians | 54,913,000 | 49.7% | 259,865,000 | 65.9% | 3.5% |
| | Roman Catholics | 19,085,000 | 17.3% | 88,281,000 | 22.4% | 3.5% |
| | Protestants | 7,747,000 | 7.0% | 73,626,000 | 18.7% | 5.1% |
| | Orthodox | 12,126,000 | 11.0% | 42,002,000 | 10.7% | 2.8% |
| | Independents | 4,377,000 | 4.0% | 30,641,000 | 7.8% | 4.4% |
| | Anglicans | 3,102,000 | 2.8% | 29,915,000 | 7.6% | 5.2% |
| | Pentecostals | 3,451,000 | 3.1% | 65,478,000 | 16.6% | 6.8% |
| | Evangelicals | 6,013,000 | 5.5% | 60,851,000 | 15.4% | 5.3% |
| Middle Africa | Total population | 40,846,000 | 100.0% | 151,952,000 | 100.0% | 3.0% |
| | Christians | 29,888,000 | 73.2% | 125,422,000 | 82.5% | 3.2% |
| | Roman Catholics | 15,596,000 | 38.2% | 70,520,000 | 46.4% | 3.4% |
| | Protestants | 5,807,000 | 14.2% | 27,460,000 | 18.1% | 3.5% |
| | Independents | 5,330,000 | 13.1% | 25,904,000 | 17.1% | 3.6% |
| | Anglicans | 102,000 | 0.3% | 625,000 | 0.4% | 4.1% |
| | Orthodox | 8,300 | 0.0% | 15,200 | 0.0% | 1.4% |
| | Pentecostals | 5,188,000 | 12.7% | 34,675,000 | 22.8% | 4.3% |
| | Evangelicals | 2,676,000 | 6.6% | 14,476,000 | 9.5% | 3.8% |
| Southern Africa | Total population | 25,454,000 | 100.0% | 62,634,000 | 100.0% | 2.0% |
| | Christians | 19,291,000 | 75.8% | 51,611,000 | 82.4% | 2.2% |
| | Independents | 4,958,000 | 19.5% | 24,352,000 | 38.9% | 3.6% |
| | Protestants | 7,257,000 | 28.5% | 12,743,000 | 20.4% | 1.3% |
| | Roman Catholics | 2,171,000 | 8.5% | 5,490,000 | 8.8% | 2.1% |
| | Anglicans | 1,347,000 | 5.3% | 3,078,000 | 4.9% | 1.9% |
| | Orthodox | 30,100 | 0.1% | 30,200 | 0.1% | 0.0% |
| | Pentecostals | 4,597,000 | 18.1% | 28,786,000 | 46.0% | 4.2% |
| | Evangelicals | 3,098,000 | 12.2% | 6,110,000 | 9.8% | 1.5% |
| Western Africa | Total population | 106,015,000 | 100.0% | 353,224,000 | 100.0% | 2.7% |
| | Christians | 30,143,000 | 28.4% | 127,638,000 | 36.1% | 3.3% |
| | Protestants | 5,529,000 | 5.2% | 45,752,000 | 13.0% | 4.8% |
| | Independents | 5,102,000 | 4.8% | 42,306,000 | 12.0% | 4.8% |
| | Roman Catholics | 7,632,000 | 7.2% | 40,655,000 | 11.5% | 3.8% |
| | Anglicans | 3,085,000 | 2.9% | 22,363,000 | 6.3% | 4.5% |
| | Orthodox | 7,100 | 0.0% | 123,000 | 0.0% | 6.5% |
| | Pentecostals | 5,537,000 | 5.2% | 73,190,000 | 20.7% | 5.9% |
| | Evangelicals | 6,209,000 | 5.9% | 48,743,000 | 13.8% | 4.7% |
| Sub-Saharan Africa | Total population | 282,743,000 | 100.0% | 962,287,000 | 100.0% | 2.8% |
| | Christians | 134,235,000 | 47.5% | 564,536,000 | 58.7% | 3.2% |
| | Roman Catholics | 44,483,000 | 15.7% | 204,946,000 | 21.3% | 3.5% |
| | Protestants | 26,339,000 | 9.3% | 159,582,000 | 16.6% | 4.1% |
| | Independents | 19,767,000 | 7.0% | 123,202,000 | 12.8% | 4.2% |
| | Anglicans | 7,635,000 | 2.7% | 55,982,000 | 5.8% | 4.5% |
| | Orthodox | 12,172,000 | 4.3% | 42,170,000 | 4.4% | 2.8% |
| | Pentecostals | 18,772,000 | 6.6% | 202,128,000 | 21.0% | 5.4% |
| | Evangelicals | 17,997,000 | 6.4% | 130,179,000 | 13.5% | 4.5% |

# Methodology and Sources of Christian and Religious Affiliation

## Todd M. Johnson and Gina A. Zurlo

Unless otherwise designated, the demographic figures in this book, both in the full colour section and in the tables throughout, are from the *World Christian Database* (Boston, MA: Brill). This essay offers a concise explanation of methods and sources related to the database. It is adapted from longer treatments in Todd M. Johnson and Brian J. Grim, *The World's Religions in Figures: An Introduction to International Religious Demography* (Oxford: Wiley-Blackwell, 2013) and David B. Barrett and Todd M. Johnson, *World Christian Trends* (Pasadena, CA: William Carey Library, 2001). The *World Christian Database* (*WCD*) includes detailed information on 45,000 Christian denominations and on religions in every country of the world. Extensive data are available on 234 countries and 13,000 ethno-linguistic peoples, as well as on 5,000 cities and 3,000 provinces. Information is readily available on religious activities, growth rates, religious literature, worker activity and demographics. Sources are evaluated and reviewed on a weekly basis by a professional staff dedicated to expanding and updating the *WCD*, and the database is updated quarterly.

### The Right to Profess One's Choice

The starting point of this methodology is the United Nations 1948 Universal Declaration of Human Rights, Article 18:

> Everyone has the right to freedom of thought, conscience and religion; this right includes freedom to change his religion or belief, and freedom, either alone or in community with others and in public or private, to manifest his religion or belief in teaching, practice, worship and observance.

Since its promulgation, this group of phrases has been incorporated into the state constitutions of a large number of countries across the world. This fundamental right also includes the right to claim the religion of one's choice, and the right to be called a follower of that religion and to be enumerated as such. The section on religious freedom in the constitutions of very many nations uses the exact words of the Universal Declaration, and many countries instruct their census personnel to observe this principle. Public declaration must therefore be taken seriously when endeavouring to survey the extent of religious and non-religious affiliation around the world.

## Religious Demography

The origins of the field of religious demography lie in the church censuses conducted in most European societies. For many years and in many countries, churches produced the most complete censuses of the population. They achieved this largely by recording baptisms and funerals. These data, however, were seen not as referring to specific religious communities, but rather to the larger homogeneous societies. With the decline of national churches in Europe beginning in the nineteenth and continuing into the twentieth century, governments began tracking births and deaths, eventually replacing churches as the main bodies collecting detailed information on human populations. Although thousands of sources for international religious demography are available, ranging from censuses and demographic surveys to statistics collected and reported by religious groups themselves, little has been done by scholars in religion, sociology, or other disciplines to collect, collate and analyse these data.

## Sources

Data for religious demography fall broadly under five major headings:

### *1. Censuses in which a religious question is asked*

In the twentieth century, approximately half the world's countries asked a question related to religion in their official national population censuses. Since 1990, however, this number has been declining as developing countries have dropped the question, deeming it too expensive (in many countries each question in a census costs well over US$1 million), uninteresting or controversial. As a result, some countries that historically included a religion question have not done so in their censuses since 1990. National censuses are the best starting point for the identification of religious adherents, because they generally cover the entire population.

### *2. Censuses in which an ethnicity or language question is asked*

In the absence of a question on religion, another helpful piece of information from a census is ethnicity or language. This is especially true when a particular ethnic group can be equated with a particular religion. For example, over 99% of Somalis are Muslim, so the number of Somalis in, say, Sweden is an indication of a part of the Muslim community there. Similarly, a question that asks for country of birth can be useful. If the answer is 'Nepal' there is a significant chance that the individual or community is Hindu. In each of these cases the assumption is made (if there is no further information) that the religion of the transplanted ethnic or linguistic community is the same as that in the home country.

*3. Surveys and polls*

In the absence of census data on religion, large-scale demographic surveys such as MEASURE (Monitoring and Evaluation to Assess and Use Results) and Demographic and Health Surveys (DHS) often include a question about the respondent's religious affiliation. In some instances, demographic surveys by groups such as UNICEF (the United Nations Children's Fund) include a religious affiliation question. Demographic surveys, although less comprehensive than a national census, have several advantages over other types of general population surveys and polls. Demographic and Health Surveys (DHS) are highly regarded by demographers and social scientists, and provide valuable nationally representative data on religion. Surveys can also be commissioned in light of a dearth of data on a particular subject and results can be used to search for correlations between different variables.

*4. Scholarly monographs*

Every year, scholars publish hundreds of monographs on particular religions or religions in particular countries or regions. Such monographs differ from other sources in that they attempt to provide an overall profile of religion in an area or country, bringing to light local sources of quantitative data as well as qualitative information that provides layers of context and background.

*5. Religion statistics in yearbooks and handbooks*

Religious communities keep track of their members, using everything from simple lists to elaborate membership reports. The most detailed data collection and analysis is undertaken each year by some 45,000 Christian denominations and their 4.7 million constituent churches and congregations of believers. The latter invest over US$1.1 billion annually for a massive, decentralised and largely uncoordinated global census of Christians. In sum, they send out around 10 million printed questionnaires in 3,000 different languages, covering 180 major religious subjects reporting on 2,000 socio-religious variables. This collection of data provides a year-by-year snapshot of the progress or decline of Christianity's diverse movements, offering an enormous body of data from which researchers can track trends and make projections. Statistics collected by religious communities often enable researchers to distinguish between two categories of religionists – practising and non-practising – based on whether or not they take part in the ongoing organised life of the religion.

In addition to the above categories, there are governmental statistical reports, questionnaires and reports from collaborators, field surveys and interviews, correspondence with national informants, unpublished documentation, encyclopaedias, dictionaries and directories of religions, print and web-based contemporary descriptions of religions, and dissertations and theses on religion. The best practices in determining the religious affiliation of any population utilise as many sources as possible.

## Affiliation

There are at least two different perspectives on what it means to be a Christian: professing Christians and affiliated Christians. Utilising the United Nations Universal Declaration of Human Rights as a foundation, 'professing Christians' means all those who profess to be Christians in government censuses or public-opinion polls, that is, who declare or identify themselves as Christians, who say 'I am a Christian' or 'We are Christians' when asked the question 'What is your religion?'

However, not all those who profess to be Christians are affiliated to organised churches and denominations. Therefore, 'affiliated Christians' are those known to the churches or known to the clergy (usually by names and addresses) and claimed in their statistics, that is, those enrolled on the churches' books or records, with totals that can be substantiated. This usually means all known baptised Christians and their children, and other adherents; it is sometimes termed the 'total Christian community' (because affiliated Christians are those who are not primarily individual Christians but who primarily belong to the corporate community of Christ), or 'inclusive membership' (because affiliated Christians are church members). This definition of 'Christians' is what the churches usually mean by the term (and thus the *WCD*), and statistics on such affiliated Christians are what the churches themselves collect and publish. In all countries, it may be assumed with confidence that the churches know better than the state how many Christians are affiliated to them. This therefore indicates a second measure of the total Christians that is quite independent of the first (government census figures of professing Christians).

## Children

The family is by far the most important instrumentality through which individuals acquire personal, cultural and social self-identification. In consequence, children of church members are more likely to remain members than those whose parents are not church members. Children of ardent and practising Christians usually are, to the extent that their years permit, ardent and practising Christians. However, many churches do not enumerate children under 15 years. One reason is that it has been widely noted that most conversion crises occur in the 13–20-year age group in Christian families or in majority Christian contexts. On this view, therefore, children who have not yet reached 15 cannot reasonably be expected to be practising and believing Christians. The *WCD* takes the opposite view: children and infants also can properly be called Christians, and can actively and regularly (to the extent of their ability) practise the Christian faith. Consequently, where Christian denominations do not count children in their membership rolls, their membership is reported in our adult category. A total community figure is calculated (in the absence of any additional information from the denomination) by adding in the average number of children reported in United Nations statistics for the given country. Thus, the total community figures are comparable from one denomination to the next whether or not they count children in their membership.

### Choice of Best Data Available

Religious demography must attempt to be comprehensive. In certain countries where no hard statistical data or reliable surveys are available, researchers have to rely on the informed estimates of experts in the area and subject. Researchers make no detailed attempt at a critique of each nation's censuses and polls or each church's statistical operations. After examining what is available, researchers then select the best data available until such time as better data come into existence. In addition, there are a number of areas of religious life where it is impossible to obtain accurate statistics, usually because of state opposition to particular tradition(s). Thus it will probably never be possible to get exact numbers of, for example, atheists in Indonesia or Baha'i in Iran. Where such information is necessary, reasonable and somewhat conservative estimates are made.

### Reconciling Discrepancies in Survey Data

There are post-survey strategies that help general population surveys better reflect the actual composition of a particular country. For instance, if in a survey of 1,000 people, 60% were women and 40% were men, but we know that women and men are each 50% of the country's total population based on a recent census, then each woman's response on the general population survey would be weighted down by a factor of 500/600 and each man's response would be weighted up by a factor of 500/400. Such adjustments are called weighting.

Other adjustments made to general population surveys may require taking into account that they are meant to be representative of only adult populations. Therefore their results require adjustments, particularly if some religious groups have more children than others in the same country. This requires either a complete roster of members of each household or some other way to estimate of the number of children living in the household with the adults. When a complete roster is unavailable, most estimates of religious affiliation of children assume that they have the same religion as their one of their parents (usually assumed by demographers to be the religion of the mother). Differences in fertility rates between religious groups are particularly useful in estimating religious differentials among children. This is because demographic projections carry forward children born to women. It may introduce some bias to the degree that the father's religion is more likely to be the religion of the children than the mother.

*Example: Coptic Church in Egypt*

At times, the results from government censuses and information from religious communities can be strikingly different. For example, in Egypt, where the vast majority of the population is Muslim, government censuses taken every 10 years have shown consistently for the past 100 years that a declining share of the population declare themselves as or profess to be Christians. In the most recent census, some 5% identified as Christian. However, church estimates point to a percentage figure three times larger (15%). This discrepancy may be due to overestimates by the churches or attributed, at least in part, to social pressure on some Christians to record themselves as Muslims. Further, according to news reports, some Egyptian Christians have complained that they are listed on official identity cards as Muslims. It also might be that church reports include Egyptian Christians working as expatriates outside of Egypt, while the census does not, or that the churches simply overestimate their numbers.

Such a lack of clarity is compounded by media reports and even Egyptian government announcements repeatedly claiming that Christians make up 10% or more of the country's approximately 80 million people, despite the fact that the census repeatedly reports only 5%. The highest share of Christians found in an Egyptian census was in 1927 (8.3%). Figures for Egyptian Christians declined in each subsequent census, with Christians seemingly making up 5.7% of the Egyptian population in 1996. The report from the most recent census, conducted in 2006, does not, however, provide data on religious affiliation, but a sample of the 2006 census data is available through the Integrated Public Use Microdata Series, International (IPUMS). They sample the same Christian share (about 5%) as the latest Egyptian Demographic and Health Survey, with a sample size of 16,527 women aged 15–49 years.

According to the Pew Forum's analysis of Global Restrictions on Religion (see www.pewforum.org), Egypt has very high scores for government restrictions on religion as well as high scores for social hostilities involving religion. These factors might lead some Christians to be cautious about revealing their identity. Regardless of the actual number, it is very likely that Christians are declining as a proportion of Egypt's population, even if their absolute numbers are not falling. On the one hand, Christian fertility in Egypt has been lower than Muslim fertility. On the other, is possible that large numbers of Christians have left the country, although a 2012 study by the Pew Forum on the religious affiliation of migrants around the world has not found evidence of an especially large Egyptian Christian diaspora.

### Dates of Statistics

It is important, in changing situations, to know the exact date (year, perhaps also month and sometimes even day) to which particular statistics apply. This methodology compares government statistics of religion with statistics from religious communities themselves; but in doing so, it must be remembered that a government census (or a public-opinion poll) is almost always taken on a single, known day; whereas, by contrast, religious statistics are compiled over a lengthy period – perhaps three, four or even five years from the local grassroots counting of heads to final compilation of totals by a large denomination or church. Denominational totals published in 2015 therefore probably refer to the situation in 2012, 2011 or even 2010.

### Counting Pentecostals

#### *Three types of Pentecostals*

For the purpose of understanding the diverse global phenomenon of Pentecostalism, it is useful to divide the movement into three kinds, or types. First are denominational Pentecostals, organised into denominations in the early part of the twentieth century. Second are Charismatics, individuals in the mainline denominations (primarily after the mid-twentieth century). Third are Independent Charismatics, those who broke free of denominational Pentecostalism or mainline denominations to form their own networks.

#### *Pentecostals (Type 1)*

Pentecostals are defined as Christians who are members of the explicitly Pentecostal denominations whose major characteristic is a new experience of the energising ministry of the Holy Spirit that most other Christians have considered to be highly unusual. This is interpreted as a rediscovery of the spiritual gifts of New Testament times and their restoration to ordinary Christian life and ministry. Classical Pentecostalism usually is held to have begun in the United States in 1901, although most scholars have moved to a 'multiple origins' theory of the birth of modern Pentecostalism, emphasising early activity outside of the Western World. For a brief period, Pentecostalism expected to remain an interdenominational movement within the existing churches, but from 1909 onwards its members increasingly were ejected from mainline bodies and so forced to begin new organised denominations.

Pentecostal denominations hold the distinctive teachings that all Christians should seek a post-conversion religious experience called baptism in the Holy Spirit and that a Spirit-baptised believer may receive one or more of the supernatural gifts known in the early church: the ability to prophesy; to practise divine healing through prayer; to speak (glossolalia), interpret or sing in tongues; to sing in the Spirit, dance in the Spirit, pray with upraised hands; to receive dreams, visions, words of wisdom, words of knowledge; to discern spirits; and to perform miracles, power encounters, exorcisms (casting out demons), resuscitations, deliverances, or other signs and wonders.

From 1906 onwards, the hallmark of explicitly Pentecostal denominations, by comparison with Holiness/Perfectionist denominations, has been the single addition of speaking in other tongues as the 'initial evidence' of one's having received the baptism of the Holy Spirit, whether or not one subsequently experiences regularly the gift of tongues. Most Pentecostal denominations teach that tongues-speaking is mandatory for all members, but in reality today not all members have practised this gift, either initially or as an ongoing experience. Pentecostals are defined here as all associated with explicitly Pentecostal denominations that identify themselves in explicitly Pentecostal terms, or with other denominations that as a whole are phenomenologically Pentecostal in teaching and practice.

Among Protestants (coded as 'P-') are Pentecostal denominations such as the Assemblies of God. Sub-categories of Oneness, Baptistic, Holiness, Perfectionist and Apostolic were retained from earlier research. Each minor tradition within Pentecostalism is considered to be 100% Pentecostal (all members of Pentecostal denominations are counted as Pentecostals).

### *Charismatics (Type 2)*

Charismatics are defined as Christians affiliated to non-Pentecostal denominations (Anglican, Protestant, Catholic, Orthodox) who receive the experiences above in what has been termed the Charismatic movement. The Charismatic movement's roots go back to early Pentecostalism, but its rapid expansion has been mainly since 1960 (later called the Charismatic renewal). Charismatics usually describe themselves as having been 'renewed in the Spirit' and as experiencing the Spirit's supernatural and miraculous and energising power. They remain within, and form organised renewal groups within, their older mainline non-Pentecostal denominations (instead of leaving to join Pentecostal denominations). They demonstrate any or all of the *charismata pneumatika* (gifts of the Spirit), including signs and wonders (but with glossolalia regarded as optional).

Type 2 recognises the existence of Pentecostal individuals within the Anglican, Roman Catholic, Orthodox and Protestant traditions. These are designated 'Charismatic' and evaluated by country as Catholic Charismatics, Anglican Charismatics and so on, designating renewal within an existing tradition. For example, the beginning of the Charismatic movement in Anglican churches is described by Episcopal priest Dennis Bennett in *Nine O'Clock in the Morning* (Alachua, FL: Bridge-Logos, 1970). Traditions are assessed to determine what percentage of adherents identify themselves as Charismatics, ranging from 0% to 100%. Self-identification percentages for Charismatics were calculated by contacting renewal agencies working within denominations.

*Independent Charismatics (Type 3)*

While the classification and chronology of the first two types is straightforward, there are thousands of churches and movements that 'resemble' the first two types but do not fit their definitions. These constitute a third type and often pre-date the first two types. For lack of a better term, these are called 'Independent Charismatics'. Part of the rationale for this term is the fact that they are largely found in the Independent category of the overall taxonomy of Christians. Thus, Type 3 includes Pentecostal or semi-Pentecostal members of the 250-year-old Independent movement of Christians, primarily in the global South, of churches begun without reference to Western Christianity. These indigenous movements, although not all explicitly Pentecostal, nevertheless have the main features of Pentecostalism. In addition, since Azusa Street, thousands of schismatic or other Independent Charismatic churches have come out of Type 1 Pentecostals and Type 2 Charismatic movements. They consist of Christians who, unrelated to or no longer related to the Pentecostal or Charismatic denominations, have become filled with the Spirit, or empowered by the Spirit and have experienced the Spirit's ministry (although usually without recognising a baptism in the Spirit separate from conversion); who exercise gifts of the Spirit (with much less emphasis on tongues, as optional or even absent or unnecessary) and emphasise signs and wonders, supernatural miracles and power encounters; but also do not identify themselves as either Pentecostals (Type 1) or Charismatics (Type 2). In a number of countries they exhibit Pentecostal and Charismatic phenomena but combine this with rejection of Pentecostal terminology. These believers frequently are identified by their leadership as Independent, Postdenominationalist, Restorationist, Radical, Neo-Apostolic or 'Third Wave.'

Thus, the third type is Independent Charismatics (also known in the literature as neo-Charismatics or neo-Pentecostals) who are not in Protestant Pentecostal denominations (Type 1) nor are they individual Charismatics in the traditional churches (Type 2). Type 3 is the most diverse of the three types and ranges from house churches in China to African Initiated Churches to white-led Charismatic networks in the Western world. It includes Pentecostals who had split off from established Protestant denominations (Type 1) and who were then labelled as Independent. Independent churches formed by Charismatic leaders (Type 2) who founded new congregations and networks are also included. Some Independent Charismatics speak in tongues, but healing and power evangelism are more prominent in this type than in the other two.

### *Three types together*

One difficulty that has plagued all researchers and historians of Pentecostalism is what to call the overarching movement. Some have used 'Pentecostalism' or 'Global Pentecostalism', while others have used 'Charismatic'. Still others have used 'Pentecostal and Charismatic'. David Barrett originally used the lengthy phrase 'the Pentecostal and Charismatic Renewal of the Holy Spirit', which he later shortened to 'Renewal'. He then coined the term 'Renewalist' to refer to all three waves or types. For the purposes of this series, we use the term 'Pentecostals/Charismatics' to refer to all three types.

A demographic overview of Pentecostals/Charismatics (all types) illustrates the complexities of both the spread of the movement across the countries of the world and the striking diversity of the churches themselves. While current ways of understanding Pentecostals, Charismatics and Independent Charismatics reveal a global movement of immense proportions, perspectives on classification, counting and assessment of the movement are likely to continue to evolve. In the meantime, hundreds of millions of Christians across all traditions will continue to participate in the movement – bringing vitality in some denominations and schism in others. They will also promote social transformation in some communities and show little participation in others. What is certain is that, for the foreseeable future, Christianity as a whole will continue to experience the growth pains of this global phenomenon.

## Counting Evangelicals

Any effective and comprehensive method for counting Evangelicals must take into consideration denominational affiliation, self-identification and theology. The results of counting Evangelicals are directly related to denominational membership figures. Strictly speaking, denominational affiliation means official membership on a church roll.

### *Method 1: Individuals in denominations that are 100% Evangelical*

The first category of Evangelicals includes individuals who are found in denominations that are coded 100% Evangelical. That is, membership of an Evangelical council (national, regional or global) is assessed for every denomination and those denominations that have Evangelical affiliations are classed as 100% Evangelical. Consequently, 100% of the members of these denominations are considered Evangelical. Using this method alone, the *WCD* estimates there are 150 million Evangelicals in the world. As of 2010, the nine largest 100% Evangelical denominations in the world were all Protestant, and the five largest 100% Evangelical denominations were found in Brazil, Ethiopia, Nigeria and Indonesia, reflecting the global scope of the movement.

### *Method 2: Individuals who self-identify as Evangelical in non-100% Evangelical denominations*

For those denominations not identified as 100% Evangelical, an estimate is made of the percentage (0–99%) of members who self-identify as Evangelical. Self-identification percentages for Evangelicals in non-100% Evangelical denominations are verified by contacting key figures within each denomination, and each estimate is sourced in documentation housed at the Center for the Study of Global Christianity. Adding together figures from both 100% and partially Evangelical denominations gives a total of 285 million Evangelicals worldwide. Looking at both 100% and non-100% Evangelical denominations reveals that the movement has a significant presence beyond Western Protestantism. Some of the denominations with the most Evangelicals are within Anglicanism in the global South, such as the Anglican Church of Nigeria and the Church of Uganda. Chinese house churches (classified as Independents) taken together constitute the denomination with the third most Evangelicals globally. The United Kingdom (the Church of England) and the United States (the Southern Baptist Convention), however, are still important locations of the movement.

### *Method 3: Evangelicals not affiliated with any denomination (Unaffiliated Evangelicals)*

To date, no studies have addressed directly how many Evangelicals are denominationally unaffiliated. However, two well known realities (in Western Christianity, in particular) appear to provide indirect evidence for this undocumented trend. The first is reflected in recent research indicating the unaffiliated are not uniformly non-religious. The Pew Research Center reported that 68% of America's unaffiliated believe in God. It is reasonable to assume that a notable proportion of Christians is among the ranks of the unaffiliated by virtue of Christianity being the largest religion in many of the countries studied. The second reality is the acknowledged fact that unaffiliated Christians often attend and are active in churches, including Evangelical churches, without becoming official members. These unaffiliated Christians profess allegiance and commitment to Christ but do not maintain church affiliation.

## Dynamics of Change in Religious Populations

The question of how and why the number of religious adherents changes over time is critical to the study of international religious demography. It is more complex than simply 'counting heads' via births and deaths – a well established area in quantitative sociological studies – but in addition involves the multifaceted areas of religious conversion and migration. The migration of religious people has only in the past few years become a more researched area of demographic study, and issues surrounding religious conversion continue to be under-represented in the field. Data on religion from a wide range of sources – including from the religious communities themselves, as well as governments and scholars – must be employed to understand the total scope of religious affiliation. Given data on a particular religion from two separate points in time, the question can be raised, 'What are the dynamics by which the number of adherents changes over time?' The dynamics of change in religious affiliation can be reduced to three sets of empirical population data that together enable enumeration of the increase or decrease in adherents over time. To measure overall change, these three sets can be defined as follows: (1) births minus deaths; (2) converts to minus converts from; and (3) immigrants minus emigrants. The first variable in each of these three sets (births, converts to, immigrants) measures increase, whereas the second (deaths, converts from, emigrants) measures decrease. All future (and current) projections of religious affiliation, within any subset of the global population (normally a country or region), will account for these dynamics, and the changes themselves are dependent on these dynamics.

### *Births*

The primary mechanism of global religious demographic change is (live) births. Children are almost always counted as having the religion of their parents (as is the law in Norway, for example). In simple terms, if populations that are predominantly Muslim, for example, have more children on average than those that are predominantly Christian or Hindu, then over time (all other things being equal) Muslims will become an increasingly larger percentage of that population. This means that the relative size of a religious population has a close statistical relationship to birthrates.

### *Deaths*

Even as births increase their memberships, religious communities experience constant loss through the deaths of members. Although this often includes tragic, unanticipated deaths of younger members, it most frequently affects the elderly members. Thus, changes in health care and technology can positively impact religious communities if members live longer.

### *Births minus deaths/total fertility rate*

The change over time in any given population is most simply expressed as the number of births into the community minus the number of deaths out of it. Many religious communities around the world experience little else in the dynamics of their growth or decline. Detailed projections rely on a number of estimated measures, including life expectancy, population age structures and the total fertility rate. This means that any attempt to understand the dynamics of religious affiliation must be based firmly on demographic projections of births and deaths.

### *Converts to*

It is a common observation that individuals (or even whole villages or communities) change allegiance from one religion to another (or to no religion at all). Unfortunately, one of the problems in studying conversion is the paucity of information on it. Reliable data on conversions are hard to obtain, for a number of reasons. Although some national censuses ask people about their religion, they do not directly ask whether people have converted to their present faith. A few cross-national surveys do contain questions about religious switching, but even in those surveys it is difficult to assess whether more people leave a religion than enter it. In some countries, legal and social consequences make conversion difficult, and survey respondents might be reluctant to speak honestly about the topic. In particular, Hinduism is for many Hindus (as is Islam for many Muslims) not just a religion but also an ethnic or cultural identity that does not depend on whether a person actively practises the faith. Thus even non-practising or secular Hindus may still consider themselves, and be viewed by their neighbours, as Hindus.

### *Converts from*

Conversion to a new religion, as mentioned above, also involves conversion from a previous one. Thus, a convert to Islam is, at the same time, a convert from another religion. In the twentieth and twenty-first centuries, the most converts from Christianity were and continue to be found largely among those in the Western world who have decided to be agnostics or atheists.

### *Converts to minus converts from*

The net conversion rate in a population is calculated by subtracting the number of 'converts from' from the number of 'converts to'. Conversion to and conversion from will likely continue to play a role in changing religious demographics in the future.

### *Immigrants*

Equally important at the international level is how the movement of people across national borders impacts religious affiliation. Once religious communities are established through immigration they often grow vigorously (for a time) via high birth rates.

### *Emigrants*

In a reversal of nineteenth-century European colonisation of Africa, Asia and parts of the Americas, the late twentieth century witnessed waves of emigration of people from these regions to the Western world. The impact on religious affiliation is significant.

### *Immigrants minus emigrants*

In the twenty-first century, international migration continues to have a significant impact on the religious composition of individual countries. One can try to anticipate the way in which expected immigration and emigration trends will affect a country's population over time. One profound change to be expected is the increase of religious pluralism in almost every country of the world. Increasing religious pluralism is not always welcomed and can be seen as a political, cultural, national or religious threat.

The six dynamics discussed above determine changes in religious demographics. Gains are the result of three positive dynamics: births, conversions to, and immigration. Losses are the result of three negative dynamics: deaths, conversions from, and emigration. The net change in religious demographics is the result of gains minus losses. The balance of dynamics can be reflected in any proportions (for example, mainly births for gains, mainly conversions from for losses) but can also be represented by pairing the gains and losses by type: births versus deaths, converts to versus converts from, and immigrants versus emigrants. In each case, the net change (either positive or negative) will be the difference between the two. This means that any attempt to understand religious affiliation in the past, present or future must be firmly based on demographic dynamics. A proper awareness of these dynamics and their significance is thus vital both for undertaking and for interpreting studies of the future of religion.

## Measuring Growth Rates

The rates of growth, increase, decrease or decline of membership in many congregations can readily be measured from their annually reported statistics. This has been done by obtaining the statistics for two different years, where possible five years apart (to minimise the effects of roll-cleaning and other annual irregularities), usually 2000–5 and 2005–10, and working out the average annual growth rate as a percentage. Great care must be taken in such computations to ensure that the statistics used are measuring exactly the same entity (especially geographically) for each of the two years concerned. Growth, as a percentage increase or decrease per year, must be measured by dividing any annual increase by the identical category of total. Thus a church, for example, in a particular country with 500,000 total adherents (including children) in 2005 which grows to 600,000 total adherents (including children) in 2010 shows an increase of 600,000 minus 500,000 = 100,000, which divided by 5 = 20,000 a year, which divided by the mean membership of 550,000 gives an increase rate of 3.64% per year. In practice, the methodology follows a more accurate method by using the 1970 to 2015 figures for each denomination to arrive at average annual growth rates.

There are different ways of measuring the growth of a religious body. First, one can measure either adults only, or total community including children. Secondly, the growth rate of a church or religious grouping can be measured over a single day, or a month, a year, a decade, or 50 years – and all will yield differing results. This survey is concerned primarily to measure long-term rates. A growth rate measured for a specific religious body over a two- or three-year period may not be sustained over a decade.

## Projecting Religious Populations

The starting point of future studies is natural growth of the total population of the country or region of interest, using demographic projections as a baseline. Three major areas beyond natural growth are utilised to improve the projections. First, birth and death rates vary among religious communities within a particular country. Secondly, increasing numbers of people are likely to change their religious affiliations in the future. Thirdly, immigration and emigration trends will impact a country's population over time. The highest-quality projections for religious communities are built on cohort-component projections – ones that use differential rates for each religion: age-specific fertility rates by religion, age structure in five-year age-and-sex cohorts by religion, migration rates by religion, and mortality by religion.

Unfortunately, this kind of detail is not yet available for many countries (half of censuses do not ask a question about religion). Fortunately, the process of filling in missing data using demographic and smaller-scale general population surveys is underway, and as these data become available through the Pew–Templeton Global Religious Futures Project, researchers will have access to these data through the *World Religion Database*, where they will be archived in full, with summary results available at the Pew Forum's website. In the meantime, projections cannot solely rely on the cohort-component method. Instead, they use a hybrid projection method. First, the 2015 religious composition of each country is established as the baseline. Then, utilising the United Nations medium variant cohort-component projections of populations for five-year periods up to 2050, future religious shares are modestly adjusted from the 2015 baseline. Adjustments are based on analysis of past differential growth rates of religious groups, factoring in historical patterns of religious switching and possible future attenuation of past trends. Finally, these projections take into account how immigrants might alter the future religious composition of country populations.

## Ethno-linguistic People Groups

A problem for social science research is the lack of available survey and polling data in non-Western countries. While the United States and many European countries have a long history of engaging in this kind of research, many – often more underdeveloped – countries can be difficult to access and/or speak languages difficult for Western researchers. The *WCD*'s method directly addresses this methodological challenge through its additional taxonomy of the world's ethnic groups, which are paired with religious statistics.

A 'peoples' taxonomy must take into account both ethnicity and language. The approach taken in 'Ethnosphere' in Part 8 of the *World Christian Encyclopedia* was to match ethnic codes with language codes, which produced over 13,700 distinct ethno-linguistic peoples. Not all combinations of ethnicity and language are possible, but nevertheless every person in the world can be categorised as belonging to an ethno-linguistic people (mutually exclusive). For example, there are ethnic Kazaks who speak Kazak as their mother tongue and ethnic Kazaks who speak Russian as their mother tongue. These, then, are two separate ethno-linguistic peoples.

The work of determining the religious breakdown of ethno-linguistic peoples was begun in the 1970s in Africa, where many Christian churches reported the ethnic breakdown of their congregations. Utilising data gathered by religious bodies and in government censuses, estimates of religious affiliation for all peoples was completed in the mid-1990s and published in the second edition of the *World Christian Encyclopedia*. These data continue to be updated and published in the *World Christian Database* and *World Religion Database*.

Each distinct ethno-linguistic group in a country is assigned varying shares of the 18 categories of religion. For example, the Japanese in Japan are reported as 56% Mahayana Buddhist, 23% various New religionist, 10% agnostic, 3% atheist, 2% Shinto and 1% Christian. Each group is traced throughout the world with the assumption that whatever their religious breakdown is in their home country will be the same abroad. This allows researchers to locate Christian people in predominantly non-Christian countries. For example, the *WCD* reports that Pakistan – a majority-Muslim country – is also home to over 2 million Christians. While Christians are found among Muslim-majority people groups (for example, Punjabi at 4% Christian), they are also present in the country as ex-pats, such as French (65% Christian) and British (70% Christian).

## Conclusion

There are a variety of issues related to finding and choosing the best data sources of religious affiliation. Censuses are generally accepted as the most reliable, but there are times when they fail to present the full picture, for example because they omit certain regions of a country or because they do not ask clear or detailed questions about religion. General population surveys can often fill the gap, but, depending on their quality, they may also have some bias. At times, religious groups may have very different estimates of their sizes than are found by censuses and surveys, but for some types of data, such as denominations of Protestantism, estimates by the groups may be the best information available. Finally, for religions such as Islam, Hinduism, Buddhism and Judaism, subgroup information is routinely missing from censuses and surveys. Estimates for the subgroups of these religions often rely on indirect measures, such as ethnic groups likely to adhere to a particular subgroup or expert analysis of multiple ethnological and anthropological sources. Thus, it is important to take into consideration many different kinds of data in order to arrive at the best estimate of a particular religious population in a country.

# Index